# Programming Python

# Programming Python

Mark Lutz

O'REILLY®

*Beijing · Cambridge · Köln · Paris · Sebastopol · Taipei · Tokyo*

**Programming Python**
by Mark Lutz



Published by O'Reilly & Associates, Inc., 101 Morris Street, Sebastopol, CA 95472.

**Editor:** Frank Willison

**Production Editor:** Nicole Gipson Arigo

**Printing History:**

October 1996: First Edition

This book is printed on acid-free paper with 85% recycled content, 15% post-consumer waste. O'Reilly & Associates is committed to using paper with the highest recycled content available consistent with high quality.

ISBN: 1-56592-197-6 [4/99]

# *Table of Contents*

*Foreword* ... *xi*

*Preface* ... *xv*

## *I: Introducing Python* ... *1*

### *1: So What's Python?* ... *3*

"And Now for Something Completely Different" ... 3
The Life of Python ... 3
What's All the Excitement About? ... 5
The Compulsory Features List ... 6
What's Python Good For? ... 7
What's Python Not Good For? ... 9

### *2: A Sneak Preview* ... *11*

"Put Your Code Where Your Mouth Is" ... 11
Shell Tools Programming ... 12
Graphical User Interfaces ... 24
Data Structure Libraries ... 28
Persistent Information ... 39
Processing Text-Based Information ... 47
Extension Language Programming ... 53
And Whatever Else You Want to Use It For ... 64
Conclusion ... 65

*3: Getting Started* ........ 66

"Scenes from Life in the Real World" ........ 66
Configuring Your Environment ........ 66
Installing Python ........ 67
And If All Else Fails ........ 71
Using the Command-Line Interpreter ........ 72
Using the Python Command Line ........ 74
Platforms Supported Today ........ 75
What's Next? ........ 75
Conclusion ........ 76

***II: Language Fundamentals*** ........ 79

*4: Writing Basic Shell Tools* ........ 81

It Was a Dark and Stormy Night . . . ........ 81
"Quick and Dirty" File Packing ........ 82
Dissecting the Code ........ 84
New Language Concepts ........ 87
"Telling the Monkeys What to Do" ........ 111

*5: Variations on a Theme* ........ 118

"How Shall I Code Thee? Let Me Count the Ways" ........ 118
Packing With File Methods ........ 118
Packing with Explicit Files ........ 121
Packing with Counter Loops ........ 123
Unpacking with Explicit Files ........ 125
Unpacking with Line-by-Line Input ........ 127
Unpacking Without File Methods ........ 130
Crunching the Code (to Death) ........ 133

*6: Adding a Functional Interface* ........ 137

"The Packing Scripts Go Public" ........ 137
Part 1: "The Middleman" ........ 138
Part 2: "The Unpacker on Steroids" ........ 138
Part 3: "The Packer Hits the Big Time" ........ 149
Building Systems with Functions ........ 152

*7: Adding a Simple User Interface* ............ *156*

"Go Ahead—Reuse My Software" ............ 156
Running Scripts Versus Calling Functions ............ 159
Running the Interface in batch Mode ............ 165
Building Systems with Modules ............ 168

*8: Adding Text-Based Menus* ............ *181*

"On Today's Menu: Packing, Unpacking, and Fresh Spam" ............ 181
Making Menus with Dictionaries ............ 181
Making Menus with Lists ............ 186
Built-In Types: Operators, Methods, and Modules ............ 196
The Zen of Python: Namespaces are Dictionaries ............ 198
Dictionaries and Keyword Arguments ............ 202
Design Concepts: Do Modules Support OOP? ............ 207

*9: Moving Menus to Classes* ............ *210*

"Here's Your Script. Here's Your Script on OOP. Any Questions?" ............ 210
A First Attempt: Generalized Menu Functions ............ 211
So Who Needs Classes? ............ 216
OOP in Action: Menus as Classes ............ 221
Exploring Python Classes ............ 226
Configuring Menu Data ............ 233
Namespaces, Part 3: Classes and Instances ............ 238
More on Zen: Class and Instance Namespace Dictionaries ............ 246
Design Concepts: Implementing Generic Functions ............ 248

*10: More Class Magic* ............ *250*

More Bells, Whistles, and Little Blinking Lights ............ 250
Deriving Menus from Simpler User Interaction ............ 250
A Simple User-Interface Subclass: Back to Where We Started? ............ 253
A Menu-Interface Subclass: Registering Methods ............ 256
Inheriting from More than One Class ............ 259
More on Exception Handling: Exception Lists ............ 262
Making Menus Expandable: Overloading Operators ............ 264
Summary: Python and the OOP Trinity ............ 279
Design Exercise: Adding Logging and Security Extensions ............ 285
Where's the Beef? ............ 290
Conclusion ............ 294

*Welcome to the Middle of the Book!* ..... 297

A Quick Summary of Topics We've Covered So Far ..... 297
Plus a Few Shell Tool Tricks ..... 300
Python in a Nutshell ..... 301
What's Next? ..... 302
Brewing Python tee ..... 302

***III: Tools and Applications*** ..... 305

*11: Graphical User Interfaces* ..... 307

"Here's Looking at You, Kid" ..... 307
Climbing the GUI Learning Curve ..... 308
Automating GUI Construction ..... 330
Case Study: "The Packer Goes GUI!" ..... 347
Avoiding Namespace Clashes ..... 358
Handling Program Errors ..... 361
A Totally RAD Language ..... 375
Other Tkinter Topics ..... 380
Summary ..... 385

*12: Persistent Information* ..... 387

"Give Me an Order of Persistence, But Hold the Pickles" ..... 387
Case Study: a Table Browser GUI ..... 393
Other Persistence Topics ..... 424
Summary ..... 436

*13: Implementing Objects* ..... 437

"Roses are Red, Violets are Blue; Lists are Mutable, and So is Class Foo" .. 437
Implementing Stacks ..... 438
Implementing Sets ..... 462
Classical Data Structures in Python ..... 480

*14: Extending Python* ..... 505

"I Am Lost at C" ..... 505
Examples We've Already Seen ..... 506
Moving Stacks to a C Extension Module ..... 508
Moving Stacks to a C Extension Type ..... 532
Now, Forget Most of the Details ..... 569

*15: Embedding Python* ........ *571*

"Add Python. Mix well. Repeat." ........ 571
Python's Embedded Call API ........ 572
Basic Embedding Strategies ........ 577
A Higher-Level Embedded Call API ........ 587
An Embedded Call API Client ........ 601
Case Study: Embedding User-Coded Validations ........ 609
Other Approaches: Registering Callable Objects ........ 620
Other Integration Topics ........ 624
Automated Integration Techniques ........ 630
Summary: Python/C Integration Techniques ........ 636

*16: Processing Language and Text* ........ *640*

"See Jack Hack. Hack, Jack, Hack" ........ 640
Strategies for Parsing Text in Python ........ 640
Case Study: A Calculator GUI ........ 675
The "Big Finish": A Real Calculator GUI ........ 684

*Conclusion: Python and the Development Cycle* ........ *697*

"That's the End of the Book, Now Here's the Meaning of Life" ........ 697
"Something's Wrong with the Way We Program Computers!" ........ 697
The "Gilligan Factor" ........ 698
Doing the Right Thing ........ 698
Enter Python . . . ........ 700
But What About That Bottleneck? ........ 701
On Sinking the Titanic ........ 708
So What's Python: the Sequel ........ 710
In the Final Analysis . . . ........ 711
"Roll the Closing Credits" ........ 712

*IV: Appendixes* ........ *715*

*A: . . . And Other Cool Stuff* ........ *717*

*B: Futurisms* ........ *754*

*C: A Mini-Reference* ..... 759

*D: An Application Framework* ..... 792

*E: A Python Tutorial* ..... 813

*F: Python Classes for C++ Programmers* ..... 854

*Bibliography* ..... 858

*Glossary* ..... 861

*Index* ..... 867

# *Foreword*

As Python's creator, I'd like to say a few words about its origins, adding a bit of personal philosophy.

Over six years ago, in December 1989, I was looking for a "hobby" programming project that would keep me occupied during the week around Christmas. My office (a government-run research lab in Amsterdam) would be closed, but I had a home computer, and not much else on my hands. I decided to write an interpreter for the new scripting language I had been thinking about lately: a descendant of ABC that would appeal to UNIX/C hackers. I chose Python as a working title for the project, being in a slightly irreverent mood (and a big fan of *Monty Python's Flying Circus*).

Today, I can safely say that Python has changed my life. I have moved to a different continent. I spend my working days developing large systems in Python, when I'm not hacking on Python or answering Python-related email. There are Python T-shirts, workshops, mailing lists, a newsgroup, and now a book. Frankly, my only unfulfilled wish right now is to have my picture on the front page of the *New York Times*. But before I get carried away daydreaming, here are a few tidbits from Python's past.

It all started with ABC, a wonderful teaching language that I had helped create in the early eighties. It was an incredibly elegant and powerful language aimed at nonprofessional programmers. Despite all its elegance and power and the availability of a free implementation, ABC never became popular in the UNIX/C world. I can only speculate about the reasons, but here's a likely one: the difficulty of adding new "primitive" operations to ABC. It was a monolithic closed system, with only the most basic I/O operations: read a string from the console, write a string to the console. I decided not to repeat this mistake in Python.

Besides this intention, I had a number of other ideas for a language that improved upon ABC, and was eager to try them out. For instance, ABC's powerful data types turned out to be less efficient than we hoped. There was too much emphasis on theoretically optimal algorithms, and not enough tuning for common cases. I also felt that some of ABC's features, aimed at novice programmers, were less desirable for the (then!) intended audience of experienced UNIX/C programmers. For instance: ABC's idiosyncratic syntax (all uppercase keywords!), some terminology (for example, "how-to" instead of "procedure"); and the integrated structured editor, which its users almost universally hated. Python would rely more on the UNIX infrastructure and conventions, without being UNIX-bound. And in fact, the first implementation was done on a Macintosh.

As it turned out, Python is remarkably free from many of the hang-ups of conventional programming languages. This is perhaps due to my choice of examples: besides ABC, my main influence was Modula-3. This is another language with remarkable elegance and power, designed by a small, strong-willed team (most of whom I had met during a summer internship at DEC's Systems Research Center in Palo Alto). Imagine what Python would have looked like if I had modeled it after the UNIX shell and C instead! (Yes, I borrowed from C too, but only its least controversial features, in my desire to please the UNIX/C audience.)

Any individual creation has its idiosyncracies, and occasionally its creator has to justify them. Perhaps Python's most controversial feature is its use of indentation for statement grouping, which derives directly from ABC. It is one of the language's features that is dearest to my heart. It makes Python code more readable in two ways. First, the use of indentation reduces visual clutter and makes programs shorter, thus reducing the attention span needed to take in a basic unit of code. Second, it allows the programmer less freedom in formatting, thereby enabling a more uniform style, which makes it easier to read someone else's code. (Compare, for instance, the three or four different conventions for the placement of braces in C, each with strong proponents.)

This emphasis on readability is no accident. As an object-oriented language, Python aims to encourage the creation of reusable code. Even if we all wrote perfect documentation all of the time, code can hardly be considered reusable if it's not readable. Many of Python's features, in addition to its use of indentation, conspire to make Python code highly readable. This reflects the philosophy of ABC, which was intended to teach programming in its purest form, and therefore placed a high value on clarity.

Readability is often enhanced by reducing unnecessary variability. When possible, there's a single, obvious way to code a particular construct. This reduces the number of choices facing the programmer who is writing the code, and increases the chance that it will appear familiar to a second programmer reading it. Yet another contribution to Python's readability is the choice to use punctuation mostly in a conservative, conventional manner. Most operator symbols are familiar to anyone with even a vague recollection of high school math, and no new meanings have to be learned for comic strip curse characters like @&$!.

I will gladly admit that Python is not the fastest running scripting language. It is a good runner-up, though. With ever-increasing hardware speed, the accumulated running time of a program during its lifetime is often negligible compared to the programmer time needed to write and debug it. This, of course, is where the real time savings can be made. While this is hard to assess objectively, Python is considered a winner in coding time by most programmers who have tried it. In addition, many consider using Python a pleasure—a better recommendation is hard to imagine.

I am solely responsible for Python's strengths and shortcomings, even when some of the code has been written by others. However, its success is the product of a community, starting with Python's early adopters who picked it up when I first published it on the Net, and who spread the word about it in their own environment. They sent me their praise, criticism, feature requests, code contributions, and personal revelations via email. They were willing to discuss every aspect of Python in the mailing list that I soon set up, and to educate me or nudge me in the right direction where my initial intuition failed me. There have been too many contributors to thank individually. I'll make one exception, however: this book's author was one of Python's early adopters and evangelists. With this book's publication, his longstanding wish (and mine!) of having a more accessible description of Python than the standard set of manuals, has been fulfilled.

But enough rambling. I highly recommend this book to anyone interested in learning Python, whether for personal improvement or as a career enhancement. Take it away, Eric, the orchestra leader! (If you don't understand this last sentence, you haven't watched enough Monty Python reruns.)

Guido van Rossum
Reston, Virginia, May 1996

# Preface

## About This Book

This book is about Python, an exciting object-oriented (OOP) programming language. Python is commonly used as both a scripting language for other systems, and a standalone rapid development tool. To address all its roles, we'll cover a broad range of topics in this book:

- The Python language itself: both introductory and advanced coverage.
- Some prominent extensions: the Tk interface, system tools, the persistence system, etc.
- Python's C integration tools, for adding new extensions and embedding Python in other systems.

As we'll see, Python provides a simple yet powerful high-level language, plus C integration facilities. Because of this combination of utility, much of the focus in Python development is on extensions that aren't part of the language itself. We'll cover all the bases in this book; both beginners and seasoned programmers should find something of interest here. But a few structural issues should be pointed out up front.

### It's a Practical Book

Although Python is interesting from a language design perspective, our main focus will be on how it can be used for day-to-day programming tasks. After all, Python is just a tool; it's really only valuable in the context of real applications. Because of that, this book emphasizes the *practical*, rather than the theoretical. The presentation is also fairly informal. Part of Python's appeal is that it's actually fun to use; as we'll see, Python is useful for serious development, but it has a down-to-earth, practical flavor.

## *It's Organized By Roles and Examples*

The book is organized by Python's major roles, not by language features. Much of it is based on incremental improvements to realistic examples. For instance, we'll get started by showing a "real world" use for Python, as a shell tools programming language. Then we'll move on to explore Python as a graphical user interface (GUI) development tool, an extension language, and cover a variety of other roles. Especially in Part 3, *Tools and Applications*, the examples are realistically scaled programs; we'll study a table browser, a calculator GUI, an embedded-call API, and more.

## *It's Not a Reference Manual*

This book is more like a tutorial than a reference manual. Of course, we'll study all the important concepts in the language along the way. The index serves as a language guide, and some reference material appears in appendixes. But this book doesn't replace Python's reference manuals. If you want an exhaustive list of language rules, the manuals do the job. Here, our goal is to show how those rules work in practice: to address the "*how*," not the "*what*." The manuals can be used to supplement the material here, if needed.

## *It Teaches the Fundamentals*

The text focuses on Python concepts that span domains. Python is being applied in some amazing areas, such as distributed programming and World Wide Web (WWW) scripting, but most of these could fill a whole book on their own. Instead, we'll stress common denominators of Python applications. We'll study a few advanced roles, and peek at more in an appendix. But this book's emphasis is on *core* Python tools. After reading this text, you'll be able to explore more advanced topics on an "as needed" basis.

## *There's an Optional Tutorial at the End*

From talks with people when this book was being planned, it became apparent that different people learn in different ways. For those who prefer a quick bottom-up introduction structured by language features, I've included a tutorial appendix, based on simple interpreter interaction. It's optional reading; the examples are artificial, and Chapter 2, *A Sneak Preview*, is probably better if you're looking for a quick overview. But the appendix may be useful for those new to dynamic languages, and for readers just getting started with programming.

## *Why Read This Book?*

Naturally, this book will teach you how to use Python. But beyond that, it provides *context* you won't find in the standard reference manuals. We'll explore topics of general interest:

- *Object-oriented programming*: Chapter 13, Part 2, etc.
- *Graphical user interfaces*: Chapters 11, 12, and 16.
- *Extending and embedding*: Chapters 14 and 15.
- *Persistent objects*: Chapter 12.
- *Shell tools programming*: Part 2, framework appendix.
- *Introductory material*: Part 2, tutorial appendix.

We'll also study things like the Python debugger, text processing, and system design concepts. But this book discusses the topics above with more depth and perspective than you'll get from reading manuals.

## *The Book's Structure*

The book's high-level structure reflects its practical orientation:

*Part 1, Introducing Python*
: Introduces some of the goals behind Python, presents some examples to give a first look at the language, and explains how to configure Python. It can be used as a quick overview.

*Part 2, Language Fundamentals*
: Covers most of the fundamentals of the Python *language*, by progressively refining relatively simple examples. It uses the shell tools application domain to introduce basic concepts.

*Part 3, Tools and Applications*
: Moves on to present other ways Python's commonly used, by exploring realistic programs. Many of its topics are tools used in larger systems: GUIs, persistence, extending and embedding, etc.

*Other*
: The *Conclusion* looks at Python's roles. The tutorial, reference material, and contributed examples of other Python tools and applications appear as appendixes.

## *How to Read the Material*

Depending on your background, a linear cover-to-cover reading of this book might not make sense. For example, the "sneak preview" chapter in Part 1, *Introducing Python* may be too advanced for beginners, and Part 2, *Language Fundamentals*'s material may move too slowly for some advanced readers. The book tries to follow a progression towards more complex topics, but it's difficult to satisfy everyone's needs at once. Here are some suggestions:

- Advanced readers may want to read cover to cover, but can read Part 2 quickly, skipping the tutorial.
- Intermediate readers might want to do the same, but should spend more time studying basics in Part 2.
- Beginners can start with the tutorial appendix, skim Part 1 quickly and return to it again after Part 2.

Again, these are just suggestions. For instance, Part 2 is really an extended tutorial, which explores language details in depth. But most of its material is critical to understanding the ideas underlying Python. Unless you've already attained Python wizard status, I'd recommend reading it.

### *Python for people in a hurry*

This book is roughly equivalent to an in-depth Python training course (or two). If you're short on time, you can still learn a lot of Python by reading just the tutorial and most of Part 1. Other parts of the book can be consulted on an as-needed basis.

For a quick start, I recommend reading Chapter 1, the tutorial in Appendix E, Chapter 2, and (perhaps) Appendix A. Naturally, this skips lots of important material, but it's probably enough to get started if you already have some programming experience.

# *Prerequisite Knowledge*

The book assumes a general familiarity with programming, but it covers basic ideas well enough to be accessible for beginners. The book is also oriented toward UNIX engineers, but UNIX development concepts apply to most platforms (Python has a following on Microsoft and Macintosh platforms, too).

There's probably no preferred language background for this text. People familiar with languages such as C, C++, Scheme, Perl, Tcl, and more have been able to learn Python quickly. In fact, some have even been able to pick up Python's core concepts in a few days; most of its features are remarkably intuitive.

Some sections assume a familiarity with C or C++ programming (extension-language work), and some assume prior knowledge of an application domain (GUIs, databases, etc.). But most of these sections contain enough information in the narrative to make new concepts approachable. Where appropriate, sources of additional information are given; a bibliography appears at the end of the book.

## About the Examples

This book is based on release 1.3 of Python. The examples should work on releases 1.3 and higher. Most examples work on release 1.2, but some 1.3-specific features are used (keywords, linking conventions). Most of the GUI examples use the *Tkinter* interface, which was based on Tk 4.0 and Tcl 7.4 in Python 1.3, but they should work with later releases as well.

Python is a growing language, and there will probably be a number of new enhancements even before this book is printed (1.4, a minor update, is already in the works). But Python's inventor takes great care to make each new release backward-compatible with prior ones. Because of this, later releases may have additional features, but the examples here should still work as advertised.

### Platform Issues

All examples in this book were run on the *Linux* operating system, a public-domain UNIX implementation for Intel-based PCs. The example C code was compiled with *gcc*, and GUI examples were run under the Linux *X-Windows* system implementation. Since Python is extremely portable, the examples should run on any UNIX system that supports Python (and that's just about all of them).

But Python is not just a UNIX tool. Except where UNIX-specific utilities are used, most of the examples should also run on other platforms with little change. Even the GUI examples should port well; they use the *Tk* API, which is now available on X11, Microsoft Windows, and Macintosh platforms. Some of the extensions shown (*dbm*, process-forking, etc.) may be less portable outside UNIX, but this depends on your system.

Module filenames in this book are sometimes more cryptic than they should be: filenames respect the eight-character limit imposed by popular PC platforms. This was done so that Python users on MS-DOS and Windows 3.1 could run the examples; Python makes a great language for PCs too. Someday (we all hope), the "8.3" limit will go away completely; until then, it's still a lowest common denominator.

### *How to Get Source Code for the Examples*

If you have access to a machine with Python installed, I strongly recommend working along with the text, by running the examples on your own. Python is a dynamic, interactive language, and there's really no substitute for experimenting with the system. If you don't have Python on your machine, Chapter 3, *Getting Started*, shows how to get the system and install it.

Of course, you can learn Python without running programs, but working through the examples can be a great supplement to the material here. All the program examples in this book can be found in the "examples" directory on the accompanying CD-ROM. See the "README" file in the CD examples directory for more details. In addition, the examples will also be available from O'Reilly's FTP Site. Check *http://www.ora.com* for more details.

### *Using This Book's CD-ROM*

Besides the examples, the CD in the back of this book also contains Python binaries, source-code packages, and a large collection of extra tools. For instance, the CD includes about 50 ready-to-run Python executables, for a wide variety of platforms; some have *Tk* and *dbm* preinstalled. See the top-level "README" file on the CD for information on what's available and how to use its packages.

The CD was added late in the project, so you may see references in the text to FTP files which are more readily available on the CD. When in doubt, check the CD first. Directions for getting Python files by FTP are still present; you may find them useful if you need to fetch updated releases or newly contributed packages.

## *Where to Look for Updates*

If there's one constant in the software world, it is change. Updates to this book will probably be posted on the author's web page before they make it into future printings of the book. With your web browser, check URL: *http://rmi.net/~lutz* for links to new material, corrections, and examples.

Unfortunately, URLs have a way of changing over time, too. If the above address doesn't work, this information might also be accessible from O'Reilly's web site: *http://www.ora.com*, and/or Python's home page: *http://www.python.org*.

### *About the author*

*"Hello. My name is Mark, and I'm a Python-aholic."*

I've been involved with Python since 1992. Among other things, I wrote an expert-system shell in Python, developed an integration code generator, designed a portable GUI development tool based on Python, and used Python as an embedded scripting language in a large C++ framework. And I wrote this book. Naturally, I think Python is a pretty amazing tool, and I hope to show you some of the reasons why.

But first, a disclaimer. When I was growing up, I had a friend whose family had migrated from China. After school, we used to stop off at a restaurant they owned, to bum sodas and chicken from his parents. Sometimes, his grandmother, an endearing older woman, would stop by. She had a favorite expression, which she regularly employed on these occasions in accented English: "Mock [Mark], you a funny boy!" And so you've been warned: if you think something in this book sounds odd, you're probably right. :-)

## *Acknowledgments*

Writing a book like this is a major undertaking. Here are some of the people who contributed in one way or another to this one; apologies in advance to anyone I've missed.

I'd first like to thank the gang in Boulder that took time to read early drafts, point out errors, and offer advice: Louis Krupp, Dave Gottner (a.k.a. Amrit Prem), Pat West, Smitha Sundaresan, and the rest of you. Thanks to XVT for giving me a chance to play with Python, and to KaPRE Software for letting me take a leave of absence to write this book. And thanks go to my editor Frank Willison, and the people at O'Reilly, both for helping me write a technical book and for believing in the project.

This book's look and feel is largely the product of O'Reilly's amazing production department. They may not be lumberjacks, but they're definitely okay :-). Frank Willison was the technical editor. Nicole Gipson Arigo was the project manager, with production help from Michael Deutsch, Mary Ann Faughnan, John Files, Nancy Wolfe Kotary, Mary Anne Weeks Mayo, and Julie Nudler. Joseph Pomerance copyedited the book. Kismet McDonough-Chan and Clairemarie Fisher O'Leary performed quality checks. Seth Maislin wrote the index. Chris Reilly prepared the illustrations. Erik Ray, Ellen Siever, and Lenny Muellner worked with the tools to create the book. Nancy Priest and Mary Jane Walsh designed the interior book layout, and Edie Freedman and Hanna Dyer designed the front cover.

The CD-ROM in the back of this book was put together with the help of Jessica Perry Hekman, Norm Walsh, and Frank Willison at O'Reilly, along with Guido van Rossum and Ken Manheimer at Python's Internet sites. Many other people contributed packages and executables for the CD; most are identified on the CD.

I also want to acknowledge the people who took part in the formal technical review of the book: Guido van Rossum, Aaron Watters, and Michael McLay. Various people inspired or contributed examples in this book (especially in Appendix A); they're credited in the text. Whether they knew it or not, everyone in the Python community played a role in this project too by spurring discussion and popularizing the language. I hope those involved with Python accept this book as one reward for all their efforts.

And of course, I'd like to thank Guido van Rossum individually, both for giving us such a remarkable tool, and for fostering a community that's been genuinely fun and exciting to be a part of. Without his vision and profound dedication, we'd all be using Perl or Tcl for some time to come (not that there's anything wrong with that :-). Keep dodging those crazy buses, Guido!

Finally, I find myself once again indebted to my wife Lisa, and my kids, a set that currently consists of Michael and Samantha. As usual, they've been unbelievably patient, and helped me keep at least one foot in reality during this project. Such is life with a curly-haired blond.

May all your objects be persistent,

Mark Lutz
October 1996
somewhere near Boulder, Colorado

# I

# *Introducing Python*

- Chapter 1, *So What's Python?*
- Chapter 2, *A Sneak Preview*
- Chapter 3, *Getting Started*

In this section we'll touch briefly on Python's structure and goals, before jumping into details. Some aspects of Python will be familiar to users of other language tools. But in many ways Python represents a significant departure from older approaches, and we'll point out some of its distinctions here.

In Chapter 1 we'll try to define Python's roles. In Chapter 2 we'll take a quick first look at some Python code in action. These examples foreshadow chapters in later sections of the book. Finally, Chapter 3 presents some of the bare essentials of Python use, to help you get set up to run Python programs on your machine.

If you're already familiar with similar tools, Chapter 1 and Chapter 2 might be used as a quick overview of the language. But this part of the book is only intended to give you a brief introduction to Python. We'll save most of the details for later.

# 1

# So What's Python?

*In this chapter:*

- *"And Now for Something Completely Different..."*
- *The Life of Python*
- *What's All the Excitement About?*
- *The Compulsory Features List*
- *What's Python Good For?*
- *What's Python Not Good For?*

## *"And Now for Something Completely Different..."*

This book is about using Python, a public-domain programming language. In acronyms, Python is both a very-high-level language (VHLL), and an object-oriented dynamic language (OODL). As a preliminary definition, Python can be described as a new kind of language tool. For many users, its

- Support for object-oriented development
- Powerful programming constructs
- Extendible and embeddable architecture
- Remarkably clear syntax and coherent design

make it almost ideal as both a *scripting* interface for modern systems, and a *stand-alone* rapid-development language. For example, Python's object-oriented nature mixes well with frameworks written in C++. And as a standalone tool, Python is commonly used in domains such as system administration, graphical user interfaces, internet scripting, and database programming. We'll refine this description in a moment.

## *The Life of Python*

Python was invented around 1990 by Guido van Rossum, at CWI in Amsterdam. Despite the reptiles, it's named after the BBC comedy series *Monty Python's Flying*

*Circus.* Guido was also involved with the Amoeba distributed operating system and the ABC language. In fact, the original motivation for Python was to create an advanced scripting language for the Amoeba system.

But Python's design turned out to be general enough for a wide variety of domains. It's now used by a growing number of engineers around the world, in increasingly diverse roles. For instance, a number of companies use Python in commercial products, for tasks such as GUI development tools, WWW scripting, interactive television, rapid program development, on-site customization of C++ class libraries, and more.

Since it first appeared on the public domain scene in 1991, Python has continued to attract a loyal following, and spawned a dedicated Internet newsgroup, *comp.lang.python*, in 1994. And as this book was being written, Python's home-page debuted on the WWW at *http://www.python.org/*.

To help manage Python's growth, an informal organization aimed at supporting Python developers has begun taking shape: the Python Software Activity, or PSA for short. Despite its public domain status, Python is a well-supported system, thanks to the dedication of its inventor and the Python community. For example, the PSA facilitates Python workshops, and maintains a software and resources locator service.

### *"Buses considered harmful"*

The PSA was originally formed in response to a thread on the Python newsgroup, which posed the semiserious question: "What would happen if Guido was hit by a bus?" Guido van Rossum still manages most new developments in Python, but the PSA and Python's user-base help support the language, work on extensions, etc. Given Python's popularity, and the PSA infrastructure, bus attacks seem less threatening now; of course I can't speak for Guido . . .

Finally, Python is true *freeware*: there are no restrictions on copying it, or distributing it with your products. It comes with complete source code, a debugger and profiler, built-in interfaces to common external services, plus tools for adding other interfaces. System functions, GUIs, and databases are supported "out of the box." Python programs run on most platforms, including nearly all flavors of UNIX, PCs (DOS, Windows, OS/2), the Macintosh, and others. And by the time you read this, Python should be part of most Linux distributions.

# *What's All the Excitement About?*

Back to our description. Python has been called a "next-generation scripting language." This definition probably summarizes the language's distinctions, and the theme of this book, better than most. Although different people like different things about Python, there are some common reasons underlying its popularity. Some of the central points in the "Python philosophy" are:

*Coherence*
: A scripting language doesn't have to be hard to read, write, and maintain. Issues of aesthetics and readability need not be sacrificed in the interest of utility. With the right tool, there's no reason to abandon normal standards of quality, even for "quick and dirty" code.

*Power*
: An extension language doesn't have to have limited functionality. The design goals of embeddability and semantic power aren't necessarily contradictory: an extension tool can also be a full-featured programming language.

*Scope*
: A dynamic language can be used for more than trivial tasks. There's no reason that a language can't both provide rapid response during the development cycle and also have features that make it useful for building more advanced systems.

*Objects*
: Object-oriented programming *can* be a useful paradigm, given the right tool. When easy to apply, OOP can be a powerful tool for structuring and reusing code. An object-oriented language doesn't necessarily also have to be complex or difficult to use.

*Integration*
: No language is an island. By providing both a powerful dynamic language, and well-defined interfaces to other languages, Python fosters hybrid systems that simultaneously leverage the rapid turnaround of Python, and the efficiency of C.

Python's *integration* support is a crucial property: as we'll see, much of Python's power comes from its open design, and its interfaces to external services. In fact, some consider Python's library of existing interfaces to be among its greatest assets. As we'll see, embedding APIs in a high-level language like Python makes them easier to use. Moreover, Python's integration tools make it practical to embed Python in products, and to apply paradigms such as rapid prototyping and rapid development.

But compared to other public-domain scripting languages, the first two points here—coherence and semantic power—may be Python's biggest distinctions. Aesthetic issues such as readability and design coherence are always hard to define, but crucial in a programming tool. As one Python user put it,

> "Python looks like it was designed, not accumulated."

Python's inventor has done a extraordinary job of balancing the goals of simplicity and utility. We'll see that Python's clear syntax and high-level tools encourage the creation of easy-to-read, reusable software.

We'll also find that Python programs tend to resemble traditional languages such as C and Pascal, rather than scripting languages like Perl or Tcl. In fact, Python is something of a scripting language in the guise of a traditional language. Another observer summarized this fusion of ideas well:

> "Python bridges the gap between scripting languages and C."

By providing a full-featured programming language and supporting modern development paradigms, Python brings programming tools used for more substantial systems to the scripting world. For example, C is poor for fast prototyping, and *awk* is almost useless for designing large systems, but Python does both well. In short, Python is a simple but powerful language, suitable both for "quick and dirty" scripts and medium-to-large-scale systems development.

### *Is it a "scripting language" or an "extension language"?*

The terms "scripting language" and "extension language" are often used interchangeably to refer to an embedded, interpreted language component. Unfortunately, "scripting language" sometimes denotes system administration languages, used for writing shell tools. Since Python can be used in both roles, we'll use both terms too. But the term "scripting" isn't meant to imply that Python is just a shell tools language. For instance, we'll see that embedded Python code can take many forms: character strings, objects in module files, executable script files, and more.

## *The Compulsory Features List*

One way to describe a new language is by listing its features. Of course, this will be more meaningful after we've seen Python in action; the best we can do now is speak in the abstract. And it's really how Python's features work together, that make it what it is. But looking at some of Python's attributes may help us define it.

To some extent, what Python is depends on your perspective. If you're approaching Python from a scripting language background, you might find that some of its features are more powerful than what you're used to. On the other hand, if your background is in static languages like C, you may be amazed at how much coding Python eliminates. In fact, some have gone so far as to call Python programs "executable pseudocode." Here are some of the reasons why:

*Table 1-1: Python language features*

| Features | Benefits |
|---|---|
| No compile or link steps | Rapid development cycle turnaround |
| No type declarations | Programs are simpler, shorter, and more flexible |
| Automatic memory management | Garbage collection avoids bookkeeping code |
| High-level datatypes and operations | Fast development using built-in object types |
| Object-oriented programming | Code structuring and reuse, C++ integration |
| Embedding and extending in C | C integration, mixed-language systems |
| Classes, modules, exceptions | Modular "programming-in-the-large" support |
| Dynamic loading of C modules | Simplified extensions, smaller binary files |
| Dynamic reloading of Python modules | Programs can be modified without stopping |
| Universal "first-class" object model | Fewer restrictions and special-case rules |
| Run-time program construction | Handles unforeseen needs, end-user coding |
| Interactive, dynamic nature | Incremental development and testing |
| Access to interpreter information | Metaprogramming, introspective objects |
| Wide portability | Cross-platform programming without ports |
| Compilation to portable byte-code | Execution speed, protecting source code |
| Built-in interfaces to external services | System tools, GUIs, persistence, databases, etc. |

To be fair, Python is really a conglomeration of features borrowed from other languages. It includes elements taken from C, C++, Modula-3, ABC, Icon, and others. For instance, Python's modules came from Modula, and its slicing operation from Icon. And because of Guido's background, Python borrows many of ABC's ideas, but adds practical features of its own, such as support for C-coded extensions.

Roughly, Python falls into the same tools family as dynamic scripting languages such as Perl, Tcl, Scheme, REXX, and some BASIC languages. But Python's *combination* of features makes it unique: it opens up new possibilities for scripting language users.

## *What's Python Good For?*

Because Python is used in an increasingly wide variety of ways, it is hard to give an authoritative answer to this question. For instance, some use it as an embedded extension language, while others use it exclusively as a standalone programming tool. And to some extent, this entire book will be an attempt to answer this very question—we'll take an in-depth look at some of Python's most common roles. For now, here's a summary of some of the ways Python is being used today:

*Shell tools*
: System-administration tasks, command-line programs

*Extension-language work*
: Frontends to C/C++ libraries, customization

*Rapid-prototyping/development*
: Throw-away or deliverable prototypes

*Language-based modules*
: Instead of writing special-purpose parsers

*Graphical user interfaces*
: Using simple and advanced GUI APIs

*Database access*
: Persistent object stores, SQL system interfaces

*Distributed programming*
: Using integrated client/server mechanism APIs

*Internet scripting*
: CGI scripts, HTTP interfaces, WWW applets, etc.

Of course, Python is not really tied to any particular application area. For example, Python's integration support makes it useful for almost any system which can benefit from a frontend, programmable interface. In general terms, Python provides services that span domains:

- A *dynamic* programming language, for situations in which a compile/link step is either impossible (on-site customization), or inconvenient (prototyping, rapid development, shell tools)
- A powerful but *simple* programming language, for situations in which the complexity of larger languages is sometimes a liability (prototyping, end-user coding)
- A *generalized* language tool, for situations where we might otherwise need to invent and implement yet another "little language" (programmable system interfaces, configuration tools)

Given these general properties, Python can be applied to any area we're interested in, by extending it with domain libraries, embedding it in an application, or using it standalone. For instance, Python's role as a shell tools language is due as much to its built-in interfaces to system services, as to the language itself.

In fact, *any* external service can be used in Python programs by wrapping it in integration logic. By providing an easily extended architecture, Python has fostered a growing library of extensions, available as off-the-shelf components to Python developers. To name just a few:

*Table 1-2: Popular Python extensions*

| Domain | Extensions |
|---|---|
| Systems programming | Sockets, threads, signals, pipes, RPC calls, POSIX bindings |
| Graphical User Interfaces | X11, Tk, Tix, MFC, STDWIN |
| Database interfaces | Oracle, Sybase, PostGres, mSQL, persistence ("pickling"), *dbm* |
| Microsoft Windows tools | MFC, OLE |
| Internet tools | Grail web browser (applets), HTML parsers, CGI interfaces |
| Distributed objects | ILU (CORBA) |
| Other popular tools | Expect, regular expressions, numerical extensions, cryptography |

As we'll see later, Python's *open architecture* supports flexible development modes and products. With Python, we can arbitrarily mix prototyping, rapid-development, and traditional software engineering, according to the demands of the current project. And by using Python as a *scripting tool*, we can open up parts of our systems to end-user customization, in ways we might have otherwise never considered.

### *The ultimate Python exception handler?*

At a prominent WWW search engine company that uses Python extensively, one developer is rumored to have a Python exception-handler programmed to dial his pager automatically. Although this is a great example of how Python is being applied in real products, most programmers find it to be considerably less intrusive. :-)

## *What's Python Not Good For?*

To be fair again, some tasks are outside Python's scope. Like all dynamic languages, Python (as currently implemented) isn't as fast or efficient as static, compiled languages like C. In many domains, the difference doesn't matter. But in others, efficiency can be a high priority.

Because it's interpreted, Python usually isn't the best tool for delivery of performance-critical components. Instead, computationally intensive operations can be implemented as compiled *extensions* to Python, and coded in a low-level language like C. Python can't be used as the sole implementation language for such components, but it works well as a frontend scripting interface to them.

For instance, numerical programming was being added to Python as this was written, by combining optimized extensions, and a higher-level model for use in Python (see the bibliography). The net result is a numerical programming tool that's both efficient and easy to use.

Moreover, Python can still serve as a prototyping tool in such domains. Systems may be implemented in Python first, and later moved in whole or piecemeal, to a language like C for delivery. C and Python have distinct strengths and roles; a hybrid approach, using C for compute-intensive modules, and Python for prototyping and frontend interfaces, can leverage the benefits of both.

In some sense, Python solves the efficiency/flexibility tradeoff by not solving it at all. It provides a language optimized for usability, along with tools needed to integrate with other languages. While it's unlikely that it'll ever be as fast as C, Python's speed of development is at least as important as C's speed of execution.

### *"My language can beat up yours! :-)"*

Programming language virtues are notoriously subjective. Some would even call them religious issues; they're debated tirelessly on the Net by those who care about such things. The debates, sometimes known as "language wars," are generally spawned by an innocent query ("How do Perl, Python, and Tcl compare?"), but digress rapidly (nudge, nudge; know what I mean? ;-).

Certainly users of other languages have found enough to be excited about in Python to make them almost evangelical about the language. Some see it as a step up from current scripting languages. To others, it's a simpler alternative to traditional languages like C++. And still others will remain devoted to assembler language until retirement!

But it's not my intent to preach about language design here. I'd rather show how Python can be used for real development tasks, and let you be the judge. If this book achieves its goals, Python's distinctions should be obvious by the time you've finished reading it. We'll return to some observations about Python's scope at the end, after you've had a chance to see it in action. Of course, I have some opinions on all this (I'm writing a Python book, after all :-), but I'll keep them discreetly tucked away for now.

# 2

# A Sneak Preview

*In this chapter:*


- *"Put Your Code Where Your Mouth Is"*
- *Shell Tools Programming*
- *Graphical User Interfaces*
- *Data Structure Libraries*
- *Persistent Information*
- *Processing Text-Based Information*
- *Extension Language Programming*
- *And Whatever Else You Want to Use It For*
- *Conclusion*


## *"Put Your Code Where Your Mouth Is"*

Okay, enough rhetoric. Although we can't get into many details in this introductory section, examples usually speak louder than words. Let's take a brief look at some of the ways you might use Python in your day-to-day work, by studying examples from some of Python's most common roles:

- Shell tools
- Graphical user interfaces
- Data-structure libraries
- Persistent objects
- Text processing
- Extension-language work

We'll cover these topics in more detail, in upcoming chapters. And although this list is representative, it's certainly not exhaustive. Later in the book, we'll also explore other ways Python is being used, in domains such as internet scripting, and distributed objects. In fact, since Python's a true *general-purpose* language, there are almost as many Python roles as Python programmers.

But if you're like me, you probably like to see some real code right away, when approaching a new language (without having to wade through a few hundred pages first!). That's what this section is for: to see what Python programs *look like*, and to introduce some basic concepts we'll expand on later.

### *"Nobody expects the Spanish Inquisition"*

Unless you're already a Python guru, some of these examples probably won't make much sense yet. This is just an overview, intended to spark your interest, and hint at some of the exciting things you can do with Python.

On the other hand, if you're familiar with similar tools, this chapter can be used as a quick introduction to the language. But we won't explain much here: don't be concerned with details in the code at this point. We'll study the concepts in these examples in depth, later in the book. For now, let's jump right in . . .

# *Shell Tools Programming*

For many, Python's interfaces to operating system services, together with its support for advanced programming paradigms, make it an ideal language for writing portable shell tools (sometimes called "system administration scripts"). Here are a few ways Python can be applied in this domain.

## *Packing Files*

The following script copies files listed on the command-line to standard output, separated by markers:

*Example 2-1: file: packer.py*

```
#!/usr/local/bin/python
import sys                          # load the system module
marker = '::::::'

for name in sys.argv[1:]:           # for all command-line arguments
    input = open(name, 'r')         # open the next input file
    print marker + name             # write a separator line
    print input.read(),             # and write the file's contents
```

The first line in this file is a Python comment ("# . . . "), but it also gives the path to the Python interpreter using the UNIX "pound-bang" trick. If we give *packer.py* executable privileges, we can pack files by running this program from the system command line (a UNIX "csh" prompt here):

```
% packer.py spam.txt eggs.txt toast.txt  >  packed.txt
```

Running the program this way creates an output file called *packed.txt*, which contains all three input files, with a header line before each.

### *Python program structure*

Now, here's the first big concept to notice about Python. The *packer.py* script is a file of Python code. More accurately, it's a Python *module*; its statements are executed when it is imported, or run as a script. In Python, all code exists in modules, which import services from other modules.

For instance, module *packer* gets command-line arguments by importing the built-in *sys* module. The operation *sys.argv[1:]* fetches the "argv" arguments list from module *sys*, and slices off the program name at the front (more on slicing later). The net result is to make the *for* loop in this script step through all the filenames listed on the command line.

In general terms, Python programs are composed of modules, which contain statements, which operate on objects:

- *Modules* are the biggest program unit. They are created by writing Python source files or C extensions. And as we'll see, clients can import modules as a whole with *import* statements, fetch their top-level components with *from*, and reload modules at run-time with *reload*.
- *Statements* do the real work inside a Python module. Most of them are fairly standard: assignments (=), tests (*if*), and loops (*for*, *while*). Some create new objects: *def* makes a new function, *class* makes a class. And others are more exotic: *try* and *raise* for exceptions, *exec* to run strings, etc.
- *Objects* are processed by statements. Our packer script uses three kinds of objects: strings (the *marker* and *name* variables), lists (*sys.argv*), and file objects (*input*). Strictly speaking, the *sys* module is an object too; in fact, everything is an object in Python. Objects are automatically reclaimed when no longer used.

Watch for these components in the examples in this chapter. As we'll see, Python provides both powerful built-in object types, and statements and tools for creating new ones.

### *Where's the rest of this program?*

If you use compiled languages, the first thing you might notice about the packer's code is its lack of variable declarations and block markers. In fact, this turns out to be a key concept in Python. Variables (and object members) come into existence by assigning values to them, and block boundaries are detected automatically. For now, hold that thought: we'll see why it matters after a few more examples.

## *Packing Files "++"*

The *packer* script gets the job done. But as we'll see, Python's support for code reuse allows us to write scripts that inherit functionality which might have to be recoded (or omitted) otherwise. Later, we'll look at an application *framework* based on Python classes, which provides interfaces to system components. By using it for our file-packer, we get a packing *class*, which is much more useful:

*Example 2-2: file: PackApp.py*

```
#!/usr/local/bin/python
from apptools import StreamApp          # get the superclass
from textpack import marker             # get a marker constant

class PackApp(StreamApp):               # define a class
    def start(self):                    # define some methods
        if not self.args:
            self.exit('use: packapp.py [-o target]? src src...')

    def help(self):
        StreamApp.help(self)            # show superclass args
        print '<file> <file>...'        # then show my args

    def run(self):
        for name in self.restargs():
            try:
                self.message('packing: ' + name)
                self.pack_file(name)
            except:
                self.exit('error processing: ' + name)

    def pack_file(self, name):
        self.setInput(name)
        self.write(marker + name + '\n')
        while 1:
            line = self.readline()
            if not line: break
            self.write(line)                      # copy until eof
```

*Example 2-2: file: PackApp.py (continued)*

```
if __name__ == '__main__':  PackApp().main()    # if run as a script
```

Here, *PackApp* inherits members and methods that handle:

- Operating system services
- Command-line processing
- Input/output stream redirection
- Help message interfaces

from the *StreamApp* class, imported from another Python module file. *StreamApp* also provides a standard "start/run/stop" execution protocol; *PackApp* redefines the *start* and *run* methods locally, for its own purposes. Most of the low-level system interfaces are hidden by the *StreamApp* class. In OOP terms, it *encapsulates* system services.

This module can both be run as a program, and imported by a client. Python sets a module's name to `__main__` when it's run directly, so it can tell the difference. When run as a program, the last line creates an instance of the *PackApp* class, and starts it by calling its *main* method (defined in *StreamApp*).

So why go to all this trouble? For one thing, *StreamApp* clients won't need to remember all the system interfaces in Python; *StreamApp* exports a unified view. For another, such a framework can provide extra precoded utility we'd otherwise have to recode in every script we write. And since file access isn't hard-coded in *PackApp*, it can take on new behavior, by changing the class it inherits from: *PackApp* could just as easily read and write to strings or sockets, as to text files and streams.

### *Python classes in a nutshell*

The PackApp class makes use of logic in the imported *apptools* module not shown here; see Appendix D for the superclass's source code. We'll study Python classes in depth later, but here's a quick overview for readers familiar with object-oriented languages.

*Classes*

Like C++, classes are Python's main OOP tool. In Python, class objects are created with the "class" statement. Superclasses are listed in parenthesis after the new class's name, and multiple-inheritance is implemented by listing more than one.

*Instances*

Objects created from a class are called instance objects. They are generated by calling the class like a function: `object=class()`. Each instance inherits class attributes, and gets its own namespace; instance members are created by assignment: `object.member=value`.

*Inheritance*

Instance objects inherit attributes (both methods and members) from their class, and all accessible superclasses, according to a depth-first, left-to-right search though superclass links. Inheritance occurs when an object is qualified: `object.attribute`.

*Methods*

Class methods are just nested function *def* statements, with a special first argument named *self* (by convention). When a method is called, the *self* argument receives the instance object which is the subject of the call: `object.method(...)` becomes `method(object,...)`. Methods qualify the *self* argument to access or create instance data.

*Protocols*

In Python, special protocols like constructors, destructors, operator overloading, and metaclass hooks, are implemented as specially-named methods. We'll see examples of these in a moment.

Both classes and modules support software reuse, but in different ways: classes implement new objects, and modules are packages of logic and data. Classes always live inside a module.

## Generalized File Scanners

One of the first things we usually need to know when writing shell tools is how to interface with external data sources. Python doesn't have an implicit file-scanning loop, but it's simple to write one. The following module defines a general file-scanning routine, which applies a passed-in Python function to each line in an external file:

*Example 2-3: File: scanfile.py*

```
def scanner(name, function):
    file = open(name, 'r')              # create a file object
    while 1:
        line = file.readline()          # call file methods
        if not line: break              # until end-of-file
        function(line)                  # call a function object
    file.close()
```

Once we've coded this module, we can use it any time we need to step through a file line-by-line. For example, here's a client script that does simple line expansion:

*Example 2-4: File: commands.py*

```
#!/usr/local/bin/python
from scanfile import scanner

def processLine(line):                  # define a function
    if line[0] == '*':                  # applied to each line
        print "Ms.", line[1:-1]
    elif line[0] == '+':
        print "Mr.", line[1:-1]         # strip 1st and last char
    else:
        raise 'unknown command', line   # raise an exception

scanner("people.txt", processLine)      # start the scanner
```

If, for no obvious reason, the file *people.txt* contained the following lines:

```
*Granny
+Jethro
*Elly-Mae
+"Uncle Jed"
```

then our commands script could be run as follows:

```
% commands.py
Ms. Granny
Mr. Jethro
Ms. Elly-Mae
Mr. "Uncle Jed"
```

As a rule, we can usually speed things up by shifting processing from Python code to built-in tools. For instance, if we're concerned with speed (and memory space isn't tight), we can make our file scanner faster by using the *readlines* method to load the file into a list, instead of the manual *readline* loop above:

```
def scanner(name, function):
    file = open(name, 'r')              # create a file object
    for line in file.readlines():       # get all lines at once
        function(line)                  # call a function object
    file.close()
```

And if we have a list of lines, we can work more magic with the *map* built-in function. Here's a minimalist's version; the *for* loop is replaced by *map*, and we let Python close the file for us:

```
def scanner(name, function):
    map(function, open(name, 'r').readlines())
```

But what if we also want to change a file while scanning it? Here are two approaches: one uses explicit files, and the other uses the standard input/output streams, to allow for redirection on the command line.

*Example 2-5: File: filter.py*

```
def filter_files(name, function):         # filter file through function
    input  = open(name, 'r')              # create file objects
    output = open(name + '.out', 'w')     # explicit output file too
    for line in input.readlines():
        output.write(function(line))      # write the modified line
    input.close()
    output.close()                        # output has a '.out' suffix

def filter_stream(function):
    import sys                            # no explicit files
    while 1:                              # use standard streams
        line = sys.stdin.readline()       # or: raw_input()
        if not line: break
        print function(line),             # or: sys.stdout.write()
```

Since the standard streams are preopened for us, they're often easier to use. Finally, we could use classes to hide some of the details here; the next module defines a *File* object that "wraps" a real file:

*Example 2-6: File: filescan.py*

```
class File:
    def __init__(self, filename):
        self.file = open(filename, 'r')      # open and save file

    def __getitem__(self, i):                # overload indexing
        line = self.file.readline()
        if line:
            return line                      # return the next line
        else:
            raise IndexError                 # end 'for' loops, 'in'
```

This class defines two specially-named methods:

- The `__init__` method is called whenever a new object is created.
- The `__getitem__` method intercepts indexing operations.

Each time a *File* object is indexed, it returns the next line in the actual file. Since *for* loops work by repeatedly indexing objects, we can iterate over a file as though it were an in-memory list:

```
for line in File("spam.txt"): print '\t', line,
```

### *Flying first class*

In Python, functions (and everything else) are "*first-class*" data objects: they can be passed around programs just like simple data items (numbers, strings). Here, this means there are no special rules or syntax to follow, when passing a line-processing function to a scanner or filter. We'll see more powerful applications of this later; for instance, since *classes* are first-class objects too, we can pass them to functions that generate arbitrary objects.

## *A Regression Test Script*

Python provides interfaces to a variety of system services, along with tools for adding others. Here's a script that shows some commonly used services. It implements a simple regression-test system, by running a program with a given input file and comparing the output to the last run's results.

*Example 2-7: File: RegTest.py*

```
#!/usr/local/bin/python
import os, sys                          # get unix, python services
from stat import ST_SIZE                # file stat record
from glob import glob                   # file-name expansion
from posixpath import exists            # file exists test
from time import time, ctime            # time functions
print 'RegTest start.'
print 'user:', os.environ['USER']       # environment variables
print 'path:', os.getcwd()              # current directory
print 'time:', ctime(time()), '\n'
program = sys.argv[1]                   # two command-line args
testdir = sys.argv[2]

for test in glob(testdir + '/*.in'):    # for all matching input files
    if not exists('%s.out' % test):
        # no prior results
        os.system('%s < %s > %s.out 2>&1' % (program, test, test))
        print 'GENERATED:', test
    else:
        # backup, run, compare
        os.rename(test + '.out', test + '.out.bkp')
        os.system('%s < %s > %s.out 2>&1' % (program, test, test))
        os.system('diff %s.out %s.out.bkp > %s.diffs' % ((test,)*3) )
        if os.stat(test + '.diffs')[ST_SIZE] == 0:
            print 'PASSED:', test
            os.unlink(test + '.diffs')
        else:
            print 'FAILED:', test, '(see %s.diffs)' % test

print 'RegTest done:', ctime(time())
```

For each file with a *.in* suffix in the test directory, this script runs the program and looks for deviations in its results. Output and difference files are generated in the test directory, with appropriate suffixes. For example, if we have an executable program or script called *shrubbery*, and a test directory called *test1* containing a set of *.in* input files, a typical run of the tester might look something like this:

```
% regtest.py shrubbery test1
RegTest start.
user: mark
path: /home/mark/stuff/python/testing
time: Mon Feb 26 21:13:20 1996

FAILED: test1/t1.in (see test1/t1.in.diffs)
PASSED: test1/t2.in
FAILED: test1/t3.in (see test1/t3.in.diffs)
RegTest done: Mon Feb 26 21:13:27 1996
```

Most of the interfaces in this script are similar to C's:

- *os.system* runs a shell command.
- *os.stat* gets a file's statistics.
- *os.unlink* deletes a file, *os.rename* moves it.
- Python's "%" operator works like C's *sprintf* string-formatting function.
- The *time* module exports C's time-processing utilities.

But the equivalent program in C would be much longer: it would need to declare variables, handle data structures, etc. In C, all external services exist in a single global scope (the linker's scope); in Python, they're partitioned into module namespaces (*os*, *sys*, etc.) to avoid name clashes. And unlike C, the Python code can be run immediately, without compiling and linking.

### *Is Python compiled or interpreted?*

Technically speaking, Python programs are "compiled" to a machine-independent form, called "byte-code". The byte-code is then interpreted by the Python system. Compilation occurs at run-time, when a module is first imported or run, unless a compiled version of the module already exists. But since the compilation step is hidden (and fast), Python is usually considered to be an interpreted language, as currently implemented.

## *Redirecting Streams to Objects*

Besides built-in system interfaces, some features of the Python language make it well suited for writing shell tools. For example, because Python is deeply object-oriented, we can redirect the standard input/output streams to instances of *classes*, which provide methods to "fake" real files.

Redirecting file streams is usually done at the shell level. But it can be useful inside a Python program too: for instance, to make a GUI text box's screen act like an input/output file. Here's an implementation of this idea: the following module simulates files with in-memory character strings.

*Example 2-8: File: redirect.py*

```
import sys, string                              # get built-in modules


class Input:                                    # simulated input file
    def __init__(self, input=''):               # default argument
        self.text = input                       # save string when created

    def read(self, *size):                      # optional argument
        if not size:                            # read N bytes, or all
            res, self.text = self.text, ''
        else:
            res, self.text = self.text[:size[0]], self.text[size[0]:]
        return res

    def readline(self):
        eoln = string.find(self.text, '\n')
        if eoln == -1:
            res, self.text = self.text, ''
        else:
            res, self.text = self.text[:eoln+1], self.text[eoln+1:]
        return res


class Output:                                   # simulated output file
    def __init__(self):
        self.text = ''                          # empty string when created

    def write(self, string):                    # add a string of bytes
        self.text = self.text + string

    def writelines(self, lines):
        for line in lines: self.write(line)


def redirect(input, function, args):            # redirect stdin/out
    std_streams = sys.stdin, sys.stdout         # run a function object
    sys.stdin   = Input(input)                  # return stdout text
    sys.stdout  = Output()
```

*Example 2-8: File: redirect.py (continued)*

```
try:
    apply(function, args)
except:
    sys.stderr.write('error in function! ')
    sys.stderr.write(`sys.exc_type` + ',' + `sys.exc_value` + '\n')
result = sys.stdout.text
sys.stdin, sys.stdout = std_streams
return result
```

This module defines two classes and a function. *Input* and *Output* instances can be read and written just like normal external files. The result of a *redirect* call is the text written to the standard output stream, during a call to the passed-in function. Some file methods are omitted here: "readlines," "flush," etc.; a more complete version appears later. This module uses ideas we'll explore later:

*Tuple packing*
: Multiple assignment form: "`name1, name2 = value1, value2`" pairs targets on the left of = with values on the right. *std_streams* becomes a two-item tuple.

*Slicing*
: Slices extract sections of sequences: "`string[low:high]`" fetches items *low* through *high-1* from *string*. If missing, slice limits default to zero and the object's length.

*Exceptions*
: The *try* statement catches exceptions raised by the system or a *raise* statement. Exceptions are roughly like higher-level versions of C's *setjmp/longjmp*.

Let's test this module from Python's interactive command-line, by typing a function that reads lines from standard input, and writes a message to standard output. In the following, function *seuss* is run interactively, and then with streams redirected to objects. Messages are built up using + and `*`, to concatenate and repeat strings; like slicing, both work on any sequence object (strings, lists, etc.).

```
% python
>>> def seuss(letter, repeat):
...     line = '=>'
...     while 1:
...         next = raw_input('Word? ')           # read from stdin
...         if not next:
...             break
...         else:
...             line = line + ' ' + next
...     print line + (', ' + letter) * repeat    # write to stdout
...
>>> seuss('Z', 3)
Word? Zizzer
Word? Zazzer
```

```
Word? Zuzz
Word?
=> Zizzer Zazzer Zuzz, Z, Z, Z
>>>
>>> import redirect
>>> output = redirect.redirect("Zizzer\nZazzer\nZuzz\n\n", seuss, ("Z!", 3))
>>> output
'Word? Word? Word? Word? => Zizzer Zazzer Zuzz, Z!, Z!, Z!\012'
```

Again, we'll study the details in this code later. For the moment, simply note that Python's object-oriented nature makes it easy to change fundamental parts of the language. In this example, we are able to alter the behavior of the *raw_input* function and *print* statement, without changing the programs that use them. Python is extensible "to the core."

## *Python versus csh*

If you're familiar with other common UNIX shell script languages, it might be useful to see how Python compares. Here's a simple *csh* script, which mails all the files in the current directory with a suffix of *.py* (i.e., all Python source files) to a fictitious address.

```
#!/bin/csh
foreach x (*.py)
    echo $x
    mail stuff@psa.org -s $x < $x
end
```

The equivalent Python script looks similar:

```
#!/usr/local/bin/python
import os, glob
for x in glob.glob('*.py'):
    print x
    os.system("mail stuff@psa.org -s %s < %s" % (x, x))
```

but is slightly more verbose. Since Python, unlike csh, isn't meant just for shell scripts, system interfaces must be imported, and called explicitly. And since Python isn't just a string-processing language, character strings must be enclosed in quotes as in C.

Although this can add a few extra keystrokes in simple scripts like this, being a general-purpose language makes Python a better tool, once we leave the realm of trivial programs. Python scripts are also usually more portable to other platforms than csh. And like C, we don't need $ to use variables; what else would you expect in a free language?

# Graphical User Interfaces

Because of Python's rapid turnaround during development, it turns out to be an excellent tool for prototyping GUI applications. And due to Python's very high-level nature, GUI programs are surprisingly simple to write. Both of these factors support rapid GUI development; the effects of program changes can be observed almost immediately.

## "Hello GUI World"

There are a number of GUI extensions for Python, both simple and advanced: X11, MFC, Tk, WPY, wxPython, and more. An integration to the Tk GUI library (developed initially for the Tcl language) is a standard part of Python. Roughly, Tk is an abstraction of the X-Windows system, though it also runs on MS-Windows, and the Macintosh. Here's a GUI "hello world" program in Python, using the Tk interface:

*File: gui1.py*

```
from Tkinter import *
widget = Label(None, text='Hello GUI world!')
widget.pack()
widget.mainloop()
```

The *from** import statement copies over *all* the names in another module. This code simply:

- Loads a Label widget class from the *Tkinter* module
- Makes a Label object, passing a parent widget and a configuration option
- Packs (arranges) the label in its parent widget
- And starts the *Tk* event loop

Because this label isn't attached to anything specifically (its parent is *None*), it's put on a default parent window. When we call the label's *mainloop* method, a window with our message pops up on the screen; it looks like Figure 2-1.

*Figure 2-1: Hello GUI world*

This window probably isn't anything to write home about! But if you've ever written GUIs in C, using traditional window APIs like Motif, you can appreciate what's happening here: it took just four lines to build and display a completely functional window. The corresponding "hello world" GUI program in C would be much longer, and more complex. And there's no need to compile the Python code first. In fact, if we wanted to get complicated and tricky, we could write this GUI in two lines, using the dictionary-based interface that was supported in Python 1.2:

```
from Tkinter import *
Label(None, {'text': 'Hello GUI world!', Pack: {}}).mainloop()
```

or pack the widget in-place without saving it:

```
from Tkinter import *
Label(None, text='Hello GUI world!').pack()
mainloop()
```

---

*NOTE* As of Python 1.3, keyword arguments are the accepted standard for *Tkinter* coding, and the style used in this book. The older dictionary-based scheme is still supported. As we'll see, dictionaries are Python's built-in access-by-key object; keyword arguments are matched by name, not by position.

---

## *Running GUI Programs*

Like all Python code, this example could be run as an executable *script* file,

*Example 2-9: File: gui1*

```
#!/usr/local/bin/python
from Tkinter import *
widget = Label(None, text='Hello GUI world!')
widget.pack()
widget.mainloop()
```

```
% gui1
```

or put in a Python *module* file and run as a program (or imported by another module),

*Example 2-10: File: gui1.py*

```
from Tkinter import *
widget = Label(None, text='Hello GUI world!')
widget.pack()
widget.mainloop()
```

```
% python gui1.py
```

or entered interactively, at the Python interpreter's command line:

```
% python
>>> from Tkinter import *
>>> widget = Label(None, text='Hello GUI world!')
```

```
>>> widget.pack()
>>> widget.mainloop()
```

It could also be executed as a character string or a module-file reference, from inside a program written in another language (for instance, a C or C++ program). This is called *embedded* programming, which we'll look at in a moment.

## *Using Widget Frameworks*

Naturally, this example doesn't really do justice to the *Tk* interface. The *Tkinter* module defines an object-oriented framework for building GUI applications. It exports the "flat" Tk API as a set of general classes of GUI objects (usually called *widgets*), which we can specialize for our application's purposes. In effect, *Tk* becomes an object-oriented tool in Python, because Python is object-oriented.

For example, the *Frame* class serves as a container for other GUI objects. Interfaces composed of multiple widgets can be implemented as a subclass of *Frame*:

*Example 2-11: File: hello.py*

```
from Tkinter import *                    # get widget classes

class Hello(Frame):                      # subclass our GUI
    def __init__(self, master=None):     # constructor method
        Frame.__init__(self, master)
        self.pack()
        self.make_widgets()

    def make_widgets(self):              # attach a button to 'me'
        widget = Button(self, text='Hello world', command=self.quit)
        widget.pack(side=LEFT)

if __name__ == '__main__':  Hello().mainloop()
```

As mentioned earlier, inheritance is specified by listing superclasses in parentheses after a new class's name. Here, *Hello* is a specialized *Frame*. And within the class's methods, the first argument is the implied subject of the call: it is the object that's being processed. Here, *self* gets attributes from both *Hello* and *Frame*.

When a *Hello* object is created, it makes a button, and attaches it to itself (i.e., to the frame). The new *Button* object declares an action to perform when it's pressed by the user: *self.quit*, an inherited method that closes the GUI's windows. Finally, when we run this module as a program, the last line creates a *Hello* object, and calls its *mainloop* method to start catching user-generated events. We get a one-button window, shown in Figure 2-2.

```
% python hello.py
```

*Figure 2-2: Hello framework world*

## *Changing Behavior by Subclassing*

As we'll see, Python's OOP features are a natural fit for GUI development. Each screen object is modeled by a *class*, and larger interfaces are built up as *trees* of class instances. Moreover, by creating *subclasses*, we can build up complex GUI systems, which can themselves be reused, extended, and attached to other widgets. For instance, here's an extension of our *Hello* class, which adds more buttons, and redefines the *quit* method to make sure the user really wants to exit:

*Example 2-12: File: hellobye.py*

```
from Dialog  import *                     # get dialog object
from Tkinter import *                     # get Tk widgets
from hello   import Hello                 # get the 'Hello' class

class HelloGoodbye(Hello):
    def really_quit(self):
        Hello.quit(self)                  # do superclass quit

    def quit(self):                       # redefine quit here
        ans = Dialog(self,
                  title   = 'Verify exit',
                  text    = "I can't let you do that, Dave.",
                  bitmap  = 'question',
                  strings = ('Yes', 'No'), default = 1)
        if ans.num == 0:
            self.really_quit()

    def make_widgets(self):               # extend superclass method
        Hello.make_widgets(self)
        extra = Button(self, text='Goodbye', command=self.really_quit)
        extra.pack(side=RIGHT)

if __name__ == '__main__':  HelloGoodbye().mainloop()
```

Now, when we make a *HelloGoodbye* object and call its *mainloop*, we'll get a window with two buttons: one created by the *Hello* class, and one we add here in *HelloGoodbye*. Pressing the new *Goodbye* button exits the program immediately as before. But pressing the "*Hello world*" button now pops up a dialog to verify the quit operation instead of quitting directly, since we've redefined what the *quit* method does. We get the window shown in Figure 2-3.

```
% python hellobye.py
```

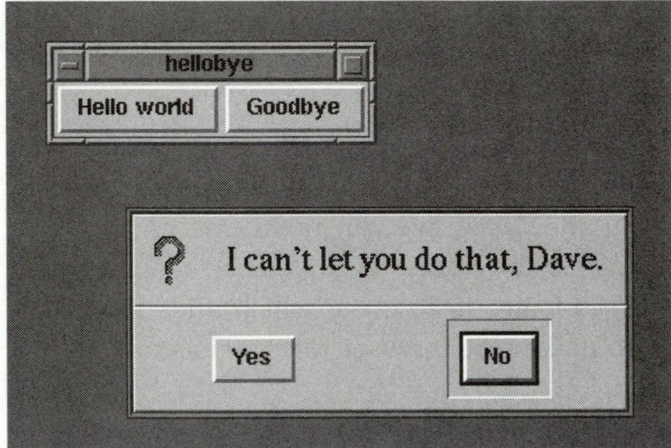


*Figure 2-3: Hello subclass world*

Later on, we'll see that the concepts in these simple examples scale up to more realistic GUI structures. The main point here is to start thinking in terms of objects, and specialization. When applied well, programming can become a simple matter of selecting existing classes, and defining how your needs differ.

# Data Structure Libraries

One way to see Python's utility as a general programming language is to look at implementations of data structures in Python. And two common examples from this domain are stacks and sets.

## Implementing Stacks Two Ways

A simple kind of object we'll use frequently later is the stack: a last-in-first-out (LIFO) list. Here's a shared stack object, implemented as a Python module:

*Example 2-13: File: stack1.py*

```
stack = []                          # when first imported

def push(object):
    global stack                    # add item to the front
    stack = [object] + stack        # use 'global' to change

def pop():
    global stack                    # remove item at front
    top, stack = stack[0], stack[1:]    # IndexError if empty
    return top
```

### *"Braces? We don't need no stinking braces!"*

By now, if your background is in languages like C or Pascal, you're probably wondering how Python knows where statements end. The short answer: in Python, blocks of code are indented under the block's header line, and statements usually end at the end of a line. Since Python is able to notice when statements end without having to be told, there's no need to type `{}`, `begin/end`, `;`, etc.

This usually seems unusual to C programmers at first glance, but most Python users come to consider it an important feature. It works well in a rapid-development language: there's less to write and read, and it makes a whole family of coding errors impossible. For example, the infamous *dangling else* problem goes away in Python. Notorious C mistakes such as:

```
if (notSafe())
    if (condition()) {
        doCautiousAction1();
        doCautiousAction2();
    }
else
    doDangerousAction();        /* paired with inner if! */
```

can't happen in Python. Since Python uses the information already conveyed by indentation, the equivalent code can never be misleading or ambiguous:

```
if notSafe():
    if condition():
        doCautiousAction1()
        doCautiousAction2()
else:
    doDangerousAction()        # matches outer if
```

In fact, Python's syntax has been called the "what you see is what you get" of programming languages. Consistent use of indentation makes code both less error-prone, and easier to read.

We'll look at how this works in more detail later. For now, keep in mind that Python is a minimalist language; its emphasis is on fast development, and its syntax is just one way it attacks this goal.

*Example 2–13: File: stack1.py (continued)*

```
def empty():                                # is the stack []?
    return not stack                        # no 'global' to access
```

This module manages a local object called *stack* (a Python list), and exports functions to operate on it. In functions, assigned names are *local* unless declared *global*; referenced names can be either. *stack* is initialized once, when the module is first imported anywhere. Every module that imports *stack1* shares the stack it manages. If instead we want to make multiple stacks, we'd probably code it as a *class*:

*Example 2-14: File: stack2.py*

```
class Stack:
    def __init__(self):                  # when instance created
        self.stack = []                  # self is the instance
    def push(self, object):
        self.stack = [object] + self.stack
    def pop(self):
        top, self.stack = self.stack[0], self.stack[1:]
        return top
    def empty(self):
        return not self.stack
```

*Stack2* also uses a Python list internally, to represent the stack. Items are added to the top of a Stack by calling its *push* method, and deleted with *pop*. To add an item to the front, we use the + operator on the current list; to delete the front item, we use the list slicing expression *[1:]* to extract all items past the first.

By implementing stacks as a class, we allow for future customization in subclasses. Moreover, we're able to make multiple, distinct stacks in client programs. Each has its own *stack* attribute, because each instance is a new "namespace." And since Python lists can contain any kind of objects, stacks can hold anything too: numbers, lists, strings, functions, and even other stacks. Unlike strongly typed languages like C or C++, there's no need for a different kind of stack for each kind of object:

```
% python
>>> from stack2 import Stack
>>> x = Stack()
>>> x.push('string')
>>> x.push(123)
>>> x.stack
[123, 'string']
>>> y = Stack()
>>> y.push(x.pop())
>>> x.stack, y.stack
(['string'], [123])
```

Here, we create a Stack instance *x*, add a string and a number, and then move the top item over to a new Stack *y*. From an abstract perspective, Figure 2-4 shows what *x* and *y* look like, as they shrink and grow.

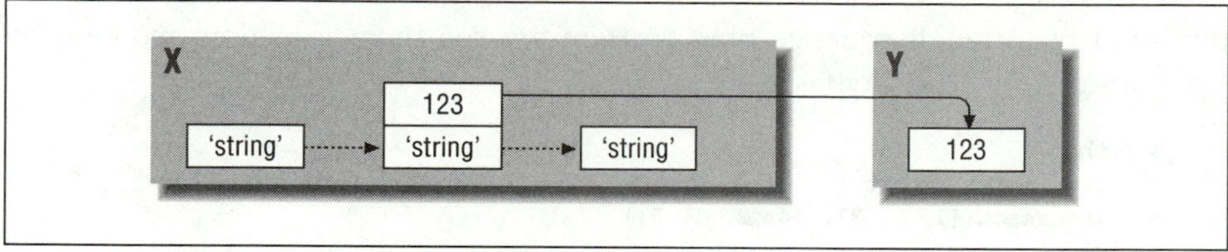


*Figure 2-4: The ups and downs of stack objects*

The stack class above uses concatenation and slicing to push and pop objects. But as we'll see, it's usually more efficient to use in-place change operations on lists; here's a variant that grows the stack at the end:

*Example 2-15: File: stack3.py*

```
class Stack:
    def __init__(self):
        self.stack = []                # initialize list
    def push(self, object):
        self.stack.append(object)      # change in-place
    def pop(self):
        top = self.stack[-1]           # top = end
        del   self.stack[-1]           # delete in-place
        return top
    def empty(self):
        return not self.stack
```

## *Implementing Sets with Operators*

Roughly, *sets* are collections of objects that support operations like *intersection*—finding items in common—and *union*—collecting items that appear in either set. There are a variety of ways to implement these operations in Python. It is straightforward to code intersection and union algorithms as functions.

*Example 2-16: File: inter.py*

```
def intersect(list1, list2):
    res = []                          # start with an empty list
    for x in list1:                   # scan the first list
        if x in list2:
            res.append(x)             # add common items to the end
    return res

def union(list1, list2):
    res = map(None, list1)            # make a copy of list1
    for x in list2:                   # add new items in list2
        if not x in res:
            res.append(x)
    return res
```

Since Python programs don't need type declarations, these functions can intersect any kind of ordered-sequence objects. Here we see them in action, working on lists, strings, and mixed-types:

```
% python
>>> from inter import *
>>> intersect([1, 2, 3], [4, 2, 1, 5])
[1, 2]
>>> intersect('abcd', 'xabyz')
['a', 'b']
>>> union([1,2,3], (1,4))
[1, 2, 3, 4]
```

But it would really be more in the Python way of thinking to implement sets as a class. This allows us to use object-oriented-programming features to hide implementation details, overload expression operators to work on sets, and support future customizations. In other words, classes let us implement new object types:

*Example 2-17: File: set.py*

```
class Set:
    def __init__(self, value = []):        # on object creation
        self.data = []                     # manages a local list
        self.concat(value)

    def intersect(self, other):            # other is any sequence type
        res = []                           # self is the instance subject
        for x in self.data:
            if x in other:
                res.append(x)
        return Set(res)                    # return a new Set

    def union(self, other):
        res = self.data[:]                 # make a copy of my list
        for x in other:
            if not x in res:
                res.append(x)
        return Set(res)

    def concat(self, value):               # value: a list, string, Set...
        for x in value:
           if not x in self.data:
                self.data.append(x)

    def __len__(self):            return len(self.data)
    def __getitem__(self, key): return self.data[key]
    def __and__(self, other):     return self.intersect(other)
    def __or__(self, other):      return self.union(other)
    def __repr__(self):           return '<Set:' + `self.data` + '>'
```

This module defines a *Set* type that can hold any kind of objects; even objects of different types. It provides intersection, union, and concatenation methods. It also provides a few specially named methods to overload (intercept) Python operations, when applied to Sets:

*Table 2-1: Special method names*

| Method | Operation | Called for . . . |
|---|---|---|
| `__init__` | Constructor | Creation of a new instance: *Set ()* |
| `__len__` | Length | The "len" function, and truth testing (empty means "false") |
| `__getitem__` | Indexing | Iteration (*for*), membership tests (*in*), and *[i]* indexing |
| `__and__` | Operator & | Sets used in & expressions |
| `__or__` | Operator \| | Sets used in \| expressions |
| `__repr__` | Printing | Print statements, and other conversions to strings (`set`) |

By defining these methods, *Set* instances participate in Python's object model. They respond to all the operations mentioned in this table, as though they were built-in types. As we'll see later, Python provides special method "hooks" for most operations in the language. A more complete set class would include other operator overloads, and more primitive operation methods. Here's how this *Set* class is used:

```
% python
>>> from set import Set
>>> users1 = Set(['Bob', 'Emily', 'Howard'])
>>> users2 = Set(['Jerry', 'Howard', 'Carol'])
>>> read, write = users1 | users2, users1 & users2
>>> print write, read
<Set:['Howard']> <Set:['Bob', 'Emily', 'Howard', 'Jerry', 'Carol']>
```

We make two sets of users, for computing access permissions. The & and | operators trigger the Set's intersect and union methods. Sets can also be used like normal lists: they can be indexed, iterated over, etc. In fact, to their clients, Set objects look like built-in collections:

```
>>> for name in users1: print name,
...
Bob Emily Howard
>>> for i in range(len(users1)): print users1[i],
...
Bob Emily Howard
```

Here, the first *for* loop uses Set's `__getitem__` method, and the second uses Set length and indexing; *range* generates a list of integers that we can iterate over in counter loops. The Set class also takes care to filter out duplicate items, following the mathematical definition:

```
>>> bobs = Set(['Bob', 'Bob', 'Bob'])
>>> print users1 & bobs, users1 | bobs
<Set:['Bob']> <Set:['Bob', 'Emily', 'Howard']>
>>> users1.concat(bobs)
>>> users1
<Set:['Bob', 'Emily', 'Howard']>
>>> users1.data
['Bob', 'Emily', 'Howard']
```

## *Optimizing Sets with Dictionaries*

One problem with this *set* implementation is that it becomes pathologically slow for larger sets, because it uses linear lists (the items in square brackets) to represent sets, and linear scans to look for items. An easy way to optimize sets is by using Python dictionaries, which are associative arrays, implemented with fast hash tables. Here's a specialization (subclass) of Set which does just that.

*Example 2-18: File: fastset.py*

```
import set                                  # fastset.Set extends set.Set
class Set(set.Set):
    def __init__(self, value = []):
        self.data = {}                      # manages a local dictionary
        self.concat(value)                  # hashing: linear search times

    def intersect(self, other):
        res = {}
        for x in other:
            if self.data.has_key(x):
                res[x] = None
        return Set(res.keys())              # a new dictionary-based set

    def union(self, other):
        res = {}
        for x in other:                     # scan each set just once
            res[x] = None
        for x in self.data.keys():
            res[x] = None
        return Set(res.keys())

    def concat(self, value):
        for x in value: self.data[x] = None

    # inherit and, or, len
    def __getitem__(self, key):  return self.data.keys()[key]
    def __repr__(self):          return '<Set:' + `self.data.keys()` + '>'
```

This set behaves like the original, except that intersection and union are faster, and items aren't stored in the same order (dictionaries are unordered). Python dictionaries grow on demand, and allow most types of objects to be used as *keys*—

identifiers used to store and fetch values. *fastset.Set* keeps a dictionary of values, but only uses their keys; the dictionary values are always empty, so we set them to *None.*

Because the two set classes have distinct strengths, both are called *Set,* but they're implemented in different module files. Set users can switch between set variants by simply changing the module name in their import statements. *fastset.Set* redefines everything except the *set.Set*'s `&`, `|`, and length operation-overload methods; given a more complete *Set* base class, *fastset.Set* might inherit more. Here's *fastset* at work:

```
% python
>>> from fastset import Set
>>> users1 = Set(['Bob', 'Emily', 'Howard'])
>>> users2 = Set(['Jerry', 'Howard', 'Carol'])
>>> read, write = users1 | users2, users1 & users2
>>> print write, read
<Set:['Howard']> <Set:['Jerry', 'Carol', 'Howard', 'Emily', 'Bob']>
>>> users1.data
{'Howard': None, 'Emily': None, 'Bob': None}
```

For maximum performance, we could also move the set type to a C language implementation, using an extension module. As we'll see later, Python lets C extension types overload operations too, using a convention similar to special method names in classes.

But because the set class hides implementation details, in both cases we're safe: we don't have to change code that uses sets, if they only use set methods and operators. As long as the methods and operators stay the same, set clients can remain happily ignorant of how they work. This is just another instance of encapsulation at work. In Python, it's a convention: we were able to access the *users1.data* member above, but it shouldn't be changed outside the class (unless supported).

## *Searching Graphs of Objects*

The next two examples are aimed at the more mathematically minded readers. Here's a Python program that finds paths through a cyclic graph of objects. The graph is represented as a set of class-instances, which embed other class-instances. Each node has an *arcs* attribute that holds a list of accessible nodes, visited by *generate.* In effect, Graph objects "know" how to search their own arcs.

*Example 2-19: File: graph.py*

```
class Graph:
    def __init__(self, label):
        self.name = label
        self.arcs = []
```

### *"I knew C++. I used C++. Python's no C++."*

C++ users may have already guessed this: in Python classes, data-members and methods are all *virtual* and *public* in the C++ sense. This policy makes sense in a rapid-development language like Python; it's simpler, and there's no extra syntax.

Many of the concepts in C++ either aren't needed, or have simpler analogues in Python. For instance, "members" and "methods" are both just attributes. And method-references (both with and without a "self") are first-class objects. As we'll see, by providing classes in a simple dynamic language, Python makes OOP easy to apply. For readers interested in digging a bit deeper, Appendix F compares Python and C++ classes in more detail.

*Example 2-19: File: graph.py (continued)*

```
    def __repr__(self):
        return self.name

    def search(self, goal):
        Graph.solns = []
        self.generate([self], goal)
        Graph.solns.sort(lambda x,y: cmp(len(x), len(y)))
        return Graph.solns

    def generate(self, path, goal):
        if self == goal:
            self.solns.append(path)
        else:
            for arc in self.arcs:
                if arc not in path:
                    arc.generate(path + [arc], goal)

if __name__ == '__main__':
    S = Graph('s')
    P = Graph('p')
    A = Graph('a')          # make nodes
    M = Graph('m')

    S.arcs = [P, M]         # S leads to P and M
    P.arcs = [S, M, A]      # arcs: embedded objects
    A.arcs = [M]
    print S.search(M)       # find paths from S to M
```

The *generate* method performs a depth-first, left-to-right search, and traps cycles by keeping track of the "path-so-far" so it can avoid visiting a node twice. The "search" method is the top-level entry: it sorts the solutions list by increasing path length, using the built in list *sort* method. Notice the *solns* member here; it's a class attribute, shared by all instances of the class (much like C++ "static" data-members). Figure 2-5 shows the graph constructed by *graph.py*.

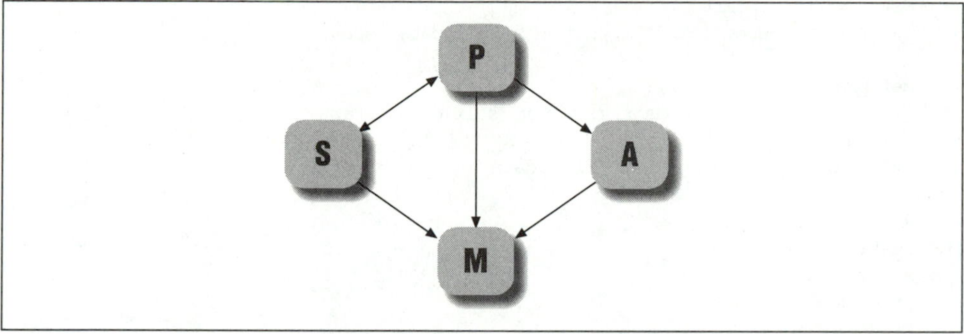


*Figure 2–5: A graph of spam*

When we run this module as a script, its self-test code (at the bottom) builds the object-graph in this figure, and reports all paths from *S* to *M* sorted by path length. Naturally, this is a simple test; but the idea of representing problems as graphs applies to a variety of domains. Later in the book we'll expand the graph-searcher to support user interaction when each solution is found.

```
% python graph.py
[[s, m], [s, p, m], [s, p, a, m]]
```

## *Fun with Vectors!*

Finally, another way operator-overloading may be used: a *Vector* implements operators (+, *), methods (*sum*, *prod*), and type operations (construction, printing). The operators apply a value to each item in the vector, and the methods collapse the vector's items into a single value.

*Example 2–20: File: vector.py*

```
class Vector:
    def __init__(self, start=[]):
        self.data = start

    def __add__(self, value):
        res = []
        for x in self.data: res.append(x + value)
        return Vector(res)
    __radd__ = __add__

    def __mul__(self, value):
        res = []
        for x in self.data: res.append(x * value)
        return Vector(res)
```

*Example 2-20: File: vector.py (continued)*

```
    __rmul__ = __mul__

    def sum(self, start=0):
        return reduce(lambda x,y: x + y, self.data, start)

    def prod(self, start=1):
        return reduce(lambda x,y: x * y, self.data, start)

    def __repr__(self): return 'self.data'


def test():
    x = Vector([2, 4, 6])
    print x + 3, 3 + x
    print x * 4, 4 * x
    print x.sum(), x.prod()

    y = Vector([1, 2, 3])
    print x + y
    print x * y
    print x * y * 2
    print x * y * x

if __name__ == '__main__': test()   # run my self-test code
```

The *sum* and *prod* methods use Python's *lambda* expression to generate anonymous functions, to be called by the *reduce* built-in function. Because *vector* defines right-side variants for the + and * operator methods, vector objects can be used as right-operands in mixed-type expressions:

*Table 2-2: Right-side operator methods*

| Method | Called for types . . . |
|---|---|
| __add__ | Vector + *any-value* |
| __radd__ | *non-vector* + Vector |
| __mul__ | Vector * *any-value* |
| __rmul__ | *non-vector* * Vector |

Python also provides a type-coercion hook; we'll learn more about mixed-type expressions later in the book. When we run the vector module as a top-level program, its self-test code is executed:

```
% python vector.py
[5, 7, 9] [5, 7, 9]
[8, 16, 24] [8, 16, 24]
12 48
[[3, 4, 5], [5, 6, 7], [7, 8, 9]]
[[2, 4, 6], [4, 8, 12], [6, 12, 18]]
```

```
[[4, 8, 12], [8, 16, 24], [12, 24, 36]]
[[[4, 8, 12], [8, 16, 24], [12, 24, 36]], [[8, 16, 24], [16, 32, 48], [24, 48,
72]], [[12, 24, 36], [24, 48, 72], [36, 72, 108]]]
```

Most of these results are straightforward. But notice what happens when adding or multiplying two vectors (`x+y`, `x*y`): as defined here, these operations generate a Vector of nested Vectors, rather than applying operators to parallel items. For `x*y`, the `__mul__` method iterates over the items in `x`, triggering a call to `__rmul__` for `y` at each step, which produces a nested Vector.

The last test is more complex (and probably belongs in the realm of unnecessarily cruel exam questions! :-) Roughly, `x*y*x` triggers recursive `__mul__` calls until we have a nonvector on the left; `__rmul__` generates an inner Vector, and the recursive `__mul__` calls collect the results.

The point to notice here is that Python classes can be a powerful way to implement object behavior. In this case, the class defines a semantics for arbitrarily dimensioned vectors. And here again, because of Python's orthogonal design Vectors can contain any object that supports the operators `+` and `*`. This includes numbers, strings, lists, instances of user-defined classes, and even extension types implemented in C.

# *Persistent Information*

Some of the database interfaces that have been developed for Python show just how far its integration tools can take us. For example, Python users have access to SQL-based relational databases, such as the public-domain *Postgres95* and *mSQL* packages, and commercial systems like *Oracle* and *Sybase*.

## *Using dbm Files*

For simpler persistent information, Python provides a variety of tools. Besides normal "flat" files, the built-in interface to the *dbm* library is one of the easiest ways to save information in Python. *dbm* is a relatively standard, hashed-file implementation: data is stored and retrieved by string keys. But in Python, *dbm* files behave exactly like normal in-memory *dictionaries* (associative arrays):

- Indexing by key fetches data from the file.
- Assigning to an index stores data in the file.

Further, *dbm* file objects support normal dictionary methods. The library itself is hidden behind this simple model. Let's create a *dbm* file interactively, to show how the interface works:

```
% python
>>> import anydbm                           get interface: dbm, gdbm, ndbm,..
>>> file = anydbm.open('movie', 'c')        make a dbm file called 'movie'
```

## *The meaning of life (without declarations)*

If you're familiar with compiled languages like Pascal or C, you may be wondering how Python can get by without data-type declarations. In Python, nothing has a predeclared type or size, and there's no need to mark variables syntactically to designate the kind of objects they can contain. Python keeps track of each object's type for you.

In technical terms, Python is a *dynamically typed* language: everything is an object, and a variable is just a name bound to an object. Variables are created when first assigned, and objects come into existence when they are used. Moreover, Python compound data types are heterogeneous, nestable, and are automatically reclaimed ("garbage-collected") when no longer needed.

Dynamic typing is a crucial feature in a rapid-development language: it reduces both the size and complexity of programs. In fact, the lack of type declarations is one of the main factors behind Python's flexibility. For instance, in many of the examples we've seen, a single data structure implementation can be used to hold any type of object. We usually only need to code a tool in Python once, to support a wide variety of objects.

Dynamic-typing shifts some errors from compile-time to run-time; but as we'll see, Python also makes finding and fixing errors fast. By eliminating memory layout and management chores, it's another way that Python optimizes speed-of-development.

```
>>> file['Batman'] = 'Pow!'          store a string under key 'Batman'
>>> file.keys()                      get the file's key directory
['Batman']
>>> file['Batman']                   fetch value for key 'Batman'
'Pow!'
>>> who  = ['Robin', 'Cat-woman', 'Joker']
>>> what = ['Bang!', 'Splat!', 'Wham!']
>>> for i in range(len(who)):
...     file[who[i]] = what[i]       add 3 more 'records'
...
>>> file.keys()
['Joker', 'Robin', 'Cat-woman', 'Batman']
>>> len(file), file.has_key('Robin'), file['Joker']
(4, 1, 'Wham!')
```

*NOTE* When the new *dbm* file is opened, *dbm* creates one or more external files, with a name that starts with the string *movie.* The examples here were tested using a version of *gdbm.* This writes two files, *movie.dir* and *movie.pag,* when a *dbm* file called *movie* is made. You normally don't need to care (unless you delete the files!)

In effect, the dictionary we're calling *file* here, is mapped to an external *dbm* file, called *movie*. Unlike normal dictionaries, the contents of *file* are retained between Python program runs. If we come back later and restart Python, our dictionary is still available; DBM files are like dictionaries that must be opened:

```
% python
>>> import anydbm
>>> file = anydbm.open('movie', 'c') open existing dbm file
>>> file['Batman']
'Pow!'
>>> file.keys()
['Joker', 'Robin', 'Cat-woman', 'Batman']
>>> for key in file.keys(): print key, file[key]
...
Joker Wham!
Robin Bang!
Cat-woman Splat!
Batman Pow!
>>> file['Batman'] = 'Ka-Boom!'     change Batman slot
>>> del file['Robin']               delete the Robin entry
```

Apart from having to import the interface and open the DBM file, Python programs don't have to know anything about DBM itself (its functions, constants, etc.). Even though *dbm* is a flat function library, DBM files look like normal Python dictionaries, stored on external files. We'll see how this integration is achieved later. As you'd expect, changes to *dbm* objects are retained indefinitely:

```
% python
>>> import anydbm                  open dbm file again
>>> file = anydbm.open('movie', 'c')
>>> for key in file.keys(): print key, file[key]
...
Joker Wham!
Cat-woman Splat!
Batman Ka-Boom!
```

## *Persistent Python Objects*

Some applications can get by with *dbm*'s simple key/value storage model. For others, we need more: *dbm* requires both keys and stored values to be character strings. We could convert values to strings manually, but this is becomes inconvenient for complex objects (class instances, large data structures, etc.). What we'd really like to have is a way to store arbitrary Python objects away, and recall them later by key.

This is where Python's *persistent object* facility comes in handy. The built-in *pickle* module converts arbitrary Python objects to character-streams, and the built-in *shelve* module writes the streams to dbm files by key. Both are external to the objects they store.

## *"Standing on the shoulders of giants"*

Strictly speaking, *dbm* isn't part of Python. Python supports the common *dbm* variants (*dbm, gdbm, ndbm*), by providing built-in *interface modules.* But like Tk, *dbm* itself is a separate library, and must be linked in to be used.

One of the main ideas behind Python is its role as an integration vehicle: a sort of "clearinghouse" for other tools. While Python can make such tools easier to use, we should give credit where credit is due. For example, many people worked on *dbm*, and the base Tk API was invented by John Ousterhout, father of the Tcl language. Tk is moving further away from its *Tcl* heritage all the time, but it's not a Python invention.

Along the way, I'll point out tools we use that are external to Python. Of course there are limits to this; anyone remember who invented text files?

Let's step through a few Python sessions, to see how this works. This time, we'll use test programs, instead of interpreter interaction. First, we'll need a class for describing objects we want to put in a shelve. Any kind of object can be put in a shelve (lists, dictionaries, etc.), but classes are sometimes more flexible.

*Example 2-21: File: person.py*

```
# a person object: fields + behavior
# class defined at outer level of file

class Person:
    def __init__(self, name = '', job = '', pay = 0):
        self.name = name
        self.job  = job
        self.pay  = pay                 # real instance data

    def tax(self):
        return self.pay * 0.25          # computed on demand

    def info(self):
        return self.name, self.job, self.pay, self.tax()
```

There's nothing special about this class. Almost any class can be used for persistence, as long as it appears at the top level of a module file, and all its constructor arguments are optional (this last rule can be relaxed). Our first test program makes instances of this class as usual, and inspects them by accessing methods and members. But it also makes the instances persistent, by assigning them to keys in a new shelve.

*Example 2-22: File: session1.py*

```
# session-1: make objects, store in shelve

from person import Person                         # get original Person class
jerry = Person('jerry', 'dentist', 50000)         # make 3 new objects
bob   = Person('bob', 'psychologist', 70000)
emily = Person('emily', 'teacher', 40000)

# extra info for bob and emily
emily.age     = (35, 40)                             # nested tuple (range)
bob.friends = [Person('howard'), Person('peeper')]   # nested objects list

# inspect in-memory objects
print bob
print bob.info()                      # tuple: name, job, pay, tax
print emily.age, emily.tax()
print bob.friends[0].info()           # access nested objects

# put them in a shelve
import shelve                         # get persistence interface
dbase = shelve.open('cast')           # make a shelve (dbm) file called 'cast'
for obj in (bob, emily, jerry):       # pickle objects to shelve
    dbase[obj.name] = obj             # use their names as file keys
```

Here, *bob* and *emily* have extra fields that reference compound data (a tuple, and a list); *bob* even owns two nested *Person* objects. Python's pickler serializes trees of objects automatically. It handles nested objects, multiple appearances of the same object, and circular references. When we run this file:

```
% python session1.py
<Person instance at e0bb0>
('bob', 'psychologist', 70000, 17500.0)
(35, 40) 10000.0
('howard', '', 0, 0.0)
```

we create a persistent shelve. Like simple *dbm* files, objects are stored in a shelve by assigning to keys. But in shelves, values stored can be arbitrary objects, not just strings. By assigning the three objects to keys in the shelve, we create a persistent-object store that endures beyond this Python session, as we see in Figure 2-6.

After we've run the test file above, the *dbm* file *cast* becomes an external database of persistent Python objects; we can use it later, as though it were an in-memory dictionary. Let's run a second test program to open the shelve, and fetch our objects back into memory. The *shelve* interface is identical to the *dbm* examples we saw earlier: key assignments store objects, and key references fetch them back.

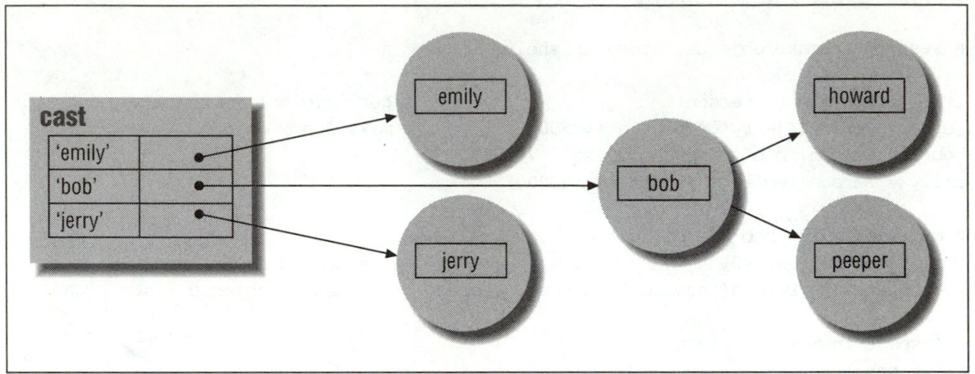


*Figure 2-6: A shelve of persistent friends*

*Example 2-23: File: session2.py*

```
# session-2: fetch objects from shelve

import shelve
dbase = shelve.open('cast')           # reopen shelve file, same class
print dbase.keys()                    # no need to import class here

bob = dbase['bob']                    # fetch bob from shelve
print bob
for who in bob.friends:               # nested objects
    print who.name, who.info()
print bob.info()                      # name, job, pay, tax

print dbase['emily'].info()           # fetch emily
for key in dbase.keys():
    obj = dbase[key]                  # fetch objects by key
    print obj.name, obj.tax()         # tax is a called method here
```

Here is *session2*'s output:

```
% python session2.py
['emily', 'bob', 'jerry']
<Person instance at e08d0>
howard ('howard', '', 0, 0.0)
peeper ('peeper', '', 0, 0.0)
('bob', 'psychologist', 70000, 17500.0)
('emily', 'teacher', 40000, 10000.0)
emily 10000.0
bob 17500.0
jerry 12500.0
```

### *Pickles without shelves*

Shelves can be thought of as *dbm* files that serialize ("pickle") stored values: values may be arbitrary objects, but keys must still be strings. Shelves require some flavor of *dbm* to be installed. If you don't have access to the *dbm* extension, it's still possible to use persistent objects in Python: the *pickle* module provides an interface for saving objects to normal, "flat" files. As we'll see, if we save and restore a complete dictionary in this way, we can get the same sort of functionality, without using *shelve* and *dbm*. And with Python's RPC or socket-based tools, we can even send pickled objects across a network.

## *Changing Persistent Object Behavior*

One of the nice things about Python's persistence system is that we can change behavior by changing classes, without having to convert stored information. Here's why this is so:

- When a class instance is stored in a shelve, Python saves its data members, but not its class.
- When the object is later fetched, Python reimports the class to recreate the instance.

Because the class is external to stored objects, we can usually change the methods of a class without affecting instances in a shelve. To see how this works, let's change the *Person* class to the version below.

*Example 2-24: File: person.py (from person2.py)*

```
# an enhanced person class
# may be used with previously-stored Person objects

class Person:
    def __init__(self, name = '', job = '', pay = 0):
        self.name = name
        self.job  = job
        self.pay  = pay                      # real instance data

    def __getattr__(self, name):             # on undefined names
        if name == 'tax':
            return self.pay * .30            # a computed member
        else:
            raise AttributeError             # others are errors

    def __repr__(self):                      # for printing myself
        return 'Person=>%s' % self.name
```

*Example 2-24: File: person.py (from person2.py) (continued)*

```
    def basic(self):
        return self.name, self.job, self.pay, self.tax

    def extra(self):                        # collect unique members
        result = []
        for field in self.__dict__.keys():
            if field not in ['name', 'job', 'pay']:
                result.append((field, getattr(self,field)))
        return result

    def info(self): return self.basic(), self.extra()
```

The special __getattr__ method here intercepts undefined attribute references; *Person* uses this hook to make *tax* look like a real data member. If we put this module file in the same directory as the original version, objects we fetch from the shelve become instances of the new class, and take on all its extended behavior. To illustrate, let's run one last test program; it's nearly the same as the second.

*Example 2-25: File: session3.py*

```
# session-3: use the new Person class
import shelve
dbase = shelve.open('cast')          # reopen shelve file
print dbase.keys()                   # uses new Person definition

bob = dbase['bob']                   # refetch bob
print bob                            # new class's __repr__
for who in bob.friends:
    print who, who.info()            # new extra fields list
print bob.info()                     # new tax-rate applied

print dbase['emily'].info()          # refetch emily
for key in dbase.keys():
    obj = dbase[key]                 # refetch objects by key
    print obj, obj.tax               # new tax is a computed member now
```

*session3* is run as follows:

```
% cp person2.py person.py
% python session3.py
['emily', 'bob', 'jerry']
Person=>bob
Person=>howard (('howard', '', 0, 0.0), [])
Person=>peeper (('peeper', '', 0, 0.0), [])
(('bob', 'psychologist', 70000, 21000.0), [('friends', [Person=>howard,
Person=>peeper])])
(('emily', 'teacher', 40000, 12000.0), [('age', (35, 40))])
Person=>emily 12000.0
Person=>bob 21000.0
Person=>jerry 15000.0
```

This time, *Person* objects are printed with the new `__repr__` format, *tax* is a data-member (not a called method), everyone's taxes were raised, and *info* calls show unique fields collected by the new *extra* method. All these differences reflect changes in the *Person* class, not the stored instances.

Under Python's persistence system, classes subsume both records and traditional programs. We create databases of arbitrary Python objects, using normal Python syntax: there's no need to map to and from a database *record* form. And since shelves act like normal dictionaries, systems can be prototyped with dictionaries, and converted to use shelves for delivery by adding a *shelve.open* call.

By some criteria, "pickling" isn't quite a full-blown persistence system. As we'll see, objects lose their link to the shelve once they are fetched, and must be stored explicitly after modifications. Moreover, we may get multiple copies of an object, if it appears in more than one *shelve* entry. The pickler has hooks that allow such limitations to be overcome with support code. In fact, pickling can be used as the basis for more advanced Object-oriented database (OODB) features. But for many tasks, a simple shelve of pickled Python objects is all we need.

# *Processing Text-Based Information*

In one form or another, text processing seems to be a pervasive task in most domains. For instance:

*Shell tools*
: Extracting information from system configuration files

*Internet scripts*
: Parsing information in input data streams

*Programming aids*
: Finding patterns in source-code and output files

to name a few. If you've ever used C to extract information from text files, you probably know how tedious such programs can be to write. In Python, there are a variety of tools for automating these tasks.

## *Splitting and Joining Strings*

The built-in *string* module exports functions for splitting strings into a list of substrings, around a "token." In many cases, this simple idea is all we need to extract information from text. To illustrate, here's a script that finds C source files that use any of the *#define* constants in a C header file. It uses the *string.split* built-in to chop each line into a list of substrings, around whitespace delimiters (spaces and tabs).

### *What Python means by "dynamic"*

In *session1.py*, we added new data members to instances of the *Person* class, outside the class itself. *bob*, *emily*, and *jerry* all have data-members called *name*, *job*, and *pay*, since the class constructor method (`__init__`) always assigns these. But *bob* has an extra *friends* member, and *emily* has an extra *age*. The new Person's *extra* method collects these unique members.

Python allows attributes to be added to objects on the fly, by assigning values to them, just as variables are created when first assigned; there's no need to declare class members either. Usually, the class itself creates members, by assigning them to *self* in its methods. But it's just as easy to create new attributes outside the class.

This might be surprising, if you're used to static languages like C++. But in Python, a class instance is, more or less, just a new dictionary with inheritance links. We make use of this in the extra method of the enhanced Person class: by fetching the instance's built-in `__dict__` attribute (*self.__dict__*), we can use its attribute dictionary explicitly.

Creating members of class instances at run-time may not be appropriate for languages like C++, used for large, multi programmer development efforts. But the extra flexibility makes sense in a rapid-development language like Python. It's useful here as a sort of "property-list" for people in our database. In typical Python development, the fewer language restrictions we have to deal with the better.

*Example 2-26: File: finder1.py*

```
#!/usr/local/bin/python
import string, glob, os, sys
try:
    srcdir = sys.argv[1]          # optional arg = directory
except:                           # scan C header, grep for constants
    srcdir = '.'
header = '/usr/local/include/Py/rename2.h'

for line in open(header, 'r').readlines():                # for all lines
    if line[:7] == '#define':                             # starts with '#define'?
        oldname = string.split(line)[1]                   # get word after #define
        print oldname
        for source in glob.glob(srcdir + '/*.[ch]'):      # for all ".c"/".h" files
            print source
            print os.popen('grep -w -n %s %s' % (oldname, source)).read()
print 'done.'
```

This script works by running the *grep* command-line program on all C files in a directory, for each constant in the C header file. It uses the *os.popen* built-in to capture and print the output of the *grep* shell command. We could also use *os.system* to run *grep*, but its output might not intermix with our script's as expected, if "stdout" is redirected to a file (*grep* runs as a separate process).

Using the search script beats running *grep* by hand for each `#define` in a header. But the algorithm is inefficient if there are many `#defines` in the header-file: it would be better to run *grep* on each file just once. We'll see a better version later in the book.

Another common use for string splitting is processing files by columns. Suppose we have a text file, with numbers arranged in columns in each line, separated by spaces and/or tabs:

*Example 2-27: File: table1.txt*

```
1       5       10    2   1.0
2       10      20    4   2.0
3       15      30    8    3
4       20      40   16   4.0
```

It's easy to sum this file's columns: we scan the file, splitting each line around spaces and tabs, and adding its values to a list of accumulators. This script does the job:

*Example 2-28: File: summer.py*

```
import string, sys

def summer(numCols, fileName):
    sums = [0] * numCols                              # make list of zeros
    for line in open(fileName, 'r').readlines():      # scan file's lines
        cols = string.split(line)                     # split up columns
        for i in range(numCols):                      # around blanks/tabs
            sums[i] = sums[i] + eval(cols[i])         # add numbers to sums
    return sums

if __name__ == '__main__':
    print summer(eval(sys.argv[1]), sys.argv[2])      # '% summer.py cols file'
```

When we run this module as a top-level script, it prints the sums for each column; we could also import the module, and call *summer* from another program. To show that Python is not just for UNIX developers, here's what happens when the script is run from an MS-DOS command line under Windows:

```
C:\stuff>python summer.py 5 table1.txt
[10, 50, 100, 30, 10.0]
```

Notice that this script uses the built-in *eval* function to convert strings to numbers. As we'll see, *eval* is more powerful than shown here. In fact, *eval* can execute an arbitrary Python expression string at run-time. For example, a file processed by *summer* can hold columns of Python expressions, not just numbers:

*Example 2-29: File: table2.txt*

```
2     1+1          1<<1          eval("2")
16    2*2*2*2      pow(2,4)      16.0
3     len('abc')   [1,2,3][2]    {'spam':3}['spam']
```

```
C:\stuff>python summer.py 4 table2.txt
[21, 21, 21, 21.0]
```

In effect, *table2.txt* is a file of Python program snippets, executed by another Python program. *eval* (and its cousin for statements *exec*) calls the Python compiler/interpreter at run-time.

As is, expressions in this file can't have embedded spaces (since they're separators), and there's not much support for variables. As we'll see later in the book, variables can be used in dynamically constructed code like this, if we pass in namespace dictionaries. And to allow embedded spaces, we could separate columns by an illegal Python character (say, `$`) instead of whitespace, and split lines on that character instead.

The *string.splitfields* function lets us select a specific separator like `$`. Python also provides inverse operations for joining substrings into a whole. In fact, the combination of splitting and joining strings can be surprisingly powerful:

*Example 2-30: File: replace.py*

```
import string
def replace(str, old, new):                  # global substitution
    list = string.splitfields(str, old)      # split around old's
    return string.joinfields(list, new)      # rejoin, inserting new's
```

This *replace* function can be used like this:

```
% python
>>> from replace import replace
>>> replace("A$B$(C + 1)$D * 2", "$", "..")
'A..B..(C + 1)..D * 2'
>>> replace("foo = foo+1", "foo", "spam")
'spam = spam+1'
```

## *Matching Regular Expressions*

Naturally, chopping strings up into pieces only takes us so far. For instance, *finder1* works for typical lines, but fails if there are any intervening spaces between `#` and `define`. To handle more general text processing requirements,

Python has a built-in regular expression module called *regex*, which provides the sort of pattern-matching found in languages like Perl and *awk*, and text editors like Emacs.

Python's *regex* allows expressions to be precompiled, and lets us extract matched substrings after a successful search. To show how the interface works, here's an example that searches for **#define** and **#include** lines in C header files, using regular expressions. By default, *regex* uses the Emacs-style syntax used in this script, but can be configured to accept a variety of standard regular expression syntaxes.

*Example 2-31: File: cheader1.py*

```
#! /usr/local/bin/python
import sys, regex
from string import strip

pattDefine = regex.compile(
    '^#[\t ]*define[\t ]+\([a-zA-Z0-9_]+\)[\t ]*')

pattInclude = regex.compile(
    '^#[\t ]*include[\t ]+[<"]\([a-zA-Z0-9_/\.]+\)')

def scan(file):
    count = 0
    while 1:                                    # scan line-by-line
        line = file.readline()
        if not line: break
        count = count + 1
        n = pattDefine.match(line)              # save length-of-match
        if n >= 0:
            name = pattDefine.group(1)          # substring for \(...\)
            body = line[n:]
            print count, name, '=', strip(body)
        elif pattInclude.match(line) >= 0:
            regs = pattInclude.regs             # start/stop indexes
            a, b = regs[1]                      # of first \(...\) group
            filename = line[a:b]                # slice out of line
            print count, 'include', filename

if len(sys.argv) == 1:
    scan(sys.stdin)                     # no args: read stdin
else:
    scan(open(sys.argv[1], 'r'))        # arg: input file name
```

This script looks for lines in the input file that match one of the two regular expression patterns. Compiling a pattern creates a regular-expression *object*. When a match is found, the substring matched by a nested pattern (inside "\(. . . \)" delimiters) can be fetched by calling the expression object's *group* method, or by using its *regs* attribute to get the substring's start/stop indexes in the line.

By using regular expressions, this script accommodates unusual yet legal lines that the string-splitting example can't. For example, suppose we have the following C header file:

*Example 2-32: File: test.h*

```
#include <stdio.h>
#include <usr/local/include/Py/Python.h>

#define SPAM
#define SHOE_SIZE 7.5

#  include   "local_constants.h"
#  define    PARROT  dead + bird
```

If we make our script executable, we get the following results when it's run over this file:

```
% cheader1.py test.h
1 include stdio.h
2 include usr/local/include/Py/Python.h
4 SPAM =
5 SHOE_SIZE = 7.5
7 include local_constants.h
8 PARROT = dead + bird
```

As is, this script still may not be quite as robust as we'd like. For instance, it doesn't handle `#define` continuation lines, and fails for `#define` lines with arguments ("macros"). We'll see an improved version that addresses these issues later in the book. We'll also see an extension of regex, *regsub*, which performs substitutions on substrings matched by a pattern.

## Language Processing

Regular expressions are useful for parsing simple data streams, but can't handle full-blown languages. For more demanding tasks, we can always write parsers in Python, as we'd do in C or C++, or use an integrated parser-generator module. But we'll also find that many language-based tasks become obsolete with Python.

In Python-based systems, the Python compiler and interpreter are always available at run-time. In both Python and C, arbitrary strings of Python code can be run with a single call: *eval* and *exec* in Python, and the embedded-call API in C. Because of that, it's often easier to use *Python itself* for language-based interfaces, instead of writing a custom parser, and inventing yet another "little language."

By embedding Python in an application, we get a powerful object-oriented scripting language. And by adding application-specific extensions, the embedded code can take on any flavor we like. As we'll see, Python provides a general way to add configurability to systems.

### *"There's objects, and then there's objects"*

You might have noticed that none of the examples in the text-processing section use classes. Strings, files, and compiled regular expressions are all first-class Python "objects," but they're not derived from classes; there's no notion of inheritance.

In fact, we've seen two versions of many of the examples so far: both with and without classes. Which underscores an important point: in Python, OOP is an *option*. It's supported, but not imposed.

For most tasks, we can get by using a simple subset of the language. Python's dynamic typing and built-in datatypes make it easy to write simple programs fast. We don't need to know about OOP and underlying object hierarchies just to get started.

On the other hand, Python's OOP model is one of the best parts of the language, and we'll cover it in depth later in the book. As we'll see, Python classes support advanced OOP ideas, such as multiple inheritance, operator overloading, and meta-object protocols. They provide a simple tool for building reusable frameworks. Unless you don't want to. :-)

## *Extension Language Programming*

Some people would argue that almost everything of practical interest in Python uses some sort of integration with external services. For instance, the shell tools, GUI, and persistence examples we've seen rely heavily on integrated libraries of external routines. This wasn't obvious in the GUI code, because the integration looks like a set of Python classes (*Frame*, *Button*, etc.). But at the bottom, there's a simple C library.

In fact, Python's library of extensions is one of its best assets. Because Python was designed to be extensible, Python programmers have access to an increasing variety of interfaces to external tools and systems. Moreover, Python provides the tools needed to add our own extensions to the language: any external library can become a new Python tool, by wrapping it in an extension module.

By modern standards, Python is comparatively simple. It's Python's ability to structure interfaces to other services that makes it useful for everything from simple file scanners, to numerical programming. By integrating external APIs into a powerful dynamic language like Python, they become more accessible. And by using Python as an embedded scripting component, we can open up parts of a system to its end users.

Of course, you need to know something about lower-level languages like C to understand how extending and embedding work. But if you're interested in using Python as part of a larger system, you probably already have the required background knowledge. Here are a few simple examples, to introduce some of the general ideas behind Python/C integration.

## Extending Python in C

Suppose we want to use the C library's *getenv/putenv* functions in Python. This may sound contrived, but there's no direct equivalent to these functions in Python 1.3. Shell environment variables are made available to Python programs in the *environ* dictionary of the built-in *os* module; but changes to *os.environ* aren't propagated outside the Python program.

We can work around this by writing a C extension for Python, which exports C's *getenv/putenv* standard-library routines. The following C file provides the "glue-logic" needed to call the functions from Python.

*Example 2-33: File: environ.c*

```
/*
 * A C extension module for Python, called "environ".
 * Wrap the C library's getenv/putenv routines for use in
 * Python programs. Inspired by an idea from Andy Bensky.
 */

#include <Python.h>
#include <stdlib.h>
#include <assert.h>
#include <string.h>

static PyObject *                                 /* returns object */
wrap_getenv(PyObject *self, PyObject *args)       /* self not used */
{                                                  /* args from python */
    char *varName, *varValue;
    PyObject *returnObj = NULL;                           /* null=exception */

    if (PyArg_Parse(args, "s", &varName))                 /* Python -> C */
        if ((varValue = getenv(varName)) != NULL)         /* call C getenv */
            returnObj = Py_BuildValue("s", varValue);     /* C -> Python */
        else
            PyErr_SetString(PyExc_SystemError, "Error calling getenv");
    else
        PyErr_SetString(PyExc_TypeError, "Usage: getenv(varName)");
    return returnObj;
}

static PyObject *
wrap_putenv(PyObject *self, PyObject *args)
{
    char *varName, *varValue, *varAssign;
```

*Example 2-33: File: environ.c (continued)*

```
    PyObject *returnObj = NULL;

    if (PyArg_Parse(args, "(ss)", &varName, &varValue))
    {
        varAssign = malloc(strlen(varName) + strlen(varValue) + 2);
        sprintf(varAssign, "%s=%s", varName, varValue);
        if (putenv(varAssign) == 0) {
            Py_INCREF(Py_None);                    /* success */
            returnObj = Py_None;                   /* reference None */
        }
        else
            PyErr_SetString(PyExc_SystemError, "Error calling putenv");
    }
    else
        PyErr_SetString(PyExc_TypeError, "Usage: putenv(varName, varValue)");
    return returnObj;
}

static struct PyMethodDef environ_methods[] = {
    {"getenv", wrap_getenv},
    {"putenv", wrap_putenv},          /* name, address */
    {NULL, NULL}
};

void initenviron()                    /* on first import */
{
    (void) Py_InitModule("environ", environ_methods);
}
```

Although this is a small C module, it illustrates the three standard parts of Python extensions:

- The module's method functions: *wrap_getenv*, *wrap_putenv*
- A name/address registration table: *environ_methods*
- An initialization function, called by Python when the module is first imported: *initenviron*

It also includes the standard Python header file, *Python.h*, which defines Python's exported API; most API names start with *Py*. Once we've compiled this C module and added it to Python, we can use it exactly as though it were written in Python. Python programs don't need to know how a module is implemented; the extension module handles all the conversion details, and Python routes the calls to C. You might call this a seamless integration:

```
% python
>>> from environ import *
>>> getenv('USER')
'mark'
>>> putenv('USER', 'gilligan')
```

```
>>> getenv('USER')
'gilligan'
>>> import os
>>> os.environ['USER']
'gilligan'
>>> putenv('USER', 'skipper')
>>> getenv('USER')
'skipper'
>>> os.environ['USER']
'gilligan'
```

So how does Python route function calls to this C code? In short, the initialization function is the hook between Python and C: when the module's imported, the *registration table* is used to build-up a Python module, with one attribute for each pair in the table. Later, a Python call to *environ.getenv* is mapped directly to the C function *wrap_getenv*, and Python dispatches to the C function's address.

One more puzzle piece: how does the module become part of Python? There are two options: we can either add it statically (when Python is built) or dynamically (at run-time). To add it statically, we simply:

1. Put (or link) *environ.c* in the *Modules* directory of the Python source tree
2. Add this new line to the *Modules/Setup* file to declare the new module: *environ environ.c*
3. Run a *make* command in the top-level of the Python source tree

Python's build system takes care of updating built-in tables, changing make-files, etc. This strategy binds the module into Python's libraries and executables directly: it becomes a new built-in module. In fact, there's really no distinction between C extensions written by Python users, and services that are a standard part of the language; Python itself is built with the same extension interfaces. To add the module dynamically:

1. Compile *environ.c* into a shareable object file (a *.so* on some UNIX platforms, a DLL under Windows)
2. Put the object file in a directory on Python's module search-path (shell variable PYTHONPATH)

If we take this route, the module will be loaded at run-time, when first imported by a Python program. Since there's no need to rebuild Python to add the module, this can be a more flexible approach, provided your platform supports dynamic object-module loading (most now do).

### *Wrapping C extensions in Python*

Whether we bind the module statically or dynamically, it gives us access to C's environment utilities in Python. Clients import the C module, and call its functions as usual; to Python programs, there's no distinction between modules implemented in C and Python.

But there's another problem: if you were reading the output above carefully, you may have noticed that the *os.environ* dictionary doesn't reflect changes we make with our new *putenv* routine. We could try to use *getenv/putenv* exclusively, but this may be hard to enforce in a large system. What we'd really like is a way to keep Python's *os.environ* in synch with C's environment.

We could implement this by running some embedded code to set *os.environ* in our *wrap_putenv* C function. Perhaps a more interesting idea is to write a Python *wrapper module* that extends the C module:

*Example 2-34: File: envmod.py*

```
import os
import environ                          # get C module's methods

def putenv(name, value):                # redefine putenv
    os.environ[name] = value            # keep os in sync
    environ.putenv(name, value)         # call C method

def getenv(name):
    value = environ.getenv(name)        # call C method
    if value != os.environ[name]:       # integrity test
        os.environ[name] = value
    return value
```

This Python module would be used exactly like the C extension module above, but its *putenv* function takes care to update *os.environ* first, to keep the two values in synch. Its *getenv* also updates *os* if needed: it's possible that another C module may call C's *putenv* outside the module's control.

```
% python
>>> import os, envmod
>>> os.environ['USER']
'mark'
>>> envmod.putenv('USER', 'skipper')
>>> os.environ['USER']
'skipper'
>>> envmod.getenv('USER')
'skipper'
```

But once we start introducing specialized behavior, we're starting to move into the domain of OOP. If we could make the C *environ* module act like a class, we could

> ### *Close, but no cigar*
>
> If you're following this discussion closely, you may have noticed a subtle problem: this code assumes we're interested in making *os.environ* reflect C's *getenv/putenv* settings, and not vice versa. If someone changes *os.environ* in a Python program, we're still out of luck: *getenv* will happily overwrite the *os.environ* changes. We can't have it both ways.

extend it to update *os.environ* by *subclassing*. In the following module, class *Environ* provides one method for each function in the extension module, which the *EnvSync* class can override to specialize. This interface is used almost like a module, but variables are accessed through a class instance object:

*Example 2-35: File: envsub.py*

```
import os, environ                           # get C module

class Environ:
    def getenv(self, name):                  # C module wrapper class
        return environ.getenv(name)          # delegate to C module
    def putenv(self, name, value):
        environ.putenv(name, value)

class EnvSync(Environ):                      # extend by subclassing
    def putenv(self, name, value):
        os.environ[name] = value
        Environ.putenv(self, name, value)    # do superclass putenv

    def getenv(self, name):
        value = Environ.getenv(self, name)   # do superclass getenv
        os.environ[name] = value             # integrity check
        return value

Env = EnvSync()                              # make one instance
```

Let's test this version interactively:

```
% python
>>> import os
>>> from envsub import Env
>>> os.environ['USER']
'mark'
>>> Env.getenv('USER')
'mark'
>>> Env.putenv('USER', 'professor')
>>> os.environ['USER']
'professor'
```

Alternatively, we can use Python's metaclass protocol system (sometimes called "meta-object protocol"), to provide a member-based interface, instead of methods. When defined, the special method `__getattr__` intercepts accesses to non-existent attributes, and `__setattr__` catches every attribute assignment. Here we use these hooks to make environment variables act like data members of a class instance:

*Example 2-36: File: envclass.py*

```
import os
from environ import *                  # get C module's methods

class EnvWrapper:                      # wrap in a Python class
    def __setattr__(self, name, value):
        os.environ[name] = value       # on write access
        putenv(name, value)

    def __getattr__(self, name):
        value = getenv(name)           # on read access
        os.environ[name] = value       # integrity check
        return value

Env = EnvWrapper()                     # make one instance
```

This version is used as follows:

```
% python
>>> import os
>>> from envclass import Env
>>> os.environ['USER']
'mark'
>>> Env.USER                      __getattr__: getenv
'mark'
>>> Env.USER = 'ginger'           __setattr__: putenv
>>> Env.USER
'ginger'
>>> Env.NEW = 'mary-anne'
>>> os.environ['NEW']
'mary-anne'
```

And finally, we can make the interface act like a dictionary, by defining a mapping class. With the following wrapper, indexing the *Env* object invokes the class's `__getitem__`, and assigning to an index triggers `__setitem__`. The index value in square brackets is passed to the method.

*Example 2-37: File: envmap.py*

```
import os
from environ import getenv, putenv     # get C module's methods

class EnvMapping:                      # wrap in a Python class
    def __setitem__(self, key, value):
        os.environ[key] = value        # on index assignment
        putenv(key, value)
```

*Example 2-37: File: envmap.py (continued)*

```
    def __getitem__(self, key):
        value = getenv(key)             # on index reference
        os.environ[key] = value         # integrity check
        return value

Env = EnvMapping()                      # make one instance
```

Here's *envmap* in action:

```
% python
>>> import os
>>> from envmap import Env
>>> Env['USER']                __getitem__: getenv
'mark'
>>> Env['USER'] = 'Mr. Howle'  __setitem__: putenv
>>> os.environ['USER']
'Mr. Howle'
>>> Env['USER']
'Mr. Howle'
```

Notice that by adding Python interfaces on top of C extension modules, we can build a variety of integration structures. For instance, the *Tkinter* GUI interface adds an object-oriented interface to the "flat" *Tk* library, by wrapping a C extension in Python classes.

Later in the book, we'll see that it's also possible to extend Python with new *datatypes*, implemented in C. The *regex* and *dbm* interfaces we looked at earlier are examples of C types. C extension types have a different structure than extension modules, and behave much like Python classes: they support multiple instances, can overload Python operators, etc.

## *Python as a rapid-prototyping tool*

C extension modules are also one of the main factors behind Python's role as a rapid-prototyping language. Systems can be prototyped in Python first, and later migrated to C for delivery. Python's simplicity lets us develop initial prototypes fast.

But because Python programs can arbitrarily mix modules implemented in Python and C, we really only need to migrate performance-critical modules to C. As we'll see later, such a strategy can leverage both Python's speed of development and C's efficiency.

## *Embedding Python in C*

So far, we've only looked at *extending* Python with C libraries. But the inverse is just as useful: there are at least five ways to embed and run Python programs in another language, as shown in the following table.

*Table 2-3: Embedding strategies*

| Method | Description | Abstraction |
|---|---|---|
| Character strings | Running expressions and statements | *"balance > 1000"* |
| Module references | Calling a function in a file by name | *module.object(args)* |
| Registered callable objects | Calling a known object by pointer | *(*object)(args)* |
| Methods of Python objects | Calling a known object's method | *object.method(args)* |
| Scripts and code files | Running a whole file of code | *system(filename)* |

Unfortunately, embedding also requires much more Python API information than we can get into here. For now, here's an example that runs embedded Python strings in C, to hint at what's to come:

*Example 2-38: File: embed.c*

```
#include <Python.h>

main(argc, argv)
int argc;
char **argv;
{
    Py_Initialize();                                      /* initialize python */
    PyRun_SimpleString("print 'Hello embedded world!'"); /* run  python code */

    /* use our C extension module */
    PyRun_SimpleString("from environ import *");
    PyRun_SimpleString(
           "for i in range(5):\n"
                "\tputenv('USER', 'T.Howle the ' + `i`)\n"
                "\tprint getenv('USER')\n\n" );

    PyRun_SimpleString("print 'Bye embedded world!'");
}

char *getprogramname() { return "embed"; }  /* not always needed */
```

If we compile this file, and link it with Python's libraries, we'll get a standalone executable program. Here's this program's (genealogically suspicious) output:

```
% embed
Hello embedded world!
T.Howle the 0
T.Howle the 1
T.Howle the 2
```

```
T.Howle the 3
T.Howle the 4
Bye embedded world!
```

The *PyRun_SimpleString* function is the simplest way to run Python code in a C program. It's also limited in some critical ways: there's a single namespace, and no real result. We'll see more powerful alternatives later in this book, including tools that let us pass data to and from Python programs, debug embedded calls, and reload code in Python modules without stopping the enclosing C application.

But for many embedded applications, it's sufficient to set Python module variables, run a string of code, and fetch a variable's value as the result. For instance, with a little extra logic to export C's *argv* array we can run embedded Python *Tkinter* GUI commands from C as strings:

```
PyRun_SimpleString("from Tkinter import *");
PyRun_SimpleString("x = Label(None, text='Embedded GUI')");
PyRun_SimpleString("x.pack()");
PyRun_SimpleString("x.mainloop()");
```

We've seen that C extensions can be bound to Python statically or dynamically. But what if C's "on top," and Python's being used as an embedded language? We'll discuss build details later in the book, but as a quick example here's a "makefile" used to build this program on a Linux (UNIX) machine:

*Example 2-39: File: makefile*

```
PY = /home/mark/python-1.3/Python-1.3

PLIBS = $(PY)/Modules/libModules.a \
        $(PY)/Python/libPython.a \
        $(PY)/Objects/libObjects.a \
        $(PY)/Parser/libParser.a

POBJS = $(PY)/Modules/config.o $(PY)/Modules/getpath.o

embed: embed.o
        cc embed.o $(POBJS) $(PLIBS) -lm -o embed

embed.o: embed.c
        cc embed.c -c -I$(PY)/Include -I$(PY)/.
```

This makefile assumes there are no extension libraries to link in. Moreover, makefile syntax varies widely, file paths differ per installation, and on Microsoft Windows, Python may be a single DLL instead of a set of static libraries. Your mileage will vary!

## *Mixing Integration Modes*

If you study *embed.c* above, you'll notice that the embedded Python code is also using our C extension module. Mixing embedding and extending in this way turns out to be a useful concept: not only can we run embedded Python code, but we can also export parts of our system for the embedded program to use, by providing C extensions. In practice, it's usually not very useful to run embedded Python code, unless it knows something about the enclosing application. An integration might be structured something like Figure 2-7.

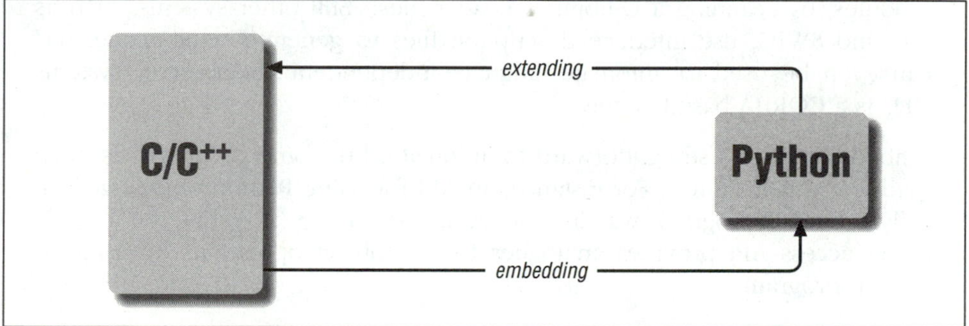


*Figure 2-7: Integration—the "big picture"*

C programs call embedded Python code, Python programs call C extensions, and so on. As we'll see, Python's open architecture makes it easy to mix Python and C arbitrarily.

Some applications don't explicitly use one or both of the interfaces in this picture. But even standalone Python code uses C integration implicitly. For example, Python's *open* function is a built-in C extension that interfaces to C's file system. In fact, all of Python's data types are really just prebuilt C extensions. Every time you use a Python number, list, class, etc., you're using an extension type.

As a rough summary, Python can be extended by adding new C modules and types, and can be embedded as character-strings, module references, or by object registration. And in an abstract sense, you extend Python every time you write reusable Python code. In fact, some built-in services are written entirely in Python. In general terms, Python systems can be extended with:

- Functions, classes, and modules written in Python
- Functions, types, and modules written in a C-compatible language

Whether we're coding Python or C, extensibility and reuse are the name of the game in Python, and themes we'll revisit often in this book.

### *Toward automated integration*

Since most C extension modules and types follow the same pattern (method functions, registration table, initialization function), you might think that C extensions would be a prime candidate for automation. And you'd be right: as of this writing, there are a number of tools that address this issue, at least partially.

The *modulator* system generates boilerplate extension code, from a GUI-based description. And the *bgen* tool tries to generate complete extension modules, by scanning a C library's header files. Still other systems, such as ILU and SWIG, use interface description files to generate "glue" code. ILU can even be used to automate language-independent client/server systems (ILU is a CORBA-based system).

Embedding is less straightforward to automate, but some progress has been made on this front too. For instance, an API for using Python objects generically from a C program, was introduced in Python 1.3. Roughly, the abstract object-access API provides analogues for the object operations available to Python programs.

Automated integration is still an evolving area, and this issue really goes beyond Python itself. For instance, a number of component-based models, and distributed-object systems are currently competing for mind-share among engineers. Don't touch that dial . . .

## *And Whatever Else You Want to Use It For*

Like C, Python is a completely general programming language: it can be used for just about any application you could mention. For example, it's also been used in such diverse roles as:

- Distributed object systems
- WWW programming: CGI scripts, browser applets
- Compiler development
- Artificial Intelligence (AI): expert systems, neural simulations
- Windows scripting: OLE, MFC
- Numerical programming and image processing

and many more. We'll explore some of these later in the book. See Appendix A, *. . . And Other Cool Stuff*, for a quick tour of some advanced Python domains.

# Conclusion

By now, I've probably completely confused you, unless you've already used Python! But the only real goal of this chapter was to give some sense of the rationale behind Python: the "view from 30,000 feet." Let's come down to where the air is a bit thicker, and move on to study the language in more reasonable detail in the body of this book.

If you'd like a more basic introduction first, this is probably a good time to go through the tutorial appendix. Next, we'll study shell tools code, to learn basic rules of the language. After that, we'll look at some core applications. At the end of the book, we'll return to some of the issues of Python's roles mentioned here.

## *What's in a name?*

Python gets its name from the British TV comedy series, *Monty Python's Flying Circus*. According to Python folklore, Guido van Rossum, Python's inventor, was watching reruns of the show at about the same time he needed a name for a new language he was developing. And as they say in show-business, "the rest is history."

Because of this heritage, references to the comedy group's works often show up in examples and discussion. For instance, the name "*Spam*" has a special connotation to Python users, and discussions are sometimes referred to as "*The Spanish Inquisition.*"

As a rule, if a Python user starts using phrases that have no relation to reality, they're probably borrowed from the show. Some will even pop up in this book. Viewing movies such as "*The Holy Grail*" or "*The Meaning of Life*" certainly isn't a prerequisite for Python programming; on the other hand, it can't hurt :-).

While "Python" turned out to be a distinctive name, it's also had some interesting side-effects. For instance, when the Python newsgroup, *comp.lang.python*, came on-line in 1994, its first few weeks of activity were almost entirely taken up by people wanting to discuss topics from the TV show. And as of 1995, at least one internet directory still listed *comp.lang.python* as a site for discussion of the show.

There's still an occasional post from fans of the show on Python's news list. For instance, one recent poster innocently offered to swap Python scripts with other fans. Had he known the nature of the newsgroup, he might have at least mentioned whether the scripts ran under DOS or UNIX . . .

# 3

# *Getting Started*

*In this chapter:*

- *"Scenes from Life in the Real World"*
- *Configuring Your Environment*
- *Installing Python*
- *And if All Else Fails*
- *Using the Command-Line Interpreter*
- *Using the Python Command Line*
- *Platforms Supported Today*
- *What's Next?*
- *Conclusion*

## *"Scenes from Life in the Real World"*

In this chapter, we'll quickly cover some practical details before moving on to study the language itself. If you want to work along with the examples, the information here should be enough for you to get set up.

## *Configuring Your Environment*

Before we get started, try to locate an installed version of Python (see the next section if you can't find it on your machine). You'll probably find it helpful to enter some of the examples, so you can see their results first-hand. For many, there's really nothing like interacting with a new language, when first learning it.

Your local Python guru or system administrator can help you set up your system: minimally, you need to be able to run the interpreter. You may also need to set the Python module search-path in your environment, and can specify a start-up file if desired. We'll see why these are important in a moment, but here's a quick guide on environment-variable settings for UNIX users:

PATH

The operating system's executable search path variable. Add the directory containing the *python* interpreter executable file, according to your platform's conventions. For instance, on DOS you might set *PATH* in your *autoexec.bat* file; under UNIX, it may go in your *.cshrc* file. Alternatively, you can alias *python* to point to the file (see your system shell's manpage for more details).

PYTHONPATH

Python's module file search path. If set, it's used to locate modules at run-time, when they're imported by a Python program. Add the current directory (.), the standard library (the library directory where Python is installed), and any other directories you want to import from. For instance, to run GUI programs using the Tk interface, add Python's *tkinter* library directory too. These may be added by default already; see your installation expert, or type **import sys** and check *sys.path* in the Python command-line interpreter (discussed later).

PYTHONSTARTUP

An optional Python initialization file. If used, set this variable to the full path-name of a file of Python code (a module) you want to be run each time the Python interactive command-line interpreter starts up. This is a convenient way to change prompts (*sys.ps1*, *sys.ps2*), import commonly used modules, and so on.

Python recognizes other environment settings, but the three above are the most important. If you use extensions to the Python system, you may need to set other variables too. For example, the current Tk GUI extension requires setting *TK_LIBRARY* and *TCL_LIBRARY* variables, to point to the *Tk* and *Tcl* library file directories. See the extension's documentation for more details.

# *Installing Python*

Of course, the first step to using Python is finding it. If Python is already installed on your machine, you can probably skip most of this section. If not, you can find Python sources on the CD-ROM in the back of this book. This CD-ROM also contains pre-built binaries for a number of platforms; see the *README* file on the CD-ROM for more information about its contents.

The traditional way to get the Python distribution is by *FTP*. Names of FTP sites that carry Python vary over time; but at least as of this writing, the main Internet site for getting Python by anonymous FTP is *ftp://ftp.python.org/pub/python/src.*

Python is packaged as a "gzipped" tar file, which you must unzip and extract to use. As usual for public-domain tools, Python is shipped as a set of C source files, which you compile and link locally. Building Python is mostly an automatic process. It compiles and runs out of the box on most UNIX platforms.

## Getting Python by FTP

If you're not familiar with downloading software, here's an example of using *FTP* from a UNIX command-line shell account. FTP output lines have been omitted to save space. This is just an example; your FTP interface might be different (for instance, a GUI tool), and you may want to use a different site.

```
% ftp ftp.python.org                          connect to python's FTP site
Connected to python.org.
Name (ftp.python.org:lutz): anonymous         user name is 'anonymous'
Password: <email-id>                          password is your email ID
ftp> cd pub/python                            root: code, FAQ, old mail, etc.
ftp> cd src                                   goto source directory
ftp> bin                                      use binary transfer mode
ftp> get python1.3.tar.gz                     download python to your machine
ftp> quit                                     exit FTP
```

## Building Python from Source Code

Once you've pulled down Python to your machine by FTP (or loaded it off a CD-ROM), building and installing is a simple process. Here's a UNIX command-line example; the build procedure assumes you have a C compiler installed on your machine.

```
% gzip -d python1.3.tar.gz                    unzip (decompress) file
% tar xvf python1.3.tar                       extract tar file contents
...[output]...
% cd Python-1.3                               goto the build-tree root
% ./configure                                 run auto-config script
% make                                        build python
...[output]...
% make test                                   run self-test system
% make install                                put python in standard places
% ./python                                    and now you're in business...
```

Again, this is just an example: check the *README* file in the top-level directory of the Python distribution for more accurate build instructions. After you've built Python, you can add or remove extension modules, by modifying the *Setup* file in the *Modules* directory of the build-tree, and re-making Python. We'll see how this process works in a moment.

If you're on a non-UNIX platform, there are other ways to install Python, including precompiled executables, and special download versions on the FTP site. And if you'll be using extensions, you'll need to find these libraries, and modify Python configuration files. The "frequently asked questions" (FAQ) file described below lists sources of supported extension libraries.

## *Installing Extensions Used in This Book*

Some of the examples in this book require the Tk and DBM (or related filesystem) extensions.

- To run the GUI code, you'll need to enable the *tkinter* extension module in the *Modules/Setup* file, and link with *Tk*, *Tcl*, and *X* libraries (under UNIX).
- To run the *dbm* and persistence examples, you'll need to enable one of the *dbm* extension modules, and link it with the referenced external library.

If you already have a prebuilt Python binary with both of these tools enabled, you can skip most of this section. See the CD-ROM for Python executables with *Tk* and *dbm* support. The CD also contains source code for *Tk*, *Tcl*, and *gdbm*. But to show how adding extensions works, let's go through the process for the *tkinter* extension. Python 1.3 requires Tk4.0 and Tcl7.4, or higher versions. As for Python itself, the first step is getting the packages, either by FTP or from another medium (CD-ROM, etc.). Here's how the *Tcl* and *Tk* libraries were fetched for this book; naturally paths and version numbers will vary over time.

```
% ftp ftp.sunlabs.com
Name (ftp.sunlabs.com:lutz): anonymous
Password: <email-id>
ftp> cd pub/tcl
ftp> bin
200 Type set to I.
ftp> get tcl7.4.tar.gz
ftp> get tk4.0.tar.gz
ftp> quit
```

Building and installing the two packages works the same as for Python:

1. Put both files in the same directory, and unzip them using *gzip -d*.
2. Extract their contents using *tar xvf*; this step creates two source directories.
3. Run a *./configure* command at the top level of both directories.
4. Run a *make* command at the top level of both directories, to build binaries.
5. Run a *make install* command at the top level of both directories, to copy to standard directories.

After installing *Tk* and *Tcl*, we need to activate the *tkinter* extension module to use them in Python programs. The *tkinter* module ships with Python, so all we need to do is uncomment the relevant lines in Python's *Modules/Setup* file, and rebuild Python by running a *make* command in its top-level directory. If you've run the *make install* command for *Tk* and *Tcl*, the *Setup* lines to activate will look something like this:

```
tkinter tkintermodule.c -I/usr/local/include -L/usr/local/lib -ltk -ltcl -lX11
TKPATH=:$(DESTLIB)/tkinter
```

The top-level Python *make* uses the activated *Setup* lines to update makefiles and configuration tables. If *Tk* and *Tcl* aren't installed in standard places, you may need to tweak the *Setup* entries. Here's a more complex scheme that was used at one point while developing this book:

```
tbase      = /home/mark/python-1.3
tkincludes = -I$(tbase)/tcl7.4 -I$(tbase)/tk4.0 -I/usr/X11/include/X11
tklibs     = -L$(tbase)/tcl7.4 -L$(tbase)/tk4.0 -L/usr/X11/lib
tkinter tkintermodule.c $(tkincludes) $(tklibs) -ltk -ltcl -lX11
TKPATH=:/home/mark/python-1.3/Python-1.3/Lib/tkinter
```

If you have trouble linking, you can change paths in *Setup* using the usual makefile techniques (lines are copied to makefiles). As a rule, you're better off installing packages in the standard directories.

## *Tkinter and tkinter*

Python programs actually use a module called *Tkinter* in Python, not *tkinter*. Tkinter is a Python wrapper around the *tkinter* C extension module enabled here. As mentioned above, environment variables *TK_LIBRARY* and *TCL_LIBRARY* also need to point to the *Tk* and *Tcl* source code library directories, wherever they were installed.

Activating the *dbm* extension is often simpler, since some form of DBM library is usually already present on UNIX machines. (If not, it's available on this book's CD-ROM, or by FTP.) Again, uncomment the appropriate line in the *Modules/Setup* file, and run a *make* command to rebuild Python. Here are two alternative entries:

```
#dbm dbmmodule.c -I/usr/include -L/usr/lib -ldbm
gdbm gdbmmodule.c -I/usr/local/include -L/usr/local/lib -lgdbm
```

We'll also be adding extensions of our own. For reference, here are the necessary *Modules/Setup* entries for the "environ" module we added in Chapter 2, *A Sneak Preview*, and two more we'll discuss later:

```
environ environ.c
stackmod stackmod.c
stacktype stacktyp.c
```

Most of these details are prone to change, and will vary from platform to platform. For example, if you're running *Tkinter* examples on MS Windows or a Macintosh, you'll need more recent *Tk/Tcl* versions, and won't use the X-windows library. See the *README* files in the source directories of these packages for more details. The extension installation process itself may vary over time too; see the *README* and *Setup* files in the Python distribution, for up-to-date information.

### *Getting binaries off the Web*

As this book was being written, a new system for downloading prebuilt binaries was installed on Python's WWW site. In brief, you can now get Python by visiting Python's homepage (discussed below), and answering a series of questions about your platform. The other Python distribution channels (FTP, etc.) are still available as before.

The WWW system gives step-by-step instructions on how to download and install Python binaries. At this writing, it only has binaries for common UNIX platforms and Windows configurations, but this is likely to expand over time.

One caution: if you plan on adding C extension modules and types statically, you need to get the source code distribution, and build your own binaries. Prebuilt binaries are fine if you plan on using the language as it comes out of the box, or will be adding C extensions as dynamically linked modules (described later).

## *And if All Else Fails*

Building a system like Python is a complex process; it usually works without a glitch, but not always. When you get stuck, there are a variety of places to look for help on building and using Python.

*The FAQ*

Perhaps the best source of up-to-date information on Python is the FAQ file maintained by its inventor. Among other things, it contains build hints for many platforms, and alternative FTP sites. The FAQ file is posted periodically on *comp.lang.python*, and is available at both the FTP and WWW sites named below. It's usually the best first stop when looking for information.

*README files*

The Python distribution comes with a collection of *README* files that describe how to build, install, and extend the system. They're located in the source tree itself.

*Reference manuals*
: Python's standard reference manuals are included in the distribution. The manuals are almost a book in themselves; they're also available in hypertext form on the website, and PostScript versions can be accessed via FTP separately from the FTP site. There's also a useful *QuickReference* document in Python's *Doc* directory.

*The web page*
: Python's WWW homepage is currently at the URL *http://www.python.org*. It has prebuilt binaries, PSA announcements, and hypertext versions of just about every kind of documentation that exists: the FAQ, reference manuals, mail logs, and more. If you have access to a web browser, this can be a wealth of information.

*The FTP site*
: Python's main anonymous FTP site is currently at *ftp.python.org* in the directory *pub/python* (see the example above). This site is mirrored by other FTP sites, so you might find one closer to you. The FTP site maintains copies of the FAQ, standard documentation, mail logs, some standard extensions, and the Python distribution itself. It also has some prebuilt binary versions of Python, for selected platforms.

*The newsgroup*
: Python has a dedicated newsgroup on the Internet: *comp.lang.python*. Since the news group is cross-linked to the Python email list, news shows up in the mail logs too. It's a great place to ask questions and discuss extensions.

*Mail/news logs*
: Past email from other users is archived on Python's FTP and WWW sites. If you're stuck, there's a good chance someone may have had the same problem in the past.

## Using the Command-Line Interpreter

Since many of the examples' output will be shown by running them under Python's interactive command-line interpreter, we should take a quick look at how to use it here. Although realistically scaled applications are usually run as scripts, programs, or embedded code, Python's command line is a convenient way to enter, load, and test code. As we'll see, Python is a highly interactive language. For example:

```
% python
>>> print 'Hello world!'
Hello world!
```

On the first line, the Python interpreter is started from the system command line, by typing **python**. The actual way you'll do this is system-dependent: on most

### *"Hello. Is Guido there?"*

If you post a question on the Python newsgroup today, you'll frequently get an answer directly from the language's inventor. Guido does an amazing job of supporting both new and seasoned Python users on-line. Other Python users are ready to answer questions too. Some commercial help desks could probably learn a thing or two about customer service from Guido and company.

Guido's degree of involvement may change as Python's user-base grows larger. But for the moment, he fields an incredible number of questions, not to mention all the other work he does managing the language itself. In fact, there are those who sometimes wonder whether Guido is really a single individual at all, or is instead some sort of "collective"—it may not be too off-base to refer to him as "The Guido" (for all you Star Trek fans :-).

UNIX systems, typing **python** causes the interactive interpreter to be located according to the setting of the *PATH* environment variable (see above). But under Windows, Python might be started by double-clicking on an icon or a file manager entry.

Once Python is started, it prints version information (omitted in this book, to save a few trees) and presents its own command-line prompt. By default, the prompt is ">>>" (unless we change *sys.ps1*). In our examples, things you type will be shown in bold font, and Python output will be normal.

At the ">>>" prompt, any Python code can be entered. The command-line interpreter reads code, prints its value (if any), and then prompts for more commands. Results of expressions (which are just Python data objects) are echoed back. When compound statements are typed, Python lets you know that the body must be indented, by changing the prompt to " . . . ". Finally, typing an end-of-file character exits the interpreter:

```
% python
>>> 'Hello world!'                an expression
'Hello world!'
>>> x = 12 * 2                    assign a new variable
>>> x + 1
25
>>> while x > 0:                  compound statements
...     x = x - 1
>>> <ctrl-d>                      exit by typing <ctrl-d>
```

As we'll see later, when you're typing code at the command-line, you're actually entering it in a predefined module called __main__. There's really no difference between code in module files and code typed in the interpreter, except that unassigned values of expressions are echoed back in the interpreter.

Python's interpreter also supports the GNU readline system. When enabled, readline provides command history, editing, and recall. Since readline isn't really part of Python, we won't cover it here; see Python's *README* and *FAQ* files for more details. Python also comes with a set of Emacs macros for editing Python source code; see Appendix C, *A Mini-Reference*, for information.

> ### *Python as a replacement shell*
>
> It's possible to use Python's command-line interpreter just like a normal system shell (such as sh, tcsh, or bash). In fact, you could start-up the interpreter from your initialization file, to make Python your standard shell. But Python's system interfaces are different than traditional shell languages. For instance, operating system commands are invoked through the *os* module, instead of being typed in place. Still, Python's programming features can make for a powerful system shell tool, if you can adjust to the differences.

# *Using the Python Command Line*

There are a variety of ways to invoke the interpreter:

`% python`
: Starts the interactive interpreter described above.

`% python file args . . .`
: Runs the source code file (module) named on the command-line. The filename is passed to the program as *sys.argv[0]*, and arguments are passed in *sys.argv[1:]*.

`% python -c command args . . .`
: Runs the Python command (statements) directly. The command usually has to be quoted, since Python code contains characters special to the shell. In this form, `sys.argv[0]` is `-c`.

`% python < file`
: Runs the source code file piped in through the standard input (*stdin*) stream. This works like the second form above, but is less general: *stdin* always goes to Python, not the program being interpreted.

---

*NOTE* As we'll see, Python files can also be executed directly, if we add a special `#!/...` comment line at the top and give them executable privileges. Moreover, embedded programs are invoked through an API, not the system command line.

---

## *Platforms Supported Today*

Here's a list of some of the platforms Python's been ported to. Standard Python programs will run unchanged on all the systems shown here, but most also provide platform-specific extensions.

- UNIX (most versions)
- QNX
- Macintosh
- OS/2
- MSDOS
- Microsoft Windows: win16
- Microsoft Windows: win32
- Microsoft Windows NT
- Microsoft Windows 95
- VMS
- Next
- Amiga
- Atari Mint
- Atari TOS

Naturally, this list will be out of date by the time you read it! Since new ports are announced all the time, consult the information sources above for more details.

## *What's Next?*

In the next part of the book, we'll study the Python language, by pointing out how it's used in real programs. By way of introduction, here's a preview of the language concepts we'll encounter.

### Datatypes

Python provides common datatypes as built-in tools. All its collection types support nesting, and can hold items of any type; there's no need to declare structure or types ahead of time. This basic set can be extended by writing Python modules and classes, and extension types in C.

### Operations

Python operations and expression-operators are generic: they work on a variety of data-types. For instance, the + operator adds two numbers as expected, but also concatenates lists, strings, and user-defined objects that respond to +. Similarly, qualification ("object.attribute") can be used on any object that has named attributes. Operations apply to a type according to its category (number, sequence, mapping).

### Statements

Python is a procedural, statement-based language. Its statements are typical for a structured language. As usual, program execution flows sequentially from one statement to the next, unless branching statements are used. Some statements (*def*, *class*, *import*) are used to build higher-level program structures.

### Program Organization

As we look at examples, keep their global structure in mind. Roughly, Python systems are just sets of modules. Modules are implemented in Python or C, and may contain variables, functions, classes, and types that are exported for use by other modules. As we'll see, Python is an extremely modular language.

### Run-Time Structure

Python is a run-time interpreter engine; everything it does uses some form of added logic. Our examples will use functionality that comes from a variety of sources: either predefined by Python, or something you add to it. And it may be implemented in Python, or coded as a C extension.

## Conclusion

I hope this chapter has given you enough information to get set up to run Python programs. Real-world issues like environment configuration and installation are often dismissed as trivial, but they can turn into mind-numbing problems, especially if you're on a system outside the mainstream. If you run into problems, make use of the resources listed above. Before we move on to the next section, a few reminders:

- There's a tutorial appendix, if you want to start from the bottom up.
- The index can be used to explore language features, if you forget where they're introduced.
- Reference appendixes appear at the end of this book, to collect information we'll pick up in piecemeal fashion.

And as mentioned earlier, different sections will appeal to different readers. Roughly:

- The tutorial appendix is the easiest introduction, and doesn't depend on the shell tools domain.
- Part 2, *Language Fundamentals*, is a more comprehensive language tutorial. It also discusses shell tools topics.
- Part 3, *Tools and Applications*, is advanced material. It assumes the reader is familiar with the concepts in Part 2.

See the Preface for alternative reading suggestions.

# II

# *Language Fundamentals*

## *"Buy One, Get One Free!"*

In this section, we'll use the system-administration application area to get started. Roughly, this part of the book is an extended language tutorial; most of the fundamental ideas in Python programming are presented, in the context of shell tools. For instance, a simple seven-line script appears first, but by the end of the section, we'll wind up taking a look at basic OOP concepts.

We really have two goals here: to learn about writing shell tools in Python and to study the Python language in the process. By the time we finish this section, we should have enough information to explore other application domains, without getting bogged down in language details. At the same time, we'll have learned something about using Python to write UNIX-style shell utilities.

## *"Python in Seven Easy Steps!"*

Most of the chapters in this part are fairly short. The approach taken here is to refine a simple shell utility program. Each chapter builds on the improvements of the one before:

- *Chapter 4, Writing Basic Shell Tools.* Starts us off, by exploring some simple scripts for packing and unpacking text files.
- *Chapter 5, Variations on a Theme.* Presents some ideas on alternative ways to code the scripts from Chapter 4.
- *Chapter 6, Adding a Functional Interface.* Adds functions to the scripts, to make them reusable.

- *Chapter 7, Adding a Simple User Interface.* Builds a simple user-interface on top of the functions in Chapter 6, and talks about modules.
- *Chapter 8, Adding Text-Based Menus.* Adds logic to display a menu of options on the screen, and lays a path to classes.
- *Chapter 9, Moving Menus to Classes.* Shows why in the world we'd want to use something like OOP, and gives some examples.
- *Chapter 10, More Class Magic.* Introduces more class-based tricks, to demonstrate advanced OOP concepts.

This part deals mostly with the language; Part 3, *Tools and Applications,* presents applications. The only core concepts we won't cover here are C extending and embedding techniques; we'll use extensions, but won't show how to write new ones. Since they're more like a tool than a language feature, we'll save these topics for Part 3.

## *"Plus a Free Can of Spam to the First 1000 Customers!"*

Maybe not, but read Part 2, *Language Fundamentals,* first, especially if you're new to Python. It lays the groundwork for understanding the bigger examples in Part 3, and programs you'll encounter on your own.

# 4

# *Writing Basic Shell Tools*

*In this chapter:*


- *It Was a Dark and Stormy Night...*
- *"Quick and Dirty" File Packing*
- *Dissecting the Code*
- *New Language Concepts*
- *"Telling the Monkeys What to Do"*


## *It Was a Dark and Stormy Night . . .*

Well, not really. Actually, I was stuck at home thanks to a Colorado blizzard, with nothing but my PC and a modem. Still, I had to get some work done; I needed to transfer about 100 small text files back and forth from home and my UNIX account at work.

Normally, these are trivial tasks given the right tools. There are a variety of ways to pack up files for transmitting between UNIX machines (*tar*, *cpio*, even *cat*). Unfortunately, I was stranded at home with a painfully primitive PC environment, and little or no hope for getting this job done fast.

Except for Python. In this section, we're going to look at how Python can be used for common system administration tasks: what some people call "shell tool" programming. Because of its interfaces to system services, Python can be used as a general shell tool language, for tasks you might have traditionally done with a shell language like *Perl* or *csh*. And because of Python's support for advanced programming constructs, we'll find that it raises systems programming to new levels.

In the end, we'll see that Python allows us to easily apply modern techniques such as OOP to system administration work. Perhaps more importantly, it allows us to write code that's both readable and maintainable, even for scripts we didn't plan to reuse. In Python, writing reusable code is almost automatic.

### *System administration and other acts of nature*

Of course, this "real world" scenario of being crippled by a snow storm may be more hypothetical for some of you than others! But the examples we'll look at in this section are typical of the sort of tasks software engineers perform on a regular basis. They should apply to system administration work in general, whether the disaster you're battling is natural or not.

## *"Quick and Dirty" File Packing*

So there I was, sequestered in my basement, facing the prospect of spending hours downloading roughly 100 individual text files from work over my modem (and wasting a good chunk of the free day off from work). But without any tools on my PC, there seemed no good alternatives.

Luckily, I had at least installed Python on my machine at home. With Python, I could quickly throw-together scripts that would run on both the UNIX machine at work and my PC. All I really needed was something that concatenated all the files into one big text file, so I could transfer with a single command. Naturally, I also needed a way to unpack the files at the receiving end. Here's what I coded first:

*Example 4-1: file: pack1.py*

```
#!/usr/local/bin/python

import sys                          # load the system module
marker = '::::::'

for name in sys.argv[1:]:           # for all command arguments
    input = open(name, 'r')         # open the next input file
    print marker + name             # write a separator line
    print input.read(),             # and write the file's contents
```

*Example 4-2: file: unpack1.py*

```
#!/usr/local/bin/python

import sys
marker = '::::::'

for line in sys.stdin.readlines():              # for all input lines
    if line[:6] != marker:
        print line,                             # write real lines
    else:
        sys.stdout = open(line[6:-1], 'w')      # or make new output file
```

These two scripts did the job. To transfer the files:

1. I ran the *pack* script remotely by modem on my UNIX machine at work, to bundle up the files:

```
% pack1.py *.py > packed.txt
```

2. I downloaded the output file *packed.txt* to my PC in one step (with the UNIX *sx* command):

```
% sx packed.txt
```

3. Finally, I unpacked the files by running the unpack script locally on my PC:

```
C:\TEMP> python unpack1.py < packed.txt
```

Figure 4-1 shows how the process works.

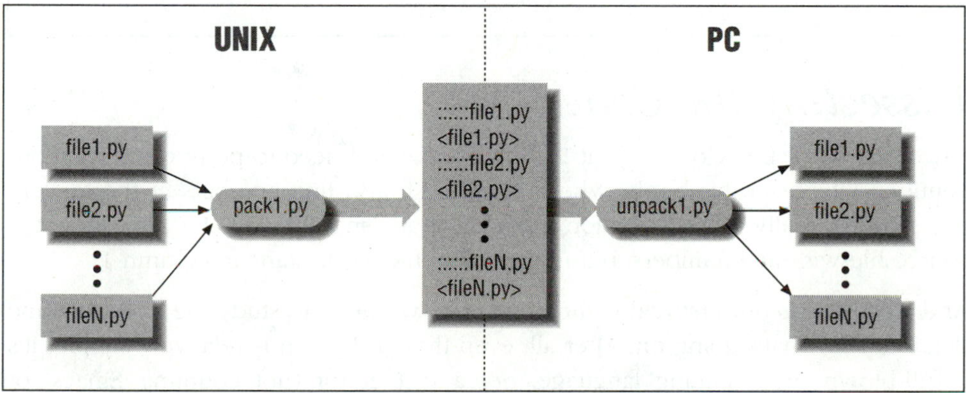


*Figure 4-1: Packing files*

Since the Python code runs on both my PC at home and the UNIX machine at work, I was able to test and debug both scripts locally on the PC, before running them on the remote UNIX system. More importantly, I was also able to use this pair of scripts to transfer the other way: to upload a group of files to the UNIX machine from my PC. I just ran the *pack* script on the PC, and the *unpack* script on the UNIX box:

```
C:\FILES> python pack1.py *.py > upload.txt
```

*...[send "upload.txt"]...*

```
% unpack1.py < upload.txt
```

Python is a portable shell tools language. Of course, I also had to transfer the two script files to the UNIX machine, but compared to about 100 downloads, that's a dramatic savings!

### *So why not use a mail script?*

Someone who read an early draft of this chapter asked why I couldn't just use a simple shell script here. For instance, the following *csh* script could mass-mail all the files automatically, if run remotely:

```
#!/bin/csh
foreach x (*.py)
    mail myself@home -s $x < $x
end
```

Besides being addicted to Python hacking, I didn't have an Internet feed at the time, so this wasn't really an option. Even if I had, Python was the only language tool on my PC, and I'd still have to extract 100 messages from my mailbox file somehow (probably an exercise in typing). Not to mention the Murphy's law corollary on email . . .

# *Dissecting the Code*

Since this is our first close look at Python programs, I need to point out some conventions I'll use in this book. Where helpful, I'll add line numbers at the far left; these aren't really part of Python code (Python isn't BASIC!). I'll also indent a source file with line-numbers; but in the actual file, code starts in column 1.

And since this is our first real Python example, we need to study the code in some detail to see what's going on. After all, even though Python is relatively simple, it's a full-blown programming language, not a text editor (not counting Emacs, of course :-). First, we'll take a quick line-by-line tour of our scripts; after that, we'll dig deeper into some of the language features they use. Let's look at *pack1.py* first.

## *pack1.py, Under the Scope*

Our packing script starts out with a Python comment:

```
#!/usr/local/bin/python
```

As usual, comments document code; they start with a # and extend to the end of the line. This comment is special: it also tells the operating system where to find an interpreter, for running the rest of the file.

```
import sys
```

In Python, all code exists in a module: a set of named objects that normally corresponds to a Python source file, or a C module with registered objects.

Here, we use the *import* statement to load a module called *sys*, which happens to be a built-in module with a variety of system-level components (we need its *argv*).

```
marker = '::::::'
```

The name *marker* is assigned the Python character string ::::::. This assignment creates the variable marker, since this is the first time it's assigned a value. We'll use this string to separate files in the packed output. This isn't foolproof (what if a real line starts with ::::::?), but it's sufficient for our purposes.

```
for name in sys.argv[1:]:
```

This line is the start of a loop, which iterates over the command-line arguments. "name" is set to the next string in the argument list (the name of a file to be packed), each time through the loop. Command-line arguments are a list of strings in the *sys* module we just imported, called[*] *argv*. The notation *sys.argv* is called *qualification*; it's used to access a named attribute in a variety of object types (similar in spirit to accessing *struct* members in C). We slice off the first item in *argv* (*[1:]*), since it's the script name.

```
input = open(name, 'r')
```

The body of the loop begins at this line. It opens the next input file ("r" means "read"). In Python, *open* means: "create a new file object, attached to the external file whose name (path) is passed in." Once we have the file object, we can manipulate it by calling its attributes ("methods").

```
print marker + name
```

Here, we output a separator for each new file. The *print* statement sends text to the standard output file, *sys.stdout*. We need to redirect output to a file on the command line if we're going to save it. We could also write the packed output to another file directly, but it's traditional to use standard input/output streams in shell tool programs: this allows us to connect scripts by pipes, pipe output to processing scripts, etc.

```
print input.read(),
```

Finally, each time through the loop, we copy the entire contents of an input file to the standard output, after the separator line we just wrote. The expression *input.read()* runs the *read* attribute of the file object we created with *open*. *read* loads the entire contents of a file all at once, and returns it as a Python string.

In plain English, the packer's loop:

```
for name in sys.argv[1:]:
    input = open(name, 'r')
    print marker + name
    print input.read(),
```

means: "For each filename on the command-line: open the file, and print a separator followed by the text of the file, to the standard output stream."

The result is a single file holding all the files listed on the command line, with marker lines introducing each file's text. The packed output file that gets transferred between machines looks something like Figure 4-2:

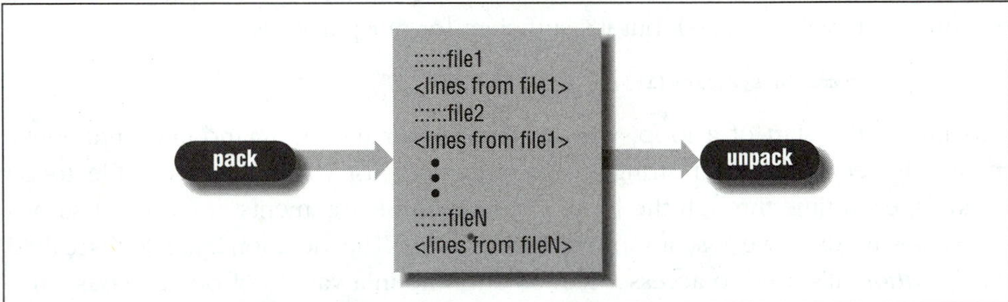


*Figure 4-2: A packed file*

## *unpack1.py, Unplugged*

After we pack our files, the unpack script simply scans the packed file, noticing the separator lines we wrote, and writing the text to the files named in the separators. Here's some of the unpack script; we'll concentrate on the ways it differs from the pack script.

```
import sys
```

For unpacking, we need items in the built-in *sys* module again: we'll read from *sys*'s *stdin* file object, and write to its *stdout* file object. These two files are preopened for us when we start a Python program (and reference the interactive input/output sources by default, as in C).

```
for line in sys.stdin.readlines():
```

To unpack, we iterate over the lines read from the standard input stream, rather than command-line arguments. We call the *readlines* attribute of the *sys.stdin* file object; *readlines* loads a whole file at once, and returns a list of strings corresponding to the lines of text in the file (or an empty list if the file is empty). Since we're using the standard input stream to read the packed file, *stdin* is redirected on the command-line.

```
if line[:6] != marker:
```

Here, we check for separator lines in the packed file. We use slicing to compare the first six characters of the next line (a Python string) to the marker string `::::::`.

Note that we're slicing a string, not a list as done in the packer: slicing works on all ordered sequence objects, built-in and user-defined.

```
print line,
```

If it's not a separator line, we print it to the standard output as is. We suppress the extra end-of-line character *print* usually adds, by ending the statement with a comma. We could instead strip off the end-of-line at the end of "line" by slicing: *print line[:-1]*.

```
else:
    sys.stdout = open(line[6:-1], 'w')
```

When a separator line introducing a new file's text is detected, we set the standard output stream to a new file. Again, we use *open* to create a file object, this time with mode *w*, so the new file's opened for writing. The target file name is embedded in the separator line, after the marker, up to the end-of-line character: slice *line[6:-1]* extracts the name. It gets characters from offset 6 (after `::::::`), and up to, but not including the last character (up to the end-of-line); an index of –1 means "1 from the end."

Taken together, the unpacker's loop:

```
for line in sys.stdin.readlines():
    if line[:6] != marker:
        print line,
    else:
        sys.stdout = open(line[6:-1], 'w')
```

means: "For all *lines* in the input stream: if it's not a new-file marker, copy it to the current output file; otherwise open a new output file with the name given in the marker line."

By scanning the packed file in this way, we recreate all the files that were packed (and save a few hours).

# New Language Concepts

Now, let's look at some of the language tools these scripts use in more detail. Throughout this part of the book, we'll use *using* and *more* sections like the ones here, to point out new language ideas in programs along the way, or expand on ideas introduced earlier. Since this is our first real look at Python code, we have to cover quite a few features here, to understand how these scripts really work.

## *Using Objects, Variables, and Expressions*

At the most primitive level, Python programs make objects, assign them to names, and use them in expressions. Let's look at these concepts first.

### *Assignment*

The = symbol is used to write assignment statements in Python. In simple terms, assignment always stores *references* to *objects*. Although = statements can take different forms, our scripts use the simplest:

```
marker = '::::::'
```

which gives a target on the left of the = symbol ("marker"), and a value on the right (::::::). Sometimes we assign to variables without using the = operation. For example, the *import* statement in both scripts:

```
import sys
```

brings a module called *sys* into the importer's namespace, by assigning that module (one kind of Python object) to the variable name *sys*. Similarly, the *for* loop implicitly assigns items in a sequence to the loop variable:

```
for name in sys.argv[1:]:      # assign to "name" each time through
```

In other cases, we use assignment to change part of a larger structure, instead of setting a named variable. For instance, we set the *stdout* attribute in the imported *sys* module in the unpacker:

```
sys.stdout = open(line[6:-1], 'w')
```

Here, *stdout* is really a variable in another namespace. As we'll see later, we also use = to change nested components of complex data structures such as lists, by assigning to indexes (`list[index] = value`).

### *Variables*

In Python, variables are simply names for objects, and new variables are created just by assigning a value to them. There are no type declarations in Python: variables can hold objects of any type or size, and don't need to be declared in advance. But they do need to have a value when used; in Python,

- *Assignment* creates a new variable, but
- *Referencing* an undefined variable is an error.

### *Assignment is not an expression*

A note for C programmers: unlike C, Python assignment is a *statement*, not an expression. We can't use the = symbol in expressions: it's not an operator. Python is really a statement-based language. Although this scheme requires separate lines for things we might squeeze onto one in C, it's intended to enhance code readability, and avoid errors: you can never mistakenly type = for == in a Python expression (it's a syntax error).

Python also doesn't directly support C's `?:` comparison expressions, or side-effect assignment operators like += and ++. But as we'll see, `?:` can be simulated in Python with "and/or" combinations, and classes can implement C-like side effect operators.

This gives us some protection from typing mistakes: if Python created a variable when it was used but not yet set, we might not detect the error in our code. So:

```
name = value          assignment: create "name" if it doesn't exist yet
if nome > 10:         reference: raise an error if "nome" doesn't exist yet
```

When we assign a value to a variable name, the variable becomes a named reference to the assigned object, not a copy of it. In fact, objects are never copied in Python unless we request it. So it's easy to pass large objects around in a program. But it can also lead to side effects: since assignment makes object references, a given object might be referenced by multiple variables and data-structures. We'll see why this can matter later, but here's the idea (refer to Figure 4-3):

```
marker = '::::::'     make "marker" a reference to a new string object
other  = marker       now "other" and "marker" share the same object
```

The pack script uses four variables to get its job done: *sys*, *marker*, *name*, and *input*. The unpacker uses three: *sys*, *marker*, and *line*. Since variables are created just by assigning to them, we can be fairly free in our use of variables in Python. But as usual, there are a few rules we have to follow when using variables:

*Reserved words*
: Programs have to avoid using a variable name that's the same as a reserved Python word such as *if*, *import*, *for*, etc. The complete list appears in Appendix C, *A Mini-Reference*.

*Legal names*
: Like C, Python variable names start with a letter or underscore (_), and can consist of any number of letters, digits, and underscores.

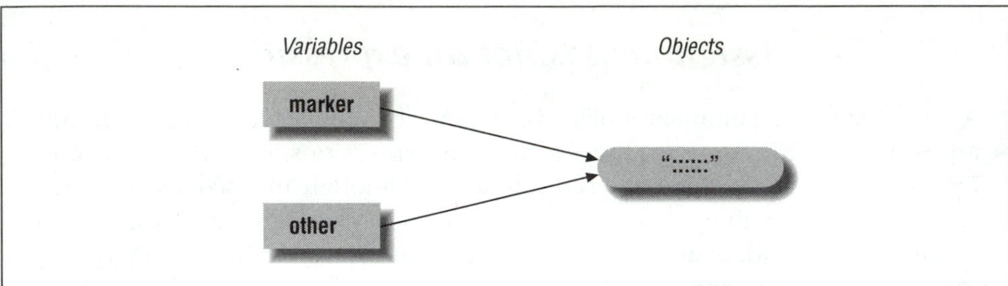


*Figure 4-3: Sharing objects*

*Case matters*
: Case (upper or lower) is always significant: `X` is a different variable than `x`. Case also matters in reserved words: they're always lowercase.

### *Namespaces, Part 1: object attributes*

As usual in lexically scoped languages, Python variables always exist in a *namespace*, sometimes called a "scope." When simple variables are assigned, Python changes or creates the name in the *closest* ("local") namespace, unless told otherwise (by using "global" statements, to be discussed later). When they're *referenced*, Python follows a search path through enclosing namespaces to find the closest version of the name.

But what about strings of names separated by dots, like *sys.stdin.readlines*? When variable names are qualified this way, we give an explicit path of namespaces to search for the attributes listed. The leftmost name (*sys*) will be looked up in the namespace where the code is written, but the rest (*stdin*, *readlines*) are looked up directly in the *object* identified by the list of names to the left. For instance, the name *sys.stdin.readlines* is evaluated in three steps, as shown in Figure 4-4.

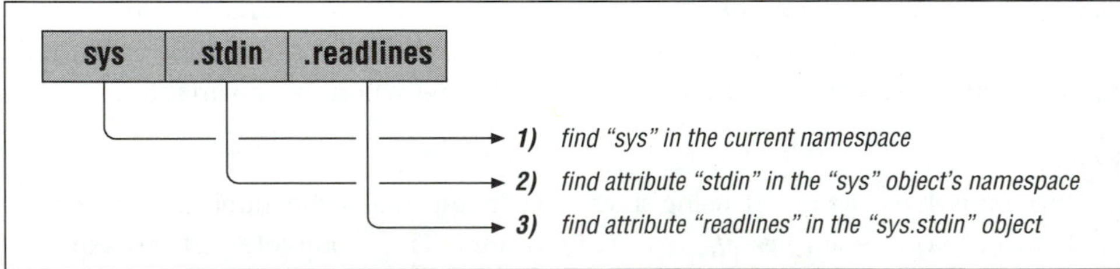


*Figure 4-4: Qualified names*

This process yields a method of a file object in the *sys* module. Qualification is just a matter of going into another namespace explicitly; as we'll see, it can be used on any object with named attributes: modules, classes, instances, lists, etc. As you might expect, qualified variables follow the same rules as simple ones:

- When we *assign* to a qualified name, it creates or changes the rightmost name in the identified object.
- When we *reference* a qualified name, it has to exist in the object, or an exception is raised.

In our scripts, namespaces are mostly a trivial issue: each has just one namespace for all its unqualified variables, since all the code is written at the top-level of the file (it's not nested in a function or class object). Technically, this is the namespace of the module corresponding to the script file. Names like *open* live in an implied built-in namespace that surrounds modules. We'll revisit scope issues later in the book, when we encounter functions and classes.

### *Calling functions and methods*

Our scripts don't create any functions or methods, but they use them four times. The packer calls the built-in *open* function, and the file-object *read* method:

```
input = open(name, 'r')       # call a function, passing 2 arguments
print input.read(),           # call an object's method, no arguments
```

The unpacker calls the file *readlines* method, and the *open* function:

```
for line in sys.stdin.readlines():
        sys.stdout = open(line[6:-1], 'w')
```

*Methods* are just functions associated with an object. As usual, arguments are passed to a function (or method), by enclosing a list of expressions in parenthesis after the name of the function. More formally, a function *object* is called by adding parentheses after a function object reference expression. For instance, when *open* is called, control transfers to the function that the variable *open* refers to, until it returns a file object back (or raises an error). (See Figure 4-5.) We'll defer more details on functions until we see how to create new ones.

### *Equality tests*

We used equality testing only once; in the unpacker, we use the != operator to see if the first six items in the *line* string are not the same as the *marker*:

```
if line[:6] != marker:
```

This is an example of *string equality* at work: Python performs a lexical, character-by-character comparison of the ASCII character codes in the two strings. If any characters don't match (or they're of different length), the comparison stops and fails.

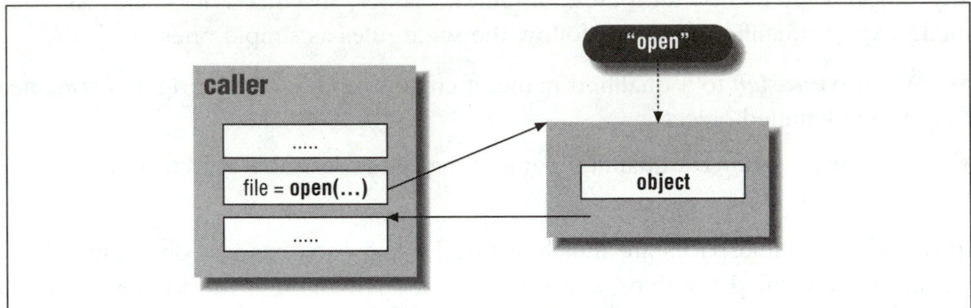


*Figure 4-5: Calling function objects*

Python equality tests (and other comparisons) are more general than those found in languages like C. When comparing built-in data structures, Python recursively compares all their parts automatically. For example, two lists of strings are equal only if all their strings are equal by string equality (more on lists in a moment).

### *A comparison of comparisons*

Python provides the usual comparison operators: >, <, >=, etc. They work on any kind of object, and return integer 1 or 0 (for true and false). They can also be strung together to test ranges: the following is true if *X* is an integer value 10 through 19:

```
10   <= X < 20          # same as "X >= 10 and X < 20"
```

The equality operator is ==, and inequality can be tested with either != or <> (they work the same: Python's inventor couldn't choose between C's and Pascal's). As noted above, you can't mistake = for ==, since assignment isn't an expression in Python. = can only appear in assignment statements. And, unlike C, all comparisons apply recursively as needed.

Because assignment creates potentially shared object references, it's sometimes useful to know if two objects are really the same object, and not just *equivalent*; Python's *is* operator tests this case. We'll see more comparisons in action as we move along.

## *Using Python Statements*

At the next level of complexity, Python programs are built up from statements. Besides = assignments, our scripts use four other kinds of statements. Some statements (*import*) hint at higher-levels of organization.

### *Loading modules with import*

Though it might not be obvious, our script files are really Python modules. In Python, programs are structured as sets of modules. In simple terms, a module is just a namespace, corresponding to a Python source file or a C extension. Modules import other modules, to use the objects and services they export:

- Modules are created by writing new source files (or C extensions).
- Modules are used by importing them (or *from* them) in other modules.

Both our scripts use another module called *sys*. By executing the statement:

```
import sys
```

they gain access to names (really, named *attributes*) exported by module object *sys*. For example, we use the exports listed in Figure 4-6.

**Module "sys"**

| | |
|---|---|
| **.argv** | *- command-line argument list* |
| **.stdout** | *- the standard output stream file* |
| **.stdin.readlines** | *- a method of the standard input stream* |

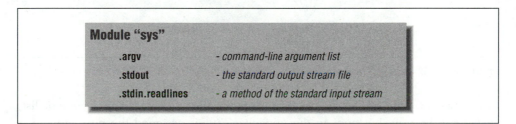

*Figure 4-6: Module services*

We'll see variations of the *import* statement as we move along. When we write a Python source file, all the variable names assigned at its top-level are available to importers. When we write a C module, we define a list of attribute names to export. Our packing scripts were designed to be run immediately, so they're not very useful to other modules (yet); but both are clients of the *sys* module.

### *Stepping through lists with for loops*

Both of the scripts use *for* loops:

```
for name in sys.argv[1:]:           # the packer's loop
for line in sys.stdin.readlines():  # the unpacker's loop
```

The packer's loop iterates over the command-line arguments, and the unpacker's steps through lines read from the input stream. The Python *for* loop is a simple way to step through items in ordered collections. More formally, it's a generic iterator, which assigns a variable (or set of variables) to each of the objects in a sequence object in turn, and executes the loop's body for each.

Its general form is:

```
for <target> in <sequence>:
        <statements using target>
```

where *sequence* is any indexable data object: *for* can be used to iterate through any sequence (lists, strings, class instances, even C types). The *target* is just a normal Python variable (or other assignment target); it's assigned consecutive items from the sequence, and doesn't go away when the loop ends. (See Figure 4-7.)

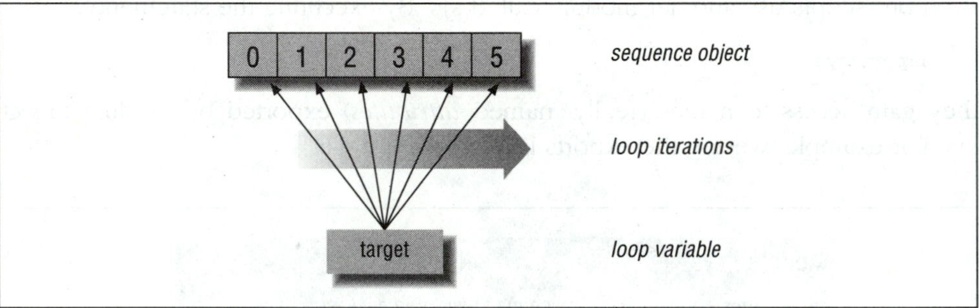


*Figure 4–7: For-loop assignments*

In the packer, *name* is set to the next string in the command-line argument list, each time through the loop. In the unpacker, *line* is assigned the next input line on each repetition.

### *Selecting actions with if tests*

The unpack script introduces Python's *if* statement:

```
if line[:6] != marker:
    print line,                          # write real lines
else:
    sys.stdout = open(line[6:-1], 'w')   # or make new output file
```

The general form of the *if* statement is fairly standard for procedural languages: an *if* test, one or more optional *elif* tests (a contraction of "else if"), and an optional *else*. Python executes the statements associated with the first test that evaluates to true, or the *else* statements if all are false:

```
if <test1>:
    <statements>
elif <test2>:
    <statements>
else:
    <statements>
```

As we'll see, in Python *true* means a nonzero number (as in C), or a nonempty data structure (as in Lisp). The *if* is Python's main selection construct. Although there are no *switch* or *case* statements in Python, multi-way branching can be coded with multiple *elif* clauses, or dictionaries (discussed later in the book).

### *Displaying text with print statements*

The Python *print* statement is a simple way to display objects on the screen. Given a list of values (objects) separated by commas, it types the textual representation of each to the standard output stream, separated by blanks. The *print* adds an end-of-line after the last item, unless we include a trailing comma. We use both forms in the pack script:

```
print marker + name          # write a separator, add an end-line
print input.read(),          # write the file, without an extra end-line
```

In the second form, we suppress an end-of-line with a comma, since the file already (presumably) has one.

## *Using System-Level Services: argv, Streams, Files*

For writing shell utilities, Python provides access to operating-system interfaces in a variety of ways. Most are relatively standard for UNIX tools. Here are some of the system services used in our scripts so far.

### *Command-line arguments*

To get the command-line arguments, we use an object in the *sys* module both scripts import, called *argv*. *sys.argv* is a Python list of character strings, representing the arguments on the command line used to run the script. It's exactly like the *argv* array passed to the *main()* function in C programs. If we have three files, *spam.py*, *eggs.py*, and *ham.py* in the directory where we run the packer, here's the correspondence:

```
Command:      % pack1.py *.py > packed.txt
sys.argv:     ['pack1.py', 'spam.py', 'eggs.py', 'ham.py']
```

As in C, the first item in *argv* is the program's name: *pack1.py*. Python's slicing operator `[1:]` is used to strip it off, leaving the list of files to be packed: `['spam.py', 'eggs.py', 'ham.py']`.

### *Standard input/output streams*

One of the basic concepts in shell programming is the use of the standard input/output streams (known as *stdin* and *stdout* in C programming). Python gives us access to these streams, both as file objects, and through higher-level input/output statements and functions. By redirecting these streams, we can make programs work both in interactive mode, and as file processors (see Figure 4-8).

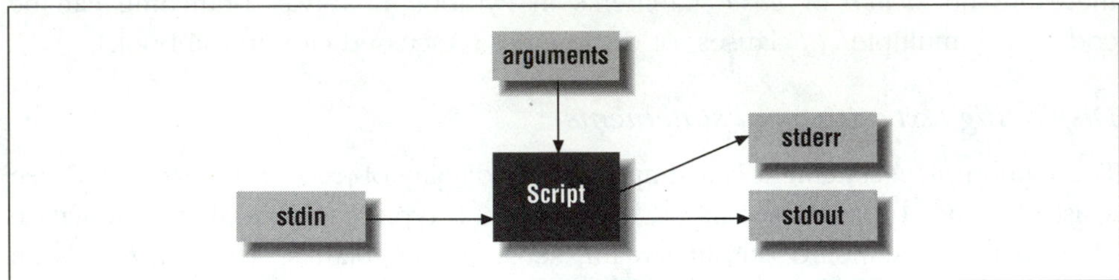


*Figure 4-8: The shell tool environment*

Internally, the *print* statement sends its output to the standard output stream, which is really a file object, available as attribute *stdout* in module *sys*. Normally, *stdout* is connected to the window where the Python program was started. But since we can redirect the output stream, we can use *print* to write to files too. In the packer script, we assume output is redirected on the system command line (as we'll see later). In the unpacker, we make *print* text go to a file, by resetting the output stream inside Python:

```
sys.stdout = open(line[6:-1], 'w')    # now "print" goes to the new file
```

As we'll see in a moment, we can always simulate *print* by writing to *sys.stdout* explicitly; *print* is really just a convenience. The standard *input* stream file object is also available as *sys.stdin*. It's also connected to the window where the program was started initially, so it can be used to get input from the keyboard. In the *unpack* script, we read from it directly:

```
for line in sys.stdin.readlines():    # read stdin lines until end-of-file
```

and assume that input was redirected from a file (a packed file) at the system-shell level, if necessary. The *raw_input* and *input* functions are higher-level interfaces to *stdin*; we'll see an example shortly.

A third standard stream, *stderr*, is available in Python as file object *sys.stderr*. The Python interpreter uses it for internally generated prompts and error messages.

### *External files: open plus methods*

The pack script reads from the files to be packed, by opening a file for each. In Python, external files are accessed by calling the built-in *open* function: *open* creates a file object, and connects it to the external file, prepared for reading and/or writing. *open* takes the name of the external file, and the mode in which we want to use it: *r* for reading, *w* for writing, and others not used here (*r* is the default).

The packer opens a file object for reading (*r*), and calls its *read* method (attribute) to load the file's text all at once, as one long character string object (refer to Figure 4-9):

```
input = open(name, 'r')          # open the next input file ('r')
print input.read(),              # read and print the file's contents
```

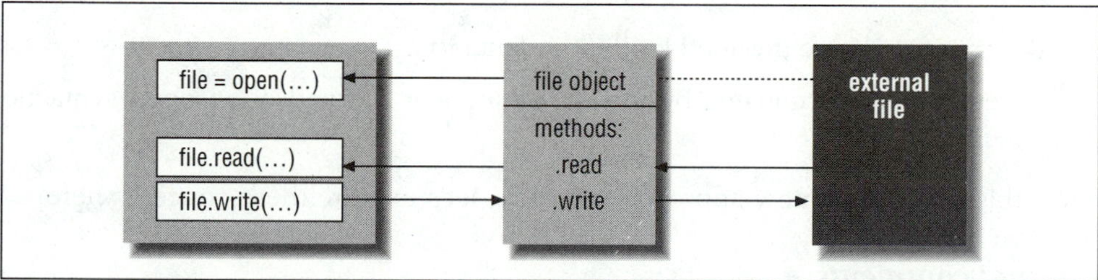


*Figure 4-9: File objects*

The unpacker reads from the standard input file, and resets the standard output file to redirect print text:

```
for line in sys.stdin.readlines():              # use the file readlines method
        sys.stdout = open(line[6:-1], 'w')      # open a new output file ('w')
```

There's one boundary case in the unpacker: since *sys.stdout* is initially connected to the default output stream (normally the screen), if there are any lines in the packed file before the first marker line, they'll be printed to *stdout*. This would only happen in our scripts if the packed file gets corrupted.

## *Python's filesystem looks a lot like C's*

If you've programmed in C, you probably recognize this: Python's file system is really just a thin wrapper (integration) over C's *stdio* filesystem. In fact, Python's *open* function is equivalent to C's *fopen*. But in Python, the *open* function makes an object which wraps the C file-pointer and has methods for common file actions.

All the usual *stdio* file operations are supported as methods of Python file objects: read, write, close, flush, seek, tell, etc. Python adds higher-level methods to the *stdio* set, like the *readlines* used here. The full set of file object methods is summarized in Appendix C, later in this book. Later in the book, we'll also see other Python file-processing tools, such as file descriptors, pipes, and shelves.

## *Using Python's Syntax*

Python is a procedural, structured programming language. By and large, its syntax is fairly conventional, when compared to some other tools (such as Scheme). But while its syntax rules are simple, Python also makes use of syntactic structures that minimize coding errors, and reduce program size. In particular, Python notices when statements and blocks end, without requiring special symbols to be typed:

- Blocks of code are grouped by their indentation.
- Statements are terminated by the end-of-line (or the end of an open syntactic pair).

Since this is usually a new approach for many, let's explore these concepts here.

### *Internal comments: #*

Both of our scripts start with a line of the form:

```
#!/usr/local/bin/python
```

which is a Python comment line. This particular comment tells the operating system shell to send the file to the Python interpreter; we'll expand on this idea in a moment, when we see how the scripts are run. Python comments start with a # character (not nested in a character string constant) and run to the end of the line.

As usual, comments serve as internal documentation for your code, and are always ignored by Python. They don't have to take up a whole line; comments can also appear to the right of executable code in our scripts, in order to help explain what's going on:

```
import sys                    # load the system module
```

### *Implicit end-of-block syntax*

As mentioned in Chapter 2, *A Sneak Preview*, Python uses the indentation of the statements in a block of code to detect where it ends. There's no need to type "begin/end" or `{}` pairs around blocks. Python compound statements usually take the form of a header line terminated by a `:`, and a block of code indented under the header. The nested block ends at the next line that's not indented as deeply as the lines in the block. Figure 4-10 gives the abstract case.

Indentation can consist of any combination of blanks and tabs, so long as it's consistent for all lines in a code block. For instance, the statements in the *for* loop in the packer script are all indented four blanks (shown here as periods to highlight):

```
for name in sys.argv[1:]:               loop header line
....input = open(name, 'r')             loop body block: 3 indented lines
....print marker + name
....print input.read(),
```

but this is arbitrary: we might use a different number of blanks, use tabs, etc. At the top level, unnested lines always start in column one; for each level of statement nesting, we just indent a block's lines further right:

```
for line in sys.stdin.readlines():                  0: 'for' header (column 1)
....if line[:6] != marker:                          4: 'for' block: 'if' header
........print line,                                 8: 'if' block line
....else:                                           4: 'for' block: 'else' header
........sys.stdout = open(line[6:-1], 'w')          8: 'else' block line
```

---

*NOTE* Notice that this is really just a description of how programmers would normally indent structured code like this in any language. Python's able to use that information itself, rather than requiring you to write extra, error-prone symbols to mark where a block starts and stops. In effect, block boundaries are detected automatically.

---

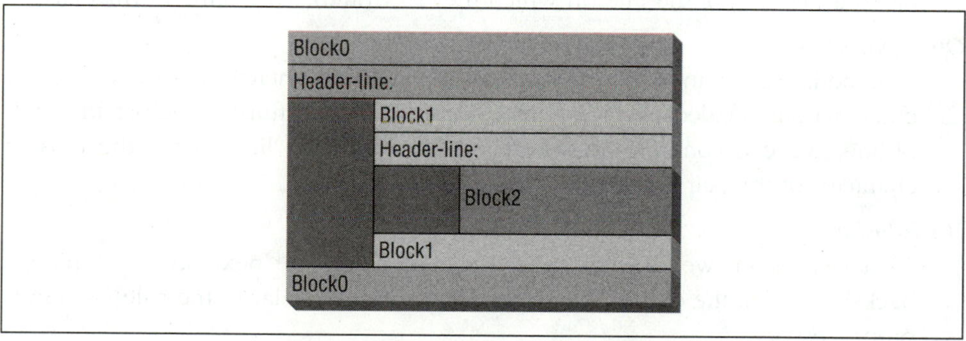


*Figure 4–10: Nesting blocks by indentation*

***Putting bodies next to headers.*** There is one useful exception to the indentation rule: a compound statement's body can appear on the same line as the statement's header, as long as the body doesn't contain any compound statements itself. For example, if we want to print the arguments passed in to a script, we could do it on one line instead of two:

```
for arg in sys.argv: print arg
```

Similarly, we could collapse the nested *if* statement in the unpacker to two lines:

```
6   for line in sys.stdin.readlines():
7   ....if line[:6] != marker: print line,
8   ....else: sys.stdout = open(line[6:-1], 'w')
```

but we can't move the *if* statement up to line 6, since it's compound too. As a rule of thumb, it's usually best to minimize compressing lines like this; as you can see, it can be less readable than the consistently indented form. But this is really a matter of style which we won't debate here.

### Implicit end-of-statement syntax

Much like implicit block delimiters, Python normally uses the end of a line to detect the end of a statement. There's no need to type a `;` after each line, as in C. Although this scheme handles most statements you may write, some are too big to fit on one line. For these cases, Python provides two additional rules for continuing lines. Here are all the line termination cases:

*End of line*
: Statements (and header lines for compound statements) are normally terminated at the end of the line on which they're written. This is the normal case.

*Open pairs*
: Statements can span lines, if there's an incomplete syntactic pair: if we start a construct surrounded by `()`, `[]`, or `{}` pairs, but can't finish it before the end-of-line, we can continue anywhere on the following lines, until the closing character of the pair is typed.

*Backslashes*
: As a last resort, we can continue a statement on the next line by typing a backslash (\) at the end of the current line. This is similar to the rule used in C preprocessors.

Although they're still supported, backslashes are never needed for continuation lines. They are a throwback to older versions of Python that didn't support the open-pairs rule. In practice, we can be fairly cavalier in our use of continuation lines. The normal end-of-line rule handles nearly all our statements. Where this fails, the open-pair rule usually applies naturally (long data structure constants are usually the only items that span lines). For instance, if we're writing a list, it can be continued until we type the last "]".

```
breakfast = ['spam',                          # open '[]' list constant pair
                  'eggs',                     # can span any number of lines
                    'toast']                  # indentation doesn't matter
```

And in the worst case, we can use a continuation line without backslashes, by enclosing the construct in parentheses to force the open-pairs rule:

```
if (thisIsOneBigHonkinVariableName   and     # open parenthesis pair
    this_is_a_bigun_too < 0          and     # 2 continuation lines
    _so_Is_This_1):
    print 'spam'
```

Similarly, function argument lists can always span lines, since they're always in parentheses anyhow:

```
result = function(argument1,                 # we're in parenthesis anyhow
                  argument2,                 # so we can continue at will
                  argument3)
```

Backslashes won't appear in this book; still, you may see them in older Python code:

```
lunch = 'spam' + \
        'eggs' + \
        'ham'
```

***Semicolons work, if you insist.*** There's one special case to mention here: if you really want to put more than one noncompound statement on a line, you can do it by separating them with semicolons. For instance, we could combine the three statements in the pack script's *for* loop:

```
input = open(name, 'r'); print marker + name; print input.read(),
```

It's hard to imagine contexts where this rule would be required, but it's sometimes used to combine simple statements to save "real estate." For example, simple assignments are occasionally combined:

```
x = 1;  y = 2;  z = 3      # a 3-statement line
```

But for multiple assignments, Python lets us use multiple targets and values too (which are really are an application of tuples, discussed later).

```
x, y, z = 1, 2, 3          # a single statement
```

### *Other syntax components*

Finally, blank lines and comments can always be used *anywhere* in a Python program; they're always ignored, regardless of indentation level or continuation line status. Blanks and tabs inside statements are optional, and can be used arbitrarily too. And some string constant forms we'll use later are allowed to span lines (triple-quoted string blocks, joined string constants, etc.). Multiline strings aren't subject to the normal continuation line rules.

### *Using implied delimiter syntax*

Implied-delimiter syntax isn't a new concept: it was part of the ABC language, and is used in a number of popular modern languages. In practice, it's remarkably simple to use: we just indent nested blocks of code as we'd do normally in a structured language, and let the end-of-line (or open-pairs) terminate our statements.

Python users find it to be an important feature in a rapid development language. There's less to type, and it adds an implicit quality control check on code indentation: a block's visual nesting is its true nesting. It's another way Python's design enhances readability (although you may occasionally forget to type `{}` and `;` in your C programs :-).

A number of systems have successfully implemented automatic Python code generation: it's usually just a matter of writing tabs instead of `{}` or `begin/end` braces. Moreover, Python's syntax works well in text-editing environments: for instance, a set of Emacs macros for working with Python code ships with the system. If you're not an Emacs user, most text editors allow you to automate indentation; do what you'd do for C or Pascal.

And finally, if you absolutely need to use end-of-block markers, or if properly indenting code is problematic, there's a standard Python tool called *pindent*, which allows special comments to be used to close blocks. Of course, this should only be used as a last resort. See the overview in Appendix A, *...And Other Cool Stuff.*

## *Using Built-In Types: Numbers, Strings, and Lists*

Our scripts use objects of three intrinsic datatypes: numbers, character-strings, and lists. We also use a built-in datatype: *files* (discussed earlier). In our scripts:

- Numbers are used as indexes in slice expressions: for example, *sys.argv[1:]*, *line[:6]*, *line[6:-1]*.
- Lists show up twice: the *sys.argv* argument list, and the result of the *sys.stdin.readlines()* call.
- Strings appear as the `::::::` marker, inside the two lists we use, and as the *input.read()* result.
- Files show up as attributes of the *sys* module, and as new files the packer opens for input.

Datatype objects are created by writing constants, or by calling built-in operations or functions. For instance, the + operation in *marker* + *name* makes a new string object. Since built-in datatypes are a primary programming tool, here's a quick overview of the ones used in our scripts; Appendix C provides additional details on built-in type operations we won't cover here.

### *Number objects*

Python provides the usual integer and floating-point number support. Python's integer is like C's "long int," and its floating-point is like C's "double." Integers are written as a string of decimal digits, and floating-point numbers have an embedded decimal point (.) and an optional exponent suffix (as in C).

*Table 4–1: Writing numbers*

| Number constants | Interpretation |
|---|---|
| 1234 | Integers |
| 3.14159 | Floating-point |
| 0177 | Octal integers |
| 0x1AFF | Hexadecimal integers |
| 99999999999L | Long integers |

Python supports C's notion of octal and hexadecimal constants: they begin with "0" and "0x", respectively. It also supports unlimited-size integers: if an integer ends with an *L* (*99L*), it's a Python *long* integer. For writing numeric *expressions*, Python provides all the usual arithmetic operators, precedence rules, grouping by parentheses, etc. In addition, Python provides a set of numerical tools, including:

- Built-in math functions: *pow*, *abs*, etc.
- Built-in *math* module: things like *tan*, *floor*, and *pi*
- Bitwise operators for integers: << does a left shift, & is bitwise-and, etc.

Appendix C, covers details on numeric operators and modules. As in C, when mixing numbers of different types in an expression, operands are coerced (i.e., converted) up to the most complex type. For mixed types, integers are converted up to long or floating-point, and longs are converted up to floating-point.

### *String objects*

Character-string objects can be written by enclosing text in single or double quotes. See the following table for an example.

*Table 4-2: Writing strings*

| String constants | Interpretation |
|---|---|
| `''` | An empty string |
| `'x'` | A one-character string |
| "*This is bob's string*" | Double quotes |
| '*this is a "string" too*' | Single quotes |
| "*with a \t tab and newline\n*" | Embedded special characters |
| """<*text spanning lines*>""" | A multiline text block |

There's no difference between single and double quotes, but having both allows for embedded quotes without backslashes. The empty string is written by putting two quotes next to each other; and as in C, special characters can appear in strings, by preceding them with a backslash. Supported backslash character codes appear in a table in Appendix C.

Python strings may span lines (the rules are like C's), and there's a triple-quoted form for writing blocks of text; we'll use both later. Strings are really *collections* of one-character strings; unlike C, there's no distinct type for individual characters. In arithmetic, strings are not converted to numbers automatically: 1+'2' is an error; 1+eval('2') works. Strings are processed with both operators and modules, but not methods.

### *List objects*

Python lists are essentially variable-length arrays. Since lists are built in, they're one of the main tools for structuring data in Python programs. They can hold objects of any type including other lists, and so naturally support nesting. Although this script doesn't use list *constants*, it may help to see what they look like. Lists are written as a set of items separated by commas, and enclosed in square brackets:

*Table 4-3: Writing lists*

| List constants | Interpretation |
|---|---|
| [] | An empty list |
| ["parrot"] | A one-item list, holding a string |
| [1, 'spam', [3.14, 'pie']] | A three-item list, with a sublist |

The last example in Table 4-3 holds a number, a string, and a nested list. But as in our scripts, lists are often created without writing them down: lists in our scripts come from using and calling objects in the *sys* module. As we'll see, Python lists can grow and shrink on demand, and items can be changed in place, without copying the list. We'll manipulate lists using sequence operations (indexing, concatenation, etc.), plus extra list-specific methods (append, sort, etc.).

***Lists are arrays of references.*** A list constant *[1,2,3,4]* can be thought of as an array of integers, as shown in Figure 4-11.

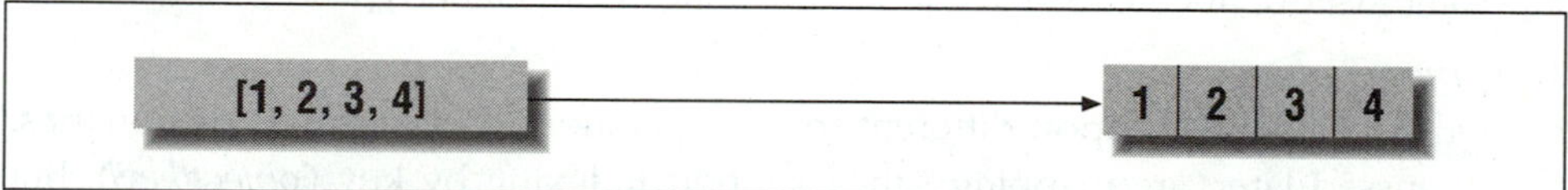


*Figure 4-11: Lists—an array of numbers*

But it's more accurate to think of lists as arrays of object references: assigning list items stores references to possibly shared objects as usual. When lists contain objects that can be changed in-place, this sharing of objects sometimes matters in larger programs; as we'll see later, lists are open to side effects. Not only may lists change, but objects they contain might be altered through other references too. Figure 4-12 shows what lists really look like internally.

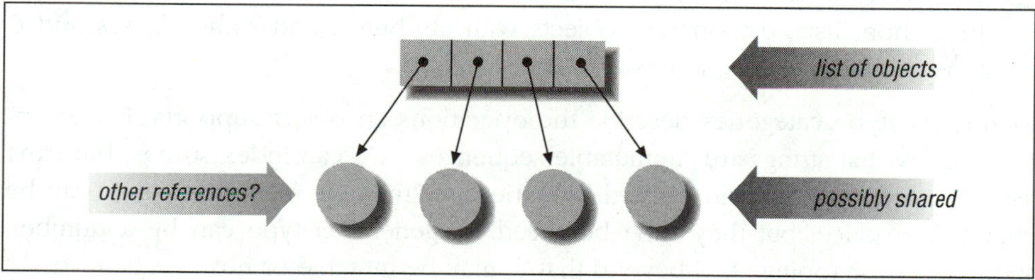


*Figure 4-12: Lists–arrays of references*

### *Just a little theory: Python type categories*

Let's introduce some of the terminology used to describe Python's datatypes:

*Numbers*

Number objects support typical numeric operators. As we've seen, this category includes the usual integer and floating-point types, plus Python's unlimited-precision ("long") integers. But instances of user-defined classes and C extension types (both discussed later) can also act as numbers, and respond to numeric expression operators.

*Sequences*

Strings and lists are examples of sequence datatypes. Roughly, a *sequence object* is any ordered collection of items that allows its items to be indexed by their relative position. This distinction matters, because sets of generic operations apply to datatypes, according to their categories. For instance, sequences support indexing (*object[i]*), concatenation (*object* + *object*), repetition (*object* * *N*), and slicing (*object[i:j]*). In Python, sequences include lists, strings, tuples, some user-defined class instances, and some C extension types.

*Mappings*

Other categories support different sets of operations. For instance, dictionaries, discussed later, are mappings; they support indexing by key (*object[key]*), but not concatenation or slicing, since there's no notion of ordering among their elements. In Python, dictionaries, class instances, and C extension types can all be mappings.

*Mutability*

Python lists can be changed in place, but strings can't. We have to make a new string object to change a string's value. More formally, we say that Python strings are immutable, and lists are mutable (changeable). For lists we can change one of the list's items, by assigning to an index: *list[i]* = *new-value*. This won't work on a string; we'll see how to get around this constraint later. In Python, lists, dictionaries, objects with attributes, and some classes and C types are all mutable; strings and tuples are not.

Python datatype categories describe the operations an object supports. For example, we say that strings are "immutable sequences": we can index strings, but can't assign to their indexes. Similarly, dictionaries are "mutable mappings": they can be changed in place, but they can't be sliced. In general, a type can be a number, sequence, or mapping. And beyond that, it may be mutable or not.

### Using sequences: slices, concatenation, iteration

Since all sequence objects share a set of operations, we'll lump them together whenever possible instead of explaining how they work for each type they apply to. We use three sequence operations in our scripts: slicing, concatenation, and iteration.

***Slicing sequences.*** Slices extract *sections* of sequence objects. Since we can index from both the front and end of a sequence, slices let us split up collections arbitrarily.

Given a pair of indexes: `[I:J]`, Python makes a *new* sequence object, containing items at offsets I through (J-1) from the object being sliced. Both the lower and upper bounds (I and J) can be omitted; they default to zero, and the length of the sequence respectively. Python indexes always start at zero, and end at one less than the length of the sequence; like C, indexes are really "offsets."

Slices are used three ways in our scripts. In the packer, we use slicing to strip off the first item in the command-line argument list:

```
for name in sys.argv[1:]:                 extract items 2 and beyond from argv
```

which deletes the program name, leaving the filenames. Since the upper bound is omitted, it defaults to the length of the *argv* list; *[1:]* is the same as *[1:len(sys.argv)]*. In the unpacker, we first use a slice to extract the first six characters in a line, at offsets 0 though 5:

```
if line[:6] != marker:                    extract items up to node 7 from line
```

Since the lower bound's missing, it defaults to zero; `[:6]` is the same as `[0:6]`. We also slice the line to extract the filename stored after the '::::::' marker:

```
sys.stdout = open(line[6:-1], 'w')        extract items after 6 up to the last
```

In Python, we can also use negative indexes, which are taken to be offsets from the end of the sequence: index –1 is the last item (one from the right), –2 is the second last, and so on. Slice *[6:-1]* extracts the seventh item at offset 6, through the second last (the item before the last at index -1). Figure 4-13 shows the relationships for the *line* string in the unpack script:

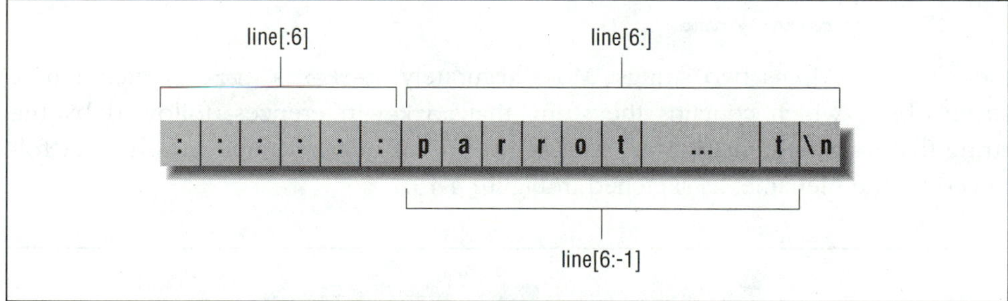


*Figure 4–13: Slicing lines*

More generally, if we have a sequence *S* that's four items long, then indexes and slices correspond as shown in Figure 4-14.

Like most Python operations, slicing is generic: the packer slices a list, and the unpacker slices a string. The meaning of slices is the same for all sequence objects, but a slice makes a new object of the type being sliced: for instance, if we slice a string, we always get back a new string.

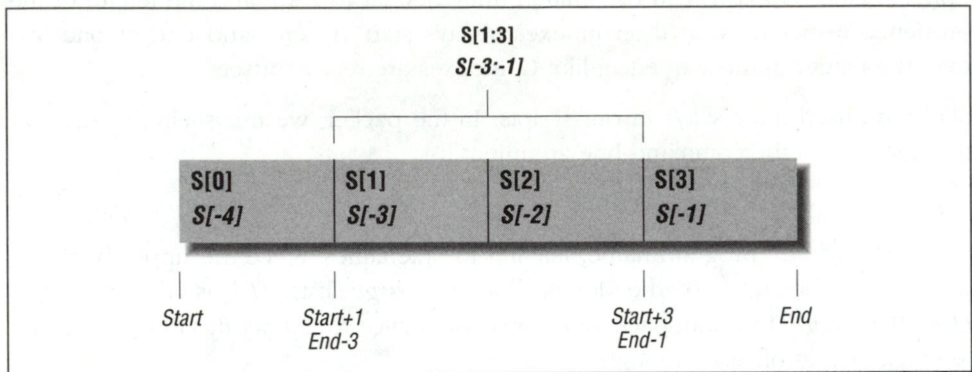


*Figure 4-14: Indexes and slicing*

> ## *Slice assignment*
>
> It's also possible to assign to slices in mutable sequence objects (lists, etc.). For instance: *list[2:4] = [8,9]*. This is one way to change, insert, and delete whole sections of a sequence. We'll see examples that use slice assignment later in the book.

***Concatenating sequences.*** We use sequence concatenation once in our scripts: in the packer,

```
print marker + name
```

the + operator joins two strings. More accurately, `marker + name` creates a new string object which contains the string that `marker` references, followed by the string that `name` references. The result is just one of our separator lines: `::::::` followed by the filename, as sketched in Figure 4-15.

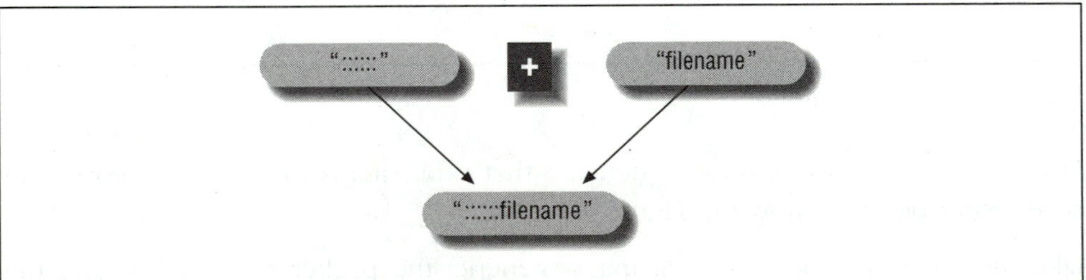


*Figure 4-15: Concatenating string objects*

As we'll see, the + operator allows us to concatenate any two sequence objects of the *same* type. It also lets us get around the "no-change" (immutable) rule for strings: to add a character to a string, we just make a new one:

```
string = string + 'x'                       # add 'x' at the end
```

To change a character in a string, slice and concatenate to make a new string:

```
string = string[:2] + 'x' + string[3:]      # change the third character to 'x'
```

***Concatenation, mutability, and side effects.*** Since lists can be changed in place (they're mutable), they are easier to modify; we can assign to indexes directly: *list[3] = 'x'*. In fact, there are methods in lists for inserting and appending in place which are actually more efficient that the "+" operation. The following have the same effect:

```
list = list + ['extra']             # concatenate 2 lists, making a new one
list.append('extra')                # add an item on the end of a list in-place
```

but *append* avoids making a new list object. Since index assignment and *append* don't create new lists, they're faster but also open to side effects as mentioned. For example, if a list is referenced in more than one place (from variables or data structures), *append* changes the list for all the references. In Figure 4-16, *X* and *Y* refer to the same list object; *X.append(4)* changes it for both:

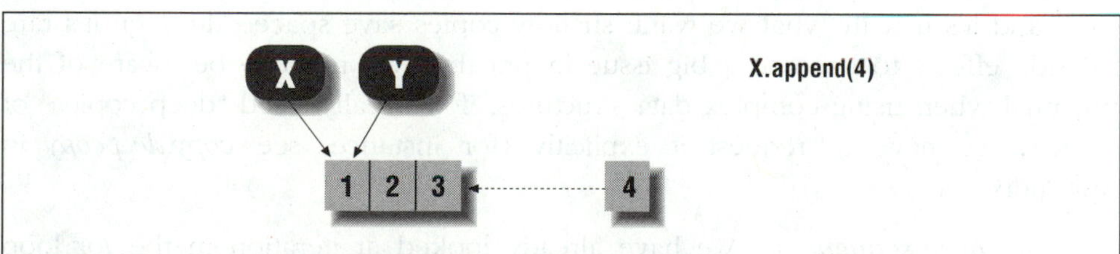


*Figure 4-16: Side effects of changing lists in place*

Such side effects can never happen if we use + concatenation, since it creates a new object. After executing *X = X + [4]*, *X* would be set to a new list, and *Y* would still refer to the old one, as shown in Figure 4-17.

Both slicing and concatenation make new sequence objects which aren't linked to the original. But not quite—the "copy" is really only one level deep. For both slicing and concatenating, Python makes a top-level copy of the original object, and copies its object references over. The new sequence references the same nested objects as the original. Figure 4-18 shows the internal effect of a top-level copy.

The copy and original share nested objects initially. Although changes to either object itself are side effect free, if we change an object nested in one object, it still may change the other object as a side effect.

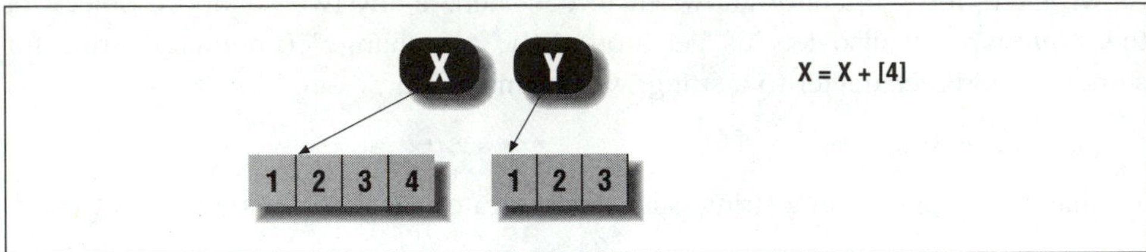


*Figure 4-17: Concatenation is side-effect free*

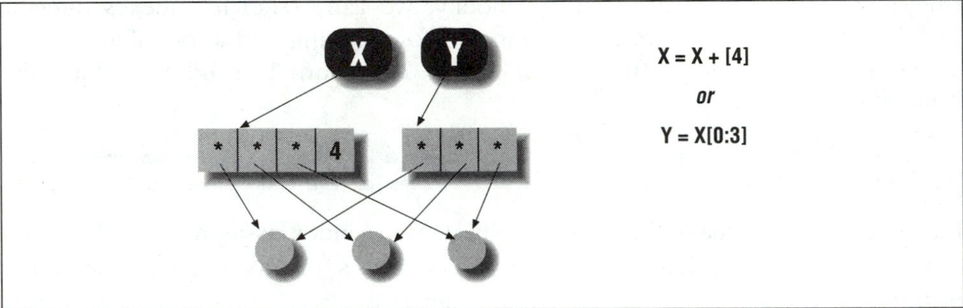


*Figure 4-18: Concatenation and slicing make top-level shallow copies*

This only matters for sequences holding mutable objects (other lists, dictionaries, etc.), and it's usually what we want: shallow copies save space. Although it's rare for side effects to become a big issue in practice, we need to be aware of the potential when using complex data structures; if we really need "deep copies" of objects, we have to request it explicitly (for instance, see *copy.deepcopy* in Appendix A).

***Iterating over sequences.*** We have already looked at iteration in the *for* loop description above. We'll just mention it here to emphasize that *for* loops iterate over any kind of sequence object: it's really a sequence operation. In our scripts,

```
for name in sys.argv[1:]:              # the packer's loop
for line in sys.stdin.readlines():     # the unpacker's loop
```

both scripts iterate over lists of strings: *name* and *line* are set to strings each time through. But we could just as easily iterate over the characters in a string:

```
for char in "spamSpamSPAM":            # for each character in the string
```

which sets variable *char* to a one-character string on each iteration.

### *Why can't strings be changed in place too?*

Strings cannot be changed in place—there's no equivalent to *append* for strings. Being unable to change strings in place is sometimes inconvenient, but it allows Python to implement some important string optimizations internally. More important, it also guarantees that a string object won't change "out from under" a reference. Since assignment creates shared references, changing a string object in place might create more unexpected side effects than we'd like. The immutability rule provides some degree of integrity for strings.

#### *in generates and tests*

In fact, we haven't seen this used yet, but the *in* reserved word in the *for* loop also works by itself as an operator for testing sequence membership:

```
if "guido" in inventors: print "found"
```

Internally *for* loops and *in* membership tests both work by repeatedly indexing the sequence object. As long as an object knows how to respond to indexing, it can be used in both contexts. We'll see why this matters when we study classes and extension types.

#### *Python has real data structures*

As you can probably tell by now, Python isn't just a string-processing language. Its built-in datatypes let us build up complex data structures, which we use for representing information in our programs. In this respect, Python is actually closer to a Lisp-like language than a traditional shell language.

We'll see additional built-in types in later chapters. We'll also see that, in addition to its rich set of built-in types, Python provides tools for adding new types beyond those provided (modules, classes, C extensions). In fact, Python's data structure tools are one of its greatest assets when we move beyond trivial programs.

## *"Telling the Monkeys What to Do"*

Finally, let's look at some of the ways these scripts can be run. In general, Python code may be run as scripts or program files, typed at the interactive prompt, or executed as embedded code.

### *"Side effects can be our friends"*

In practice, Python's built-in types are almost trivial to use. Part of the reason we went into detail on slicing and side effects here was to lay the groundwork for more advanced concepts. For instance, we'll see that dictionaries are open to side effects in the same way as lists—both themselves, and their nested objects can have side effects. And when we get to classes we'll see that the same side effect rules apply, even though we'll be changing object attributes instead of data structure components.

But we'll also find that side effects are a useful tool, as long as we plan for them. For instance, they make it possible to alter arguments passed to Python functions (discussed later in the book), and let us pass large data structures around a program, without making multiple copies. Moreover, classes depend on side effects to change data members of instance objects. And in more advanced programs, Python object-sharing is often useful as a higher-level analogue of "pointers" in languages like C.

Here's how to run them as top-level scripts, from the UNIX and MS-DOS command lines:

```
% pack1.py *.py > packed.txt

C:\TEMP> unpack1.py < packed.txt
```

Where necessary, I'll use different command-line prompts to distinguish which system a script is run under. Here, `%` is a UNIX command-line prompt, and `C:\TEMP>` is an MS-DOS prompt.

*NOTE* The above discussion assumes that a UNIX-like command-line processor is used on the MS-DOS machine. Command-line shells vary, even on the same platform. If you don't have a shell that recognizes `#!` comments, you can still run the scripts by passing them to Python manually.

```
C:\temp> python unpack1.py < packed.txt
```

Some platforms also allow Python programs to be started by clicking on GUI devices; see your documentation manual for details.

## *Using Shell Globbing and Redirection*

The commands above make use of common system shell features. The first command packs all the files in the current directory that match the pattern **.py* (i.e., all the Python source files). The system shell expands the **.py* pattern into a list of filenames; this is usually called filename *globbing*. As we've seen, items on the command line show up in the script's *sys.argv* list.

The shell is also used to redirect streams here. To pack, the > shell operator is used to route the packer's output (stdout) to a file called *packed.txt* so we can download it. To unpack, the < shell operator is used to take standard input (stdin) from the packed file.

Since the *pack* script writes to *stdout*, we can also send its output to command-line filter tools. For instance, if we want to see how many files are in a packed file, we can pipe the output to programs that find separator lines and count how many there are:

```
% pack1.py *.py | grep '::::::' | wc -l
```

The | connects output and input streams. In fact, we could attach pack output to unpack input directly:

```
% pack1.py *.py | unpack1.py
```

but there would be little point in doing so; as long as both scripts work correctly, this command would have no effect (we would pack and unpack in the same directory!).

## *Making Python Files Executable Programs*

As we saw earlier, our *pack* script starts with the comment line:

```
#!/usr/local/bin/python
```

But this comment is special: it holds the name (file directory path) of the Python interpreter. Like all scripting languages, Python source code files can be executed directly by:

1. Putting such a comment line at the top
2. Giving the file executable privileges (for instance, *chmod +x pack1.py* on UNIX systems)
3. Invoking the file from the system command line:

```
% pack1.py *.py > packed.txt
```

The operating-system shell sends the source file to the interpreter named in the first line. Running scripts this way is really a system shell feature, but it's a standard trick. Python programs can also be run by passing source code filenames to the *python* interpreter ourselves:

```
% python pack1.py *.py > packed.txt
```

In this case:

- We don't need line 1 (but it won't hurt—Python ignores comments).
- The file doesn't have to be made executable.

In all other respects, there is no difference between the two schemes. For instance, when programs are passed to the python interpreter, the *sys.argv* list contains the command-line arguments after the python command name. In the example above, sys.argv's first item would be *pack1.py*, not *python*, exactly as though *pack1* was run directly as an executable file—programs don't depend on how they're run.

### *Python source-file naming rules*

If a Python script will only be run from the system command-line, it doesn't need a *.py* extension. In fact, we could have named our script files *pack1* and *unpack1*. But as a rule, any Python file that's imported by another Python module has to end with *.py*. "Import" statements always omit the *.py* suffixes, but imported files need them.

It's usually a good idea to end all Python files with *.py*: it serves to distinguish them as Python files, and lets us use them from other modules. It's less useful to add the special `#!` comment at the top of Python files that are meant to be imported as modules, but not run as top-level scripts. But even in this case, we might use the comment to arrange for running self-test code when the file is run like a script; we'll see an example later in this book.

## *Interactive Coding and Filename Expansion*

It's also possible to run code by typing it interactively at the Python command-line prompt:

```
% python
>>> import sys
>>> marker = '::::::'
>>> and so on...
```

When entered this way, Python runs the code as you type it, in the same way the UNIX shell's command line works. It's also possible to run code as character strings, embedded in another program or language, but we'll ignore this possibility until later in the book.

But there's a problem here: the pack script won't really work if typed interactively exactly as is, since *sys.argv* won't hold the filename list. While in the *python* command-line interpreter, *sys.argv* contains the arguments passed to the *python* program. We can't list the files to be packed in the *python* command, since Python will assume they're programs to run, and will try executing each (with surprising results).

To run this code interactively, we would probably use Python's own implementation of filename globbing (expansion) to create the list of files to be packed at the prompt:

```
% python
>>> import glob
>>> marker = '::::::'
>>> for name in glob.glob('*.py'):              not sys.argv
...     input = open(name, 'r')
...     print marker + name                     or to a real file...
...     print input.read(),
...
<output shows up here>
>>>
```

After we type this code, the packed file is displayed to us on the screen, since we're using print statements and stdout isn't redirected. We probably also want to write the output to an explicit file instead of using print (we'll see how in Chapter 5, *Variations on a Theme*), or assign *sys.stdout* to a real file, as done in the unpack script.

The glob call *glob.glob* expands filename patterns into a list of matching filename strings, in the same way filename patterns get expanded in the UNIX shell command-line. For example, if there are three matching files in the directory where you start *python*, *a.py*, *b.py*, and *c.py*, the glob call would return a list of character strings: `[a.py, b.py, c.py]`.

### *Running shell commands in Python*

Python's glob module allows patterns to include most of the usual shell operators: `*` to match any substring, `?` to match one character, `[...]` for listing alternative characters, and `[!...]` for negation. But if you depend on a unique feature of the system shell's filename globbing, you can use it instead:

```
% python
>>> import os
>>> marker = '::::::'
>>> for name in os.popen("ls *.py", 'r').readlines():
...     input = open(name[:-1], 'r')
...     print marker + name,        already has end-line...
...     print input.read(),
```

The *popen* function in the *os* built-in module runs a system shell command, and connects to its standard input or output stream, as though it were a file. Here, the "readlines" method returns the output of the *ls* (list files) command as a list of character-strings, one for each line (file-name). The *popen* function is usually the easiest way to capture the output of a program or shell command in Python (see Figure 4-19).

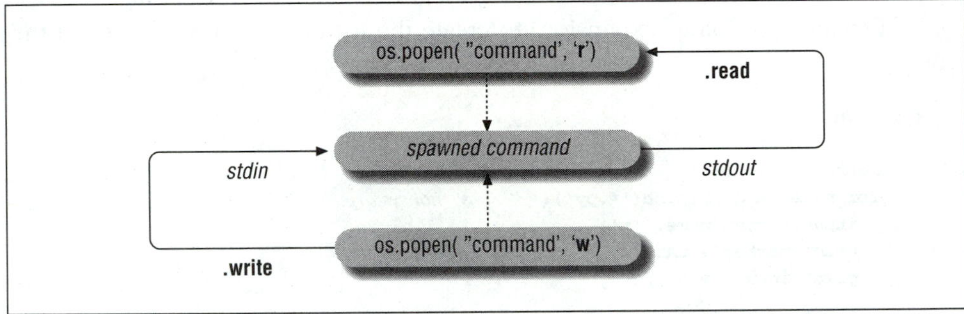


*Figure 4–19: Capturing a command's output, or sending input*

The effect of the *os.popen* call here is the almost the same as calling the *glob.glob* built-in module, but not quite: *readlines* retains the end-of-line markers on each line, and the order of names may be different. To get similar behavior, we slice off the last character in each line (*name[:-1]*), and add a comma to the first print. Here are both schemes in action:

```
% ls *.py
pack1.py    pack1c.py  pack2.py
% python
>>> import os, glob
>>> glob.glob("*.py")
['pack1.py', 'pack2.py', 'pack1c.py']
>>> os.popen("ls *.py", 'r').readlines()
['pack1.py\012', 'pack1c.py\012', 'pack2.py\012']
```

Finally, if all we really want is a list of all the files in a directory, the *os.listdir(<path>)* function simply returns a list of filenames without spawning a shell process.

### *A first look at Python interprocess communication*

Technically, the *os.popen* command spawns a new process to run the shell command, and connects a pipe to the spawned process's stdout or stdin streams, for modes *r* and *w*, respectively (*r* is the default). On multitasking machines, the spawned command runs independently of the Python program, but the two are synchronized with the data sent back and forth, by reading or writing the pipe object returned by *popen*.

The related function, *os.system(<command>)*, runs shell commands too, but there's no connection to the spawned process's input or output. Since shell stream redirection syntax may be part of the spawned command, we can often use temporary files to achieve the same result as a *popen* call:

```
>>> os.system("ls *.py > /tmp/output")
>>> for name in open('/tmp/output', 'r').readlines():
```

### *Capturing the stderr stream*

By default, calling *popen* in read (*r*) mode connects to the stdout stream of the command. On most UNIX systems, we can also capture stderr output by using shell-redirection syntax: *os.popen("command 2>&1")*. See your shell's manpages for details; *popen*, *system*, and advanced shell syntax may be unavailable on some platforms.

*popen* and *system* come straight from the standard C libraries. Both support rudimentary multitasking. For instance, we can spawn other Python programs with either of these functions, by naming another Python script in the shell command. To start a Python script called *monitor.py* we could either:

```
os.system("monitor.py &")                     # run monitor in background
x = os.popen("monitor.py", "r").read()        # capture monitor's output too
```

Here, the shell's & operator makes the program run independently; the *system* call doesn't wait for it to finish. For more sophisticated multitasking, Python includes the usual UNIX/C tools: fork/exec, pipes, signals, sockets, threads, and more.

### *What's the difference between os and sys?*

Generally, the *os* module contains operating system interfaces, and the *sys* module holds Python-related information. For instance, under UNIX, *os* is an interface to POSIX bindings. But the distinction between *os* and *sys* objects isn't always clear-cut. For example, shell command-line arguments are in list *sys.argv*, but shell environment variables are kept in a dictionary in the *os* module called *environ*: `who = os.environ['USER']` that fetches the value of environment variable *USER* as a string. Sometimes the portability of a component determines its module. In this case, the contents of the environment are platform dependent, but the *argv* list is more universal. The differences between *os* and *sys* will become clearer with use.

# 5

# *Variations on a Theme*

*In this chapter:*

- *"How Shall I Code Thee? Let Me Count the Ways..."*
- *Packing With File Methods*
- *Packing with Explicit Files*
- *Packing with Counter Loops*
- *Unpacking with Explicit Files*
- *Unpacking with Line-by-Line Input*
- *Unpacking Without File Methods*
- *Crunching the Code (to Death)*

## *"How Shall I Code Thee? Let Me Count the Ways . . . "*

As you might expect, there are many ways we might code the *packer* and *unpacker* scripts. In this chapter we'll look at a few variants that illustrate some basic input/output options, and more language concepts.

## *Packing With File Methods*

The first is a version of the packer, which still sends its output to the *stdout* stream, but writes to it directly using file methods. The original used *print* statements to write output; roughly, *print* is the same as calling the *write* method of the *sys.stdout* file object. The main difference is that the *print* statement adds a *newline*, unless told not to with a trailing comma; the *write* method writes exactly what you send. More formally:

- *print* statements write *objects*
- *write* methods write *strings*

For string objects, the two work almost the same, but *print* adds extra blanks and newlines.

*Example 5-1: File: pack1b.py*

```
#!/usr/local/bin/python

from sys import argv, stdout                # use stdout explictly
marker = '::::::'

for name in argv[1:]:
    input = open(name, 'r')
    stdout.write(marker + name + '\n')      # add an end-line
    stdout.write( input.read() )            # no end-line to strip
```

## More on Strings: "\n"

In Python, a newline can be written as the string "\n"; Python's backslash escape mechanism for special characters works exactly like C's. Other common escapes are "\t" for a tab, and "\0" for a null character (which really isn't all that useful in Python, since the end of a string is maintained internally). The full set of special backslash characters appears in Appendix C, *A Mini-Reference.*

## More on Modules: *from*

In this version, we use the *from* statement to import specific attributes (variables) of the *sys* module, instead of importing the module itself with an *import* statement. The *from* statement creates new local variables called *argv* and *stdout,* and assigns them the values of the corresponding variables in *sys.* The effect is almost as if the *pack1b* module ran these statements (but sys isn't available after the *from* statement):

```
import sys
argv   = sys.argv          like "from sys import argv, stdout"
stdout = sys.stdout        'from' assigns to local names
```

Since the *from* statement copies named objects from another module, we don't need to qualify *argv* and *stdout* with the *sys* module name to use them in this script; they become local copies of the variables in *sys.*

### *from copies names without linking them*

Although this can be convenient, *from* can also be more error-prone than loading a module with the *import* statement. With *import,* the owning module is usually obvious, and we can never inadvertently overwrite one module's names with another's. Moreover, we have to inspect *from* statements to tell where unqualified names in a file come from; this can be complex in large programs.

More dangerously, *from* might not always work as expected. Because it imports another module's attributes by assigning to local names, changing an imported variable locally doesn't change it in the module where it was imported from. For instance, if we use *from* in the original *unpack1.py* script:

```
from sys import stdin, stdout                  # instead of 'import sys'
marker = '::::::'

for line in stdin.readlines():                 # okay; references work the same
    if line[:6] != marker:
        print line,                            # to sys.stdout, not local stdout!
    else:
        stdout = open(line[6:-1], 'w')         # oops: changes local 'stdout' only
```

it won't work! The assignment to *stdout* changes the *local* variable called *stdout* in this module, not the *stdout* in the *sys* module. The two *stdout* names refer to the same object after the *from* executes, but they're no longer the same once either module changes their *stdout* variable's value. Since *print* sends to *sys.stdout*, the assignment to the local *stdout* above would have no effect.

This behavior is relatively rare. As a rule, it's usually safe to use *from* to import things from a module that aren't expected to change: functions, classes, constant variables, etc. But if we need to change names in another module, we have to use the *import* statement, and assign to qualified names: `sys.stdout = ....` Figure 5-1 shows how the two import forms access modules; *import* loads modules, and *from* copies names out.

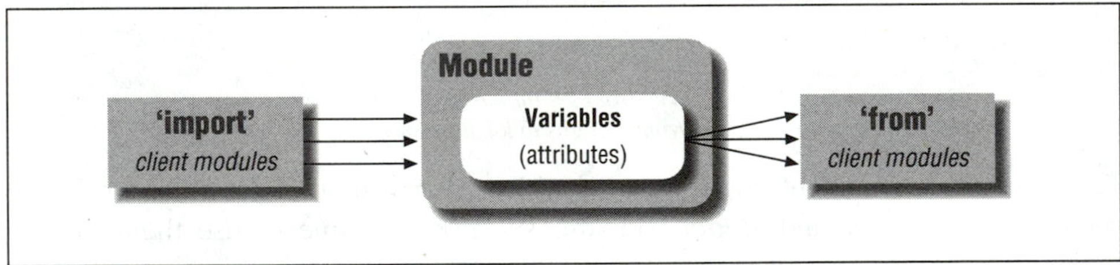


*Figure 5-1: import and from*

Since *from* is an assignment, we can also use it to import mutable data structures that are expected to change in place: the local variable shares the object with the module that owns it, so it can make and track changes. For example, if a module exports a list, any number of modules can import it with *from* and change it:

```
from server import list          # import a shared list object
list[0] = 'new value'            # changes effect the server module
```

But this is almost always a bad idea: it's better to implement interfaces to manage shared data, so clients are insulated from changes in a module's internals. We'll see how later.

### *More on Functions: Call Statements*

In Python, there's really no distinction between functions, and what some languages call *procedures*. Every function returns a value whether explicit or not; callers can choose to ignore the return value:

```
stdout.write(marker + name + '\n')        # call a "procedure"
```

calls the *write* method of the *stdout* file object, but ignores the result. Function calls like this can appear by themselves, as statements (i.e., outside a larger expression).

> **Much ado about None**
>
> *write* errors are communicated by raising exceptions, rather than returning integer status codes. The *write* file method has no return value. More accurately, it returns *None*, a special data object similar to C's *NULL*. But in Python, *None* is really the only value of a special object datatype.
>
> *None* is a Boolean false value, since it's considered to be empty. It can also be assigned to variables and data structures normally: `x = None`. Which (believe it or not) can actually be useful; we'll see how later on.

## *Packing with Explicit Files*

Once we start writing with file methods, it's a simple step to move from this version to one that uses an explicit output file, instead of the *sys.stdout* output stream:

*Example 5-2: File: pack1c.py*

```
#!/usr/local/bin/python

from sys import argv
marker = ':::::'
output = open('pack.out', 'w')              # use a real output file

for name in argv[1:]:
    input = open(name, 'r')                 # input.close() automatic...
    output.write(marker + name + '\n')
    output.write( input.read() )            # output.close() automatic...
```

This is one way we might pack files in the interactive interpreter, without having them spewed over our screen; we could also assign *sys.stdout* to a real file, and keep using *print* statements, as we did in the *unpack* scripts above. We run this version without redirecting output on the command line, since output goes to file *pack.out*:

```
% pack1c.py *.py
```

## More on External Files: "close"

Traditionally, files must be closed when we're done processing them; closing finalizes operating-system management, flushes buffers, etc. But notice that we don't close the output file at the end of the script with *output.close()*. For that matter, we never close each of the input files either. Why?

The short answer is that all the files in this program are closed by Python automatically: there's no need to call the file object "close" method. In general, we usually don't need to close files in simple scripts like this, since they're closed when the script ends. But a better answer leads to an interesting digression.

### When are files closed for you?

More specifically, Python uses a reference count garbage collection strategy to reclaim memory behind the scenes. This allows Python to release an object's space as soon as it's no longer referenced anywhere in your program (but no sooner). For instance, each time we set *input* to a new file in the *for* loop above, its previous value can be reclaimed. Reference count collection has some classic limitations (circular references can cause space to be wasted), but it never pauses a program to free space like other schemes.

Python file objects are really just wrappers around operating system files (C's file system). When a file object is reclaimed, the file is automatically closed in the operating system sense. We usually don't need to close such files manually; in the worst case, all files are usually closed by Python when a program exits, since every remaining object gets reclaimed.

Still, manual file closing is sometimes necessary. If it's impossible to know that a file object will be reclaimed, manually closing keeps us from running into system limits on the number of open files. And if an output file must be read back in by the program that made it, manual closing guarantees that its contents have been flushed out to disk.

# *Packing with Counter Loops*

So far, we've been using the *for* loop to step over items in lists. It's just as easy to iterate over lists (and other sequences) using C-style counter loops and indexing:

*Example 5-3: File: pack1e.py*

```
#!/usr/local/bin/python
from sys import argv
marker = ':' * 6                      # string repetition

for i in range(1, len(argv)):         # for (i=1; i < argc; i++)
    input = open(argv[i], 'r')
    print marker + argv[i]
    print input.read(),
```

or equivalently:

```
for i in range(len(argv)-1):          # for (i=0; i < argc-1; i++)
    input = open(argv[i+1], 'r')
    print marker + argv[i+1]
    print input.read(),
```

But unless we're shuffling items in a list, there's probably no good reason to use numbers and indexing when stepping over lists. Python's *for* loop does all the indexing logic for you behind the scenes.

## *More on Sequences: len, range, and xrange*

Python's built-in *len* function returns the number of items in any sequence object. Here, *len(argv)* is the number of command-line arguments (like C's *argc*). The *range* function constructs a list of consecutive integers:

```
>>> print range(3), range(1,5)
[0, 1, 2] [1, 2, 3, 4]
```

We use the *range* function two ways in the *packer* examples above, to compute lists of indexes:

- *range(1, len(argv))*. In the first form, we give an explicit lower bound (1).
- *range(len(argv)-1)*. In the second form, we only give an upper bound, so the lower defaults to zero.

Like C array indexes, Python's range always stops at 1 less than the upper bound. If the length of the *argv* list is *N*, then the first form makes a list of numbers with *1..N-1*, and the second makes a list with *0..N-2*. See the following example.

```
>>> L = ['s', 'p', 'a', 'm']
>>> range(1, len(L))
[1, 2, 3]
>>> range(len(L)-1)
[0, 1, 2]
```

*range* turns out to be useful for stepping through sequences by indexing, as we did here. Although we can think of these as counter-loops, we're really still stepping over a *list* (the one made by *range*). But *range* can also be used outside *for* loops, any time we need a list of numbers. For instance, it's part of a common Python idiom for setting constants to numbers:

```
[red, green, blue] = range(3)          # same as red=0; green=1; blue=2
```

using list *unpacking* assignment. When a list of targets appears on the left of =, Python assigns each one a node from the list on the right. (We'll see a tuple-based version of this later, in Chapter 8, *Adding Text-Based Menus.*)

Creating a real list of numbers can be excessive, especially if we're going to step over a huge list: *range(1000)* makes a 1000-node list! If space is a concern, there's a variant of range called *xrange*, which doesn't really build the list of numbers, but instead generates them one at a time. It's generally no faster than *range*, but saves space (this usually only matters on memory-starved machines).

## More on Sequences: Indexing

In both loops above, we visit the second through last items in the *argv* lists as illustrated in Figure 5-2.

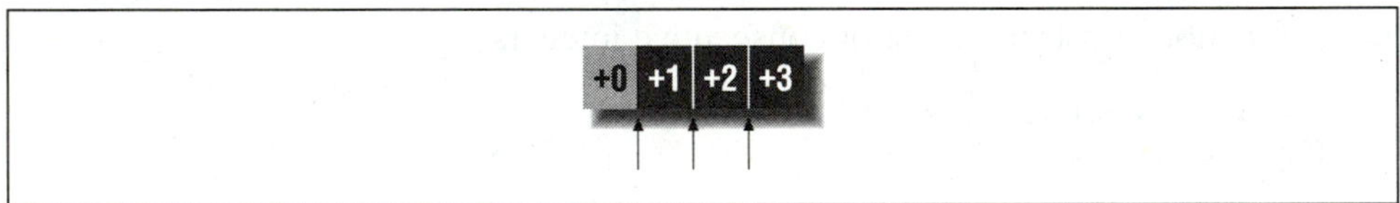


*Figure 5–2: Indexing items 2..N*

In Python, this means indexes 1 though *N*–1, since sequence indexes start at 0, and end at 1 less than the number of items present: as noted earlier, indexes are really *offsets* for sequences. They're put in square brackets, after the object being indexed: *argv[i]*.

As we'll see, indexing is more general than this example suggests. For instance, to index nested data-structures, we use a series of index operations, like C's multidimensional arrays: *S[1][2][3]*. Moreover, the index brackets notation is also used to access items in mappings (dictionaries). In fact, the meaning of an index operation depends on what sort of object is being indexed; see the following table.

*Table 5-1: Indexing objects*

| Object type | Index type | Indexing rules |
|---|---|---|
| Sequence | Offset | Referencing or assigning out-of-bounds offsets raises an exception |
| Mapping | Key | Referencing non-existent keys is an error; assigning them creates entries |
| User-defined | Arbitrary | Classes and C types can interpret the index operation arbitrarily |

Unlike the sequence indexing rule shown here, *slicing* scales out-of-bounds indexes, instead of raising an error. For example, given a two-node list `L`, `L[4]` is an error, but `L[-100:100]` is the entire list.

### *And Still More on Sequences: Repetition*

In this version, we also introduced an alternative way to write the marker string:

```
marker = ':' * 6                  # string repetition: same as '::::::'
```

which uses sequence repetition. In Python, the `*` operator is overloaded to work on all sequence data objects: strings, lists, etc. Given an expression of the form: `<sequence> * <integer>`, the result is a new sequence containing `<integer>` copies of the `<sequence>` object.

The effect is exactly like concatenating the `<sequence>` to itself, `(<integer> - 1)` times, using the `+` operator. For instance, the assignment above is equivalent to:

```
marker = ':' + ':' + ':' + ':' + ':' + ':'
```

We were able to use `*` here to make the length of the marker more explicit. Repetition is useful whenever we have a fixed-length sequence like this.

## *Unpacking with Explicit Files*

In the original unpacker script, we were careful to import *sys* instead of importing its members with the *from* import statement form. As we saw, this was required to change *sys.stdout*, so *print* would send lines to the current output file. We can get around this issue by using explicit files for the output, instead of reusing the standard output stream and *print*:

*Example 5-4: File: unpack1b.py*

```
#!/usr/local/bin/python

from sys import *                      # don't alter sys
marker = '::::::'
```

*Example 5-4: File: unpack1b.py (continued)*

```
output = stdout                              # use explicit files

for line in stdin.readlines():               # for all input lines
    if line[:6] != marker:
        output.write(line)                   # write real lines
    else:
        output = open(line[6:-1], 'w')       # or make new output file
```

## *More on Modules: from**

The from statement here shows the third way to import. It's really just a *from* special case: when we give an * operator for the names to import from a module, we get copies of *all* the names defined at the top-level of that module. The effect is similar to *sourcing* files in shell languages like *csh*, and C's *#include*. But in Python, imported names really exist in a module object at run-time; imports are not text file insertions.

The *from** form is the most convenient way to import. We get copies of everything, without having to list what we need. However, it's also the most dangerous: it can lead to serious namespace pollution.

- We usually get everything from the named module: names in the imported module might clash with variables defined in the importing module, or in other imported modules.
- Further, we might get more than we bargained for: if the imported module also uses from imports, we'll import all the names that it imports too.

Here's a summary of all three import forms:

*Table 5-2: Import forms*

| Statement | Interpretation |
|---|---|
| *import sys* | Load a module, qualify its variables (use *sys.argv*) |
| *from sys import argv* | Copy selected variables out of a module (use *argv*) |
| *from sys import ** | Copy all variables out of a module (use *argv*) |

The simple *import* statement requires name qualification, but it's always safest: there's no potential for namespace clashes, or copied variables becoming out of synch between modules. Still, *from** can be convenient, especially if we're copying many names from a module. Moreover, it's possible to design modules that support *from** well (the *Tkinter* module we'll use in Part 3, *Tools and Applications* is one such example).

### *Breaking the from* rules*

As a special case, names in a module that start with an underscore (_X) are *not* copied over to the importer when a *from** statement is used. This provides a simple access control mechanism. But its only purpose is to limit *from** namespace pollution: names with leading underscores may still be accessed by simple *from* or *import* statements.

# *Unpacking with Line-by-Line Input*

One weakness in the original unpacker is that it loads the whole file into memory all at once: the file *readlines* method builds up a list of strings, containing all lines in the file. This is convenient to use, but might be expensive when packing huge files. Here's one way around this difficulty:

*Example 5-5: File: unpack2.py*

```
#!/usr/local/bin/python

import sys
marker = ':::::'

while 1:
    line = sys.stdin.readline()               # read next line
    if not line:
        break                                 # exit on end-of-file
    elif line[:6] != marker:
        print line,                           # or copy real line
    else:
        sys.stdout = open(line[6:-1], 'w')    # or new output file
```

In this version, the packed file is read line-by-line: instead of using the file *readlines* method to load the entire file, we use *readline* to get one line at a time. This makes things slightly more complicated for us: we need to detect end-of-file manually, but if we're ever going to use our packing system for very large files (or pipes), this change could matter, especially on a PC with limited memory.

## *Using while Loops*

We use a *while* loop here, instead of a *for* loop. The *while* loop works as you might expect:

```
while <test>:
      <statements>
```

The statements in the *while* loop's body are executed repeatedly, until the *test* evaluates to a *false* result. If the test is false to begin with, the statements are never executed. The *while* and *for* loops are Python's main looping statements; some built-in functions we'll see later also imply an iteration (*map()*, *reduce()*, etc.).

## A tale of two loops

The *while* loop is more general than *for*. In fact, *for* can be simulated with *while*:

```
t = sequence
while t:                        # like: "for x in sequence: body..."
    x = t[0]
    body...
    t = t[1:]                   # strip the first item off t
```

but the *for* loop indexes the sequence instead of slicing it. Slicing is slower, since it makes copies of the sequence. To mimic the *for* loop, we can use indexing in *while* loops too, using *len*:

```
i = 0
while i < len(sequence):
    x = sequence[i]             # index sequence, like "for" does
    body...
    i = i+1
```

or use a *try* to detect the end (we'll meet the *try* statement in a moment, since it's used in the next unpacker script); this is how *for* really works internally:

```
i = 0
while 1:
    try:                        # here's the real "for"
        x = sequence[i]
    except IndexError:
        break
    body...
    i = i+1
```

But it's usually easier (and faster) to use a *for* loop to step through sequences; the *while* loop is useful for just about everything else.

## *Using Loop breaks*

As we've seen, in Python integer 0 is considered *false*; all other integers mean *true*. In this example, the header line *while 1* really means "repeat forever", since 1 is always true. So how does this program end?

```
6   while 1:
7       line = sys.stdin.readline()
8       if not line:
9           break
```

The trick is to use Python's *break* statement to exit the loop from inside its body. In this loop, we read one line from the packed file each time through. The file *readline* method gives us a line as a Python string; after the last line is read, we get an empty string. On lines 8 and 9, we use this to force an exit of the loop. Python's *break* is the same as C's: it jumps out of the closest enclosing *while* or *for* loop (see Figure 5-3).

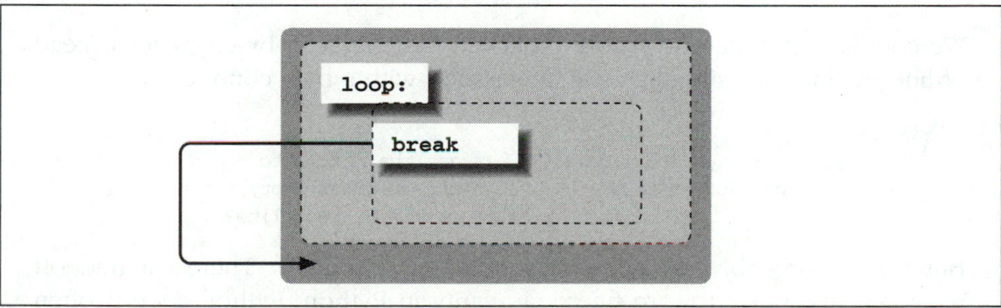


*Figure 5-3: Loop breaks*

### *On the search for truth*

Line 8 is an example of another common idiom in Python. It makes use of the fact that Python considers "empty" data structures to be false too. On end-of-file, *line* is an empty string (`''`). Because empty means false, and not-empty means true, we can just test the string itself, rather than comparing it to an empty string. Line 8 is equivalent to this:

```
8       if line == "":          same as "if not line:"
```

## *More on if Tests*

The rest of this loop (lines 10 through 13) is the same as in the original unpacker. We used an *elif* clause, as shown in the following code.

```
 8    if not line:
 9        break                                  # exit on end-of-file
10    elif line[:6] != marker:
11        print line,                            # or copy real line
12    else:
13        sys.stdout = open(line[6:-1], 'w')     # or new output file
```

but since *break* exits the loop, we'll never get to line 10 if the test on line 8 passes. We could code line 10 as the start of a new *if* to achieve the same effect:

```
 8    if not line: break                         # exit on end-of-file
 9    if line[:6] != marker:
10        print line,                            # copy real line
11    else:
12        sys.stdout = open(line[6:-1], 'w')     # or new output file
```

Which form is "better" is a question of style.

### *Letting Python do your work*

We could go further, and read the packed file character-by-character instead of line-by-line, by using the *read* file method with a byte count of 1:

```
while 1:
    character = sys.stdin.read(1)      # get the next byte
    if not character: break            # end-of-file: empty string
    ...                                # marker or real line?...
```

But there's probably no good reason to do that here. There's a tradeoff whenever we move toward finer granularity in Python. Python code is often slower than built-in tools.

For instance, although the line-by-line version of the unpacker conserves space, it's probably slower than the original *readlines* version, since we've transferred file-scanning logic from C code (the *readlines* method) to Python code (the *while* loop). Moving to a character-by-character version would be even slower.

# *Unpacking Without File Methods*

Finally, we could go to the extreme of avoiding file methods altogether, and rely on Python's higher-level input/output stream interfaces: the *print* statement for standard-stream output, and the *raw_input* built-in function for standard-stream input:

*Example 5-6: File: unpack2b.py*

```
#!/usr/local/bin/python

import sys
marker = '::::::'

while 1:
    try:
        line = raw_input()                          # sys.stdin implied
    except EOFError:                                # error at end-of-file
        break
    if line[:6] != marker:
        print line                                  # no end-line to strip
    else:
        sys.stdout = open(line[6:], 'w')            # no end-line to strip
```

Of course, we still have to reset *sys.stdout* in this example, each time we start a new file. The *raw_input* function is almost like calling *sys.stdin.readline*, except that it strips the trailing end-of-line character, and raises an exception when end-of-file is reached, instead of returning the empty string.

This policy turns out to be just as easy to handle: instead of testing for the empty string in an *if* statement as in the original unpacker, we wrap the *raw_input* call in a *try* statement, and catch the end-of-file exception if it's raised. When caught, the *break* exits the loop (it works the same, even when nested in a *try* statement).

## Using try Statement Exception Handlers

In Python, most errors aren't reported until we run a program; even syntax errors aren't detected until a module is imported. To simplify error processing, Python provides a high-level protocol for handling errors at run-time. The *try* statement lets us catch *exceptions* raised by the interpreter on errors, or generated by programs with *raise* statements. We used a relatively simple form in Example 5-6:

```
try:
    <statements1>            # run statements
except <name>:
    <statements2>            # come here if the named exception occurs
```

The *statements1* under the *try* are executed normally. While they're running,

- If an exception named in an *except* clause is raised, control jumps to that *except* and runs its *statements2*.
- If a different exception is raised, it's propagated up to an enclosing, active *try* statement (if any).

- If no exception occurs, control skips the *except* block and continues past the end of the whole *try*.

If the *except* clause catches an error, control continues past the entire *try* after the *statements2* block finishes (see Figure 5-4).

*try* statements *nest* (i.e., are stacked) at run-time: when an exception is raised, Python searches for the most recently entered *try*, with an *except* clause that matches the raised exception. If no match is found, the exception is reported by Python at the top level as an error, and the program terminates. In its most general form, try can include:

- Multiple *except* clauses, to specify a set of exceptions to catch.
- An optional target for data sent when the exception was raised.
- An empty *except* with no name, to catch all (or all other) exceptions.
- An *else* clause, with statements to run if no exceptions are raised.
- Or a *finally* clause to specify clean-up actions to always run on the way out.

We'll see examples of all these forms in later chapters. Exceptions can also be triggered manually, to signal application-specific errors or to implement alternative control flows. The *raise* statement generates exceptions:

```
raise <exception>, <optional-data>
```

but we'll defer more details until we can see *raise* in action too.

In our script, we catch *EOFError* exceptions. *EOFError* is a built-in exception name in Python: it's always defined. Exceptions are identified by objects. They are usually names of variables assigned to unique string objects in modules (but more general exception objects can be defined).

---

*NOTE* Exceptions are also part of the broader topic of handling errors in general. We'll explore this in detail in Chapter 11, *Graphical User Interfaces*, where we'll use Python's debugger.

---

## More on Input/Output Streams

The built-in *raw_input* function is a higher-level interface to *sys.stdin*, much like *print* is for *sys.stdout*. It's a simple way to get a line from *stdin*, without importing *sys* and calling methods. A similar built-in function, *input*, reads a line and converts its text to a Python object (we don't get back a 'raw' string).

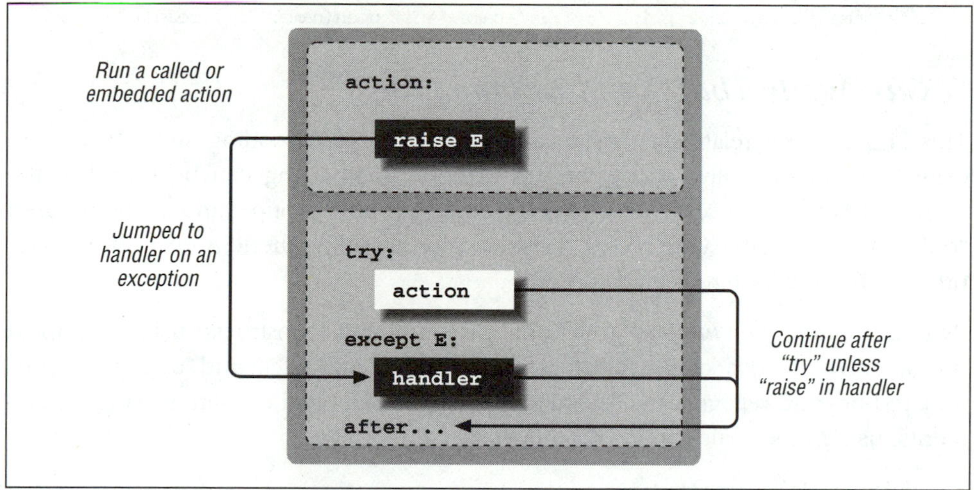


*Figure 5-4: Catching exceptions*

---

*NOTE* *raw_input* really does have to raise an exception on end-of-file. Otherwise, there'd be no way to distinguish an empty line from an end-of-file string. Since *raw_input* strips the end-of-line character from lines, an empty line would be an empty string too.

---

## *Crunching the Code (to Death)*

Of course, many of the operations in our scripts could be combined, to shorten the programs. Here's an example of a shorter packer, for anyone keeping track of line counts.

*Example 5-7: File: pack1d.py*

```
#!/usr/local/bin/python
from sys import *
for name in argv[1:]:
    print '::::::' + name + '\n', open(name, 'r').read(),
```

The main trick used here is to get rid of the *input* variable: since *open* returns a file object that is automatically reclaimed (garbage-collected), we don't have to assign it to a variable in order to call its *read* method. We also have to manually add a newline (\n) to the separator line to make this work.

And if we really wanted to be frugal, we could also move the *print* statement to the same line as the *for* loop header, to get the packer done in the following two executable lines.

```
from sys import *
for name in argv[1:]: print '::::::'+name+'\n', open(name, 'r').read(),
```

## "I Can Write That Script in One Line!"

This is actually a relatively tame example of convoluted coding style. Pathologically (and intentionally) bad examples of code compacting can be found in the Python FAQ, and occasionally surface on the newsgroup, under the subject "obfuscated Python." (One recent thread explored coding the RSA encryption algorithm to fit on a T-shirt. :-)

Python's *map* and *lambda* functional-programming constructs usually appear prominently in such code. Just for fun, here are our pack and unpack scripts, mutated beyond recognition. Technically, they're both legal one-liners: single statements, using open-pair continuation lines.

*Example 5-8: File: pmap.py*

```
import sys; map(                    # pack, the hard way
     lambda name:
        sys.stdout.write("::::::"+name+'\n' + open(name,'r').read()),
     sys.argv[1:])
```

*Example 5-9: File: umap.py*

```
import sys; files = [sys.stdout]; map(          # unpack (right?...)
     lambda line:
         (line[:6] != "::::::" and [files[-1].write(line)])
          or files.append( open(line[6:-1],'w') ),
     sys.stdin.readlines())
```

### Beauty is in the eye of the maintainer

Although some may take perverse pleasure in studying this code, it's not typical. In fact, *map*, *lambda*, and their cohorts are the only Python constructs that really support such a coding style. The rest were purposely designed to discourage unreadable programs. But as usual, code quality depends as much on a programmer, as a language. Despite the best intentions of Python's inventor, we can still write bad code if we try hard!

## The Naughty Bits

The examples above were written to illustrate coding style issues. But as we'll see later, some of the tricks they use to compact the scripts can actually be more useful than the examples here imply.

### *But you didn't hear it from me...*

Naturally, all of these coding tricks result in bad style if abused. There are many legitimate exceptions; in fact, we'll use *map* and *or* expressions frequently in this book. But it's often no more work to write simple *for* loops, *if* statements, and *def* functions. They are usually easier to code (and decode) than deeply nested expressions.

Code compactness is really a matter of taste, and there aren't any absolute rules or standards on Python coding. So I won't lecture on this more here, except to say that readability is an art worth mastering: even if you can remember what your code does six months down the road, your coworkers may not be so lucky. :-)

### *for as an expression*

The Python *map* built-in function iterates over a list (or other sequence) applying a function to each node. It returns a list of the function's result for each node, which we can use or ignore. The call:

```
map(function, list)            # like: "for all x in list: function(x)"
```

applies *function* to each node in *list*, and collects the results. *function* is often a *lambda* anonymous function expression (discussed later in this book). As a special case, if we use *None* for the function, we get back a list of the items in *list* unchanged (this is one way to convert strings and tuples to lists).

### *if as an expression*

By combining Python *and* and *or* Boolean tests, we can simulate C's `?:` expressions. In Python:

- *and* only evaluates the *right* operand if the *left* was true. It returns one of the operand objects: the left operand if it's false, or the right operand if the left was true (the result is true if both operands are).
- *or* only evaluates the *right* operand if the *left* was false. It returns one of the operand objects too: the left one if it's true, or the one on the right otherwise (*and* and *or* don't convert results to integer 1 or 0).

Because of this, the Python expression:

```
((test and [trueAction]) or [falseAction])[0]
```

works essentially the same as C's *test ? trueAction : falseAction*:

- If *test* is false—we skip *trueAction* and evaluate and return *falseAction*, whether it's true or false.
- If *test* is true—we evaluate *trueAction*. Because it's wrapped in a list, it's always true (i.e., nonempty) regardless of trueAction's result, so we won't evaluate *falseAction*.

Careful readers might have noticed that *falseAction* doesn't have to be wrapped in a list to make it true; it wasn't necessary in the unpack script above. But wrapping both results in lists makes it easy to extract the result by indexing, regardless of the outcome.

*In this chapter:*

- *"The Packing Scripts Go Public"*
- *Part 1: "The Middleman"*
- *Part 2: "The Unpacker on Steroids"*
- *Part 3: "The Packer Hits the Big Time"*
- *Building Systems with Functions*

# 6
# *Adding a Functional Interface*

## *"The Packing Scripts Go Public"*

After quickly writing the simple pack/unpack scripts, I was able to transfer my files in one step. A more reasonable person might imagine that at this point I would have turned my PC off and enjoyed the rest of my day off from work. But being a software engineer, I wasn't really happy with any of these versions.

They're all limited in some fundamental ways. For example, there's no way to monitor the scripts' progress, no way to use them except as UNIX-style scripts, and no provision for handling file errors. But perhaps more important, there's no way to make use of the scripts' logic outside the scripts themselves. So far, our scripts have been run-once, standalone files; they don't contain any notion of participation in a larger system.

In this chapter, we'll start to build on the "quick and dirty" scripts. The biggest improvements we'll see are the introduction of features that turn these scripts into reusable software:

*Modules*
: Partition parts of our system.

*Functions*
: Export the pack and unpack tools for use by other modules.

# Part 1: "The Middleman"

Let's first define an auxiliary module, to hold the separator line marker, so we're sure the pack and unpack tools are using the same string:

*file: textpak1.py*

```
marker = '::::::'        # shared by packer and unpacker
```

Even though it's just one line long, this file is an "official" Python module: it can be imported from any other module that needs to use its *marker* constant (see Figure 6-1). It's intended to be used much like a C *#include* header file: it's usually a good idea to keep common values and functions in modules shared by all the other modules of a system. Later in this book we'll expand this module to hold additional logic for our program.

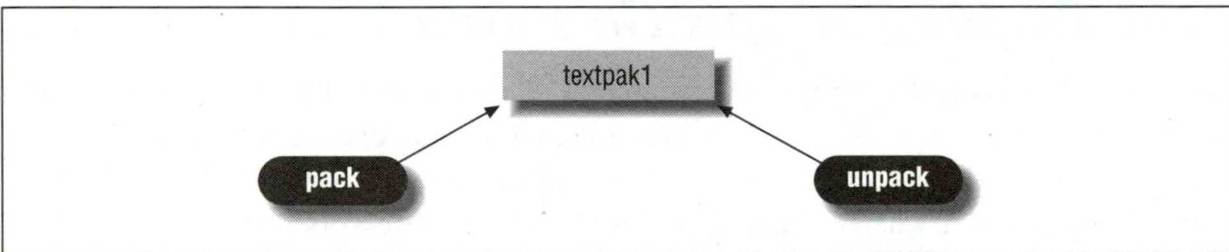


*Figure 6-1: Shared modules*

# Part 2: "The Unpacker on Steroids"

Next, let's generalize the unpacking script. Here's an enhanced version that's quite a bit different from the original unpacker. It provides some critical improvements: file error handling, a functional API, explicit files, and more.

*file: unpack3.py*

```
#!/usr/local/bin/python

from sys import *                          # system interfaces
from textpak1 import marker                # "textpak1.py" marker constant
mlen = len(marker)

def unpack_file(name):
    try:                                   # catch errors here
        input = open(name, 'r')
        unpack_stream(input)
    except:
        import sys
        print 'unpack error!', sys.exc_type, sys.exc_value

def unpack_stream(input, output=stdout):
    while 1:
```

```
17          line = input.readline()
18          if not line:                        # until end-of-file
19              break                           # copy real lines
20          elif line[:mlen] != marker:         # else, create file
21              output.write(line)
22          else:
23              name = line[mlen:-1]
24              print 'creating:', name
25              output = open(name, 'w')
26
27  if __name__ == '__main__':
28      if len(argv) == 2:
29          unpack_file(argv[1])
30      else:
31          print 'usage: unpack filename'; exit(1)
```

This module (source file) can be run like a script, as we've been doing all along. If we make it executable, it works from the system command line as earlier:

```
% unpack3.py packed.txt
```

But since this version uses explicit files for both the input and output, rather than the standard streams, the name of the packed input file is passed in as an argument on the command line, instead of being sent in to stdin with <. Executing the program when it's run as a script (or passed to the *python* interpreter) is arranged by line 27: a module's name is set to `__main__` when it's run as a top-level program.

```
27  if __name__ == '__main__':
```

This version also lets us know when it's making a new output file, so we can monitor its progress:

```
24  print 'creating: ', name
```

If we don't pass in a filename, the script prints the *usage* message, and calls *exit* to return a status code of one to the shell. Python exit status is zero by default; a nonzero status is a common script error indicator. *exit* was imported from *sys* (but you'd never know this from the code: a good example of *from* statement drawbacks). Because *sys.exit* ends a Python program (process) immediately, it's also useful for quickly terminating a program from deeply nested code.

But the major innovation in *unpack3* is the use of *functions*: it defines two functions that can be called from other modules that import *unpack3*. In other words, the unpacker's functionality has been bundled-up for reuse in other programs. It's no longer just a standalone shell script. We can unpack a file from another Python module (or the interactive command line) like this:

```
import unpack3                           # use "unpack3.py"
unpack3.unpack_file("packed.txt")        # unpack a file, given its name
```

or similarly,

```
from unpack3 import unpack_stream        # use names in "unpack3.py"
myfile = open("packed.txt", 'r')         # unpack from an open file object
unpack_stream(myfile)                    # unpack_stream(sys.stdin) works too
```

## More on Modules:__name__

Since *unpack3* has the special `#!` comment at the top, it can be run directly if it is made executable. But its logic has been packaged as functions: we need to add extra code to call the functions if the file's run directly. This *if* statement at the bottom takes care of this case:

```
if __name__ == '__main__':
```

Python supports files that are meant to both be run as scripts, and used as modules, by setting a built-in module variable called `__name__` to the string `__main__`, if and only if the file is running as a script. Both names have two underscores before and after, to avoid clashing with user-provided names. The *if* uses this trick to map command-line invocations to functions, when the file is run (but not when imported).

This is another common idiom in Python. Even for modules that aren't meant to be used as top-level scripts, it's helpful to include a self-test function, and add a line to call it if the file is run as a script:

```
<exported objects>

def test_me():
    <test my exports>

if __name__ == '__main__': test_me()   # test this module by running it
```

### Module statement order and forward-references

When a module is imported the first time (or run as a script), lines in the file are executed in the order in which they appear, from top to bottom. Some of the statements in a module create objects and names as a side-effect. In fact, this is how a module object's attributes are generated.

For instance, *def* creates a function when executed, and assignments may create variables. Subsequent imports just use the already loaded module, without running its statements again (unless you request a reload, to be discussed later).

Because of this, the *if* test for `__main__` has to appear at the bottom of the file, after the functions it calls. For example, in our script:

```
27  if __name__ == '__main__':
28      if len(argv) == 2:
29          unpack_file(argv[1])        # call a function
```

This code has to be written after the definition of *unpack_file*, or else it won't yet exist. Since the *if* statement will be run where it appears, it has to appear after the *def* statement that creates the function.

Module statement order usually only matters for imperative statements at the top level of a module, which run immediately: assignments, *if*, etc. Since statements like *def* (and as we'll see later, *class* methods) create objects to be used later, the code they contain can refer to objects defined anywhere in the module: above or below the statement. Their references aren't resolved until the object is called after all statements in the module have run.

In more traditional language terms, forward references are always allowed inside Python functions and methods, but not within statements at the top level of a module, which are executed when it's imported. If we move the *if* at line 27 to the top of the file, calling *unpack_file* will raise an undefined-name error (exception).

## *More on Functions: "Rolling Your Own"*

If you look back, you'll see that the function *unpack_stream* is similar to previous versions of the unpack script. But by wrapping its logic in a function, the unpacker can be used from another Python program: it has become a reusable component. As usual, Python functions are just a simple way to package units of code, so they can be used (called) multiple times.

### *The def statement*

In Python, *def* defines callable Python functions. Specifically, *def* is an executable statement that creates a function object, and assigns it to the function name (which becomes a variable referencing a function). Functions aren't really created until the *def* is executed. *def* takes the general form:

```
def <name>(<argument1>, <argument2>, ... <argumentN>):      # header line
    <statements using arguments>                            # function body
```

The statements in a function's body (indented under its header) aren't executed until the function is called:

```
result = <name>(<value1>, <value2>, ... <valueN>)
```

As usual, objects passed to the function in parentheses are paired with (assigned to) the argument names in the header before the function's body is run. Arguments become new variables inside the function. Normally, passed values are paired with arguments by position, as shown in Figure 6-2; in later chapters, we'll generalize this concept.

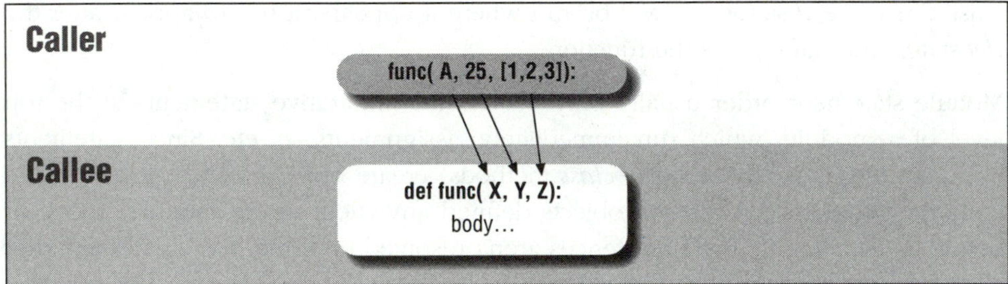


*Figure 6-2: Passing arguments*

### *Returning values from functions*

Functions pass results out by *return* statements, setting global variables, or changing arguments. Although we didn't use it here, a function's body may contain *return* statements, to send an object back to the caller, as the result of the function call. If there is no *return* statement, as in this unpacker, the return value is *None*, and is usually ignored; as we saw earlier, this is Python's *procedure*. (More on this topic later.)

### *Passing arguments: by assignment*

In Python, argument objects are passed to functions by assigning them to the argument names in the header. Just like = assignment, an argument becomes a named-reference to the object passed in, and shares the object with the caller, until the argument name is assigned a new value in the function. This is identical to the behavior of variable names copied over using *from* module imports. More specifically:

- Python arguments are passed by "object reference": arguments are names for shared objects.

- They're not passed by reference (i.e., by aliasing names, like Pascal *var* or C++ *reference* parameters).
- And they're not really passed by value (i.e., by making object copies, as in C).

In Python, passed objects are shared, but the argument names are not aliases for variable names at the point of call. Setting an argument name to a new object in the function has no effect on the caller's variables. For instance, when we change the argument *output* in *unpack_stream*:

```
output = open(name, 'w')
```

it only assigns a new object to the local variable *output*, but has no effect on the object (or variable) passed to the second argument when the function was called.

In Python, since argument names initially share objects passed in, it's possible to alter mutable data-structure objects in the caller, by changing them in place in the function (we'll see how this is used later). But since sharing simple objects like numbers and strings is usually irrelevant, in practice Python's "object reference" scheme works much like C's argument passing model:

- In C, simple objects are copied; in Python simple objects are shared, but they can't be changed.
- In C, arrays are passed by pointer; Python functions can side effect mutable objects: lists, etc.
- In C, assigning to an argument name has no effect on a variable in the caller, as in Python.

### *Using default argument values*

Normally, Python raises an error when the number of objects passed is not the same as the number of arguments in the function header. Python also includes special tools for handling variable-length argument lists, and setting default argument values when too few are passed. We'll explore variable-length argument lists in Chapter 7, *Adding a Simple User Interface*, but default argument values are used in the script here:

```
def unpack_stream(input, output=stdout):      # output defaults to stdout
```

Here, *unpack_stream* can take either one or two arguments. If two arguments are passed, the = in the header has no effect. If only one argument is passed to *unpack_stream(x)*, it's assigned to *input*, and the *output* argument is initialized to (assigned) the value *stdout*, the output-stream file imported from *sys*.

*NOTE* In general, functions can define any number of default argument values. As we'll see, default values are evaluated when the function is created, not when it's called. A default argument's value reflects the state of the assigned expression when the *def* was executed. In effect, it saves information for later use. We'll see why this matters later.

## Namespaces, Part 2: Variables in Functions

A new namespace is created for a function each time it's called. Some of the argument and variable names it uses exist only for the duration of the function call, and go away when it returns to the caller. Such names are called "local" to the function call. Names outside the function, owned by the enclosing module, are called "global." Global names exist at the top level of a module file. Inside Python functions:

- Variable *assignment* always applies to local variables, unless they're listed in "global" statements.
- Variable *references* can refer to local, global, or built-in names; the closest occurrence is used.

In other words, functions can always access global names, but need to declare global names in order to change them. More formally, for variable names in a function body, the following rules hold true:

### Reference

When an unqualified variable name (`x`) is referenced in a function, Python searches the following three namespaces for the name, and raises an error if it's not found in any:

*Local*
: Python first looks for the name in the function-call's namespace.

*Global*
: If not found, the name is next looked up in the enclosing module's namespace.

*Built-in*
: If the name still hasn't been found, Python checks the `__builtin__` module.

### *Assignment*

Assigned names are local unless declared global. When a variable name is assigned in a function, by default Python always changes (or creates) the name in the local namespace of the function call. But if the name is listed in a *global* statement earlier in the function body, Python assigns to the name in the enclosing module's namespace instead.

We'll meet the *global* statement in a moment. Function arguments are a special case: when Python assigns them to the objects passed in, it always creates new local variables for the argument names. Thereafter, referencing or assigning an argument always uses the local version of the name, by the rules above.

As illustrated in Figure 6-3, these scope rules work the same outside a function, except that there's no global namespace involved (or equivalently, no local namespace). For example, our original scripts had two scopes—the script file (module) and built-in. As we'll see in later chapters, both the assignment and three-scope reference rules work the same when we move to classes, except that the local namespace is different.

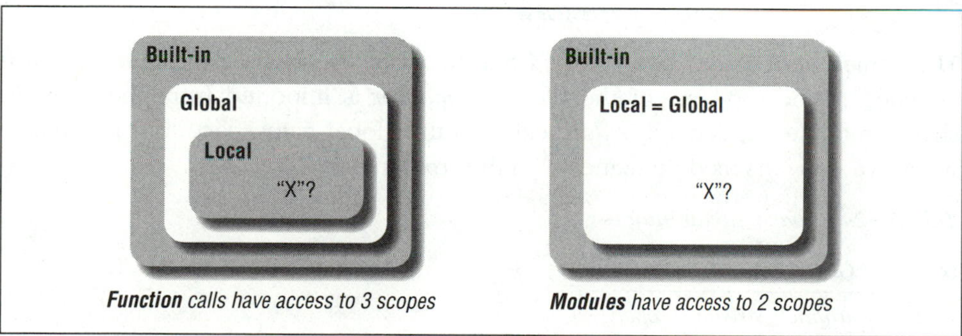


*Figure 6-3: Namespace (scope) nesting*

What does all this mean in practice? Let's classify the names in our two functions.

```
def unpack_file(name):
    try:                                    # catch errors here
        input = open(name, 'r')
        unpack_stream(input)
    except:
        import sys
        print 'unpack error!', sys.exc_type, sys.exc_value
```

Here, *name*, *input*, and *sys* are local variables: they're all assigned in the function, and not declared in a "global" statement. Every other name is a global (module-level) or built-in name.

*Table 6-1: unpack_file names*

| Local | Global | Built-in |
|---|---|---|
| *name* | *unpack_file* | *open* |
| *input* | *unpack_stream* | |
| *sys* | | |

Note that the function's name (*unpack_file*) is really a global name; this matters if the function calls itself recursively. The function *unpack_stream* uses a few more names, but the rules work the same:

```
def unpack_stream(input, output=stdout):
    while 1:
        line = input.readline()
        if not line:                          # until end-of-file
            break                             # copy real lines
        elif line[:mlen] != marker:           # else, create file
            output.write(line)
        else:
            name = line[mlen:-1]
            print 'creating:', name
            output = open(name, 'w')
```

The names *marker* and *mlen* come from the global (module) namespace: *mlen* is assigned at the top-level of the file, and *marker* is imported from the *textpak1* shared module we defined. *stdout* exists in the global namespace too: it's created when we copy *sys* module names with the *from* import.

*Table 6-2: unpack_stream names*

| Local | Global | Built-in |
|---|---|---|
| *input* | *unpack_stream* | *open* |
| *output* | *stdout* | |
| *line* | *mlen* | |
| *name* | *marker* | |

### *Nested functions aren't nested scopes*

Since *def* is an executable statement, it can appear anywhere: even in another function's body. When a nested *def* statement is executed (i.e., when the enclosing function's called), Python creates a new function object, and assigns it to the function name variable as usual, according to the assignment scope rules above.

Usually, this just results in a new local variable that references a new function object; both go away when the function returns, unless they're "passed out" somehow. In effect, this is just a convenient way to make temporary local functions (along with the *lambda* we'll see later in the book). Since functions are Python objects, they can be created by a function, and returned for use elsewhere in the program. For instance:

```
def maker():
    def new():
        print 'cool stuff'
    return new                    # return the function object

f = maker(); f()
```

But what this doesn't do is nest namespaces: a function created by a nested *def* statement still has just three namespaces: local (when it's called), global (the enclosing module), and built-in. Its global scope is always the enclosing module file, not the enclosing function's local scope namespace. We'll see that the same rule applies to functions nested in *class* objects later on.

## *A (in)sanity check*

Here's a riddle: why can't nested functions call themselves recursively without global declarations? The answer follows from the three-scope rule: the name of the nested function becomes a variable in the local scope of the enclosing function. It's not available in the nested function's own local scope or its global scope (the module outside both functions). We need to declare the function name global in the enclosing module, to get to it from the nested one:

```
def outer(x):
    global inner
    def inner(i):           # set inner in outer's global
        print i             # 'i' found in my local scope
        if i: inner(i-1)    # 'inner' found in my global scope
    inner(x)
```

Unlike Pascal, nested functions in Python don't have access to the namespaces of the functions they're enclosed by. Regardless of how deeply nested a *def* is, its global namespace is outside all the enclosing code. This policy keeps things simple on purpose: there's usually no need for deeply nested functions (or namespaces) in Python.

## More on try Exception Handlers: Catch-All excepts

The *unpack_file* function is a slightly higher-level interface: it takes a file name, opens it, and calls *unpack_stream*. *unpack_file* also arranges to trap and report any errors that get raised while unpacking: it uses a *try* statement with an empty *except* clause:

```
try:                                    # catch errors here
    input = open(name, 'r')
    unpack_stream(input)
except:
    import sys
    print 'unpack error!', sys.exc_type, sys.exc_value
```

which catches all errors that may occur in the *try* block: an error opening the named file, or any error that happens during the call to *unpack_stream*. Since this catches everything, we need to fetch information from the *sys* module to tell what happened:

- *sys.exc_type* is the name of the exception we caught
- *sys.exc_value* is the extra data (if any) passed when the exception was raised.

Because these aren't defined until an exception is caught, we have to import *sys* in the *except* clause again: the original *from sys import ** at the top of the module didn't get their new values. Moving the *import sys* statement to the top of the file would work too; but since we only need *sys* itself when a fatal error occurs, the nested import statement works just as well here.

### Catching too much?

Although catch-all *except* clauses without exception names are convenient, they should probably be used sparingly. Since they catch *everything*, they might catch an exception that's added to the system in the future, which may not designate an error condition. Conversely, they may prevent a real error from reaching its handler. More on this later.

## More on Modules: Nested Imports in Functions

But what happens to namespace scopes when an import statement appears nested inside a function like this? Again, not what you may think: the nested *import sys* simply assigns the *sys* module object to a new, local variable called *sys* in the function's namespace.

There's no notion of namespace nesting. The importer has to qualify the local *sys* variable name as usual, to access names in the *sys* module. Conversely, the module loaded by a nested import can't access names in the importing function's namespace. Importing is really just a matter of assigning module objects to variables in the current namespace.

It's also legal to nest a statement like *from sys import ** inside a function body. But this too works exactly as it does when we write it at the top-level of a module: the variable names in *sys* are copied to the local namespace where the *from* statement runs. At the module level, the local namespace is the same as the module's global namespace. In a function, the *from* statement will copy all names in *sys* to new local variables in the function's namespace, which all "go away" when the function exits (local variables are stacked internally).

### *Nested imports are cheap, but not free*

Sometimes there's a good reason to import inside functions as done here. But since importing can be expensive, it's usually better done at the top level of a module when possible. Doing so shifts import overheads from execution time to start-up time.

The simple *import* statement is relatively fast, as long as the module has already been imported elsewhere (like *sys* here); if not, Python module files must be located, compiled, and run. But *from* imports can be a bit more expensive: Python also has to copy symbols over, each time a *from* statement runs. Keeping imports outside functions makes all this happen once, when the enclosing module is loaded, instead of every time a function is called.

## *Part 3: "The Packer Hits the Big Time"*

Finally, here's a version of our pack script, with similar extensions. It's become functions in a module:

*Example 6-1: file: pack2.py*

```
#!/usr/local/bin/python

from sys import *
from textpak1 import marker

def pack_file(name, output):
    input = open(name, 'r')
    output.write(marker + name + '\n')
    while 1:
        line = input.readline()                 # add 1 file
        if not line: break                      # transfer line-by-line
        output.write(line)
```

*Example 6-1: file: pack2.py (continued)*

```

def pack_all(outname, sources):
    try:                                            # add all files
        output = open(outname, 'w')                 # write explicit file
    except:
        print 'error opening file'; exit(1)
    for name in sources:
        try:
            print 'packing:', name
            pack_file(name, output)
        except:
            print 'error processing:', name;  exit(1)

if __name__ == '__main__':
    try:
        pack_all(argv[1], argv[2:])
    except IndexError:
        print 'usage: pack output src src...'; exit(1)
```

Like *unpack3*, this version of the packer uses the shared *textpak1* marker string, defines functions that can be called externally, and arranges to run the main logic when run as a script, by checking if the module's `__name__` is `__main__` when Python's running the statements in the file.

As before, we can run this file as a script from the system command line, but the output file's name is passed in as the first command-line argument (and becomes *sys.argv[1]* in Python):

```
% pack2.py packed.txt *.py
```

and like the unpacker above, we can reuse the script's logic by calling its functions from other Python program code:

```
import pack2, glob
pack2.pack_all("packed.txt", glob.glob("*.py"))      # use Python name expansion
```

or equivalently:

```
from pack2 import pack_all
pack_all("packed.txt", ['file1', 'file2', 'file3'])  # use a list constant
```

We could call *pack_file* externally too:

```
import pack2
outfile = open("packed.txt", "w")
pack2.pack_file("file1", outfile)
```

but *pack_all* is a higher-level interface: it handles errors and opens all files for callers.

## *More on Exception Handling: "raise"*

This packer calls the *sys* module's *exit* function again, to end the program on an error. That makes sense in the final *if* statement (line 26), since its code *only* runs if the file's run as a script. But in function *pack_all*, calling *exit* is questionable. In an exported function interface, it probably makes more sense to raise an exception on errors, and let callers deal with the error as appropriate.

The module would also be more useful if it didn't print error messages in exported functions: we really don't know what the surrounding context may be. The changes we can make to get around these problems are shown in **boldface** in the listing below.

```
14  PackError = "Error packing files"                # define exception string
15
16  def pack_all(outname, sources):
17      try:
18          output = open(outname, 'w')
19      except:
20          raise PackError, 'while opening file'    # raise, with message
21      for name in sources:
22          try:
23              print 'packing:', name
24              pack_file(name, output)
25          except:
26              raise PackError, 'while processing: ' + name
27
28  if __name__ == '__main__':
29      try:
30          pack_all(argv[1], argv[2:])
31      except IndexError:
32          print 'usage: pack output src src...'; exit(1)
33      except PackError, message:
34          print PackError + '...', message; exit(1)
```

There are three changes to notice here:

1. We define an exception called *PackError* (a simple string variable) at the top level of the module, so it can be imported by client modules.
2. When an error's detected in *pack_all*, we use the *raise* statement to signal the caller, instead of exiting. The text we were printing in *pack_all* is passed to the caller as a string, along with the exception. Callers can use this as they see fit: *pack_all* signals errors, but doesn't handle them.
3. In the *if* statement, we added a second *except* clause to the *try* statement, to catch *PackError* when the file is run as a script. The message sent with the exception (by the *raise*) is printed here, since we know there's no external caller. *IndexError* is raised by Python; we raise *PackError* ourselves.

*raise* jumps to the closest matching *try* statement (if any), no matter how deeply embedded the *raise* is. In our example, it jumps out of the *pack_all* function, and possibly out of a *for* loop. Assuming we made these changes in a file called *pack2b.py*, here's how this program is run at the shell's command line:

```
% pack2b.py packed4 *.txt
packing: t1.txt
packing: t2.txt
packing: t3.txt
% echo $status                               check command's result
0
% pack2b.py packed5 t1.txt t4.txt t2.txt     t4.txt doesn't exist...
packing: t1.txt
packing: t4.txt
Error packing files... while processing: t4.txt
% echo $status
1
```

If we call the packer as a function from another module, the call may be wrapped in a *try* statement to catch pack errors (we usually ignore them in the interactive command line, since Python reports uncaught exceptions there anyhow). The exception name variable is imported from the pack module as usual:

```
# module: pack_client.py

import pack2b, glob
try:
    pack2b.pack_all("packed.txt", glob.glob("*.txt"))
except pack2b.PackError, message:
    handle the error here
```

Notice that we didn't alter the *pack_file* function at line 6, since it doesn't detect or report errors. Since *pack_all* catches errors that occur in *pack_file*, it should be used as the main external interface to the packer. Printing the name of each file as it's packed might also be inappropriate in a general-purpose function like *pack_all*, but we'll leave this as it is (adding a "verbose" flag to control messages might be needed later; we would add an argument to both the functions and the command line).

## Building Systems with Functions

When we start writing new functions in Python, we're faced with some choices about how to structure interfaces. Modular design deals with the entire structure of a program system (modules, classes, functions, etc.). But even at the function level, there are some crucial tradeoffs that impact the maintainability of systems. This is a big topic we don't have time to cover in detail here, but a few comments are in order.

Let's take a quick look at how functions interact with the "outside world." When we call a function, it receives input values, does its work, and usually passes a result value out. The term "black box" is used to describe this model: when structured well, callers send information in and get results out, but they're deliberately ignorant of the internal workings of the function. Figure 6-4 sketches the environment a function exists in.

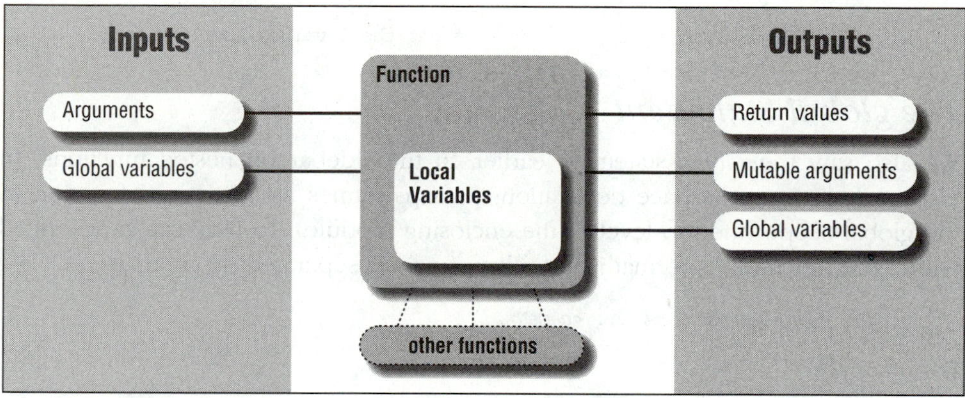


*Figure 6-4: Putting the pieces together—function interfaces*

We've already seen functions getting inputs through argument passing, and accessing global (module-level) variables, using the function namespace lookup rules. We haven't used function outputs much yet, since our scripts are mostly procedures: they do work, but don't compute values for callers.

Although we didn't go into details at the time, we saw function output with the *return* statement: in the discussion on nested functions above, it was used to pass out the local function. Functions can also influence the surrounding context by changing passed-in mutable arguments (lists, dictionaries, class instances, etc.), or by setting variables declared in *global* statements. We'll see these used later in the book, but here's a preview.

## *The return Statement*

*return* statements in a function send an object back to the caller (it becomes the result of the function call). Its format is straightforward:

```
return <expression>
```

where the expression evaluates to a Python object, of any data type: like normal variable names, functions have no type declarations or constraints.

Python functions can return *multiple values* to the caller, in lists, dictionaries, etc. One notable case: a return with multiple items separated by commas returns a "tuple" of objects (tuples show up in Chapter 7). In fact, this is one way to simulate "call-by-reference" in Python, by returning the arguments:

```
def function(x, y, z):
   ...change arguments here
   return x, y, z                      # return 3 values, as a tuple

x, y, z = function(x, y, z)            # get the 3 values from the call
```

## The global Statement

We also saw the *global* statement earlier, in the sidebar on nested functions. In fact, *global* is a namespace declaration; it maps names assigned in a function to the global scope (the top level of the enclosing module), so they can be changed within the function. Its format is just a list of names separated by commas:

```
global <name1>, <name2>, ... <nameN>
```

For example:

```
y, z = 1, 2

def all_global():
    global x             # only need to declare globals that are assigned
    x = y + z            # reference global 'y' and 'z', change global 'x'
```

Here, *y* and *z* are global by reference look-up rules. Since the name *x* is assigned directly, it is declared global to make it map to the module scope. Note that functions can change components of global variables without global declarations: in *L[i]=new*, *L* is really a reference, resolved by the three-scope lookup rule.

## Changing Mutable Arguments

Since arguments are passed by shared object references, we can alter objects passed in if they support in-place changes. This is another way to simulate "call-by-reference" in Python. For instance, if we pass in a list, assigning to one of its indexes within the function's body (*argument[i] = value*) will change the list object for the caller too; the change remains after the function returns to the caller:

```
def sideEffects(list):
    list[0] = "surprise!"              # change the passed list 'in-place'

x = ['a', 'b', 'c']
sideEffects(x)                         # on return, x[0] is "surprise!"
```

Similarly, changing an attribute of a passed-in object (*argument.name=value*) will change the caller's object in-place. When we study classes in later chapters, we'll see that this becomes a fundamental operation: methods change objects by assigning values to attributes of "self," an implicitly passed-in object.

### *Don't abuse module-level variables*

I once worked with a systems analyst who was teaching himself C. He confided that he declared all variables at the *top* of C files, so his variables were always global. "Local variables," he claimed, made programs "harder to debug." Of course, this misconception wasn't his fault: the analyst was struggling to overcome an old COBOL prejudice. But anyone who's used languages like C or Pascal knows that local variables are almost always a better idea. The same ideas hold true in Python.

As a rule of thumb, arguments are the best way to pass information into a function, and *return* statements are usually the best way to pass results out. It makes behavior more consistent, both for the caller and for the function itself. Changing module-level globals and altering mutable arguments in functions can have unexpected side effects. Moreover, using variables in another module is harmless, but changing them is dangerous. It often leads to both subtle program bugs and code that's hard (or impossible) to maintain.

Naturally, there are legitimate exceptions. For instance, Python classes depend on changing mutable arguments, and large data structures are sometimes best changed in-place. But limiting globals and argument alterations is usually a good thing. If we really wanted to, we could make all variables in Python programs global too. But that would negate decades of progress in software engineering. Python is not COBOL, either . . .

# 7

# Adding a Simple User Interface

*In this chapter:*

- *"Go Ahead—Reuse My Software"*
- *Running Scripts Versus Calling Functions*
- *Running the Interface in batch Mode*
- *Building Systems with Modules*

## *"Go Ahead—Reuse My Software"*

Adding functions to our scripts may not seem very useful at first glance, but here's one way they might be used. Suppose we want to provide access to all the shell tools we write, from a common interface. One way to do this is to add top-level logic to the common *textpak* module we started earlier. Here's an example which does just that.

*Example 7-1: File: textpak2.py*

```
#!/usr/local/bin/python

marker = '::::::'

from glob import glob
from sys import argv
import pack2, unpack3                                 # warning: circular!

def pack():
    output  = raw_input("output file name? ")
    pattern = raw_input("files to pack? ")            # expand filenames
    pack2.pack_all(output, glob(pattern))             # call as a function

def unpack():
    unpack3.unpack_file( raw_input("input file name? ") )

def interact():
    while 1:
        name = raw_input("tool?  [pack, unpack, stop] ")
        if name == 'pack':
            pack()
        elif name == 'unpack':
            unpack()
        elif name == 'stop':
```

*Example 7-1: File: textpak2.py (continued)*

```
            break
        else:
            print 'what? - try again'

if __name__ == '__main__':
    try:
        if len(argv) == 1:
            interact()
        else:
            if   argv[1] == '-i': interact()
            elif argv[1] == '-p': pack()
            elif argv[1] == '-u': unpack()
            else: print 'usage error'
    except EOFError: pass                          # ctrl-D exits anything
    print 'bye'
```

This script (module) imports the *unpack3* and *pack2* modules we just saw, and calls the functions they define. Really all we're doing here is adding user interaction logic on top of the pack scripts: we use *raw_input* to gather the information needed to run a utility, and then call the utility's exported function.

## *Running the Interface*

If we run *textpak2* with no arguments (so *len(argv)* is 1), it starts the main loop in function *interact*. We can also pass in one of three command-line *switches* (arguments used as flags) to select a particular utility instead (*–i*, *–p*, *–u*). Here's an example of interacting with this program.

```
% textpak2.py
tool? [pack, unpack, stop] unpack
input file name? packed1
creating: file1.txt                              (unpack output)
creating: file2.txt
tool? [pack, unpack, stop] pack
output file name? packed2
files to pack? *.py
packing: pack2.py
packing: unpack3.py                              (pack output)
packing: textpak2.py
tool? [pack, unpack, stop] unpack
input file name? packed3
unpack error! IOError (2, 'No such file or directory')
tool? [pack, unpack, stop] stp
what? - try again
tool? [pack, unpack, stop] stop
bye
```

### *Updating textpak's clients*

To switch over to the new *textpak2* version, the import statements in the *pack2.py* and *unpack3.py* scripts seen in Chapter 6, *Adding a Functional Interface*, can be changed to name the new *textpak2* file (not *textpak1*). In both files, line 4 becomes:

```
4   from textpak2 import marker        # marker constant
```

Since this is the only line changed, I won't repeat these two scripts here. This change isn't strictly needed if we keep the 1-line *textpak1* around too, but for now, let's assume that *textpak1.py* is being replaced by *textpak2.py*. I'll explain why it matters later in this chapter.

## *More on Exception Handling: EOFError Isn't Always an Error*

We can exit by typing **stop**, or typing an end-of-file character (usually the key combination control + **d**) anytime we're prompted for input. Because everything the script does is embedded in (or called from) the *try* statement at line 30, typing an end-of-file raises an exception caught by the *except* at line 38. In this context, the *EOFError* exception isn't really an error condition. It's a signal to end the program, and works something like C's *longjmp*: we jump up to the exception handler immediately.

## *Using the pass Statement*

When we catch the end-of-file exception, we execute a *pass* statement:

```
38   except EOFError: pass
```

which does nothing except tell Python to continue at the next statement. *pass* is really just a place-holder for cases where we need a statement syntactically, but don't really have anything to do. Here, the *except* clause requires one or more statements (a "body"), but there's no special exception-handling to be done: the *except* clause is only there to catch the *EOFError*. By using a *pass* statement here, we make sure the program moves on to print *bye* and exit, whether an *EOFError* is raised or not.

## *More on if Tests: Multiway Branching*

At line 34, we use an *if* statement to run one of the three functions in this file, according to the value of the command-line "switch":

```
if   argv[1] == '-i': interact()
elif argv[1] == '-p': pack()
elif argv[1] == '-u': unpack()
else: print 'usage error'
```

Here, we compare the switch string (*argv[1]*) to three string constants to see which the user wants to perform. A similar construct is used at line 20. As I hinted at earlier, this is one of the ways we can implement *switch* or *case* statements in Python. In the next chapter's examples, we'll see other techniques based on data structures.

# *Running Scripts Versus Calling Functions*

As we've seen, Python has interfaces for running shell commands too. In fact, our scripts can also be run as separate programs (processes), instead of calling their exported functions. We just change lines 7–15 in *textpak2.py* to the following code (if you're running the examples, this version is called *textpak3*).

```
7   import os                              # no need to import pack/unpack
8
9   def pack():
10      output  = raw_input("output file name? ")           # run as a script
11      pattern = raw_input("files to pack? ")              # slower than call
12      os.system('pack2.py %s %s' % (output, pattern))    # system glob's
13
14  def unpack():
15      os.system('unpack3.py %s' % raw_input("input file name? "))
```

But it's quite a bit slower to run scripts than to call functions: not only does Python have to reparse and reload a script each time it's called, but on UNIX systems, a new process is also spawned to run the command passed to the *os.system* function.

Since importing and calling functions is more direct, and therefore almost always faster, it's usually a better way to link programs. But such a tight coupling isn't always practical. For instance, distributed client/server applications depend on much looser integration mechanisms. The *os.system* and *os.popen* functions handle some multiprocessing tasks, but we'll look at other tools later in the book.

## More on Built-In Types: % String Formatting

We've introduced the % operator in this example. For numbers, % is the modulus operation. For string objects, % works much like C's *sprintf* function. It allows us to format strings, according to a format pattern, and a set of input objects. Its general form is:

```
<string with '%' format codes>  %  <object, or 'tuple' of objects>
```

Objects on the right of the % operator are paired with conversion codes starting with % in the string on the left. The objects on the right side are converted to a character string representation according to the % format codes in the string on the left, and are then inserted into the string in the, replacing the conversion code. We use % twice:

```
os.system('unpack3.py %s' % raw_input("input file name? "))
```

In this instance, the *%s* format code is replaced with the string returned by *raw_input*, to construct the shell command-line run by *os.system*. The *%s* code means: "insert a string's text here." *%s* converts any object to its string representation. The other % expression:

```
os.system('pack2.py %s %s' % (output, pattern))
```

makes use of two *%s* conversion codes in the format string on the left, and a *tuple* holding two objects on the right. `output` is inserted at the first *%s*, and `pattern` is inserted at the second, as shown in Figure 7-1.

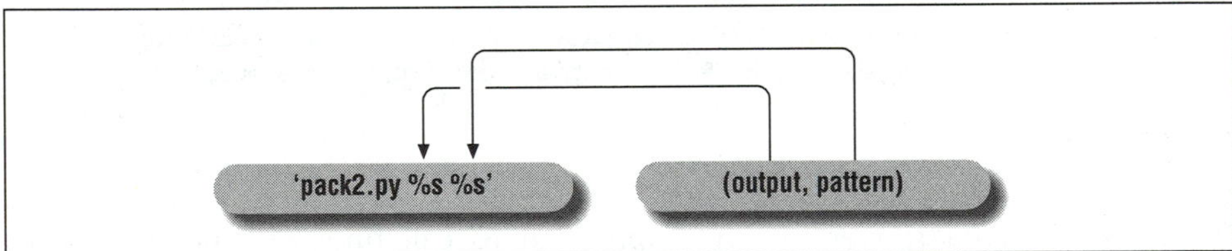


*Figure 7-1: String formatting*

Since Python objects can be converted to strings using back-quotes (`` `object` ``), % can usually be replaced by concatenations, or by lists in `print` statements:

```
concatenation  'pack2.py ' + output + ' ' + pattern
print lists    print "the sum of", x, "+", number, "=", (x + number)
back-quotes    "the sum of " + `x` + " + " + `number` + " = " + `(x + number)`
```

but % is sometimes clearer:

```
print "the sum of %d + %d = %d" % (x, number, (x + number))
```

## *Other string format codes*

*%* supports the usual C *printf* conversion codes. For instance, *%d* converts integers to strings, *%f* and *%g* convert floating-point numbers, and *%s* converts anything. Precision and width modifiers are supported too: `'%1.2g' % 3.1415` creates string *3.1.* Appendix C, *A Mini-Reference* lists all the conversion codes available. As we'll see, there's also an extension for pulling objects into a format string by name, using dictionaries.

## *More on Built-In Types: Tuples*

We've mentioned tuples in passing, and finally used them in this example; let's introduce them here. In simple terms, Python tuples are a way to group objects into a collection. They're similar to Python lists, except that tuples are written differently, and are immutable sequences: like strings, we can't change tuples in place by assigning to indexes. Tuple objects are processed with sequence operators; they don't have methods or dedicated modules, but play a role in some special operations discussed below.

To change a tuple item, we need to make a new tuple by slicing and concatenating. This has some performance benefits, and provides some degree of integrity constraints: we can be sure a tuple won't change, if it's passed around a program. Tuples are written as a list of items, separated by commas and enclosed in parentheses:

```
os.system('pack2.py %s %s' % (output, pattern))
```

When it's not ambiguous, we can sometimes omit the enclosing parentheses. This is commonly done in assignments and return statements (tuple assignments are discussed in the next chapter):

```
x, y, z = 1, 2, 3                          # tuples on both sides
return value1, value2, value3              # return 3 items as a tuple
```

If commas are significant, we need to enclose tuples in parentheses; for instance, inside a function's argument-list or a list constant. One special case: empty tuples are written as an empty parenthesized list, but a tuple with one item requires a trailing comma so it's not confused with a parenthesized expression:

*Table 7-1: Writing tuples*

| Tuple constants | Interpretation |
|---|---|
| `()` | An empty tuple |
| `(1,)` | A tuple with one item |
| `(1)` | An expression, not a tuple |
| `(1, 2, 3)` | A three-item tuple |
| `1, 2, 3` | A three-item tuple too, unless ambiguous |
| `('name', (first, last))` | A two-item tuple, with a nested tuple |

### *Why both lists and tuples?*

Since lists do everything tuples do and more, this is a common question. As a guideline, Python lists are useful for collections we need to change often. Python tuples come in handy if we just want to group a number of items together, but don't plan on changing the structure of the grouping itself.

Beyond these abstract distinctions, the choice between lists and tuples is often a matter of style. However, some built-in operations require tuples to be passed-in or return tuple results (%, *apply*, etc.), and some constructs may be easier to understand with tuples (for instance, the multiple-target assignment above).

---

*NOTE* Strictly speaking, we can't change the tuple itself, but we can change items inside it, if they're mutable. Just like lists, tuples are really arrays of object references; nested objects in a tuple can be changed if they allow it. For instance, lists nested in tuples can change.

---

### *Tuples and argument lists*

One particular place where tuples come into play is Python's support for variable-length function argument lists. If we prefix an argument name with a `*` in the function header, the name will be assigned to a tuple holding the rest of the passed argument objects (or an empty tuple if there's none left). We haven't seen this used yet, but here's the general idea:

```
def function(*arguments):
    for arg in arguments:
        <process each argument 'arg'>
```

When *function* is called, *arguments* is assigned all the passed objects (enclosed in parentheses at the call), as a tuple. Figure 7-2 shows how this works. Since tuples are sequences, we can iterate over the argument list using a *for* statement, etc. If there are real argument names before the * catch-all, then the * argument gets a tuple of the remaining arguments:

```
def function(x, y, *rest):
```

Here, *x* and *y* are assigned the first two arguments passed, and *rest* gets a tuple of arguments three and beyond (or an empty tuple, if there are only two). * arguments work much like C's *varargs* system, but Python's version is simpler to use: it's based on tuple objects.

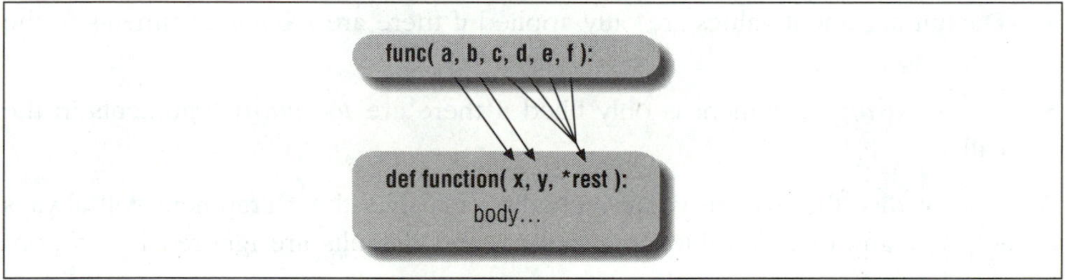


*Figure 7-2: Catching variable-length argument lists*

The inverse, calling a function with a tuple of arguments, is also possible, as illustrated in Figure 7-3. The *apply* built-in function takes a function object, and a tuple of objects, and makes the tuple an argument-list in a call to the function:

```
def function(x, y, z):
...
apply(function, (arg1, arg2, arg3))        # same as function(arg1,arg2,arg3)
```

*apply* is useful for calling functions, when the length of the argument list can't be predicted ahead of time. In such cases, a call can't be hard-coded; instead, we can put the arguments in a tuple built at run-time, and call the function generically with *apply*. We'll use both *apply* and "*" arguments in later examples.

***Mixing defaults and variable-length argument lists.*** In Python, passing the wrong number of arguments to a function is normally trapped as a run-time error. Python raises an exception if the number of arguments passed isn't the same as the number of nondefault arguments. The * argument gets around this rule by accepting an arbitrary number of arguments.

Earlier, we used default arguments in function-headers too: `name=default`. The question naturally comes up: how do defaults and * arguments mix? When a list of objects is passed to a function, Python only assigns "left-over" arguments to the * name, after all other names in the header have been resolved.

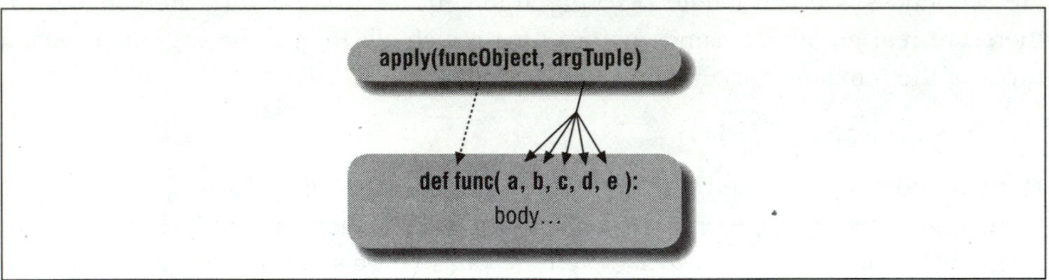


*Figure 7-3: Sending variable-length argument lists*

- Default argument values are only applied if there are *too few* arguments in the call.
- The * *varargs* argument is only filled if there are *too many* arguments in the call.

Because of this, the two ideas are mutually exclusive: the * argument will always be empty if any default values are applied, and defaults are ignored if * is non-empty. Here's a simple example.

```
% python
>>> def f(a, b, c=1, *d): print a, b, c, d
...
>>> f(3)
Traceback (innermost last):
  File "<stdin>", line 1, in ?
  File "<stdin>", line 1, in f
TypeError: not enough arguments
>>> f(3, 4)
3 4 1 ()
>>> f(3, 4, 5)
3 4 5 ()
>>> f(3, 4, 5, 6)
3 4 5 (6,)
>>> f(3, 4, 5, 6, 7, 8)
3 4 5 (6, 7, 8)
```

We always have to pass at least two arguments here, to match *a* and *b*, or Python raises an error. If we only pass two, *c* will default to 1, and *d* will get an empty tuple. If we pass three, *c* isn't set to 1, but *d* is still empty. In fact, *d* is only nonempty when we pass four or more arguments.

In Chapter 8, *Adding Text-Based Menus*, we'll see one more argument passing extension: keyword arguments. Since it involves dictionaries, we'll defer details for the moment.

## *Running the Interface in batch Mode*

Although this script was written to interact with an interactive "user", it can just as easily be run in *batch* mode. This is really more of a UNIX trick than a Python feature, but it illustrates standard stream redirection. If we put the input lines we typed in the interaction listing above into a text file:

*Example 7-2: File: input1*

```
unpack
packed1
pack
packed2
*.py
stop
```

then we can run the script in silent mode by piping this file in to *stdin*, and sending the output to another file. Python reads *raw_input* from the file instead of asking you:

```
% textpak2.py < input1 > output1
```

This isn't all that useful here, but the technique can be used to capture script output and compare it to expected results (more on this in a moment). To redirect files programmatically, we can change *textpak2.py* itself, and run it without shell redirection:

```
if __name__ == '__main__':
    import sys
    sys.stdin  = open('input1', 'r')          # redirect stdin internally
    sys.stdout = open('output1', 'w')
    ...rest unchanged...
```

```
% textpak2.py
```

But here's a more interesting idea: why not write another Python script to do all this for us?

*Example 7-3: File: batch.py*

```
#!/usr/local/bin/python

import os, sys                          # unix, python services
from posixpath import exists            # file exists test
from time import time, ctime            # time functions

if len(sys.argv) != 4:
    print 'use: batch <program> <input> <output>'
    sys.exit(1)

print 'batch run start.'
print 'what: ', sys.argv[1]
```

*Example 7-3: File: batch.py (continued)*

```
print 'who:  ', os.environ['USER']          # environment variables
print 'where:', os.getcwd()                 # directory
print 'when: ', ctime(time())

if exists(sys.argv[3]):
    os.rename(sys.argv[3], sys.argv[3] + '.bkp')        # backup output

os.system('%s < %s > %s 2>&1' % tuple(sys.argv[1:]))    # run command
print 'batch run done.'
```

This script prints information about the run, and runs the program in the shell, redirecting input and output to the files named on the command line. It also backs up the last run's output (if it exists) by moving it to a *.bkp* suffixed file-name. There aren't many new ideas in this script, just a few new built-in services:

*os.environ*
: The shell-variable dictionary mentioned before (we'll discuss dictionaries in Chapter 8).

*os.getcwd*
: Returns the current directory name, where the script is being run.

*os.rename*
: The POSIX file rename function (like the *mv* UNIX command).

*posixpath.exists*
: An easy way to test whether a filename exists.

*time*
: This built-in module implements most of C's time-processing functions.

*tuple*
: This built-in function makes a new tuple out of the items in any sequence; % requires one.

This script can run any Python script. In fact, it can be used to run any executable program (not just Python scripts) and redirect its standard streams to files. But to be completely general, the script could also allow for command-line arguments to be passed to the program being run. We could support such arguments on the command-line after the output-file name, by changing the usage test and the *system* call:

```
import string
if len(sys.argv) < 4:
    print 'use: batch <program> <input> <output> <arguments>?...'
...
os.system('%s %s < %s > %s 2>&1' %
              (sys.arv[1], string.join(sys.argv[4:]), sys.argv[2], sys.argv[3]) )
```

Here, the *join* function in the built-in *string* module concatenates arguments 5 and beyond into a single substring, that gets inserted in the command after the program's name. *join* takes a list of strings and inserts a blank between them. Here's a log of a batch *textpak2* run and the resulting output file:

```
% batch.py textpak2.py input1 output1
batch run start.
what: textpak2.py
who:  mark
where: /home/mark/stuff/python.src/test
when: Sat Jul 15 19:05:34 1995
batch run done.

% cat output1
tool? [pack, unpack, stop] input file name? creating: file1.txt
creating: file2.txt
tool? [pack, unpack, stop] output file name? files to pack? packing: batch.py
packing: textpak2.py
packing: pack2.py
packing: unpack3.py
tool? [pack, unpack, stop] bye
```

## *Almost a regression tester*

The *output1* file may not look very interesting, but notice that its content won't change unless we change one of the three module files it reflects (*textpak2*, *pack2*, *unpack3*). In fact, with a little extra logic in *batch.py*, we could also compare the output file to the one we backed up. By running a *diff* command on files *output1* and *output1.bkp*, we can detect deviations from the prior run's output, and hence changes in the scripts.

This turns out to be a simple way to test programs: a more sophisticated regression-test system could build on this idea, by running a set of tests automatically, looking for changes in output. Suggested exercise: enhance the *batch.py* script to compare outputs and report differences. (Hint: define a standard directory structure for files: inputs, outputs, and scripts; one possible solution appears in Chapter 2, *A Sneak Preview*.)

# Building Systems with Modules

Let's step back for a moment and look at how the interface program is "glued" together. Our file packing system is now composed of three modules (source files):

*pack2.py*
: The packer with a functional interface.

*unpack3.py*
: The unpacker with a functional interface.

*textpak2.py*
: The interactive user-interface logic file.

The *pack* and *unpack* modules import *textpak* to load the *marker* constant, and *textpak* imports the other two to use their functional interfaces. All three import Python-provided services (*sys*, *glob*), and implicitly import items in the `__builtin__` module, where names like *open* and *raw_input* are found.

In terms of the packing logic, *textpak* is a "client" of *pack* and *unpack*; in terms of the *marker* string, textpak is a "server." Figure 7-4 shows how the modules in our system are related by import statements.

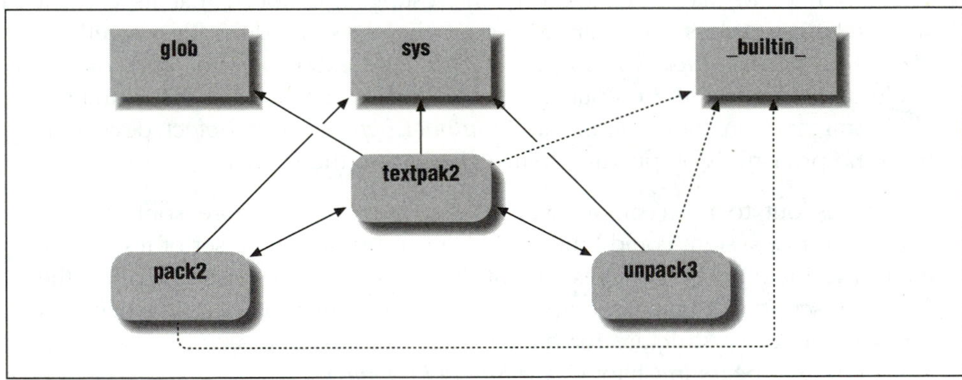


*Figure 7-4: Putting the pieces together–import dependencies*

## How import Statements Affect Module Dependencies.

Figure 7-4 only shows how modules reference each other, not how the imports are actually performed. When the *import* statement is used, the importer has direct access to the imported module's contents. The importer can use (and change) the imported module's variable names at will, by attribute qualification. Encapsulation is an informal agreement in Python: there's no way for a module to restrict access to its contents, when the import statement is used.

But when the *from* import statement is used, module dependencies don't endure beyond the point of import. Names are copied over once when the *from* is run, but the bond between the importing and imported module is broken after that. The copied names share objects initially, but there's no link to the imported module itself. As we saw earlier, the importer can change imported "mutable" objects in place, but there's no way to change variables in the module where names were imported from.

## *There's No Escaping Modules!*

In the general case, Figure 7-5 shows how the components of Python programs fit together. We've already seen variables, modules, and functions; we'll see classes in an upcoming chapter.

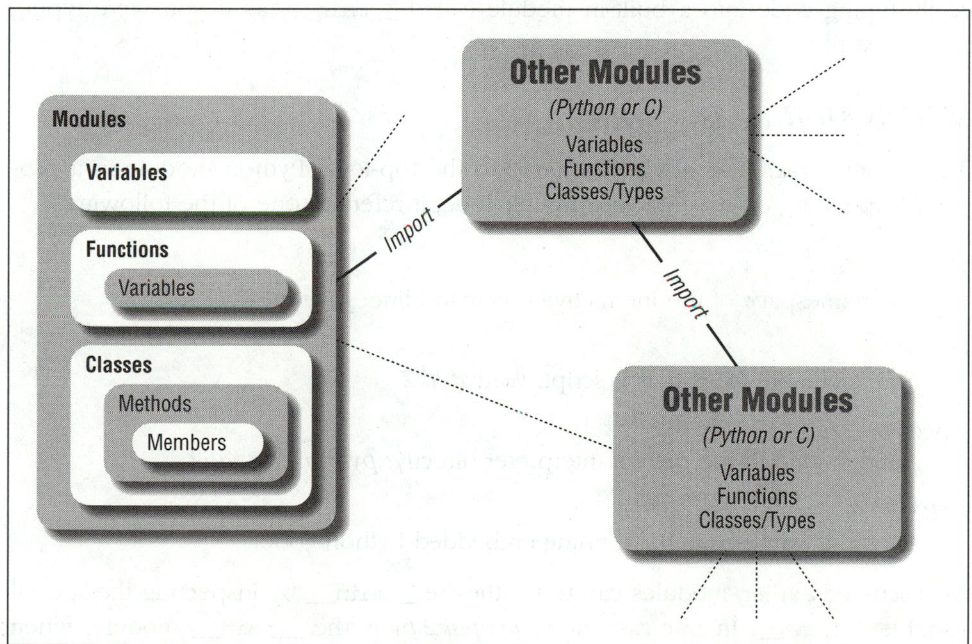


*Figure 7-5: Modular program organization*

At the highest level of abstraction, Python programs are just sets of modules:

*Functions*
Used to divide a large task into its procedural components.

*Classes*
Used to model objects (in the abstract sense of the word) in the application

*Modules*
Tie the whole thing together into larger, reusable packages of related components.

Inside a class, functions implement its methods, and variables are its data members. Inside modules, variables, functions, and classes implement exported services.

There are no absolute rules about how to structure code, but larger systems are often built as sets of modules containing classes, with a few utility functions thrown in. Modules are the biggest program unit: in fact, you're never not in a module when working in Python. Even at the interactive command-line, you're really typing code into a built-in module called `__main__`, as if you were typing into a text file.

## Which Module Is __main__?

The name `__main__` is always assigned to the top-level Python module in a process. Depending on how you're running code, it refers to one of the following:

*Prompt*
The namespace of the interactive command line: *python*

*Scripts*
An executable file run as a script: *% textpak2*

*Programs*
A file passed to the *python* interpreter directly: *python textpak2*

*Embedded*
A default namespace for running embedded Python code.

As discussed earlier, modules can test if they're `__main__` by inspecting the special variable `__name__`. In our case here, *textpak2.py* is the `__main__` module, when we run it as a script.

## C Modules Look the Same as Python Modules

As we'll see in Chapter 14, *Extending Python*, modules are also the unit of C extensions and integration: modules in the picture above may be implemented in Python or C (or any C-compatible language). Modules implemented in C can define variables, functions, and new built-in data types, which behave just like Python objects.

When we import a module, we don't have to know which language it's written in. For instance, we've been using the built-in open function, and things in the *sys* module (the *stdout* file, the *argv* list, etc.), which are really implemented in C. At the same time, we've also been using the *glob* module's *glob* function, which is coded in Python. But to Python programs, there's no way (or need) to tell the difference.

In fact, this is a important feature of Python: because Python and C modules are used exactly the same way, the clients of a module don't need to be changed if it's later moved from a Python implementation, to a C one. This concept lets us be fairly cavalier when prototyping systems: we can start them in Python, and move selected parts to C as needed to speed things up for delivery. We'll expand on this idea when we explore C extensions in Chapter 14.

### *But C types are not Python classes*

As we'll also see later, new data types implemented in C modules are usually exported by a function that creates objects of the type. Once created, C data type objects are manipulated by calling a set of exported methods and/or applying overloaded expression operators to the objects.

But what is a C data type? Actually, we've been using one without knowing it: the file type is implemented in a C module. The built-in *open* function creates file objects, which are manipulated by calling file methods (*read*, *write*, etc.). For instance:

```
input = open("/tmp/spam", "r")    # make a file-type object (in C)
line  = input.readline()          # call its methods (in C)
```

In later chapters, we'll find that this scheme is very close to how we make and use instances of Python classes. But not quite: there's no notion of inheritance for C data types, and we can't subclass a C type to change its behavior. Types don't participate in a bigger organizational framework. But we'll also see that C types can be made to look more like classes by adding Python wrapper classes. Stay tuned.

## *Handling Circular import Dependencies.*

Our three modules are an example of "circular imports": *textpak* imports *pack* for its functions, but *pack* imports *textpack* for the "marker" constant. Python is smart enough to avoid getting into endless cycles when resolving such imports, but they can still get us into trouble if we're not careful.

To see why, we need to know more about how imports work. When a Python module is imported the first time from anywhere in a program, Python follows this sequence of steps:

1. Compile the file's source code, or load a precompiled version.
2. Create a new module object with an empty namespace, and put it in the *sys.modules* dictionary.
3. Execute the module's statements one by one, from the top of the file to the bottom.

On subsequent imports, the module is found already loaded in *sys.modules*, and Python just uses the existing module object. As we've seen, some of the statements executed in step 3 create new named objects in the module's namespace, as a side effect: assignments, *def* and *class* statements, etc.

Import statements are part of this process too: they're not executed until all statements before them are run. When an import statement runs, any statements below it that create named objects as side effects won't have been run yet. In effect, a module is only partially complete when it imports another module—some of its names may not yet exist.

But because the module itself already exists (by step 2 above), an incomplete module won't be finished if it is imported while one of its own import statements is running. The importer will get the module as it exists "so far," and Python won't try to load or run statements in the cyclically imported module, since the module object already exists. In fact, this is the only thing preventing circular imports from looping forever!

Because of this, the order of statements in a module sometimes matters, when circular imports run. For example, we have to assign to the variable "marker" in the *textpak2* module before it imports *pack2* or *unpack3*, because they in turn import marker from *textpak2* with a "from" statement. "marker" must already be created when we run the imports in *textpak2*, or we'll get an undefined name error.

In Figure 7-6, *textpak2* imports *pack2*, which imports *textpak2* circularly. When it executes the *import-2* statement, *pack2* can only copy names already created in *textpak2* before the *import-1* statement. Everything created by statements below the level of *import-1* in *textpak2* does not yet exist.

In other words, *pack2* only has *from* access to names created in *textpak2* by statements above the one that imported *pack2*; it has *import* access to *textpak2* itself, since it already exists (in an incomplete state).

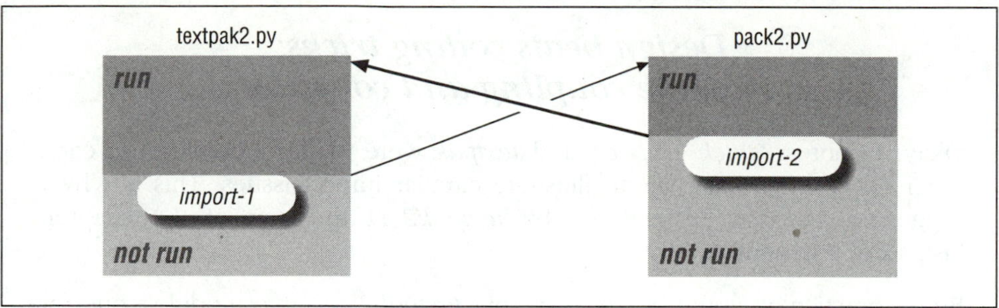


*Figure 7-6: Circular imports*

### *Avoiding circular import problems*

Such concerns are fairly rare in practice, but the potential for problems becomes greater as you move toward larger systems. As a general rule, try to avoid using circular imports, by careful design. Failing that, one of the following approaches can be used.

- Some conflicts can be avoided if import statements appear near the bottom of your source files. In this case, most of a module will already be defined when it's imported recursively.
- Putting import statements in functions which use imported names can also solve some problems, by delaying imports. However, this approach incurs the overhead of repeated imports.
- As a heuristic, circular import problems can often be avoided by minimizing *from* imports. If you use the *import* form instead, you're usually safe, because you won't access names in the imported module until later. Since the imported module will probably be complete by then, its exports will usually be present when needed.

## *Incremental Development and Module Reloads*

So far, we've seen that modules are loaded with either the *import* or *from* statements. Both let us link modules into larger systems, and develop components separately. This is usually called "incremental development": programs are developed and tested piece by piece. In fact, we can both test components individually (*unit testing*), and test the system as a whole when all pieces are coded (*integration testing*).

But it's also sometimes useful to be able to change a component without having to stop programs that use it. For instance, if a program takes a long time to start up, we'd like to be able to change its parts and see the effect immediately. In Python,

### *Design beats coding tricks: module coupling and cohesion*

Okay, I confess. *pack*, *unpack*, and *textpak* were made dependent on each other like this on purpose, to illustrate circular import issues. This is why I suggested *textpak1* be replaced by *textpak2* at the start of the chapter, instead of augmenting it.

But in practice, it would be better to split *textpak2* into two modules: one for constants (like *marker*), and one for the new top-level interaction logic. Such a structure breaks the circular dependency altogether. Combining the two components in a single module file isn't good design: different functionality should appear in different modules.

More generally, the concept of cohesion applies to Python modules, just as it does to other program units like functions: items in a module should have a strongly related role. If we follow this practice, module coupling (import dependencies) is naturally kept to a minimum, and circular import problems are rare.

Here, *pack* and *unpack* should really get the *marker* constant from the original *textpak1* module, as coded in Chapter 6. From here on, we'll assume they do, and omit *marker* constants in new textpak mutations. If you're working along with the examples, you may want to change the import statements in *pack2* and *unpack3* to reference *textpak1*; the *marker* assignment in *texpak2* will become unnecessary but harmless.

this is accomplished with the *reload* built-in function. After a module is imported, a *reload* call reimports the source file: we can edit a module to test changes, without having to stop the program that imports it. Here are two simple examples to demonstrate the idea.

*Example 7-4: File: knight.py*

```
def says(rept):
    return 'Ni!...' * rept      # change me
```

*Example 7-5: File: lines.py*

```
import knight                   # changes out from under this module

def text():
    print knight.says(3)        # get most recent version (fails if "from" used)
```

When we test the modules interactively, we get the expected behavior:

```
% python
>>> import knight, lines
>>> knight.says(2)              # test a component
'Ni!...Ni!...'
>>> lines.text()                # test an enclosing system
Ni!...Ni!...Ni!...
>>>
```

But now, let's go to another window, and change the *knight.py* module file (or suspend the *python* interpreter and change it in the same window, if your system allows it). The Python interpreter program stays active while we're editing. The *vi* text-editor is used to change the file here:

```
% vi knight.py
% cat knight.py
def says(rept):
    return 'A shrubbery!...' * rept     # change me
```

When we go back to the Python interpreter and reload the module, we get the following new behavior:

```
>>> reload(knight)
<module 'knight'>
>>> knight.says(2)
'A shrubbery!...A shrubbery!...'
>>> lines.text()
A shrubbery!...A shrubbery!...A shrubbery!...
```

Notice that the change to the *knight* module impacted both the command-line interpreter's namespace, and the imported *lines* module. When a module is reloaded, the module *object* is changed in place. Any client that accesses its attributes by qualification ("module.attribute") will get new versions after a reload. This doesn't work if we use *from* imports, since the module object isn't qualified; more on this later.

Of course, this is an artificial example; it's probably just as fast to exit the interpreter here. But in practice the importing program might be a large Python application, instead of the command-line interpreter. Moreover, *reload* can be useful at the command line too; with reloading, testing can take the form:

```
import system's top-level module
start-up the system
repeat:
    test the system
    edit component modules
    reload component modules
until the system works
```

There's no need to stop and restart each time we need to change a module.

> ### *reload requires a module object*
>
> Unlike *import* and *from*, *reload* requires a module *object*, not a name. It's sometimes necessary to import the module in the namespace where *reload* is run. Imported modules can also be accessed by-name in the *sys.modules* dictionary, without importing: `reload(sys.modules['knight'])`. But then we may have to import *sys* instead. We will see how to use dictionaries later, in Chapter 8.

### *More on reload*

In effect, *reload* forces a module to be imported again, and changes it for every module that imports it. Roughly, *reload* overwrites everything in the module's namespace in place, including its functions, variables, etc. Here are a few more details on the module reloading process.

***reload = load + import.*** Python modules are always loaded the first time they're imported. But once loaded, future imports just use the already-loaded version (found in *sys.modules*), rather than loading the source file again. Since the same module may be imported in many places in a large program, and many times if imported in a function, reloading the module on each import could be expensive.

By contrast, *reload* forces a module to be reloaded, even if it has already been imported. In effect, *reload* is like an *import*, with forced loading of the module source file. In some contexts this simple idea supports more rapid turnaround after program changes.

***reload reruns statements in an existing module object.*** Like normal imports, after the module source file is read, *reload* executes all the new statements in the file, in the module's namespace dictionary. Because of this, the old values of names in the module are replaced:

- Prior values of its variables are replaced by running assignment statements again.
- Prior values of functions and classes are replaced by running *def* and *class* statements.
- Import statements in the module are executed once again and replace nested modules.

The effect is that the module is replaced in-line by the new file's definition. But there are three special cases to watch out for when using *reload*. All of these cases are fairly obscure, but worth a look here.

***1. Reloading active code is handled gracefully.*** If any clients are running code in a module's function when it's reloaded, the active calls aren't impacted immediately: the active code is finished first (or they would almost certainly crash!). Internally, references to active code objects are kept on the execution stack until they exit, so code isn't reclaimed while it's running. Luckily, this case is so rare that, it's hard to demonstrate. Here's the abstract case:

*Example 7-6: File: M.py*

```
def F():
    import M
    reload(M)           # reload myself...
    <do more stuff>
```

Here, when function *F* reloads module *M*, it's reloading *itself* too: F's definition will be replaced when the *def* is rerun. But the old version of *F* is retained until the call finishes: the *<do more stuff>* part runs in the old function's code. Later calls to *M.F* get the new version.

***2. Transitive imports aren't followed.*** Reload doesn't *transitively* load modules that a reloaded module imports. Import statements in the reloaded module are reexecuted, but if they name modules already loaded (in *sys.modules*), they won't cause the nested modules to be loaded. In the example above, if *knight* imports another module that's been imported before, that other module won't be reloaded when we *reload(knight)*. We'll get the already loaded version unless we reload knight's imports too.

***3. from clients aren't always affected.*** This is probably the most significant reload issue: as we've seen, if a client module uses the *from* import statement at its top level, it copies names out of a server module once, when the client is imported. If the server module is later reloaded, the client will retain the old values of the names copied out, since there's no link back to the module they came from; *from* is a simple assignment, not a name-aliasing operation. For example, if we change the *import knight* statement in the *lines* module above to a *from*:

*Example 7-7: File: lines.py*

```
from knight import says          # copy name from knight

def text():
    print says(3)                # use the name unqualified
```

then editing and reloading *knight* will have no effect on the behavior of *text* calls: *lines*' copy of *knight*'s *says* variable will still be a reference to the prior function object.

This occurs because names created by the *from* are evaluated when it runs, and before the reload. In Python, variable names aren't evaluated until they're used (evaluation is deferred until execution). For instance, names in a function aren't resolved until the function is called: if we reload a module, calls to a function in the module from other functions in the same module will access the new versions after the reload:

```
def function1():
    ...new definition     # replaces prior version when module reloaded

def function2():
    function1()           # name not evaluated till call: finds new global
```

But in the *from* case, names are evaluated too soon—when the module is imported. Using *import* and name-qualification defers the evaluation until the name is actually used; the new versions are picked up correctly.

### Avoiding from reload problems

There are really two ways to fix this *from* reload problem:

- A *reload* always has an impact if we use *import* statements instead. In Example 7-5 above, we refetched names in *knight* each time they were qualified (*knight.says*).
- *reload* also works if we use a *from* statement inside a function: since it runs on every call, the *from* will recopy (i.e., reevaluate) all of the imported variables each time it runs.

For example, this version works too:

*Example 7-8: File: lines.py*

```
def text():
    from knight import says    # copy name from knight on each call
    print says(3)
```

But given the cost of *from* statements, the original *import* version is usually a better approach. This is yet another good reason to avoid *from* when possible.

---

*NOTE* We'll revisit module reloading in Chapter 11, *Graphical User Interfaces*, as a way to change a running GUI program. And in Chapter 15, *Embedding Python*, we'll use it to update Python code embedded in C.

---

## *Transitive Import Concepts*

In some sense, modules nest when *import* statements are kicked off transitively. Since we usually just use the names at the *top* of an imported module, this isn't always apparent. But if we want to follow module links we can, provided we're not using *from* to import names.

For instance, if some module *X* imports a module *Y*, which imports another module *Z*, we can get to names in *Z* when we import *X*, by normal attribute qualification: *X.Y.Z.name*. Figure 7-7 shows how.

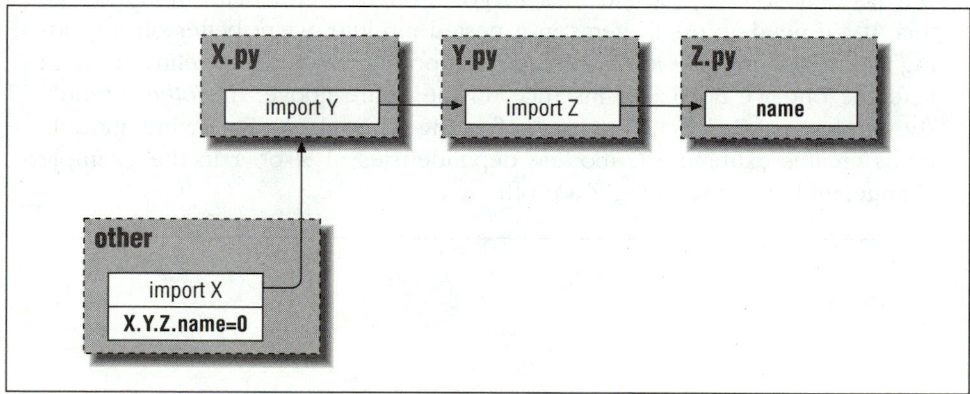


*Figure 7-7: Transitive import links*

To summarize, here's how module nesting pertains to some of the concepts we've seen:

*scopes*
: Nested modules aren't nested namespace scopes: we're only qualifying nested module objects in the example. In all three modules, the import statements assign module objects to local variable names, which we qualify as usual. For instance, module *Y* doesn't have access to names in module *X* (unless it imports and qualifies *X* too).

*from*
: When *from* statements are used, module nesting doesn't occur: for instance, if *X* imports *Z from Y*, it gets *Z* directly, but has no access to the module *Y* itself. In effect, *from* collapses qualification lists. Only *import* creates links to other modules.

*reload*

Finally, when *reload* is used we don't follow the import links to other modules: reloading *X* doesn't reload *Y* or *Z* if they've already been imported (by *X*, or any other module). And when *from* is used, there's no link to the module that owned the imported names: reloading *Y* has no effect on *X* if it imports *Z* *from Y*.

### *Transitive imports are (well . . . ) transitive*

But it's almost always a bad idea to go through intermediate modules like this. If we need access to items in a nested module, we're better off importing the nested module itself, instead of importing one and traveling through it to the one we need. For instance, in the figure above, the *other* module should import *Z* directly, instead of going through *X*. Following module paths creates extreme intermodule dependencies: if *X* or *Y* in the example change, all bets on reaching *Z* are off!

*In this chapter:*

- *"On Today's Menu: Packing, Unpacking, and Fresh Spam"*
- *Making Menus with Dictionaries*
- *Making Menus with Lists*
- *Built-In Types: Operators, Methods, and Modules*
- *The Zen of Python: Namespaces are Dictionaries*
- *Dictionaries and Keyword Arguments*
- *Design Concepts: Do Modules Support OOP?*

# 8

# *Adding Text-Based Menus*

## *"On Today's Menu: Packing, Unpacking, and Fresh Spam"*

In the interactive interface we looked at in the last chapter, legal commands are listed in the prompt for input: *[pack, unpack, stop]*. It doesn't take much extra work to show the user options in the form of a menu, one per line. We could do this using the *if* multiway branch structures we used earlier. But we can avoid having redundant lists of option names, by automating the menu process with menu data structures. Dictionaries and lists both work well for representing command-menus.

## *Making Menus with Dictionaries*

One way to automate menu logic is to store option names and functions in Python dictionaries:

*File: textpak4.py*

```
#!/usr/local/bin/python

from sys import argv, exit
from textpak2 import pack, unpack           # reuse textpak2 stuff

menu = { 'pack':   pack,                    # interactive menu
```

```
          'unpack': unpack,                # 'key' : function
          'stop':   exit }                 # sys.exit on 'stop'

def interact():
    while 1:
        for name in menu.keys():           # could do list.sort
            print '\t' + name              # show options
        tool = raw_input('?')
        try:
            menu[tool]()                   # run function
        except KeyError:                   # let eof-error pass
            print 'what? - try again'      # key not found

if __name__ == '__main__':
    flags = {'-i':interact, '-p':pack, '-u':unpack}
    try:
        if len(argv) == 1:                          # no flags: interact
            interact()
        else:
            if flags.has_key(argv[1]):              # test key first
                flags[argv[1]]()                    # run function
            else:
                print 'usage error: -i | -p | -u'  # not found
    except EOFError: pass                           # ctrl-D exits anything
```

When we run this script, we have access to the same pack/unpack utilities. In fact, we're reusing the *pack* and *unpack* basic user interaction functions we wrote in *textpak2* above. Since the *textpak2* functions handle calling functions in the *pack2* and *unpack3* modules, we don't need to import those modules here. In effect, this module is just an extension of *textpak2*. But this time we're shown a menu of option names, to help us see what's available:

```
% textpak4.py
        stop
        pack
        unpack
?unpack
input file name? packed1
creating: file1.txt
creating: file2.txt
        stop
        pack
        unpack
?pack
output file name? packed2
files to pack? text*5*.py
packing: textpk5b.py
packing: textpak5.py
        stop
        pack
        unpack
?stop
```

We don't get the *bye* message when we type **stop** this time: typing **stop** triggers the *sys.exit* function, which ends the program immediately.

## *More on Built-In Types: Dictionaries*

The biggest innovation in this version is the use of dictionaries to represent menus. Python dictionaries are sometimes called "associative arrays": unordered collections of objects, indexed by key instead of relative position. Dictionaries can be written as *key : value* pairs, separated by commas, inside curly-braces (`{}`).

*Table 8-1: Writing dictionaries*

| Dictionary constant | Interpretation |
|---|---|
| `{}` | An empty dictionary |
| `{key : value}` | A one-item dictionary |
| `{'spam': 2, 'eggs': 1, 'toast': 3}` | A three-item dictionary |
| `{'python':['shell','glue','rad']}` | A dictionary with a nested list |

Dictionaries are processed with both operators (indexing) and methods (*keys*, *has_key*, etc.). They are classified as "mutable mappings." Like lists, we can change them in-place, by assigning to keys. Unlike lists, assigning to a new key creates a new entry (out-of-bounds indexing is an error for sequences like lists):

```
dictionary['spam'] = value          change (or create) the entry for 'spam'
```

And since they're unordered collections, there's nothing like *append* or "+" concatenation for dictionaries.

In our script, we use two dictionaries. One represents the program's menu:

```
menu = { 'pack':   pack,
         'unpack': unpack,
         'stop':   exit }
```

and the other maps the command-line switch arguments:

```
flags = {'-i': interact, '-p': pack, '-u': unpack}
```

The *menu* dictionary is essentially a table of function objects, which looks something like Figure 8-1.

The names *menu* and *flags* are assigned dictionary objects, with three entries in each. In both, a reference to a function object is stored under each of the three keys, for mapping a command to an action. For instance, `menu['pack']` fetches the

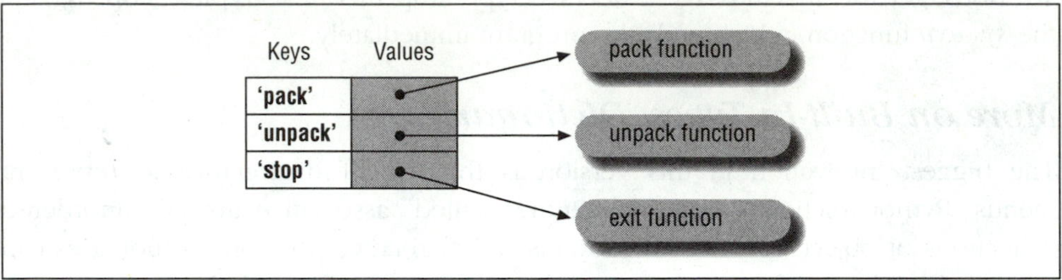


*Figure 8-1: Dictionaries*

function assigned to variable *pack*, and `flags['-u']` gets the function referenced by *unpack*. For menus, we first scan the dictionary's keys to display menu options:

```
for name in menu.keys():            # get dictionary keys list
    print '\t' + name               # print tab+key, one per line
```

using the dictionary's *keys* method. *keys* returns a list of the keys of all items in the dictionary. We then index the dictionary on the input command-name, to select the associated function; *flags* is used similarly.

## *Multiway Branching with Dictionaries*

One way to understand how dictionaries work, is to note their similarity to the *if* statements we used to implement multiway branching in the last chapter. In this script, we use two dictionary-based techniques, to replace the *switch* logic coded with *if*s earlier. In the first case:

```
try:
    menu[tool]()                    # index dictionary
except KeyError:
    print 'what? - try again'       # 'default' case: not found
```

we just index the dictionary to get the function to run. If the key (*tool*) isn't found, we catch the *KeyError* built-in exception and perform the default action. In the second case:

```
if flags.has_key(argv[1]):                  # key exists?
    flags[argv[1]]()                        # fetch/run function
else:
    print 'usage error: -i | -p | -u'       # 'default' case
```

we use the dictionary's *has_key* method first, to see if the command-line switch (*argv[1]*) exists before trying to index the dictionary with it to fetch a function. Both techniques have the same result; catching an exception versus testing for a key first is mostly a matter of style.

### *A "look under the hood": dictionaries are hash tables*

Internally, dictionaries are really dynamically-sized hash tables. Since they start small and are expanded as you add items, there's very little space overhead, even for very small dictionaries. Dictionaries use optimized lookup algorithms, which make them ideal for almost any Python program that needs to do some sort of searching. And as we'll see later, almost any kind of object can be used as a key (not just strings), as long as it can yield a unique, hashable identifier.

Because dictionaries are based on hashing, there's no notion of order among the items in a dictionary: items are randomly ordered, for quick lookup. This usually doesn't matter; but since dictionaries are unordered, we can't predict the order of the items returned by *keys*. But we can always sort the *keys* result manually, using the list *sort* method:

```
names = menu.keys()
names.sort()                    # sort the key list in-place
for name in names: ...
```

Notice that we can't use "for" or "in" to iterate over items in dictionaries directly—they are not sequences. Instead, we call the "keys" method to fetch a dictionary's keys list, and iterate over that, indexing the dictionary to fetch items from keys.

## *More on Functions: "Strictly First Class"*

Our menu contains three function objects:

```
menu = { 'pack':   pack,
         'unpack': unpack,
         'stop':   exit }
```

We store functions in a dictionary, so we can call them by key later. More specifically, we store references to shared function objects imported from modules *textpak2* (pack, unpack), and *sys* (exit). As usual assignment creates object references (not copies), whether we're assigning to variable names, or values in dictionaries. In general, setting a part of any data structure (lists, tuples, etc.) stores a reference.

In Python, functions are just another type of object: we can assign them to variables, and store them in data structures just like numbers and strings. The names *pack*, *unpack*, and *exit* in the dictionary are just references to function objects. Later, we call the stored functions "anonymously," using the key we input:

```
menu[tool]()              # fetch and call a function
```

But this is really no different than calling a function by the name used in a *def* statement: as we've seen, *def* assigns a function object to a variable name. We use the name to call the object later, by adding parenthesis. Here, we store away an object made by an earlier *def* in our dictionary, and call it later (see Figure 8-2):

```
menu[tool]              is a reference to the function object
menu[tool]()            calls the referenced function object
```

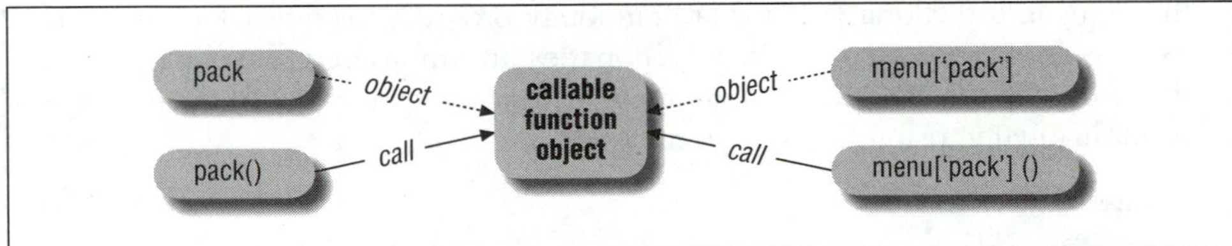


*Figure 8-2: Function references and calls*

In Python, functions, modules (and we'll see later, classes) are all "first-class" objects: they're really data items, which we can pass around programs just like simpler data type objects. In our script, that means there are no special rules to follow when storing callable functions in a dictionary.

# *Making Menus with Lists*

Of course, forcing users to type command-names is not exactly user-friendly. In the interactive interfaces we looked at so far, commands have to be typed verbatim. One better approach would be to let the first letter of a utility's name identify a command. Here's a way to implement that idea, using lists to represent our menus.

*Example 8-1: File: textpak5.py*

```
#!/usr/local/bin/python

from sys import argv
from string import upper, lower                 # case converters
from textpak2 import pack, unpack               # reuse textpak2 stuff

menu = [ ('pack',   pack),                      # 'key', function
         ('unpack', unpack),                    # procedures return None
         ('stop',   lambda:1) ]                 # return 1 to break loop

def interact():
```

*Example 8-1: File: textpak5.py (continued)*

```
    while 1:
        for name, func in menu:                         # show menu items
            print '\t' + upper(name[0]) + ')' + name[1:]
        tool = lower(raw_input('?'))
        for name, func in menu:
            if tool == name[0] or tool == name:         # matches menu key?
                exitflag = func()                       # run function
                break                                   # exit for, not while
        else:
            print 'what? - try again'                   # didn't break: not found
            continue                                    # goto top of while
        if exitflag: break                              # exit while if 'true'

if __name__ == '__main__':
    flags = ['-i', interact, '-p', pack, '-u', unpack]
    try:
        if len(argv) == 1:                               # no flags: interact
            interact()
        else:
            try:
                option = flags.index(argv[1])            # search for flag
            except ValueError:
                print 'usage error: -i | -p | -u'        # not found
            else:
                flags[option+1]()                        # found: run function
    except EOFError: pass                                # ctrl-D exits anything
```

We're still reusing the *pack* and *unpack* user-interface functions in *textpak2* here. But when we run this version, we only have to type the first letter of a command in upper- or lowercase to select it; we can also still type the full name if we want.

```
% textpak5.py
        P)ack
        U)npack
        S)top
?U
input file name? packed1
creating: file1.txt
creating: file2.txt
        P)ack
        U)npack
        S)top
?pack
output file name? packed2
files to pack? *.txt
packing: file1.txt
packing: file2.txt
        P)ack
        U)npack
        S)top
?pk
what? - try again
```

```
            P)ack
            U)npack
            S)top
?s
```

When we type **stop** this time, we trigger an anonymous function (made by the *lambda* expression, discussed in the next chapter) which forces control to break out of the "interact" loop and return to the top-level *if*, instead of calling *sys.exit*. And as before, we can use command-line switches to select specific tools too:

```
% textpak5.py -o
usage error: -i | -p | -u
% textpak5.py -p
output file name? packed3
files to pack? *.txt
packing: file1.txt
packing: file2.txt
%
```

### A peek ahead: friendlier interfaces

This still isn't exactly what we'd call "state of the art" in ergonomic interfaces! It would be better to associates numbers with commands, so we can handle two commands that start with the same letter. Better still would be a GUI device, such as a list box, which allows users to select a shell tool with a pointing device like a mouse. Which should give you a hint about where we're headed later in the book.

## More on Lists: Object Trees

Here again, we're using two menu representations. The first uses a list with nested tuples:

```
menu = [ ('pack',   pack),
         ('unpack', unpack),             # ('key', function)
         ('stop',   lambda:1) ]
```

and the second use a simple list, with a series of *name, function* pairs at the top level:

```
flags = ['-i', interact, '-p', pack, '-u', unpack]
```

### Nested data structures

As you might expect, Python data structures can be nested arbitrarily. Here, we've used a list of tuples. But since strings are really sequences too, there are actually three levels of data structure nesting in *menu*. Figure 8-3 shows what *menu* looks like internally.

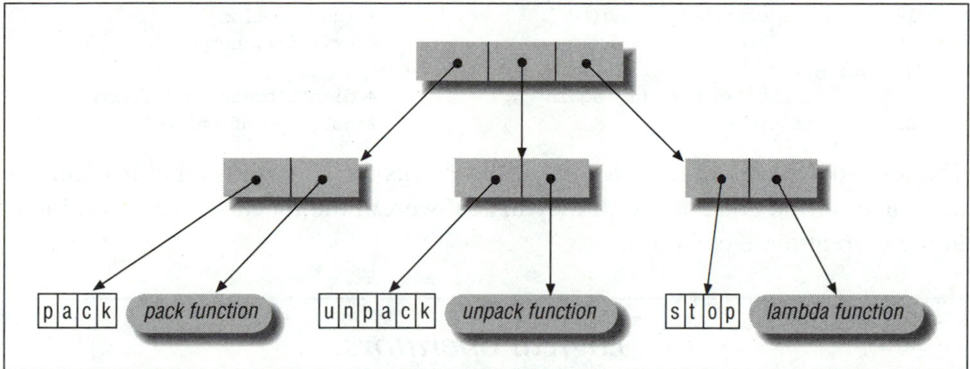


*Figure 8-3: Nested sequences*

We use a series of consecutive index operations to access nested sequence items. For instance:

- *menu[1]* is the tuple: ('unpack', *unpack*)
- *menu[2][1]* is the *lambda* function
- *menu[0][0][0]* is the character *p* at the front of the string *pack*
- *menu[1][0][1:-1]* is the string *npac* in the middle of string *unpack*

We really have a *tree* of Python objects here. When we test *tool == name[0]* at line 17, it's equivalent to the *menu[0][0][0]* index case: the *for* loop already iterates through the *menu* list (the leftmost index), and the tuple assignment (*name, func*) in the *for* header splits the nested tuples apart (the middle index).

### *Searching lists two ways*

To implement multiway branching by key, this version uses *manual searching* of the menu lists, to find a function. For the *menu* list, we first iterate over the list's tuples, and display the first item in each:

```
13   for name, func in menu:
14       print '\t' + upper(name[0]) + ')' + name[1:]
```

We then search through the menu to find a name matching the input:

```
for name, func in menu:
    if tool == name[0] or tool == name:     # matches menu key?
        exitflag = func()                   # run function
        break                               # exit for, not while
else:
    print 'what? - try again'               # didn't break: not found
    continue                                # goto top of while
```

The test: *tool == name[0] or tool == name* checks for a match on the first letter of the name, or the entire name. If they match, we call the function: the second item in the current tuple of the list.

## *Logical operators*

Another note for C programmers: in Python, logical (sometimes called boolean) operators are written out as *and*, *or*, and *not*. We saw *and* and *or* in Chapter 5, *Variations on a Theme*; Python logical operators work like C's &&, ||, and ! respectively, but *and* and *or* return objects, not integer 1 and 0. Python uses the same operator symbols as C, for bitwise logical operations on integers: &, |, etc. And as usual, complex expressions can be built up by using logical operators, grouping with parenthesis, etc. A summary of all of Python's operators and precedence rules appears in Appendix C, *A Mini-Reference*.

For the *flags* list, we instead call the built-in list method *index* to do the list search for us:

```
try:
    option = flags.index(argv[1])        # search for flag
except ValueError:
    print 'usage error: -i | -p | -u'    # not found
else:
    flags[option+1]()                    # found: run function
```

*index* scans a list, looking for a complete match on the argument passed in. If the command-line argument is found, *index* returns its offset, and we call the function that follows it in the list: *flags[option+1]*. If it's not found, *index* raises a *ValueError* exception which we catch here, and use like a default case in a *switch* statement.

### *Exceptions versus return values*

Like *raw_input*, *index* raises an exception to signal that the key wasn't found, rather than returning a special value. It could just as easily return a special value or type.

But as a general rule, raising exceptions is usually better than designating special return values as errors, as is commonly done in C programming. With exceptions, it's impossible to ever clash with real, valid results. Moreover, exceptions can often eliminate code that tests return values after each operation; a single *try* statement is sometimes enough.

### *More on performance: index beats for (probably)*

Since the list *index* method is implemented in C internally, it's usually faster at searching lists than a manual *for* loop (as done for the *menu* list). But it can only search for an exact match by equality; if we need to do special comparisons (like looking for a match on the first letter, as with *menu*), we usually need to scan the list in a *for* loop.

However, the penalty for using *for* loops instead of *index* is not necessarily that clear-cut: performance analysis in Python is harder than you might expect, due to its dynamic nature. We'll come back to this in Chapter 13, *Implementing Objects*, when we explore Python's profiler tool.

## *More on try Exception Handlers: else Clauses*

At line 35, we use an *else* clause on the *try* statement. This makes Python execute the call at line 36 if and only if the *ValueError* was *not* raised. In other words, we fall into the *else* if the command-line argument was found by *index*. In the general case, *else* clauses on *try* statements are executed if no exception is raised while the *try* block was running.

## *More on Built-In Types: Tuple Assignments*

When we use a list of names as the target in a *for* loop header:

```
16    for name, func in menu:
```

there's really no "magic" involved. Recall that the *for* loop just assigns items in a sequence to the target. Since *menu* is a list of tuples, this works exactly like the tuple assignments we've already seen:

```
name, func = 'pack', pack           same as:  name='pack'; func=pack
```

When assigning one tuple to another, Python "unpacks" the tuple, and assigns its items to corresponding names in the target tuple. In effect, the target of this *for* header is just a tuple. The enclosing parentheses can be omitted in this context; adding them probably makes it clearer:

```
16    for (name, func) in menu:
```

Tuple assignment is also used in another Python idiom: to swap the values of two variables (or data structure components), we assign them in "reverse" order: *X, Y = Y, X* (see Figure 8-4). Because Python transfers the tuple on the right to targets on the left, we don't need a temporary to save one of the values (*T = X; X = Y; Y = T*).

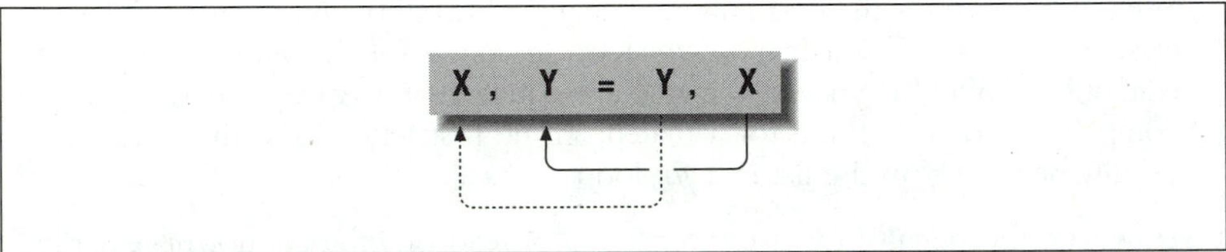


*Figure 8–4: Swapping with tuples*

## *Python is not Prolog either*

Tuple unpacking can be used any place assignment is applied. For instance, if we pass a tuple to a function argument:

```
func(99, (1,2,3), 'spam')
```

the function's header can extract the items of the passed tuple, by writing a tuple constant in the function header:

```
def func(number, (item1, item2, item3), string):
```

which, if you've done any AI work, may look suspiciously like pattern-matching in the Prolog language. But it's really not: since passed arguments are assigned to items in the function header's list, this is again just tuple-assignment.

## *More on Loops: the Loop else*

Note the use of the *else* block at line 20: it's associated with the *for* loop, not the *if* in the *for* (its indentation matches the *for* header). The statements under the *else* are executed if we exit the *for* normally, i.e., without running into the *break* statement at line 19. In effect, the *else* works much like a default case in a *switch* statement:

- If a matching key is found in the menu list, we execute the *break* to leave the loop, and skip the *else.*
- If we don't find a matching key, we fall into the *else* to report the error.

*else* clauses like this can be used on both *for* and *while* loops; in many cases, they avoid having to set and analyze exit condition variables after we exit a loop.

## *(Ab)Using the continue Statement*

The loop at line 12 is fairly complex: it uses a loop *else*, a nested *break*, and a *continue* statement. Python's *continue* statement works just like C's: it transfers control to the top of the closest enclosing loop. In this example, it makes us jump to the top of the *while* at line 12, and skip line 23:

```
12    while 1:
      ...
16        for name, func in menu:
17            if tool == name[0] or tool == name:    # matches menu key?
18                exitflag = func()                  # run function
19                break                              # exit for, not while
20        else:
21            print 'what? - try again'              # didn't break: not found
22            continue                               # goto top of while
23        if exitflag: break
```

Here are some of the control transfers that go on inside the loop:

*nested break*
: When we find a matching command name, the *break* at line 19 exits the *for* loop at line 16, since it's the closest enclosing loop (i.e., not the *while* at line 12).

*loop else*
: If no match is found, we instead fall into the *for*-loop's *else* clause at line 20: since the *break* at line 19 didn't run, the *for* loop exited normally.

*continue*
: The *continue* at line 22 send us to the top of the *while* loop, so we don't test the *exitflag* at line 23: if no match is found, *exitflag* is never set in the *for* loop.

*simple break*

Finally, if the *exitflag* is returned as *true* from the function, the *break* at line 23 exits the outer *while* loop, and interaction stops.

In effect, although there's no *goto* statement in Python, the results are similar:

- The *break* at line 19 is like a *goto* to line 23
- The *continue* at line 22 is like a *goto* to line 12

Figure 8-5 diagrams the complexities of break, continue, and loop-else.

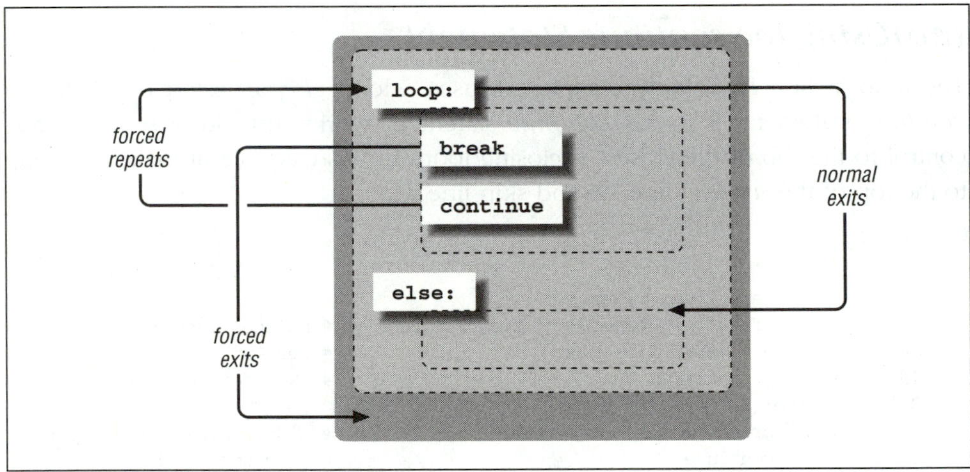


*Figure 8-5: Break, continue, and loop-else*

### *Simplification: avoiding continue and break*

As you can probably guess, programs that use *continue* statements like this can become difficult to understand. In fact, this example is arguably bad Python style! It was written as it is, to illustrate how nested *break* and *continue* statements work. Usually, we can get the same effect with simpler code. Here's an equivalent loop, without *continue* or the second *break*:

```
exitflag = 0
while not exitflag:
    ...
    for name, func in menu:
        if tool == name[0] or tool == name:    # matches menu key?
            exitflag = func()                  # run function, set flag
            break                              # exit for, not while
    else:
        print 'what? - try again'              # didn't break: not found
```

Of course, *break* and *continue* are both sometimes useful. But since they jump around a program, they can make programs difficult to understand if misused.

This is really another style issue, but as a suggestion: avoid using *continue* when possible, and minimize *break* use, except where its meaning is obvious. Overuse of either can lead to good old-fashioned "spaghetti" code.

### *Simplification: splitting up complex logic*

When functions start getting deeply nested or large, it may also help to split their logic up into a set of smaller functions. Again, this is mostly a matter of style. But as a rule of thumb, if functions become longer than a page, or too deeply nested to understand, splitting is probably a good idea. Here's how we might split up the complex loop in *textpak5*: Replace code starting at line 11 in *textpak5.py* with the following example.

*Example 8-2: File: textpak5.py (altered)*

```
11  def get_option():
12      for (name, func) in menu:                    # show menu items
13          print '\t%s)%s' % (upper(name[0]), name[1:])
14      return lower(raw_input('?'))
15
16  def run_option(tool):
17      for (name, func) in menu:
18          if tool == name[0] or tool == name:      # matches menu key?
19              return func()                        # run function
20      print 'what? - try again'                    # name not found
21      return None                                  # not really needed...
22
23  def interact():
24      while 1:
25          tool = get_option()
26          if run_option(tool): break               # func returned 'true'?
```

Instead of one complicated *while* loop, we now have a simpler one (just two lines long), and two simple utility functions. Even though these functions aren't likely to be useful outside this module file, they help make the logic easier to understand, and can enhance maintainability.

## *More on Functions: Returning None*

We didn't really have to *return None* on line 21 above: as we've seen, functions return *None* if they exit without running into a *return* statement. Since *None* is a *false* value in Python tests, this prevents us from executing the *break* at line 26, and the main *while* loop at line 24 continues, even if we return nothing (well, *None*), from *run_option*. This same trick keeps interaction going when we call the *pack* and *unpack* procedures imported from *textpak2*. Only the *stop* menu option returns a *true* value (integer 1).

### *"How 'bout a little KISS?"*

Simplicity is an important design goal, when writing reusable software. Both of the preceding loop simplification examples try to simplify list-based menu processing. But even with the suggested improvements, it's still fairly complicated code. The main reason that the list-based menu interface is more complex than the dictionary-based one, is that it replaces dictionary *indexing* with manual *searching* of lists for a key.

As a rule of thumb, dictionaries are the best tool for search-based algorithms, and lead to much simpler (and faster) code. Naturally, dictionaries sometimes aren't enough. They aren't much help here, since we want to match on the first letter of a key too. The list-based approach also lets us specify an explicit *order* on the menu items displayed. Classes (coming up) will address some of these concerns, by hiding complexity from clients.

For what it's worth, if you haven't seen this acronym: *KISS* is usually translated to mean "Keep It Simple, Sir!" (although the last word is sometimes replaced with a more colorful phrase :-).

## *Built-In Types: Operators, Methods, and Modules*

In the list-based menu module, string case converters are imported from the built-in *string* module:

```
4   from string import upper, lower              # case converters
```

We also used the *string* module's *join* method in the last chapter. The *string* module contains a set of extra string-processing functions. String objects have no callable *methods*, unlike lists and dictionaries; instead, most of their unique operations are imported from the built-in *string* module. In general, built-in types package their operations in different ways:

*Table 8-2: Operation sources*

| Type | Operators? | Methods? | Modules? |
|---|---|---|---|
| Tuples | Yes | No | No |
| Strings | Yes | No | Yes |
| Lists | Yes | Yes | No |
| Dictionaries | Yes | Yes | No |
| Numbers | Yes | No | Yes |

*Tuples*

For tuples, only sequence operations (concatenation, slicing, indexing, etc.) are supported. There are no tuple methods or support modules. Some built-in functions use tuples, e.g., *apply*.

*Strings*

String objects support sequence operations. But instead of methods, the built-in *string* module provides extra utilities for strings. In addition, there are related modules for matching patterns, built-in string functions, and conversion tools we'll see later in the book.

*Lists*

For lists, we can use the usual sequence operations, plus list-object methods. We've already seen some list methods: *append*, *sort*, and *index*. There's no list-specific module.

*Dictionaries*

For these, we can use mapping operations (indexing) plus dictionary-specific *methods*. We've seen some of these too: *keys*, *has_key*. There's no dictionary-specific module.

*Numbers*

Number objects support numeric operators. Like strings, they have no qualifiable methods, but Python provides modules (like *math*) and functions (like *abs*) for extra operations.

Other object types provide methods too (files). And types share generic operations according to their categories. Here's a summary of the types we've seen:

*Table 8-3: Summary of built-in types*

| Type | Constants | Indexing | Sequence? | Mutable? | Extras |
|---|---|---|---|---|---|
| Numbers | 123, 3.14, 0177, 99L | n/a[a] | No | No | *x+y pow(x, y)* |
| Strings | " '123' ", "it's" | `S[1]` | Yes | No | *format % (x, y)* |
| Lists | [ ] [1, [2, 3], 4] | `L[1]` | Yes | Yes | *L.append(x)* |
| Tuples | () (1,) (1,2,3) | `T[1]` | Yes | No | *x, y = y, x* |
| Dictionaries | {} {'a':1, 'b':2} | `D['key']` | No | Yes | *D.keys()* |
| Extensions | *constructor*: open(..) | (Some) | (Some) | (Some) | *methods: file.read()* |

[a] n/a = not applicable

We've also seen other object types that serve more specific roles: functions, modules, *None*, etc. And as we'll see later, instances of C extension types, and Python classes, may also be sequences or mappings, and mutable or not, depending on the operations they support. Both can implement methods and operators. (See Appendix C for more details on type-specific operations, modules, and functions.)

## The Zen of Python: Namespaces are Dictionaries

Now that we've seen dictionaries, I can let you in on one of the major secrets in Python's design. When we introduced dictionaries, you may have noticed that assigning and referencing dictionary keys follows the same rules as variable names: keys are created when first assigned, but must exist when referenced by indexing. Which may give you a hint about how Python implements variables behind the scenes; usually,

- Namespaces are really just dictionaries.
- Qualification is the same as indexing dictionaries.

For instance, variables (attributes) in a module's namespace are recorded as keys in an associated dictionary. In fact, most objects with attributes provide a way to access their namespace's dictionary explicitly. Module attributes can be reached by qualifying the module object or by indexing its dictionary:

```
>>> import string
>>> string.uppercase                          qualify module's attribute
'ABCDEFGHIJKLMNOPQRSTUVWXYZ'
>>> string.__dict__['uppercase']              index the module's dictionary
'ABCDEFGHIJKLMNOPQRSTUVWXYZ'
```

Modules, classes, and class instances (classes are coming up next) all have a built-in `__dict__` attribute that refers to their namespace dictionaries, which we can index by key as usual. We can even carry this indirection a step further: as mentioned in Chapter 7, *Adding a Simple User Interface*, Python records all imported modules in a dictionary called *modules* in the *sys* module. To fetch a module that's already loaded, we can either import it again, or go through the *sys* dictionary manually:

```
>>> import sys                                         get string through sys
>>> sys.modules['string']                              fetch a module object
<module 'string'>
>>> sys.modules['string'].uppercase                    qualify module object
'ABCDEFGHIJKLMNOPQRSTUVWXYZ'
>>> sys.modules['string'].__dict__['uppercase']        get uppercase the long way
'ABCDEFGHIJKLMNOPQRSTUVWXYZ'
>>> sys.__dict__['modules']['string'].__dict__['uppercase'] 3 dictionaries...
'ABCDEFGHIJKLMNOPQRSTUVWXYZ'
```

Of course, *string.uppercase* is noticeably simpler than the last line we typed here! And since it starts at the *string* module's namespace, it's also faster: Python doesn't have to follow the path starting at *sys*. But the fact that namespaces are dictionaries makes things uniform in Python. It also lets us write programs that manage other programs (see later), by accessing this sort of exposed system data.

## *Fetching Function Namespaces*

This concept of namespaces as dictionaries applies to *unqualified* names too: the local, global, and built-in scopes (namespaces) can be thought of as implicitly searched dictionaries. A function's global and built-in scopes really are dictionaries: the `__dict__` attributes of the enclosing and `__builtin__` modules, respectively. For instance, if we make a function,

```
>>> def func(x, y): print pow(x, y)      define a new function
...                                      which raises 'x' to the power 'y'
>>> func(2, 4)
16
```

we can use its built-in attributes to inspect its compiled-code (another object type), and access its global scope's dictionary (which is just the `__dict__` dictionary of the enclosing module):

```
>>> func                                                        a function object
<function func at 3e7f8da4>
>>> func.func_code                                              its compiled code
<code object func at 3e7f8d1c, file "<stdin>", line 1>
>>> func.func_globals                                           its global scope:
{ 'sys': <module 'sys'>, 'string': <module 'string'>,           module's __dict__
 'func': <function func at 3e7f8da4>, '__name__':'__main__',  ...etc... }
```

Things aren't quite as simple for the local scope, since the current implementation puts a function's locals in a stacked array for efficiency; we have to call the *vars* built-in inside a function, to create a dictionary for its local scope. But locals can usually be thought of as a dictionary without getting into too much trouble.

## *Fetching Built-In-Type Attributes*

Some objects' namespaces are exposed in different ways; built-in C extension types usually don't have a `__dict__` attribute. For instance, a module's attribute names can be fetched by calling the *keys* method on its `__dict__` dictionary, or by calling the *dir* built-in function on the module itself:

```
sys.__dict__.keys()       return a list of attribute names
dir(sys)                  same, but the list is sorted too
```

But a file-object's method names are exported in a list attribute called `__methods__`:

```
>>> file = open('temp', 'w')
>>> file                                                    make a file object
<open file 'temp', mode 'w' at ad77684>                     fetch its method list
>>> file.__methods__
['close', 'fileno', 'flush', 'isatty', 'read', 'readline', 'readlines',
'seek', 'tell', 'write', 'writelines']
```

We access its methods by name, using the *getattr* built-in function, instead of indexing a dictionary. The method name can still be a string created at run-time:

```
>>> getattr(file, 'close')                                  same as "file.close"
<built-in method close of file object at ad77684>
```

## A First Look at Metaprogramming

Hooks like these let us use modules and their exports anonymously: objects may be accessed by indexing system data-structures with character-string keys computed at run-time. This lends itself to highly dynamic systems; we can write programs that use objects without knowing their names beforehand, and ask questions about an object's state. In effect, we can write programs about programs, usually called metaprogramming.

When more indirection is needed, we can also build entire expressions and statements at run-time as strings, and run them using the *eval* and *exec* built-ins. For instance, if we don't know the name of a certain module we will need to import, we can execute a character-string to do the import, instead of hard-coding an *import* statement:

```
statement = "import " + name    # create an import statement string
exec statement                  # run the code string in this scope
```

*exec* runs statements, and *eval* runs expressions. Roughly, both are run-time calls to the compiler: Python's parser is always available for use from Python (and C) programs. We'll use dynamically constructed code strings like this later in the book. But here's a brief look at an example that illustrates *sys.modules*, module dictionaries, and *exec*.

Given a module's name as a string, the *fix* function below runs a text-editor on a module's source-file, and then imports or reloads it in module `__main__` (the interactive command line's namespace). We can tell whether a module has been imported yet, by checking the *sys.modules* dictionary keys list. *exec* is used to run an import or reload *string*, and `__main__.__dict__` is passed for the string's local and global scopes. The effect is as if we had typed the string at the >>> prompt.

*Example 8-3: File: fixer.py*

```
editor = 'vi'  # your editor's name

def python(cmd):
    import __main__
    exec cmd in __main__.__dict__, __main__.__dict__

def edit(filename):
    import os
    os.system(editor + ' ' + filename)

def fix(modname):
    import sys                               # ex: fix('textpak4')
    edit(modname + '.py')                    # assumes in '.'
    if modname in sys.modules.keys():
        python('reload(' + modname + ')')    # reload in __main__
    else:
        python('import ' + modname)          # first load in __main__
```

This utility may be used to edit and load modules from the Python command line. In fact, *fix* can be used as a higher-level import/reload command, which also lets us browse and edit source code:

```
% python
>>> from fixer import fix
>>> fix("spam")                   browse/edit and import by string name

[edit "spam.py" here]

>>> spam.function()               spam was imported in __main__
>>> fix("spam")                   edit and reload() by string name
[edit "spam.py" here]
>>> spam.function()               test new version of function
>>> etc...
```

We'll cover *exec* and its relatives in greater detail later in the book.

---

*NOTE* Utility functions like this can be loaded into the interactive namespace automatically whenever you start the command-line, by importing them in the file referenced by environment variable *PYTHONSTARTUP*. See Chapter 3, *Getting Started*, for details.

---

# Dictionaries and Keyword Arguments

And now that we've seen dictionaries, we can also discuss the last extension to argument-passing in Python: keyword arguments. Python 1.3 introduced a new way to pass arguments to functions. By default, arguments are still passed by the usual positional correspondence: values in a call are matched to arguments in the function header, from left to right.

But with keywords, callers can also give the name of the argument in the function's header that is to receive a passed value. When names are used, arguments don't need to appear in the same order as in the function header. Further, keywords and positional arguments can be mixed, and the function itself may collect arbitrary keyword arguments in a dictionary for processing explicitly. There are two sides to the interface: the caller (a call expression), and the callee (a function's header-line).

*Caller*
: A function (or method) call specifies keywords using an assignment-like syntax. For example, *function(name=value)* passes *value* to the argument called *name* in the header for *function*. When using keyword arguments, the name isn't evaluated; it acts like a string constant, and becomes a dictionary key internally.

*Callee*
: The function (or method) doesn't need to do anything to support keyword arguments. Python automatically matches keywords in the call to the names of arguments in the function's header. But a function can also collect arbitrarily many keyword arguments in a dictionary, by using the ***name* argument form in its header. It's similar in spirit to the **name* form we saw earlier, but ***name* gets unmatched keyword arguments only. If used, **name* still gets a tuple of all the unmatched positional arguments in the call.

## A Quick Example

Since keyword arguments are matched by name, we can pass them in any order we like. The following function can be called in a variety of ways.

*File: keywords.py*

```
def func(spam, eggs, toast=0, ham=0):  print (spam, eggs, toast, ham)

func(1, 2)                         # output: (1, 2, 0, 0)
func(1, ham=1, eggs=0)             # output: (1, 0, 0, 1)
func(spam=1, eggs=0)               # output: (1, 0, 0, 0)
func(toast=1, eggs=2, spam=3)      # output: (3, 2, 1, 0)
func(1, 2, 3, 4)                   # output: (1, 2, 3, 4)
```

As before, all nondefault arguments must still be assigned a value in the call (here, *spam* and *eggs*). However, the assignments can come from either a positional or keyword argument.

## *Argument Mode Order Rules*

When passing both positional and name-based arguments, we need to follow some ordering rules:

- *Function call.* Keyword arguments must appear after all nonkeyword arguments.
- *Function header.* The special **name* argument must appear after normal arguments.
- *Function header.* The special ***name* argument must appear last.

For example, nonkeyword arguments after keywords in the call generate an exception:

```
% python
>>> def f(a, b, c, d): print a, b, c, d
...
>>> f(2, a=1, 4, c=3)
SyntaxError: non-keyword arg after keyword arg
>>> f(1, 2, d=4, c=3)
1 2 3 4
```

And anything after the keyword ***name* argument in a function header does too:

```
>>> def f(a, **kw, *va): print a
  File "<stdin>", line 1
    def f(a, **kw, *va): print a
                   ^
SyntaxError: invalid syntax
>>> def f(a, *va, **kw): print a, va, kw
...
>>> f(1)
1 () {}
```

Moreover, we can't assign a parameter both ways:

```
>>> f(3, 4, a=1, b=2)
TypeError: keyword parameter redefined
```

## Mixing Argument-Matching Modes

With keywords, there are five argument-matching concepts:

*Normal*
: Arguments in the call are matched by position.

*Keyword*
: Arguments in the call are matched by name.

*Default*
: Argument values in functions are used when arguments are omitted in the call.

**name*
: Arguments in functions collect extra nonkeyword arguments in a tuple.

***name*
: Arguments in functions collect extra keyword arguments in a dictionary.

So how do all these special argument-matching tools work when combined? At first glance, the last example above seems almost ambiguous: *a* could be assigned by position or keyword! But the algorithm Python uses to resolve calls is straightforward. When a function (or method) is called, the following steps are followed to consume passed arguments:

1. Assign nonkeyword arguments by relative position, left to right.
2. Assign keyword arguments by matching names.
3. Assign any extra nonkeyword arguments to the **name* tuple.
4. Assign any extra keyword arguments to the ***name* dictionary.
5. Unassigned arguments in the header are assigned default values.

Nonkeyword arguments are always resolved before any keyword arguments are matched. Since they must appear before keywords in the call, they normally are applied to the leftmost arguments in the function header, before any keyword arguments are matched by name.

In other words, positional and keyword arguments are handled separately; keywords are just an extension to our earlier argument-passing discussion. Steps 3 and 4 above are only applied if too many arguments are passed. If there are too few, step 5 applies defaults for unassigned arguments in the header.

Notice that a *name=value* form provides an argument default in a function header, but specifies a keyword argument in a call. Despite the similar syntax, they mean different things. The following table shows which argument forms in calls and function-headers match.

*Table 8-4: Matching argument forms*

| Function call | Function header | Match type |
|---|---|---|
| *value* | *name* | By position |
| *value* | *name=default* | By position |
| *value, . . .* | **name* | Extra positionals |
| *name=value* | *name* | By name |
| *name=value* | *name=default* | By name |
| *name=value, . . .* | ***name* | Extra keywords |
| *<omitted>* | *name=default* | Default if absent |
| *<omitted>* | **name* | Empty if absent |
| *<omitted>* | ***name* | Empty if absent |

## The apply Function with Keywords

To support dynamically constructed keyword argument lists, the built-in *apply* function we saw earlier also accepts an optional third argument, which is a dictionary specifying keyword arguments to be passed. For example, given a function header:

```
def spam(item, count): ...
```

the following two calls are equivalent:

```
spam(count=20, item='pigs')
apply(spam, (), {'count': 20, 'item': 'pigs'})
```

---

*NOTE* Functions and methods defined in C extension modules can get a dictionary of their keyword arguments too. By default, extension functions don't receive keywords, since their argument names aren't available to Python. There will be more details on extensions in Chapter 14, *Extending Python.*

---

## Argument Passing Examples

Let's step through some simple examples to show how these special passing modes work when combined. We'll start with a simple function header.

```
% python
>>> def func1(a, b, c): print a, b, c
...
>>> func1(1, 2, 3)                    matched by position
1 2 3
>>> func1(c=3, a=1, b=2)              matched by name
1 2 3
```

```
>>> func1(1, c=3, 2)                keywords must be last
SyntaxError: non-keyword arg after keyword arg

>>> func1(1, c=3, b=2)              matches positionals first
1 2 3                               then keyword args by name
```

Next, let's try out the ***name* argument; it gets a dictionary holding the name and value of all unmatched keyword arguments.

```
>>> def func2(a, **rest): print a, rest
...
>>> func2(1, b=2, c=3)              'rest' gets unmatched keyword args
1 {'b': 2, 'c': 3}
>>> func2(b=2, c=3, a=1)            'a' is consumed first by name matching
1 {'b': 2, 'c': 3}
```

When defaults are used, they're applied last. And a default can be overridden by either a positional or keyword argument.

```
>>> def func3(a, b=0, **rest): print a, b, rest
...
>>> func3(1, c=3)                   1 is positional, c is unmatched, b is omitted
1 0 {'c': 3}
>>> func3(1, 2, c=3)                the positional 2 overrides b's default
1 2 {'c': 3}
>>> func3(1, c=3, b=2)              b's keyword argument overrides the default
1 2 {'c': 3}
```

Finally, here's a complex function header that uses all four modes. Positional and keyword arguments are resolved in separate steps. Then **varargs* gets leftover positionals, and ***kwargs* gets leftover keywords. ***kwargs* must be last, and **varargs* must be second to last.

```
>>> def func4(a, b=0, *varargs, **kwargs): print a, b, varargs, kwargs
...
>>> func4(1, 2, 3, 4)                   all positional: kwargs is empty
1 2 (3, 4) {}
>>> func4(b=2, c=3, d=4, e=5, a=1)      all keywords; a and b match by name
1 2 () {'d': 4, 'e': 5, 'c': 3}
>>> func4(1, c=3)                       b's default used; no extra positionals
1 0 () {'c': 3}
>>> func4(1, 2, 3, 4, e=5, f=6)         both extra keywords and positionals
1 2 (3, 4) {'e': 5, 'f': 6}
>>> func4(1, b=2, c=3)                  b consumed by name match first
1 2 () {'c': 3}
```

Notice that the **name* and ***name* forms allow programs to process variable-length argument lists (both positional and keyword) explicitly, using normal tuple and dictionary operations. In Chapter 11, *Graphical User Interfaces*, we'll see the keyword argument mode applied in the *Tkinter* GUI extension. In *Tkinter*, keywords are used to set (pass) widget configuration options. The *Tkinter* extension processes passed argument lists like dictionaries.

> ### *Complexity alert!*
>
> As you can probably tell from the examples above, things can get confusing when we mix positional, keyword, and default argument matching. The usual complexity warnings apply here: as a rule, it's best to limit the number of protocols used for a function's arguments. Also notice that this discussion only deals with the way passed arguments are matched to arguments in a function header. Once matched, the header's arguments are assigned the passed values. The underlying argument-passing scheme is still just simple assignment.

# *Design Concepts: Do Modules Support OOP?*

Here's a bit of philosophy, to foreshadow the next chapter. In both the menu modules, we import and reuse the *pack* and *unpack* interactive functions in the older version, *textpak2*. In some sense, the menu modules extend *textpak2* with menus. By adding their own *interact* function and top-level `__main__` logic, they add new functionality to what was already available in textpak2.

As we'll see in Chapter 9, *Moving Menus to Classes*, this is one of the main concepts in OOP: specializing and extending existing components, for new requirements. In OOP, we determine how our needs differ from existing services, and replace or extend parts as needed. In the example here, we only needed to replace the interact function and `__main__` logic, to switch to a menu-based interface.

So is this OOP? Maybe. As we'll see, Python's main OOP construct is the *class* statement (and object). Although we're using modules here instead of classes, the concepts are similar. In fact, modules can be thought of as single-instance classes, with one-level inheritance. Modules "inherit" from other modules by importing, and can specialize by locally redefining imported functions and variables. For instance, *textpak4* and *textpak5* both import *textpak2*'s pack and unpack, but redefine its interact and `__main__` logic.

But there's a critical distinction: while a module can be imported from multiple clients, multiple imports are not multiple instances: each client shares the module's single namespace. For example, it's not enough to redefine the interact function in our menu modules: when the original version's top-level logic calls interact, it's calling the locally defined version of the function. We also need to redefine the top-level logic redundantly in the menu modules (*textpak4*, *textpak5*), to call their own versions of interact.

## *Specializing Modules is Risky Business*

It's possible to change a module's behavior from the outside, but dangerous. For instance, if we put *textpak2*'s top-level logic in a function called *main* so it's not executed when the module is imported, we could reset its "interact" attribute to a local function. Here are the changes for dictionary-based *textpak4*:

*Example 8-4: File: textpak2.py*

```
def main():
    try:
        if len(argv) == 1:                # top-level logic unchanged
            interact()                    # calls textpak4.interact if reset
        else:
            if   argv[1] == '-i': interact()
            elif argv[1] == '-p': pack()
            elif argv[1] == '-u': unpack()
            else: print 'usage error'
    except EOFError: pass
    print 'bye'

if __name__ == '__main__': main()
```

*Example 8-5: File: textpak4.py*

```
from textpak2 import pack, unpack, main          # get items from textpak2
import textpak2                                  # and get the module itself
...
... the rest of textpak4.py                    # define local "interact"
...
textpak2.interact = interact                   # change interact to the local version
if __name__ == '__main__': main()              # run top-level logic in textpak2 now
```

In effect, this manually *overrides* a function defined in another module. It only works because *interact* is a variable that isn't evaluated until run-time. But really, it's a kludge of epic proportions! Because there's only one copy of each module, resetting *textpak2.interact* in *textpak4* like this changes *textpak2* for every other module that imports it. If we later import and run *textpak5*, it may get *textpak4*'s *interact* by mistake, as shown in Figure 8-6.

Because a module's namespace is shared by all its clients, it's usually bad practice to change its attributes from the outside. As we'll see in the next chapter, this is exactly the sort of thing that's hard for modules, but simple with classes. With classes, we'd redefine an "interact" *method*, and inherit the rest. Since classes define extension "frameworks," changing *interact* in one version doesn't change others: it's looked up according to a class hierarchy, not by a flat module structure.

As a rule, classes support specialization much better than modules. Still, if we need to implement a shared data structure, and don't expect multiple copies to be made, the choice between a class and a module file is arbitrary.

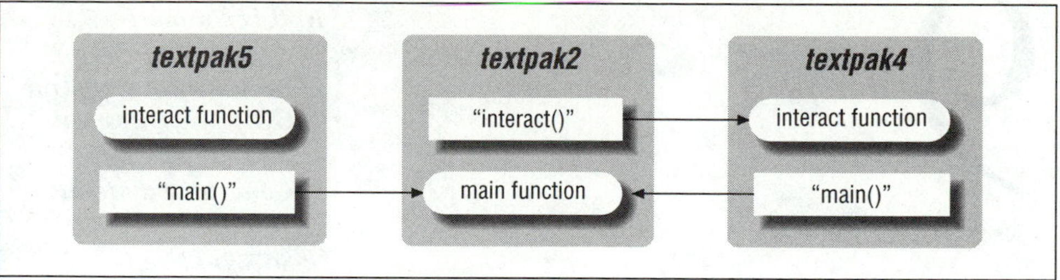


*Figure 8-6: Changing modules externally—"just say no"*

## *What is a Python "object"?*

So far, we've used the term "object" somewhat loosely. In an abstract sense, every Python data-item is a generic object. In more technical terms, everything is a first-class object; since variables have no type constraints, they can be assigned any kind of object: numbers, strings, lists, modules, etc. We used this property to store and call functions anonymously in our menu interface scripts above.

In fact, the notion of objects is carried to an extreme in Python: even datatypes are a type of object. For example, if we call the built-in *type* function, we get back the argument's datatype as a type object:

```
>>> type("hello")           # a string's type is a type object!
<type 'string'>
```

Although this may be confusing if you're used to types being something that's only used by a compiler, type objects are useful for testing an object's type at run-time. For instance, to test if a variable *X* refers to a string object:

```
if type(X) == type(''):    # same type object as an empty string?
```

But when we get to classes, the term "object" refers more to an instance of a Python class, used in object-oriented-programming. We will usually use the term "instance" to refer to a class instance (i.e., an OOP "object"), and keep using the term "object" to refer to Python data items in a generic way. Only class and instance objects support true inheritance.

# 9

# *Moving Menus to Classes*

*In this chapter:*


- *"Here's Your Script. Here's Your Script on OOP. Any Questions?"*
- *A First Attempt: Generalized Menu Functions*
- *So Who Needs Classes?*
- *OOP in Action: Menus as Classes*
- *Exploring Python Classes*
- *Configuring Menu Data*
- *Namespaces, Part 3: Classes and Instances*
- *More on Zen: Class and Instance Namespace Dictionaries*
- *Design Concepts: Implementing Generic Functions*


## *"Here's Your Script. Here's Your Script on OOP. Any Questions?"*

By now, we've taken our packing scripts almost as far as we can. We wrote simple scripts, added functions, packaged them in a user interface, and finally extended the interface to display a menu of options. This is far more than I ever needed to get my files transferred (remember those files?).

But there's one more issue that makes the code we've seen so far less useful than it might be. In Chapter 8, *Adding Text-Based Menus*, we wrote two menu interfaces: one to handle menus represented as dictionaries (mappings), and one for menus written as lists (sequences) of tuples. By taking things this far, we wound up with code we could only use in the scripts we wrote.

Every time we want to write a new menu interface, we'd have to cut and paste most of the menu scripts' logic. Since menu-based interaction would clearly be a generally useful tool to have, this is unsatisfactory. What we'd really like is a generalized menu processing system, which we can reuse arbitrarily.

In this chapter, we'll make the intellectual leap from using functions to structure our logic, to using classes that structure the objects in our problem domains. As we'll see, the result of this last transformation will be software that minimizes redundancy and maximizes extendibility, maintainability, and reuse.

## *A First Attempt: Generalized Menu Functions*

Of course, now that we know about functions, we could implement generalized menu managers by packaging the menu scripts' logic as functions in a general module. This is a relatively simple change: instead of defining menus as global variables, we pass them as arguments to the menu interaction functions.

---

*NOTE* To simplify the examples here, we'll ignore the command-line switches logic used in earlier versions, and concentrate on the interactive menu functions (i.e., the *interact* functions of the menu scripts in the last chapter). Extending the examples here to handle command-line switches too would be an interesting exercise, but uses the same ideas.

---

More specifically: we extract the *interact* menu functions from the two menu scripts we saw in the last chapter, and make the *menu* variable an argument, instead of a global. By bundling the functions in a module, we provide a menu management utility, useful outside the *textpak* interface:

*Example 9-1: File: menu0.py*

```
from string import upper, lower

def interact_dict(menu):                        # pass in menu (not global)
    while 1:
        for name in menu.keys():
            print '\t' + name                   # show options
        tool = raw_input('?')
        try:
            menu[tool]()                        # run function
        except KeyError:
            print 'what? - try again'           # key not found

def interact_list(menu):                        # pass in menu here too
    while 1:
        for name, func in menu:
            print '\t' + upper(name[0]) + ')' + name[1:]
        tool = lower(raw_input('?'))
        for name, func in menu:
            if tool == name[0] or tool == name:   # matches menu key?
```

*Example 9-1: File: menu0.py (continued)*

```
                exitflag = func()                       # run function
                break
        else:
            print 'what? - try again'                   # not found: goto while
            continue
        if exitflag: break                              # exit while if 'true'

def interact(menu):
    try:
        if type(menu) == type([]):                  # do type-testing
            interact_list(menu)
        elif type(menu) == type({}):                # 'switch' on the menu's type
            interact_dict(menu)
        else:
            print "bad menu: must be a list or dictionary"
    except EOFError: pass
```

The *interact_dict* and *interact_list* functions in this module handle dictionary and list-based menus. They're exactly the same as the *interact* functions we saw earlier (in fact, they were copied verbatim from *textpak4.py* and *textpak5.py*, respectively). But here, *menu* is a passed-in argument, so the functions can be used to show different menus.

## Using Type Tests

A top-level "*interact*" function was also added to dispatch to one of the other two functions, based on the menu object's datatype. It uses the trick that was mentioned at the end of Chapter 8: the *type* built-in function returns the datatype object of its argument. Since datatypes are a type of object in Python, we can compare an object's type to the type of a known object to see what it is. Here,

```
if type(menu) == type([]):                  # same type as a (empty) list?
    interact_list(menu)
elif type(menu) == type({}):                # same type as a (empty) dictionary?
    interact_dict(menu)
```

we compare the menu's type object to the type objects of a list and a dictionary, written as empty constants. The result is that *interact* becomes a generic function that can handle both kinds of menus.

### *The types module*

Python also provides a library module called *types*, which defines and names all the valid type objects. But all it really does is assign the results of *type* calls like the ones used here to module variables. For instance:

```
IntType    = type(0)
StringType = type('')
...
```

It's used like any other module:

```
from types import *
if type(object) == StringType:
```

There really aren't any guidelines on which type testing approach is "better." As a general rule, use whatever general rule works best for you.

## *Testing the Menu Functions*

Let's test this module interactively on some new menus. First we write a file (module) with some test menus, so we don't have to reenter them at the command line:

*Example 9-2: File: testmenu.py*

```
from sys import stdout, exit

dmenu = { 'spam': lambda:stdout.write('SPAM\n'),
          'stop': exit }

lmenu = [('eggs', lambda:stdout.write('EGGS\n')),
         ('stop', lambda:1)]
```

Next, we start up the interactive interpreter, import the test and menu modules, and run some tests.

```
% python
>>> from testmenu import *
>>> from menu0 import interact
>>> interact(lmenu)               test a list menu
        E)ggs
        S)top
?e
EGGS
        E)ggs
        S)top
?s
>>> interact(dmenu)               test a dictionary menu
        spam
        stop
```

```
?spam
SPAM
        spam
        stop
?stop
%                              sys.exit ends the interpreter too
```

## Using "lambda": Functions Without Names

We used *lambda* in our test menus, and earlier for *stop* actions: Python's *lambda* expression creates anonymous function objects. Its general form is:

```
lambda <arg1>, <arg2>, ...<argN>:  <expression using arg's>
```

*lambda* only allows *expressions* after the :, not statements (we're able to print by using *sys.stdout* methods, instead of *print* statements). But in general, the *lambda* expression works exactly like the *def* statement, except the new function isn't assigned to a variable name unless you request it. For instance, the *lambdas*:

```
temp1 = lambda:1
temp2 = lambda:stdout.write('SPAM\n')          # save lambda result
```

are really the same as:

```
def temp1(): return 1
def temp2(): stdout.write('SPAM\n')            # run a def statement
```

but:

- The *def* statements assign the created function objects to names in function headers.
- The *lambda* expressions return the new function objects as their results.

Neither runs the functions immediately. Since *def* statements can be nested in Python, *lambda* is never strictly needed: calling the following *maker* function has the same effect as *lambda:1*:

```
def maker():
    def temp(): return 1
    return temp
```

But *lambda* is sometimes a convenient shorthand for writing *def*'s. So far, we've been using it as a way to create functions 'in place' in menus, without writing an extra *def*. Since *lambda* is an expression, it can be used in places the *def* statement can't: for instance, embedded in the dictionary and list constants here.

### *lambda scope issues*

As we'll see, *lambda* is often used with Python's functional-programming built-ins: *map*, *reduce*, etc. Python *lambda*s follow the normal three-scope lookup rule for function objects. By default, *lambda* expressions have access to their arguments' names, but not to names in an enclosing function's scope (i.e., names in the function where a *lambda* expression was written). But in Chapter 11, *Graphical User Interfaces*, we'll see how to retain information from the enclosing scope, using default lambda arguments.

## *Reusing the Menu Functions in the textpak Scripts*

While we're at it, *textpak4* and *textpak5* from Chapter 8 can be rewritten to use this module too: they become much simpler (though partially due to the fact that command-line switches have been dropped):

*Example 9-3: File: textpk4m.py*

```
#!/usr/local/bin/python

from sys import exit
from textpak2 import pack, unpack          # reuse textpak2 tools
from menu0 import interact                 # get the menu manager

menu = { 'pack':   pack,                   # interactive menu
         'unpack': unpack,                 # 'key' : function
         'stop':   exit }                  # sys.exit on 'stop'

if __name__ == '__main__': interact(menu)
```

*Example 9-4: File: textpk5m.py*

```
#!/usr/local/bin/python

from textpak2 import pack, unpack
from menu0 import interact                    # get the menu manager

menu = [ ('pack',   pack),                    # 'key', function
         ('unpack', unpack),                  # procedures return None
         ('stop',   lambda:1) ]               # return 1 to break loop

if __name__ == '__main__': interact(menu)
```

These variants are now clients of both the *textpak2* user interface module (for the *pack* and *unpack* functions), and our *menu0* menu-manager module (for *interact*).

## So Who Needs Classes?

This function-based approach works well: we can write any sort of menu we want, and the functions handle all the display and invocation logic. Certainly, if we can be absolutely sure that we'll never have to change the menu-processing code again, there's really no reason to change things at this point. What was that phrase: "if it ain't broke, don't fix it"?

But in most software development scenarios, we're not quite so lucky: programs are used by others, expand and evolve over time, etc. From this perspective, there are still major weaknesses in the function-based approach. In particular, there are at least three issues that limit this code's reusability:

*Redundancy*
: Having two versions of the menu interaction logic quickly leads to maintenance problems.

*Granularity*
: The solution's centralized model forces extensions to be lumped into the same functions.

*Type-switches*
: Logic such as that used by the *interact* function can also cause some growth problems.

### Redundancy: Changing Core Behavior

Both the list and dictionary-based menu functions implement their own interaction logic. Although they differ slightly, we still have two functions to change, if we ever need to change the way interaction happens. More seriously, we'll have to add each future extension in two places instead of one. Ultimately, this leads to an explosion in code size. For our simple functions, this isn't a major consideration. But for larger systems, we clearly need a way to factor out common logic, so it only appears in one place.

### Granularity: Adding Special Processing

Perhaps worse than the redundancy problem, every time we add an *extension* to the menu system, we'll probably wind up embedding special-case logic in our functions. Functions naturally centralize all the logic related to the behavior they implement. Because of this, each change in the behavior mutates the function "in-place," which can make for overly-complex code over time.

For instance, suppose we wanted to add support for logging a user's menu selections, and validating selections using a security module. We really only have two choices with functions:

*Copying*
: We can make a new copy of each function for each extension, which leads to massive code redundancy. Under this scenario, we would have multiple functions to update for a change in the core behavior.

*Embedding*
: But in practice, we would probably just add support logic for every new extension in the same function, which leads to a mess. We wind up with so much extra code, that the original purpose of the function is all but lost.

By the time we've added a handful of extensions, the original meaning of the function disappears; it becomes an unmanageable, tangled web of special-case rules. Consider what the dictionary menu function might look like after we've added logging and validation:

*Example 9-5: File: menu0b.py*

```
def interact_dict(menu, logFlag=0, secFlag=0):        # menu + extension flags
    import os, security, logger                       # utility modules
    user = os.environ['USER']
    if secFlag:                                       # any allowed?
        for name in menu.keys():
            if security.allow(name, user):
                break
        else:
            print "You're not authorized for any menu selections"
            return
    while 1:
        for name in menu.keys():                      # show legals
            if (not secFlag) or security.allow(name, user):
                print '\t' + name
        tool = raw_input('?')
        if logFlag:
            logger.record(user, tool)                 # log it, validate it
        if secFlag and not security.allow(tool, user):
            print "You're not authorized for this selection - try again"
        else:
            try:
                menu[tool]()                          # run function
            except KeyError:
                print 'what? - try again'             # key not found
```

Which may not be the most convoluted code ever written. But the original meaning—basic menu interaction—is obscured, if not lost altogether. Keep in mind that this is a simple example; extending the *list* menu function would be worse, and additional extensions would compound the problem over time.

The redundancy problem makes this phenomenon even worse: each extension has to be added to two functions: the list and dictionary versions. And we have to hope both versions somehow stay in sync with respect to all our extensions, over time (anyone care to make odds?).

## Type-Switching: Adding New Menu Types

Our *menu0.interact* is a *generic* function. It uses a multiway branch on the type of the menu object passed in. In effect, we're adding a level that interprets the menu objects, to decide how they should be handled. As is, we'll have to add a few lines to the *interact* function each time we add a new kind of menu. For example, adding a menu based on splitting strings requires a new entry in the *interact* interpreter.

But in practice, a generic function like *interact* would probably be built up over time. Because we won't be able to plan out all the possible menu types in advance, it would probably use nested logic rather than separate functions as done above. We might start with the dictionary *interact* function, later add an *if* clause to handle lists, etc. This is the sort of embedded structure we would usually wind up with:

*Example 9-6: File: menu0c.py*

```
def interact(menu):
    try:
        if type(menu) == type({}):              # dictionaries first
            while 1:
                for name in menu.keys():
                    print '\t' + name           # show options
                tool = raw_input('?')
                try:
                    menu[tool]()                # run function
                except KeyError:                # sys.exit to end
                    print 'what? - try again'

        elif type(menu) == type([]):            # lists added later...
            from string import upper, lower
            while 1:
                for name, func in menu:
                    print '\t' + upper(name[0]) + ')' + name[1:]
                tool = lower(raw_input('?'))
                for name, func in menu:
                    if tool == name[0] or tool == name:
                        exitflag = func()
                        break                   # run function
                else:
                    print 'what? - try again'   # not found: goto while
                    continue
                if exitflag: break              # exit while if 'true'
```

*Example 9-6: File: menu0c.py (continued)*

```
        elif type(menu) == type(''):
            pass # handle string-based menus in the future...

        else:
            print "bad menu type: not a list, dictionary, or string"

    except EOFError: pass
```

Which still probably isn't enough to have us put behind bars. But by the time we add a few more menu types, and some of the extensions we saw earlier, we'll have another mess: a long code segment that's both hard to understand and dangerous to modify. Even if we're careful to put each menu type's interaction in a separate function, we still have to update the generic type-switch logic for each new kind of menu, and hope it stays in sync with the menu functions, and doesn't spread to other parts of the program.

## Welcome to Object-Oriented Programming!

As you may have guessed by now, these are exactly the kinds of problems OOP was designed to address. Here's how OOP answers these code reuse challenges.

*Redundancy*
: Under OOP, programs are developed by defining core behaviors, and then specializing them for new requirements. Common behavior is factored-out and stored just once. Specialized versions are written as separate packages that inherit the core behavior and extend it externally, instead of copying it (or changing it directly, as we did to modules at the end of the last chapter). When used well, behavior is never implemented redundantly.

*Granularity*
: Unlike functions, OOP specifies a deliberately decentralized model. Systems are extended by defining deviations from packaged behavior. Rather than adding an extension's logic to an existing package in place, we write a new package that inherits the existing package's behavior, and modifies or extends it with logic added locally.

*Type-switches*
: Any time we see a function like *interact*, a mental alarm should go off: manual object-type testing is usually one of the primary symptoms of a program that can benefit from OOP. Because functions deal in the *how*—procedures for operating on objects, they really have no other options when dispatching to behavior that varies per data-type.

> By contrast OOP deals with the *what*—the objects being operated on. Rather than selecting an action by checking object types, we make the objects responsible for "doing the right thing" on their own. In effect, by embedding actions in objects, the choice of action is delegated to the objects themselves. Programs work by asking objects to do some work, and objects in turn ask other objects to perform services.

By definition, OOP is just a way to structure programs: we define generic "base" behavior, and specialize it by specifying how extensions deviate from the base. Although it is possible to implement generic behavior by passing menu objects to simple functions that test their data types manually, OOP provides a better solution for writing reusable and maintainable software.

### *Classes are a tool*

In Python, the tool behind all this magic is the *class*. Classes are just a way to describe the objects in our program. More specifically, classes bundle up:

- The behavior of an object (methods)
- The information associated with an object (data-members)
- The rules for inheriting behavior from other classes (superclasses)

By defining inheritance rules, classes construct an external framework where extensions can be added without changing more general logic in place. But as we'll see, classes don't embody many new concepts; they're really just namespaces. Methods are named functions, and data-members are variables. In fact, classes aren't much more than modules, with support for attribute inheritance and multiple copies.

### *Objects are a paradigm*

But the real magic of OOP is the way we use it to structure our problem domain. Instead of writing a set of functions, we implement a set of objects, to model the system's components. In our simple menu-functions example, we have just one object: a *menu*. Yet we can get around all three problems above by restructuring the system as a superclass that implements a generic menu interaction loop, plus two subclasses that extend the generic class to handle dictionary and list-based menus.

In a moment we'll see an implementation of this idea: a *Menu* superclass, and subclasses for the two menu types: *DictMenu* and *ListMenu*. As a preview:

- Since the main logic exists only in the Menu superclass, there's no redundancy.

- OOP's naturally decentralized model lets us extend Menu's core logic in separate subclasses.
- The program is organized by menus, not functions: menu logic is moved to the menus themselves.

In effect, the subclasses essentially make dictionaries and lists *know* how to do menu interaction. Instead of the type-switch, the generic Menu class asks the subclasses to handle portions of the interface that differ from type to type; the subclasses fill in the blanks, to implement specialized menu behavior.

There's more to OOP than eliminating redundancy, decentralized granularity, and getting rid of type switches. OOP is really a set of concepts that derive from the basic idea of associating procedures with data. In fact the class model we'll use here: filling in the blanks in subclasses is just one of many ways to structure OOP code. We'll explore other OOP threads, like information hiding, composition, and data encapsulation, later in this book.

### *OOP works, despite the hype*

Because it's the current software "solution du jour", some claims about OOP are almost certainly exaggerated. In fact, there seems to be no shortage of purported OOP benefits, or vague OOP terminology ("object" is about as abstract as it gets!) There are clearly situations where the extra complexity of OOP isn't warranted; for example, it may not help if you're writing a few lines of code that you'll never use again.

Still, for all but the simplest jobs, applying OOP can pay off. For instance, we'll study an application framework later that "wraps" system-level components, and provides a standard way to do input/output redirection, argument list processing, etc. Such a class-based tool can even benefit scripts knocked off in a hurry. And as we'll see, for nontrivial programs, OOP can be an indispensable tool for structuring and reusing code.

## *OOP in Action: Menus as Classes*

The best way to see how OOP works is to see it in action. Now that we know something about the goals behind OOP, let's expand our menu functions to use classes. First we define a general menu class to handle interaction, and two subclasses to handle list- and dictionary-based menu representations.

*Example 9-7: File: menu1.py*

```
class Menu:                                     # the menu superclass
    def run(self, prompt='?'):
        try:
            while 1:                            # common interactive loop
                print '\n\tMENU...'
                self.showOptions()
                command = raw_input(prompt)
                try:
                    flag = self.runCommand(command)
                except (IndexError, KeyError):
                    print "what: '%s'?" % command
                else:
                    if flag: break
        except EOFError: pass                   # ctrl-d still exits all


class DictMenu(Menu):                           # a Menu subclass
    def showOptions(self):
        options = self.menu.keys()              # menu = mapping
        options.sort()
        for cmd in options: print '\t\t' + cmd

    def runCommand(self, cmd):
        return self.menu[cmd]()                 # call method/function


class ListMenu(Menu):                           # menu = nested sequences
    def showOptions(self):
        for i in range(len(self.menu)):
            print '\t\t%d) %s' % (i, self.menu[i][0])

    def runCommand(self, cmd):
        try:
            index = eval(cmd)                   # convert string to number
        except:
            raise IndexError
        return self.menu[index][1]()            # selected by number
```

*ListMenu* and *DictMenu* are both specializations of the *Menu* superclass. In effect, both tell us how what they do is different from the generic behavior of *Menu*. Although they both "know" how to show and run menu options for their types, the main interaction logic only exists in *Menu*. In OOP terminology, *ListMenu* and *DictMenu* inherit the *run* method from the *Menu* superclass: they're both subclasses of *Menu*.

*Menu* contains the main interaction loop, but it is deliberately naive about how to actually show a menu's options, or invoke its functions. Those jobs are delegated to subclasses, by calling the *showOptions* and *runCommand* methods. Subclasses are expected to implement these methods, according to their menu's type; when called, they're looked up in the framework implied by class inheritance rules. None of the three classes define the *menu* attribute: it must be provided at a lower level, by other classes or an instance.

## *Putting the Classes to Work by Subclassing*

These three classes don't really do anything yet—they're just exported services. Before we get into details, let's see how they might be used; one way is to import and specialize them in other modules. Here are two client modules, which use our menu classes by defining subclasses with attached menus, making instances of them, and calling the *run* method inherited from the *Menu* class to start the interaction process.

*Example 9-8: File: textpak6.py*

```
#!/usr/local/bin/python

import sys
from menu1 import DictMenu                     # get menu interaction
from textpak2 import pack, unpack              # reuse textpak2 funcs

class TextPak(DictMenu):                          # subclass this menu
    menu = { 'pack':   pack,                      # my interactive menu
             'unpack': unpack,                    # static class data
             'stop':   sys.exit }

if __name__ == '__main__': TextPak().run()  # make one and run it
```

*Example 9-9: File: textpak7.py*

```
#!/usr/local/bin/python

from menu1 import ListMenu                        # get menu interaction
from textpak2 import pack, unpack                 # reuse textpak2 funcs

class TextPak(ListMenu):
    menu = [ ('pack',   pack),                    # ('key', function)
             ('unpack', unpack),
             ('stop',   lambda:1) ]

if __name__ == '__main__': TextPak().run()  # inherit from ListMenu
```

These two modules roughly correspond to our dictionary and list-menu modules above, *textpk4m* and *textpk5m*. In fact, they look a lot alike, but here, we're making class instances instead of calling functions. Both modules create a local class called *TextPak*, which is a subclass of (i.e., inherits from) the appropriate superclass imported from *menu1*. The subclasses define *menu* data members, which are managed by the imported superclass. The rest of the menu's behavior is inherited from superclasses.

## Running the Subclass Scripts

Here are our scripts in action, run from the system command line. We're mapping scripts to OOP here: as soon as the scripts start up, they make an instance of their class, and call its *run* method. We've also added some of the features suggested in Chapter 8: dictionary entries are sorted before they're displayed, and *list* entries are numbered when displayed; they are selected by typing the number associated with them.

```
% textpak6.py

         MENU...
                  pack               run the textpak6 script
                  stop               make a DictMenu subclass instance
                  unpack
?pack
output file name? packed1
files to pack? *.txt
packing: file1.txt                   pack some files
packing: file2.txt                   reuses the original textpak2...
                                     which uses original pack2/unpack3
         MENU...
                  pack
                  stop
                  unpack
?stop
% textpak7.py                        run the textpak7 script
                                     make a ListMenu subclass instance
         MENU...
                  0) pack
                  1) unpack
                  2) stop
?1
input file name? packed1
creating: file1.txt                  unpack some files
creating: file2.txt                  reuses chapter6/7 stuff too

         MENU...
                  0) pack
                  1) unpack
                  2) stop
?2

% textpak6.py
                                     raise some exceptions...
         MENU...                     across module and class boundaries
                  pack
                  stop
                  unpack             KeyError caught in Menu superclass
?s                                   raised in DictMenu.runCommand
what: 's'?
```

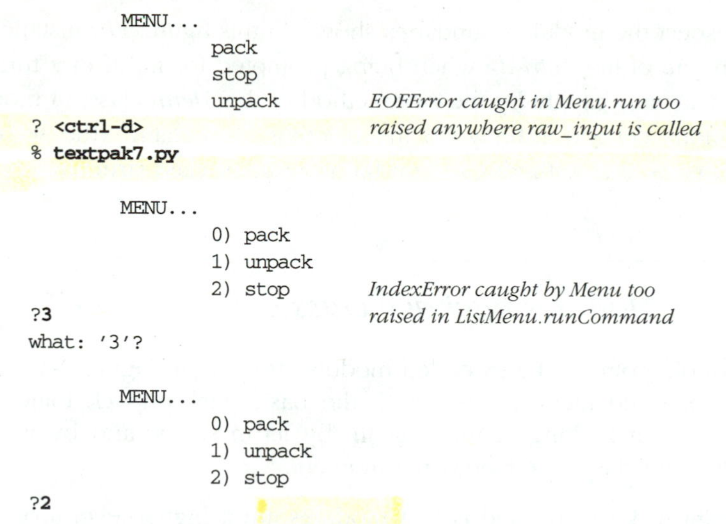

```
        MENU...
                pack
                stop
                unpack          EOFError caught in Menu.run too
? <ctrl-d>                      raised anywhere raw_input is called
% textpak7.py

        MENU...
                0) pack
                1) unpack
                2) stop         IndexError caught by Menu too
?3                              raised in ListMenu.runCommand
what: '3'?

        MENU...
                0) pack
                1) unpack
                2) stop
?2
```

## *"A Fist Full of Modules"*

To understand what's going on here, let's first get a clear picture of all the modules involved. Modules *texpak6* and *textpak7* both import a menu superclass from module *menu1*, plus the pack and unpack functions from module *textpak2*. Module *textpak2* in turn imports the primitive packing and unpacking functions from modules *pack2* and *unpack3*, which both get *marker* from *textpak1*.

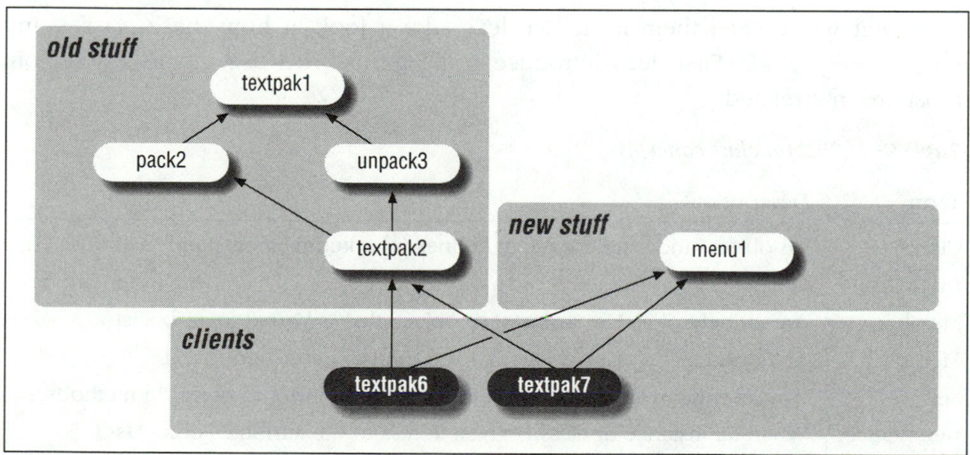


*Figure 9-1: The module view—textpak6/7 import dependencies*

Figure 9-1 shows the relationships. Everything from *textpak2* on up was developed in earlier chapters. In this section, we've only added classes to handle menu-based interaction.

Exceptions don't respect the module boundaries shown in this figure. For instance, if the user types an end-of-file <*ctrl-d*> when being prompted for input in a function in *textpak2*, it's actually caught by the *run* method of the *Menu* class, in module *menu1*. Exceptions depend entirely on the run-time "call-chain" (the set of currently active functions and methods), not on the module or class structures of a program.

### *Modules package classes*

Of course, the whole point of the extended module structure in Figure 9-1 is to combine the exported menu classes, with the basic pack/unpack logic. There are two ways of looking at this system: by its modules, and by its classes. We'll study the class-based view in a moment.

For now, the point to keep in mind is that modules are a higher-level tool, for organizing and partitioning other tools. For instance, the classes in *menu1* are totally independent of the activity menus perform. By putting our menu classes in a module, they become a generally-useful class library; any client that imports the enclosing module can use its classes to interact with users. With modules, we get code reuse automatically.

## *Exploring Python Classes*

Now that we've seen them in action, let's take a look at how these classes and scripts really work. First, let's introduce some terms we'll use in this discussion; most are interrelated.

*Table 9–1: Python class concepts*

| Term | Description |
|---|---|
| Class | An object (and statement) that defines inherited members and methods |
| Instance | Objects that are created from a class, and inherit its members and methods |
| Member | An attribute of a class or instance object, that is bound to an object |
| Method | An attribute of a class object that is bound to a function object |
| Self | By convention, the name given to the implied instance object in methods |
| Inheritance | When an instance or class is given access to the attributes of a class |
| Superclass | The class or classes another class inherits attributes from |
| Subclass | A class that inherits attributes from another class [also: to specialize (verb)] |

## *Using the class Statement*

Much like the *def* statement, *class* is an executable statement that creates a class object and assigns it to a variable name. The name used in the class statement becomes a variable in the scope where the class statement appears. Its general form is:

```
class <name> ( <superclass>, <superclass>,...):
        <statements>
```

The class header line gives the class's name, followed by a list of classes separated by commas that the new class will inherit attributes from. In our example, the *Menu* class doesn't have a superclass list: it's a top-level *root* class. But *DictMenu* and *ListMenu* both inherit attributes from *Menu*.

### *Methods: functions, with a place holder*

The *Menu* class begins with:

```
class Menu:                                     # the menu superclass
    def run(self, prompt='?'):
```

Menu has one method: *run*, which uses a default argument to allow the `?` prompt to be overridden when *run* is called: `object.run(">")`. In Python, class methods are written as function *def* statements, nested in a *class* statement (i.e., indented under the class header). As usual, *def* creates a function and assigns it to the method name, this time in the class's namespace. They become attributes of the class.

Methods really are functions, with one crucial exception: the first (leftmost) argument is used as a place-holder, to accept the implied instance object when the method is called. Since there may be multiple instances of a class, we need a way to refer to the one that's the subject of a method call.

***Mapping method-calls to classes.*** Here's how this dilemma is resolved. When a method is called, Python adds a reference to the object being qualified, to the front of the argument list. This is the "hook" that makes it possible to change the implied subject instance inside a class method. It also provides access to attributes defined in a lower class or instance. If *object* is an instance of *class*, the mapping from method-calls to class methods is as shown in Figure 9-2.

In this figure, *object* is the instance that we're manipulating, by calling its method. Python makes it the implied first-argument in the call to the class method function. In fact, both kinds of method calls are valid, but we usually call through the instance instead of the class (except when extending a method, as we'll see later). Otherwise code would be dependent on the structure of the classes used by the objects it processes.

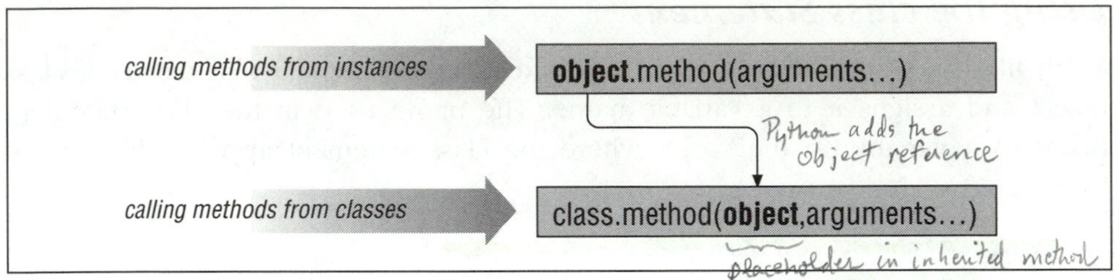


*Figure 9-2: Calling methods*

***Using the self argument.*** By convention, the added method argument is usually called *self*. It provides access to everything associated with the class instance object being processed. When calling a method we never pass the first argument ourselves, but we always use it inside the method:

- The *self* argument is always implied at the point of call: it's the object that was qualified.
- The *self* argument is always explicit in the method: it is used to access the instance's attributes.

For instance, if *object* is an instance of the *DictMenu* class above, a call to its *run* method becomes a call to *Menu.run*:

```
object.run()            ...becomes...    Menu.run(object)
```

Later, while inside Menu's *run* method, *self* still refers to the original *object*. A call to *self*'s *showOptions* method becomes a call to a *DictMenu* class method, passing a reference to *object*:

```
self.showOptions()      ...becomes...    DictMenu.showOptions(self)
```

Python knows to pick *DictMenu's* method, because of self's inheritance rules (this will be discussed in a moment). Methods qualify *self* to access anything that might *vary* from instance to instance. In fact, both methods and members can vary, according to the type of the *self* instance object:

*Methods*

When *Menu.run* calls *self.showOptions()*, it's requesting a look up of the *showOptions* attribute, in the Menu instance that's the subject of the call. Since *showOptions* is different in *DictMenu* and *ListMenu* subclasses, we have to qualify the instance to get the right one.

*Members*

Similarly, when *DictMenu.showOptions* uses the expression: *self.menu.keys()*, it's accessing the *menu* attribute of the instance whose *run* method was called. If we make more than one menu object, *menu* might be different in each.

By qualifying *self* to fetch members and methods, classes implement behavior in a generic fashion: the meaning of an attribute depends on the type of the instance object passed to *self*. This is usually called polymorphism; in Python, it's really just a matter of looking up attributes in objects. As we'll see below, methods also assign *self*'s attributes to *change* an instance.

### *More on self: almost this, but not quite that*

By convention, this special first argument is usually called *self*, but we can really use any name we want. If you've used C++, you've probably noticed that Python's *self* is exactly like the implicit *this* pointer in C++ methods. But in Python, we must always go through *self* to get instance members: there are no special scoping rules for searching the instance's namespace when unqualified names are used.

The rationale behind this policy is that it prevents confusion about where a name inside a method comes from: instance members are always obvious, since they're *self*-attribute qualifications. There's no implicit, hidden object scope, on top of the others.

### *Members: variables plus inheritance*

When DictMenu references the *menu* attribute of *self*: *self.menu.keys()*, it's using a data member of the object. But there's really nothing special here: data members are just named attributes of the instance object, or one of its classes. They exist in an instance or class namespace, but are qualified like variables defined at the top-level of a module.

As is the case for all variable names, members come into existence when first assigned, and must exist when referenced. But unlike module variables, undefined member attribute references are resolved by inheritance, exactly like methods. References to undefined module attributes raise exceptions immediately.

Usually, data member attributes are created by assigning to them in the methods of a class. This is the only way we can enforce uniformity on the data associated with objects created from a class. However, as we'll see later, *menu* can be set in a variety of ways: any code that has access to an object can set its members, by assigning its attributes to any kind of object: numbers, lists, functions, even other instances.

## *Making Class Instances*

Of course, the whole point of writing classes is to support creation of one or more instance objects. The last line of both the *textpak6* and *textpak7* scripts is the same:

```
if __name__ == '__main__': TextPak().run()
```

which creates an instance of the local subclass, and calls its *run* method inherited from *Menu*. In Python, we make an instance of a class, by calling the class as though it were a *function*: *TextPak()* creates an instance of the *TextPak* class. As we'll see in a moment, we sometimes also pass arguments to the class name, if it accepts extra details when making instances.

Here, we immediately call the *run* method of the class, by qualifying the new instance's *run* attribute. Since we didn't assign the created instance to a variable, it goes away (is garbage-collected) after the *run* method returns. But because our script exits immediately after the call, saving the instance isn't an issue here.

### *Classes versus instances*

It's important to note the distinction between classes and instances. In Python, they are different object types:

- Classes are templates for creating instances; they implement shared behavior.
- Instances are the concrete realizations of a class; each has a unique attribute namespace.

Classes provide behavior for their instances, as method and member attributes. Instances are the "real" objects; they inherit the behavior or their class in the same way that subclasses inherit from superclasses.

We can make as many instances of a given class as we want: each gets its own *attribute namespace*, which starts out empty, but inherits all the class's attributes. By assigning to instance attributes, the instances of a class diverge over time. Instance attributes are usually assigned in class methods, by changing the mutable *self* argument: *self.member=value*. But since instances are just namespaces, we can also assign an instance's attributes outside its classes (we'll see how to do both in a moment).

## *How Inheritance Rules Work*

In simple terms, Python inheritance makes attributes of a class's namespace appear as though they are true members of another class or instance namespace. But instead of copying a class's attributes over, they're fetched from the class each time they are accessed through a subclass or instance. In Python:

- A class inherits attributes from the classes listed in its header, and all classes above.
- An instance inherits attributes from the class it's created from, plus all classes above.

When an instance or class is qualified (*object.attribute*), Python searches for the attribute name in the namespaces of the object and its superclasses, and always uses the first occurrence it finds. The search proceeds from the bottom up, where an *instance* is at the bottom, its *class* is above, and class *superclass* lists define higher ancestors. For instance, class relationships in our menu system define a class hierarchy, shown in Figure 9-3.

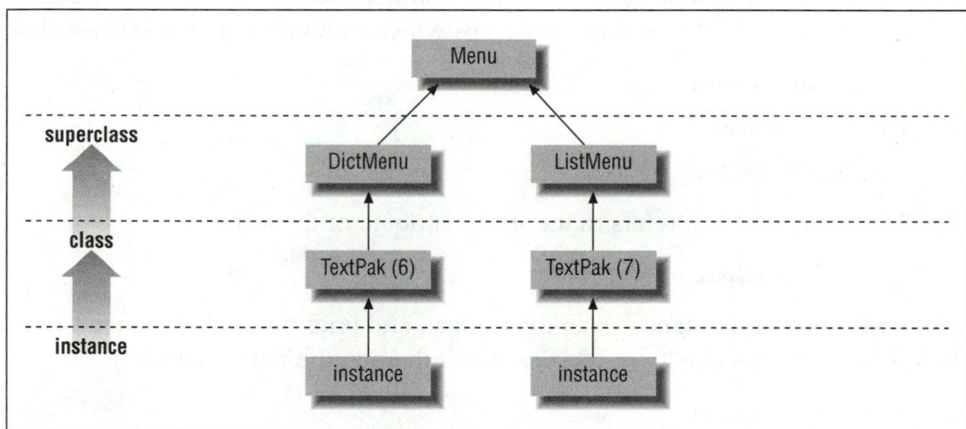


*Figure 9-3: The class view—an inheritance hierarchy*

In this figure, the arrows represent attribute inheritance search paths. If a qualified attribute name isn't found in an instance's namespace, the search begins climbing the class tree. An error is reported only if the attribute name can't be found in any class above the object qualified.

### *Inheritance in action*

Here are some concrete examples to illustrate how hierarchy searching works in practice. In the *textpak6* script above, when we make an instance and execute its *run* method:

```
TextPak().run()
```

Python searches for an attribute *run*, by looking in four accessible namespaces:

1. The instance object
2. The *TextPak* class
3. The *DictMenu* class
4. The *Menu* class

and finds the name *run* in the *Menu* class. Later, when we use a qualified attribute name in the *run* method of the *Menu* superclass:

```
self.showOptions()
```

Python searches for *showOptions* in the *instance* (*self* is the implied instance-object), then in the *TextPak* class, and stops when it's found in the *DictMenu* class:

1. The instance object
2. The *TextPak* class
3. The *DictMenu* class

Finally, when *DictMenu* refers to the *menu* attribute of the instance:

```
options = self.menu.keys()
```

Python looks in the instance's namespace first, and finds an attribute named *menu* in the *TextPak* class (we'll see why it's stored there in the next section):

1. The instance object
2. The *TextPak* class

And in other cases, attributes might be found in the instance immediately. As we'll see, this searching of class hierarchies is the basis of specialization: by adding same-named attributes at lower levels of the hierarchy, subclasses and instances can override inherited behavior. The lower versions are found first.

### *Multiple inheritance search*

Technically, Python inheritance uses a depth-first, left-to-right search of the class hierarchy for an attribute name. It always search from bottom to top first. The left-to-right part comes into play when classes list more than one superclass in their headers (this is called "multiple inheritance"; we'll explore it in the next chapter). In this case, it's possible that multiple superclasses may define the same member or method name: Python uses the first one found searching the tree toward the right (instead of treating this as an error).

# *Configuring Menu Data*

There are a variety of ways we can initialize the *menu* attribute expected by our menu manager classes: static subclass data, attribute assignment outside the class, and assignment within constructor methods. In fact, there are two places where an object's attributes can exist: in the instance itself, or in one of its classes.

## *Attribute Assignment Changes Instances*

When an instance's attribute is assigned, the name is always created or changed in the namespace of the instance object itself, not its class. This happens both outside the class and within class methods:

```
object.attribute = value      # outside the class: change the instance
self.attribute   = value      # in a class method: change the instance
```

In both cases, the attribute is altered in the instance namespace. This is how classes manage data that vary per instance: assignments to *self* attributes refer to a particular object. Although it's possible to assign to class attributes too (*class.attr=value*), it changes the attribute for every instance of the class.

## *Attribute Reference Searches Hierarchies*

As we've seen, a reference to a class-instance's attribute is located by inheritance rules. Namespace objects are searched in this order:

1. *Instance.* The instance's namespace is searched first.
2. *Class.* The namespace of the instance's class is searched next.

3. *Superclasses.* Classes accessible from the instance's class are searched depth-first, left-to-right.

Here too, these rules apply regardless of whether the object is qualified outside the class or within a class method:

```
object.attribute        # outside the class: search an arbitrary instance
self.attribute          # in a class method: search an instance of the class
```

Because of the way attribute search rules work, the *menu* attribute may be created in either the instance, or a specialized subclass. If stored in the instance, it will be located by step 1; if created in a subclass, step 2 will find it. Here are some ways to apply these techniques in our menu system.

## Using Class Data: static Members

In the initial versions shown earlier, the menu is assigned inside the *class* statement of local subclasses, so it becomes a data member of the *class* itself. For instance, *textpak6* assigns a dictionary to *menu*:

```
class TextPak(DictMenu):                    # subclass this menu
    menu = { 'pack':   pack,                # my interactive menu
             'unpack': unpack,              # static class data
             'stop':   sys.exit }
```

Here, *menu* is assigned in the namespace (scope) of the class statement. Like methods, it becomes an attribute of the *TextPak class* object, and will be inherited by all instances we make from *TextPak*, by step 2 above. In effect, *menu* will be *shared* by all instances and subclasses of TextPak. Such attributes are usually called static class data (and correspond to C++'s static members).

## Setting Instance Data Outside Classes

Since we're not making subclasses of *TextPak* here, the extra class isn't really needed. We could just as easily assign the *menu* attribute to the instance directly. The following code works the same as the earlier *textpak6* version, but uses direct instance attribute assignment, instead of subclassing:

*Example 9-10: File: textpk6b.py*

```
#!/usr/local/bin/python

import sys
from menu1 import DictMenu                  # get menu interaction
from textpak2 import pack, unpack           # reuse textpak2 stuff

mymenu = { 'pack':   pack,                  # interactive menu
           'unpack': unpack,                # not static class data
           'stop':   sys.exit }
```

*Example 9-10: File: textpk6b.py (continued)*

```
if __name__ == '__main__':
    instance = DictMenu()                     # make a DictMenu directly
    instance.menu = mymenu                    # assign instance member
    instance.run()
```

This time, the name *menu* becomes an instance attribute. When the menu classes reference *self.menu*, inheritance finds *menu* by step 1 above. But to the class methods, instance and class members look the same; in both cases, they just qualify *self* to access attributes. Since *self* is the instance object, the search for *menu* starts at the instance's namespace, and travels up through the class tree if needed.

Notice that we assign the instance's *menu* attribute *outside* the classes here: members can always be added or changed on the fly from anywhere in a program. Of course, this technique can be dangerous if abused; but as shown here, it can also be useful when used well.

## *Configuring Instances with Class Constructors*

Since every instance derived from the *Menu* superclass is expected to have a *menu* attribute, we could also make the assignment part of the instance creation protocol. Here are the changes:

*Example 9-11: File: menu1.py*

```
class Menu:
    def __init__(self, menu):           # pass a menu object to the constructor
        self.menu = menu                # assign argument to instance attribute

    def run(self, prompt='?'):
        ...rest of the module unchanged...
```

*Example 9-12: File: textpk6c.py*

```
#!/usr/local/bin/python

import sys
from menu1 import DictMenu                    # get menu interaction
from textpak2 import pack, unpack             # reuse textpak2 stuff

mymenu = { 'pack':   pack,                    # interactive menu
           'unpack': unpack,                  # not static class data
           'stop':   sys.exit }

if __name__ == '__main__': DictMenu(mymenu).run()
```

The `__init__` constructor method is inherited by subclasses and instances, just like any other class attribute name. But if defined, `__init__` will be run automatically, when the class-name is called to create an instance. Arguments passed to the class-name are sent to the `__init__` method's argument list, along with the newly created instance object, *self*. By assigning attributes to *self*, `__init__` methods initialize instance objects.

When we make a *DictMenu* instance, Python finds the `__init__` method in *Menu*'s namespace, and runs it with the *mymenu* object as its second argument. Since `__init__` assigns the argument's value to the *menu* attribute of *self*, it becomes an *instance* attribute again. As in the last example, it will be located by search step 1 above, when later referenced in menu class methods as *self.menu*.

By defining the `__init__` constructor method here, it forces a menu to be passed in whenever a *Menu* instance is created: if a menu isn't passed, we'll get a *wrong-number-arguments* error when we call the class. This is probably what we want; since *Menu* and its subclasses assume that a *menu* attribute exists below, putting it in the constructor ensures that it will be available.

### *Special names for special methods*

We'll see other special method names like `__init__` later in the book. Python uses specially named methods as "hooks" for providing extra class behavior. For example, `__del__` is the instance destructor, `__add__` overloads the + operator, and `__getitem__` intercepts indexing. All hook methods have names that start and end with two underscores to avoid clashing with attributes we add (just like `__name__` and `__dict__` in modules), and all follow the normal attribute inheritance search rules.

To summarize: *instance* attributes may be assigned outside a class, or by qualifying *self* in methods; *class* attributes can be assigned by statements in a *class* statement, or by qualifying a class object. Because of the way inheritance works, the two have different effects: changing an instance alters a particular instance only, but assigning *class* attributes impacts all instances created from the class, as well as its subclasses. Figure 9-4 shows both cases.

#### *Extending superclass methods*

Since `__init__` is inherited, Python finds and runs just one `__init__` constructor when making an instance, not the constructors of *all* classes above the instance. Unlike C++, there are no special rules for passing a subclass's arguments to a superclass's constructor; constructors follow the normal rules for attribute inheritance. If we want other `__init__` methods to run during creation, we can call them explicitly.

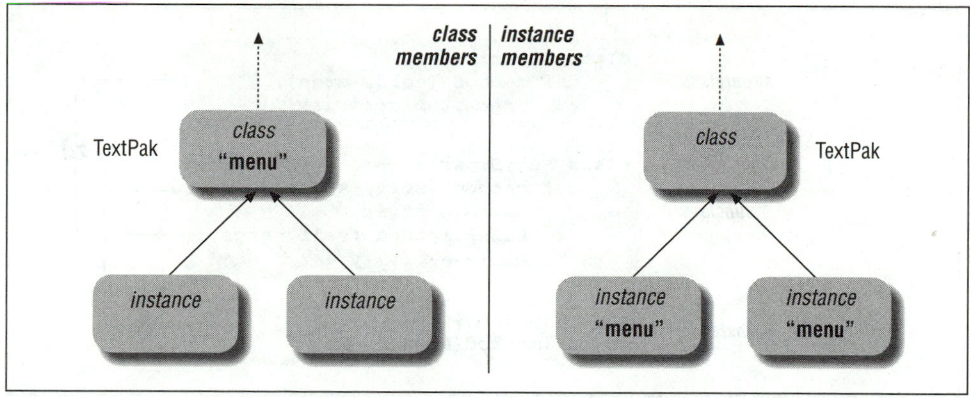


*Figure 9-4: Class data versus instance data*

For example, if we needed to do extra construction time activity in *DictMenu*, we can define an `__init__` which would probably have to call the *Menu* superclass's `__init__`, so our menu is recorded in the instance. But handling this is simple; we just use the equivalence of instance qualification to class method calls.

```
class DictMenu(Menu):
    def __init__(self, menu, other):        # override superclass init
        Menu.__init__(self, menu)           # do superclass init first
        <use 'other' here>                  # do local init logic here
```

Inheritance finds the `__init__` name in *DictMenu*, and runs that version: to make the *Menu* constructor run too, we have to call it manually from *DictMenu*.`__init__`. Although we're just working with constructor methods here, we'll see that this technique applies to extending superclass methods in general (see Figure 9-5).

### *Using inheritance to specialize behavior*

In Figure 9-5, the subclass extends the inherited method with extra logic. But if it didn't call the superclass's version explicitly, it would replace the inherited method completely. In general, we can utilize inheritance rules to reuse and modify inherited behavior in a variety of ways:

- *Providing* methods and members superclasses expect: filling in the blanks
- *Adding* new methods or members to the inherited set, by defining them locally
- *Replacing* inherited methods or members completely, by redefining them locally

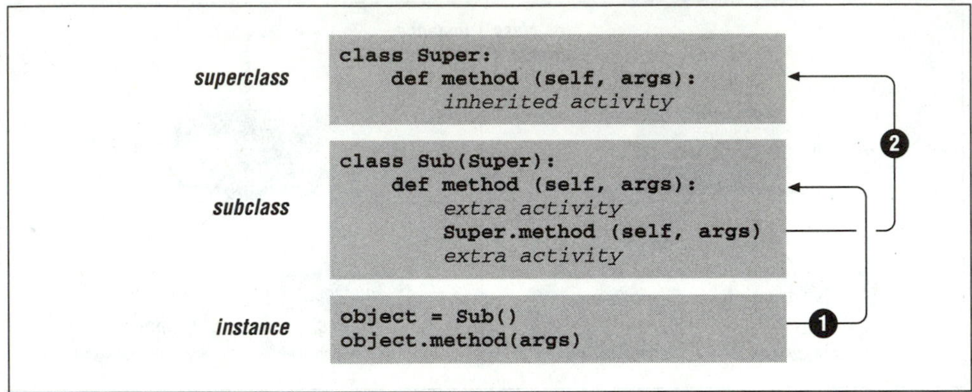


*Figure 9-5: Extending inherited methods*

- *Extending* inherited methods, with local redefinitions that call the inherited version explicitly
- *Inheriting* members and methods verbatim, without redefining them locally

We'll see examples of all these techniques throughout this book.

# Namespaces, Part 3: Classes and Instances

By now, you've probably noticed that namespaces are central to much of what we do in Python. Here's how some of the namespace concepts we've already seen apply to classes and instances:

- Like modules, classes and instances are mostly just namespaces for defining attributes.
- Like functions, classes add a third local scope to search when unqualified names are used.
- Unlike modules, classes and instances add inheritance of qualified attribute names.
- Unlike module imports, each instance of the same class gets a new, empty namespace.

### *A class by any other name . . .*

Since functions are first-class objects, there are other ways to associate data and logic with objects without using classes. For instance, we can simulate our classes by representing each instance as a dictionary, and each attribute as a key. Here's a rough sketch:

```
def Menu(menu):                             # a superclass
    obj = {}                                # start an instance
    def run(prompt='?', self=obj):          # a method: nested func
        while 1:
            self['showOptions']()           # call subclass method
            ...etc.
            flag = self['runCommand'](command)
    obj['menu'] = menu                      # assign data-member
    obj['run']  = run                       # assign methods
    return obj

def DictMenu(menu):                         # subclass constructor
    obj = Menu(menu)                        # extends superclass
    def showOptions(self=obj):              # subclass methods
        options = self['menu'].keys()
        ...etc.
    def runCommand(cmd, self=obj):          # saves this call's "obj"
        return self['menu'][cmd]()
    obj['showOptions'] = showOptions        # assign methods
    obj['runCommand']  = runCommand         # can over-ride Menu keys
    return obj

def ListMenu(menu): ...etc.

if __name__ == '__main__': DictMenu(mymenu)['run']('>')
```

This code builds up a dictionary, and sets its keys to the nested method functions. It makes use of the fact that default arguments retain the value assigned when a *def* or *lambda* is run. Here, the nested function's *self* argument still refers to the *obj* dictionary that is built up when the construction functions are run.

Besides being incredibly complex, this approach isn't really a replacement for classes. Attributes must be set manually, each instance creates new method functions, and dictionaries don't support extra class features like operator overloading (to be discussed in Chapter 10, *More Class Magic*).

Moreover, because there's just one namespace here (the dictionary), there's no easy way to extend inherited behavior: changing a key replaces its prior value. Although dictionaries are similar, classes provide a more convenient way to define and encapsulate behavior.

## *Scopes Versus Object namespaces*

One way to understand how namespaces apply to classes is to notice the distinction between scopes and namespaces in Python. We've been using the terms interchangeably but they serve different purposes:

- *Scopes* are used to resolve *unqualified* names, and correspond to *source file* units.
- *namespaces* are searched when resolving *qualified* names, and correspond to *objects.*

The two concepts are disjoint when resolving names. For example, a name *X* is resolved according to the scopes surrounding its appearance in a source-file. But when we qualify names—*X.attribute*—the attributed is looked-up in the qualified object's namespace.

But in some contexts, scopes and namespaces merge. For example, a module file defines a scope for names referenced in the file. But it also creates a module object with a namespace: we can later access attributes in an imported module by qualifying it (*module.name*). Classes work the same way: they define a new scope, but nested statements create attributes in the namespace of a class object.

In other words, statements in some scopes serve to initialize object namespaces. Each class and instance object is a distinct namespace: they have attributes we can qualify. But class statements are also a scope for the statements it encloses. Instances are just namespaces, but classes are both namespaces and scopes.

## *Class Statement Scope*

The *class* statement introduces a new local scope, extending to the end of the class statement. As in functions, statements nested in a class that create names as a side effect (assignment, *def*, *import*, etc.), store new names in the class's local scope. But in classes, names stored in the class statement's local scope become attributes in the class object it creates. In fact, any Python statement can appear nested in a *class*:

```
from config import platform

class GuiManager:
    if platform == 'unix':
        gui = 'X11'
    else:
        gui = 'Windows'

    def display(self):
        if self.gui == "X11": pass # ...etc...
```

Here, we nest an *if* in a *class*, to set a class attribute according to the setting of *platform*:

- The name *platform* exists in the global scope: the module enclosing the class statement.
- Name *gui* is assigned in the class's local scope: it becomes a class data member attribute.
- Name *display* is created in the local scope too: it becomes a class method attribute.

Unlike functions, the local scope of a class becomes a namespace shared by all class instances and subclasses; it's not recreated for each instance (call). Further, class scope is used to implement inheritance: all instances and subclasses of a class inherit attributes from the class's local scope (namespace).

## *Scoping Rules: the Rest of the Story*

We are finally in a position to summarize the entire set of scope rules in Python. We've seen parts of this set of rules before, but we'll collect all the rules here. Table 9-2 summarizes the local and global scopes searched when an unqualified name (i.e., one not preceded by a period) is used in various contexts. We'll study the functions in the last table entry later in the book.

*Table 9–2: Local and global scope rules*

| Symbol context | Global scope | Local scope |
|---|---|---|
| Module | Same as local | The module itself |
| Script, Interactive prompt | Same as local | The module `__main__` |
| Class | The enclosing module | The class statement |
| Function (and method) | The enclosing module | The function call |
| exec, eval, execfile, input | The caller's global | The caller's local |

### *Unqualified names search scopes*

Let's review some namespace ideas we saw earlier. Unqualified names are resolved by their location in a source file: the enclosing statement-type or context determines the local and global scopes searched for a name. On a name reference, Python searches at most three scopes for the name, in this order:

1. The *local* scope at the spot where the reference appears in the file (or code string)

2. The *global* scope which always turns out to be the enclosing module's namespace
3. The *built-in* scope where Python built-in functions and exceptions are kept

The global and local scopes for various name contexts are given in Table 9-2 above. Local names override global ones, and both local and global names override built-in's (you can redefine *open* and *range* if you want, but it's usually not a good idea!). As we've seen, *assignment* to an unqualified name always sets the name in the local namespace, unless it's declared *global* (to map it to a module name).

### Qualified names search object namespaces

For both reference and assignment, the path of namespaces to search is explicit when qualification is used. Python only searches the namespaces of objects along the path (not their global scopes). In a attribute reference path: "X.Y.Z":

- The leftmost name ("X") is resolved like an unqualified name, according to the surrounding scopes.
- The rest (".Y.Z") refer to attributes in the namespaces of the object identified by the path to the left.

There's no notion of scope searching when attributes are referenced. However, if the object qualified is a class instance, then Python also will search for the attribute in the namespaces of accessible class objects. In fact, this is just the definition of attribute inheritance in Python. When a qualified attribute is assigned, the name is created (or changed) in the namespace of the object that was qualified.

### Using name resolution rules

Table 9-3 summarizes the rules for qualified and unqualified name references.

*Table 9-3: Name reference and assignment rules*

| Usage form | Symbol type | Access mode | Action |
|---|---|---|---|
| *name* | Unqualified | Reference | Searches up to three scopes: local, global, built-in |
| *name* = value | Unqualified | Assignment | In the local scope, unless declared global |
| object.*name* | Qualified | Reference | Searches one or more objects' namespaces |
| object.*name* = value | Qualified | Assignment | Assigns attribute in the object's namespace |

In practice, Python namespace rules are trivial to use. But here are a few consequences that illustrate some fundamental class concepts.

***Instances don't have access to class globals.*** Notice that Python's lexical scope rules only apply to code inside a construct (*class*, *def*, module), not when we qualify an object from the outside. As one consequence, there's no way to access a class's global-scope names, by qualifying an instance of a class, or the class itself. For example:

*Example 9-13: File: module.py*

```
globalVar = 99                  a global variable in this module
class C:
    member = globalVar          okay: globalVar visible inside the class statement
I = C()
I.globalVar, C.globalVar        both are undefined attribute errors
```

But this is really what we want. If all names in a class's global scope were accessible as attributes:

- Every variable name in the enclosing module would look like a data member of the class.
- Every function name in the module would look like a method of the class.

The global scope of a class is really only intended for use by its methods; instances only need access to the class's attributes, created by statements in its local scope.

***Accessing class attributes from a method.*** A function in a class (i.e., a method) only has access to its own local scope, and the class's global scope. Note that methods don't have unqualified access to the enclosing class's local namespace, and this is where names of all the class's methods and static members are defined.

Methods follow normal function scope rules: the local scope is the method call, and the global scope is the module surrounding the method's class, not the enclosing class (or the instance subject). But since class locals become attributes in the class object, methods can access class data by either:

- Qualify the *self* argument: *self.member*, since the instance inherits the class's attributes.
- Qualify the *class* object: *class.member*, since classes can be qualified directly.

We've been using both techniques; in general, methods usually qualify *self* to get attributes defined in classes, unless they need to override the inheritance rules that locate the name from the instance. Figure 9-6 illustrates how this works.

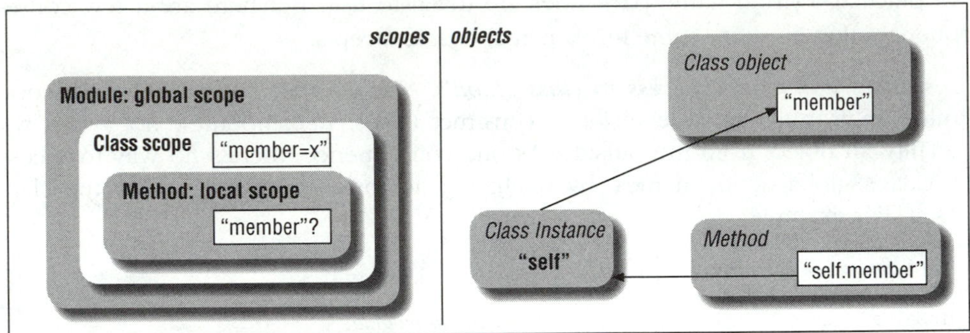


*Figure 9-6: Accessing class data through instances*

Because the method's global scope is the same as the class's global scope, methods can access names global to the class without going through *self*. Use the global name *unqualified*, instead of qualifying *self*. Methods (like all functions) retain a reference to their global namespace, so it can be searched on each call.

***Extending scopes dynamically.*** Since modules and classes are also objects, namespaces aren't really carved in stone: they may contain more attributes than those created by nested statements. Statements just provide initial values for namespace objects. For instance, if we add names to a module's namespace by assigning them to its attributes, functions nested in the module will have access to the new names as global scope variables:

*Example 9-14: File: spam.py*

```
def func(): print message    # not defined in this module file/scope
```

```
% python
>>> import spam
>>> spam.message = 'hello'
>>> spam.func()
hello
```

Although we can change class attributes too, this change only affects instances and subclasses: unlike modules, classes aren't an enclosing scope for deferred code in functions.

***Nested class statements aren't nested scopes.*** Like functions, nested class statements don't imply nested namespaces. A class nested in another scope context (*def*, or another *class*) still has a single local and global scope. Its local scope refers to the statements it directly encloses, and its global scope is the module outside all statements it's nested in. As Figure 9-7 shows, statements in the class don't have unqualified access to names in surrounding statements.

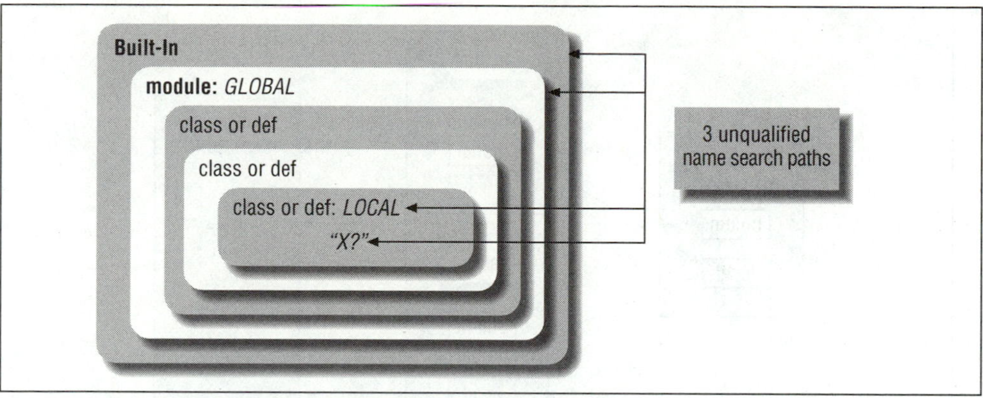


*Figure 9-7: Nested statements aren't nested scopes*

### *Putting namespaces together*

Figure 9-8 and Figure 9-9 summarize namespace link concepts. The first gives the scope view for unqualified references in lexical constructs. The second gives the object namespace view for qualified references. Notice the following points:

*Built-in links*
: All lexical scope constructs (functions, classes, modules) get the names in the `__builtin__` module/scope automatically; it's searched last.

*Class links*
: For classes and modules, the local scope becomes the object's attribute namespace. Class built-in and global scopes only exist for statements nested in the *class* statement.

*Inherit links*
: In classes and instances, the *inherit* component is followed if an attribute name doesn't exist in the object's namespace. Instance type and class-headers define *inherit* links.

*Type instances*
: Instances of built-in or extension datatypes (files, etc.) have an attribute namespace, but they don't participate in either lexical scoping or attribute inheritance.

In the object view seen in Figure 9-9, module and class local scopes become object attribute namespaces. Instances are linked to classes they're created from, and classes are linked to superclasses listed in their statement headers. As we'll see later in the book, datatype attributes are actually implemented in C.

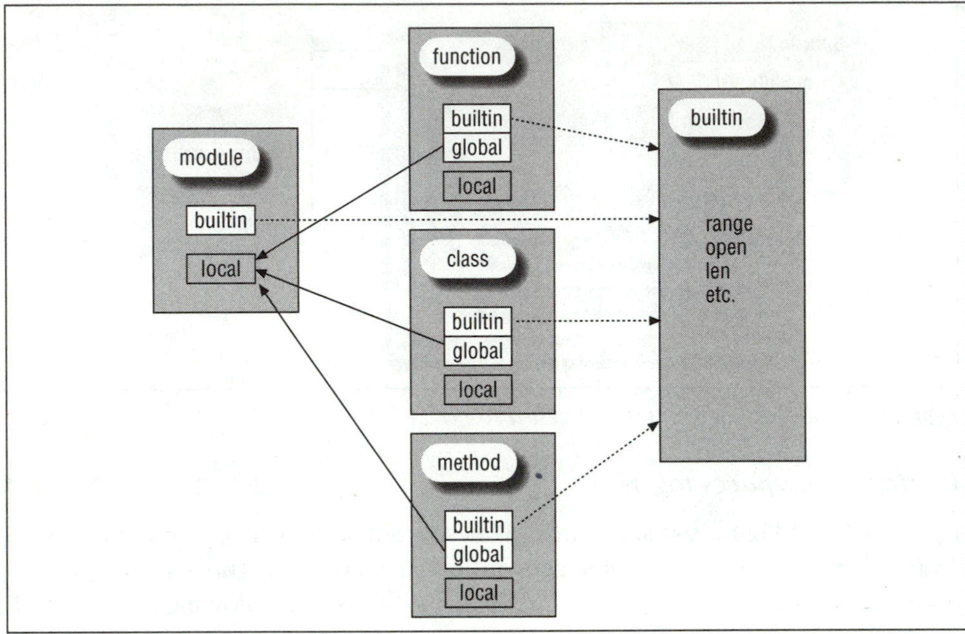


*Figure 9-8: Scope links for unqualified names*

# More on Zen: Class and Instance Namespace Dictionaries

At the end of Chapter 8, we saw that a module's `__dict__` attribute gave access to the module's namespace dictionary. It works exactly the same for classes and class instances: a class `__dict__` is its attribute namespace, and an instance `__dict__` holds attributes assigned to *self* by methods after it's created (or assigned outside the class). To show what happens to names-spaces when using classes and instances, here's an interactive session that tracks the `__dict__` built-in attribute of both.

```
>>> class super:
...     def change(self): self.member = 1
...
>>> class sub(super):
...     def change2(self): self.member2 = 2
...
>>> instance = sub()                              make a 'sub' instance
>>> instance.__dict__                             its namespace starts empty
{}
>>> sub.__dict__                                  class namespaces have methods
{'change2': <function change2 at b7140>}
>>> super.__dict__                                inherited names not copied
{'change': <function change at b76a0>}            but are looked-up when used
```

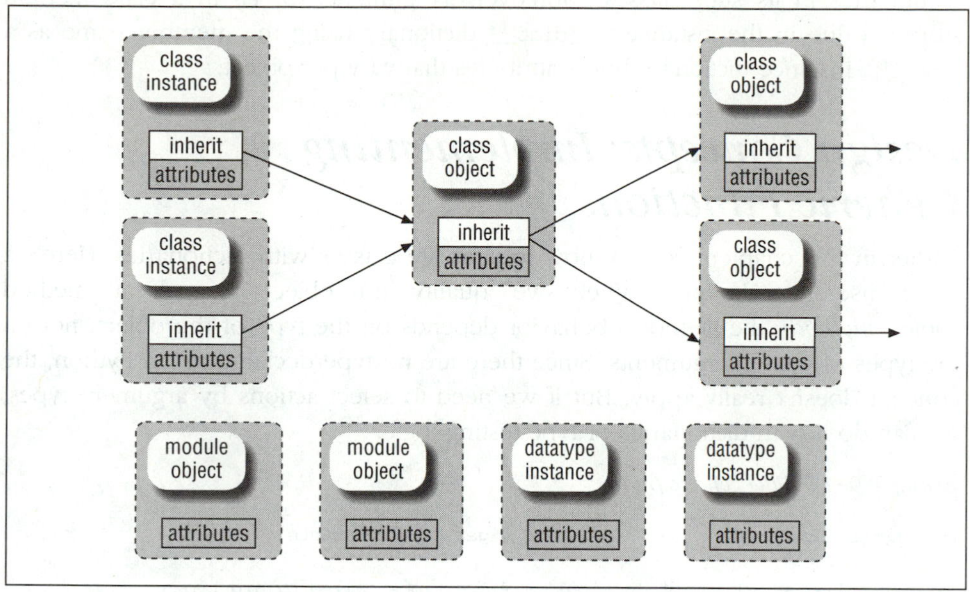


*Figure 9-9: Namespace links for qualified names*

```
>>> instance.change()                              calling inherited methods
>>> instance.__dict__                              changes self's namespace
{'member': 1}
>>> instance.change2()
>>> instance.__dict__                              qualification looks here first
{'member': 1, 'member2': 2}                        then climbs to class __dict__


>>> super.__dict__                                 class namespaces unchanged
{'change': <function change at b76a0>}


>>> sub.change                                     subclasses inherit too
<unbound method super.change>
>>> sub.change(instance)                           call a method manually
>>> instance.__dict__                              changes existing names
{'member': 1, 'member2': 2}


>>> instance
<sub instance at cfb90>
>>> instance.change                                bound methods: instance+method
<method super.change of sub instance at cfb90>     may be called, passed, etc.
```

Class and instance namespaces are almost dictionaries, but inherited attributes aren't copied to lower `__dict__`s. Instead, they're looked up dynamically from classes when referenced. In fact, inheritance is just a matter of searching dictionaries: the instance `__dict__` is searched first, then those of its class, then all the dictionaries in its superclasses. Moreover, assignments to *self* in a class method store a value in the instance's `__dict__` dictionary using the member name as a key. The instance dictionary holds attributes that vary per object.

## Design Concepts: Implementing Generic Functions

Earlier in this chapter, we saw how to simulate classes with dictionaries. Here's a more useful technique. When we qualify an object to call a method (*object.method*), the method's behavior depends on the type of the object, not on the types of passed arguments. Since there are no type declarations in Python, the concept doesn't really apply. But if we need to select actions by argument types, we can do it with dictionaries or type-testing logic:

*Example 9-15: File: generic.py*

```
from types import *                          # get type constants

def action1(x, y, z): print 'action1'    # functions called by arg types
def action2(x, y, z): print 'action2'
def action3(x, y, z): print 'action3'
def action4(x, y, z): print 'action4'
def action5(x, y, z): print 'action5'

Actions =  {                                 # type dispatch table
    IntType:                                 # Actions[type1][type2]
        { IntType:    action1,
          StringType: action2 },
    StringType:
        { ListType:   action3,               # actions can be lambda's too
          StringType: action4 },
    ListType:
        { ListType:   action5 }
}

def action(x, y, z):
    try:
        Actions[type(x)][type(y)](x, y, z)
    except KeyError:
        print 'bad types for action'

if __name__ == '__main__':
    for arg1 in (123, 'ABC', [3]):
        for arg2 in (456, 'XYZ', [4]):
            print arg1, arg2,
            action(arg1, arg2, 'hello')
```

When we run this file as a top-level program, it tests these nine argument type combinations:

```
% python generic.py
123 456 action1
123 XYZ action2
123 [4] bad types for action
ABC 456 bad types for action
ABC XYZ action4
ABC [4] action3
[3] 456 bad types for action
[3] XYZ bad types for action
[3] [4] action5
```

This code relies on the fact that functions are first-class objects again; they're stored in nested dictionaries. It also applies the rule that dictionary keys may be any immutable object. In this instance, the dictionary keys are *type* objects: the result of *type(object)* calls. In a later chapter, we'll see that classes and instances which conform to hashing protocols can be keys too.

We can also use manual type testing in methods, like the *interact* function at the start of the chapter:

```
class Action:
    def action(self, x, y, z):
        if type(x) == IntType:
            if type(y) == IntType:
                ...
            elif type(y) == StringType:
                ...
        elif type(x) == StringType:
            ....
```

or define one subclass per type combination, and make instances of the one we want:

```
class ActionIntInt:
    def action(self, x, y, z): ...

class ActionIntString:
    def action(self, x, y, z): ...

object = ActionIntString().action(x, y, z)
```

In fact, this is the approach we used for menu classes: type-specific subclasses (*DictMenu*, *ListMenu*) handle behavior that varies per type. It's usually possible to implement generic-function behavior with simpler attribute inheritance. For example, rather than analyzing the combination of two objects, it may work better to pass one to a method of the other. Naturally, the best approach depends on your application.

# 10

# *More Class Magic*

*In this chapter:*

- *Deriving Menus from Simpler User Interaction*
- *A Simple User-Interface Subclass: Back to Where We Started?*
- *A Menu-Interface Subclass: Registering Methods*
- *Inheriting from More than One Class*
- *Making Menus Expandable: Overloading Operators*
- *Summary: Python and the OOP Trinity*
- *Where's the Beef?*

## *More Bells, Whistles, and Little Blinking Lights*

In this chapter, we'll introduce a few more features of the menu classes we discussed in Chapter 9, *Moving Menus to Classes.* Although the menu classes are fairly simple examples of applied OOP, they're still candidates for some advanced Python OOP features like operator overloading and multiple inheritance. Many of the OOP topics introduced here will be used extensively in Part 3, *Tools and Applications.*

We'll also study ways to generalize the classes, briefly discuss object-oriented design, and take a look at how Python rates in terms of some common OOP ideas. This chapter ends Part 2, *Language Fundamentals,* and closes with a summary of everything we've learned.

## *Deriving Menus from Simpler User Interaction*

Now that we've looked at classes (the *tool*), there's still the issue of how to model the objects in a problem domain. In general, besides the alternative ways to write classes which we just saw, there is also a wide variety of ways to structure the objects (and hence classes) that participate in any given program. Some structures are better than others: in fact, entire paradigms have sprung up to address these issues.

We won't be able to spend much time on object-oriented design in this book. But to give you an idea of the tradeoffs involved, here's a mutation of the menu system. Suppose we expect to have to support non-menu-based user interaction too, along the lines of the first user interface we built. If this were known ahead of time (and that's usually the "big if"), it might be a better idea to structure our classes with basic interaction at the top, and menus defined as a specialization of the basic interaction class.

*Example 10-1: File: interact.py*

```
class Interact:
    def __init__(self):
        self.prompt = '?'

    def run(self):
        while 1:
            command = self.readCommand()
            if not command:
                break
            result = self.evalCommand(command)
            if result:
                break

    def readCommand(self):
        try:
            return raw_input(self.prompt)
        except:
            return None                          # break loop on ctrl-d


class Menu(Interact):
    def readCommand(self):                       # extend superclass read
        print '\n\tMENU...'                      # print menu items first
        self.showOptions()
        return Interact.readCommand(self)

    def evalCommand(self, cmd):
        try:
            return self.runCommand(cmd)          # catch bad key/index, etc.
        except (EOFError, SystemExit):           # let sys.exit, ctrl-d pass
            return 1                             # but break main loop
        except:
            print "what: '%s'?" % cmd            # return None implicitly
```

*Example 10-1: File: interact.py (continued)*

```
# the rest is exactly the same as menu1.py
# subclasses repeated here for convenience


class DictMenu(Menu):
    def showOptions(self):
        options = self.menu.keys()                    # menu = dictionary
        options.sort()
        for cmd in options: print '\t\t' + cmd

    def runCommand(self, cmd):
        return self.menu[cmd]()                       # call action by name

class ListMenu(Menu):                                 # menu = nested sequences
    def showOptions(self):
        for i in range(len(self.menu)):
            print '\t\t%d) %s' % (i, self.menu[i][0])

    def runCommand(self, cmd):
        try:
            index = eval(cmd)                         # convert string to number
        except:
            raise IndexError
        return self.menu[index][1]()                  # selected by position
```

Here, we've just added an extra superclass above *Menu*, and changed *Menu* to use the hooks defined by this new *Interact* class. The main interaction loop is moved to *Interact*, and *Menu* implements the *readCommand* and *evalCommand* methods, so it works with *Interact*'s protocol. *ListMenu* and *DictMenu* are the same as in module *menu1*, but they're repeated here just for illustration purposes.

In fact, the *DictMenu* and *ListMenu* subclasses we wrote in *menu1.py* will work unchanged, with the new *Menu* class here. We'll get the exact same behavior, if we put them in a separate file, and import *Menu* from this *interact* module, instead of using the original *menu1* Menu. The new *Menu* superclass still calls these subclass's *showOptions* and *runCommand* methods to do type-specific work, as before.

## *New Methods to Extend*

*Menu* extends the *Interact* superclass's *readCommand* menu. Its default action is to read a response from standard input; in *Menu*, we redefine readCommand to first display the menu of options (done in a lower class) but still call *Interact*'s *readCommand* to get the reply. We're really just adding logic to *readCommand*, not replacing it.

## New Blanks to Be Filled

By contrast, Menu's *evalCommand* implements a method that Interact expects but does not define: if it's not defined in a subclass of Interact, we'll get an undefined error when Interact calls it. Such methods are "pure virtual" in the C++ sense: they're not defined in a class, but must be provided by a subclass.

## Interclass Method Calls

When a menu object's *run* method is called, it sets off a series of interclass method calls (sometimes called "messages"). For instance, the *Interact.run* method calls a *readCommand* method to interact with the user. If we're using menus, this winds up calling the *Menu* class's method. This method in turn delegates control to the *showOptions* method. Figure 10-1 shows the way method calls nest in this class system when a *ListMenu* instance is run; the call graph is determined by *ListMenu*'s inheritance rules:

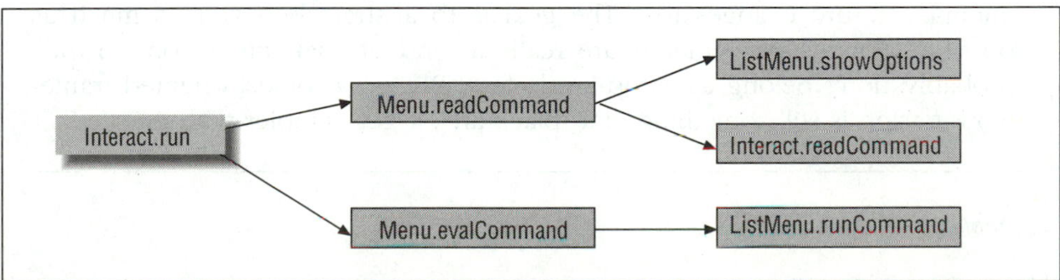


*Figure 10–1: Nested method calls with menus*

Notice that we're really only dealing with a single object here: all of these calls are applied to the same instance, but are routed to different classes it inherits from. In more complex systems, methods may also call methods of objects derived from disjoint class hierarchies (see the discussion of composition later in the chapter).

# A Simple User-Interface Subclass: Back to Where We Started?

Now that simple user interaction is part of our class system, we can use it to rewrite our first user interface script (which we've known as *textpak2*). To simplify, command-line switches have been dropped here too.

## A first stab at object-oriented design

Although we didn't need to change *DictMenu* or *ListMenu* to add the *Interact* class, we did have to change *Menu* radically. *Menu* was completely restructured to use the hooks Interact provides for its subclasses. Interact calls *readCommand* and *evalCommand* methods looked up from the *self* instance: it provides a default *readCommand*, but expects *evalCommand* to be defined below.

In more complex programs, restructuring classes to fit in with new method protocols like this might be a costly transformation. So how can we know what sort of shape our class hierarchies should take? Of course, large frameworks are usually designed ahead of time: it helps to know your requirements early on. If requirements are known, there are a number of design techniques for translating them to class hierarchies.

In more dynamic environments, building in generality and flexibility can minimize future changes too. The goal is to abstract behavior as much as possible. For instance, menus are really a kind of user interaction, so they probably don't belong as a top-level class. But good object-oriented framework design is still something of a "black art"; it gets simpler with practice.

*Example 10-2: File: textpak8.py*

```
#!/usr/local/bin/python

from glob import glob
import pack2, unpack3
from interact import Interact

class TextPak(Interact):
    def __init__(self):
        self.prompt = "tool?  [pack, unpack, stop] "

    def evalCommand(self, name):
        if name == 'pack':
            self.pack()
        elif name == 'unpack':
            self.unpack()
        elif name == 'stop':
            return 1
        else:
            print 'what? - try again'

    def pack(self):
        output  = raw_input("output file name? ")
        pattern = raw_input("files to pack? ")
        pack2.pack_all(output, glob(pattern))
```

*Example 10-2: File: textpak8.py (continued)*

```
    def unpack(self):
        unpack3.unpack_file( raw_input("input file name? ") )

if __name__ == '__main__': TextPak().run()
```

This script defines a subclass of the *Interact* top-level class, and makes an instance of it: we're allowed to make instances of classes anywhere in a hierarchy (not just from the classes at the bottom, as we've done so far). Here, class *TextPak*:

- *Replaces Interact*'s constructor (__init__) with a local version that sets the prompt string.
- *Fills in the blank* in *Interact*, by providing a local *evalCommand* method to process the user's reply.
- *Adds* extra methods locally, to perform the extra user-interaction needed to get pack/unpack details.
- *Inherits Interact*'s *readCommand* method, since it's not redefined here.

Since we've eliminated menus, the method-call nesting picture is simpler when a *TextPak* instance is run, but we've also added extra menu-specific pack/unpack methods, as sketched in Figure 10-2.

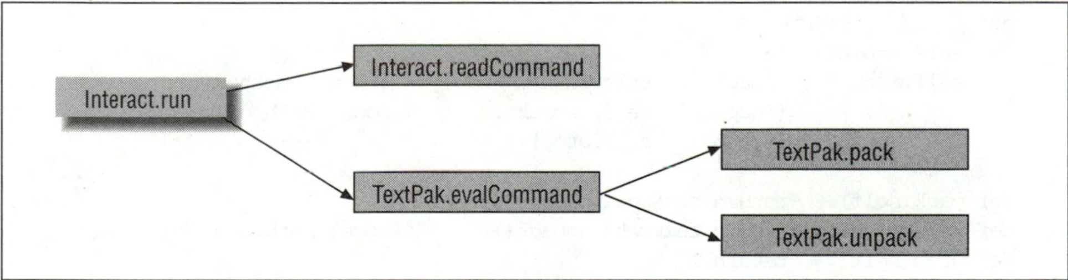


*Figure 10-2: Nested method calls without menus*

When we interact with this script, we get the same behavior as in Chapter 7, *Adding a Simple User Interface*; see the following interaction.

```
% textpak8.py
tool? [pack, unpack, stop] pack
output file name? packed1
files to pack? *.txt
packing: file1.txt
packing: file2.txt
packing: file3.txt
tool? [pack, unpack, stop] s
what? - try again
tool? [pack, unpack, stop] stop
```

### *A method (or two) to the madness*

We seem to have come full circle here: the *textpak8* script doesn't use menus at all! But besides illustrating how we can make instances from more abstract superclasses, this example also moves the pack and unpack functions to methods. As we'll see in a moment, this structure has some interesting consequences.

## A Menu-Interface Subclass: Registering Methods

Here's another subclass of the Interact hierarchy, which carries the local method idea further.

*Example 10-3: File: textpk7b.py*

```
#!/usr/local/bin/python

import textpak2                              # reuse textpak2 funcs
from interact import ListMenu                # get menu interaction

class TextPak(ListMenu):
    def __init__(self):
        self.prompt = '>'
        self.menu = [ ('pack',   self.pack),         # ('key', method)
                      ('unpack', self.unpack),       # bound method objects
                      ('stop',   self.stop) ]

    def pack(self):   return textpak2.pack()
    def unpack(self): return textpak2.unpack()       # local method defs
    def stop(self):   return 1

if __name__ == '__main__': TextPak().run()
```

This TextPak class replaces the superclass's __init__ method, to change the prompt character and assign the menu attribute. To make *menu* an instance attribute containing *self* methods like this, the assignment really has to occur in the class's constructor: we need access to *self* to change the instance, and it's not available at the class level (i.e., outside method *defs*), since there's no instance until a method's called.

This version also introduces bound methods. In Python, even methods are objects (as you might have predicted by now). Since calling a method requires an implicit subject object (*self*), method objects come in two varieties: *bound* or *unbound*, depending on whether the *self* object is known or not. Method objects work something like method pointers in C++, but the concept is simpler to apply in Python: since methods are first-class objects, there is no special syntax or rules.

## *Unbound Methods*

If we access a method function from its class without calling it, we get an unbound method object. We can pass it around, and assign it as usual, but we need to supply a subject object when it's called:

```
method = Menu.run              # assign an unbound method (a function object)
instance = TextPak()           # make an instance object
method(instance)               # call the method with an explicit subject
```

All we're really doing here is making use of the equivalence of instance method calls, and direct class method calls again: when calling methods through the class, we have to supply the instance (*self*) manually, whether the call is delayed like this or not. The three lines above are the same as:

```
instance = TextPak()
Menu.run(instance)
```

## *Bound Methods*

In Example 10-3 above, our menu structure contains method objects that already have an associated subject object (*self*). When we fetch a method by qualifying an instance, Python packages a reference to the instance with the method function, and returns the pair as a bound method object. If we later call this object, we don't need to supply the instance, since it's part of the method object:

```
instance = TextPak()           # make an instance object
method = instance.run          # make a bound-method object
method()                       # call it without an explicit 'self'
```

Our menu structure in the example above includes a bound method:

```
self.pack                      # extract a bound-method object
```

which refers to the *pack* method of the class, plus the instance that *self* refers to while the `__init__` constructor is running. When the *ListMenu* class later calls the object associated with the name *pack*:

```
self.menu[index][1]()          # call a function or bound-method
```

it treats it like a simple function: no instance has to be provided, since it's part of the bound method object. Bound methods let us use simple functions and methods interchangeably: code that's written to call functions can be used to call bound methods without any modifications. In effect, we register an object to be called when an option in the menu list is selected; *ListMenu* doesn't need to know about our classes.

*NOTE* In fact, we'll see later that bound methods like this are used to register callback handlers, to respond to events. In Chapter 11, *Graphical User Interfaces*, we'll associate bound methods with user interface events. On an event (button press, etc.), the *Tk* interface calls back to the registered object to do application-specific processing, as though it were a simple function: it doesn't need to keep track of the instance object that will catch the call.

### *Bound type methods*

Bound methods actually come in two flavors too: class methods, and built-in type methods. For example, methods of *list* objects can be passed around like simple functions:

```
fab4 = ['john', 'paul', 'george']
method = fab4.append                # a bound built-in type method
method('ringo')                     # same as: fab4.append('ringo')
```

The subject list (*fab4*) is bundled with the method-function ("append"), to produce a bound-method object. Methods of all other built-in types (files, dictionaries, etc.) can be used the same way.

Type methods work exactly like class-instance methods. But unlike classes, there's no way to get unbound methods for built-in types; for instance, we can't get to the list *append* method without having a list object to qualify.

***Callable object types.*** In general, there are a variety of callable object types in Python:

- Functions
- Classes
- Unbound class methods
- Bound methods of class instances
- Bound methods of type instances
- Class instances that inherit a `__call__` method

but all are called in the same way: adding parentheses after an object expression. As we've seen, functions are implemented in Python or C; they're used the same way, regardless of the implementation language (*range* and *open* are C functions).

# *Inheriting from More than One Class*

This last version (*textpk7b*) provides pack and unpack methods, which do nothing but call the *textpak2* pack/unpack user interface functions. But we've already made these functions methods, in the *textpak8* simple user interface class above. Is there some way to reuse *textpak8*'s methods, instead of writing new pack and unpack methods locally?

That question leads us naturally to the concept of *multiple inheritance*: by listing more than one superclass in a class's header, we can use methods defined by all listed superclasses. In this case, we can rewrite *textpk7b* to inherit methods from both the list-based menu class (*ListMenu*), and the *textpak8* class. Instead of providing our own pack and unpack methods, we mix them in by inheritance:

*Example 10-4: File: textpk7c.py*

```
#!/usr/local/bin/python

from interact import ListMenu                     # get menu interaction
import textpak8                                   # get pack/unpack methods

class TextPak(ListMenu, textpak8.TextPak):               # Menu's evalCommand,...
    def __init__(self):                                  # textpak8's pack/unpack
        self.prompt = '>'
        self.menu = [ ('pack',   self.pack),             # call inherited methods
                      ('unpack', self.unpack),           # not textpak2 functions
                      ('stop',   self.stop) ]

    def stop(self): return 1

if __name__ == '__main__': TextPak().run()
```

*TextPak* inherits from both *ListMenu* in *interact*, and the TextPak class defined in module *textpak8*. It gets menu-related behavior from *ListMenu*, and the pack and unpack methods from *textpak8*'s *TextPak*. In a sense, the class here is a composite of behaviors taken from the two superclasses, and adds some behavior of its own (*stop*, and __init__).

---

*NOTE* Note the qualification *textpak8.TextPak* in the class header here: we can't use *from* to get *textpak8*'s *TextPak* name, since we're using the same name locally in the importer.

---

So far so good. But there's something "fishy" going on here. If you look back at the *textpak8* module, you'll notice that its *TextPak* class inherits from class *Interact*. But so does the *ListMenu* class we're using here. Along the way, some methods are defined differently.

*evalCommand*

Both *textpak8.TextPak* and *interact.Menu* define a method called *evalCommand*: *textpak8*'s version implements simple interaction, but *Menu*'s does the menu-related processing we need. Climbing up from the new *TextPak* class reaches both versions.

*readCommand*

Because *textpak8's TextPak* inherits from *interact.Interact*, its *readCommand* is the simple version in class Interact. But *ListMenu* inherits Menu's extended version we want here. Both can be reached from the new *TextPak* class.

So which versions of all these methods are really used? Let's first get a clear picture of the modules and classes that play a part in this program. Our module dependencies are shown in Figure 10-3.

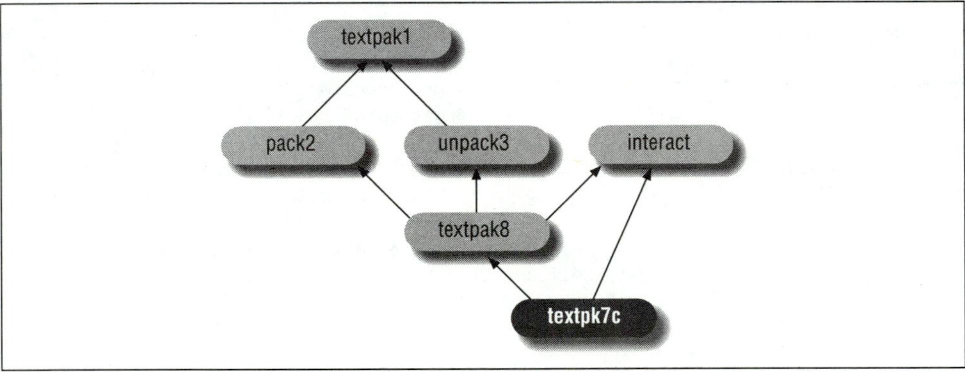


*Figure 10–3: textpk7c's module dependencies*

Note that module *interact* is imported twice: this is one reason Python only loads a module once when first imported, unless you use *reload*. The class-hierarchy is built with classes imported from modules; it's sketched in Figure 10-4.

The rule for resolving attribute-name conflicts has already been mentioned in passing: in Python, inheritance uses a depth-first, left-to-right search. When an attribute's defined in more than one place in the hierarchy implied by superclass lists, Python takes the *closest* and *leftmost* version from the perspective of the object qualified. The solution lies in the order of superclasses in the class statement's header:

```
class TextPak(ListMenu, textpak8.TextPak):
```

By putting *interact.ListMenu* before *textpak8.TextPak* in the superclass list, we make it the *leftmost* branch above the new *TextPak* class here. In terms of inheritance, this makes Python always choose names found in the *ListMenu* branch before looking in the *textpak8.TextPak* branch.

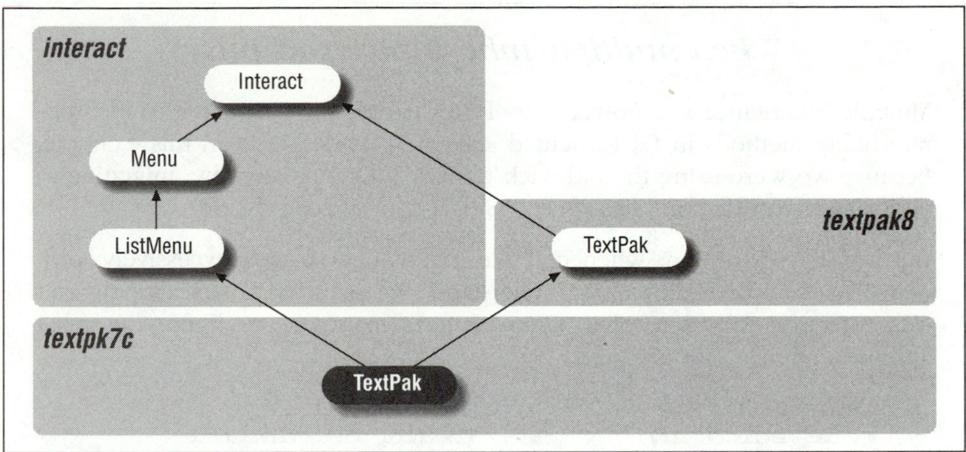


*Figure 10-4: textpk7c's class hierarchy*

In other words, when there's a conflict, we'll use the names found by searching up from *ListMenu*: methods *evalCommand* and *readCommand* come from the *ListMenu* branch, so we get menu-based interaction. *textpak8.TextPak* can really only add attributes that aren't present in *ListMenu*'s hierarchy: *pack* and *unpack* come from this branch, since they don't appear in *ListMenu*'s branch.

In effect, the inheritance link from *textpak8.TextPak* to the *Interact* class is never used here, since we reach *Interact* from *ListMenu* first.

Here's a summary of where all of *textpk7c.TextPak*'s class method attributes come from:

*Table 10-1: Class attribute resolutions*

| Local methods | textpak8.TextPak | ListMenu | Menu | Interact |
|---|---|---|---|---|
| `__init__` | *pack* | *showOptions* | *evalCommand* | *run* |
| *stop* | *unpack* | *runCommand* | *readCommand* | |

The *menu* and *prompt* attributes become instance attributes, so they're not shown in this class inheritance table. The `__init__` constructor is redefined (i.e., replaced) locally by *textpk7c*'s *TextPak* to set the prompt and menu attributes, even though it appears in both Interact and textpak8's TextPak. *stop* is the only new method added to the set of names inherited from listed superclasses.

### *When multiple inheritance gets busy*

Multiple inheritance is a powerful tool. In Chapter 11 we'll use it to incorporate utility methods in GUI oriented classes. It made sense in this example, because we were using the old pack/unpack functions anyhow; migrating to class-based versions of these (*textpak8*) is a natural progression.

But a word of caution: when multiple inheritance is used excessively, programs may become difficult to understand. We may have to search disjoint class hierarchies and resolve name conflicts manually, to figure out what attributes refer to. For instance:

```
class Super1:
    def method2(self):...              # method1 not defined here

class Super2:
    def method1(self):
        self.method2()                 # calls Super1.method2
    def method2(self):...              # not the version here!

class Sub(Super1, Super2):...          # mix Super1 and Super2

object = Sub()
object.method1()                       # call Super2.method1
```

Here, *Super2.method1* will call *Super1*'s *method2*, not its own. This may be what we want, but can lead to confusion when trying to analyze *Super2* by itself. Moreover, when mixing classes developed independently, accidental name clashes may occur. Here, if we really want *Super2*'s *method2*, we need to resolve the conflict manually:

```
class Sub(Super1, Super2):          # use Super1, except its method2
    method2 = Super2.method2        # resolve conflict: class data
```

Like all advanced programming tools, multiple inheritance should be handled with care.

# *More on Exception Handling: Exception Lists*

Let's take a short break from the OOP topics we've been studying to discuss the way these examples catch exceptions. The two *Menu* classes shown in Example 10-5 and Example 10-6 demonstrate different exception-handling techniques. Both use *try* statements with *except* clauses that have a list of exception names, which are enclosed in parentheses.

*Example 10–5: menu1.Menu:*

```
try:
    flag = self.runCommand(command)
except (IndexError, KeyError):
    print "what: '%s'?" % command
else:
    if flag: break
```

*Example 10–6: interact.Menu:*

```
28  try:
29      return self.runCommand(cmd)       # catch bad key/index, etc.
30  except (EOFError, SystemExit):        # let sys.exit, ctrl-d pass
31      return 1                          # but break main loop
32  except:
33      print "what: '%s'?" % cmd         # return None implicitly
```

When exceptions are listed like this, the *except* block is executed if any of the listed exceptions are raised. This is equivalent to listing each exception in a separate *except* clause, but we only have to write the block to be executed once. It is perhaps more interesting that the two Menus use different strategies for catching errors.

*menu1.Menu*
: Catches errors that designate user-entry errors: (a bad sequence index or a bad mapping key), and lets the rest pass: *EOFError*'s percolate to the outer *try* statement, while others are uncaught (and so are fatal). The *else* only runs if *no* exception occurs.

*interact.Menu*
: Catches errors that signal an end of the program and returns 1 to end the interaction loop (Ctrl-D presses, *sys.exit* calls), and assumes the rest are user-entry errors. The *except* at line 32 runs if any other exception occurs.

In effect, *menu1* looks for user-errors, and *interact* looks for exit signals. Neither scheme is foolproof:

- The *menu1* version may assume too few exceptions are user errors: if we add more menu types in the future, it may have to be updated to recognize more exception names as user-entry errors.
- On the other hand, the *interact* version may assume too many exceptions are user-entry errors: if there's a numeric error or misspelled variable in some menu handling code, it may be caught by the empty *except* at line 32 and treated like a user entry error.

If we want to catch exceptions in deeply nested logic or function call chains, we need to be careful not to be too exclusive or inclusive when deciding which exceptions we're interested in.

# Making Menus Expandable: Overloading Operators

One weakness of our menu classes as they currently exist is that we can't access the *menu* object inside without going "behind the back" of the class. For example, if we need to expand a menu, all we can do right now is modify the *menu* attribute inside the Menu instance, and hope nothing breaks in the process.

Of course, we could try to predict everything a client may ever want to do with *menu* and write a method for each. But a simpler idea would be to somehow make menus behave like the type of object *menu* is. For example, to make menu access easier, *ListMenus* could imitate normal lists, and *DictMenus* could respond to the usual dictionary operations. Clients would process menus with familiar but controllable operations.

In this section, we introduce some special methods, previewed in the table below. By defining such methods, our classes can intercept (*overload*) common object operations and perform specialized activities. The end result will be menu objects that support expansion and act more like built-in object types.

*Table 10-2: Special methods for menus*

| Method | Example usage | Role |
|---|---|---|
| `__getattr__` | *menu.append(newOption)* | Delegate method calls to embedded objects |
| `__add__` | *menu + moreOptions* | Overload the + operator to work on menus |
| `__getitem__` | *menu[index]* | Allow menu entries to be fetched by indexing |
| `__setitem__` | *menu[index] = newValue* | Allow menus to be changed by index assignment |

## Catching Attribute Access with Special Methods

In Python, some of this sleight of hand is performed by providing a class method called `__getattr__`. If defined, this method is called whenever an instance is qualified with an attribute name that doesn't exist in the instance or any of its classes (normally an undefined-name error). We can use this as a hook to catch qualifications, and route them to another object that can handle the request.

Since `__getattr__`, like all other methods, is inherited by subclasses, we only have to add it to the *Menu* superclass, to make the hook work for both *ListMenu* and *DictMenu* instances. Here's the new method; the rest of *Menu* and its subclasses remain the same (we'll collect these extensions in a new version below).

```
class Menu:                                 # the menu superclass
    def __getattr__(self, name):            # pass off to 'menu'
        return getattr(self.menu, name)     # keys, append, sort...
```

The *getattr* built-in function fetches a named attribute from any object with attributes. The call *getattr(object, name)* works just like the qualification *object.name*, but *getattr* helps when we don't know the *name* ahead of time: it can be a string created when the program's run. Here, *__getattr__* is passed the attribute-name string when an undefined attribute is accessed, and we use *getattr* to delegate the access to the embedded menu object inside the instance; in general terms:

```
instance.undefined    ...becomes...    instance.__getattr__("undefined")
```

For instance, when we add this method, calls to a *keys* method of a *DictMenu* instance are passed to the dictionary inside the *DictMenu* instance object. Figure 10-5 shows the mapping from qualifications, to classes, and finally to embedded objects:

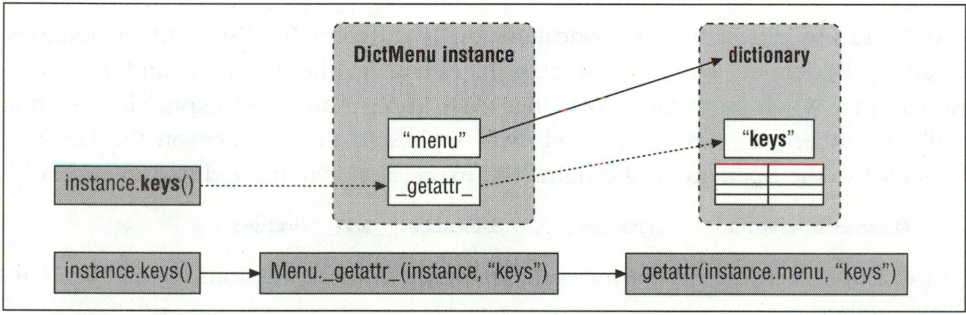


*Figure 10-5: Delegating to embedded objects with __getattr__*

## *Overloading Operators with Special Methods*

The `__getattr__` trick works for *qualifications*: *ListMenu* objects respond to list attributes like *append* and *sort*, and *DictMenu* objects accept qualifications on dictionary attributes like the *keys* and *has_key* methods. But methods are only half the picture when integrating classes into Python's object model: we can also use class instances in expressions by defining specially named class methods.

For instance, it would be convenient to use the + operator to add a set of options to an existing menu, regardless of the kind of menu it is. Python lets us use class instances in expressions if we define methods it can call when the instance appears as an operand. For the + operator, the `__add__` method provides the hook we need.

Here are the required changes. Again, we'll just show methods that are added to the classes: the *Menu* superclass, and other parts of the classes shown here are unchanged. (If you're working along with the examples, a version called *menu1b.py* incorporates the changes so far.)

```
class DictMenu(Menu):                          # a Menu subclass
    def __add__(self, other):                  # on 'menu + other'
        new = DictMenu()                       # make a new instance
        new.menu = {}
        for key in self.menu.keys():
            new.menu[key] = self.menu[key]     # copy 'self' dict
        for key in other.keys():
            new.menu[key] = other[key]         # add other dict
        return new


class ListMenu(Menu):                          # menu = nested sequences
    def __add__(self, other):
        new = ListMenu()                       # make a new instance
        new.menu = self.menu + other           # copy 'self' list
        return new                             # add other list
```

Since the implementation of concatenation is different for lists and dictionaries, `__add__` is defined lower in the class hierarchy, in the *ListMenu* and *DictMenu* subclasses. When an instance of either class appears in a "+" expression, Python calls the inherited `__add__` method, with *self* set to the instance on the left, and *other* set to the operand on the right. The expression is translated to a method call:

```
(instance + value)    ...becomes...    instance.__add__(value)
```

For example, Figure 10-6 illustrates the mapping from expressions to the *DictMenu* class method.

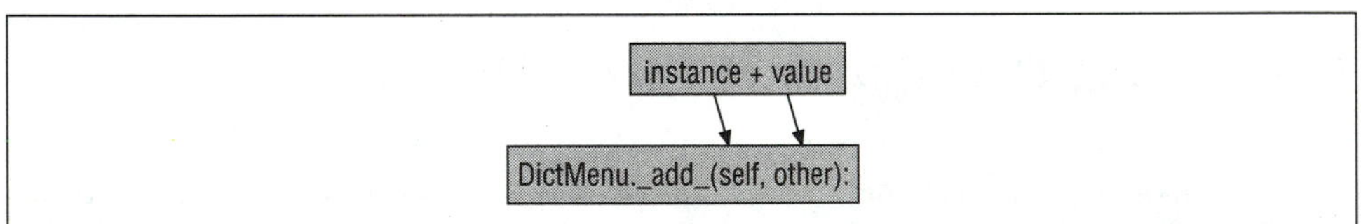


*Figure 10-6: Operators and methods*

### *Making new class-instances, versus changing in place*

To allow menu addition in a larger expression, the `__add__` methods above make and return new class instances, instead of changing the operand (*self*) in-place. Even though methods can change *self* (since it's a mutable argument), it's usually a bad idea to let + change its operands directly. But if we really want to alter the menu used in an expression (for example, to simulate C's += operator), we can do the following.

```
class DictMenu(Menu):
    def __add__(self, other):
        for key in other.keys():                    # change my-self
            self.menu[key] = other[key]             # add other dict
        return self                                 # return me

class ListMenu(Menu):
    def __add__(self, other):
        self.menu = self.menu + other               # change self in-place
        return self                                 # I'm the result too
```

We also went out of our way to copy the *menu* data structure too: since dictionaries and lists are both mutable objects, we need to be careful to accommodate the object-sharing semantics of Python assignment. If we would have assigned *self.menu* to the new instance's *menu* attribute instead of copying it over:

```
class DictMenu(Menu):
    def __add__(self, other):
        new = DictMenu()                            # make a new instance
        new.menu = self.menu                        # the 2 share a dictionary
        for key in other.keys():
            new.menu[key] = other[key]              # add other dict- to both!
        return new

class ListMenu(Menu):
    def __add__(self, other):
        new = ListMenu()                            # make a new instance
        new.menu = self.menu                        # the 2 share a list
        for item in other:
            new.menu.append(item)                   # add item- to both!
        return new
```

then the new instance and *self* would share the same list or dictionary; changing it for the new instance would also change it for the *self* operand. In effect, we would be altering the original menu, as though we hadn't made a new instance at all.

## Making Menus Respond to Indexing Operations

So far, menus can be processed using the methods of the underlying object, and by using the + operator to concatenate additional options. The `__getattr__` method lets us apply list and dictionary methods to menu instances, and `__add__` overloads +. But we can't yet change items in dictionary-based menus in place: *append* (and other) methods alter list-based menus, but there's no equivalent methods for dictionaries.

We might get around this, if indexing could be overloaded too: *menu[index]* would fetch an item out of a wrapped menu, and *menu[index]=value* would assign to an index. Such an extension would let us expand dictionary-based menus by assigning to new keys, and change menus by assigning to existing keys or offsets.

## Copying lists and dictionaries

The *append* list method is used here to extend the list in place. Copying a list is easy, if we're also expanding it. The + concatenation operator always creates a new list object, instead of extending an existing one. But if we ever really need to copy a list to avoid sharing objects, it's simple. Because slicing always makes a new object, we just assign a slice of the whole list, instead of the list itself. *list[:]* extracts all items and puts them in a new list object.

```
X = [1, 2, 3]       # a new list
Y = X               # a reference: X and Y share the same list
Z = X[:]            # make a copy: X and Z differ (or X+[], or X*1)
Y[0] = 4            # changes X[0] too
Z[0] = 5            # only changes Z
```

*X+[]* and *X*1* would copy *X* too. Copying dictionaries requires an explicit loop over its contents: since dictionaries aren't sequences, we can't use the + operator to concatenate them. *DictMenu*'s `__add__` iterates over the old dictionary and the extension, assigning all keys in both to the new dictionary.

Notice that strings and tuples can be copied with sequence operations too, but it's usually not as important as for lists. Since they are both immutable, their components won't be changed unexpectedly even if they're referenced elsewhere in a program.

Again, special methods do the trick. To intercept class-instance indexing, we define another specially-named method: `__getitem__`. If defined, Python maps index operations to method calls, much like the + operator we saw earlier. To catch assignment to indexes, we provide a `__setitem__` method; the mapping from assignment statements to class methods is similar, but the value assigned is passed to the method too:

```
instance[index]            ...becomes...   instance.__getitem__(index)
instance[index] = value    ...becomes...   instance.__setitem__(index, value)
```

Since the indexing operation is used for both sequences and mappings (we can put either *offsets* or *keys* in the square brackets ([]) ), we only need to define these methods once, at the *Menu* superclass level. The list and dictionary menus inherit it as usual:

```
class Menu:
    def __getitem__(self, index):               # on 'menu[index]', 'in'
        return self.menu[index]
    def __setitem__(self, index, value):        # on 'menu[index] = value'
        self.menu[index] = value
```

These new methods just pass off the index operation to the embedded list or dictionary referenced by the *menu* attribute. Figure 10-7 shows the mapping from index operations to Menu class methods.

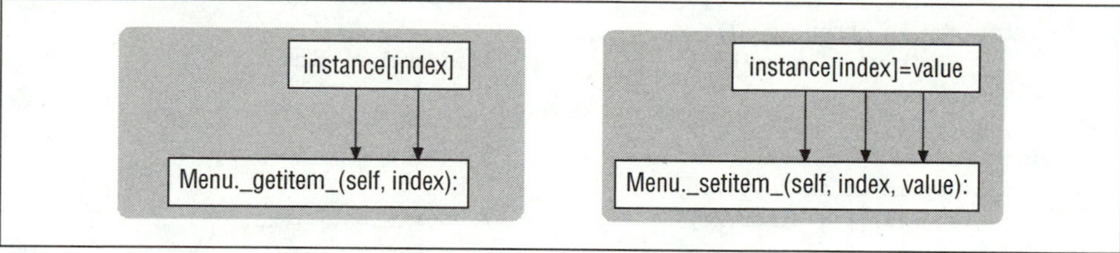


*Figure 10-7: Indexing and methods*

## *Coding the Enhancements*

Let's pull these ideas together: here's a version of the *menu1* classes, which illustrates our three new extensions and other concepts we've talked about. We'll discuss its features following the code below.

*Example 10-7: File: menu1c.py*

```
class Menu:
    def __init__(self, start=None):              # inherited constructor
        self.menu = start or self.empty()        # passed-in or default

    def __getitem__(self, index):                # on 'menu[index]', 'in'
        return self.menu[index]                  # index a wrapped menu

    def __setitem__(self, index, value):         # on 'menu[index] = value'
        self.menu[index] = value                 # set a menu's key/index

    def __getattr__(self, name):                 # on 'menu.other'
        return getattr(self.menu, name)          # keys, append, sort...

    def run(self, prompt='?'):                   # a 'real' method
        try:
            while 1:                             # common interactive loop
                print '\n\tMENU...'
                self.showOptions()
                command = raw_input(prompt)
                try:
                    flag = self.runCommand(command)
                except (IndexError, KeyError):
                    print "what: '%s'?" % command
                else:
                    if flag: break
        except EOFError: pass                    # ctrl-d still exits all

class DictMenu(Menu):
    def empty(self): return {}                   # new dict each time
```

*Example 10-7: File: menu1c.py (continued)*

```
    def __add__(self, other):                # on 'dictmenu + other'
        new = DictMenu()                     # make a new instance
        for key in self.keys():
            new[key] = self[key]             # copy 'self' dict
        for key in other.keys():
            new[key] = other[key]            # add other dict
        return new

    def extend(self, other):                 # change menu in-place
        for key in other.keys():
            self[key] = other[key]           # uses __setitem__

    def showOptions(self):                   # more 'real' methods
        options = self.keys()                # uses __getattr__
        options.sort()
        for cmd in options: print '\t\t' + cmd

    def runCommand(self, cmd):
        return self[cmd]()                   # uses __getitem__

class ListMenu(Menu):
    def empty(self): return []

    def __add__(self, other):                # on 'listmenu + other'
        return ListMenu(self.menu + other)   # make a new instance

    def extend(self, other):                 # change menu in-place
        self.append(other)                   # uses __getattr__

    def showOptions(self):
        i = 0                                # 'in' uses __getitem__
        for name, func in self:
            print '\t\t%d) %s' % (i, name); i=i+1

    def runCommand(self, cmd):
        try:
            index = eval(cmd)                # convert string to number
        except:
            raise IndexError
        return self[index][1]()              # uses __getitem__
```

### Points to ponder

These classes are used in exactly the same way as the prior *menu1* examples. Here are some points to notice:

*self by itself*

The `__getattr__` and `__getitem__` hooks are used inside the methods of these classes too. Since *self* is a *Menu* instance too, we can index it directly, and call menu object attributes, without qualifying the *menu* attribute. Because of this, the `__add__` methods here are simpler than the previous versions.

*Expanding in place*
: The + operator still makes new instances as before, but an extra *extend* method is provided as a convenience, for changing menus in place.

*Menu iteration*
: *for* loops and *in* membership tests both work by indexing an object repeatedly, starting at offset 0, until an *IndexError* is raised. Because of this, `__getitem__` lets us iterate through *ListMenu* instance items like normal sequences (*showOptions*). We can't iterate through *DictMenus*, since dictionaries aren't sequences.

*Default values*
: Instead of extending the `__init__` method inherited from *Menu*, we define an *empty* method in the subclasses, to build a default initial value for menus; it varies per menu type. The *start or self.empty()* expression in *Menu*'s constructor picks the subclass default, if a value isn't passed in. The *empty* methods always make a new default value each time it is needed; we'll see why this matters later.

*Menu concatenation*
: Since menus now respond to indexing, we can concatenate two *DictMenus* with a + expression: *menu1* + *menu2*. The `__add__` method just indexes through the keys of *menu2*, regardless of what kind of object it is. For *ListMenus*, this won't work: we need to add a `__radd__` method to handle cases where a ListMenu appears on the right of a +. We'll fix this problem too.

With these extensions, there's now more to menus than what our classes define. Menus can be processed by using +, indexing, and all the methods defined for lists and dictionaries (and other menu types we might add in the future). The methods defined in these classes are just a part of the operations menus support. In fact, to clients, menus look like lists and dictionaries, with extra menu-specific methods added by the classes.

## Testing Expandable Menus

Finally, let's test the extensions in *menu1c* interactively to see how they work. We'll use a simple test module again to define menus:

*Example 10-8: File: menutest.py*

```
d = { 'spam': lambda:1, 'ham': lambda:1 }
l = [('eggs', lambda:0), ('toast', lambda:0)]
```

## *Other special method names*

Although these classes imitate much of the behavior of real lists and dictionaries, there's still a bit more work to do, to make the equivalence complete. We've only seen two operators overloaded so far: `__add__` has a set of relatives for overloading the rest of Python's operator set, and `__getitem__` has cousins that handle slicing, calculating lengths, etc. Binary operators have versions for right-side appearances too (`__radd__`).

Methods like `__getattr__` are part of Python's metaclass protocol: methods that deal with a class's internal implementation, instead of its exported behavior. There are other metaclass methods for catching assignments to attributes, calling a class instance, etc. Other special methods do things like printing, converting to other types, and more. Here's a sampling of some of the other common hooks:

| | |
|---|---|
| `__and__` | Intercepts & operator expressions |
| `__rand__` | Intercepts appearances on the right side of the "&" operator |
| `__setattr__` | Catches assignment to all attributes |
| `__getslice__` | Intercepts *[i:j]* slicing operations |
| `__cmp__` | On comparisons (<, ==, etc.), returns -1, 0, or 1, like C's *strcmp* |
| `__hash__` | Computes a unique identifying integer for adding to dictionaries |
| `__str__` | Converts an instance to a string for printing |
| `__del__` | Is called when a instance is deleted (garbage-collected) |
| `__call__` | Intercepts calls on an instance object (*instance()*) |
| `__len__` | Responds to the *len* built-in function |

The complete list of special methods appears in Chapter 13, *Implementing Objects*; we'll use most later.

Here's how the example menus are grown:

*ListMenu*
: We can expand a list menu by using the + operator with a list of tuples, or by calling the list *append* method on a *ListMenu*. They can be changed by assigning to their offsets.

*DictMenu*
: Similarly, *DictMenus* can be expanded by using + and a dictionary of new options, but there's no *append* equivalent: they expand or change in-place by assigning to keys, as shown.

```
>>> import menutest
>>> from menu1c import DictMenu, ListMenu
>>> x = DictMenu(menutest.d)                MAKE A DICTIONARY-MENU...
>>> x.run()                                 menu set in Menu.__init__

        MENU...
                ham
                spam
?<ctrl-d>
>>>
>>> x.keys()                                use "keys" dictionary method:
['spam', 'ham']                             calls Menu.__getattr__
>>> x.has_key('spam')
1
>>> x['ham']                                index a DictMenu directly:
<function <lambda> at b7280>                calls Menu.__getitem__
>>> x = x + { 'toast' : lambda:0 }          use overloaded "+" operator:
>>> x.keys()                                calls DictMenu.__add__
['ham', 'spam', 'toast']
>>> x.run()

        MENU...
                ham
                spam
                toast
?<ctrl-d>
>>>
>>> x['eggs'] = lambda:1                    expand by key assignment:
>>> x.run()                                 calls Menu.__setitem__

        MENU...
                eggs
                ham
                spam
                toast
?eggs
>>>
>>> y = ListMenu()                          MAKE A LIST-MENU...
>>> y.menu                                  menu set to 'empty' in __init__
[]
>>> y.run()

        MENU...
?<ctrl-d>
>>>
>>> y = y + menutest.l                      use overloaded '+' operator:
>>> y.run()                                 calls ListMenu.__add__

        MENU...
                0) eggs
                1) toast
?<ctrl-d>
>>>
>>> y.append(('spam', lambda:0))            use list methods: __getattr__
```

```
>>> y.sort()                                    expand with 'append'
>>> y.run()

        MENU...
                0) eggs
                1) spam
                2) toast
?<ctrl-d>
>>> y[1]                                        use list indexing: __getitem__
('spam', <function <lambda> at c33a0>)
>>> y[1][0]
'spam'
>>> y[1] = ("SPAM", y[1][1])                    change part of the ListMenu
>>> y.run()

        MENU...
                0) eggs
                1) SPAM
                2) toast
?<ctrl-d>
>>>
>>> y = y + [('ham', lambda:0), ('stop', lambda:1)]
>>> y.run()

        MENU...
                0) eggs
                1) SPAM
                2) toast
                3) ham
                4) stop
?4
>>>
```

### *Testing menu concatenation*

Now we'll see menu concatenation in action. This section also shows why making multiple *DictMenu* instances can be a useful thing: client programs can combine menus as needed. The methods of the Menu class really do make *DictMenus* look like normal mappings: *DictMenu.*__add__ indexes the right operand by key as usual.

```
>>> m1 = DictMenu(menutest.d)
>>> m2 = DictMenu({'eggs': lambda:0, 'toast': lambda:1})
>>> m1.run()

        MENU...
                ham
                spam
?<ctrl-d>
>>> m2.run()

        MENU...
                eggs
```

```
                    toast
?<ctrl-d>
>>> m3 = m1 + m2                      concatenate two menus...
>>> m3.run()                          __add__ does the right thing

        MENU...
                    eggs
                    ham               we have three DictMenus now
                    spam              each has its own "menu" attribute
                    toast
?toast
>>>
```

Of course, expandable menus will be more useful when applied inside another program that builds up menus dynamically. But by testing classes interactively like this, we're able to isolate problems early. This is another example of incremental testing at work.

## *Two Final Tweaks: Supporting General + Expressions*

Although the extended menu classes already handle most operations as they currently exist, they still have two subtle limitations we'll touch on briefly here before leaving this example.

### *Making ListMenu concatenation work*

As noted earlier, we can't concatenate two *ListMenus* yet, because the `__add__` method doesn't handle cases where a *ListMenu* appears on the right. When the current `__add__` runs: "self.menu + other", there's no conversion if *other* is a *ListMenu* too. One way to fix this is to iterate over the right operand, instead of using + concatenation. Here's the method to change in *menu1c*:

```
class ListMenu(Menu):
    def __add__(self, other):                # on 'listmenu + other'
        new = self.menu[:]                   # copy my list
        for x in other:                      # loop over other: a menu too?
            new.append(x)                    # like DictMenu.__add__
        return ListMenu(new)                 # make a new instance
```

### *Making menus work on the right side of a +*

This new `__add__` handles both *ListMenu* + *list* and *ListMenu* + *ListMenu* cases now. If *other* is a *ListMenu* too, we iterate over it like a sequence using `__getitem__`. But *list* + *ListMenu* cases still won't work: Python raises an error, because it expects to find a different method. To handle this case, we define a symmetric `__radd__` method in *ListMenu* too. Since we know *other* isn't a *ListMenu*, it's simpler, as shown in the following code example.

```
class ListMenu(Menu):
    def __radd__(self, other):                # on 'non-listmenu + listmenu'
        return ListMenu(other + self.menu)    # order matters for sequences
```

*DictMenu*'s code handles *DictMenu* + *dictionary* and *DictMenu* + *DictMenu* cases. Supporting *dictionary* + *DictMenu* cases is even simpler than for lists: since the order of insertion doesn't matter for dictionaries, we can reuse the existing __add__ method, by assigning it to the __radd__ attribute:

```
class DictMenu(Menu):
    def __add__(self, other):
        ...as is
    __radd__ = __add__                        # '+' is transitive for mappings
```

When a *DictMenu* is on the right and the left operand isn't a *DictMenu*, *other* will be the left operand. But since it usually doesn't matter whether *other* or *DictMenu* is added to the new menu first, __add__ does the trick. In the general case, expressions are mapped to __add__ and __radd__ methods (and their relatives) as shown in Figure 10-8.

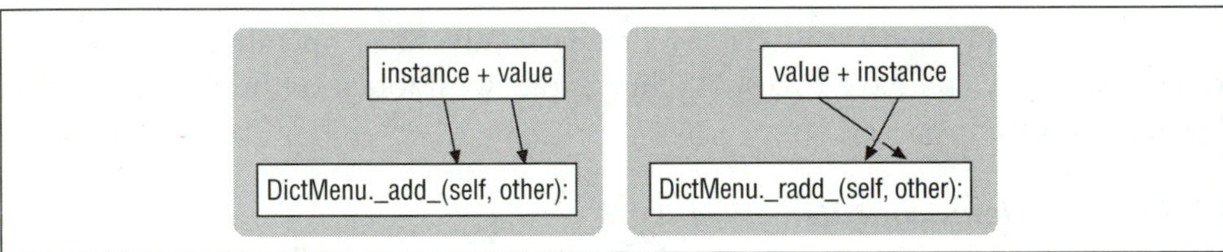


*Figure 10–8: Right-side operators and methods*

When both operands are instances (*instance* + *instance*), Python tries to run the __add__ method first, if it can be found from the instance. Our menu __add__ methods handle these cases too. In general:

- __add__ handles: *Menu* + *any-value* expressions
- __radd__ handles: *nonmenu* + *Menu* expressions

where *any-value* can also be another Menu instance. There are other protocols for supplying conversions to be run when operators are applied, but we won't deal with them until later in the book.

## Avoiding Shared Mutable Objects in Defaults

In the *menu1c* classes discussed above, we were careful to create default initial menu values using methods. Here are the relevant lines from the example.

```
class Menu:
    def __init__(self, start=None):              # inherited constructor
        self.menu = start or self.empty()        # passed-in or default

class DictMenu(Menu):
    def empty(self): return {}                   # new dict each time

class ListMenu(Menu):
    def empty(self): return []
```

Each time the Menu class's constructor calls one of the *empty* methods, it generates a new default-value object. At first glance, this might seem excessive. But it's essential, and illustrates an important concept. For instance, suppose we tried to save a method call by using the class members, as follows:

```
class Menu:
    def __init__(self, start=None):
        self.menu = start or self.empty          # save a method call

class DictMenu(Menu):
    empty = {}                                   # class data

class ListMenu(Menu):
    empty = []                                   # set during "class" run
```

This procedure won't work. As we learned in Chapter 9, assigning to names in classes creates class attributes. Since *empty* will be shared by all instances in this version, every instance that passes no arguments to the constructor will get the same dictionary or list. And as we saw earlier, changing a shared mutable object changes it for every reference. When we expand a menu in place, we'll change the underlying menu object for every class instance created with the default:

```
>>> m1 = DictMenu(); m2 = DictMenu()        make 2 empty DictMenus
>>> m1 = m1 + menutest.d                    changes m2 too!

>>> l1, l2 = ListMenu(), ListMenu()         make 2 empty ListMenus
>>> l2.extend(('spam', lambda:1))           changes list object in both
```

Putting the default in a method's header:

```
def __init__(self, menu={}):        # doesn't make a new '{}' when called
```

won't help either: the default argument value is evaluated once, when the *def* statement runs, not when the function is called. When you code a default this way, it still won't make a new dictionary object each time a menu is created without arguments; instances would still share the empty default object.

### *Create defaults by executing code*

When we want to avoid object sharing, programs should be written such that default values are created by code that's actually executed when a constructor runs. By returning defaults from a method, the original version guarantees that we get a new object for each default instance. Another way to ensure unique objects is to define constructors in the subclasses to create a default value for *menu*:

```
class Menu:
    def __init__(self, start):                # inherited constructor
        self.menu = start                     # 'start' menu required here

class DictMenu(Menu):
    def __init__(self, menu=None):
        Menu.__init__(self, menu or {})       # makes a new dict each time

class ListMenu(Menu):
    def __init__(self, menu=None):
        Menu.__init__(self, menu or [])       # makes a new list each time
```

Because the default value has been moved to code that's really executed each time an instance is made, we get a new empty object for each one that uses the default.

### *Making mutable objects work for you*

These issues are subtle but rare in practice. If we apply a few common sense conventions (like creating mutable defaults in methods), we're always safe. By understanding Python's object semantics, side effects are easy to recognize, and even become a useful tool. In fact, sometimes we really want shared objects.

Here's an example. We've seen that there's no direct equivalent to call-by-reference argument passing in Python. Instead, arguments are passed by assignment: since assignment just creates references to shared objects, there's no alias between an argument name in the caller and callee. But we can use the notion of assignment as a tool, to simulate the call-by-reference effect in a variety of ways:

- By passing a mutable list object, which can be changed in place:

```
def func(a):
    a[0] = 'new-value'          # 'a' references a list
    a[1] = a[1] + 1             # change a shared object

args = ['old-value', 99]
func(args)
use args[0], args[1]            # args is ['new-value', 100]
```

- By passing a mutable dictionary object:

```
def func(args):
    args['a'] = 'new-value'      # args is a dictionary
    args['b'] = args['b'] + 1    # change it in-place

args = {'a': 'old-value', 'b': 99}
func(args)
use args['a'], args['b']
```

- Or by bundling values in a mutable class instance:

```
class callByRef: pass            # an empty class

def func(args):
    args.a = 'new-value'         # args is a callByRef
    args.b = args.b + 1          # change object in-place

args = callByRef()
args.a = 'old-value'
args.b = 99
func(args)
use args.a, args.b
```

Of course, there's usually no reason to get this complicated. As we saw earlier, the easiest way to simulate call-by-reference is by returning a tuple containing the final values of arguments:

```
def func(a, b):
    a = 'new-value'          # a and b are local names
    b = b + 1                # names assigned new objects
    return a, b              # return new objects

x, y = 'old-value', 99
x, y = func(x, y)            # use tuple assignment
use x, y
```

The point to notice is that once you understand that assignment simply creates references to shared objects, all its uses start to look the same. Moreover, shared objects are often exactly what we need.

# *Summary: Python and the OOP Trinity*

OOP is typically characterized as supporting three concepts: inheritance, polymorphism, and encapsulation. We've mostly dealt with inheritance so far, but we have used polymorphism without discussing it much. And depending on which definition you prefer, we may or may not have applied encapsulation already. Let's put on our theorist hats for just a moment, and see how Python stacks up in terms of these concepts.

### *Packaging objects: members, methods, operators, and metaclass support*

So how do all the extra features we added here tie in with OOP's goals? They are really just extra encapsulation tools. When we write generally useful classes, operator overloading and metaclass protocol are often a normal part of the package, along with more basic methods and members.

Operator overloading is probably a familiar concept, if you've used C++. Metaclass protocol is a more dynamic concept, but `__getattr__` is roughly like overloading the -> dereferencing operator in C++. Technically, we could write classes without both. For example, we might require method calls instead of allowing menus in expressions, and could define wrappers for the methods relevant to a menu type (*append*, *keys*, etc.), instead of using `__getattr__`:

```
class ListMenu:
    def append(self, other):
        self.menu.append(other)     # wrap list methods...
    def sort(self):
        self.menu.sort()            # instead of __getattr__
    def index(self, index):
        return self.menu[index]     # L.index(i) versus L[i]
    def add(self, other):
        return ListMenu(self.menu + other)  # L.add(v) versus L+V
```

But operators and metaclass methods can enhance a class's usability dramatically. `__getattr__` is much more convenient, if there are many methods in a wrapped object: a single `__getattr__` suffices for all. And operator overloading lets us manipulate objects with familiar Python operations. The end result is a simpler, more consistent interface.

## *Inheritance*

This was the real secret behind our menu classes. We've already discussed what inheritance means in detail. By using inheritance, we were able to eliminate redundancy and move toward a decentralized granularity, where extensions were packaged as separate subclasses, instead of being mixed together in a function.

As we've seen earlier, classes inherit attributes from the superclasses they list in their headers, and instances inherit from the classes they're created from. We've also seen that Python supports multiple inheritance, and that it resolves name conflicts by taking the first occurrence of a name found during a depth-first, left-to-right search of the instance's class hierarchy.

## *Polymorphism*

Roughly, *polymorphism* refers to generic operations whose behavior is determined by the type of the operation's subject. Although we didn't point it out, polymorphism allowed us to get rid of the type-switch logic of the generic *interact* function in the function-based menu module. In Python, every time an object is qualified:

```
object.attribute
```

the meaning of *attribute* depends on the type of *object*. In C++ terms, Python methods and data members are all virtual: i.e., their behavior depends on the object being qualified. We used this notion in our menus to delegate type-specific behavior to more specific subclasses. When the *menu1.Menu* class calls:

```
self.showOptions()
self.runCommand(command)
```

the behavior of *showOptions* and *runCommand* depends on what *self* is: a *ListMenu* or *DictMenu*. Although these methods vary depending on whether a list or dictionary menu is used, Menu doesn't have to know which version is used. In fact, it shouldn't—we might add more menu types later (see Figure 10-9). Since logic is associated with objects, the type of the menu object will determine the correct action automatically.

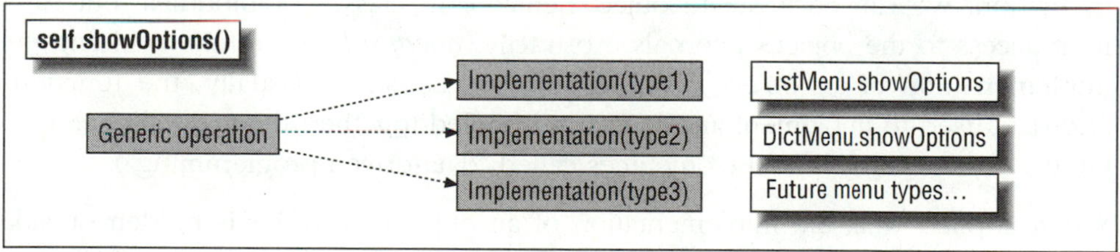


*Figure 10-9: Polymorphism*

Python's lack of type declarations almost forces polymorphism to be a basic property of the language. Because attribute names are never resolved until run-time, Python is heavily polymorphic by nature. Instances and classes are both first-class objects that can be passed around and used generically. For example, suppose we pass an instance of the *Menu* class to a routine that calls objects' *run* methods:

```
def doit(x): x.run()          # execute this object's "run"

x = TextPak()                 # make an instance derived from "Menu"
doit(x)                       # pass it to doit
```

Here, *doit* has no idea what sort of object is passed in: the call to *run* depends completely on the type of *x*. In fact, run-time attribute lookup accounts for much of the dynamic nature of OOP in Python. Not only is it inconvenient to know what qualifying an object will do, it is also often impossible: subclasses may be added in the future, attributes might be added on the fly, etc.

### *Virtual methods versus generic functions*

On an abstract level, Python polymorphism is implemented by attribute inheritance. Since qualifications are resolved by inheritance, an object's behavior is determined by its own attributes, plus its inheritance rules. Because it is a typeless language, Python doesn't support the notion of generic function polymorphism used in some other languages—multiple definitions of a function, selected according to the *types* of arguments passed in.

In Python, the type of the single qualified object determines the action. This policy is simpler to use: generic functions imply *strong typing* (with all its associated complexity), and usually apply complicated resolution rules to pick a function. As we saw in Chapter 9, generic functions can be implemented in Python if needed; but it's often possible to accomplish the same effect with much simpler instance qualification polymorphism.

## *Encapsulation*

In Python, we can encapsulate object behavior in classes or modules, but can't limit access to the object's internals. Abstractly, *encapsulation* refers to hiding the implementation of an object within a software construct. Usually, the functions and data used to implement an object are bundled together; this naturally leads to OOP's object-centric model (sometimes called "data-driven programming").

When applied well, the implementation of an object's behavior is hidden outside the package. Externally, clients follow protocols (an API) for manipulating an object—method calls, expression operators, etc.—without having to know anything about the internals of the object package itself. Encapsulation in the OOP sense is just a step up from the black box model of functions: objects are black boxes too, but they use both functions and data to implement behavior.

In Python both modules and classes can be used to implement behavior. Both can contain logic and data used to model an object (see Figure 10-10). Both export a set of methods that may be used to manipulate the modeled object. But classes take encapsulation even further: by overloading operators, instances integrate more closely with other objects. In fact, given a complete set of class operators, clients often don't need to know that they're processing class instances at all: they look like normal built-in types (lists, dictionaries, etc.).

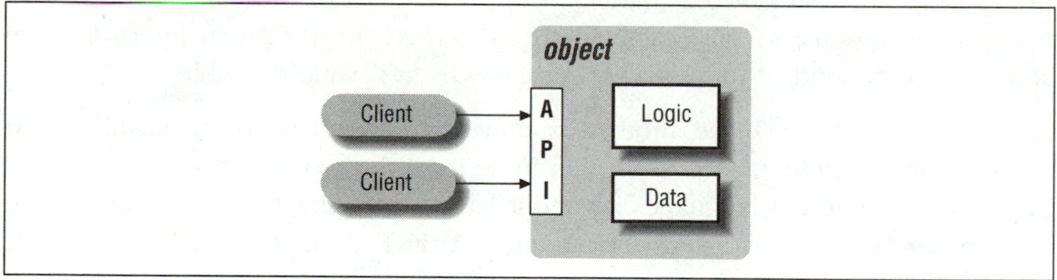


*Figure 10-10: Encapsulation*

But in general, modules and classes can both implement abstract data types: objects with encapsulated implementations.

To some extent, polymorphism and encapsulation go hand in hand. For example, when the *menu1.Menu* superclass calls methods implemented by its subclasses:

```
self.showOptions()
self.runCommand(command)
```

their behavior depends on the type of *self* (polymorphism). But *Menu* is ignorant about what these calls really do: their effects are hidden inside the subclass's implementation of the methods (encapsulation).

---

*NOTE* Some texts use the term encapsulation to refer to hiding logic, some use it for hiding data, and some use both meanings. Encapsulating logic is sometimes called procedure abstraction, and hiding data might be called data abstraction, or information hiding. Procedure abstraction is what we do with functions; data abstraction requires a way to store information along with procedures. In this book, *encapsulation* is defined to mean "packaging an object's behavior (logic and data) for external use." (Any resemblance to other definitions is purely coincidental. :-)

---

### *Exposing your private parts*

Depending on which author you cite, the definition of encapsulation sometimes deals not only with what clients *can* do, but also with what they *can't* do. In particular, some languages have special syntax and rules to limit access to components of an object's implementation: *export* statements, *private* declarations, and so on. In Python, object access is a convention, instead of an imposed rule. As we have seen earlier, all attributes in modules, classes, and instances are visible (and changeable) from the "outside world."

In practice, however, the convention works as well as the rules do. As long as clients restrict themselves to an object's methods and operators, they're insulated from changes in the object's implementation. This is one reason we introduced operators to menus: to protect clients from changes in the menu internals; they shouldn't be dependent on the *menu* attribute always being available.

Later in this book, we'll see another example that makes use of encapsulation to allow an object's internal representation to be moved to completely different types (and even to different languages), without having an impact on its clients. While we can't prohibit access to an object's internals in Python, such extra constraints and language rules may not make sense in a language designed for speed of development.

### *"We're all consenting adults"*

That's how Python's inventor once replied to questions about the lack of access controls in Python. This is a another point of philosophy that we probably shouldn't debate here. In short, Python takes the position that imposing access rules isn't necessary or desirable in a rapid-development tool. If the programmers of an object's clients really want to break its implementation, they can; whether or not this justifies adding special rules to a language is beyond the scope of this book.

## *Modules Versus Classes: The Rest of the Story*

Since Python has both classes and modules, and their roles can sometimes overlap, the difference is often confusing for new users of the language. We've hinted at some of the ways they differ along the way, but now that we've seen classes at work, let's summarize. Classes and modules are both useful for implementing encapsulated data structures. Also, both are namespaces, with attribute names we qualified to use. But there are also some major distinctions:

*Features:*

- Classes support *inheritance* of attribute names from other class's namespaces.
- Classes support *multiple copies*: each instance gets a distinct attribute namespace.
- Classes can *overload* operators, so instances can be manipulated outside method calls.
- Classes can provide other *metaclass* hooks to modify their own interpretation.

*Structure:*

- Modules correspond to files (or extensions); classes are statements in a file.
- Classes exist inside a module file and namespace; modules aren't enclosed in anything.
- Classes are created with the *class* statement; modules are made just by writing files.
- Classes are used by instance calls and superclass lists; modules are used by *import* statements.
- Modules are the unit of C-compatible extensions; classes are for writing extensions in Python.

In terms of source code, classes are always written as statements inside a module file, just like functions. In terms of namespaces, a class object's global namespace is always the enclosing module; for modules, there's no notion of an enclosing global namespace. Except for the implied built-in namespace, modules are always the top level of the namespace nesting model.

In general, classes are a better way to implement abstract datatypes, because of their support for multiple instances, and their extra features. Modules are really only useful for managing shared objects. Of course, there are exceptions; but as a rule, here's how to summarize the distinctions between classes and modules:

*Classes*
: Designed for implementing object behavior, to model items in an application domain.

*Modules*
: Packages of objects (code and data) used to organize a program system.

# *Design Exercise: Adding Logging and Security Extensions*

In Chapter 9 we showed how functions can get overly convoluted when adding extensions *in place*, by adding hypothetical extensions for logging and validating menu selections (e.g., *menuOb.py*, *interact_dict*). We won't go into detail about how to do this with classes here, since there will be better examples applying the same techniques later in the book. But the extensions illustrate the kinds of design problems that come up when building larger hierarchies. The last time we met our menu functions earlier in this chapter, they were evolving out of control. Figure 10-11 shows how.

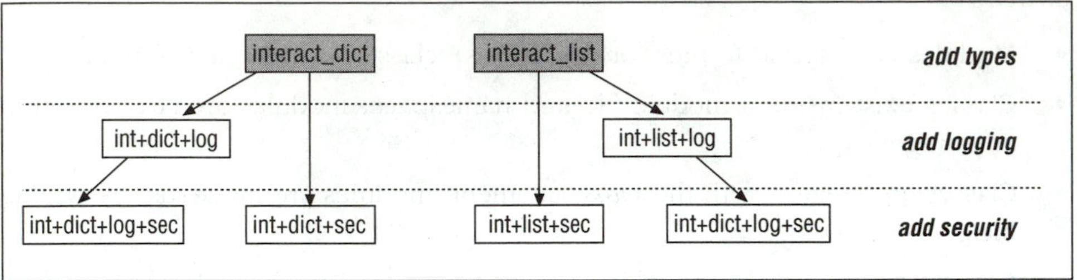


*Figure 10-11: Extending functions in place*

In the end, we would have had two functions containing the union of all changes added on each branch, and control flag arguments to select extensions. As we saw, we needed a way to factor out common behavior. Although these are probably trivial issues for such small functions, on a larger scale the complexity and duplication of logic introduced by extending the two functions can lead to serious maintenance problems.

*Multiple inheritance* may be a better approach here: define a base set of behavior, and add subclasses that extend it. Instead of embedding more code each time we make a change, we define how a variant differs from the base, and let clients pick and choose from the set of deviations.

In our examples, we defined a base behavior (*Menu*) that handles basic menu interaction. We extended *Menu* by adding variants for list and dictionary menus, and defined how these kinds of menus differ from the base. Later, we might also define an extension that logs selections, and one that validates them.

As we've seen, composite objects can be built up by selecting methods from a set of variants: the multiple-inheritance example we saw earlier combined the methods of two classes. If we also define logging and security subclasses, clients could pick the list and validation variations, or just the dictionary extension, etc. Figure 10-12 illustrates this scheme.

In this figure, the arrows point up to represent behavior that's inherited from base sets. As we go lower in the figure, we're either adding extensions by defining how they deviate from higher base sets, or combining existing extensions to package composite behavior. For instance, a *DictMenu* is like a *Menu*, but defines how it's different when a dictionary is used to record menu options. *SecLogDictMenu* adds no new extensions, but it packages the logging, dictionary, and security extensions for use together.

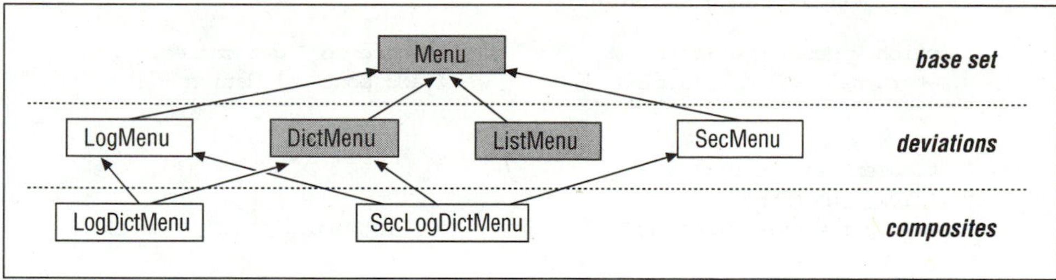


*Figure 10-12: Deviation-based programming: extending and combining classes*

## *Adding Logging and Validation by Subclassing: A First Cut*

Can our classes really coexist in such an idealistic world of mix-and-match software extensions? In principle, yes; but in practice, supporting a wide range of extensions takes careful planning and hierarchy design. As our menu classes currently exist, they're not yet appropriate for adding these extensions.

Here's a rough sketch of how the classes might be restructured for logging and security extensions. The initial check to see if any items are valid can be done just by extending the existing *run* method, adding preprocessing logic. Similarly, logging can be added by extending the *runCommand* method.

*Example 10-9: File: securlog.py*

```
from menu1 import Menu, ListMenu
import os, security, logger

class SecureMenu(Menu):
    def __init__(self):
        self.user = os.environ['USER']          # call 'Menu.__init__' here?...

    def run(self):
        for tool in self.menu.keys():           # add a pre-validation step
            if security.allow(tool, self.user):
                break
        else:
            print "You're not authorized for any menu selections"
            return
        Menu.run(self)

    def validate(self, tool, verbose=0):        # where do I get called?...
        if not security.allow(tool, self.user): # what's 'tool' here?...
            if verbose:
                print "unauthorized - try again"
            return 0
        return tool

    def input(self):
```

*Example 10-9: File: securlog.py (continued)*

```
        option = Menu.input(self)                   # where do I get called?...
        return self.validate(option, 1)             # add post-validation


class ListLogMenu(ListMenu):
    def __init__(self):
        self.user = os.environ['USER']              # 'ListMenu.__init__' here?...

    def runCommand(self, cmd):
        logger.record(self.user, cmd)               # add pre-logging
        ListMenu.runCommand(self, cmd)              # do normal list runCommand
```

### *Problem 1: Redesigning superclass protocols*

For other extensions, some rethinking of our approach is needed. We'll mention the issues here, but won't try to solve them. We first need to change the *Menu* superclass protocol (what it expects subclasses to implement), to provide additional hooks we can override in subclasses to modify default behavior. For instance, we need a way to intercept input requests so we can augment them with validation; the *input* and *validate* methods need to be called at strategic spots in *Menu* methods. This is the same sort of framework restructuring we did to add a top-level *Interact* class at the start of this chapter.

### *Problem 2: Defining type-specific boundaries*

Other issues are less clear-cut. For instance, if the option we get back from *Menu.input* varies per menu (a string for dictionaries, a number for lists, etc.), then *validate* must be delegated to type-specific methods, or must be moved to type-specific classes. We need to encapsulate type deviations better.

### *Problem 3: Resolving inheritance conflicts*

Adding the logging extension is simpler: it is only called from Menu in one place. But combining security, logging, and type-specific subclasses takes some care. For example, *SecureMenu* has to be mixed with a type-based menu class to be used: since it doesn't define *showOptions* or *runCommand*, we can't make a *SecureMenu* instance directly.

Depending on the protocol used, we may need to write control methods that manually select same-named methods from superclasses. For instance, the *ListLogMenu* is list-specific: to make a general *LogMenu* class, we need a way to distinguish the extended *runCommand* from one inherited in another class (do we call *ListMenu*'s or *DictMenu*'s *runCommand* to perform superclass defaults?). Alternatively, we might restructure *runCommand* itself to call an initial action before the real one.

### *Problem 4: Initialization protocols*

*Menu*'s `__init__` constructor (if present) should probably only be called once: we don't want every class derived from *Menu* to call *Menu*.`__init__` from their own `__init__` methods. Of course, *Menu* could keep a record of whether it's been initialized yet or not (in an instance attribute), but an initialization convention would be better. Normally, this is simple: a class calls its immediate superclass's constructors. But when multiple inheritance is used, more than one class may have the same superclass.

Again, we'll see examples of complex multiple inheritance later in the book. For now, we'll leave the completion of these extensions as an advanced exercise for the interested reader.

## *Inheritance Versus Composition*

Another way to approach this problem, is to avoid multiple inheritance altogether. Instead, we can sometimes add behavior by separating components into distinct objects, controlled by a top-level container object. In OOP terminology, this is usually called *composition*: an aggregate object embeds other objects, and invokes their messages to coordinate activity among them.

For example, suppose we just want to add a single security validation step, before allowing menu interaction. Here's a rough sketch of how this might be coded using composition.

```
import os

class Menu:
    as before...

class User:
    def __init__(self, name):
        self.user = name or os.environ['USER']
    def authorized(self):
        validate self.user...

class Interface:                                # an aggregate object
    def __init__(self, tools, who=None):
        self.user = User(who)                   # embed two other class instances
        self.menu = Menu(tools)
    def run(self):
        if self.user.authorized():              # invoke embedded object methods
            self.menu.run()

if __name__ == '__main__': Interface().run()    # make the controller object
```

In this module, the *Interface* class serves as an aggregate: it embeds instances of two other classes, *Menu* and *User*. *User* is independent of the *Menu* class hierarchy, and encapsulates security issues. Similarly, *Menu* is independent of the *User* class's logic, and only deals with menu interaction.

Rather than adding validation by forming an inheritance association, Interface implements a composition relationship. In this case, the result is a cleaner separation of logic. Of course, we simplified the problem for this example; if validation must also occur for each menu operation, the division-of-labor may require interaction between Menu and User.

Composition is a central OOP concept; in fact, it's sometimes as important as inheritance, especially in larger systems. Watch for examples of composition and object embedding in action, later in the book.

### *A second stab at object-oriented design*

As we've noted before, object-oriented design issues like these aren't always simple to resolve. Some go beyond the Python language. In fact, some of the problems listed here have little to do with Python itself: they're really broader design issues we won't cover in this book.

Again, object-oriented design issues are easier to address if we know what we want from a hierarchy beforehand. Therein lies one of the main reported benefits of OOP: it forces us to think through our designs ahead of time.

Of course, the bigger the program, the more planning we need to do: some programming scenarios really don't justify exhaustive up-front analysis. In such cases, Python's simplicity and rapid turnaround support a more experimental mode of development.

Still, reusable tools require some degree of planning. We can throw together class-based programs fast in Python, if we want to; changing them later may be another story.

## *Where's the Beef?*

Finally, some perspective. With functions, classes, modules, and all the built-in tools Python provides, it can be confusing to keep track of where services come from, and what has to be imported. For instance, when we used the *glob* filename expansion function in the *textpak* module, how did we know it was in a standard module called *glob*? And how did we know module *glob* had to be imported?

As you might expect, Python's toolset becomes more familiar with use. But to help you understand the general framework, Figure 10-13 gives the global picture. When Python is running, functionality is already available from a variety of sources, and you add more by writing Python modules and C extensions, as shown in the chart below.

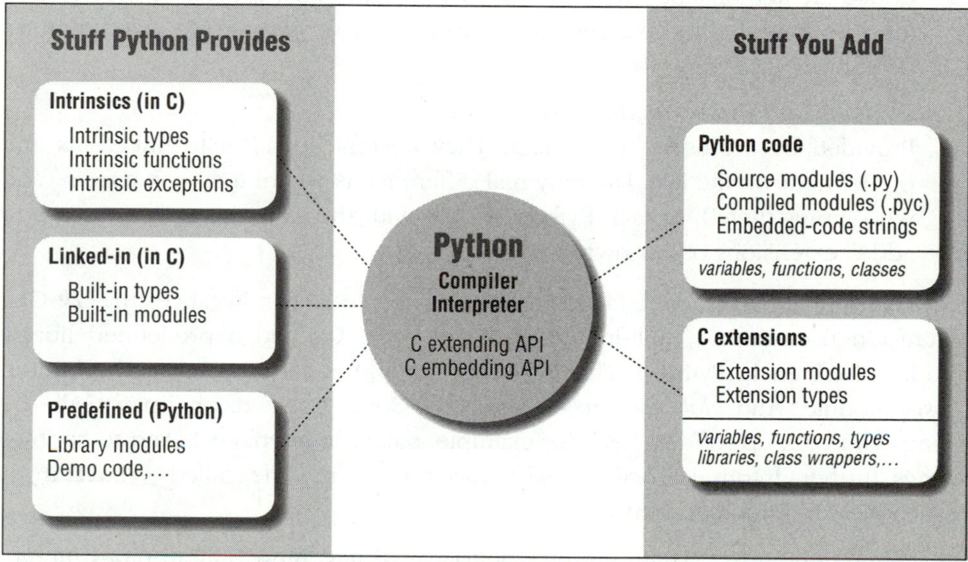


*Figure 10–13: A chart of Python's functional structure*

On the left are all the tools that Python provides; by adding components on the right, you extend Python for your application's purpose. A few definitions:

*Intrinsic types*
: Coded in C and always available. Most have a syntactic representation, and respond to operators and methods. Examples: numbers, strings, lists, modules, functions, classes.

*Intrinsic functions and exceptions*
: Available without imports. They belong to the preimported module `__builtin__`; every module gets its contents "for free." Examples: *open, range, EOFError.*

*Built-in types*
: Coded in C and linked in to the system like intrinsics, but must be imported to be used in Python programs. Examples: dbm (hashed files), array (C arrays).

*Built-in modules*
Implemented in C too, and must be imported to be used. The set of linked-ins can be configured when Python is installed. Examples: *sys*, *posix*, *regex* (regular expressions), *strop*.

*Library modules*
Coded in Python and shipped with the system (in the *Lib* directory). They must be imported to be accessed too. Examples: *os*, *glob*, *string*, *pdb* (Python's debugger).

*C extensions and Python modules*
Provided by the user on the right. They become identical to linked-ins and predefineds on the left. The only real difference is where they come from (and who writes them!). In fact, Python is built with the same interfaces we use to add C extensions of our own.

These distinctions are rarely absolute for a given tool. For instance, the *Tk* GUI extension uses both a built-in module (written in C), and a predefined library module (written in Python). The *os* library module is a front end to the built-in *posix* module. And *glob* uses *regex* internally. Some C extensions may really be things you pick up "off the Net" (for example, database interfaces). And to confuse things further, intrinsic functions exist in a built-in module called `__builtin__`, which we can import and inspect.

As a rule, you always have to import built-in modules, most built-in types, library modules, Python modules you write, and C extensions you link in. Generally, Python's toolset is layered: the most common tools are intrinsic, and less common ones are built-in or predefined (and must be imported).

Common Python services are summarized in Appendix C, *A Mini-Reference*, at the end of this book. Since Python's prebuilt toolset changes over time, the Python library manual is probably the best source of information on what's available, and in what form. But here's another trick: since `__builtin__` contains all the intrinsic functions and exceptions, we can find out what's available without imports by the following code:

```
>>> import __builtin__          get the built-in module "__builtin__:"
>>> dir(__builtin__)            list its contents: intrinsics
```

The intrinsic function *dir* can be used as a quick way to see what's available inside any module. For instance, if we forget what's in the *sys* module, we can check it interactively:

```
>>> import sys
>>> dir(sys)
```

If we know where to look, we can always find prebuilt tools in the source code of the Python system. For example, predefined library modules currently all reside in the *Lib* directory of the Python build tree, and built-in C extensions are in the *Modules* and *Objects* directories. But scanning source code isn't useful for everyone; Python's manuals are the best source of up-to-date documentation on prebuilt tools.

## An Extra Slice of Onion

It may also be helpful to remember that your Python programs run embedded in a number of systems, whether you notice it or not. The immediate system you interact with is the Python interpreter itself. Outside the Python system, extensions and interfaces are accessed from a layer of C-compatible services. And outside everything, you're running and interfacing with an operating system (see Figure 10-14).

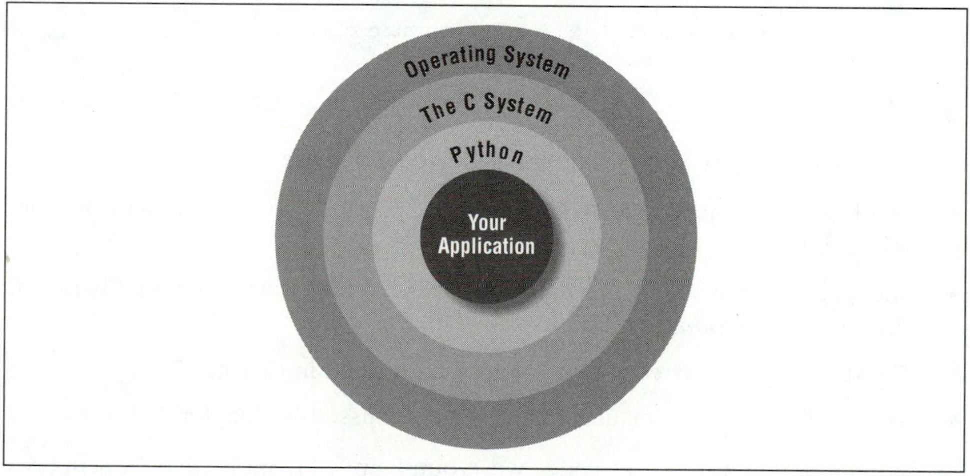


*Figure 10–14: Python process structure*

For example, when we use the *os.system* function to run a shell command in a Python program, we first call a Python function, which routes the call to a C extension module, which finally invokes an operating-system service. Since Python itself is a C program (or library), your Python programs are ultimately running in a C process.

The routing of calls from Python to the operating system is very fast (as we'll see in Chapter 14, *Extending Python*, C services are registered function pointers). Normally, you don't notice these layers when writing Python programs, but they may become important if you start extending Python, or using it as a component of larger systems.

# Conclusion

By now, our original packing scripts have become sophisticated tools. Really, they're a system of modules, which implement a variety of services: file packing and unpacking, user interfaces, and menu management. Some of these modules can also be run as scripts, to pack files. For instance, the original quick and dirty pack scripts mutated into a class instance in Chapter 9:

*Example 10-10: File: textpak6.py*

```
#!/usr/local/bin/python

import sys
from menu1 import DictMenu                  # get menu interaction
from textpak2 import pack, unpack           # reuse textpak2 funcs

class TextPak(DictMenu):                       # subclass this menu
    menu = { 'pack':   pack,                   # my interactive menu
             'unpack': unpack,                 # static class data
             'stop':   sys.exit }

if __name__ == '__main__': TextPak().run() # make one and run it
```

which uses a variety of services we implemented along the way:

- The basic packing and unpacking logic we wrote in Chapter 4, *Writing Basic Shell Tools*
- The packer scripts' functional interfaces that were developed in Chapter 6, *Adding a Functional Interface*
- The user interface extension functions that evolved in Chapter 7
- And finally, the menu-manager classes we discussed in Chapter 9

By progressively refining the code, we wound up with more than a script we would use once and then throw away. And by exporting functionality at each step, we ended up with a set of modules that could be reused for similar programs in the future. The results are in: our file packing system is really only two imperative statements: we simply define a subclass, and call the *run* method of its instance. The rest of the logic is encapsulated in the classes and modules imported.

## Room for Improvement

Later in the book, we'll revisit the packing scripts in the context of a shell tools GUI interface (see Chapter 11). And for those interested in pursuing further enhancements, versions of these scripts that use a class-based application framework appear in Appendix D, *An Application Framework*.

## *What is a "compiled" Python module? Packaging Python code*

As we saw earlier, Python source files (modules) must have a *.py* suffix to be imported. When a module is imported by another module, Python internally compiles its code to an intermediate, portable form called byte-code, and stores it in a file with a *.pyc* suffix if possible. Later, when the module is imported again, Python loads the *.pyc* file directly if it's found on the module search-path, and it's not older than the corresponding *.py* source file. This avoids the byte-code compile step and can speed program startups.

It's also the only "make" dependency system Python programs require: since imported modules aren't loaded until run-time, there's no need for nested dependencies when compiling a module. Roughly, *.pyc* files correspond to *.so* or *.DLL* dynamically loaded library files used for C development. But since Python interprets the compiled byte-code, there isn't as clear a distinction between *source* and *object* modules in Python: *.py* files are really dynamically loaded modules too.

Because Python compiles code at run-time (when imported), making sure files are precompiled is one way to speed up Python programs that import many modules. To minimize startup time, make sure your source-code files are kept in directories where you have write-access permissions so Python can store their compiled form in *.pyc* files.

*.pyc* files are also a way to ship Python programs without sending source code: a precompiled module file is stored in portable binary form, and will be loaded if no *.py* file can be found for an imported module. Precompilation can be forced by importing a module at the interactive command line (or with the *–c* command line flag). *.pyc* files can't be run as scripts (they're binary files), but can be sent to the interpreter:

```
% python textpak2.pyc ...
```

The standard *freeze* tool provides another way to ship Python programs without source, by packaging them as C files or binaries. Unlike *.pyc*'s, Python doesn't have to be installed to run "frozen" programs (see Appendix A, *. . . And Other Cool Stuff*, for more details).

In fact, there are at least three ways to ship Python programs: as source-code files (*.py*), as precompiled byte-code (*.pyc*), or as "frozen" binaries. Some applications that embed Python code stored as strings may use more specific mediums: database entries, etc. And as we'll see later in this book, pickled objects can be transferred between Python systems too.

Among other things, the framework wraps the details of system interfaces, behind a common API. In other words, it encapsulates operating-system services. The interested reader may study the framework examples as an additional exercise.

Part of the goal of the last two chapters was to prepare you for the object-oriented tools we're going to turn to next: the *Tkinter* GUI extension uses a class-based model, classes will be used to model persistent database objects, etc. But before we move on, let's summarize what we've seen so far.

# *Welcome to the Middle of the Book!*

Congratulations! If you've gotten this far, you've already learned most of the Python language. Of course, there are a few more tricks to pick up along the way, but we've already covered most of Python's core features, enough for you to write substantial programs. By modern standards, it's a fundamentally simple language.

## *A Quick Summary of Topics We've Covered So Far*

We've covered a lot of concepts in this part of the book. To review, here's a summary of some of the topics we've studied, from a language feature perspective:

### *Variable Names are Object References*

- Variables are created when assigned.
- Referencing undefined variables is an error.
- Names always exist in a *namespace*, sometimes called a *scope*.
- Unqualified assignments change the local scope, unless a name is declared global.
- Unqualified references search three scopes: local (if any), global, and then built-in.
- Attributes in namespace objects are qualified: *sys.stdin.readline*.

## *Syntax Rules Are Typical, with a Few Exceptions*

- Comments start with # and continue to the end-of-line.
- The ends of blocks are usually implied by their level of indentation.
- The ends of statements are usually implied by the end of a line (or a continued open pair).

## *Built-In Datatypes Are the Subjects of Python Programs*

- Numbers work as expected.
- Strings are collections of characters; a character is a string of length 1.
- Lists are variable-length collections of objects, indexed by position.
- Dictionaries are unordered collections, indexed by key.
- Tuples are like lists, but they can't be changed in place.
- Extension types define functions for making instances, plus methods and operators.
- Sequence objects can be indexed, sliced, concatenated, and repeated.
- Mapping objects can be indexed, and support key tests.
- Mutable objects can be changed in place; immutables require making a new object.
- Most types have unique operators, modules, or methods: *list.sort()*, *string % objects.*
- Operators apply according to type category: `+`, `*`, `%`, `==`, `>`, `and`, `or`, `not`, `in`, `is`, etc.
- *True* means a nonzero number value, or a nonempty collection data structure.
- Everything is an object type: functions, classes, instances, modules, methods, code, and even types.

## *Statements Are the Basic Building Blocks of Python Programs*

- Assignments create references to objects.
- Function calls can be statements if the return value is ignored.
- *print* statements write objects to the standard output stream.

- *if* statements are Python's main selection construct.
- *for* statements iterate over sequence objects.
- *while* loops are general iteration statements.
- *break*, *continue*, and *pass* are used in special contexts.
- *try* statements catch exceptions, and *raise* statements trigger them.

## Functions Group Statements and Program Logic for Reuse

- *def* statements create function objects and assign them to variables.
- *return* statements send a value (or values) back to the caller.
- Assigned names in functions are local unless declared global.
- Referenced names in functions may be local, global, or built-in.
- Each function call is a new, local namespace.
- Arguments are passed by assignment to arguments; i.e., by object reference.
- Functions support default argument values, "varargs", and keyword matching.
- Functions can change mutable arguments in place, and can set global variables or return values.

## Classes Implement New Objects, with Data + Behavior

- *class* statements create class objects and assign them to variables.
- Classes add a local namespace, much like functions.
- Methods of a class are nested functions, with a first argument for the instance object.
- Members are normal qualified attributes of an instance or one of its classes.
- Classes are templates for making multiple instance objects.
- Calling a class-name like a function makes an instance object of the class.
- Instances inherit class attributes and get their own attribute namespaces.
- Classes inherit attributes from other classes listed in their headers.
- Inheritance searches for an attribute in a class hierarchy, depth-first and left to right.
- Encapsulation is supported, but information hiding is a convention.

- Polymorphism is automatic, based on attribute reference not generic functions.
- Specially named methods handle construction, operator overloads, and metaclass protocol.
- Good OOP hierarchy design takes some planning.

### *Modules Tie Everything Else Together into Program Systems*

- Modules are packages, created by writing Python source files or C extensions.
- Variables, functions, and classes exist in modules—they are module attributes.
- *import* gets a whole module.
- *from module import x* copies selected variable names from a module.
- *from module import ** copies all names from a module.
- *reload()* forces a module to be imported again.
- *from* statements copy names: they don't copy objects or make name aliases.
- Modules are executed line-by-line the first time they're imported.
- Precompiled modules load faster than source modules, until the source is changed.

### *Built-In Services Are C Extensions or Predefined Python Modules*

- Intrinsic types, functions, and exception names are always available.
- Built-in modules must be imported to be used.
- Predefined Python library code must always be imported to be used.
- The built-in service set is extended by adding Python and C modules.
- Python programs run inside a C process; Python itself is usually a C executable program and library.

## *Plus a Few Shell Tool Tricks*

We also saw some application-specific concepts from the system administration domain:

- Python source files can be made executable from the system shell.
- Python code can be run as scripts, program files, imported modules, interactively typed code, or embedded code.

- Command-line arguments are available as a list of strings in the *sys* module.
- Standard input/output streams are available in the *sys* module as preopened file objects.
- *print* and *raw_input* are higher-level standard-stream interfaces.
- External files are accessed with the built-in *open* function (like C's *fopen*).
- *print* statements write objects; *write* file-methods write strings.
- The *os* module has methods for spawning shell commands and for getting command results.
- Filename expansion is provided by the *glob* module.
- Shell environment variables reside in the *environ* dictionary of the *os* module.
- The `__name__` attribute can be tested to see if a file is being run as a script.
- Python isn't just a string processing language; it has real data structures.
- Python isn't just a system administration language; it has general development tools.

*Table 1: Common built-in Python tools*

| Functions | Modules | Shell tools |
|---|---|---|
| *open* | *sys* | *sys.stdin* |
| *len* | *glob* | *sys.stdout* |
| *range* | *os* | *sys.argv* |
| *raw_input* | *string* | *os.popen* |
| *eval* | *time* | *os.system* |
| *apply* | *posix* | *os.environ* |
| *reload* | *regex* | *sys.exit* |

# *Python in a Nutshell*

But now you can forget most of the details above. Python's simplicity is one of its best qualities; thanks to its coherent design, a few core concepts are enough to capture most of the language:

*Assignment*

The idea of assignment adds a surprising amount of consistency to the language. It works the same for variables, data structure components, *for* loop targets, *from* imports, function argument-passing, and more. Even statements usually thought of as definitions—*def* and *class*—are just assignments in Python.

*Dictionaries*

As we've seen, dictionaries are both a built-in type and an implementation mechanism. For instance, variables in modules are really attributes in the module's dictionary. And classes are mostly just dictionaries that inherit attributes from other dictionaries; each instance is a new dictionary. Dictionaries seem to pop up everywhere.

*Type categories*

Operations are generic (polymorphic); they apply to objects according to their type category. For example, + adds numbers, but also concatenates sequences: lists, tuples, strings, and some user-defined classes and C extension types. Within a type category, operations always have the same meaning.

*Object model*

There are no type constraints in Python. Variables and data structure components can be bound to any kind of Python object: numbers, lists, functions, modules, classes, methods, and more. Since objects can be passed around a program at will, there are no special type rules to keep in mind; everything is first-class object, even types coded in C.

Naturally, there are other important ideas besides these (or else I could have written a pamphlet, instead of a book :-). For example, we'll see in Chapter 14, *Extending Python*, that the C extension system allows for remarkably seamless integrations. But by and large, a handful of kernel ideas describe most of the language. This is one of the hallmarks of a well-designed tool.

## What's Next?

Appendix C, *A Mini-Reference*, provides additional summary information. The rest of the book really deals with how to apply these features in application domains. Part 3, *Tools and Applications*, presents more advanced concepts, plus realistically scaled programs and case studies. For instance, we'll study GUI programming, object persistence, extension topics, and other concepts. Along the way, we'll still point out new language concepts that appear in the examples. But the rest of the book deals mostly with application level details; we've already seen most of the Python language itself.

## Brewing Python tee

Finally, a bit of fun. Most UNIX systems have a standard command-line program called *tee*; among other things, *tee* copies its standard-input stream to its standard-output stream. Which may not sound all that useful! But let's use it to summarize some of the file-processing ideas we've seen. Here are six ways to code *tee* stream-copying as Python scripts.

*Example 1: File: tee1*

```
#!/usr/local/bin/python
import sys
while 1:
   ch = sys.stdin.read(1)                # read character-by-character
   if not ch: break
   sys.stdout.write(ch)                  # print adds a space after
```

*Example 2: File: tee2*

```
#!/usr/local/bin/python
import sys
while 1:
   line = sys.stdin.readline()           # read line-by-line
   if not line: break
   print line,                           # print adds a '\n'
```

*Example 3: File: tee3*

```
#!/usr/local/bin/python
import sys
for line in sys.stdin.readlines():       # load lines into a list
   print line,
```

*Example 4: File: tee4*

```
#!/usr/local/bin/python
import sys
map(sys.stdout.write, sys.stdin.readlines() )      # apply method
```

*Example 5: File: tee5*

```
#!/usr/local/bin/python
import sys
sys.stdout.write(sys.stdin.read())       # run method on whole file
```

*Example 6: File: tee6*

```
#!/usr/local/bin/python
import sys
print sys.stdin.read(),                  # print sends to stdout
```

We could also use explicit file objects (with *open*), but there's no real need for them when using standard streams: *stdin* and *stdout* are preopened by Python. Usually:

- Reading character-by-character (*read(1)*) is the slowest method.
- Reading line-by-line (*readline*) works well if connecting processes with pipes.
- Reading all at once (*read*, *readlines*) might entail waiting until a producer process is done.

- Reading all at once may be fastest, but the increased speed isn't always significant.
- Reading all at once may require a big memory space for big files.

# III

# *Tools and Applications*

- Chapter 11, *Graphical User Interfaces*
- Chapter 12, *Persistent Information*
- Chapter 13, *Implementing Objects*
- Chapter 14, *Extending Python*
- Chapter 15, *Embedding Python*
- Chapter 16, *Processing Language and Text*

Now that we've had a chance to study Python itself, we're going to explore some of the common roles Python plays by looking at some realistically scaled programs. Some of these topics aren't really ends in themselves, but rather are tools you will probably use in larger systems. In fact, later chapters will use tools introduced by earlier chapters.

In these chapters we'll also look at some larger case studies of Python in action. By now, we've seen the majority of Python's language features; the idea here is to show how they come together in bigger applications. Because of that, we'll spend most of our time on application-level details in this section.

The domains here aren't an exhaustive list of Python's application areas, but they are representative of typical Python roles and techniques. People are doing some amazing things with Python today, but some of it is too complex to present here. For instance, we can't really teach Internet protocols or distributed programming in this book, despite the fact that they're both current hot topics in the Python world. Appendix A, *...And Other Cool Stuff*, hints at other work that's going on, so you have a place to start if you're interested in looking further.

### *The quest for the "killer app"*

It's impossible to predict Python's future roles. So far, we have concentrated on Python basics, which apply to every domain. Here we'll look at common Python applications, but the emphasis is still on tools and techniques that span domains. Although real-world applications are probably as important as the language itself, some Python applications are still emerging, and new ones are likely to appear during the shelf life of this book.

For instance, while this book was being written, Guido van Rossum (Python's inventor) released the *Grail* WWW browser. *Grail* is based on Python and the *Tkinter* GUI extension. Roughly, web pages may include Python code ("applets") that is run on the local machine when a page is accessed. Among other things, this lets web pages be extended with Python code that displays GUI widgets, interacts with users, etc.

It's possible that *Grail* (and Python's role in commercial WWW systems) will make Python popular as a WWW scripting language. But because Python is a general-purpose language, it is unlikely that it will ever become a "one-application" language. For some, the ILU system makes Python a great client/server language; to others, *Tkinter* makes it useful for building GUIs. Many use it as a general extension tool; for others it serves other purposes.

# 11

# *Graphical User Interfaces*

*In this chapter:*

- *"Here's Looking at You, Kid"*
- *Climbing the GUI Learning Curve*
- *Automating GUI Construction*
- *Case Study: "The Packer Goes GUI!"*
- *Avoiding Namespace Clashes*
- *Handling Program Errors*
- *A Totally RAD Language*
- *Other Tkinter Topics*
- *Summary*

## *"Here's Looking at You, Kid"*

For most software systems, a GUI interface has become an expected part of the package. Even simple UNIX tools usually have some sort of graphical component. In this chapter, we'll explore how to write such interfaces in Python by studying examples of programming with the *Tkinter* extension module, a GUI API that's a standard part of the Python system.

*Tkinter* is an interface to the *Tk* library, originally written for use with the *Tcl* programming language. The *Tk* API is a wrapper over the X Window system. In Python, *Tk* is packaged as an object-oriented tool: the *Tkinter* layer exports *Tk*'s function-based API as Python classes. With *Tkinter*, we can either use a simple function-like approach to create widgets (screen objects), or apply OOP techniques such as inheritance and subclassing to extend the base set of classes, and construct frameworks of linked widgets.

Since a GUI API is more of a tool than an end in itself, we'll defer some details until later chapters, where we can show *Tkinter* being used in other applications. And since this book isn't really about *Tcl* or *Tk*, we'll concentrate on using Python's *Tkinter* interface. For basic *Tkinter* development, we don't need to know much about *Tk* itself. We also won't look at the entire *Tk* widget-set in this book, but we'll see enough to write substantial GUIs. The standard book on *Tcl* and *Tk* (written by their author, John Ousterhout), the *Tkinter* manual, and other sources provide more information than we can cover here.

## *Other GUI Options*

*Tkinter* is one of a number of GUI alternatives for Python. For instance, there are interfaces to the raw X11 API, the MFC class framework, and more (MFC interfaces are discussed in Appendix A, *...And Other Cool Stuff*). Other extensions such as *STDWIN*, *WPY*, and *wxPython* all aim to be portable GUI toolkits for Python. *Tk* itself was originally written for the X Window API, but it now runs on Microsoft Windows on PCs and the Macintosh; on these systems, *Tkinter* is a portable GUI solution.

At present, the *Tkinter* system we'll use here is the dominant public domain GUI toolkit. In fact, *Tk* is something of a de facto standard, due to its *Tcl* heritage. Other languages besides Python provide *Tk* interfaces too (notably, *Perl*). And at this writing, it seems likely that the *Tk* API will evolve away from its *Tcl* legacy completely (see the entry on *Rivet* in Appendix A). While predicting the future in a field like software engineering is next to impossible, *Tk* seems destined to be a long-lasting standard.

### *Has anyone noticed that "GUI" are the first three letters of "GUIDO"?*

Python's inventor didn't originally set out to build a GUI development tool, but Python's high-level nature and rapid turnaround have made this one of its primary roles. From an implementation perspective, GUIs in Python are really just instances of C extensions, and extendibility was one of the main ideas behind Python.

But from a practical point of view, GUIs are a critical part of modern systems, and an ideal domain for a tool like Python. As we'll see, Python lets us experiment with alternative layouts and behavior rapidly, in ways not possible with traditional development techniques. In fact, we can usually make a change to a Python-based GUI, and observe its effects in a matter of seconds. Don't try this with C or C++.

# *Climbing the GUI Learning Curve*

Let's start out by quickly stepping through a few small examples that illustrate basic concepts, and show the windows they create on the screen. The examples will become more sophisticated as we move along.

### *"If you let me play"*

GUIs are really highly dynamic interactive interfaces; the best we can do here is to show static screen shots of the interfaces that result from each program example. This really won't do justice to most examples. If you're not working along with the examples already, I'd encourage you to run the GUI examples in this (and later) chapters on your own. You may need to install *Tk* (see Chapter 3, *Getting Started*), but experimenting with these programs is a great way to learn about GUI programming and Python in general. See this book's CD-ROM for *Tk* and for Python executables with *Tk* installed.

## *"Hello World" in Four Lines (or Less)*

The usual first example for GUI systems, is to show how to display a "Hello World" message in a window. As coded here, it's just four lines in Python:

*Example 11-1: File: gui1.py*

```
from Tkinter import *
widget = Label(None, text='Hello GUI world!')
widget.pack()
widget.mainloop()
```

This is a complete GUI program. When we run it we get a simple window with a label in the middle; it looks like Figure 11-1.

*Figure 11-1: Hello GUI world*

Naturally, this is a trivial example, but it illustrates steps common to most *Tkinter* programs. The code:

1. Loads widget classes from the *Tkinter* module
2. Makes an instance of the imported *Label* class
3. Packs (arranges) the new *Label* in its parent widget
4. Starts the *Tk* event loop, to bring up the window

The *mainloop* method called last puts the label on the screen and enters a *Tkinter* wait state, which waits for user-generated GUI events. To display a GUI's window, we need to call *mainloop*; to display widgets in the window they must be *packed* (or "placed"). We pass two arguments to the *Label* class constructor:

- The first is a parent-widget object, which we want the new label to be attached to. Here, *None* means: "attach the new Label to the default top-level window."
- The second is a configuration option for the Label, passed as a keyword argument: a text string for the label message. Most widget constructors accept multiple keyword argument options.

As we'll see, the parent-widget argument is the hook we use to build-up complex GUIs as widget trees. *Tkinter* works on a "what-you-build-is-what-you-get" principle: we construct widget object trees as models of what we want to see on the screen, and then ask the tree to display itself (by calling its *mainloop*).

The *pack* widget method calls the *packer* geometry manager, one of two ways to control how widgets are arranged in a window. If we don't pass any arguments to *pack*, we'll get default packing (which attaches to side *top*). We'll use the packer in all the examples in this book. An alternative *placer* system is described in *Tk* documentation; it's less popular than the packer, and difficult to use for larger GUIs.

### *Running GUI programs*

Like all Python code, this module can be started up as a top-level program in a number of ways:

*Table 11–1: Running top-level GUI code*

| Method | Description | Command |
|---|---|---|
| *Program file* | By passing it as a program file to *python* interpreter. | *% python gui1.py* |
| *Module file* | By importing the module from another Python module. | *import gui1* |
| *Shell script* | As a UNIX executable, if we add the "#!" comment line. | *% gui1.py &* |
| *Interactively* | By typing the code at the Python command line prompt. | *% python ...* |
| *Embedded* | In an enclosing C application, as a code string, etc. | *PyRun_String(...)* |

In fact, there are no special rules to follow when running GUI code. The *Tkinter* interface (and *Tk* itself) are linked into the Python interpreter. When a Python program calls GUI functions, they're passed to the embedded GUI system behind the scenes. For example, we can write shell scripts that pop up windows, and run them just like the text-based scripts we studied in Part 2, *Language Fundamentals*. Similarly, embedded Python code can create windows too: we can use Python with *Tkinter* linked-in as an embedded GUI language, from C applications (embedding is covered in Chapter 15, *Embedding Python*).

### *Tkinter coding alternatives*

As you might expect, there are a variety of ways to code this example. In this book, we'll use the Python 1.3 convention of passing keyword arguments for configuration options, and using string constants imported from *Tkinter* for option values. But under Python 1.2, widget configuration options were passed to *Tkinter* in a dictionary; the interface is concise, but more error-prone:

*Example 11-2: File: gui1b.py*

```
from Tkinter import *
Label(None, {'text': 'Hello GUI world!', Pack: {'side': 'top'}}).mainloop()
```

In this scheme, packer options can be sent as values of the key *Pack* (a class in *Tkinter*). The dictionary calling scheme is dated, but it is still supported; dictionaries can be useful if we want to compute a set of options dynamically. As we saw earlier, keyword arguments are passed in a dictionary, so the two schemes are similar internally (see Chapter 8, *Adding Text-Based Menus*). If we don't need to save a widget, we can pack it in place, to eliminate a statement:

*Example 11-3: File: gui1c.py*

```
from Tkinter import *
root = Tk()
Label(root, text='Hello GUI world!').pack(side=TOP)
root.mainloop()
```

We'll use this form when a widget is attached to a larger structure. The *TOP* constant is imported from *Tkinter*; it's just a preassigned name (*TOP = "top"*) in *Tkconstants*, a module automatically loaded by *Tkinter*. We also use a *Tk* instance as the parent here, instead of *None*. *Tk* is the default parent widget, if we don't pass a real parent explicitly. Finally, some widget methods are exported as functions too:

*Example 11-4: File: gui1d.py*

```
from Tkinter import *
Label(text='Hello GUI world!').pack()
mainloop()
```

The *Tkinter mainloop* can be called with or without a widget. We didn't pass a parent argument here either: it defaults to *None* when omitted. Widgets are attached to the "top" of their parent by default, and top-level windows can be resized by the user. Figure 11-2 shows how our window looks when it's expanded:

*Figure 11-2: Expanding gui1*

### *Using objects as dictionary keys*

Notice that *Pack* is a class object used as a dictionary key in *gui1b.py*. Dictionaries support arbitrary key objects, as long as the object can be mapped to a constant key value. Classes are hashed on their *id* (address). The only objects that cannot be dictionary keys are things containing lists, dictionaries, or other mutable types, since key hash values must not change (and mutable objects do).

By default, class *instances* hash by *id* too, but classes can define `__hash__` methods to compute an integer key. Most instance objects can be used as keys, if we provide a hash method. One special case: instances can't be keys if they inherit a `__cmp__` comparison method but not a `__hash__`; they're then presumed to be mutable.

## *Adding Buttons*

Usually we want to provide widgets that actually respond to users. The program below creates the window in Figure 11-3.

*Example 11-5: File: gui2.py*

```
from Tkinter import *
widget = Button(None, text='Hello widget world', command='exit')
widget.pack()
widget.mainloop()
```

Here, instead of making a label, we create an instance of the *Button* class. It's attached to the default top level as before. In the button's configuration arguments,

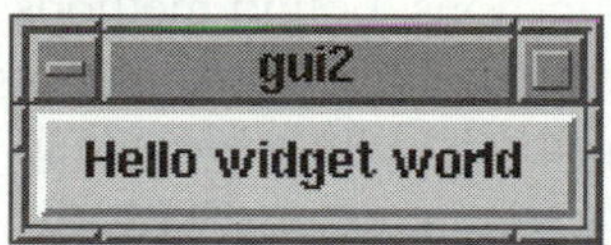


*Figure 11-3: Hello widget world*

we set an option called *command* to the string *exit*. The *command* option specifies a handler action to be run, when the button is pressed. In effect, we use *command* to *register* an action for *Tkinter* to call when a widget's event occurs.

Because *Tkinter* calls back to an action we register with the *command* option, such actions are usually known as *callback handlers*. The callback handler used here isn't very interesting: the string *exit* triggers a built-in action that shuts down the GUI program. Pressing the button makes the window go away.

## Adding User-Defined Callback Handlers

The next program produces the window shown in Figure 11-4.

*Example 11-6: File: gui3.py*

```
from Tkinter import *
def quit():                                   # instead of 'exit' action
    print 'Hello, I must be going...'         # a custom callback handler
    import sys; sys.exit()                    # kill process (and gui box)

widget = Button(None, text='Hello event world', command=quit)
widget.pack()
widget.mainloop()
```

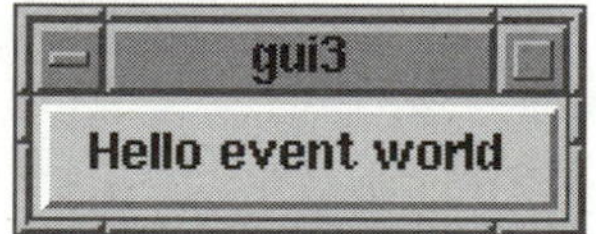


*Figure 11-4: Hello event world*

This is almost identical to the last example. But here, the *command* option specifies a *function* we've defined locally. When the button is pressed, *Tkinter* calls the *quit* function in this file, to handle the event. Inside *quit*, the *print* statement types a message on the program's *stdout* stream, and the GUI process exits as before. As usual, *stdout* is normally the window that the program was started from, unless it's been redirected to a file (see Chapter 4, *Writing Basic Shell Tools*).

In general, callback handlers can be any callable object: functions, bound methods of class or type instances, or *lambda* anonymous function expressions. They always receive no arguments (other than *self* for bound-methods). But we can register *lambda* expressions with default argument values to specify extra data to be passed in; we'll see how later in this chapter. As we'll also see, bound methods work particularly well as callback handlers: they record both an instance to send the event to, and an associated method to call.

### *Event-driven programming*

*command* options are usually the hook we use to intercept and process user-generated events: button-presses, menu selections, etc. Later, we'll see an event *bind* mechanism that registers callbacks too. When we write GUI programs, we create widget objects, register actions to handle widget events, and then do nothing: calling the *mainloop* method pauses a program until there are events to handle.

Because of this structure, GUI programs take the form of a set of event handlers. Application-specific logic is triggered by events, instead of being called explicitly. As we'll see, information can be saved between events, in global (module-level) variables or class instance attributes.

## *Attaching Widgets to Frames*

Now, let's add multiple widgets. The next example makes the window in Figure 11-5.

*Example 11-7: File: gui4.py*

```
from Tkinter import *

def greeting():
    print 'Hello stdout world!...'

win = Frame()
win.pack()
Label(win,  text='Hello container world').pack(side=TOP)
Button(win, text='Hello', command=greeting).pack(side=LEFT)
Button(win, text='Quit',  command=win.quit).pack(side=RIGHT)

win.mainloop()
```

This example makes a *Frame* widget (another *Tkinter* class), and attaches three other widget objects to it: a label and two buttons. Pressing the *Hello* button trig-

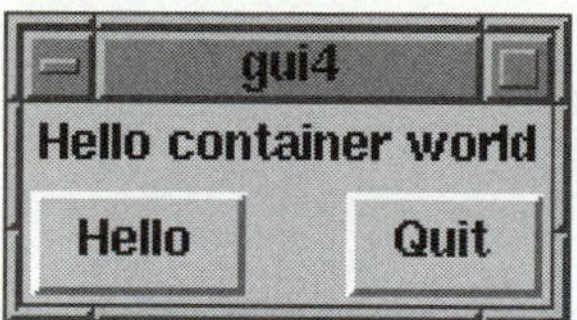


*Figure 11-5: Hello container world*

gers the *greeting* function defined in this file, which prints to *stdout*. Pressing the *Quit* button calls the standard *quit* method, which is inherited by *win* from the *Frame* class; the *win.quit* bound method has the same effect as the *exit* string.

The critical innovation here is the use of frames: by attaching widgets to frames, and frames to other frames, we can build up arbitrary GUI layouts. Frame widgets are just containers for other widgets. Here, *win* serves as an enclosing window for the other three widgets.

By specifying *win* in the first argument to the *Label* and *Button* constructors, they're attached to the *Frame* by *Tkinter* (they become children of *win*). *win* itself is attached to the default top-level window, since it doesn't pass a parent to the Frame constructor. When we ask *win* to run itself (by calling *mainloop*), *Tkinter* draws all the widgets in the tree we've built.

The three child widgets also provide *pack* options now: the *side* arguments tell which part of the containing frame (i.e., *win*) to attach the new widget to. The label hooks onto the top, and the buttons attach to the sides. *TOP*, *LEFT* and *RIGHT* are all preassigned string variables imported from *Tkinter*. Figure 11-6 shows the widget tree that's constructed by the calls, and its packing relationships:

When the tree is displayed, child widgets appear inside their parents, and are arranged according to the order of creation, and packing options. As we'll see in a moment, frames can be *nested* in other frames, to make complex layouts. Note that the widget tree is implicit here; *Tkinter* records the relationships internally. In OOP terms, this is a composition relationship—the *Frame* contains a *Label* and *Buttons*; let's look at inheritance relationships next.

## Subclassing Widgets

In *Tkinter*, GUIs are built up as class-instance object trees. Here's another way Python's OOP features can be applied to GUI models: specializing widgets by inheritance. The next program builds the window in Figure 11-7.

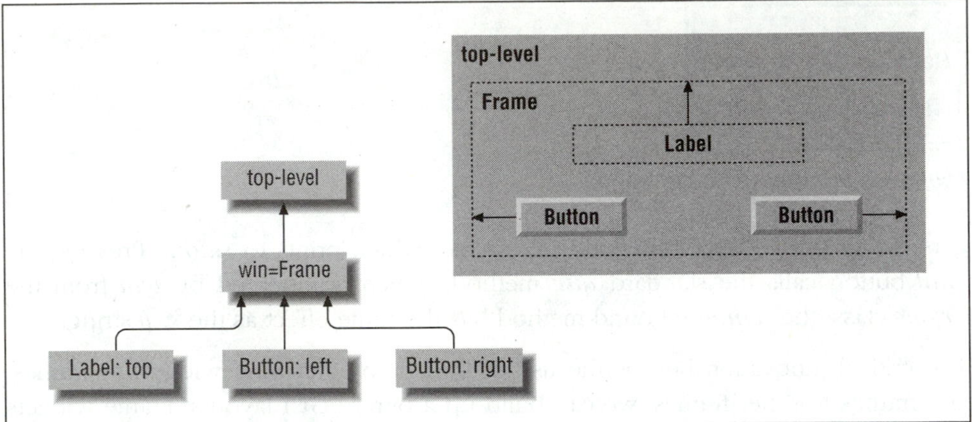


*Figure 11-6: A widget tree*

*Example 11-8: File: gui5.py*

```
from Tkinter import *

class HelloButton(Button):
    def __init__(self, parent=None, **config):      # add callback method
        Button.__init__(self, parent, config)       # and pack myself
        self.pack()
        self.config(command=self.callback)
    def callback(self):                             # default press action
        print 'Goodbye world...'                    # replace in subclasses
        self.quit()

if __name__ == '__main__':
    HelloButton(text='Hello subclass world').mainloop()
```

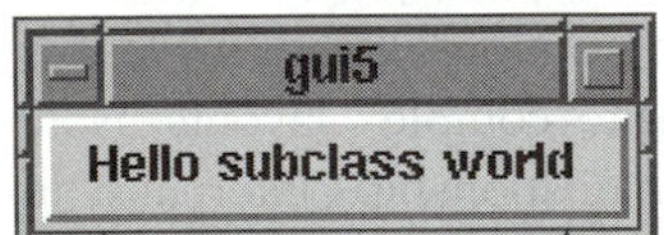


*Figure 11-7: Hello subclass world*

This example isn't anything special to look at: it just displays a single button. But this time, it's a button widget we created on our own. The *HelloButton* class inherits everything from *Button*, but adds a *callback* method and constructor logic to set the *command* option to *self.callback*: a bound method of the instance. When the button is pressed, the new widget class's *callback* method is invoked.

The ***config* argument here is assigned unmatched keyword-arguments; they're passed along to the *Button* constructor. The *config* widget-method called in *HelloButton*'s constructor is just an alternative way to pass configuration options after the fact (instead of passing them to the widget's constructor).

So what's the point of subclassing widgets like this? It allows widgets to be configured by *subclassing*, instead of passing in options. *HelloButton* is a true button; we pass in configuration options as usual, when one is made. But we can also specify callback handlers by overriding the *callback* method in subclasses:

*Example 11-9: File: gui5b.py*

```
from gui5 import HelloButton

class MyButton(HelloButton):          # subclass HelloButton
    def callback(self):               # redefine press-handler method
        print "Ignoring press!..."

if __name__ == '__main__':
    MyButton(None, text='Hello subclass world').mainloop()
```

Instead of exiting, this button prints to *stdout*. Whether it's simpler to customize widgets by subclassing or passing in options is probably a matter of taste. But the point to notice is that *Tk* becomes object-oriented in Python, just because Python's object-oriented: we can specialize widget classes using normal class-based techniques. The next example provides a different way to arrange for specialization.

## *Subclassing Frames*

Larger GUI interfaces are often built up as subclasses of *Frame*, with callback handlers implemented as methods. This structure gives us a place to store information between events: instance attributes record *state*. It also allows us to *specialize* GUIs by overriding their methods in new subclasses, and lets us attach them to larger GUI structures. Here's a simple example to illustrate. *gui6.py* produces the window in Figure 11-8.

*Example 11-10: File: gui6.py*

```
from Tkinter import *                         # get the Tk module

class Hello(Frame):                           # subclass our gui
    def __init__(self, parent=None):
        Frame.__init__(self, parent)          # do superclass init
        self.pack()
        self.make_widgets()                   # attach widgets to self

    def make_widgets(self):
        widget = Button(self, text='Hello framework world!', command=self.quit)
        widget.pack(side=LEFT)

if __name__ == '__main__': Hello().mainloop()
```

This example pops up a single button window again. When pressed, the button triggers the *self.quit* bound method, which is just the standard *quit* widget method this class inherits from Frame.

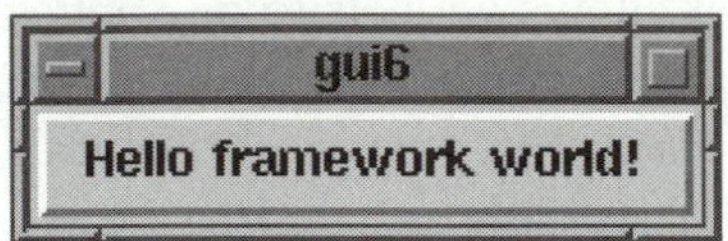


*Figure 11-8: Hello framework world*

This may seem like a roundabout way to show a Button (we did it in fewer lines above). But the *Hello* class provides an enclosing organizational structure for building GUIs. In most examples so far, we've been making GUIs using a functionlike approach: we call widget constructors as though they were functions, and hook widgets together manually. There's been notion of an enclosing context. This works for simple GUIs, but can make for brittle code when building up large GUI structures.

By subclassing *Frame* as we've done here, the class becomes an enclosing context for the GUI:

- Widgets are added by attaching objects to *self*, an instance of a *Frame* container subclass.
- Callback handlers are registered as bound methods of *self* (instance/method pairs).
- State information is retained between events by assigning to attributes of *self*.

In a sense, entire GUIs become specialized *Frame* objects, with extensions for an application. Classes can also provide protocols for building widgets (the *makeWidgets* method here), handle standard configuration chores (like setting window manager options), etc. In short, *Frame* subclasses provide a simple way to organize collections of other widget-class instances.

Perhaps more important, subclasses of *Frame* are true widgets: they can be further extended and customized by subclassing, and can be attached to enclosing widgets. For instance, to attach the entire package of widgets a class builds to something else, we create an instance with a real parent widget passed in:

*Example 11-11: File: gui6b.py*

```
from Tkinter import *                      # get Tk widget classes
from gui6 import Hello                     # get the subframe class

parent = Frame(None)                       # make a container widget
parent.pack()
Hello(parent).pack(side=RIGHT)             # attach Hello instead of running it

Button(parent, text='Attach', command='exit').pack(side=LEFT)
parent.mainloop()
```

Here, this code just adds *Hello*'s button to the right side of *parent*. In more complex GUIs, we might attach large *Frame* subclasses to other containers, and develop each independently. To extend *Hello*, we just override its methods in a new subclass (which itself becomes a specialized *Frame* widget):

*Example 11-12: File: gui6c.py*

```
from Tkinter import *
from gui6 import Hello

class HelloSubclass(Hello):
    def quit(self):                              # redefine quit here
        print 'hello'

    def make_widgets(self):                      # extend method here
        Hello.make_widgets(self)                 # make superclass widgets
        Button(self,                             # and add another button
               text    = 'Extend',
               command = lambda x=self: Hello.quit(x)).pack(side=RIGHT)

if __name__ == '__main__': HelloSubclass().mainloop()
```

This subclass adds a second *Extend* button on the right. Since it redefines the *quit* method, pressing the original button just prints *hello* to stdout, instead of exiting. But pressing the new *Extend* button exits immediately as before, since the superclass's *quit* (inherited from Frame) is called directly. Figure 11-9 shows our two extensions in action.

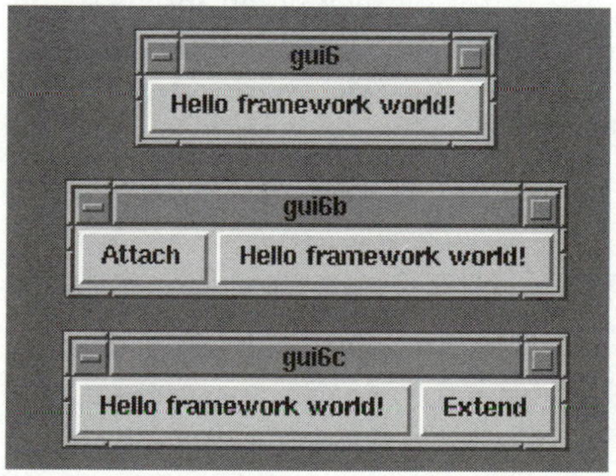


*Figure 11-9: Attaching and extending GUIs*

### *Lambdas with defaults: deferred calls and callback data*

Note the use of *lambda* with a default-argument in *gui6c*: it works just like a default argument in functions created with *def* statements. Defaults are evaluated when a lambda expression is executed; the results are saved for use when the function created by the lambda expression is later called. Since callback handlers are passed no arguments, *x* retains its default value when the lambda function is called; it refers to the original *self*.

Class methods can only be registered as callback handlers if they're bound (i.e., if *self* is known). But there's no way to associate a *self* with *Hello.quit* without calling it. To defer the call, we need to wrap it in another function. Here, *x=self* saves the original *HelloSubclass* instance, so it can be passed to the *Hello.quit* class method later. In effect, the *lambda* expression both defers the call and sets extra data to be used on the callback.

Using *lambda*s with default arguments to save information from the surrounding scope, is one way to simulate closures in Python. Appendix A discusses closures in more detail. But in practical terms, it's just a way to save data to be used during a callback.

## *Adding Canned Popup Dialogs*

Here's a bigger example, which displays two pop-up dialogs. It's written as a class framework: the entire GUI is a single class. We run it by making an instance and calling its inherited *mainloop* method. The organizational context we get by using a class comes in handy given the size of this program. This will become even more critical as our GUIs get more sophisticated.

*Example 11-13: File: gui7.py*

```
from Tkinter import *
from Dialog import Dialog

class Hello(Frame):
    def __init__(self, master=None):
        Frame.__init__(self, master)
        Pack.config(self)
        self.createWidgets()

    def greet(self):
        print "hi"

    def createWidgets(self):
        Label(self,  text='Hello popup world').pack(side=TOP)
        Button(self, text='Pop1', command=self.dialog1).pack()
        Button(self, text='Pop2', command=self.dialog2).pack()
```

*Example 11-13: File: gui7.py (continued)*

```
        Button(self, text='Hey',  command=self.greet  ).pack(side=LEFT)
        Button(self, text='Bye',  command=self.quit   ).pack(side=RIGHT)

    def dialog1(self):
        ans = Dialog(self,
                     title   = 'Popup Fun!',
                     text    = 'An example of a popup-dialog '
                               'box.  "Dialog.py" has a simple '
                               'interface for canned dialogs.',
                     bitmap  = 'questhead',
                     default = 0,
                     strings = ('Yes', 'No', 'Cancel'))
        if ans.num == 0:
            self.dialog2()

    def dialog2(self):
        Dialog(self,
               title   = 'HAL-9000',
               text    = "I'm afraid I can't let you do that, Dave...",
               bitmap  = 'hourglass',
               default = 0,
               strings = ('spam', 'SPAM'))

if __name__ == '__main__': Hello().mainloop()
```

The *createWidgets* method (called when an instance is made) attaches a *Label* and four *Button* objects to the instance (a *Frame* subclass object). We've also defined two methods to pop-up dialog boxes. The *Pop1* and *Pop2* buttons bring up dialogs, *Hello* prints to *stdout*, and *quit* runs the inherited *Frame.quit* method, which kills the GUI as before.

*Dialog* is a *Tkinter* utility, which provides a simplified interface for bringing up windows to interact with the user. We supply a list of button labels and a message, and get back the index of the button pressed (the leftmost is index zero). *Dialog* windows are modal: the rest of the application's windows are disabled until the *Dialog* receives a response from the user. The *Dialog* call works like a function call; it doesn't return until a button has been pressed. When we press the *Pop1* button, the first dialog pops up, as shown in Figure 11-10.

---

*NOTE* We provided a *title* option for this dialog, but it doesn't show up here. *Tkinter* tries to conform to the standard look and feel of the windows system it's running under. Since the examples in this book were run under X-windows, dialogs have no border or title. On other platforms (Microsoft Windows, Macintosh), they might have a border and/or title.

---

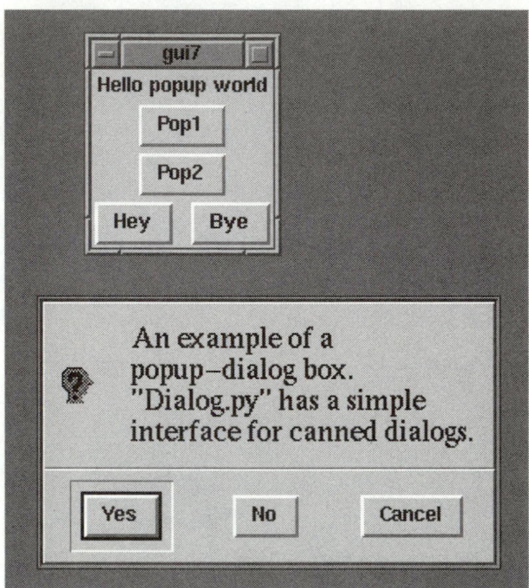


*Figure 11-10: Pop-up dialogs, scene one*

Now, if we then press the *Yes* button (or hit return to select the default), the second dialog comes up. Figure 11-11 shows what it looks like.

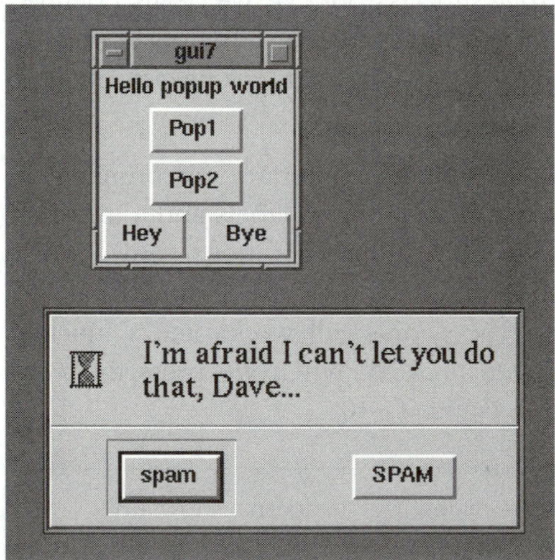


*Figure 11-11: Pop-up dialogs, scene two*

Of course, many applications require more sophisticated user interactions than we can provide with these canned *Dialog* calls. We'll see how to build-up more complex dialog boxes in a later example.

## *Adding Menus and Toolbars*

Here's a more comprehensive example that pulls together some ideas we've already seen, and introduces menu building widget classes and methods. It adds a menu bar at the top and a toolbar at the bottom.

*Example 11-14: File: gui8.py*

```
#!/usr/local/bin/python
from Tkinter import *                               # get widget classes
from Dialog  import Dialog

class Hello(Frame):                                 # an extended frame
    def __init__(self, parent=None):                # attach to top-level?
        Frame.__init__(self, parent)                # do superclass init
        self.pack()
        self.createWidgets()                        # attach frames/widgets
        self.master.title("Buttons and Menus")      # set window-manager info
        self.master.iconname("tkpython")            # label when iconified

    def createWidgets(self):
        self.makeMenuBar()
        Label(self, text='Hello menu/toolbar world').pack(padx=30, pady=30)
        self.makeToolBar()

    def makeToolBar(self):
        toolbar = Frame(self, cursor='hand2', relief=SUNKEN, bd=2)
        toolbar.pack(side=BOTTOM, fill=X)
        Button(toolbar, text='Quit',  command=self.quit    ).pack(side=RIGHT)
        Button(toolbar, text='Hello', command=self.greeting).pack(side=LEFT)

    def makeMenuBar(self):
        self.menubar = Frame(self, relief=RAISED, bd=2)
        self.menubar.pack(side=TOP, fill=X)
        self.fileMenu()
        self.editMenu()

    def fileMenu(self):
        mbutton = Menubutton(self.menubar, text='File', underline=0)
        mbutton.pack(side=LEFT)
        menu = Menu(mbutton)
        menu.add_command(label='New...',  command=self.notdone)
        menu.add_command(label='Open...', command=self.notdone)
        menu.add_command(label='Quit',    command=self.quit)
        mbutton['menu'] = menu
        return mbutton
```

*Example 11-14: File: gui8.py (continued)*

```
    def editMenu(self):
        mbutton = Menubutton(self.menubar, text='Edit', underline=0)
        mbutton.pack(side=LEFT)
        menu = Menu(mbutton)
        menu.add_command(label='Cut',   command=self.notdone)
        menu.add_command(label='Paste', command=self.notdone)
        menu.add_separator({})

        submenu = Menu(menu)
        submenu.add_command(label='Spam', command=self.notdone)
        submenu.add_command(label='Eggs', command=self.greeting)
        menu.add_cascade(label='Stuff', menu=submenu)

        menu.add_command(label='Delete', command=self.greeting)
        menu.entryconfig(2, state=DISABLED)
        mbutton['menu'] = menu
        return mbutton

    def greeting(self):
        Dialog(self, title  = 'greeting',
                     text   = 'Howdy',
                     bitmap = '', default=0, strings=('hi',))

    def notdone(self):
        Dialog(self, title  = 'Not implemented',
                     text   = 'Not yet available',
                     bitmap = 'error', default=0, strings=('OK',))

    def quit(self):
        ans = Dialog(self, title   = 'Verify quit',
                           text    = 'Are you sure you want to quit?',
                           bitmap  = 'question',
                           default = 1,
                           strings = ('Yes', 'No'))
        if ans.num == 0: Frame.quit(self)

if __name__ == '__main__':  Hello().mainloop()   # if I'm run as a script
```

When we make a *Hello* instance and call its *mainloop* method, we get a window with a menubar at the top, a label in the middle, and a toolbar at the bottom, as shown in Figure 11-12. The toolbar is just a frame with attached buttons; just for fun, the cursor changes to a hand (*cursor=hand2*) when the mouse pointer enters the tool-bar. If we select the *Quit* menu-option in the *File* menu, or press the *Quit* button on the toolbar, we get a Dialog that verifies our intentions, and calls the *Frame* superclass's *quit* only if we press *Yes*.

The window's *title* has been set in the constructor: *self.master* is the top-level window here (a *TopLevel*). It provides access to window manager attributes: window title, icon label, border protocols, etc. Menubar entries are pull-down menus: clicking on them drops down a list of menu options, and pointing at a menu option runs its *command* callback handler. For instance, Figure 11-13 shows the *Edit* menu.

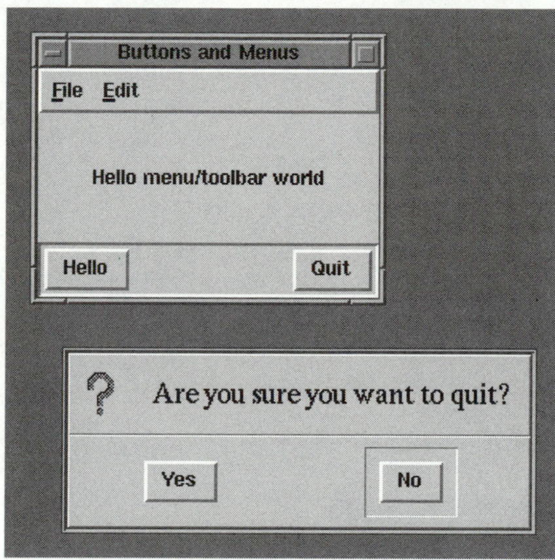


*Figure 11-12: Menus and toolbars*

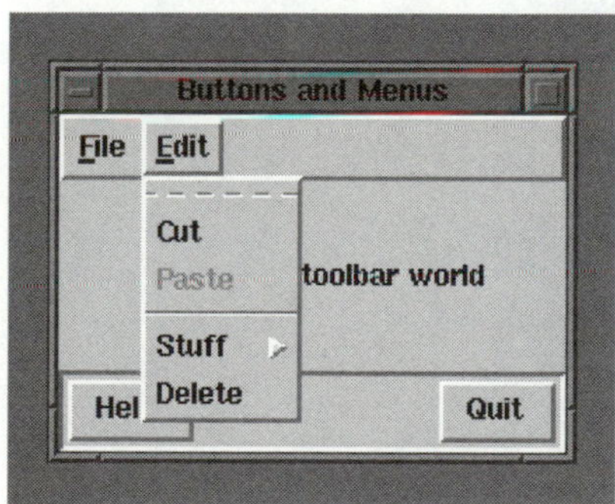


*Figure 11-13: Pull-down menus*

Note that the *Paste* option is disabled (light), and there's a separator before *Stuff*. The *Stuff* entry leads to a submenu of options; when we point at it, another list of options pops up to the right, as seen in Figure 11-14. This type of menu entry is usually called a *cascading* menu. Cascades can contain more options and more cascades.

*Tkinter* also supports tear-off menus: clicking on the dashed line at the top of a menu's item list creates a new top-level window, containing all the menu's items.

Once we tear off a menu, we can select its options faster, by clicking in the new window; there's no need to pull down the menu again. Figure 11-15 shows the scene after tearing off the *Edit*, *File* and *Edit.Stuff* menus. We've clicked on *Spam* in the rightmost window.

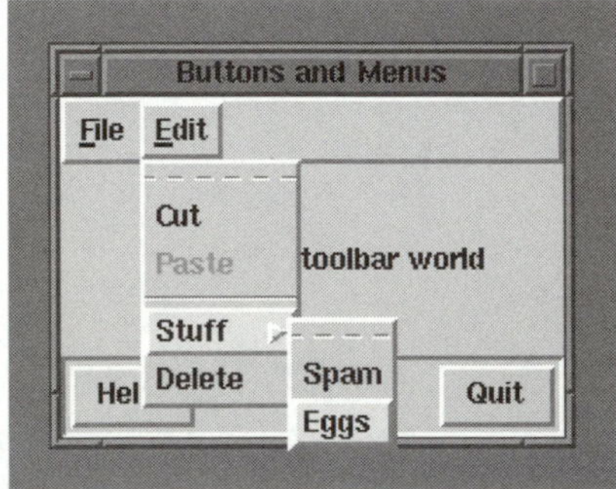


*Figure 11-14: Cascading menus*

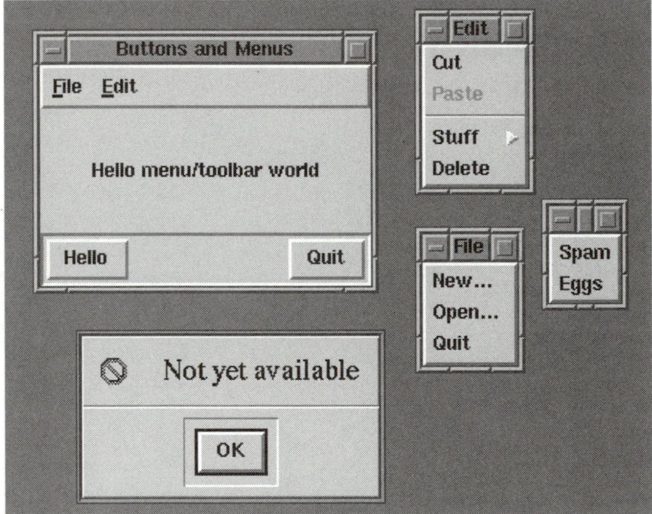


*Figure 11-15: Tear-off menus*

At this point, this example is essentially a skeleton interface. Most menu options just run the *notdone* method, which pops up a dialog to tell the user the feature is not available. This is one way to prototype a GUI's look and feel, before application logic has been written. Real callback handlers can be installed later, when the general appearance has been hashed out.

But a main goal of this example is to show how to construct menus. The menubars and toolbars are both built as *Frames*, nested in, and attached to *self*, which is a *Frame* instance too. The toolbar is straightforward: we make a *Frame*, attach it at the bottom, and insert two buttons on its left and right sides. The menu-bar is a *Frame* with buttons too, but we need to use special classes and methods for building up menus:

*Frame*
: The top-level menu-bar itself is just a Frame.

*Menubutton*
: Each entry on the menu-bar frame is an attached *Menubutton* instance.

*Menu*
: A *Menu* instance is attached to the *Menubutton*; *Menu* is a container for options.

*add_command*
: Options are inserted into Menus by calling *add_command*.

*add_separator*
: Adds a line between options listed in a *Menu*.

*add_cascade*
: Adds a menu entry that contains a list of more options (another Menu) to be popped-up.

As usual, the *command* configuration option is the hook we use to register a callback handler for menu option selections, in *add_command*. Pressing a menubutton opens the associated pull-down menu. Pressing a cascade entry in a menu opens the associated submenu. Menubuttons are linked to menus (*mbutton['menu']=menu*), and Menus are linked to cascading menus.

Menu entries can have an underlined character (the *underline* option), to allow selection from the keyboard. We also specify a *relief* mode for the menu and toolbars, and add a border (*bd=2*) to offset them. There are additional options not shown here, but this example is representative of the general approach. Figure 11-16 and Figure 11-17 show what the instance tree and its associated packing relationships look like.

The dialogs popped up by this example are attached to the main frame too; unlike its other children, they're really separate windows, not embedded in the main frame; dialogs are created on demand. Notice that the top-level Menu instances are children of a Menubutton, but cascade menus are children of another Menu. Parents have links back to the Menu they pop up (in their *menu* attributes). Menus are linked, not packed.

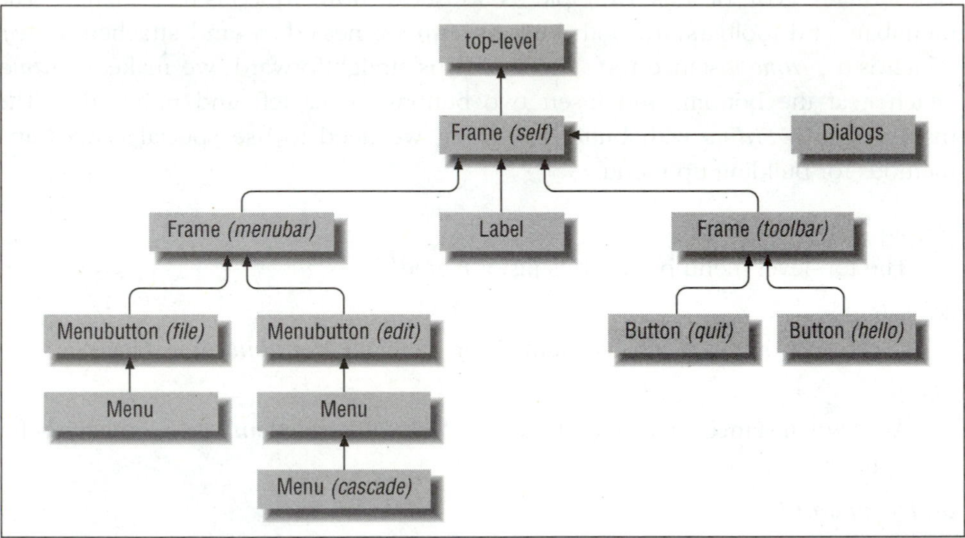


*Figure 11-16: A widget tree with menus and toolbars*

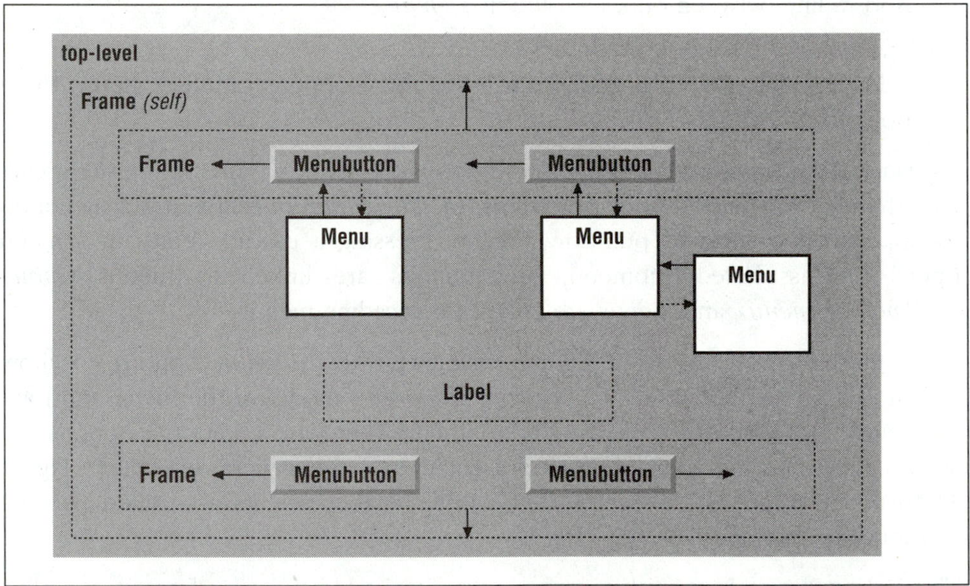


*Figure 11-17: Arranging menus and toolbars*

The *Label* instance isn't explicitly attached to any side. Since it's added (created) after the menubar and before the toolbar, it's arranged between them by default. In the absence of arrangement options, the packer arranges widgets according to their creation order, and attempts to fit widgets to make the best use of available space. The *Label* adds padding around itself to offset it from the two subframes; the packer options *padx=30, pady=30* add horizontal and vertical space around the widget, respectively.

### *Setting options three ways*

Notice that menubutton-to-menu links are stored in *menu* attributes, by assigning to a key. *Tkinter* allows configuration options to be set in a variety of ways:

- At widget creation time, using keyword arguments:

  ```
  Label(self, text='Hello world!')
  ```

- After creation, by calling the *config* widget method:

  ```
  self.config(command=self.quit)
  ```

- After creation, by indexing on the option name key:

  ```
  mbutton['menu'] = menu
  ```

We can mix the three styles arbitrarily. To allow options to be set with key indexing, *Tkinter* intercepts index operations by defining the `__getitem__` and `__setitem__` metaclass methods we explored in Chapter 10, *More Class Magic*.

## *Design Exercise: Handling Configuration Options*

In earlier examples, we finessed some of the complexities of supporting configuration options. For example, the *HelloButton* subclass in *gui5* should probably accept a *side* argument, if it packs the button:

*Example 11-15: File: gui5c.py*

```
from Tkinter import *

class HelloButton(Button):
    def __init__(self, parent=None, side=TOP, **config): # add callback method
        Button.__init__(self, parent, config)            # and pack myself
        self.pack(side=side)                             # allow passed side
        self.config(command=self.callback)
    def callback(self):
        print 'Goodbye world...'
        self.quit()

if __name__ == '__main__':
    HelloButton(side=LEFT, text='Hello subclass world').mainloop()
```

Here, ***config* will only get the *text* option, since *side* matches a real keyword. Notice the *side=side* keyword parameter: the *side* on the right is the real passed-in argument; the one on the left isn't evaluated, but becomes a key in the dictionary used to pass arguments to *self.pack*. Add a similar extension to *gui6*, to support a *side* argument for the *Frame*. Is this more convenient than calling *pack* outside the class? Since *Tkinter* still supports configuration dictionaries, we could also code this without keywords at all:

*Example 11-16: File: gui5d.py*

```
from Tkinter import *

class HelloButton(Button):
    def __init__(self, parent=None, config={}):   # add callback method
        Button.__init__(self, parent, config)     # use a real dictionary
        self.pack()
        self.config(command=self.callback)
    def callback(self):
        print 'Goodbye world...'
        self.quit()

if __name__ == '__main__':
    HelloButton(None, {'text': 'Hello subclass world'}).mainloop()
```

Is there any advantage to this approach? Suppose you're writing a GUI builder tool, which allows users to specify configuration options interactively. Does this form work any better if you don't know the set of options ahead of time? Keyword arguments become a dictionary, but they must be listed in the call. What about using the three-argument form of "*apply*" here? Recall that it accepts keyword arguments in a dictionary (see Chapter 8).

# Automating GUI Construction

As you can probably tell already, the code used to construct non-trivial GUIs gets to be enormous, if we make each widget by hand (i.e., by calling the actual *Tkinter* classes). Not only do we have to manually link up all the widgets, but there are dozens of options to be set (and remember!). If we stick to this strategy, GUI programming becomes an exercise in typing (or at least, in cut-and-paste operations).

## GuiMixin: Wrapping Shared Behavior in mixin Classes

A better idea would be to wrap or automate as much of the GUI construction process as possible. One approach is to code functions that provide typical widget configurations; for instance, we could define a button function that handles configuration details (we'll use this idea in Chapter 12, *Persistent Information*).

Alternatively, we can implement common methods in a class, and inherit them everywhere they're needed. Such classes are commonly called *mixin* classes: their methods are "mixed in" with other classes. Mixins serve to package generally useful tools as methods. The concept is almost like importing a module, but mixin classes can access the subject instance *self*. Here's an example.

*Example 11-17: File: guimixin.py*

```
########################################################
# a "mixin" class for other frames
# common methods for canned-dialogs, spawning, etc.
# must be mixed with a class derived from Frame
########################################################


PDIR = '/home/mark/python-1.3/Python-1.3'     # path to 'python' for demos

from Tkinter import *
from Dialog import Dialog
from ScrolledText import ScrolledText

class GuiMixin:
    def question(self, title, text, bitmap='question', strings=('Yes', 'No')):
        return Dialog(self,
                      title  = title,
                      text   = text,
                      bitmap = bitmap,
                      default= 1, strings=strings).num

    def infobox(self, title, text, bitmap='', strings=('OK',)):
        Dialog(self,
            title=title, text=text, bitmap=bitmap, default=0, strings=strings)

    def quit(self):
        ans = self.question('Verify quit', 'Are you sure you want to quit?')
        if ans == 0:
            Frame.quit(self)

    def notdone(self):
        self.infobox('Not implemented', 'Option not available', 'error')

    def help(self):
        self.infobox('RTFM', 'See figure 1...', 'info')    # override this

    def errorbox(self, text):
        self.infobox('Error!', text, 'error')

    def clone(self):
        new = Toplevel()                    # make a new version of me
        myclass = self.__class__            # instance's (lowest) class object
        myclass(new)                        # attach/run instance of my class

    def spawn(self, demo, fork=0):
```

*Example 11-17: File: guimixin.py (continued)*

```
        import os                                      # run /Demo program by name
        try:
            pbase = os.environ['PYTHONBASE']           # env var overrides
        except:
            pbase = PDIR
        python = pbase + '/python'
        if not fork:
            os.system('%s %s/Demo/tkinter/%s' % (python, pbase, demo) )
        else:
            pid = os.fork()
            if pid == 0:
                os.execv(python, (python, pbase+'/Demo/tkinter/'+demo))

    def browser(self, file):
        new  = Toplevel()
        text = ScrolledText(new, height=30, width=90); text.pack()
        new.title("Poor-man's Text Editor")
        new.iconname("browser")
        text.insert('0.0', open(file, 'r').read() )


if __name__ == '__main__':
    class TestMixin(GuiMixin, Frame):                # stand-alone test
        def __init__(self, parent=None):
            Frame.__init__(self, parent)
            self.pack()
            Button(self, text='quit',  command=self.quit).pack(fill=X)
            Button(self, text='help',  command=self.help).pack(fill=X)
            Button(self, text='clone', command=self.clone).pack(fill=X)
    TestMixin().mainloop()
```

The *GuiMixin* class implements common operations: typical dialogs, window spawning, and text browsing. More can be added later, if we find ourselves coding the same methods repeatedly. *GuiMixin*'s methods can be inherited and used as is, or redefined in subclasses (*help* should probably be specialized). Here are some new concepts this module introduces.

### *Making new top-level windows*

The *clone*, *browser*, and *spawn* methods make new, top-level windows.

*clone*
: Attaches a new instance of the GUI's class to a new *Toplevel* window.

*browser*
: Attaches a new *ScrolledText* widget to a new *Toplevel* window.

*spawn*

Runs a GUI program as a new process, and waits for it to end (*system*) or not (*fork*).

Making a new instance of the *Toplevel* widget class creates a new, independent window (in the window manager), and adds it to the *Tkinter* event-processing stream; we don't have to call its *mainloop* method. We can make as many *Toplevel* windows as we like, but *Toplevel* windows aren't really separate processes: they don't run in parallel with the spawning GUI, and are destroyed when their spawner is.

To make a truly independent window, the *spawn* method starts a new process. We've seen how to do this with *os.system* in Chapter 4: it spawns a process, but the spawner waits for it to exit (the call is modal, since the caller is blocked). The *fork* and *execv* functions spawn a program (command) as a completely independent window: it runs in parallel with the spawner, and lives on after the spawner is destroyed.

### *The ScrolledText widget*

The *ScrolledText* class lets us view and edit text. To store text in the widget, we call its *insert* method. The *browser* method inserts a text file's contents fetched by opening and reading the file, at the start of the widget (position 0.0). As is, the spawned window is just a browser; to make it a full-blown text-file editor, we need to add more logic to the interface. Suggested exercise: add editing features.

### *Other things to notice*

The *GuiMixin* class is useless by itself; in fact, it must be mixed with a *Frame*-based class to be used: *quit* assumes it's mixed with a *Frame*, and *clone* assumes it's mixed with a widget class.

The `__class__` special attribute is a reference to a class instance's class object—the one that the instance was made from. The *clone* method uses it to create a copy of the GUI's main window.

The *spawn* method here is set up to run a program file in Python's *Demo* directory. To run other Python programs, we'd have to change spawn to accept an absolute path to the program file. Suggested exercise: change this by subclassing. (Hint: an absolute path can be a default value argument.)

### *Testing the class by itself*

This module includes a self-test at the bottom, executed when the file is run as a script. To test mixin methods, the test code creates a *TestMixin* class, which mixes *Frame* and *GuiMixin*. Buttons invoke selected methods. Figure 11-18 shows the scene after we've pressed *clone* twice, and then *help* in one of the three copies. *clone* attaches a new copy of the *TestMixin* class to a new top-level window and *help* brings up the help dialog inherited from *GuiMixin*.

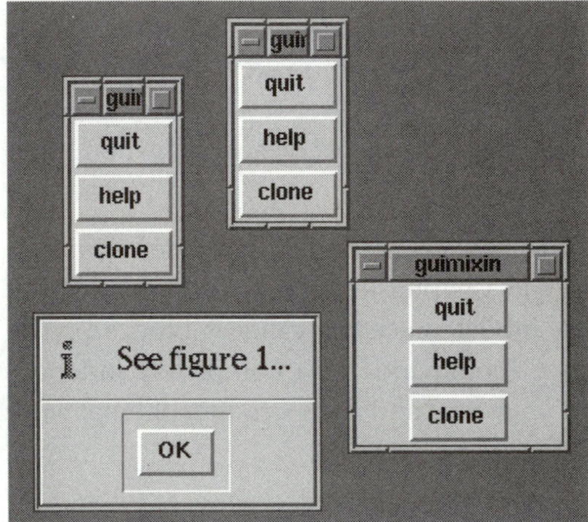


*Figure 11-18: GuiMixin self-test*

The *TestMixin* class is nested in an *if* statement here: it's only executed if the file is run as a script. Notice that one of the copies was resized (stretched). Although the buttons allow for filling horizontal space (*fill=X*), they are not configured to expand. Moreover, the frame they're attached to isn't configured to expand with the window either. We'll see how to make resizing work uniformly in the next example.

## GuiMaker: A Menu/Toolbar Tree Interpreter Class

This *mixin* class makes common tasks simpler, but it still doesn't address the complexity of linking up menus and toolbars. This can still be a lot of tedious work. Of course, if we had access to a GUI layout tool that generated Python code, this would be a nonissue. We'd design our widgets interactively, press a button, and fill in the blanks, to add callback handlers.

But for now, a programming-based approach can work just as well. What we'd like is to be able to inherit something that does all the "grunt" work of construction for us, given a template for the menus and toolbars in a window. Here's one way it can be done, using trees. The following class interprets datastructure representations of menus and toolbars, and builds the widgets automatically.

## *More on spawning processes in Python*

The *GuiMixin* class's *spawn* method starts a new process. In Chapter 4, we saw the *os.system* and *os.popen* built-ins, for running shell commands. The *fork* and *exec* built-ins provide lower-level multitasking. Here are some details.

Python's *fork* and *execv* work like their standard C-library counterparts; in fact, they're just wrappers over the C functions. *fork* copies the current process, and returns zero in the new copy of the process only. If its result is zero we're in the copy: we call *execv* to replace the current program with the one to be run.

When we call *fork* in a Python program, we're really forking the Python interpreter (a C program). But since the interpreter records everything about our program, we can think of *fork* as copying the Python program that called it. In the example above, *execv* starts a new Python interpreter, but it can start any program.

*fork* is often used in conjunction with the *pipe* and *dup2* functions in the *os* module to redirect standard streams (see Appendix A). We can usually achieve the same effect as *fork* by calling *system* with an ampersand at the end: `os.system('command &')`. This may be slower, since an extra process is spawned along the way. It's also a UNIX shell trick; see a UNIX programming book for more details on fork and system.

*Example 11-18: File: guimaker.py*

```
###############################################################
# an extended Frame that makes menu/tool-bar's automatically
###############################################################


from Tkinter import *                  # widget classes
from types   import *                  # type constants

class GuiMaker(Frame):
    def __init__(self, master=None):
        Frame.__init__(self, master)
        self.pack(expand=YES, fill=BOTH)         # make frame stretchable
        self.start()                             # subclass: set menu/toolBar
        self.makeMenuBar()                       # here: build menu-bar
        self.makeWidgets()                       # subclass: add middle-part
        self.makeToolBar()                       # here: build tool-bar
```

*Example 11-18: File: guimaker.py (continued)*

```
    ########################################
    # make expandable menu bar at the top
    ########################################

    menuBar    = []        # class defaults
    toolBar    = []        # change in subclasses
    helpButton = 1         # in 'start' if need 'self'

    def makeMenuBar(self):
        menubar = Frame(self, relief=RAISED, bd=2)
        menubar.pack(side=TOP, expand=YES, fill=X)

        for entry in self.menuBar:
            mbutton = Menubutton(menubar, text=entry[0], underline=entry[1])
            mbutton.pack(side=LEFT)
            menu = self.addMenuItems(mbutton, entry[2])
            mbutton['menu'] = menu

        if self.helpButton:
            Button(menubar, text    = 'Help',
                            cursor  = 'gumby',
                            relief  = FLAT,
                            command = self.help).pack(side=RIGHT)

    def addMenuItems(self, parent, items):
        menu = Menu(parent)
        for item in items:                       # scan nested items list
            if item == 'separator':              # string: add separator
                menu.add_separator({})
            elif type(item) == ListType:         # list: disabled item list
                for num in item:
                    menu.entryconfig(num, state=DISABLED)
            elif type(item[2]) != ListType:
                menu.add_command(label     = item[0],         # command:
                                 underline = item[1],         # add command
                                 command   = item[2])         # cmd=callable
            else:
                submenu = self.addMenuItems(menu, item[2])     # sublist:
                menu.add_cascade(label     = item[0],          # make submenu
                                 underline = item[1],          # add cascad
                                 menu      = submenu)
        return menu

    ########################################
    # make expandable button bar at bottom
    ########################################

    def makeToolBar(self):
        toolbar = Frame(self, cursor='hand2', relief=SUNKEN, bd=2)
        toolbar.pack(side=BOTTOM, expand=YES, fill=X)
        for item in self.toolBar:
            Button(toolbar, text=item[0], command=item[1]).pack(item[2])
```

*Example 11-18: File: guimaker.py (continued)*

```
    ########################################
    # default 'middle' part: override me
    ########################################

    def makeWidgets(self):
        name = Label(self,
                     text   = self.__class__.__name__,
                     cursor = 'crosshair')
        name.pack(padx=50, pady=50, expand=YES, fill=BOTH)

##############################################################
# self test when file run stand-alone: 'python guimaker.py'
##############################################################

if __name__ == '__main__':
    from guimixin import *                  # GuiMixin: help, quit
    class TestApp(GuiMixin, GuiMaker):
        #helpButton = 0
        def start(self):
            self.menuBar = [
                ('File', 0,
                    [('Quit',  0, self.quit)]
                )]
            self.toolBar = [
                ('Quit', self.quit, {'side': LEFT})
                ]
    TestApp().mainloop()
```

### *Testing the class by itself*

Like *guimixin*, when we run this file as a top-level program, we trigger the self-test logic at the bottom; Figure 11-19 shows the window we get. A simple window comes up, with a menu and toolbar, containing the options specified in the *menuBar* and *toolBar* attributes of the *TestApp* class: a *File* menu with a *Quit* entry, plus a *Quit* tool-bar button. Tool-bar buttons are packed with dictionaries, not keywords: we're dealing with a data-structure here.

### *Multiple inheritance: order matters*

*GuiMaker* adds a *Help* button on the right side of the menubar. The cursor changes to a "Gumby" figure when it's over the *Help* button, and pressing the button triggers the instance's "help" method. In TestApp, this method is inherited from *GuiMixin*, and pops up the *See figure 1* dialog; in real applications, "help" should be redefined locally.

We also get *quit* from *GuiMixin* in *TestApp*: it pops up the verification dialog. Note that *GuiMixin* comes before *GuiMaker* in *TestApp's* superclass list. Since *GuiMaker* is a Frame, placing it first in the list would make TestApp inherit *Frame*'s *quit*

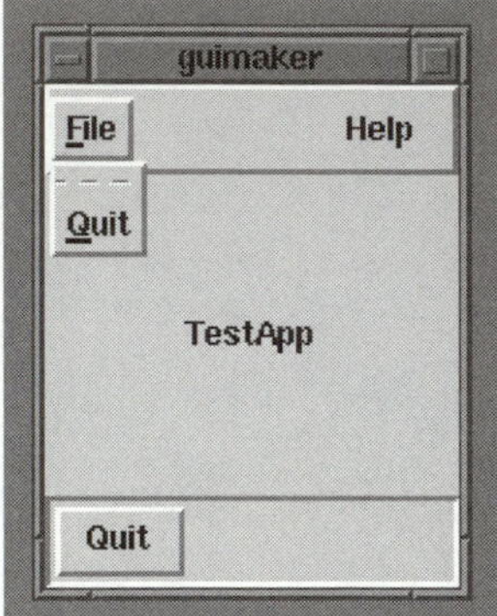


*Figure 11-19: GuiMaker self-test*

method instead of *GuiMixin*'s, due to the left-to-right search rule of multiple inheritance; *quit* would exit silently. To make sure *GuiMixin*'s methods are selected, it should usually be listed before a superclass derived from real widgets.

### *Subclass protocols*

*GuiMaker* handles constructor logic: it calls the *Frame* superclass constructor, packs the frame, and implements a system for window construction. In OOP terms, the *GuiMaker* class defines a protocol for its subclasses to follow:

- The *menuBar* attribute should be set to a menubar template tree.
- The *toolBar* attribute should be set to a toolbar template tree.
- The *start* method must be defined; this is where the two attributes can be initialized.
- The *makeWidgets* method can be redefined, to construct the middle part of the window.

By default, *makeWidgets* adds a label in the middle with the name of the most specific class: the one that the *self* instance was created from. The special instance attribute `__class__` refers to an instance's class object, and the class attribute `__name__` gives a class's name-string.

Subclass clients need to conform to *GuiMaker*'s protocol; for instance, they should use *start* to initialize themselves, not `__init__`. But in return, subclasses get a Frame that knows how to build up its own menus and toolbars from template data structures provided in subclasses.

### *Handling window resizing*

By default, new top-level windows can be resized interactively by the user. When we make a standalone instance of GuiMaker, it can be resized: it's parent is *None*, which puts it in a new top-level window. But to handle resizes gracefully, we also need to make all the widgets in a window resizable too. Widgets can specify two packing options related to resizing:

*fill* Determines how the widget should grow within its allocated area.

*expand*
: Determines if the area allocated to a widget should grow when its parent window does.

*fill* is sometimes used by itself, to give widgets a uniform size; for instance, buttons with differing text-string lengths. But the *fill* and *expand* options are often used together, so that a widget's space expands, and the widget fills the expanded space. All the widgets added by GuiMaker can be *expanded*, but menu and toolbars only grow *horizontally* (*expand=YES, fill=X*). Notice that the enclosing Frame is expandable too: in general, children aren't resizable unless their parents are.

### *More on expand and fill*

Why are there two options here? It has to do with the packer's algorithm. Widgets are assigned a size, based on what they contain (text string lengths, etc.). The packer allocates space for a widget, possibly based on the sizes of other widgets in the GUI: *fill* expands the widget to occupy its size, but *expand* asks the packer to expand the allocated space too. Combinations of the two options produce different effects. For example, using *expand* without *fill centers* the widget in the expanded space. When in doubt, try it out.

### *Template tree format*

Roughly, menu and toolbars are laid out as lists (trees) of tuples:

- *Menubar templates* are lists and nested sublists of *(label, underline, handler)* triples. If a *handler* is a sublist instead of a function or method, it's assumed to be a cascading submenu.
- *Toolbar templates* are a simple list of *(label, handler, pack-options)* triples. *pack-options* is a dictionary of packer options, following Python 1.2's coding convention.

The next module shows how to use templates to build up more sophisticated interfaces.

## *A Client GUI Demo Program*

Let's look at a program that makes use of the two automation classes we just saw. The *Hello* class here is a subclass of both *GuiMixin* and *GuiMaker*. *GuiMaker* provides the link to the *Frame* widget, plus the menu/toolbar construction logic. *GuiMixin* provides the extra common-behavior methods.

*Hello* is really another kind of extended *Frame*, because it's derived from *GuiMaker*. It follows the construction protocol defined by *GuiMaker*: it sets the *menuBar* and *toolBar* attributes in the *start* method, and overrides *makeWidgets* to put a label widget in the middle. Here's the code:

*Example 11-19: File: big_gui2.py*

```
#!/usr/local/bin/python

from Tkinter  import *             # widget classes
from guimixin import GuiMixin      # mix-in methods
from guimaker import GuiMaker      # frame, plus menu/tool-bar builder

class Hello(GuiMixin, GuiMaker):
    def start(self):
        self.hellos = 1
        self.master.title("GuiMaker Demo")
        self.master.iconname("GuiMaker")

        self.menuBar = [                                 # a tree: 3 pulldowns
          ('File', 0,                                    # (pull-down)
              [('New...',  0, self.notdone),             # [menu items list]
               ('Open...', 0, self.fileOpen),
               ('Quit',    0, self.quit)]                # label,underline,action
          ),

          ('Edit', 0,
              [('Cut',  -1, lambda:0),                   # no underline|action
               ('Paste',-1, lambda:0),
               'separator',                              # add a separator
               ('Stuff', -1,
                   [('Clone', -1, self.clone),           # cascaded submenu
                    ('More',  -1, self.more)]
               ),
               ('Delete', -1, lambda:0),
               [5]]                                      # disable 'delete'
          ),

          ('Play', 0,
              [('Hello',     0, self.greeting),
               ('Popup...',  0, self.dialog),
               ('Demos', 0,
                  [('Hanoi', -1, lambda x=self: x.spawn('guido/hanoi.py', 1)),
                   ('Pong',  -1, lambda x=self: x.spawn('matt/pong-demo-1.py'))]
               )]
```

*Example 11-19: File: big_gui2.py (continued)*

```
        )]

        self.toolBar = [
          ('Quit',  self.quit,     {'side': RIGHT}),          # add 3 buttons
          ('Hello', self.greeting, {'side': LEFT}),
          ('Popup', self.dialog,   {'side': LEFT, 'expand':YES}) ]

    def makeWidgets(self):                                    # override default
        middle = Label(self, text='Hello maker world!', cursor='pencil')
        middle.pack(padx=50, pady=50, expand=YES, fill=BOTH)

    def greeting(self):
        self.hellos = self.hellos + 1
        if self.hellos % 3:
            print "hi"
        else:
            self.infobox("Gotcha'", 'HELLO!')     # on every third press

    def dialog(self):
        button = self.question('OOPS!',
                               'You typed "rm*" ... continue?',
                               'questhead', ('yes', 'no', 'help'))
        [lambda:0, self.quit, self.help][button]()

    def fileOpen(self):
        self.browser('big_gui2.py')        # browse my source file

    def more(self):
        new = Toplevel()
        Label(new,  text='A new non-modal window').pack()
        Button(new, text='Quit', command=self.quit).pack(side=LEFT)
        Button(new, text='More', command=self.more).pack(side=RIGHT)

if __name__ == '__main__':  Hello().mainloop()
```

---

*NOTE* Note that this module is called *big_gui2*. Its predecessor, *big_gui1*, used *GuiMixin*, but built up the GUI manually instead of using GuiMaker. It was also about twice as long.

---

### *Running the demo*

When we run *big_gui2* as a top-level program, we get a box with four menu-buttons on top, and a three-button toolbar on the bottom, as shown in Figure 11-20 and Figure 11-21. The menus have separators, disabled entries, and cascading submenus, as defined by the *menuBar* template.

When we select one of the *Demos* in the *Play* menu, we spawn another GUI program, which runs as an independent process (using the *fork* or *system* calls in

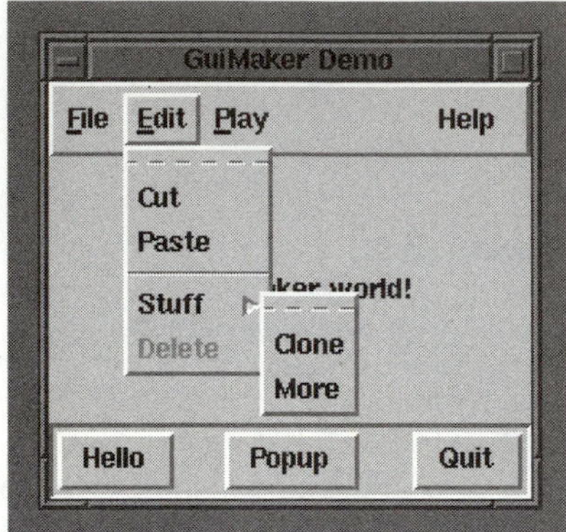


*Figure 11-20: big_gui2 main window*

*GuiMixin*). When we select *Hanoi*, the program runs in parallel with our GUI, and must be killed separately; *Pong* suspends our GUI while it runs. Menus can be torn off as usual, and *lambda*s defer the call to the "spawn" method, since extra data (here, arguments) has to be added to the call.

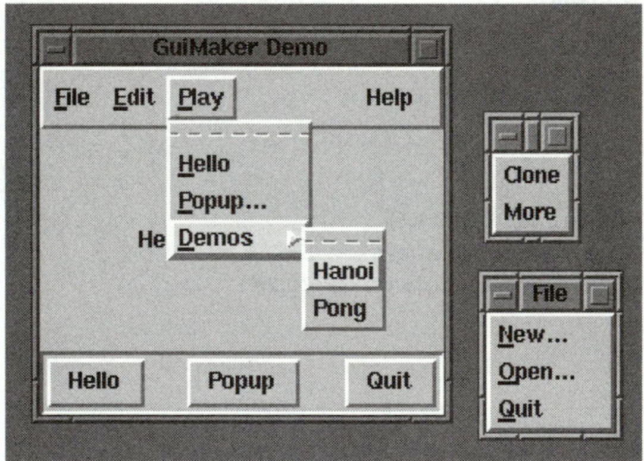


*Figure 11-21: big_gui2 menus*

Figure 11-22 is a shot after the *Hanoi* menu option has been selected, and the *Popup* button is pressed; *hanoi* keeps running even though the modal pop-up dialog blocks the rest of our GUI's windows. Note the *[lambda:0, self.quit, self.help][button]()* expression after the pop-up dialog returns: it selects one of three actions to run, based on which button is pressed in this *Dialog* box (it works like an *if*).

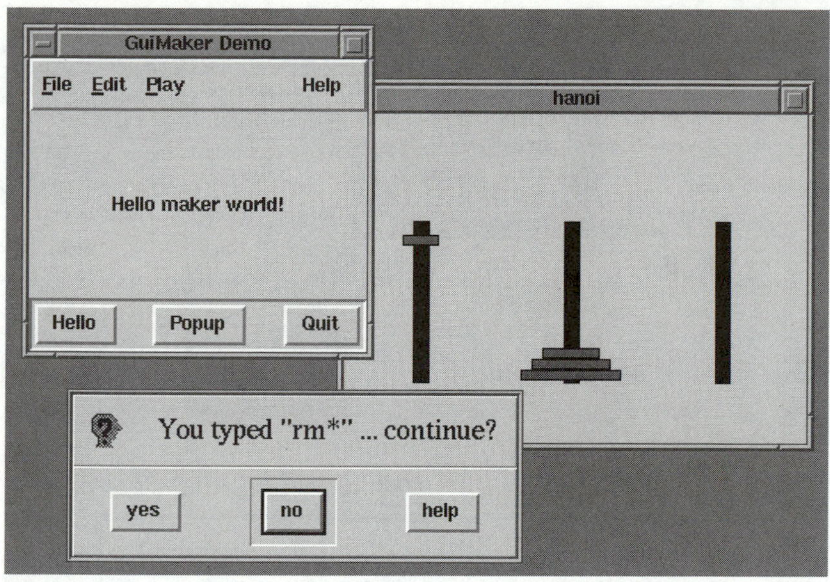


*Figure 11–22: Spawning hanoi demo*

---

*NOTE* *hanoi* was written by Guido van Rossum, and is shipped in Python's *Demo/tkinter* directory, along with other example programs. They're a good source of additional GUI examples. *hanoi* is a *Tkinter* program that gives animated solutions to the classic *towers of Hanoi* problem.

---

Finally, Figure 11-23 captures some of the *Toplevel* functionality of the GUI. We've spawned some new windows by pressing the *Edit+Stuff+More* option, and *More* buttons in the new windows, cloned the *Hello* GUI itself by pressing menu option *Edit+Stuff+Clone*, popped up a text browser on the program's source file (*File+Open*), and pressed the *Help* button on the far-right side of the menubar, triggering the inherited help default. Pressing *Quit* in any of these windows can kill them all.

### *Design exercise: alternative menu layout schemes*

As is, *GuiMaker* uses a tree data structure to represent menus and toolbars, based on built-in *lists* and *tuples*. It performs type tests to analyze layouts, as it traverses the trees. But when we introduced classes in Chapter 9, *Moving Menus to Classes*, we noted that type testing is usually a symptom of a program that could benefit from OOP.

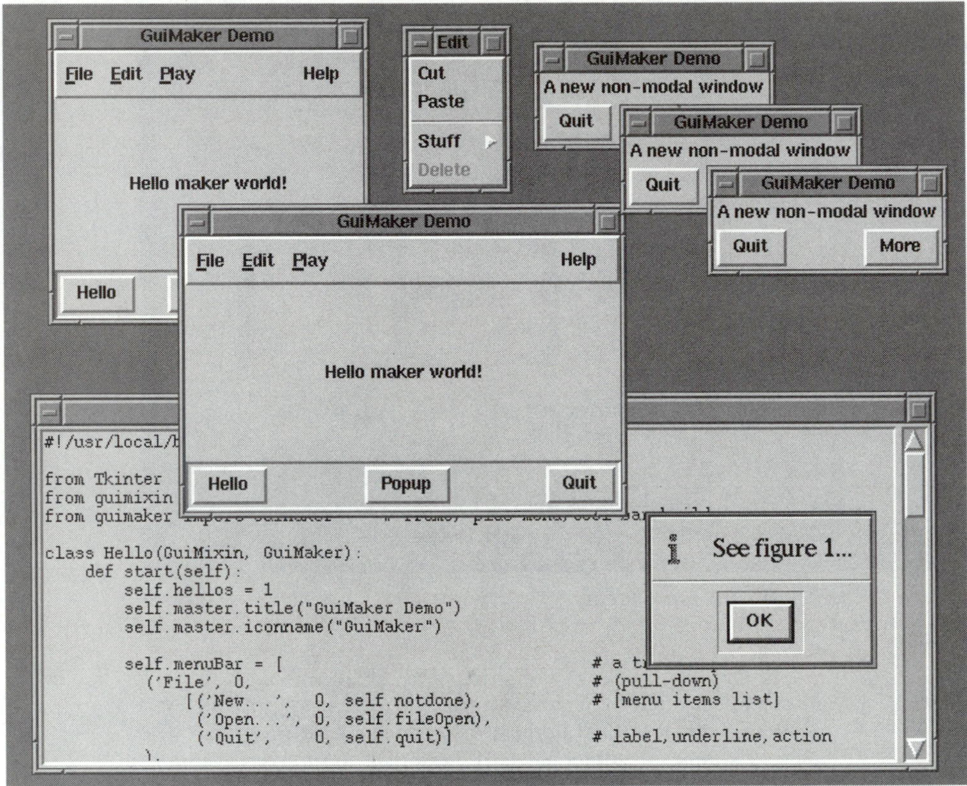


*Figure 11-23: TopLevel windows*

GuiMaker can be redesigned to use trees of embedded class instances, that "know" how to apply themselves to the *Tkinter* widget tree being constructed. One way to code this scheme appears below. Menu class *action* methods apply instances to the menu widget tree. Compare this scheme to the original. Which approach is "better"? Is there any reason to get rid of the lists and tuples in this version too?

*Example 11-20: File: guimakr2.py*

```
#####################################################################
# uses menu classes for layouts, instead of type tests
#####################################################################

from Tkinter import *              # widget classes

#######################
# menu layout classes
#######################

def addMenuItems(parent, items):
```

*Example 11-20: File: guimakr2.py (continued)*

```
    menu = Menu(parent)
    for item in items:
        item.action(menu)
    return menu

class MenuCascade:
    def __init__(self, label, underline, cascade):
        self.label     = label
        self.underline = underline
        self.cascade   = cascade
    def action(self, menu):
        submenu = addMenuItems(menu, self.cascade)
        menu.add_cascade(label     = self.label,
                         underline = self.underline,
                         menu      = submenu)

class MenuItem:
    def __init__(self, label, underline, command):
        self.label     = label
        self.underline = underline
        self.command   = command
    def action(self, menu):
        menu.add_command(label     = self.label,
                         underline = self.underline,
                         command   = self.command)

class MenuSeparator:
    def action(self, menu):
        menu.add_separator({})

class MenuDisabler:
    def __init__(self, indexList):
        self.indexes = indexList
    def action(self, menu):
        for num in self.indexes:
            menu.entryconfig(num, state=DISABLED)

#####################
# new guimaker class
#####################

class GuiMaker(Frame):
    def __init__(self, master=None):
        Frame.__init__(self, master)
        self.pack(expand=YES, fill=BOTH)        # make frame stretchable
        self.start()                            # subclass: set menu/toolBar
        self.makeMenuBar()                      # here: build menu-bar
        self.makeWidgets()                      # subclass?: add middle-part
        self.makeToolBar()                      # here: build tool-bar

    menuBar    = []    # Menu list (class data)
    toolBar    = []    # default button list
```

*Example 11-20: File: guimakr2.py (continued)*

```
    helpButton = 1     # change in subclasses

    def makeMenuBar(self):
        menubar = Frame(self, relief=RAISED, bd=2)
        menubar.pack(side=TOP, expand=YES, fill=X)
        for entry in self.menuBar:
            mbutton = Menubutton(menubar, text=entry[0], underline=entry[1])
            mbutton.pack(side=LEFT)
            menu = addMenuItems(mbutton, entry[2])
            mbutton['menu'] = menu
        if self.helpButton:
            Button(menubar, text    = 'Help',
                            cursor  = 'gumby',
                            relief  = FLAT,
                            command = self.help).pack(side=RIGHT)

    def makeToolBar(self):
        toolbar = Frame(self, cursor='hand2', relief=SUNKEN, bd=2)
        toolbar.pack(side=BOTTOM, expand=YES, fill=X)
        for item in self.toolBar:
            Button(toolbar, text=item[0], command=item[1]).pack(item[2])

    def makeWidgets(self):
        name = Label(self,
                     text   = self.__class__.__name__,
                     cursor = 'crosshair')
        name.pack(padx=50, pady=50, expand=YES, fill=BOTH)


############################
# new big_gui2 layout code
############################

from guimixin import GuiMixin      # mix-in methods

class Hello(GuiMixin, GuiMaker):  # use new GuiMaker
    def start(self):
        self.hellos = 1
        self.master.title("GuiMaker Demo")
        self.master.iconname("GuiMaker")

        self.menuBar = [
          ('File', 0,
              [MenuItem('New...',  0, self.notdone),
               MenuItem('Open...', 0, self.fileOpen),
               MenuItem('Quit',    0, self.quit)]
          ),

          ('Edit', 0,
              [MenuItem('Cut',  -1, lambda:0),
               MenuItem('Paste',-1, lambda:0),
               MenuSeparator(),
```

*Example 11-20: File: guimakr2.py (continued)*

```
                MenuCascade('Stuff', -1,
                     [MenuItem('Clone', -1, self.clone),
                      MenuItem('More',  -1, self.more)]),
                MenuItem('Delete', -1, lambda:0),
                MenuDisabler([5])]
          ),

          ('Play', 0,
               [MenuItem('Hello',     0, self.greeting),
                MenuItem('Popup...',  0, self.dialog),
                MenuCascade('Demos', 0,
                   [MenuItem('Hanoi', -1,
                                lambda x=self: x.spawn('guido/hanoi.py', 1)),
                    MenuItem('Pong',  -1,
                                lambda x=self: x.spawn('matt/pong-demo-1.py'))
                   ])
                ]
          )]

# [rest is the same as big_gui2.py]
```

### *Speaking of abstraction . . .*

The choice between list/tuple trees and class instances for menu layout is mostly a matter of style. But either way, we're getting further away from the underlying *Tk* API all the time. One of the nice things about using Python is that it's easy to wrap (abstract) system interfaces, to make them behave as we like. For example, clients of our two menu builders will be fairly independent of the underlying GUI API. Among other things, moving to higher-level abstractions can enhance portability.

# *Case Study: "The Packer Goes GUI!"*

Let's look at a more useful application of the menu/toolbar builder tool. In Chapter 10, we left off with our file packing/unpacking scripts migrated to classes that managed text-based menus. The next logical step for these scripts is to package them in a GUI interface. In fact, we could use the two automation modules we just wrote, to provide a general interface for any shell tools we might write.

Here's a comprehensive example that provides a front end GUI interface to tools passed in in a data structure. As in Part 2, it allows both dictionaries of functions and lists of *(name, function)* tuples to be used to represent the options to display. Each option is added to a pull-down menu, a toolbar (unless told otherwise), and a listbox that's displayed in the middle of the GUI.

We're mostly using ideas we've already seen; the only new widget used here is a scrollable listbox. For listboxes, we provide a general event handler, instead of registering one callback handler per entry. The event handler fetches the selected name from the listbox, and dispatches to the corresponding action. This system is composed of classes, functions, and variables taken from a number of modules:

*guimixin*
: The utility-method class developed above.

*guimaker*
: The menu/tool-bar builder class developed above.

*shellgui*
: (New) a generic interface manager class, with type-specific subclasses.

*menugui2*
: (New) subclasses for specific tool sets.

*packdlg*
: (New) a data entry dialog for pack parameters.

*unpkdlg*
: (New) a data entry dialog for unpack parameters.

*pack2, unpack3, textpak1*
: The file-packing function modules we developed in Part 2 of the book.

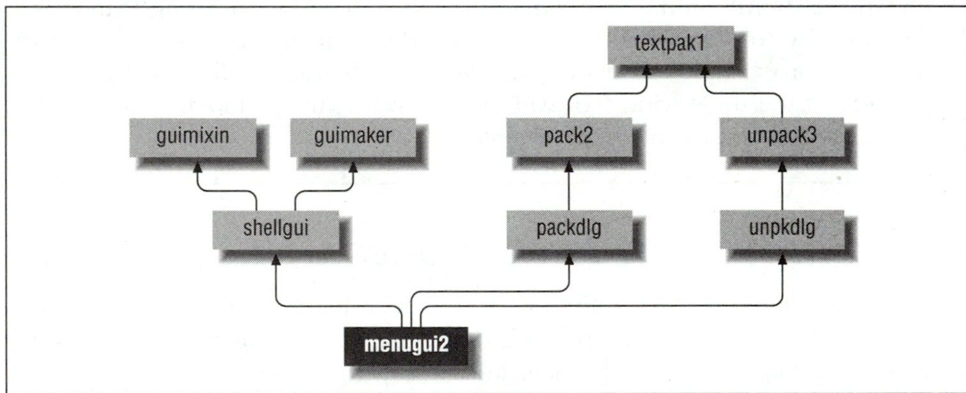


*Figure 11-24: Shell-tools GUI module relationships*

Figure 11-24 shows the module import relationships. The *menugui2* module is the main entry point for the program, since it defines the most specific subclasses of *ShellGui* (and the ones we'll make instances from). Let's look at each of the new modules, before seeing how this interface is run; it may help to peek ahead to the screens as you read through the code.

## *The shellgui Module: a Generic Shell-tools GUI*

The interface class is another *GuiMixin/GuiMaker* combination; we're getting a lot of "mileage" out of code reuse with this pair. ShellGui conforms to GuiMaker's protocol as usual; *start* sets the *menuBar* and *toolBar* attributes, and *makeWidgets* is redefined to put something in the middle—this time, a scrollable listbox. Options are added to the *Tools* menu on the menubar, to the listbox in the middle, and to the toolbar at the bottom (which may be overkill, but it's illustrative here).

Since the options to display aren't known in advance, ShellGui builds up the menu and toolbar template data structures dynamically. Its *setMenuBar* and *setToolBar* local methods construct the trees from a list of *(label, action)* tuples returned by the *fetchCommands* method, which must be defined in a lower subclass. In fact, ShellGui defines a protocol for its subclasses too:

- *fetchCommands* must return a list of *(label, action)* tuples.
- *runCommand* should run a command associated with a label (an option name).
- *forToolBar* can be used to selectively prevent options from being added to the toolbar.

This module also provides two subclasses to handle menus written as lists and dictionaries, along the lines of the menu data structures used in Part 2. Both expect a *myMenu* attribute to be set in a lower subclass or instance. Since they provide most of ShellGui's protocol, they're the classes we will use to run the GUI.

*Example 11-21: File: shellgui.py*

```
#!/usr/local/bin/python

from Tkinter  import *                                # get widgets
from guimixin import GuiMixin                         # get quit, notdone
from guimaker import GuiMaker                         # menu/toolbar builder

class ShellGui(GuiMixin, GuiMaker):                   # a frame + maker + mixins
    def start(self):
        self.setMenuBar()
        self.setToolBar()
        self.master.title("Shell Tools Listbox")
        self.master.iconname("Shell Tools")

    def handleList(self, event):
        index = self.listbox.curselection()            # on listbox double-click
        label = self.listbox.get(index)                # fetch selection text
        self.runCommand(label)                         # and call action here

    def makeWidgets(self):                             # add listbox in middle
        frame  = Frame(self)
        scroll = Scrollbar(frame)
```

*Example 11-21: File: shellgui.py (continued)*

```
        list   = Listbox(frame)
        frame.pack(side=TOP, expand=YES, fill=BOTH)

        list.config(yscrollcommand=scroll.set, relief=SUNKEN)
        list.pack(side=LEFT, expand=YES, fill=BOTH)

        scroll.config(command=list.yview, relief=SUNKEN)
        scroll.pack(side=RIGHT, fill=BOTH)
        pos = 0
        for (label, action) in self.fetchCommands():      # add to list-box
            list.insert(pos, label)                        # and menu/toolbars
            pos = pos + 1
        list.config(selectmode=SINGLE, setgrid=1)          # select,resize modes
        list.bind('<Double-1>', self.handleList)           # set event handler
        self.listbox = list

    def forToolBar(self, label):                           # put on toolbar?
        return 1                                           # default = all

    def setToolBar(self):
        self.toolBar = []
        for (label, action) in self.fetchCommands():
            if self.forToolBar(label):
                self.toolBar.append((label, action, {'side': LEFT}))
        self.toolBar.append(('Quit', self.quit, {'side': RIGHT}))

    def setMenuBar(self):
        toolEntries  = []
        self.menuBar = [
            ('File',  0, [('Quit', -1, self.quit)]),      # pull-down name
            ('Tools', 0, toolEntries)                     # menu items list
            ]                                             # label,underline,action
        for (label, action) in self.fetchCommands():
            toolEntries.append((label, -1, action))       # add app items


#####################################################
# delegate to type-specific subclasses again...
#####################################################

class ListMenuGui(ShellGui):
    def fetchCommands(self):              # subclass: set 'myMenu'
        return self.myMenu
    def runCommand(self, cmd):
        for (label, action) in self.myMenu:
            if label == cmd: action()

class DictMenuGui(ShellGui):
    def fetchCommands(self):   return self.myMenu.items()
    def runCommand(self, cmd): self.myMenu[cmd]()
```

### *Using listboxes*

The biggest innovation here is the addition of a listbox widget in the middle of the window. It's built as a *Frame*, with attached *Scrollbar* and *Listbox* widgets. Items are inserted into the listbox by calling its *insert* method, with successive offsets (slots). The scrollbar and listbox are linked to each other through configuration options, which refer to bound methods of the other:

```
list.config(yscrollcommand=scroll.set, relief=SUNKEN)
scroll.config(command=list.yview, relief=SUNKEN)
```

By cross-linking, the two widgets stay in-sync with each other. This listbox only allows a single item to be selected (*selectmode=SINGLE*), but multiple-selection lists are supported too.

The *handleList* method is registered to intercept all mouse double-clicks (*<Double-1>*) on items in the listbox. When called, *handleList* fetches the current selection, and runs the associated action (by delegating to the subclass). This differs from menu and toolbar processing, where an action is directly associated with each selectable item: for listboxes, we call *bind* to associate a general handler with an event.

In fact, there are two ways to install callbacks in *Tkinter*: by using a widget's *command* option (if supported), or by calling a widget's *bind* method to intercept lower-level events. *bind* supports a rich variety of user events: mouse movement, keyboard operations, etc. See *Tk* documentation on the accompanying CD-ROM for details.

### *More on window resizing: gridded mode*

As we saw earlier, a top-level window is expandable by default, and embedded widgets inside it can be made expandable selectively by using the *expand* and *fill* packing options. Normally, resizing is performed in terms of pixels. But for text-based widgets like our listbox, we want resizing to be done in terms of lines of text; in *Tkinter* terminology, we want gridded expansion. To enable gridded expansion, we set the *setgrid* configuration option to 1 ("on") for the listbox.

---

*NOTE* Notice the use of *toolEntries* in *setMenuBar*: the list is changed in place after it's been inserted into the menu template. Sometimes, side effects can be a useful tool.

---

## *The menugui2 Client Module: Specific Tool Sets*

Here's an example of how the *ShellGui* class is used. This module is the one we'll actually run, to bring up the GUI. It defines subclasses of the list and dictionary-based GUI menu subclasses in *shellgui*, which set the *myMenu* attribute they expect to find.

Everything else is implemented in superclasses and imported functions: the classes here get lots of behavior for free. The actions in the menus here are either imported functions or inherited methods:

- Functions imported from two auxiliary modules that create data entry dialogs
- The *notdone* method inherited from *GuiMixin* (which comes from the *shellgui* superclasses)

*Example 11-22: File: menugui2.py*

```
#!/usr/local/bin/python

from shellgui import *                  # type-specific shell interfaces
from packdlg  import packDialog         # dialogs for data entry
from unpkdlg  import unpackDialog


class TextPak1(ListMenuGui):
    def __init__(self):
        self.myMenu = [('Pack',    packDialog),
                       ('Unpack',  unpackDialog),     # simple functions
                       ('Mtool',   self.notdone)]     # method from guimixin
        ListMenuGui.__init__(self)

    def forToolBar(self, label):
        return label in ['Pack', 'Unpack']


class TextPak2(DictMenuGui):
    def __init__(self):
        self.myMenu = { 'Pack':    packDialog,        # or use input here...
                        'Unpack':  unpackDialog,      # instead of in dialogs
                        'Mtool':   self.notdone }
        DictMenuGui.__init__(self)


if __name__ == '__main__':                            # self-test code...
    from sys import argv                              # 'menugui.py list|^'
    if len(argv) > 1 and argv[1] == 'list':
        print 'list test'
        TextPak1().mainloop()
    else:
        print 'dict test'
        TextPak2().mainloop()
```

*NOTE* Notice that this module is called *menugui2*. It had a predecessor too, *menugui1*, that we won't show here. *menugui1* was essentially the same, except that the actions in the menus just printed a message to *stdout* specifying which option was selected. Such *stub* callbacks let us develop GUI's one piece at a time. For instance, *menugui1* served to test the main window, before the two data-entry dialogs were written.

## The Data Entry Dialog Modules

The classes in the last two modules below define custom data entry *dialogs*, popped up on demand from *menugui2*. Once they get the user's input, they call the simple pack/unpack functions we wrote in Part 2.

### Something old, something new

And once we call the pack/unpack functions, we've left the realm of GUI interaction: their messages appear on the *stdout* window of the application (the window where it was started). Suggested exercise: intercept this text and put it in a popped-up *ScrolledText* window instead. Hint: *sys.stdout* can be reset to a file or filelike object; see Chapter 2, *A Sneak Preview*.

*Example 11-23: File: packdlg.py*

```
import pack2                    # part-2 functions
from glob import glob           # filename expansion
from Tkinter import *           # gui widget stuff

class PackDialog(Toplevel):
    def __init__(self, target1, target2):
        Toplevel.__init__(self)                    # a new top-level window
        self.title('Enter Pack Parameters')        # 2 frames plus a button

        f1 = Frame(self)
        f1.pack(anchor=N, expand=YES, fill=X)
        Label(f1, text='output file?', relief=RIDGE, width=15).pack(side=LEFT)
        e1 = Entry(f1, relief=SUNKEN)
        e1.pack(side=RIGHT, expand=YES, fill=X)

        f2 = Frame(self)
        f2.pack(anchor=CENTER, expand=YES, fill=X)
        Label(f2, text='files to pack?', relief=RIDGE, width=15).pack(side=LEFT)
        e2 = Entry(f2, relief=SUNKEN)
        e2.pack(side=RIGHT, expand=YES, fill=X)

        Button(self, text='OK', command=self.destroy).pack(anchor=S)
```

*Example 11-23: File: packdlg.py (continued)*

```
        e1['textvariable'] = target1
        e2['textvariable'] = target2

        self.grab_set()          # make myself modal:
        self.focus_set()         # mouse grab, keyboard focus, wait...
        self.wait_window()       # till destroy; else returns to caller now

def packDialog():
    s1, s2 = StringVar(), StringVar()         # run class like a function
    PackDialog(s1, s2)                        # pop-up dialog: sets s1/s2
    output, pattern = s1.get(), s2.get()      # whether 'ok' or wm-destroy
    print 'pack:', output, pattern
    pack2.pack_all(output, glob(pattern))     # should make output gui too

if __name__ == '__main__':
    class Outer(Frame):
        def __init__(self):
            Frame.__init__(self)
            self.pack()
            Button(self, text='pop', command=self.pop).pack()
            Button(self, text='hey', command=self.hey).pack()
        def pop(self):
            packDialog()
        def hey(self): print 'HEY'      # make sure dialog is modal
    Outer().mainloop()
```

*Example 11-24: File: unpkdlg.py*

```
import unpack3               # part-2 functions
from Tkinter import *        # widget classes

def unpackDialog():
    input = UnpackDialog().input
    print 'unpack:', input
    unpack3.unpack_file(input)    # do the non-gui file stuff

class UnpackDialog(Toplevel):
    def __init__(self):
        Toplevel.__init__(self)                   # resizable root box
        self.title('Enter Unpack Parameters')     # a label and an entry

        Label(self, text='input file?', relief=RIDGE, width=11).pack(side=LEFT)
        self.entry = Entry(self, relief=SUNKEN)
        self.entry.pack(side=RIGHT, expand=YES, fill=X)
        self.entry.bind("<Key-Return>", self.gotit)

        self.grab_set()                      # make myself modal
        self.focus_set()
        self.wait_window()                   # till I'm destroyed on return key

    def gotit(self, event):                  # on return key: event.widget==Entry
        self.input = self.entry.get()        # fetch text, save in self
```

*Example 11-24: File: unpkdlg.py (continued)*

```
        self.destroy()                          # kill window, but instance lives on

if __name__ == "__main__":
    Button(None, text='pop', command=unpackDialog).pack()
    mainloop()
```

### Things to notice

These modules mostly use concepts we've already seen; for instance, the pack dialog uses nested Frames to build up the layout. Here are some new concepts illustrated by these files.

***Linking variables to entry fields.*** The pack dialog uses linked variables: *StringVar* instances are linked to the *Entry* text-entry fields. Changes in a StringVar automatically update the Entry's contents. Conversely, changes in the Entry field update the StringVar variable. A text entry field is linked to a *StringVar* by setting its *textvariable* option.

In *Tkinter*, variables currently must be instances of *StringVar* (or one of its relatives) to be linked to screen widgets; we can't link raw variable names to screen widgets. Reading and writing *StringVars* follows a *get/set* method-call protocol. Alternatively, a linked-variable's values can be fetched and stored by calling it with and without an argument:

```
value = s1.get()    ...same as...    value = s1()
s2.set('new')       ...same as...    s2('new')
```

***Catching button presses and return keys: command versus bind.*** The *pack* dialog installs a button, and catches a press event to know when to fetch the values of linked-variables. The *unpack* dialog instead binds the return keypress event to a callback handler. It uses the same *bind* method to register a handler, that we used for the listbox double-click event.

These dialogs demonstrate the two ways to catch GUI events: the pack dialog's button uses a *command* option, and the unpack dialog's entry-field uses a *bind* call. Instead of using buttons and linked variables, the unpack dialog fetches the result from the Entry widget directly, when a *<Key-Return>* occurs.

***Making windows modal.*** Both the dialogs block (prevent) other activity in the GUI while they're displayed; users need to interact with the dialog itself, before they can do anything else. Such windows are usually called *modal* dialogs. They impose a function call model on an event-driven system. Because it's unnatural to assume anything happens in a linear fashion in GUIs, enforcing it takes extra work.

Here's how these dialogs do it. To make the data entry dialogs new windows, they're built as subclasses of the *Toplevel* widget, discussed earlier. To make the dialogs modal, both dialogs grab the mouse, get the keyboard focus, and wait until the window is destroyed (i.e., until the inherited *destroy* method runs):

```
self.grab_set()          # make myself modal:
self.focus_set()         # mouse grab, keyboard focus, wait...
self.wait_window()       # till destroyed; else returns to caller now
```

The *wait_window* call works like a function call: it doesn't return until the window is destroyed. Both dialogs pause until *self* (the dialog) is destroyed, before returning from the class constructor. The effect is to make the class constructor behave like a function call: we can be sure there's been a response, after the constructor call returns.

If we didn't call the wait method, the new dialog would pop-up and be added to the *Tkinter* event loop as usual. But the program would return from the dialog-class constructor immediately. There'd be no way to guarantee that interaction had really occurred. To force interaction, we need to explicitly wait.

***Using anchors to pack widgets.*** The pack dialog uses *anchor* packing options instead of *sides* to arrange its widgets. Anchors are like sides, but accept all eight points of the compass (*n*, *ne*, *nw*, ...) and "center" as relative positions.

***Insert magic here.*** Both of these dialogs use quite a bit of configuration code. In fact, *most* of the dialogs' code is devoted to constructing widgets. It would be better to wrap the widget construction in functions; we'll see one way to do this later. Better still, would be a way to automate custom dialog construction, like we did for menus and tool-bars. Suggested exercise: design a dialog construction system.

## *Running the Shell Tools Interface*

Finally, when we run the *menugui2.py* module as a top-level program (*% python menugui2.py*), our menu options appear in a GUI interface. Figure 11-25 shows the *dictionary-based* menu as a GUI.

Tools can be selected by double-clicking on listbox entries, pressing the buttons at the bottom, or selecting pull-down menu entries. The GUI inherits menu and tool-bar widget *resizability* from GuiMaker, and makes its own widgets resizable (the listbox and its frame); it can be stretched interactively (see Figure 11-26).

When we run the program with a *list* command-line argument, we use the list-based menu; *Mtool* is kept off the toolbar (it has not yet been implemented). When we select the *Pack* option from any of the three sources, a modal (blocking) dialog pops up for entry of parameters. As seen in Figure 11-27, pressing its *OK* button makes the program fetch the entered values, and run the packer function.

*Figure 11-25: menugui2 main window*

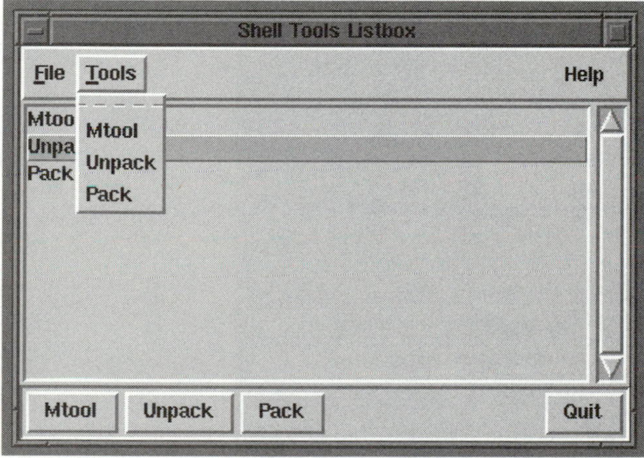


*Figure 11-26: Resizing with listboxes*

The packer function's messages show up in the *stdout* window for the application (usually, the one where we started *menugui2*). Selecting *Unpack* pops up the *unpkdlg* module's dialog (see Figure 11-28); this time, we press the return key when we're done, to make the system fetch the entered filename.

The data entry dialogs can be tested in isolation too, by running their modules as top-level files; both can be resized. Figure 11-29 shows the widgets we get when *packdlg* is run as a program file (*% python packdlg.py*). If we press the *hey* button while the pack dialog box is up, nothing happens: the parent window is blocked until the modal dialog box receives a reply.

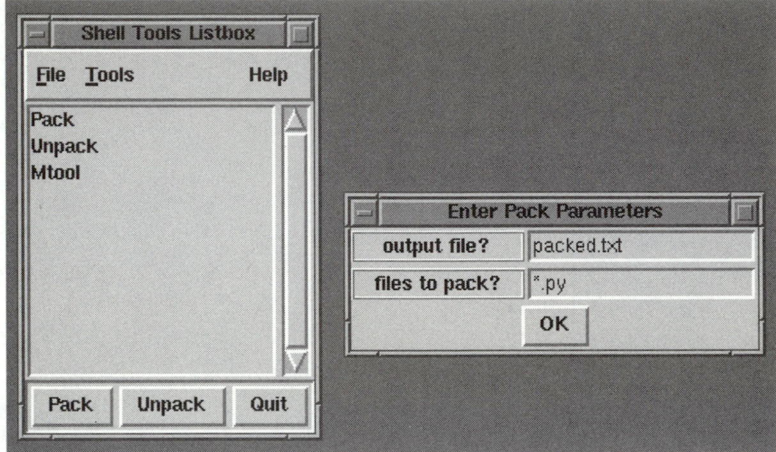


*Figure 11-27: Pop-up packing form*

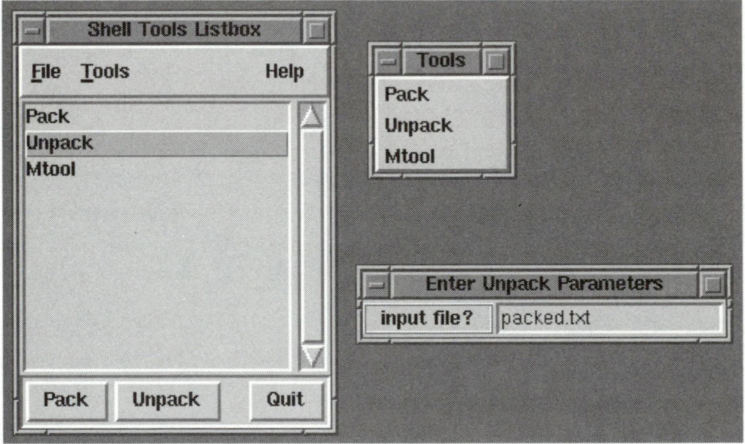


*Figure 11-28: Pop-up dialogs: unpacking form*

# Avoiding Namespace Clashes

Now we'll briefly discuss namespaces in complex programs. Since we've built our GUIs as subclasses of *Frame*, it's not impossible that methods we define locally might clash with methods *Tkinter* adds to *Frame*. If that happens, our local method will *replace* the *Tkinter* method of the same name. Careful use of names (for instance, adding a prefix or an uppercase letter) solves the problem.

As a rule, it's a good idea to minimize adding attributes to instances derived from widget classes. For example, *Tcl/Tk* programmers are accustomed to concatenating names with periods, to give a path; in Python/*Tkinter*, this translates to nested class instances, and new attribute names:

```
class GuiApp(Frame):
    def makeWidgets(self):
        self.frame = Frame(...)
        self.frame.toolbar = Frame(self.Frame)
        self.frame.toolbar.button1 = Button(self.frame.toolbar, ...)
```

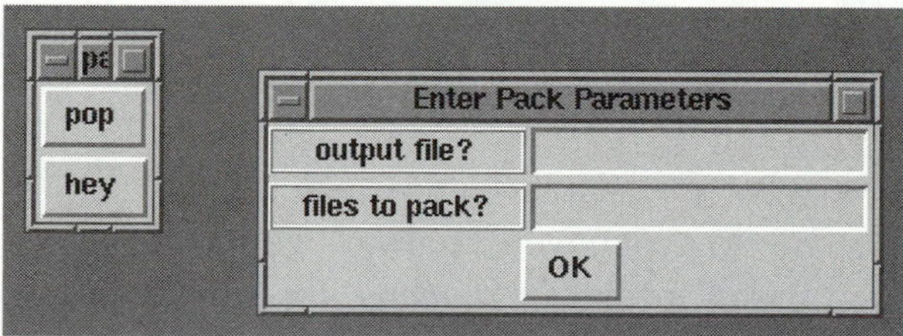

*Figure 11-29: Pack dialog self-test*

## *Another way to be modal: recursive mainloop calls*

Typically, modal dialogs are implemented by waiting for a destroy event. But other schemes are possible. For example, if we call the *mainloop* method recursively, it won't return until the *quit* widget-method has been invoked. Normally, *quit* ends the GUI program, but it will simply exit a recursive *mainloop* level if one is active. Because of this, modal dialogs can also be written without *wait* method calls:

```
class MyDialog:
    ...                                  # make window, root=TopLevel
    def show(self):
        self.root.grab_set()             # block other widgets
        self.root.mainloop()             # recusive mainloop call
        self.root.destroy()              # destroy window on return
        return self.value                # value set in callbacks

    def ok(self):
        print "ok"                       # 'ok' button callback
        self.value = 1
        self.root.quit()                 # end mainloop() call

    def cancel(self):
        print "cancel"                   # 'cancel' button callback
        self.value = 0
        self.root.quit()                 # end mainloop() call
```

But unless we need to later access embedded widgets, there's no reason to assign them to qualified attribute names like this. In fact, doing so increases the chance of name clashes (what if *Frame* has a *button1* member?). Instead, local variables can be used to link widget instances in methods:

```
class GuiApp(Frame):
    def makeWidgets(self):
        frame = Frame(...)
        toolbar = Frame(frame)
        Button(toolbar, ...)
```

If we're not sure which attribute names to avoid, we can always go look at Frame (and other widget classes): they're coded in the *Lib/tkinter/Tkinter.py* file. There are other class-based structures which get around the problem too; if we don't subclass a widget, we're always safe:

```
class GuiApp:
    def __init__(self):
        self.frame = Frame()
        self.frame.pack()
        self.makeWidgets()
    def makeWidgets(self):
        Button(self.frame, command=self.onPress,...)
    def onPress(self):
    ...etc.
    def mainloop(self): self.frame.mainloop()
```

We attach nested widget instances to *self.frame*, instead of *self*, since it's no longer a widget subclass. This solves the widget name-clash issue, and still gives us an organizational structure for GUIs. But as is, we can't use this *GuiApp* as though it were a real *Frame*, since it's not a true widget. Such a class can still be specialized and extended by overriding its methods. And we can still attach the class's instances to passed-in parent widgets:

```
class GuiApp:
    def __init__(self, parent):          # I'm not a widget
        self.frame = Frame(parent)       # but I attach new widgets to one
    ...etc.
```

But we may run into limitations, if we try to use the class like a widget from the outside:

```
subgui = GuiApp(parent)         # attach the class instance
subgui.pack(side=LEFT)          # but it has no pack method: not a real widget!
```

Naturally, the difference won't matter in many applications. Suggested exercise: what would it take to make this last *GuiApp* act more like a real widget? Would the `__getattr__` method help here?

# *Handling Program Errors*

So far, we've made the completely unrealistic assumption that our examples work the moment we type them. (It happens, but it's rare! :-) But what do we do when things don't work as planned? This may be more critical in a dynamic language like Python, since some errors aren't caught until run-time. For instance, misspelled variable names aren't detected until the offending line is executed. Even syntax errors aren't reported until you import the buggy module file at run-time.

Luckily, Python also makes finding and fixing errors simple and fast; it takes less time to repair mistakes in Python code than in compiled languages like C. And Python traps many errors at run-time that languages like C don't. For instance, out-of-bounds indexes are caught and reported instead of quietly corrupting memory. In Python, errors are part of a high-level exception-handling system.

Since error handling can be especially confusing in GUI work (callbacks are nested in an event-stream processor), this is probably a good time to discuss the topic. When program errors occur, there are a variety of ways to deal with them, from figuring out what a stack dump means, to starting up the Python debugger and stepping through the program interactively. Let's look at some options.

## *Exception Handlers, Stack Dumps, and Print Statements*

In a sense, we've already addressed error handling basics: when a program error occurs, Python raises a built-in exception, which we can catch with *try* statements. For instance, we've already used the *KeyError* (key not found), *IndexError* (out of bounds index), and *EOFError* (end of file) exceptions. There's no difference between exceptions we raise ourselves (with *raise* statements), and exceptions Python raises on real errors.

Because of this, we can always catch program errors manually and process them ourselves, using *try* statements. For some programs, this is all the error-handling logic we need. For example, to catch all errors, we could write a *try* at the top-level of our program:

```
def doit(entry):
    try:                        # catches all errors not caught in entry()
        entry()                 # sys.exc_type/value are the raised exception
    except:
        import sys
        print 'error!', sys.exc_type, sys.exc_value
```

But if an exception isn't caught by any *try* statement, it propagates up to the top level of the Python interpreter process, and Python reports the exception name, along with a call-stack trace. This stack dump gives the names, arguments, and source file lines for all functions and methods that were active when the exception occurred. For instance, suppose we're trying to run the program file:

*Example 11-25: File: stackdmp.py*

```
def function3(a, b):
    return (a / b) * a

def function2(l, m, n):
    x = function3(l, m - m)

print function2(2, 4, 8)
```

Here's the stack trace we'll get when this program file is run (we get the same stack display if we run this as a standalone script):

```
% python stackdmp.py

Traceback (innermost last):
  File "stackdmp.py", line 7, in ?
    print function2(2, 4, 8)
  File "stackdmp.py", line 5, in function2
    x = function3(l, m - m)
  File "stackdmp.py", line 2, in function3
    return (a / b) * a
ZeroDivisionError: integer division or modulo
```

We see all the lines and functions that were active when the error occurred. The bottom one is the line where the error really happened. Often, this is more than enough information to determine what went wrong. For instance, we can tell that *b* was zero in *function3*; that leads us to the *m – m* expression in *function2*.

If we need to know more, it's sometimes enough to insert *print* statements into the code, to display variables and status as it executes, and rerun. For instance:

```
debugme = 1
...
if debugme:
    print 'here I am...', a, b
...
```

Since Python programs run immediately (no compile or link steps), this is often a quick and reasonable way to get more information about a sick program.

---

*NOTE* In fact, *print* statements may be the only way to monitor execution, if the standard input, output, and error streams have been redirected. This is rare, but since debugger interaction uses streams, it can be misled. For example, *print* statements were needed to debug the stream redirection classes, in an application framework we'll see later (see Appendix D, *An Application Framework*).

---

## *A Close Encounter with Python's Debugger*

But when we need even more information to isolate a problem, we can also run the program under Python's standard *pdb* debugger. *pdb* is an interactive source code debugger, with a command-line interface similar to C debuggers such as *dbx* and *gdb*. Essentially, *pdb* works like a probe for Python programs: we can stop the program at strategic spots, step through it line by line, inspect program variables, and even test a hypothesis by changing variables and resuming execution. Pdb gives much more information about a program than a simple stack-trace. *pdb* also provides postmortem analysis, after a program crashes.

### *A quick example*

Let's first look at a simple example: printing variables in the *stackdmp* module above. We'll explain the commands used in a moment. This is also an example of how to run a *script* file (one that executes immediately) under *pdb*: since scripts are also modules, we *import* them to make them run.

```
% python
>>> import pdb                                 load the debugger module
>>> pdb.run('import stackdmp')                 load/run the script under pdb
> <string>(0)?()
(Pdb) cont                                     run up to the error occurrence
> <string>(1)?()
(Pdb) cont
ZeroDivisionError: 'integer division or modulo'
> <string>(1)?()                               post-mortum analysis:
(Pdb) where                                    print the call-stack
> <string>(1)?()
  ./stackdmp.py(7)?()
-> print function2(2, 4, 8)
  ./stackdmp.py(5)function2()
-> x = function3(1, m - m)
  ./stackdmp.py(2)function3()
-> return (a / b) * a
(Pdb) down                                     go down the call-stack
> ./stackdmp.py(7)?()                          to lower (later) functions
-> print function2(2, 4, 8)
(Pdb) down
> ./stackdmp.py(5)function2()
-> x = function3(1, m - m)
(Pdb) down
> ./stackdmp.py(2)function3()
-> return (a / b) * a
(Pdb) p a, b                                   print variable values
(2, 0)                                         sure enough; b's zero...
(Pdb) up                                       go back up the stack
> ./stackdmp.py(5)function2()
-> x = function3(1, m - m)                     this should be m - n!
(Pdb) p l, m, n
(2, 4, 8)
(Pdb) quit
```

As usual, *pdb* prints a prompt (*(Pdb)*) when it expects a command. Source context in is given by two lines of the form:

```
> file-path(line-number)function-name
-> source-line
```

The > marks the current line; it's absent for other lines in stack displays. The most recently executed (top) line is listed at the bottom, when the call stack is shown.

## *pdb versus dbx*

If you've used *dbx* (or *gdb*) for C debugging, you already know how to use most *pdb* commands; in fact, much of the following example will probably be familiar. But *pdb* also has some major distinctions: commands are debugged by running code strings, and any Python statement or expression can be run from the debugger's command line. For instance, to call functions and methods we type call expressions, and to change variable values, we type normal assignment statements.

Pdb uses the *eval* and *exec* built-ins to call the Python parser/compiler at run-time (more on these later). Expressions and statements typed at the debugger's command-line work exactly as if they were inserted into the code being debugged. This makes for a dynamic and flexible debugger. As we'll see, we can import a new module and call its functions, reload a module that's part of the program being debugged by typing a *reload* call, and even change a function in the debugged code to a new one created by typing a *def* at *pdb*'s command-line. (Try doing that in *dbx*!)

### *Debugging GUI callbacks*

Now let's look at a more complex example of *pdb* interaction, and study *pdb*'s command set. When an error occurs in a callback handler, it raises an exception in Python code that's really embedded in the *Tkinter* C system (an extension module). Since this can be confusing, let's get a clear idea of the architecture.

When you run a *Tkinter* Python program, you're actually using quite a few layers of software (though *Tkinter* hides the details). Figure 11-30 shows the layers that typical GUI calls are routed through.

The *Tkinter* module resides in the standard library directory, (usually, *Lib*). All the C components are linked in to the Python executable (or an executable that embeds Python), either statically or dynamically. When events occur, they're dispatched from the bottom layer (*Xlib*) to the top (your program):

- When we build a GUI, we register callable objects with *Tkinter* in *command* options or *bind* calls.
- When we call the *Tkinter mainloop* method, we pass control to the C-based *Tk*/X system, and wait.
- When an event occurs, *Tkinter* calls the Python object we registered to handle the callback.

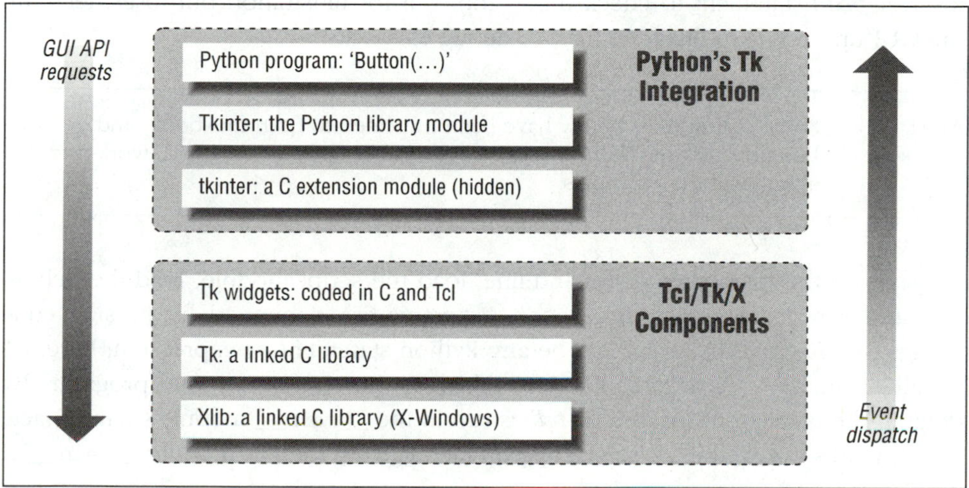


*Figure 11-30: Tkinter run-time structure*

Because of this structure, when we debug callback handlers, we only see Python code triggered by the event; above this, there's a C library/module layer.

Let's work through an example; we'll point out debugger concepts along the way. First, change file *packdlg.py*, line 24 (or assume it's started as this):

```
e2['textvariable'] = trget2
```

Next, run the buggy script normally: *Tkinter* prints a stack trace when callbacks raise uncaught errors, but the GUI itself continues.

```
% menugui2.py
dict test

<push the "pack" button>

Exception in Tkinter callback
Traceback (innermost last):
  File "/usr/local/lib/python/tkinter/Tkinter.py", line 492, in __call__
    return apply(self.func, args)
  File "./packdlg.py", line 32, in packDialog
    PackDialog(s1, s2)                          # pop-up dialog: sets s1/s2
```

```
  File "./packdlg.py", line 24, in __init__
    e2['textvariable'] = trget2
NameError: trget2
```

*<push the "quit" button>*

You can probably tell what the problem is from this information: we've misspelled a variable name. Usually, we'd fix this up and have our GUI going again in less than a minute. If we weren't sure (maybe we didn't write this code?), we could insert a *print* statement to check things too. But for illustration purposes, let's run the GUI under *pdb* to illustrate how to debug callbacks.

---

*NOTE* Some output lines below have been truncated to fit in this book, and line-numbers in *Tkinter* code will vary. For greater accuracy, work along with the examples.

---

We start up the interactive command line, load the script module, load the debugger, and run the program under *pdb*. Programs are debugged by passing code strings to *pdb.run*. The string can be any Python statement or expression; here, it's a call to make a *TextPak2* instance, which is how we start our program. By default, the code-string passed to *pdb* is run in the __main__ module's namespace, which works out well if we're calling *pdb* interactively (i.e., in module __main__).

```
% python
>>> import menugui2
>>> import pdb
>>> pdb.run('menugui2.TextPak2().mainloop()')
```

*Pdb* stops initially, to let us set breakpoints. Let's set one on the function that builds the pack dialog, and continue; *menugui2.packdialog* evaluates to a function object in the current module (__main__).

```
> <string>(0)?()
(Pdb) b menugui2.packDialog
(Pdb) c
> <string>(1)?()
(Pdb) c
```

The GUI pops up as before, with the window shown in Figure 11-31.

When we press the *pack* button, the program stops at line 30 and switches to the *pdb* command-line window. Now we can enter more commands (or first-letter abbreviations) to monitor execution. Table 11-2 lists *pdb*'s commands.

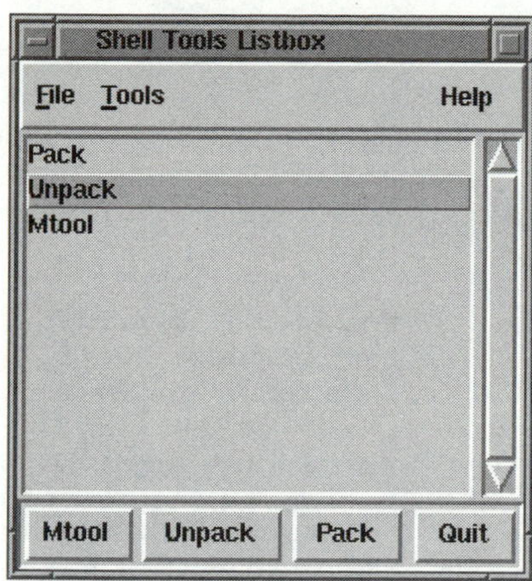


*Figure 11-31: menugui2 run under the debugger*

*Table 11-2: pdb debugging commands*

| Commands | Description |
|---|---|
| *p(rint) expression* | Inspect variables/attributes, evaluate expressions, call functions/methods |
| *w(here)* | Dump the call stack: the context of the current program location |
| *u(p), d(own)* | Travel up (to newer) or down (to older) frames in the namespace/call stack |
| *l(ist) first?, last?* | List the current context's source code file: 11 lines, or around line numbers |
| *b(reak) (line \| name)?* | Set more breakpoints on functions or line numbers, or list active breaks |
| *cl(ear) line?* | Clear a specific breakpoint (or all of them) |
| *s(tep)* | Run the next line and stop; stop in called functions |
| *n(ext)* | Run the next line and stop, but don't stop in functions it calls |
| *r(eturn)* | Continue silently until the current function returns |
| *c(ont(inue))* | Continue program execution until an error, breakpoint, or exit |
| *a(rgs)* | Print arguments passed to the current context's function |
| *q(uit)* | Quit the debugger; also terminates the code being debugged |
| *! statement, statement* | Run a Python statement in the current stack frame: *calls, assignment, reload,* ... |
| *<enter-key>* | Repeat the last command |
| *h(elp) command?* | Get command help; you can forget the rest if you remember *h* |

In the source code listed below, breakpoints are marked *B*, and the current position is ->.

```
> ./packdlg.py(30)packDialog()
-> def packDialog():
(Pdb) l
 25
 26              self.grab_set()              # make myself modal:
 27              self.focus_set()             # mouse grab, keyboard focus, wait...
 28              self.wait_window()           # till destroy; else returns to caller
 29
 30 B-> def packDialog():
 31          s1, s2 = StringVar(), StringVar()               # run class like a funct
 32          PackDialog(s1, s2)                              # pop-up dialog: sets s1
 33          output, pattern = s1.get(), s2.get()            # whether 'ok' or wm-des
 34          print 'pack:', output, pattern
 35          pack2.pack_all(output, glob(pattern))           # should make output gui
```

Now dump the call stack. Note that most of the active calls on the stack have to do with *Tkinter* support code. Only the last two lines describe our callback code—the source context and current line.

```
(Pdb) w
  <string>(1)?()
  /usr/local/lib/python/tkinter/Tkinter.py(391)mainloop()
-> self.tk.mainloop(n)
  /usr/local/lib/python/tkinter/Tkinter.py(492)__call__()
-> return apply(self.func, args)
> ./packdlg.py(30)packDialog()
-> def packDialog():
```

Run the current line: the function header counts as a line too.

```
(Pdb) n
> ./packdlg.py(31)packDialog()
-> s1, s2 = StringVar(), StringVar()            # run class like a function
```

Run the assignment: use *n* to avoid stopping in the *StringVar* constructor method.

```
(Pdb) n
> ./packdlg.py(32)packDialog()
-> PackDialog(s1, s2)                           # pop-up dialog: sets s1/s2
```

Use *s* here: we want to step into PackDialog's constructor.

```
(Pdb) s
> ./packdlg.py(6)__init__()
-> def __init__(self, target1, target2):
(Pdb) l
  1      import pack2                   # part-2 functions
  2      from glob import glob          # filename expansion
  3      from Tkinter import *          # gui widget stuff
  4
  5      class PackDialog(Toplevel):
  6  ->      def __init__(self, target1, target2):
  7              Toplevel.__init__(self)                   # a new top-level wind
  8              self.title('Enter Pack Parameters')       # 2 frames plus a butt
```

```
  9
 10                 f1 = Frame(self)
 11                 f1.pack(anchor=N, expand=YES, fill=X)
(Pdb) s
> ./packdlg.py(7)__init__()
-> Toplevel.__init__(self)                       # a new top-level window
```

Use *n* to run the line: we don't care what's in *Toplevel*. Since it's predefined, it's probably not the culprit, so skip over the constructor call.

```
(Pdb) n
> ./packdlg.py(8)__init__()
-> self.title('Enter Pack Parameters')       # 2 frames plus a button
(Pdb) l
  3     from Tkinter import *         # gui widget stuff
  4
  5     class PackDialog(Toplevel):
  6         def __init__(self, target1, target2):
  7             Toplevel.__init__(self)                  # a new top-level wind
  8  ->         self.title('Enter Pack Parameters')      # 2 frames plus a butt
  9
 10             f1 = Frame(self)
 11             f1.pack(anchor=N, expand=YES, fill=X)
 12             Label(f1, text='output file?', relief=RIDGE, width=15).pack(sid
 13             e1 = Entry(f1, relief=SUNKEN)
(Pdb) l
 14             e1.pack(side=RIGHT, expand=YES, fill=X)
 15
 16             f2 = Frame(self)
 17             f2.pack(anchor=CENTER, expand=YES, fill=X)
 18             Label(f2, text='files to pack?', relief=RIDGE, width=15).pack(s
 19             e2 = Entry(f2, relief=SUNKEN)
 20             e2.pack(side=RIGHT, expand=YES, fill=X)
 21
 22             Button(self, text='OK', command=self.destroy).pack(anchor=S)
 23             e1['textvariable'] = target1
 24             e2['textvariable'] = trget2
```

We probably don't care about all this form configuration code. Set a breakpoint at line 22 and continue to get past this code.

The *b* command can take a function object or a file line number. We can set breaks on any sort of Python function: simple functions, unbound class methods, even bound methods. For instance, we can set breaks on class `__init__` and `__del__` methods to stop on instance creation and destruction.

```
(Pdb) b 22
(Pdb) c
> ./packdlg.py(22)__init__()
-> Button(self, text='OK', command=self.destroy).pack(anchor=S)
```

Now we're stopped at line 22; let's print some variables. We have access to local variables, globals and built-ins, classes, and instance-attributes through *self*. The *p* expression is evaluated in the current source position's namespace: anything visible there can be printed (and assigned).

We can also call functions and methods as *p* expressions or "!" statements, and set variables in the running program by running assignment statements in the current namespace with `!`. In fact, if we type a command *pdb* can't recognize, it assumes it's a statement, so the `!` prefix is rarely needed.

```
(Pdb) p f1
<Frame instance at 1ce9f0>
(Pdb) p PackDialog
<class PackDialog at 163c60>
(Pdb) p self
<PackDialog instance at 1ce840>
(Pdb) p self.__class__.__name__
'PackDialog'
```

Back to our bug hunt: lets *n* around the *Button* call, and run the *e1* assignment.

```
(Pdb) n
> ./packdlg.py(23)__init__()
-> e1['textvariable'] = target1
(Pdb) s
> /usr/local/lib/python/tkinter/Tkinter.py(746)__setitem__()
-> def __setitem__(self, key, value):
```

Oops—we stepped into some *Tkinter* support code that catches assignments to an *Entry* widget's key; use *r* (return) to exit functions without stepping through.

```
(Pdb) r
--Return--
> /usr/local/lib/python/tkinter/Tkinter.py(747)__setitem__()->None
-> Widget.config(self, {key: value})
(Pdb) s
> ./packdlg.py(24)__init__()
-> e2['textvariable'] = trget2
```

Aha: what's *trget2*?

```
(Pdb) p trget2
*** NameError: 'trget2'
(Pdb) p target2
<StringVar instance at 1cee70>
```

Wrong variable name. But run the line to make sure; first *pdb* catches the error, then the function (class call) exits, and finally *Tkinter* catches the exception and prints a stack traceback.

```
(Pdb) n
NameError: 'trget2'
> ./packdlg.py(24)__init__()
-> e2['textvariable'] = trget2
(Pdb) n
```

```
NameError: 'trget2'
> ./packdlg.py(32)packDialog()
-> PackDialog(s1, s2)                         # pop-up dialog: sets s1/s2
(Pdb) c
Exception in Tkinter callback
Traceback (innermost last):
  File "/usr/local/lib/python/tkinter/Tkinter.py", line 492, in __call__
    return apply(self.func, args)
  File "./packdlg.py", line 32, in packDialog
    PackDialog(s1, s2)                        # pop-up dialog: sets s1/s2
  File "./packdlg.py", line 24, in __init__
    e2['textvariable'] = trget2
NameError: trget2
```

All right; we've seen enough. Kill the window, exit the interpreter, and fix the script.

## *Strategies for debugging mixed-language systems.*

Under *pdb*, we can only break on Python code: we can't set breaks or step through methods of built-in types (*list.append*) or built-in functions (*range*), since they're implemented in C. This is an advanced topic, and only matters when Python is used in larger systems (C integration is discussed later). But here are a few debugging issues.

In this example, we debugged a Python GUI. But really, when we stop in callback-handler code, we're debugging Python code embedded in (called from) the *Tk* interface C module. It worked in this example, because Python is "on top": we can run the whole program under *pdb*. But what if we have a different structure? How do we debug C extension code called from Python, or the C and Python code in a system when Python's embedded?

Approaches for debugging a mixed Python/C system depend on how the system is structured, and what we want to debug. If Python is embedded, we can run the enclosing C part under a C debugger (like *dbx*), and route embedded Python code to pdb by passing it to *pdb.run* calls from C (described later). If Python is "on top," we can run the *python* executable under a C debugger, to debug embedded C extensions.

For instance, under *Tkinter*, Python code calls C code (*mainloop*), which later calls registered Python code (callback handlers). To debug the *Tkinter* C code, we can run the *python* interpreter under a C debugger, and run the Python program under *pdb*.

### Debugging with classes

Here's another log of debug session with a smaller program. It illustrates some advanced debugging concepts: breaking on methods, stack navigation, changing instance attributes, etc. Comments to the right of commands in the log explain the command sequences.

*Example 11-26: File: debugtst.py*

```
def ftest(obj, val):
    obj.set(val)
    print obj.get()

class Ctest:
    def set(self, x):  self.x = x
    def get(self):     return self.x

def doit():
    inst = Ctest()
    ftest(inst, 99)

    % python

    >>> import pdb
    >>> import debugtst
    >>> debugtst.doit()                          run normally
    99
    >>> pdb.run('debugtst.doit()')              run under debugger
    > <string>(0)?()
    (Pdb) b debugtst.ftest                       break on a function
    (Pdb) b debugtst.Ctest.set                   break on an unbound class method
    (Pdb) t = debugtst.Ctest()                   could also break on __init__ if present
    (Pdb) b t.get                                break on a bound class method (same)
    (Pdb) s
    > <string>(1)?()
    (Pdb) c
    > ./debugtst.py(1)ftest()
    -> def ftest(obj, val):
    (Pdb) w                                      stopped at debugtst.ftest breakpoint
      <string>(1)?()
      ./debugtst.py(11)doit()
    -> ftest(inst, 99)
    > ./debugtst.py(1)ftest()
    -> def ftest(obj, val):
    (Pdb) s
    > ./debugtst.py(2)ftest()
    -> obj.set(val)
    (Pdb) p obj                                  'obj' in top stack-frame/namespace
    <Ctest instance at df5d0>                    'obj' is a 'ftest' local name
    (Pdb) u
    > ./debugtst.py(11)doit()
    -> ftest(inst, 99)
    (Pdb) p inst                                 'inst' in older/prior stack-frame
    <Ctest instance at df5d0>                    'inst' is a 'doit' local name
```

```
(Pdb) d
> ./debugtst.py(2)ftest()
-> obj.set(val)
(Pdb) c
> ./debugtst.py(6)set()
-> def set(self, x): self.x = x
(Pdb) w                                          stopped at Ctest.set breakpoint
  <string>(1)?()                                 now we're three levels deep...
  ./debugtst.py(11)doit()
-> ftest(inst, 99)
  ./debugtst.py(2)ftest()
-> obj.set(val)
> ./debugtst.py(6)set()
-> def set(self, x): self.x = x
(Pdb) b                                          'b' with no argument lists breakpoints
{'./debugtst.py': [1, 6, 7]}
(Pdb) l                                          list source, show breakpoints
  1 B   def ftest(obj, val):
  2         obj.set(val)
  3         print obj.get()
  4
  5     class Ctest:
  6 B->     def set(self, x): self.x = x
  7 B       def get(self):    return self.x
  8
  9     def doit():
 10         inst = Ctest()
 11         ftest(inst, 99)
(Pdb) s
> ./debugtst.py(6)set()
-> def set(self, x): self.x = x
(Pdb) c
> ./debugtst.py(7)get()
-> def get(self):    return self.x
(Pdb) s                                          program stopped in Ctest.get
> ./debugtst.py(7)get()
-> def get(self):    return self.x
(Pdb) p self                                     'self' is a local name in the method
<Ctest instance at df5d0>
(Pdb) p sel.x                                    pdb catches interactive errors
*** NameError: 'sel'
(Pdb) p self.x                                   qualification expression: attributes
99
(Pdb) self.x = 88                                change instance attribute with '='
(Pdb) c
88                                               ftest prints a different result!
--Return--
> <string>(1)?()->None
(Pdb) quit
>>> <ctrl-d>
```

***Namespace considerations in pdb.*** At the *pdb* prompt, expressions and statements run in the namespace of the line where execution is currently stopped, as if it were typed in the debugged code directly. We need to be aware of namespace context when printing variables. For instance, *Ctest* must be called *debugtst.Ctest* when *pdb* first stops (in `__main__`), but it's just *Ctest* once we get into the *doit* function. In *doit*, *Ctest* is a global, and the module name *debugtst* isn't accessible.

Here's a more interesting illustration: to change a global variable in the module enclosing a function or method we're stopped in, we have to use *global* statements along with the assignment. Otherwise the assignment goes in the function's local scope (following the usual rules for assignments: see Part 2). For instance, here's how to change a function when stopped inside another:

```
% python
>>> import debugtst, pdb
>>> pdb.run('debugtst.doit()')
> <string>(0)?()
(Pdb) s                        <and step-to or stop-at the call to ftest in doit...>
> ./debugtst.py(11)doit()
-> ftest(inst, 99)
(Pdb) def new(x, y): print 'SURPRISE'           make a new function in 'doit'
(Pdb) global ftest; ftest = new                 reset 'ftest': a global here
(Pdb) c
SURPRISE                                        calls the new function
--Return--
> <string>(1)?()->None
(Pdb)
```

***Reloading modules during pdb sessions.*** Sometimes it can be useful to load new versions of modules while we're debugging. Since *pdb* runs arbitrary Python code, we can always type *reload(<module>)* expressions at *pdb*'s command line. For example, if we isolate a problem, but want to continue the current debugging session, we might edit the file in another window, and reload the module without leaving *pdb*.

But notice that *pdb* runs expressions in the namespace of the current source position: if we're stopped in a function, a *reload* runs in that function's scope. Usually the module named doesn't exist there; for instance, it's in the namespace of module `__main__` if it was imported interactively. But *reload* expects a module object (not a string) to be passed it; here are some ways we might access the module:

- Just type *reload(module)* if the module is really available in the current scope:

  ```
  (Pdb) reload(module)
  ```

- Issue *up* commands until we're at the top, and then type *reload* (if it's imported in `__main__`):

```
(Pdb) up ...
(Pdb) reload(module)
```

- Type an import statement before the *reload* expression:

```
(Pdb) import module
(Pdb) reload(module)
```

- Import *sys*, and use its modules table directly:

```
(Pdb) import sys
(Pdb) reload(sys.modules['module-name'])
```

In the third approach, the module name is added to the current stack frame's namespace, and may clash with a local name; to avoid possible problems, we could go *up* to `__main__` before typing the *import* statements. The fourth approach adds name *sys*, but is probably less dangerous.

---

*NOTE* Like many C debuggers, the current version of *pdb* caches source files for listings. You may not see the new version of your file if you reload and list it in the debugger.

---

Suggested exercise: experiment with reloading the *debugtst* module under *pdb*. Stop execution in the *doit* function, change *ftest* in the source file, reload *debugtst*, and continue. Is the new *ftest* called? Why? (Hint: see Chapter 7, *Adding a Simple User Interface*; *reload* overwrites module namespaces, and names aren't evaluated until they're used).

# A Totally RAD Language

Python development in general, and Python GUI development in particular, can be described by a currently-popular acronym: RAD for Rapid Application Development. By definition, Python is a RAD language. It provides both:

- A very high-level, object-oriented language
- Rapid turnaround after program changes

In fact, the effects of program changes can usually be observed almost immediately. Because of this quick feedback, Python development is more than fast enough for typical GUI work.

But what about GUI programs that take a long time to start up? Perhaps we have to connect to databases, or initialize a large system. Or maybe it takes a long series of steps to retrigger a callback we want to change. In any event, it's sometimes inconvenient to stop and restart each time we need to make a change, even if restarting is fast in Python.

## How the debugger works

Python's debugger is coded in Python (evidence of the language's utility). In fact, *pdb* is structured as an extendible Python class system; it can be subclassed to create different debugger "flavors." See the library module *Lib/pdb.py* for more information. In this book, we've used the command-line debugging interface; a GUI-based interface exists (*wdb*), but it currently depends on the *STDWIN* extension, which isn't widely used. (A new Python debugger GUI, based on *Tkinter*, was announced just before this book was finished; see the reference in Appendix A).

To support debuggers, the Python interpreter defines a hook where Python objects can be registered to be called on relevant events: function calls/returns, line changes, and exceptions. The *sys.settrace* built-in is called to set the event-handler; when the handler's called, it receives the current stack-frame (another type of Python object), which gives access to the current namespace dictionaries, line number and source file information, higher (older) stack-frames, etc.

*Pdb* registers a handler for these events, and maps them to source code debugging activities. This differs from common C debugger techniques that instrument the compiled program itself (by swapping trap op-codes into the code, using symbol tables, etc.). But Python's approach supports a variety of tools. For instance, the same event handler hook is used to implement the Python profiler (covered later in the book).

*Pdb* defines a handful of top-level interfaces, for instance:

`pdb.run(stmt, ?global, ?local)`
: *runs a statement; the namespaces default to __main__*

`pdb.runeval(expr, ?global, ?local)`
: *runs an expression, and returns its result*

`pdb.runcall(func, argument...)`
: *calls a function with arguments, and returns its result*

`pdb.pm()`
: *start a postmortem debugging session after an exception*

Since *pdb*'s written in Python, it has access to everything in the running program's environment. And because its interfaces are Python functions, *pdb* can be called anywhere in a Python program (for instance, from a programming environment manager). It can even be called from C, to debug embedded Python code: instead of running a code string directly, run a *pdb* call string with the real code string as an argument: *pdb.run('code')*. *Pdb* stops before the code starts running (see Chapter 15).

## *Changing a GUI's Callbacks While It Is Running*

With a little extra work, Python can handle these cases too: we can avoid stops by using *reload* to update parts of a GUI program while it's running. The catch is that we have to explicitly request reloading of the modules that we plan to change dynamically. We explored *reload* in Chapter 7.

Here's an example that reloads a module file of callback actions without stopping the GUI. It builds the window in Figure 11-32. After editing the *actions.py* file, re-pressing the GUI's buttons prints a different message. This example is deliberately simple, to illustrate the concept. But in practice, the actions reloaded in this fashion might build pop-up dialogs, new top-level windows, etc.; reloading would let us change their appearance dynamically.

*Example 11-27: File: actions.py*

```
# callback handlers: reloaded each time triggered

def message1():                  # change me
    print 'spamSpamSPAM'        # could build a dialog...

def message2(self):
    print 'Ni! Ni!'             # change me
    self.method1()              # access the 'Hello' instance...
```

*Example 11-28: File: rad2.py*

```
from Tkinter import *
import actions                # get initial callback handlers

class Hello(Frame):
    def __init__(self, master=None):
        Frame.__init__(self, master)
        self.pack()
        self.make_widgets()

    def make_widgets(self):
        Button(self, text='message1', command=self.message1).pack(side=LEFT)
        Button(self, text='message2', command=self.message2).pack(side=RIGHT)

    def message1(self):
        reload(actions)         # need to reload actions module before calling
        actions.message1()      # now new version triggered by pressing button

    def message2(self):
        reload(actions)         # changes to actions.py picked up by reload
        actions.message2(self)  # call the most recent version; pass self

    def method1(self):
        print 'exposed method...'       # called from actions function

Hello().mainloop()
```

*Example 11-28: File: rad2.py (continued)*

```
% cat actions.py
# callback handlers: reloaded each time triggered

def message1():                    # change me
    print 'spamSpamSPAM'           # could build a dialog...

def message2(self):
    print 'Ni! Ni!'                # change me
    self.method1()                 # access the 'Hello' instance...

% python rad2.py &
[1] 150


<The GUI comes up and stays up...>
```

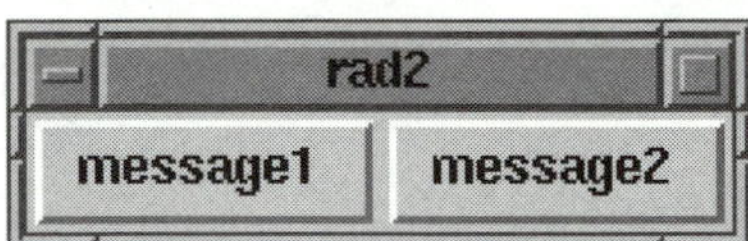


*Figure 11-32: Buttons for changeable actions*

```
%
spamSpamSPAM                       <message1 press>
Ni! Ni!                            <message2 press>
exposed method...
                                   <edit (vi) the file>
% vi actions.py
% cat actions.py
# callback handlers: reloaded each time triggered

def message1():                    # change me
    print 'parrot'                 # could build a dialog...

def message2(self):
    print 'shrubbery'              # change me
    self.method1()                 # access the 'Hello' instance...

%
parrot                             <message1 press>
shrubbery                          <message2 press>
exposed method...
```

We can change file *actions.py* any number of times; each time we do so, we'll change the behavior of the GUI when a button press occurs. But why the unusual structure here? The actions are split off into a separate file, instead of being embedded in the *Frame* subclass, as we've done so far. The answer has to do with the way that *Tkinter* works, and illustrates some interesting points about dynamic reloading.

As we've seen, *Tkinter* builds widgets on program requests, and routes callbacks to registered objects. After a program builds a window (by creating widget instances), and installs event handler objects (by using *command* or *bind*), *Tkinter* won't notice a reload of the program's file. The window isn't updated, and callbacks are still routed to old versions of functions and methods:

*Displayed windows*
: Reloading the file that created a window that is currently displayed won't update the screen. Displayed windows can be changed by explicit *Tkinter* method calls, to add new widgets or menu options, disable options, etc. Also, reloading a module that contains GUI construction code at its top level may add to a window, or create a new one. But a reload won't normally change widgets that are already displayed.

*Registered handlers*
: Reloading a module file that redefines a callback handler that is already registered won't change what the callback does: *Tkinter* holds on to the object registered earlier. For instance, changing the *message1* and *message2* methods in *rad2.py* and reloading *rad2* has no effect: the prior versions of the methods are still recorded in *Tkinter*'s object registration tables.

### *Changing event-handlers*

The callback handler effect is similar to the *from* reload problems we studied in Chapter 7. Since *Tkinter* uses objects that exist when widgets are created, there's no link back to the containing file: they're evaluated too soon for *reload* to have an impact. For instance, when *rad2* registers button-press handlers:

```
Button(self, text='message1', command=self.message1).pack(side=LEFT)
```

*self.message1* is a bound method object, recorded in the *Tkinter* system, and called directly later. There's no notion of an enclosing module.

To work around this, we can add a level of indirection, and reload something the registered callback handler objects call. Here, we split off the actions to another file, and made the calls to them qualified, so that the names are reevaluated each time. The registered handlers are just stubs that call the real, reloadable actions. Notice that the *message2* handler passes *self* to the action; it has access to all the *Hello* instance's methods and data, as though it were a real class method.

Suggested exercise: consider other ways to change a callback-handler while a GUI is running. For instance, what happens if you call the *config* method of a widget, passing in a new *command=action* option value? Where would you make the call after a reload? Would this approach be easier to code?

Suggested exercise: design a way to selectively reload callback handlers. For instance, a *reload* toggle button could be displayed, to enable callback reloads during development only, since it's expensive to reimport files. How about reloading on a module-by-module basis?

### *Changing window layouts*

The displayed-window limitation is harder to work around. Once a widget instance is created, there's no link from the object back to the creating code; reloading the module that made it has no effect on the window. If a window is created in response to an event, we can change its appearance by editing the callback handler that builds it; the next time it pops up, it will look different. For instance, the pack/unpack dialogs we saw earlier are made in modules that could be changed and reloaded dynamically.

But a window that is being displayed can't be easily changed without destroying and recreating it. There are ways to work around this problem too, but the ultimate solution will probably have to wait until there is a GUI layout tool for designing *Tkinter* GUI layouts interactively.

Suggested exercise: change *menugui2*, seen earlier, to dynamically reload *packdlg* and *unpkdlg*, and experiment with changing the appearance of the pop-up dialogs while the main window remains active.

Suggested exercise (difficult): consider ways to change GUI layouts. How would you go about structuring GUIs so that changing a file changes the structure of the currently displayed widgets?

## *Other Tkinter Topics*

*Tk* and *Tkinter* are full-featured GUI systems, and we've really only scratched the surface of these tools. We'll see two more GUI examples in upcoming chapters; some topics will appear later, but others won't be covered in this book. The bibliography lists sources of additional information.

The goal of this book is to teach you just enough to write some useful programs, and provide a basis for learning more. As with most large systems, you can pick up more *Tkinter* details on an as-needed basis. Matt Conway's *Tkinter* "life-preserver" reference manual provides more information, and *Tk* documentation provides even more. To summarize, here's a look at some topics we've studied and others we've skipped.

## *Tkinter Widget Classes*

Table 11-3 provides a list of the widget classes exported by the *Tkinter* module in Python 1.3. This list is likely to expand over time: see *Tkinter* documentation for up-to-date details. This table only includes basic widget classes; as we've seen, there are additional *Tkinter* classes for things like:

Geometry management
: *Pack, Place*

Linked variables
: *StringVar, IntVar, DoubleVar, BooleanVar*

Composite widgets
: *Dialog, ScrolledText, FileDialog*

Other tools
: *Event, Tk*

*Table 11-3: Tkinter widget classes*

| Widget class | Description |
|---|---|
| *Toplevel* | A new window managed by the window manager |
| *Button* | A simple labeled push-button widget |
| *Canvas* | A drawing area, which supports lines, circles, arcs, text, etc. |
| *Checkbutton* | Multiple-choice, two-state button widget |
| *Entry* | Simple single-line text entry field |
| *Frame* | A container for attaching and arranging other widget class instances |
| *Label* | A simple message area |
| *Listbox* | A list of selection names |
| *Menu* | A collection of options associated with a Menubutton |
| *Menubutton* | The menubar entry which opens a Menu of options |
| *Message* | A multiline label |
| *RadioButton* | Select one from a set of choice buttons |
| *Scale* | A slider widget with scalable positions |
| *Scrollbar* | A control for scrolling other widgets' contents |
| *Text* | A multiline text browse/edit widget, with support for fonts, etc. |
| *OptionMenu* | A specialized menu: select from an options list |
| *Image* | A general image-display widget |
| *BitmapImage* | A subclass of Image for displaying bitmap images |
| *PhotoImage* | A subclass of Image for displaying full-color images: GIF, etc. |
| *Studbutton* | A stylized button |
| *Tributton* | A three-state button |

Most *Tkinter* widgets are familiar user interface devices. Some are remarkably rich in functionality. For instance, the *Text* class implements a sophisticated multiline text widget, which supports fonts, colors, and special effects. And the *Canvas* class provides extensive drawing tools. Additional higher-level widgets are provided by the *Tix* extension (see Appendix A).

Many of these *Tkinter* widgets aren't demonstrated by the examples in this book. Moreover, we won't see many of the available options and methods for widgets used. The *Tkinter* manual provides further details. But one way to see all the widgets supported by *Tkinter* is to run the *widgets* demo in the Tk4.0 distribution. The *Tk wish* program can be used to launch the demo script. Although the demo is written in the *Tcl* language, the widgets it displays will look the same under Python's *Tkinter*.

## *Translating Tcl/Tk Commands to Python/Tkinter Classes*

In the *Tcl* language, *Tk* GUIs take the form of *Tcl* scripts. This book isn't about *Tcl*, but the mapping to Python's *Tkinter* may help *Tcl* programmers make the transition. The following table shows how *Tcl* command forms map to Python for some common operations:

*Table 11-4: Tk/Tkinter mappings*

| **Operation** | *Tcl/Tk* | **Python/*Tkinter*** |
|---|---|---|
| Creation | *button .fred* | *fred = Button()* |
| Masters | *button .panel.fred* | *fred = Button(panel)* |
| Options | *button .fred -fg red* | *fred = Button(fg="red")* |
| Configuration | *.fred configure -fg red* | *fred["fg"] = "red"; fred.config(fg="red")* |
| Actions | *.fred invoke* | *fred.invoke()* |
| Packing | *pack .fred -side left* | *fred.pack(side=LEFT)* |

Some of the main distinctions in Python are:

*Creation*
: Widgets are created as class instance objects by calling a widget class.

*Masters*
: Parents are previously created objects, passed to widget-class constructors.

*Options*
: Options take the form of keyword arguments or assigned keys.

*Actions*
: Widget actions become class instance method calls.

*Callbacks*
: Callback handlers may be any callable object: function, method, lambda, etc.

*Extension*
: Widgets are extended using Python class inheritance mechanisms.

*Composition*
: Interfaces are constructed by attaching objects, not by concatenating names.

Again, see the *Tkinter* manual for more information.

## *Tkinter Class Hierarchy*

As we've seen, *Tkinter* is an object-oriented framework: all its widgets are exported as classes, which inherit from a common *Widget* superclass. The *Toplevel* widget is unique, in that it also inherits from the *Wm* window manager superclass. *Mixin* classes are used extensively, in the current framework.

The class hierarchy itself is fairly flat, but we won't describe it further here (it's extremely prone to change). See the *Tkinter* manual for details on the class hierarchy's structure, or study file *Tkinter.py* in Python's source library directory.

## *Scheduled Callbacks*

Some GUI applications need to perform background activities periodically. For example, to "blink" a widget's appearance, we'd like to register a callback handler to be invoked at regular intervals. Similarly, it's not a good idea to let a long-running file operation block other activity in a GUI; if the system could invoke a callback handler when a file's ready for processing, the rest of the GUI could continue without waiting. *Tkinter* has many tools for scheduling delayed actions:

*widget.after(milliseconds)*
: This tool pauses the program for *N* milliseconds. For example, an argument of 5000 pauses for 5 seconds. This is essentially the same as Python's library function *time.sleep*.

*widget.after(milliseconds, function)*
: This tool schedules the function to be called after *N* milliseconds. *function* can be any callable Python object: a function, bound method, etc. This form of the call does not pause the program.

*widget.after_idle(function)*
  This tool schedules the function to be called when there are no more events to process. *function* becomes an idle handler, which is invoked when the GUI isn't busy doing anything else.

*tkinter.createfilehandler(file, mask, function)*
  This tool schedules the function to be called when a file's status changes. The function may be invoked when the file has data for reading, is available for writing, or triggers an exception. File handlers are often used to process pipes or sockets, since normal input/output requests can block the caller.

There's also an *after_cancel* widget method, to cancel a pending callback event before it occurs. We won't go into many details on these tools here: see *Tk* and *Tkinter* documentation for more information.

For a quick example of these tools, the following script builds the window in Figure 11-33 and calls the *Tkinter bell* method periodically. The *repeater* method beeps once, and schedules a callback to be invoked after a specific amount of time. But *after* doesn't pause the caller: callbacks are scheduled to occur in the background, while the program performs other processing. Notice that *repeater* calls *after* each time through, to reschedule the callback: delayed events are *one-shot* callbacks. To repeat the event, we need to reschedule.

*Example 11–29: File: alarm.py*

```
#!/usr/local/bin/python
from Tkinter import *

class Alarm(Frame):
    def repeater(self):                          # on every N millisecs
        self.bell()                              # beep now
        self.after(self.msecs, self.repeater)    # reschedule handler
    def __init__(self, msecs=1000):              # default = 1 second
        Frame.__init__(self)
        self.msecs = msecs
        self.pack()
        self.repeater()
        Button(self, text='Stop the beeps!', command=self.quit).pack()

if __name__ == '__main__': Alarm(50).mainloop()
```

```
% alarm.py
```

When we run this program, it starts beeping once our one-button window pops up. And it keeps beeping. And beeping. And beeping. Other activities and GUI operations don't affect it. Even if the window is iconified, the beeping continues (the events occur in the background). You need to kill the window or press the button to stop the alarm. And you probably won't want to run this script in a crowded office!

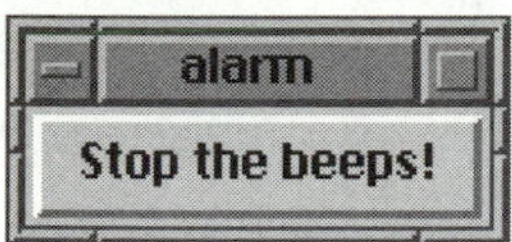


*Figure 11-33: Stop the beeps!*

### *"Engineers love to change things!"*

As mentioned in the Preface, the examples in this book are based on Python 1.3, which uses *Tk*4.0. Because we've stressed general concepts in this chapter, most of the material here should apply to future releases of *Tkinter*. Python and *Tk* are both mature systems, and won't change drastically from release to release.

Still, you may come across older *Tkinter* code that uses the Python 1.2 dictionary-based configuration scheme we saw at the start of this chapter. In fact, many of the *Tkinter* examples in the 1.3 distribution still use the Python 1.2 scheme. Python 1.3 can run most 1.2 *Tkinter* code, but not vice versa: most of the examples here won't work on 1.2.

If you're using Python 1.2, the best course of action is to upgrade to 1.3 or higher. If that's not an option, you'll need to tweak some of the examples to get them to work under Python1.2. For instance, replace keyword-arguments with dictionary constants, and add *self.master.minsize(1,1)* calls to top-level frames to make them expandable.

Although API details like this will vary over time, the underlying concepts won't. In fact, many of the ideas we've studied here should apply to any object-oriented GUI interface you might use with Python. As systems like *Tk* and MFC become available on multiple platforms, the choice of API may become largely a matter of personal preference.

# *Summary*

We've covered many topics in this chapter:

- Basic ideas: callbacks, constructing GUIs, etc.
- Abstraction techniques: *GuiMixin*, *GuiMaker*
- A generic shell tools GUI

- Useful widgets: menus, toolbars, listboxes, modal dialogs, etc.
- Using the Python debugger
- Reloading code dynamically

We'll revisit *Tkinter* later in the book. For instance, we'll study tables of persistent objects in Chapter 12, by building a generic table browser GUI. And in Chapter 16, *Processing Language and Text*, we'll write a calculator program using *Tkinter*. Both of these will be largely based on ideas we've covered in this chapter.

But there's also been something of a hidden agenda in this chapter. Although *Tkinter* is one of the most commonly used Python extensions, it's also an example of how far C extensions can take us in general. Later in the book we'll study the tools used to add *Tkinter* to Python.

*In this chapter:*

- *"Give Me an Order of Persistence, But Hold the Pickles"*
- *Case Study: A Table Browser GUI*
- *Other Persistence Topics*
- *Summary*

# 12

# *Persistent Information*

## *"Give Me an Order of Persistence, But Hold the Pickles"*

In Python programming there are four traditional ways to save information between program executions:

- Flat files
- Database systems
- *dbm* keyed files
- Persistent object stores

The main focus of this chapter is on using *dbm* files and persistent objects. We've already used flat files, and won't really cover relational database systems here. But let's look at each of the strategies briefly.

### *Flat Files*

We studied flat files in some detail in Part 2, *Language Fundamentals.* Python's file system is almost exactly like C's, because it's just a thin wrapper over it. Python supports the usual *stdio* system (with the built-in *open* function), plus lower-level file descriptor based processing, pipes, binary files, etc. As a general rule, if you can do something with flat files in C, you can do it in Python too.

#### *File objects*

There are two ways to process external files in Python: file objects and file descriptors. File objects are just an interface to C's *stdio* system; they're created by the *open* function we've been using, as well as the POSIX *os.fdopen* and *os.popen* functions:

```
file = open(name, mode, bufsize)              the standard file open: stdio
file = os.fdopen(fd, mode, bufsize)           make file object from descriptor
file = os.popen(command, mode, bufsize)       spawn command with a pipe file
```

*open* is the same as C's *fopen* function. In all three, *mode* and *bufsize* are optional. *mode* can be *r* (read), *w* (write/create), *a* (append), and any of these with `+` and `b` appended, if the underling stdio system supports it. For instance, `r+`, `w+`; and `a+`; open the file in *read/write* mode, and *rb* and *wb* open binary files (strings are used to hold raw bytes). *bufsize* can be zero, to force unbuffered processing; this avoids *flush* calls when using pipes. File-objects are processed by calling their methods:

```
string = file.read(bytes?)       plus: readline, readlines
file.write(string)               plus: writelines
file.seek(offset, whence)        same as C's stdio fseek; plus: tell
file.close()                     also closed when object is reclaimed
file.flush()                     flush output buffer; C's fflush
```

*seek* allows for random access: a *whence* can be 0 (seek from the front), 1 (seek from the current position, plus or minus), or 2 (seeks from the end).

### File descriptors

File descriptors are created by the POSIX *os.open* and *os.pipe* functions, and are processed with *os* module *functions*, instead of object methods:

```
fd = os.open(name, flags, mode)      open a low-level file (fd is an integer)
(fd1, fd2) = os.pipe()               create 2 linked descriptors: (read, write)
string = os.read(fd, N)              read N bytes, returned in a string
os.write(fd, string)                 write a string of bytes
os.close(fd)                         also closed when Python ends
os.fstat(fd)                         get file info tuple; also: os.stat(path)
```

We'll see a *pipe* example in Appendix A, *...And Other Cool Stuff.* As a rule, file objects are the preferred approach; descriptors are only needed for special features not supported by *stdio* files. The *os* module has additional POSIX functions for common file operations (deletion, etc.), and there are other file features not shown here: see Appendix C, *A Mini-Reference*, and Python's library reference manual for more information. And since these are all just wrappers for standard UNIX/C functions, see C file system documentation for additional background information.

## Database Systems

Full-blown database systems are also supported, with integration modules for commercial relational databases like *Sybase* and *Oracle*, and the shareware *mSQL* system. These are advanced, independent systems; Python only adds an integration layer, so they can be accessed in Python programs. But Python's interfaces can make them easier to use. Here's a hypothetical example of *mSQL* use:

### *os versus posix*

On UNIX systems, the *os* module is mostly just a wrapper over the *posix* module (*os* also adds a few attributes of its own). Both are built-in, and you may occasionally see programs that use *posix* directly, instead of *os*. In fact, *os* just imports everything in *posix* using a *from ** statement (see *Lib/os.py*). So why use *os* at all?

As a rule, *os* is the preferred way to access *posix* functions, because it provides some degree of platform-independence. Since many *posix* functions aren't available, or work differently on different hosts, *os* automatically imports the platform-specific module (*posix*, *mac*, etc.) that's present, to provide a consistent interface.

There's no performance penalty for using *os* instead of a more specific module. Of course, platform independence breaks-down if you use *os* features unique to a given machine (for instance, *fork* is missing on MS-DOS). See Appendix C, and Python's library manual for more information on specific *os* functions.

```
import msql
db = msql.connect("host")
db.selectdb("spam")

db.query("create table food ( x int, y int, z char(20) )")
db.query("insert into food ( x, z ) values(2, 'toast')")

records1 = db.query('select z from food where x=%d' % value)
records2 = db['select x,z from food where x=2']

print db["select * from food"]
print db.listfields("food")
print db.listdbs()
print db.listtables()
```

The *query* method (and indexing a msql object on an SQL query string) returns a Python list of tuples, *listdbs* returns a list of database names, *listtables* returns a list of table names, and *listfields* returns a list of: *(field-name, table-name, type, length, flags)* tuples, one per field.

Since Python's interpreted, we get rapid turnaround when developing database programs with these interfaces. But since they require an understanding of how the underlying database systems work, we won't cover them further here. For more information, see the *mSQL* interface in the contributions directory, on Python's *ftp* site, or the Python FAQ file. (Also see the new *Postgres95* database interface, *PyGres*, mentioned in Appendix A.)

## *Key-Based Files: dbm and shelve*

Our main focus in this chapter will be on the last two techniques: *dbm* files, and persistent-object stores called shelves. We looked at the two techniques briefly in Chapter 2, *A Sneak Preview*. Both systems integrate keyed files in Python as *mappings*, with access by string keys. And both connect to external files when an open function is called: *anydbm.open* for dbm, and *shelve.open* for shelves. But there's one major difference between them:

- *dbm* files only allow character string data to be stored.
- Persistent object shelves allow almost any kind of Python object to be stored.

Shelves are really just *dbm* files that automatically serialize objects into character streams (this is called pickling), when they're transferred to and from the dbm file. As we'll see, if we don't need keyed access to stored objects, they can also be written to flat files by using pickling without shelves.

But the similarities between dbm and shelve files are more important than their differences: once either type of file is opened, it's processed exactly as though it were an in-memory Python dictionary. Items are fetched by indexing the file object by key and stored by assigning to a key. Table 12-1 lists *dbm* operations.

*Table 12-1: dbm (and shelve) file operations*

| Python code | Action | Description |
|---|---|---|
| `import anydbm` | Import | Get *dbm*, *gdbm*, . . . whatever is installed |
| `file = anydbm.open('filename')` | Open | Create or open an existing dbm file |
| `file['key1'] = value` | Store | Create or change the entry for *key1* |
| `value = file['key2']` | Fetch | Load the value for entry *key2* |
| `count = len(file)` | Size | Return the number entries stored |
| `index = file.keys()` | Index | Fetch the stored keys list |
| `found = file.has_key('key3')` | Query | See if there's an entry for *key3* |
| `del file['key4']` | Delete | Remove the entry for *key4* |
| `file.close()` | Close | Manual close, usually optional |

Using a persistent shelve is identical, except that *anydbm* is replaced by *shelve*, and *value* can be almost any kind of Python object. For *dbm* files, we can pass mode (*r*, *w*, etc.) and protection (access mode) parameters to *open* if desired, but Python supplies reasonable defaults in all cases. One exception worth noting: in Python versions 1.5.2 and later, be sure to pass a 'c' as a second argument when calling anydbm.open, to force Python to create the file if it does not yet exist, and simply open it otherwise.

## *Conclusion?*

And that's almost as much as needs to be said about the two storage systems. In fact, since they imitate dictionaries so closely, it's nearly enough to remember that dbm files and persistent-object shelves are dictionaries that must be opened.

Both provide all the usual dictionary methods (*keys*, *has_key*), and the normal dictionary operations (indexing, the *len* function, etc.). Because this interface is so seamless, the examples we saw in Chapter 2, are virtually all we need to know about the two systems.

Since they're so simple to use, *dbm* and *shelve* are convenient ways to save information in Python. For instance, persistent object shelves let us build up databases of native Python objects: there's no need to deal with another API, manage database-specific record structures, or convert to and from them when interfacing with the database. For many applications, persistent object databases are sufficient.

So is this chapter over already? As you might expect, there are a few special rules and concepts that should be considered when using *dbm* files and persistent objects:

*Dbm files*

- Can only store string values: others must be converted to or from strings
- Require that keys must be strings too

*Persistent shelves*

- Can store arbitrary values
- Require that keys must be strings
- Must be treated as load/store mappings: *shelve[x][y] = z* won't update the file
- Aren't always necessary: persistence can also be implemented by manual pickling to flat files

*Persistent class instances*

- Usually require classes with no (or all default) constructor arguments
- Require classes that appear at the *top level* of an importable module file
- Only record instance attribute dictionaries: their classes can be changed

Apart from these, dbm and shelve files really are just dictionaries that must be opened; we can usually get by with that simple concept, and forget the exceptions. But instead of going into lots of details here, let's study a system that illustrates most of these issues, and explores object-oriented design concepts. We'll point out *dbm* and *shelve* special cases along the way, and return to some of these topics after the example. (For a simpler introduction, see the section on persistence in Chapter 2; we won't repeat that material here.)

## *How the integration works*

In Python, objects become persistent just by storing them in shelves: there's no other protocol to follow. But persistence demonstrates some common integration techniques. Both dbm and shelve files are implemented as one or more flat files (you'll see them after opening a new shelve). Internally, persistence uses three components:

*dbm* is integrated as a C extension datatype: *anydbm.open* returns a C extension-type object, much like the built-in *open*. The dbm extension type overloads the indexing operation to intercept fetch/store operations, and map them to external file operations. It also provides standard dictionary methods (*keys*, etc.) as methods of the extension-type object. We'll study C extension types in Chapter 14, *Extending Python*.

*Shelve* is just a *combination* of the dbm interface, plus the object pickling module *pickle*. It's currently implemented entirely in Python: *shelve.open* returns an instance of a class that embeds a dbm file object, overloads indexing using the `__getitem__` and `__setitem__` methods, and implements the standard dictionary methods as class methods. Because it's just a dbm file wrapper, *shelve* requires some flavor of *dbm* to be installed.

*Pickle* is the module that actually converts objects to character streams, handles circular and embedded objects, etc. It's also written completely in Python at present. This makes it relatively slow (though file access time accounts for some of the overhead). Object fetch/store operations should be kept to a minimum if speed is a concern; in the current implementation, each time you *index* a persistent shelve, the dbm file is accessed.

Python's creator considered the 1.3 implementation of persistence to be a prototype. Optimizations are being designed as this book is being written. It's possible that the *pickle* module may eventually be moved to a C-based implementation as it evolves, but the client-level interfaces shown in this book will remain the same. The pickler itself is discussed in more detail near the end of this chapter; for the present we'll use shelves.

# *Case Study: A Table Browser GUI*

In most realistic applications, users can't be expected to process records in a persistent store directly, with Python dictionary operations. One way to make processing simpler is to provide a GUI-based interface for browsing, changing, and adding records. Here's the start of a program that lets users browse and edit items in a mapping (*table*). It illustrates persistence ideas, and some additional GUI concepts.

The browser works under the assumption that items in the table being browsed are dictionaries; in other words, it browses mappings of mappings. Since dictionaries, dbm files, and persistent shelves are all mappings, in principle a single GUI program should be able to operate on all three kinds of tables. But as is, the code can only handle mappings of nested dictionaries; we'll expand on this concept in a moment.

## *The guitools Utility-Function Module*

Let's first define a utility module to simplify basic widget construction. It makes some assumptions about how we want the widgets to look and expand, but they're reasonable defaults, and can save us lots of typing. It also demonstrates another way to automate GUI construction. All the widgets it creates expand both horizontally and vertically, when the parent widget (root) is resized.

*Example 12-1: File: guitools.py*

```
from Tkinter import *

def frame(root, side):
    widget = Frame(root)
    widget.pack(side=side, expand=YES, fill=BOTH)
    return widget

def label(root, side, text):
    widget = Label(root, text=text, relief=RIDGE)
    widget.pack(side=side, expand=YES, fill=BOTH)
    return widget

def button(root, side, text, command):
    widget = Button(root, text=text, command=command)
    widget.pack(side=side, expand=YES, fill=BOTH)
    return widget

def entry(root, side, linkvar):
    widget = Entry(root, relief=SUNKEN, textvariable=linkvar)
    widget.pack(side=side, expand=YES, fill=BOTH)
    return widget
```

## The FormGui Class

Here's the main GUI interface program itself. As in earlier examples, it's structured as a *Frame* subclass. The mapping table to be browsed is passed in as an argument to the *FormGui* class constructor; in a sense, the table object is embedded in the GUI object itself but the GUI is independent of the table browsed.

*FormGui* inherits common methods from the *GuiMixin* class described in Chapter 11, *Graphical User Interfaces*, but doesn't use *GuiMaker*: there's no menu or toolbar in this interface. Instead, the program manages three independent windows:

- A *main window*, popped up initially, with buttons for navigation, storing, deletion, etc.
- A *listbox window*, containing the keys of records in the table, allowing selection by double-clicks
- A *form display window*, containing field names on the left, and field values on the right.

The main window has a row of buttons on the top, a field for display and entry of the current table *key* in the middle, and a row of buttons on the bottom. The listbox-window is popped-up on request (by the *index* button in the main window), and the form-window is popped-up to display an entry in the table. Since entries may have disjoint sets of fields (keys), the form window is erased and a new one comes up if the next record's fields are different than those of the current record.

This is a fairly long program. To keep the code simple, it uses the *GuiMixin* and *guitools* utilities. It also uses a naming convention to offset callback handlers: their name start with "*on*" ("onNext" handles "Next" button presses, and so on). Again, GUI behavior is difficult to capture in words and pictures; if possible, interacting with this example is highly recommended.

*Example 12-2: File: formgui.py*

```
#!/usr/local/bin/python

from Tkinter  import *                                 # Tk widgets
from guitools import frame, label, button, entry       # widget builders
from guimixin import GuiMixin                          # common methods

class FormGui(GuiMixin, Frame):
    def __init__(self, mapping):                       # an extended frame
        Frame.__init__(self)                           # on default top-level
        self.pack(expand=YES, fill=BOTH)               # all parts expandable
        self.master.title('Python Browser 0.1')
        self.master.iconname("pbrowse")
        self.makeMainBox()
        self.table     = mapping                 # a dict, dbm, shelve,..
        self.index     = mapping.keys()          # list of table keys
```

*Example 12-2: File: formgui.py (continued)*

```
        self.cursor    = -1                          # current index position
        self.currslots = []                          # current form's (key,text)'s
        self.currform  = None                        # current form window
        self.listbox   = None                        # index listbox window

    def makeMainBox(self):
        frm = frame(self, TOP)
        frm.config(bd=2)
        button(frm, LEFT, 'next',  self.onNext)          # next in list
        button(frm, LEFT, 'prev',  self.onPrev)          # backup in list
        button(frm, LEFT, 'find',  self.onFind)          # find from key
        frm = frame(self, TOP)
        self.keytext = StringVar()                       # current record's key
        label(frm, LEFT, 'KEY=>')                        # change before 'find'
        entry(frm, LEFT,  self.keytext)
        frm = frame(self, TOP)
        frm.config(bd=2)
        button(frm,  LEFT,  'store',  self.onStore)      # updated entry data
        button(frm,  LEFT,  'new',    self.onNew)        # clear fields
        button(frm,  LEFT,  'index',  self.onMakeList)   # show key list
        button(frm,  LEFT,  'delete', self.onDelete)     # show key list
        button(self, BOTTOM,'quit',   self.quit)         # from guimixin

    def onPrev(self):
        if self.cursor <= 0:
            self.infobox('Backup', "Front of table")
        else:
            self.cursor = self.cursor - 1
            self.display()

    def onNext(self):
        if self.cursor >= len(self.index)-1:
            self.infobox('Advance', "End of table")
        else:
            self.cursor = self.cursor + 1
            self.display()

    def sameKeys(self, item):
        keys1 = item.keys()
        keys2 = map(lambda x:x[0], self.currslots)
        keys1.sort(); keys2.sort()                    # keys list order differs
        return keys1 == keys2                         # if insertion-order differs

    def display(self):
        key = self.index[self.cursor]
        self.keytext.set(key)                         # change key in main box
        item = self.table[key]                        # in dict, dbm, shelf, classes
        if self.sameKeys(item):
            self.currform.title('Key: ' + `key`)
            for (field, text) in self.currslots:
                text.set(`item[field]`)               # same fields? reuse form
        else:
```

*Example 12-2: File: formgui.py (continued)*

```
        if self.currform:
            self.currform.destroy()          # different fields?
        new = Toplevel()                     # replace current box
        new.title('Key: ' + `key`)           # new resizable window
        new.iconname("pform")
        left  = frame(new, LEFT)
        right = frame(new, RIGHT)
        self.currslots = []                  # list of (field, entry)
        for field in item.keys():
            label(left, TOP, `field`)        # key,value to strings
            text = StringVar()               # we could sort keys here
            text.set( `item[field]` )
            entry(right, TOP, text)
            self.currslots.append((field, text))
        self.currform = new
        new.protocol('WM_DELETE_WINDOW', lambda:0)   # ignore destroy's
    self.selectlist()                                # update listbox

def onStore(self):
    if not self.currform: return
    key = self.keytext.get()
    if key in self.index:                    # change existing record
        item = self.table[key]               # not: self.table[key][field]=
    else:
        item = {}                            # create a new record
        self.index.append(key)               # add to index and listbox
        if self.listbox:
            self.listbox.insert(len(self.index)-1, key)
    for (field, text) in self.currslots:
        try:
            item[field] = eval(text.get())   # convert back from string
        except:
            self.errorbox('Bad data: "%s" = "%s"' % (field, text.get()))
            item[field] = None
    self.table[key] = item                   # add to dict, dbm, shelf,...
    self.onFind(key)                         # readback: set cursor,listbox

def onNew(self):
    if not self.currform: return
    self.keytext.set('?%d' % len(self.index))  # default key unless typed
    for (field, text) in self.currslots:       # clear key/fields for entry
        text.set('')
    self.currform.title('Key: ?')

def onFind(self, key=None):
    target = key or self.keytext.get()            # passed in, or entered
    try:
        self.cursor = self.index.index(target)    # in keys list?
        self.display()
    except:
        self.infobox('Not found', "Key doesn't exist", 'info')
```

*Example 12-2: File: formgui.py (continued)*

```
    def onDelete(self):
        if not self.currform or not self.index: return
        currkey = self.index[self.cursor]
        del self.table[currkey]                        # table, index, listbox
        del self.index[self.cursor:self.cursor+1]      # like "list[i:i+1] = []"
        if self.listbox:
            self.listbox.delete(self.cursor)           # delete from listbox
        if self.cursor < len(self.index):
            self.display()                             # show next record if any
        elif self.cursor > 0:
            self.cursor = self.cursor-1                # show prior if delete end
            self.display()
        else:                                          # leave box if delete last
            self.onNew()

    def onList(self,evnt):
        if not self.index: return                     # empty
        index = self.listbox.curselection()           # on listbox double-click
        label = self.listbox.get(index)               # fetch selected key text
        self.onFind(label)                            # and call method here

    def onMakeList(self):
        if self.listbox: return               # already up?
        new = Toplevel()                      # new resizable window
        new.title("Table Key Index")          # select keys from a listbox
        new.iconname("pindex")
        frm    = frame(new, TOP)
        scroll = Scrollbar(frm)
        list   = Listbox(frm)
        list.pack(side=LEFT, expand=YES, fill=BOTH)
        list.config(yscrollcommand=scroll.set, relief=SUNKEN)
        scroll.pack(side=RIGHT, fill=BOTH)
        scroll.config(command=list.yview, relief=SUNKEN)
        pos = 0
        for key in self.index:                         # add to list-box
            list.insert(pos, key)                      # sort list fist?
            pos = pos + 1
        list.config(selectmode=SINGLE, setgrid=1)      # select,resize modes
        list.bind('<Double-1>', self.onList)           # on double-clicks
        self.listbox = list
        if pos > 0 and self.cursor >= 0:               # highlight position
            self.selectlist()
        new.protocol('WM_DELETE_WINDOW', lambda:0)     # ignore destroy's

    def selectlist(self):
        if self.listbox:
            self.listbox.select_clear(0, self.listbox.size())
            self.listbox.select_set(self.cursor)       # list box tracks cursor

if __name__ == '__main__':
    from formtest import cast                      # self-test code
```

*Example 12-2: File: formgui.py (continued)*

```
    for k in cast.keys(): print k, cast[k]       # get dict of dict's
    FormGui(cast).mainloop()
    for k in cast.keys(): print k, cast[k]       # show modified table on exit
```

### Some things to notice

Before we see the interface in action, let's explore some new concepts in this code. Much of the code is self-explanatory, but we'll highlight a few points here.

***State information.*** *FormGui* stores the table passed in (*table*) and its *keys* list (*index*) as instance data. Since the order of items in the table may change after adding or deleting new records, the *keys* list is stored separately to maintain its original order. *FormGui*s also record the current position in the keys-list (*cursor*), a list of field-name/linked-variable tuples for slots in the current form-window (*currslots*), and references to the currently displayed form window and the listbox window's list (*currform, listbox*).

***Tables of dictionaries only.*** There really are two levels of mappings here. FormGui assumes the table item passed-in is a dictionary-like mapping. But it also assumes the table contains dictionary-like mappings too: it uses key-indexing to fetch and set fields in the records. Since dictionary items and class instance members are accessed differently (*dict[key]* versus *instance.member*), the program can only be used for mappings (tables) of dictionaries at present:

- It works for in-memory dictionaries of dictionaries, and shelve-files that contain dictionaries.
- It doesn't work for dictionaries or shelves of class instances, or *dbm* files of strings.

*dbm* files fail, because FormGui tries to index the stored value by key: dbm file values are always strings. Class instances fail whether the table is in memory or a persistent shelve, because indexing isn't the same as attribute qualification. We'll see how to work around this limitation later.

***Mapping key-list order varies.*** *FormGui* tries to reuse the current form window, if the next record has the same keys (fields) as the last one displayed (or else we need to erase and make a new one). But there's a subtle problem: we can't compare *keys* lists with ==: even if two mappings have the same set of keys, the order of their *keys* lists may vary, depending on the order in which the keys were assigned.

Instead, the *sameKeys* method sorts the two key-lists, using the built-in list *sort* method, before using == to compare them. The list *sort* method calls C's *qsort* function behind the scenes, so sorting is faster than a manual comparison here.

Note the use of *lambda* in a *map* call in this method:

```
keys2 = map(lambda x:x[0], self.currslots)
```

The *lambda* extracts the first item from a (*field-name,linked-variable*) tuple, and the *map* applies the generated function to each tuple in the *currslots* list and collects the results. In relational terms, the combination projects (extracts from) the list on its first column.

***Catching window manager events.*** Both the listbox window and form window are created as instances of the *Toplevel* widget, and become independent windows on the screen. Neither has a *quit* button, but they could be destroyed interactively by selecting the window-manager's *delete* operation. This varies from window manager to window manager; usually it's a selection in a pop-up menu associated with a window.

Since *FormGui* depends on these windows being around, we can't let them be destroyed outside our control: future accesses would reference nonexistent windows, and probably crash the program. To prevent this, we disable the *delete* event, by calling the *protocol* method of the new Toplevel widgets:

```
new.protocol('WM_DELETE_WINDOW', lambda:0)    # ignore destroy's
```

*protocol* is an interface to window-manager events. This call replaces the standard destroy action with a handler that does nothing (the *lambda* just returns 0). As before, we need to have a *Toplevel* widget to access window manager methods like *protocol*.

***Deleting data structure components.*** Data structure objects that can be changed in place (i.e., *mutable* objects) support deletion of nested items. This includes lists, dictionaries, and some built-in type and class instances. To delete such components, we can:

- Use the *del* statement
- Assign an empty value to a slice (for sequences only)
- Call special deletion methods of the object's type

For instance, *FormGui* responds to *delete* button presses by using the *del* statement, as in:

```
del self.table[currkey]                        delete mapping entry by key
del self.index[self.cursor:self.cursor+1]      delete sequence slice by indexes
```

For sequences, there usually are a variety of equivalent deletion operations:

```
del x[i]              delete item at offet 'i' directly
del x[i:i+1]          delete the slice containing slot 'i' only
x[i:i+1] = []         assign a slice (or index) an empty list to delete
x.remove(value)       if 'value' appears at position 'i' first
```

Slice deletions and assignments can actually delete large sections of a list: *x[10:20] = []*. Note that deleting an entire object (*del x*) decrements its reference count; the object is reclaimed only if the count drops to zero (no more references). This is one way to force reclamation of circularly referenced objects.

## *Catching deletions of components in classes and types*

Classes define more special methods to intercept *del* operations: `__delitem__` (on *del i[k]*), `__delslice__` (on *del i[a:b]*), and `__delattr__` (on *del i.m*). Built-in and user-defined C extension types (discussed in Chapter 14) detect *del* operations by intercepting assignments of *NULL* values to indexes, slices, and attributes; as we'll see later, their assignment handlers are registered function pointers instead of specially named methods.

Both also supply distinct handlers for deletion of the whole object: `__del__` for classes (on *del instance*), and function pointers for types. They're not called until the object is about to be reclaimed (when the reference count reaches zero, not on each *del* operation).

***Avoiding nested component assignment.*** *FormGui* goes out of its way to avoid assigning to fields inside a record individually. Instead, it makes a new dictionary, fills in its keys (fields), and only then assigns the entire dictionary to the table's key. It never goes through the table to access a record's key. In the *onStore* method:

```
item = self.table[key]          not self.table[key][field]= <newvalue>
```

we change an *item* by fetching it, changing it, and then storing it back; we never use more than one index when assigning to an existing record.

Why the restriction? Because we want to support shelves and dbm files. Each time we fetch an item from a shelve by key, Python creates a new object in memory, reflecting the values stored in the shelve file. In effect, fetching shelved dictionaries or class instances "thaws out" a new copy from the file, which we can use like a normal Python object.

But once the "thawed" copy is created, it loses its association with the persistent file. If we assign to components of a fetched persistent object, it only changes the in-memory copy, *not* the version in the file. To update the file, we need to store back the modified in-memory object as a whole. For instance, for a persistent shelve called *file*, assigning nested components doesn't update the file:

```
file['key']['field'] = value              no effect on persistent dictionary
file['key'][i] = value                    no effect on persistent list
file['key'].field = value                 no effect on persistent instance
file['key'].__dict__['field'] = value     no effect on persistent instance
```

Once we index on `['key']`, the connection to the file is lost. Instead, we need to treat shelves as one-level-deep mappings, when assigning to components of stored objects. FormGui follows a fetch/change/store protocol, when nested field values must be changed:

```
object = file['key']                      indexing fetches a stored object
object['key'] = value                     change in-memory dictionary object
object[i] = value                         change in-memory list object
object.attr = value                       change in-memory instance object
file['key'] = object                      create/store an object as a whole
```

## *Why nested shelve assignments can't work*

Notice that this constraint doesn't have to be followed if we're browsing in-memory dictionaries of objects: assigning to nested components works as you'd expect in this case. The reason it fails for shelves is that indexing returns a normal Python object, with no knowledge of its persistence. We get back the same type of object that was stored, which is what we probably want in a seamless persistence system.

We might work around this limitation by returning a special wrapper-class instance when a shelve is indexed, which knows how to route further index/qualification operations back to the file (by defining `__setitem__` and `__setattr__`). The fetched instance would record both the real object and the persistent file association.

But if we did this, shelve indexing wouldn't return the same kind of object that was stored. It would be an instance of the wrapper-class, not a normal Python object. Although metaclass protocols would help some here, we can't really have it both ways.

## Testing the FormGui Interface

Let's run *formgui.py* as a top-level program, to invoke its self-test code. First, we need to define another auxiliary module, to hold some objects we'll use to test the form GUI, and later extensions.

*Example 12-3: File: formtest.py*

```
# definitions for testing formgui and formtbl

cast = {
    'rob':   {'name': ('Rob', 'P'),   'job': 'writer', 'spouse': 'Laura'},
    'buddy': {'name': ('Buddy', 'S'), 'job': 'writer', 'spouse': 'Pickles'},
    'sally': {'name': ('Sally', 'R'), 'job': 'writer'},
    'laura': {'name': ('Laura', 'P'), 'spouse': 'Rob',   'kids':1},
    'milly': {'name': ('Milly', '?'), 'spouse': 'Jerry', 'kids':2},
    'mel':   {'name': ('Mel', 'C'),   'job': 'producer'},
    'alan':  {'name': ('Alan', 'B'),  'job': 'comedian'}
}

class Actor:                                   # file-level class: not nested
    def __init__(self, name=(), job=''):       # need no args or defaults
        self.name = name                       # for browser and pickle
        self.job  = job
    def __setattr__(self, attr, value):        # on setattr(): validate
        if attr == 'kids' and value > 10:
            print 'validation error: kids =', value
        if attr == 'name' and type(value) != type(()):
            print 'validation error: name type =', type(value)
        self.__dict__[attr] = value
```

*cast* is a dictionary of dictionaries; in terms of the browser, it's a *table* of *records*. We'll use it to initialize various tables along the way. *Actor* will be used (and discussed) in the next example. Both of these objects are put in this separate file, to avoid exporting them to *FormGui* clients.

To be used for shelves, the *Actor* class must be at the top level of a module file like this. We put it here instead of in *formgui* (or *formtbl*, to be discussed later), so it's not in the top-level program file (module `__main__` can't be reimported later, when fetching persistent instances). Actor validates the *kids* and *name* attributes whenever they're assigned, and makes sure that all instances have at least *name* and *job* attributes.

But for now, we'll use *cast* here to test in-memory tables; this is a quick way to experiment with the interface, without using external files. As is, we could also use *formgui* on shelves of existing dictionaries. For instance, if we had an existing, open shelve of dictionaries called *file*, we could browse it by calling: *FormGui(file).mainloop*. But since *formgui* self-test code doesn't have logic to initialize a shelve from *cast* yet, we'll test the interface with dictionaries initially.

Given the *cast* dictionary, we get the following behavior when we run *formgui.py* as a top-level script (*% formgui.py*). When the FormGui instance starts up, the main window pops up initially (see Figure 12-1).

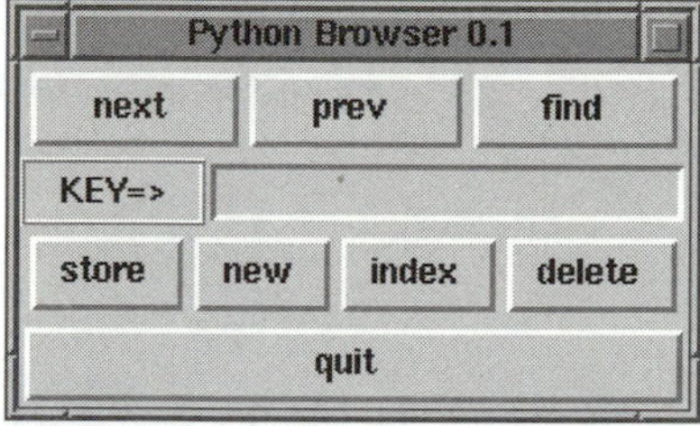


*Figure 12-1: Table browser main window*

---

*NOTE* You may need to extend your *PYTHONPATH* environment variable to run this example. Be sure it includes the directories containing all the modules used here: *guimixin.py*, *guitools.py*, *formtest.py*, and *formgui.py*. You could also copy all the modules to a test directory, and just add ., but this is a less general approach.

---

Since the main frame and all the widgets on it are expandable, we can resize this interface interactively. In fact, all the windows in this interface can be resized (except the pop-up *Dialog* instances). Figure 12-2 shows the main window after stretching.

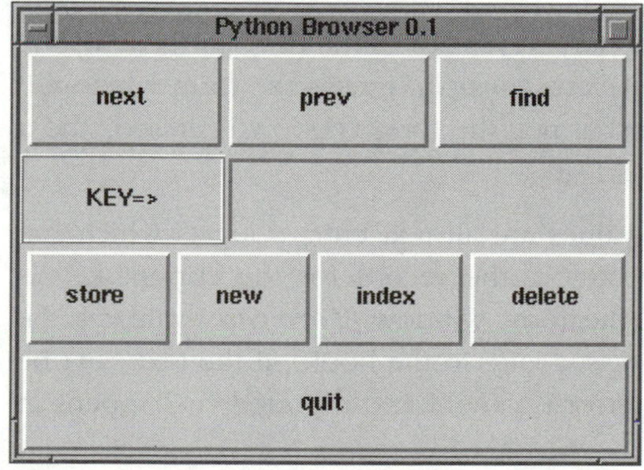


*Figure 12-2: Ssttrreeeettcchh*

When we press the *next* button, we move ahead to the next (or first) entry in the table, and an independent form display window pops up. We can also type a key in the *KEY=>* entry field, and press *find* to bring up a particular table entry directly. All the table entries in this session come from the *cast* dictionary imported from *formtest*; Figure 12-3 shows how the windows look when we're at the entry for key *laura*.

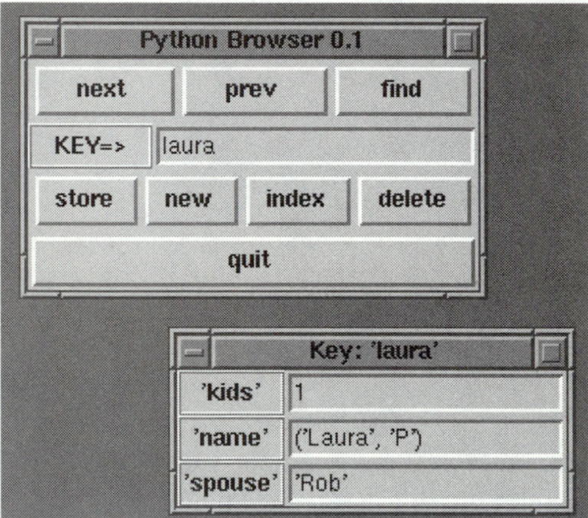


*Figure 12-3: Pop-up form window*

When the *index* button is pressed, the table key scrollable listbox window in Figure 12-4 pops up, giving an ordered list of keys we can use to select entries. The listbox stays up for the rest of the session; its window manager *destroy* event is caught and disabled by *FormGui*. *FormGui* synchronizes the main window's key entry, the form display window, and the key listbox window: when we move to a new table entry, all three are updated at once, and the new record's key is highlighted in the listbox.

Note that this entry's field names (dictionary keys) are different from those of the prior entry. When a new record is displayed, *FormGui* reuses the form window if the fields match those of the prior record; if not, the form window is erased, and a new one is brought up with different field slots.

In the form display window, the field values are all text entry widgets which can be overwritten. If we press the *store* button, the record for the current key is updated with the new field values in the form window. *FormGui* evaluates the text with the built-in *eval* function (discussed later in the book); if the text can't be translated to a valid Python object, the error is caught and reported, as happens in Figure 12-5.

When this type of validation error occurs, the field is filled with *None* (the *void* object in Python). New table entries can be added by changing the *KEY=>* entry in the main box, filling in new values for all the fields in the form box, and pressing *store*.

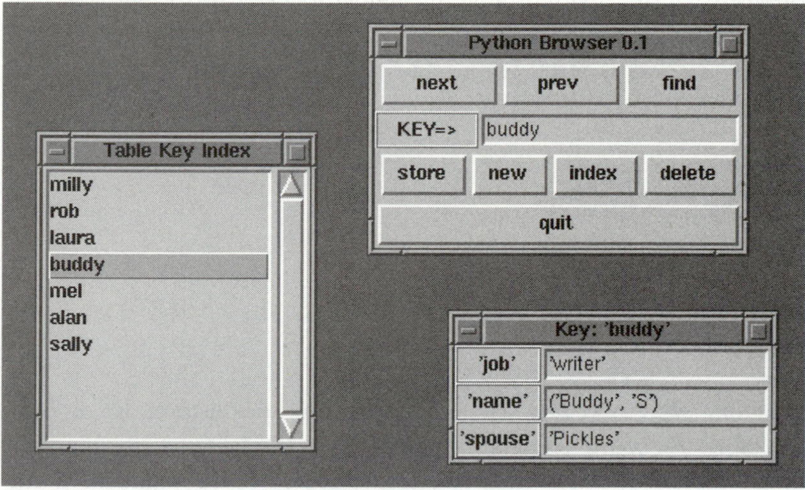


*Figure 12-4: Pop-up index listbox window*

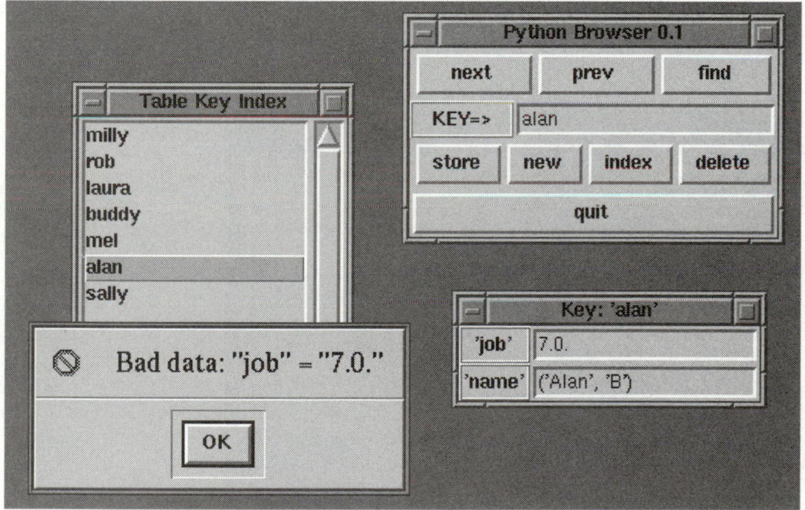


*Figure 12-5: Data entry error dialog*

---

***WARNING*** *eval* is a powerful tool. We can enter any kind of Python object with a syntactic representation: numbers, strings, lists, dictionaries, etc. But be careful not to type something destructive in a field here (*os.system('rm *')* may work too!). Python's restricted-execution mode eliminates some danger, but it's an optional feature.

---

The *new* button clears out the current key and fields, to prepare for entry of new data. When a new record is stored, its key is added to the end of the listbox, and the current position (*cursor*) is reset. Figure 12-6 shows *alan* after our data entry error.

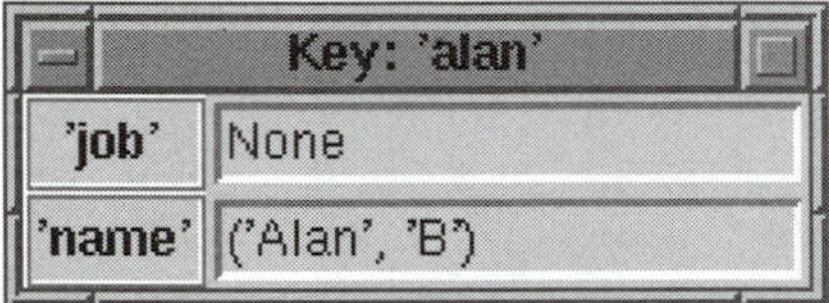


*Figure 12-6: Null values: None*

The top buttons (*find*, *next*, and *prev*), together with the keys listbox, let us navigate through the table. *FormGui* keeps an ordered list of the table's keys internally (the keys might be reordered when new entries are stored), and maintains a cursor into it (the current position's offset). Pressing a navigation button or double-clicking on a listbox entry resets the cursor and updates the form window. Dialogs inherited from *GuiMixin* pop up at the end and beginning of the table; we see one in Figure 12-7.

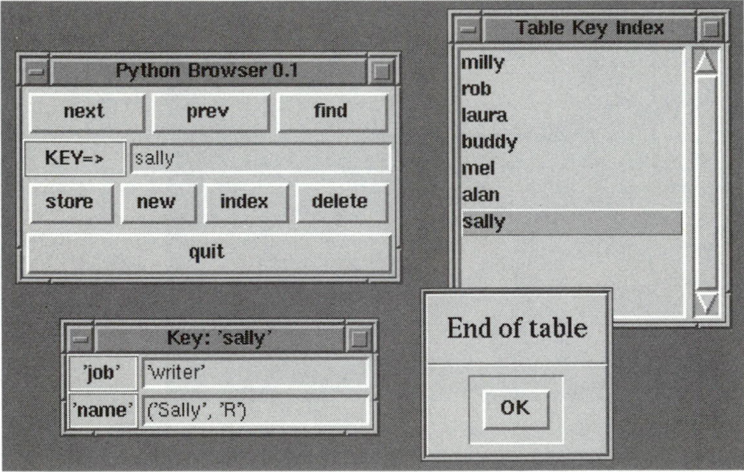


*Figure 12-7: Table navigation dialogs*

Finally, the *delete* button simply deletes the currently displayed entry from the table (and the GUI displays). Since *delete* removes the current record, we have to position the browser at a record before deleting it; double-click on it in the listbox, or enter its key and press *find* first.

To test the browser on a shelve of dictionaries, we need support logic. Here are three utility scripts: *initcast* loads the shelve with dictionaries, *viewcast* browses it under the GUI, and *dumpcast* dumps it to *stdout*. We'll defer an interaction example until we see how to browse shelves of class-instances too.

*Example 12-4: File: initcast.py*

```
import shelve
from formtest import cast
db = shelve.open('castfile')          # create a new shelve
for key in cast.keys():
    db[key] = cast[key]               # store dictionaries in shelve
```

*Example 12-5: File: viewcast.py*

```
import shelve
from formgui import FormGui           # after initcast
db = shelve.open('castfile')          # reopen shelve file
FormGui(db).mainloop()                # browse existing shelve
```

*Example 12-6: File: dumpcast.py*

```
import shelve
db = shelve.open('castfile')          # reopen shelve
for key in db.keys():                 # show each key,value
    print key, db[key]
```

### *Plenty of room for improvement*

As is, *FormGui* is something of a "first-cut" solution: it could be improved in a variety of ways. Here are some suggested exercises, ordered roughly by increasing complexity.

1. Add a pop-up dialog to validate *delete* requests. Also, pop up a warning box on *delete* if the key entry field's value isn't the same as the key of the current position's record. Why?
2. Test *FormGui* on *shelve* files. Use the three utility scripts above to initialize a shelve file from the *cast* dictionary in *formtest*, and pass the shelve into the *FormGui* constructor. Run multiple sessions of the browser, changing the table each time. Generalize *initcast* to allow an arbitrary dictionary to be passed in.
3. Keep the table keys list sorted. If we start using large shelves, it might be hard to find a record unless the listbox is sorted. How about sorting the field names in the form display box too?
4. What happens if the table changes outside *FormGui*'s control? As is, it makes a copy of the table's keys-list internally, which won't reflect outside changes. This won't matter for in-memory dictionaries, but shelve files (and we'll see later, dbm files) might be changed while being browsed.

5. Support creation of new records better. As coded, *FormGui* only allows storing new records based on existing ones. We have to bring up an existing prototype record first, since there's no way to enter a new key/field list from scratch. This approach fails when starting with an empty table: the first record must be made manually. Develop an interface for making new, empty form windows, for new records.
6. Handle nested dictionaries better. Currently, if a record field is another dictionary, we'll get its printed representation in the *field*s slot of the form window. A better idea would be to pop up another form window for displaying nested compound data like this. What about handling nested lists and tuples?
7. Consider nonprintable objects. *FormGui* can only store field values that can be printed: it converts objects to strings with back-quotes for display, and converts back from strings using *eval* to store. This fails on things like files, functions, modules and class instances. Is there some way to fix this problem?
8. Study the coding alternative for the *guitools* module in Example 12-7. It's used exactly like the function-based version used earlier. Is there any advantage to using classes over functions here?

*Example 12–7: File: guitool2.py*

```
from Tkinter import *

class frame(Frame):
    def __init__(self, root, side):
        Frame.__init__(self, root)
        self.pack(side=side, expand=YES, fill=BOTH)

class label(Label):
    def __init__(self, root, side, text):
        Label.__init__(self, root, text=text, relief=RIDGE)
        self.pack(side=side, expand=YES, fill=BOTH)

class button(Button):
    def __init__(self, root, side, text, command):
        Button.__init__(self, root, text=text, command=command)
        self.pack(side=side, expand=YES, fill=BOTH)

class entry(Entry):
    def __init__(self, root, side, linkvar):
        Entry.__init__(self, root, relief=SUNKEN, textvariable=linkvar)
        self.pack(side=side, expand=YES, fill=BOTH)
```

### *Prototyping in Python: for better or worse*

As is, the GUI lets us browse and change any mapping object. Thanks to Python's generic nature, this includes *dbm* files, persistent shelves, and anything else that responds to dictionary operations. The GUI is not perfect yet, but it does the job.

But this example illustrates another critical point: I was able to throw this interface together in less than one day. I went from an idea ("Wouldn't it be cool to have a GUI browser that could work on mappings like *dbm* and shelf files?"), to the current implementation in a matter of hours. And this includes going through a number of initial iterations that were completely inappropriate, experimenting with new features, etc.

Such rapid response makes prototyping reasonable. For instance, at this point, if someone was actually paying me to develop this GUI, I'd probably get up and walk to their office to demonstrate what the interface looks like now, instead of trying to resolve the remaining issues on my own. The conversation might go something like this:

(*knock, knock*)

*Me*: "Hey—guess what: remember that interface we talked about this morning?"

*Client*: "Yes?"

*Me*: "It's done; at least in preliminary form."

*Client*: "Wow! You must be kidding; I expected to wait at least a week."

*Me*: "Nope; I threw it together with this rapid development language called Python."

*Client*: "Cool."

*Me*: "Anyhow; here's how it looks now. Tell me what needs to be changed."

*pause, while I demonstrate the GUI*

*Client*: "Hmm; close, but there's some things that I really don't like about it as is. That button should go here (pointing). I'm not sure I like what happens when you show nested objects; maybe you could just show a button that would pop up another form to display it better. You really need to handle data entry errors better; and what about security?"

Which may not be the optimal outcome from an engineer's perspective! But this sort of interaction between developers and end users is critical for designing successful systems. By showing results earlier, users can get much more involved in the design.

We might eventually go through a series of demonstrate/fix cycles like this, until the GUI was acceptable. But since GUI work is fast in Python, each cycle will go quickly. And because GUI performance is often irrelevant (most of the time is spent waiting for the user to trigger events) the GUI could probably be delivered as is. If needed, selected callback actions might be moved to C if they're too slow (we'll see how in Chapter 14).

Ultimately, we might even let the end user start writing some GUI code too, if he or she is programming-literate. Because Python is relatively simple, we can open up parts of a system to its users. Depending on the user's skill level, this might involve anything from delegating selected simple actions to user customizable code, to actually coauthoring the GUI with users. (Of course, then I might not get paid! :-)

## *Adding Support for Class Instance Records and dbm Files*

As coded, the *FormGui* interface only handles tables of dictionaries. The tables themselves can be dictionaries or shelves, but we're out of luck if we want to browse tables that contain class instances. Class instance attributes are accessed differently than dictionary keys: `x.attr` versus `x['attr']`.

Worse, since *dbm* files only allow values to be character strings, *FormGui* can't handle *dbm* files at all: it assumes that the values in the table are dictionaries, not simple strings. We can store string representations of dictionaries in *dbm* files (back-quotes convert these dictionary keys to strings, and *eval* converts them back to dictionaries), but there's nothing in *FormGui* to do the translations.

At this point, we might be tempted to start hacking up *FormGui* itself to try and support these two other cases. But that would lead to brittle, convoluted code. A better approach is to apply OOP techniques to extend *FormGui*, rather than changing it in place. Let's consider the situation carefully:

- *FormGui* works on arbitrary mapping objects passed in, but assumes their values are dictionaries.
- Mappings of class instances could work, except that their fields are attributes, not dictionary keys.
- *dbm* files could work too, except that their values are strings, not real dictionaries.

What we need to do is extend the mapping that *FormGui* browses, not *FormGui* itself. In OOP terms, we want to specialize the mapping object that *FormGui* contains, rather than inheriting and extending *FormGui*. In other words, we need to generalize the notion of mappings, not browsing. As we saw in Chapter 10, *More Class Magic*, this implies a *composition* relationship, not interitance.

Here's one way to code this idea. Module *formtbl* defines two classes to wrap the mapping passed in to the *FormGui* constructor:

- *DbmTable* converts stored strings to dictionaries using *eval*, and converts dictionaries back to strings using back-quotes.

- *ClassTable* maps stored class instances to and from dictionaries by accessing instance attribute dictionaries.

Both use the `__getitem__` and `__setitem__` index-operator overloading methods we saw earlier, to intercept fetches and stores to the wrapped table, and to translate the stored data to and from dictionaries.

And since both classes imitate dictionaries, their instances can be used in *FormGui*, without any changes to *FormGui* itself. *ClassTable* can wrap a dictionary *or* persistent shelve of class-instances. *DbmTable* can wrap dbm files of dictionaries (but not class instances—they can't be easily mapped to or from strings).

*Example 12-8: File: formtbl.py*

```
# wrap special mappings for use in the form-browser
# convert strings and class-instances to/from dictionaries
# FormGui *contains* a mapping: these aren't subclasses


class DbmTable:
    def __init__(self, mapping, fileName=None):   # wrap table of strings
        if mapping == None:                        # can be dicts but not class
            import anydbm                          # open file (mapping)
            mapping = anydbm.open(fileName, 'c')   # unless passed-in
        self.proxy = mapping

    def __getitem__(self, key):                    # self.table[key]
        return eval(self.proxy[key])               # convert string to dict

    def __setitem__(self, key, value):             # self.table[key] = value
        self.proxy[key] = `value`                  # convert dict to string

    def __delitem__(self, key):                    # del self.table[key]
        del self.proxy[key]                        # delete from wrapped dbm file

    def keys(self): return self.proxy.keys()


class ClassTable:                                  # wrap table of instances
    def __init__(self, Class, mapping):            # mapping is dict or shelf
        self.Class = Class                         # save class for new
        self.proxy = mapping                       # save the real mapping

    def __getitem__(self, key):                    # make dict from instance
        instance = self.proxy[key]                 # use instance dictionary
        return instance.__dict__

    def __setitem__(self, key, value):             # make instance from dict
        instance = self.Class()                    # like pickle: no init args!
        for attr in value.keys():
            setattr(instance, attr, value[attr])   # set instance attributes
        self.proxy[key] = instance                 # store in wrapped mapping
```

*Example 12-8: File: formtbl.py (continued)*

```
    def __delitem__(self, key):                          # delete record by key
        del self.proxy[key]                              # from wrapped mapping

    def keys(self): return self.proxy.keys()

if __name__ == '__main__':
    from sys import argv
    from formgui  import FormGui                         # get dict-based gui
    from formtest import Actor, cast                     # get class, dict-of-dicts

    if len(argv) == 1 or argv[1] == 'shelve':            # "python formtbl.py"
        print 'shelve-of-class test'
        import shelve
        shelf = shelve.open("test2/shelve1")             # path = ./directory/file'
        table = ClassTable(Actor, shelf)                 # wrap shelf in classtable
        if len(argv) <= 2:
            for key in cast.keys():                      # "python formtbl.py shelve -"
                table[key] = cast[key]                   # initialize? - if no arg3
        FormGui( table ).mainloop()
        shelf.close()
        shelf = shelve.open("test2/shelve1")
        for key in shelf.keys():
            print key, shelf[key].__dict__               # instance dictionary

    elif argv[1] == 'dbm':                               # "python formtbl.py dbm"
        print 'dbm-of-dict test'
        import anydbm
        file = anydbm.open("test2/dbm1", "c")
        if len(argv) <= 2:                               # "python formtbl.py dbm -"
            for key in cast.keys():
                file[key] = `cast[key]`                  # store as a string
        FormGui( DbmTable(file) ).mainloop()
```

By passing in instances of these two classes, *FormGui* becomes the general mapping browser we're after: we can browse in-memory dictionaries, dbm files, and persistent-object shelves. Further, browsed dictionaries and shelves can contain instances of arbitrary *classes*, and dbm files can hold *dictionaries*. Here are the table types that the system can now browse, and the *FormGui* calls for each:

*Table 12-2: Supported table-types*

| Table type | records = dictionaries | records = class-instances |
|---|---|---|
| Dictionary | *FormGui(mapping)* | *FormGui(ClassTable(class, mapping))* |
| Shelve file | *FormGui(mapping)* | *FormGui(ClassTable(class, mapping))* |
| *dbm* file | *FormGui(DbmTable(mapping))* | *[not supported]* |

*DbmTable* also allows a filename to be passed in, if the mapping-argument is passed in as *None*: *FormGui(DbmTable(None, filename))*. In this case, it opens the file for us. *FormGui* still assumes tables contain dictionary-like records; format differences are handled automatically by the table subclasses:

*Fetches*
: When *FormGui* fetches a record from the table, the `__getitem__` methods here intercept the index operation, access the file, and perform appropriate data conversions.

*Stores*
: When *FormGui* stores a record in the table, the data is caught by the `__setitem__` methods here, and is written to an underlying dictionary, shelve, or dbm file in an appropriate format.

### *Constructor arguments not allowed*

*ClassTable* saves the wrapped table's class object. The *Class* argument passed in is just a reference to an existing class (classes are first-class objects in Python). When *ClassTable* fetches a record, the `__getitem__` method just extracts the instance's attribute dictionary (`__dict__`). When *ClassTable* is asked to store a dictionary of values, the `__setitem__` method:

1. Makes a new instance of the class originally passed in.
2. Assigns its attributes from the dictionary keys, using the *setattr* built-in function.
3. Stores the new instance in the underlying mapping table (a dictionary or shelve).

To make the new class instance, *ClassTable* calls the class as usual:

```
instance = self.Class()
```

but it doesn't pass any arguments to the class's constructor. There's no way to know what the argument list looks like, or where the values to be passed-in should come from. Because of this, instances browsed using the ClassTable wrapper class, must be made from a class with either:

- no `__init__` constructor method
- an `__init__` method with *no* arguments besides "self"
- default values for all nonoptional arguments expected by `__init__` except *self*

For example, the *Actor* class imported by the self-test code in *formtbl*:

```
class Actor:                                    # file-level class: not nested
    def __init__(self, name=(), job=''):        # need no args or defaults
        self.name = name                        # for browser and pickle
        self.job  = job
```

has two arguments besides *self*, but they both have default values. If they didn't have defaults, we'd get an argument count exception when *ClassTable* calls *Actor* with no arguments.

### *Persistence class constraints*

Prohibiting constructor arguments may seem like a severe limitation, but the *pickle* module imposes the same rule: class instances can normally only be pickled (and added to a shelve) if they're made from classes that have no constructor arguments, or all defaults. Class instances are mapped to shelve files as follows:

*Store*
: When Python stores a class instance to a shelve, it saves the instance's attribute dictionary (`__dict__`), plus a reference to the instance's class (its source file information).

*Fetch*
: When Python fetches a class instance from a shelve, it recreates the instance object by reimporting the class, and assigning the saved attribute dictionary to a new empty instance of the class.

In fact, this is similar to how our *ClassTable* translates instances to and from attribute dictionaries. Of course, the pickler has to do much more to translate objects to character streams, but since persistence imposes the same rule about constructor arguments, we can't write instances of nonconformant classes anyhow; the "no arguments" rule isn't an extra constraint in *ClassTable*.

Notice that *ClassTable* saves a class object, but persistence stores source file information for the class in the shelve. Because of this, the class used to make persistent instances must be importable: it has to appear at the *top-level* of an **importable module file**. In other words, a persistent instance's class can't be nested in other code, and can't appear in a file run as a top-level program or script (i.e., in module `__main__`).

The *Actor* class used here appears at the top level of file *formtest.py*, so it can be reimported when instances are fetched from a shelve. This importability rule isn't imposed by *ClassTable*, since it has access to an already created class object. But *ClassTable* inherits the persistence rule, when wrapping shelve files.

### *Why the special class persistence rules?*

The *class importability* rule buys us flexibility. Since pickling doesn't store an instance's class-object directly, we're able to change classes without impacting stored instances. For example, we can add or change methods while instances are stored in a shelve; when we later reload the instances, they'll inherit all the changes made to their classes, since the classes are re-imported from separate source files.

The *no arguments* rule is actually optional. Normally, there's no way for Python to tell how to pass in arguments to a class's constructor. However, classes with constructor arguments can still be used for persistence, by defining some special methods. If defined, the method `__getinitargs__` returns a tuple of arguments to be passed later to the class's `__init__` constructor.

Classes may also define two other methods to control how their instances are pickled. If a `__getstate__` method is defined, it's called when an object is stored, and its return value is used as the value to pickle for the instance (instead of pickling the instance's `__dict__` attribute-dictionary). If `__setstate__` is defined, it's called when the object is fetched, with the unpickled instance value (instead of assigning a saved attribute dictionary to the new instance).

Note that these three special methods are only used by the persistence system, and only apply to pickled *class* instances (nonclass objects can be pickled too: lists, dictionaries, etc.). They're intended to give some control over the persistence process to classes. Refer to Python's library reference manual for more information on these special hooks.

### *Setting attributes with strings: setattr and __setattr__*

When a new record is stored in a table of class-instances, three classes come into play:

1. *FormGui.onStore*
```
self.table[key] = item                        store a record in the table
```
2. *ClassTable.__setitem__*
```
setattr(instance, attr, value[attr])          set fields in an instance
```
3. *Actor.__setattr__*
```
self.__dict__[attr] = value                   really set instance field
```

*ClassTable* uses the built-in *setattr* function to assign attributes from keys in a dictionary:

```
for attr in value.keys():
    setattr(instance, attr, value[attr])
```

*setattr* is the assignment equivalent of the *getattr* built-in we saw earlier in the book. The call *setattr(object, attr, value)* is the same as *object.attr=value*, but *setattr* allows the attribute name to be a *string* computed at run-time. Like *getattr*, *setattr* can be used to set an attribute in any object that has assignable attributes: modules, classes, class-instances, etc.

Since we can access an instance's attribute dictionary through the `__dict__` attribute, the *setattr* call in *ClassTable* is almost equivalent to: *instance.__dict__[attr] = value[attr]*, with one critical exception. If the class-instance inherits a `__setattr__` metaclass method, the *setattr* function calls it, instead of assigning to `__dict__`. Direct assignment to the `__dict__` dictionary doesn't trigger `__setattr__`.

Similarly, *getattr(instance, attr)* is almost the same as *instance.__dict__[attr]*, but the *getattr* function searches the instance's classes too (i.e., it uses inheritance rules), and calls a `__getattr__` method if one is inherited, when an attribute's not found. Indexing `__dict__` directly only searches the instance's attribute-dictionary. Since using `__dict__` for assignment or lookup subverts both inheritance and metaclass protocol, the *getattr* and *setattr* functions are usually best for accessing attributes with strings.

*Table 12-3: __setattr__/__getattr__ mappings*

| Expression | Translation |
|---|---|
| *instance.attr = value* | *instance.__setattr__(attr, value)* |
| *setattr(instance, "attr", value)* | *instance.__setattr__(attr, value)* |
| *instance.undefined* | *instance.__getattr__(undefined)* |
| *getattr(instance, "undefined")* | *instance.__getattr__(undefined)* |

The `__setattr__` special method is roughly equivalent to the `__setitem__` method we've already seen, except that `__setattr__` intercepts assignments to attributes instead of indexes. If an instance inherits a `__setattr__` method from one of its classes, it's called each time an attribute is assigned, by normal qualification or the *setattr* function. If there's no `__setattr__` method, assignments are routed to `__dict__`.

In our browser system, *setattr* allows classes to define optional creation-time validations. For instance, the *Actor* class defines a `__setattr__` method to check for data errors when a new instance is added to the table. If we assigned to `__dict__` directly, these checks would never be called.

### *More on using `__getattr__` and `__setattr__` methods*

`__getattr__` and `__setattr__` have slightly different semantics. `__getattr__` is called only if a referenced attribute can't be found in the instance or its classes; this would normally be an exception. `__getattr__` should return an object, or raise an exception.

But if a `__setattr__` method is inherited, it's called on every assignment to an instance's attribute. Further, Python won't assign the attribute for us: if a `__setattr__` is defined, we must put the value in the instance dictionary manually, if we want the assignment to occur. For example, notice how *Actor* sets the attribute after error checks:

```
self.__dict__[attr] = value
```

It doesn't try to call *setattr* again: this would trigger an infinite recursion loop. In fact, we must assign attributes in a `__setattr__` method by going through `__dict__`. Any direct attribute assignment by *setattr* or qualification (*self.attr=value*) will loop. `__setattr__` is a powerful feature, but it should be handled with care.

## *Testing the formtbl Extensions*

Here's an example of *formtbl*'s classes in action. The file's self-test code just runs *FormGui* with specialized tables. Each shot was taken after the prior, to show how the effects of changes in one session are retained for the next. We'll step through three sessions, to give the flavor of the interaction.

### *Session 1*

The first time we run *formtbl* as a top-level program without arguments, it loads a new shelve-file (*test2/shelve1*) from the imported *cast* dictionary. The self-test code creates new instances of the *Actor* class imported from *formtest*, and stores them in the new shelve initially.

```
% python formtbl.py shelve
```

The browser comes up, and we click on *index* to pop up the listbox. Bring up the form window for the *laura* record, by double-clicking on *laura* in the listbox (or type **laura** in the key field and press *find*).

The resulting windows are shown in Figure 12-8.

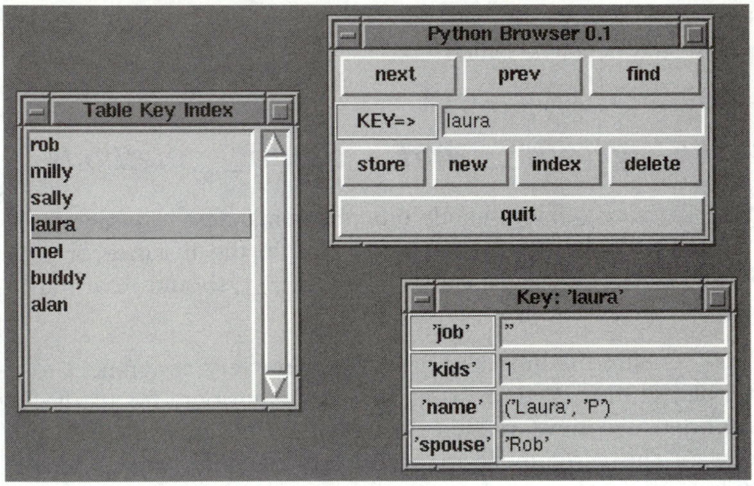

*Figure 12-8: Browsing a shelve of Actors—start state*

Notice that *laura* gets a "job" from the Actor class's `__init__` method. *laura* didn't have this field when we used a table of simple dictionaries, since it's not present in the *cast* initialization dictionary. In a persistent store, classes can provide consistency, and manage access.

We start out with all the records in the *cast* table. Now, make a few changes, and then *quit*:

- Delete *milly* by double-clicking on it and then pressing *delete*.
- Change *buddy* and *alan*: bring their records up, change the *job* field, and press *store*.
- Add a new *guido* record: bring up *alan*, press *new*, fill-in the form fields, and press *store*.

Type *guido* in the main window key field before storing. Use *The Guido* for guido's "name". This triggers a validation error in the Actor class's `__setattrr__` method when we press *store*: *Actor* expects names to be tuples. The error message is generated when the new record is actually stored in the table by *FormGui* (when a new *Actor* instance is created by *ClassTable*).

This is another example of what classes can do in persistent stores: here, the class detects an application-level data error, implemented as a test in the *Actor* class (not in *formgui*). Note that the class sets the name to the bad data anyhow; data entry errors caught by the *GUI* itself fill the field with *None* instead.

We get the following messages during this session in the *stdout* window (where *formtbl* was started); the validation error shows up when we press *store* for *guido* (it probably should pop up a dialog box, or be logged to a file), and the table's contents is dumped before the program exits.

```
% python formtbl.py
shelve-of-class test
validation error: name type = <type 'string'>

rob {'job': 'writer', 'name': ('Rob', 'P'), 'spouse': 'Laura'}
sally {'job': 'writer', 'name': ('Sally', 'R')}
guido {'job': 'inventor', 'name': 'The Guido'}
laura {'job': '', 'kids': 1, 'name': ('Laura', 'P'), 'spouse': 'Rob'}
mel {'job': 'producer', 'name': ('Mel', 'C')}
buddy {'job': 'hacker', 'name': ('Buddy', 'S'), 'spouse': 'Pickles'}
alan {'job': 'demigod', 'name': ('Alan', 'B')}
```

### *Session 2*

Next, let's start a second session, using the *test2/shelve1* shelve created by the first run: add a dash ("-") at the end of the command line to suppress reloading from the *cast* dictionary. As expected, *Actors* are persistent: all the changes we made in the last run are present.

```
% python formtbl.py shelve -
```

*Figure 12-9: Session 2—after changes*

This command gives us the windows in Figure 12-9 and Figure 12-10. Note that the validation error for *guido* isn't reported when reloading here for a second session: it's only reported the first time *guido* is stored. Persistence doesn't use the usual *setattr* protocol when recreating an instance from its saved attributes, so Actor's `__setattr__` isn't called.

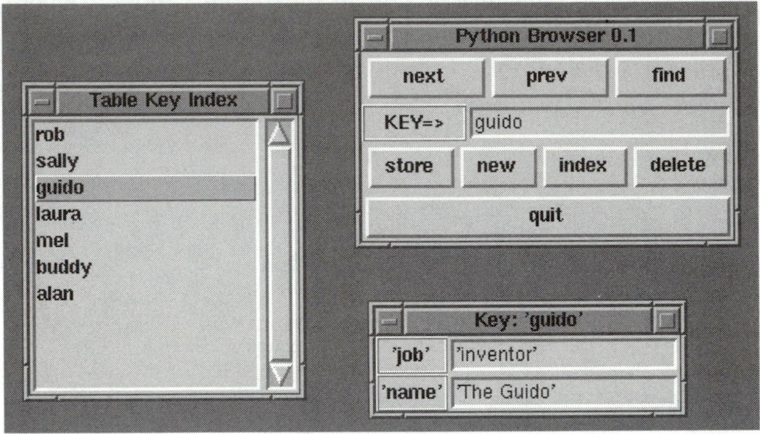


*Figure 12-10: Session 2—added record*

This time, delete *sally*, *mel*, and *alan*. Here's the second session's *stdout* log:

```
% python formtbl.py shelve -
shelve-of-class test

rob {'job': 'writer', 'name': ('Rob', 'P'), 'spouse': 'Laura'}
guido {'job': 'inventor', 'name': 'The Guido'}
laura {'job': '', 'kids': 1, 'name': ('Laura', 'P'), 'spouse': 'Rob'}
buddy {'job': 'hacker', 'name': ('Buddy', 'S'), 'spouse': 'Pickles'}
```

### *Session 3*

Finally, run the program one more time to verify results, do more updates, etc. The shelve file created on the first run (*test2/shelve1*) retains the *Actor* instances between Python runs, indefinitely.

```
% python formtbl.py shelve -
shelve-of-class test
```

The browser now looks like Figure 12-11. Of course, we could keep changing records like this forever, but you probably get the idea from these examples: the *FormGui* is working as an interface to a real persistent shelve of *Actor* class instances. We can browse, add, and change instances interactively, instead of writing programs, or entering commands at the Python command line.

Further, this same interface can be use to process dbm files of dictionaries, in the exact same ways. We just have to pass in a different sort of table to the *FormGui* constructor: a *DbmTable* object (see *formtbl*'s self-test code). In fact, since interaction is identical, there's no reason to step through an example here. To test dbm files, just use *dbm* as the first command-line argument: *python formtbl.py dbm.*

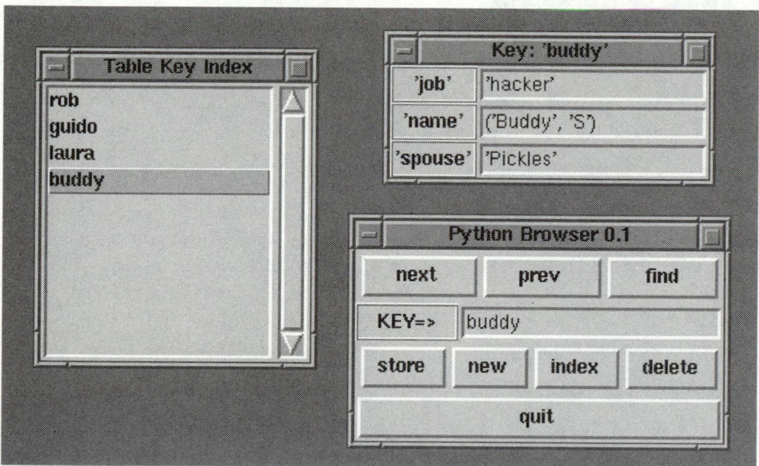


*Figure 12-11: Session 3—after deletions*

## *Generalizing Table Wrapper Classes*

Here's one last improvement to the classes that wrap mappings for use in *FormGui*. Since both the *DbmTable* and *ClassTable* classes are designed to make a mapping look like a mapping of dictionaries, we can abstract some of their processing into a common superclass. Class *Table* in this new version imitates a dictionary directly. *DbmTable* and *ClassTable* override its *getitem/setitem* methods, to change what happens when an item is fetched or set by key, and inherit the rest.

Besides the obvious benefits of code size reduction, the elimination of redundancy reduces chances of errors, and provides a better framework for adding new mapping wrappers in the future. For instance, we've also added a *ShelveTable* class that handles opening files, for shelves of objects. Here's the new module; it behaves exactly like *formtbl.py* earlier.

*Example 12-9: File: formtbl2.py*

```
# add subclassing and shelve class


class Table:
    def __init__(self, mapping):
        self.proxy = mapping                    # wrap some kind of mapping

    def storeItems(self, items):                # init from dictionary
        for key in items.keys():                # do subclass __setitem__
            self[key] = items[key]

    def printItems(self):                       # print wrapped mapping
        for key in self.keys():                 # do subclass __getitem__
            print key, self[key]
```

*Example 12-9: File: formtbl2.py (continued)*

```
    # defaults: to proxy
    def __getitem__(self, key):          return self.proxy[key]
    def __setitem__(self, key, value):   self.proxy[key] = value
    def __delitem__(self, key):          del self.proxy[key]
    def keys(self):                      return self.proxy.keys()


class ShelveTable(Table):                         # or use a shelve directly
    def __init__(self, mapping, fileName=None):   # since shelve works as-is
        if mapping == None:                       # could be a simple function
            import shelve
            mapping = shelve.open(fileName)       # open file (mapping)
        self.proxy = mapping


class DbmTable(Table):
    def __init__(self, mapping, fileName=None):   # wrap table of strings
        if mapping == None:                       # can be dicts but not class
            import anydbm                         # open file (mapping)
            mapping = anydbm.open(fileName, 'c')  # unless passed-in
        self.proxy = mapping

    def __getitem__(self, key):                   # self.table[key]
        return eval(self.proxy[key])              # convert string to dict

    def __setitem__(self, key, value):            # self.table[key] = value
        self.proxy[key] = `value`                 # convert dict to string


class ClassTable(Table):                          # wrap table of instances
    def __init__(self, Class, mapping):           # mapping is dict or shelf
        self.Class = Class                        # save class for new
        self.proxy = mapping                      # save the real mapping

    def __getitem__(self, key):                   # make dict from instance
        instance = self.proxy[key]                # use instance dictionary
        return instance.__dict__

    def __setitem__(self, key, value):            # make instance from dict
        instance = self.Class()                   # like pickle: no init args
        for attr in value.keys():
            setattr(instance, attr, value[attr])  # set instance attributes
        self.proxy[key] = instance                # store in wrapped mapping


if __name__ == '__main__':
    from sys import argv                          # also: formgui,formtbl tests
    from formgui  import FormGui                  # get dict-based gui
    from formtest import Actor, cast              # get class, dict-of-dicts

    def load_and_go(table):
        if len(argv) <= 2:                   # python formtbl2.py ?<opt> ?'-'
```

*Example 12-9: File: formtbl2.py (continued)*

```
        table.storeItems(cast)          # (re)load cast if no arg3
    FormGui( table ).mainloop()         # run gui on the table
    table.printItems()                  # tell table to print itself

if len(argv) == 1 or argv[1] == 'class':
    print 'dict-of-class test'
    load_and_go( ClassTable(Actor, {}) )          # map instance<->dict

elif argv[1] == 'dbm':
    print 'dbm-of-dict test'                        # open dbm file
    load_and_go( DbmTable(None, 'test2/dbm2') )   # map string<->dict

elif argv[1] == 'shelve':                           # just opens shelve
    print 'shelve-of-dict test'
    load_and_go( ShelveTable(None, 'test2/shelve21') )

elif argv[1] == 'class-shelve':
    print 'shelve-of-class test'
    inner = ShelveTable(None, 'test2/shelve22')   # open shelve file
    outer = ClassTable(Actor, inner)                # wrap it in classtable
    load_and_go( outer )
```

This version adds a *ShelveTable* which opens files like the *DbmTable* shown earlier; to browse a shelve of *Actor* class instances called *test2/shelve1*, all we need to do is this:

```
FormGui( ClassTable(Actor, ShelveTable(None, 'test2/shelve1')) ).mainloop()
```

The *ClassTable* wraps the *ShelveTable*, which wraps a real, open *shelve* object:

- *FormGui* browses a mapping of dictionaries.
- *ClassTable* translates a wrapped mapping's class instances to/from dictionaries.
- *ShelveTable* wraps a shelve mapping that fetches/stores class instances from/to a real *dbm* file.

ShelveTable doesn't do any data format translation; it's just a thin wrapper over the real *shelve* mapping; in fact, we can still browse a shelve without wrapping it in a ShelveTable, if we open it ourselves.

Suggested exercises:

1. Change the self-test code to also accept a filename on the command-line. How could classes be passed in from the command line too (instead of hard-coding *Actor*)? Hint: classes could be imported by the script, but you need *exec* and *eval*, since the module and class names will be strings: build and execute an *import* statement string to fetch the module by name, and use *getattr* to fetch the class from the module object by name. See the graph searcher in Chapter 13, *Implementing Objects*, for an import example.

2. When the fields differ on the next record, change the current form window instead of deleting and rebuilding. Hint: attaching new widgets to windows makes them show up immediately.
3. Change the *Actor* class to pop up a dialog box when data validation errors are detected. Also, write a message to a log file, with the record key, time, and user's name (use *os.environ['USER']*). Will the change in *Actor* affect stored instances? Why or why not?

# Other Persistence Topics

The table browser illustrates most of the special dbm/shelve concepts we listed at the beginning of this chapter. There are two final points we'll mention here briefly.

## Persistence Without Shelve

As we mentioned earlier, persistence is structured as two components: the *pickle* module converts objects to character streams, and the *shelve* module reads and writes those streams to a *dbm* file, based on associated keys. Because of this structure, we can implement object persistence without *shelve* and *dbm* files by using *pickle* directly. For instance, we can write manually pickled objects to flat files, send them across a network with Remote Procedure Calls (RPC), etc. Here are a few details on this interface:

`P = pickle.Pickler(file)`
: Make a new pickler, for pickling to open output file-object *file*.

`P.dump(object)`
: Write an object onto the pickler's file/stream.

`pickle.dump(object, file)`
: Same as the last two instances combined: pickle an object onto an open file.

`U = pickle.Unpickler(file)`
: Make an unpickler, for unpickling from open input file object *file*.

`object = U.load()`
: Read an object from the unpickler's file/stream.

`object = pickle.load(file)`
: Same as the last two instances combined: unpickle an object from an open file.

`string = pickle.dumps(object)`
: Return the pickled representation of *object*, as a character string.

`object = pickle.loads(string)`
: Read an object from a character string instead of a file.

*Pickler* and *Unpickler* are exported classes. In all of these, *file* is an open file object, or any object that implements the same attributes as file objects:

- *Pickler* calls the file's *write* method with a string argument.
- *Unpickler* calls the file's *read* method with a byte count, and *readline* without arguments.

Any object that provides these attributes can be passed in to the "file" parameters. In particular, *file* can be an instance of a Python class that provides the read/write methods. This lets us map pickled streams to in-memory objects, for arbitrary use. (In fact, this is how *shelve* maps objects to/from strings for *dbm*.) See Chapter 2 and Appendix D, *An Application Framework*, for examples.

In normal use, to pickle an object to a flat file, we just open the file in write-mode, and call the *dump* function. For instance, if we don't have a *dbm* interface, we can simulate shelves by pickling and unpickling entire dictionaries to simple flat files:

```
% python
>>> import pickle
>>> table = {'a': [1, 2, 3], 'b': ['spam', 'eggs'], 'c':{'name':'bob'}}
>>> fakeShelve = open('dbase', 'w')
>>> pickle.dump(table, fakeShelve)
>>> <ctrl-d>
% ls
dbase ...
% python
>>> import pickle
>>> fakeShelve = open('dbase', 'r')
>>> table = pickle.load(fakeShelve)
>>> table
{'b': ['spam', 'eggs'], 'a': [1, 2, 3], 'c': {'name': 'bob'}}
```

It may take longer to load and store a big dictionary like this (*shelve* loads/stores individual entries on demand), but once the dictionary's loaded, processing it is fast. Python can pickle just about anything, except instances of classes that don't follow the constraints we saw earlier, code objects, and instances of some built-in and user-defined types coded in C (file objects, etc.). A *PicklingError* is raised if an object can't be pickled. There are additional details we won't cover here; refer to Python's library manual for more information on the pickler.

*NOTE* Also see the *marshal* module: It supports portable binary code objects. In Python 1.3, *marshal* is faster than *pickle*, but also much more limited.

## Changing Classes of Stored Persistent Instances

As we've seen, the persistence system normally only records the instance attribute-dictionary for persistent class-instances. This scheme lets us change the classes an instance is derived from, without impacting instances stored in a shelve file. Of course, we have to avoid changing the class in a non-backward-compatible way (for instance, to expect attributes not present in older instances).

But if we're careful, this lets us modify database behavior dynamically, by changing the classes which manage its contents. By modifying external classes, we can change the way stored objects' data is interpreted and used. In effect, classes replace traditional file-processing records and programs.

### Case study: generalizing a persistent-object class

Here's an example. In Chapter 2, we made instances of a *Person* class, and stored them in a shelve; here's a version that's similar (but we'll drop computed data members here).

*Example 12-10: File: person.py*

```
# a person object (data-record manager)

class Person:
    def __init__(self, name = '', job = '', pay = 0):
        self.name = name
        self.job  = job
        self.pay  = pay                    # instance ('self') data

    def basic(self):
        return self.name, self.job, self.pay

    def extra(self):                       # class methods never saved
        result = []
        for field in self.__dict__.keys():
            if field not in ['name', 'job', 'pay']:
                result.append((field, getattr(self,field)))
        return result

    def info(self): return self.basic(), self.extra()
```

This class is fairly specific: its constructor defines attributes tailored for the *Person* instances we want to create. Now suppose we've been using this class for some time, and have an existing database of objects. But we decide that its methods would also be useful for other kinds of objects. Maybe we want to create *Student* objects, with a different set of attributes than *Person.*

Because we can change a class without affecting stored instances, we can generalize *Person* into a reusable superclass (*Record*), and redefine *Person* in terms of the new superclass. Example 12-11 shows one way to do this; *Person* becomes a one-line class, and inherits its prior methods from *Record.*

When existing instances are fetched from the shelve, Python will reimport *Person* as usual, and make new instances with the pickled attribute-dictionaries. It doesn't matter how extensively *Person* changes between runs: there's no need to convert the stored data, to change its interpretation.

There's one catch: since Python saves source file information for an instance's class, we have to make the change in the *same file* where the Person existed before: *person.py.* The new *Record* class could be coded in a new file and imported, but the new version of the *Person* class must appear in *person.py.* For both the variants below, assume the code is in the file *person.py* (copy it over if you're testing this).

*Example 12–11: File: person.py (record1.py)*

```
class Record:
    def __init__(self, *args):                          # use varargs list
        for field, default in self.fields:              # for all common fields
            if args:                                    # defined in subclass
                setattr(self, field, args[0])
                args = args[1:]                         # assign next argument
            else:
                setattr(self, field, default)           # or take default value
    def basic(self):
        result = []
        for field, default in self.fields:              # collect common fields
            result.append((field, getattr(self, field)))
        return result
    def extra(self):
        result = []
        for attr in self.__dict__.keys():               # collect unique fields
            for field, default in self.fields:          # or map/lambda here
                if field == attr: break
            else:
                result.append(attr, getattr(self, attr))
        return result
    def info(self):
        return (self.basic(), self.extra())             # collect all fields

class Person(Record):
```

*Example 12-11: File: person.py (record1.py) (continued)*

```
    fields = [('name', ''), ('job', ''), ('pay', 0)]     # static: common fields

class Student(Record):
    fields = [('name', ''), ('id', 0), ('year', 0), ('age', 20)]
```

Later we might decide that an alternative implementation using dictionaries of fields would be better (Example 12-12); a second change doesn't affect stored instances either. We can change the class as often as we want.

*Example 12-12: File: person.py (record2.py)*

```
from string import upper

class Record:
    def __init__(self, args={}):                         # keys not ordered...
        for field in self.fields.keys():
            setattr(self, field, self.fields[field])  # start with defaults
        for key in args.keys():
            setattr(self, key, args[key])                # add from dictionary
    def basic(self):
        result = []
        for field in self.fields.keys():
            result.append((upper(field), getattr(self, field)))
        return result
    def extra(self):
        result = []
        for attr in self.__dict__.keys():
            if not self.fields.has_key(attr):
                result.append(upper(attr), getattr(self, attr))
        return result
    def info(self):
        return (self.basic(), self.extra())          # collect all fields

class Person(Record):
    fields = {'name':'', 'job':'', 'pay':0 }

class Student(Record):
    fields = {'name':'', 'id':0, 'year':0, 'age':20 }
```

***Testing the class variants.*** Let's start off using the original *person.py* file interactively. We create some instances and store them in a shelve file called *folks*, much like we did in Chapter 2. Both circular and embedded objects are created.

```
% python
>>> from person import Person
>>> jerry = Person('jerry', 'dentist')                  make some objects
>>> bob   = Person('robert', 'psychologist', 70000)
>>> emily = Person('emily')
>>> bob.spouse  = emily;  emily.spouse = bob            circular reference
```

```
>>> bob.friends = ['howard', jerry]                  embedded object
>>>
>>> jerry.info()
(('jerry', 'dentist', 0), [])
>>> bob.info()
(('robert', 'psychologist', 70000), [('friends', ['howard',
<Person instance at b0b70>]), ('spouse', <Person instance at b0bd0>)])
>>> bob.basic()
('robert', 'psychologist', 70000)
>>> bob.extra()
[('friends', ['howard', <Person instance at b0b70>]), ('spouse',
<Person instance at b0bd0>)]
>>>
>>> import shelve
>>> db = shelve.open('folks')                        create a shelve file
>>> db['star']   = bob                               store objects in shelve
>>> db['costar'] = emily                             now they are persistent
>>> db['other']  = jerry
```

Next, leave Python, and check the shelve's contents in a new session.

```
% python
>>> import shelve
>>> db = shelve.open('folks')
>>> for id in db.keys():
...     print db[id].basic()
...
('jerry', 'dentist', 0)
('emily', '', 0)
('robert', 'psychologist', 70000)
>>> db['star'].spouse.name
'emily'
>>> db['star'].friends[1].basic()
('jerry', 'dentist', 0)
```

Now, we'll replace *person.py* with the *record1.py* version; for testing, the file was copied over. In practice, you'd probably change *person.py* in place. We get the same data (instance-objects), but slightly different behavior: this *Person* class returns a list of *(name,value)* tuples for each attribute in an instance, not just a tuple of values.

```
% python
>>> import shelve
>>> db = shelve.open('folks')
>>> db['star'].friends[1].basic()
[('name', 'jerry'), ('job', 'dentist'), ('pay', 0)]
>>> db['costar'].info()
([('name', 'emily'), ('job', ''), ('pay', 0)], [('spouse',
<Person instance at b0820>)])
>>> for id in db.keys():
...     print db[id].basic()
...
[('name', 'jerry'), ('job', 'dentist'), ('pay', 0)]
```

```
[('name', 'emily'), ('job', ''), ('pay', 0)]
[('name', 'robert'), ('job', 'psychologist'), ('pay', 70000)]
>>>
>>> from person import Person
>>> db['extra'] = Person('Peeper')
```

And finally, copy *record2.py* over to *person.py*, to test the third *Person* class version. Here, the attribute names are capitalized in the method results. Since the order of the *fields* dictionary keys isn't predictable, constructor arguments are passed in as a dictionary (just like *Tkinter* options under Python 1.2).

```
% python
>>> import shelve
>>> db = shelve.open('folks')
>>> db['star'].friends[1].basic()
[('PAY', 0), ('JOB', 'dentist'), ('NAME', 'jerry')]
>>> db['costar'].info()
([('PAY', 0), ('JOB', ''), ('NAME', 'emily')], [('SPOUSE',
<Person instance at b0860>)])
>>> for id in db.keys():
...     print db[id].basic()
...
[('PAY', 0), ('JOB', 'dentist'), ('NAME', 'jerry')]
[('PAY', 0), ('JOB', ''), ('NAME', 'emily')]
[('PAY', 0), ('JOB', ''), ('NAME', 'Peeper')]
[('PAY', 70000), ('JOB', 'psychologist'), ('NAME', 'robert')]
>>>
>>> from person import Person
>>> db['neighbor'] = Person({'name': "Howard", 'job': "navigator"})
>>> db['neighbor'].info()
([('PAY', 0), ('JOB', 'navigator'), ('NAME', 'Howard')], [])
```

***Circular and embedded objects: duplicates in shelves.*** There's one other issue we haven't touched on yet, but it may become a factor in our Person examples above. Python's pickling system handles embedded objects, and circular references properly. When an object is stored, all occurrences of its embedded objects map to the same instance, and circular references don't send the pickler into a loop.

However, when storing objects to shelves, objects are only mapped to unique instances within a shelve entry. In other words, if the same object appears in multiple shelve entries, multiple copies are stored (and later fetched); shelves don't notice appearances of the same object in different shelve slots.

This becomes apparent when storing objects that reference each other, under different keys. For example, when we make *bob* and *emily* reference each other circularly, and store each in a separate slot, Python handles the cycle correctly:

```
% python
>>> from person import Person
>>> bob   = Person('bob')
>>> emily = Person('emily')
>>> bob.spouse = emily; emily.spouse = bob                circular reference
>>> bob.spouse.name
'emily'
>>> import shelve
>>> file = shelve.open('cast')
>>> file['star']   = bob                                   store bob and emily
>>> file['costar'] = emily
>>> x = file['star']                                       fetch bob
>>> x.spouse.name
'emily'
>>> x.spouse.name = 'carol'                                change bob's embedded emily
>>> file['star'] = x                                       store back modified bob
```

But since emily is stored as part of bob, and then again individually, the object we get back for key *costar* won't be the same as the object we get back embedded in *bob* (key *star*). Figure 12-12 sketches the internal situation.

```
% python
>>> import shelve
>>> file  = shelve.open('cast')
>>> bob   = file['star']                                   fetch top-level objects
>>> emily = file['costar']                                 each key is a distinct tree
>>> bob.spouse.name
'carol'
>>> emily.name                                             two versions of emily!
'emily'
```

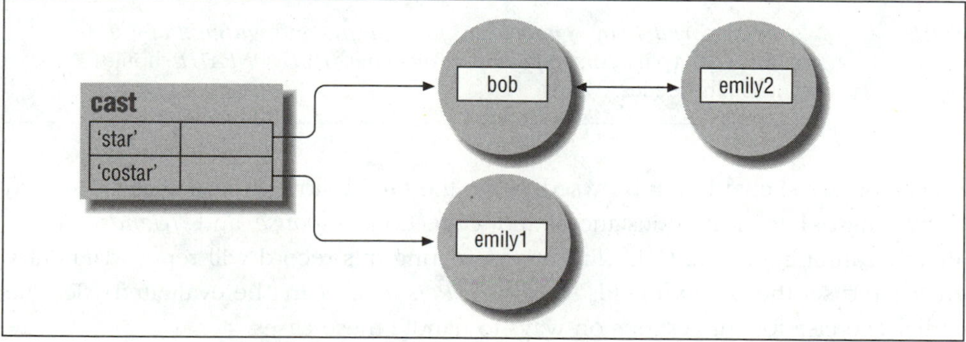

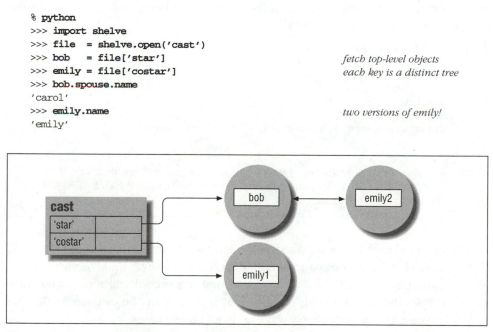

*Figure 12-12: Duplicate objects in a shelve*

The same thing happens in the earlier examples for *jerry*: bob's *jerry* isn't the one stored under key *other*. Because of this, shelves are best used when the objects stored in key slots are independent: in other words, all the objects in each slot shouldn't appear in any other slot. If not, we'll get multiple object copies when fetching and updating; depending on how the shelve is used, this may or may not be important.

---

*NOTE* Duplicate objects are really a limitation of shelves, not of Python's pickler. Shelves are adequate for many applications, but they're really just one way to use the pickling system. For special requirements, the pickler provides hooks to work around such limitations (see the *pickle.py* module in Python's library directory). In fact, the shelve module itself is extensible too; if needed, we can add logic to map objects to unique instances across an entire shelve, by subclassing (see *shelve.py* for details).

---

***Browsing Person instances with FormGui.*** Since we already wrote a GUI interface for browsing and updating shelves of class instances, there's no point to using the Python command-line to test these classes. Here's a script that brings up our *FormGui* table browser, on the *folks* shelve we've been testing, passing-in the *Person* class for store operations.

*Example 12-13: File: browse.py*

```
#!/usr/local/bin/python
from formgui  import FormGui
from formtbl2 import *
from person   import Person
FormGui(ClassTable(Person, ShelveTable(None,'folks'))).mainloop()
```

---

*NOTE* We need *formtbl2.py*, *guitools.py*, *formgui.py*, and *guimixin.py* to run the GUI (plus *person.py* and *browse.py*). *PYTHONPATH* should point to all the files.

---

Scenes of our shelve being browsed under the GUI follow. Notice that the record shown here has nested instances and collections (*spouse* and *friends*). We're already running into the GUI's limitations: storing this record will report data-entry errors, and set the last two fields to *None* (*<Person . . .* can't be evaluated). See the earlier exercise for suggestions on ways to handle these cases.

```
% browse.py
```

Figure 12-13 shows the windows we get. Note that *ClassTable* will create and store an instance of whatever class object is passed in: since *Person* is passed, the new record becomes a *Person* in the shelve. The GUI works with all three *Person* versions: *ClassTable* fetches and builds instance attribute dictionaries directly. Any class works, as long as its constructor requires no arguments. Person constructor

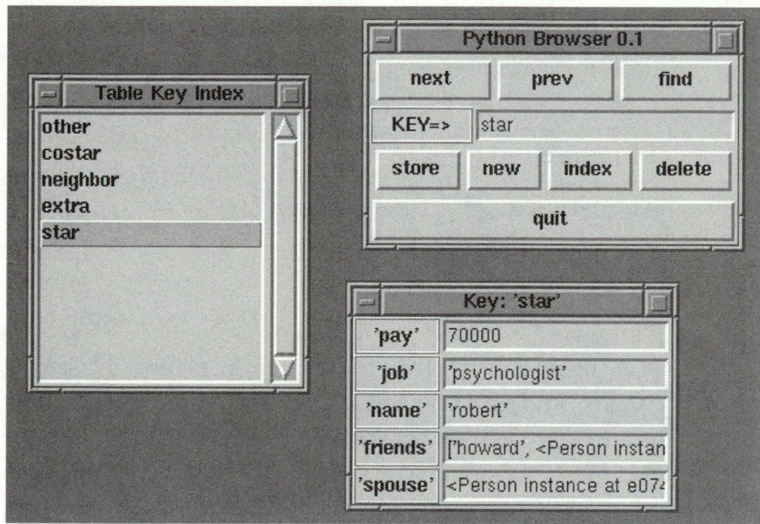


*Figure 12-13: Browsing a Person shelve*

variations are irrelevant, and method differences are only important when the methods are called. Figure 12-14 shows the scene after adding a new record based on *costar*.

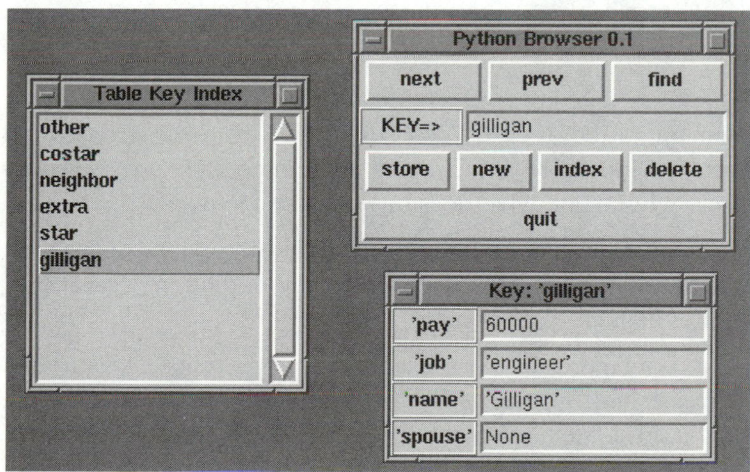


*Figure 12-14: A new Person*

Let's verify edits we made in the GUI, using the command-line. File *person.py* is the *record1.py* version at this point. Notice that the *costar* record's *spouse* field was set to *None* when it was updated; it generated a data error dialog, since it had been a *Person* instance (without a string representation).

```
>>> import shelve
>>> db = shelve.open('folks')
>>> for id in db.keys():
...     print db[id].basic()
...
[('name', 'Gilligan'), ('job', 'engineer'), ('pay', 60000)]
[('name', 'jerry'), ('job', 'dentist'), ('pay', 0)]
[('name', 'emily'), ('job', 'teacher'), ('pay', 50000)]
[('name', 'Howard'), ('job', 'navigator'), ('pay', 9999888L)]
[('name', 'Peeper'), ('job', ''), ('pay', 0)]
[('name', 'robert'), ('job', 'psychologist'), ('pay', 70000)]
>>> db['costar'].info()
([('name', 'emily'), ('job', 'teacher'), ('pay', 50000)], [('spouse', None)])
```

Finally, if we change the class-name from *Person* to *Student* in *browse.py*, storing new or updated records creates *Student* instances in the same shelve, instead of *Persons*. Existing *Person* instances are loaded as *Persons* from the shelve, but new entries use the *Student* fields list. This can lead to strange behavior: *Persons* can become *Students* if updated, records can have both classes' fields, etc. In practice, the instances of different classes should probably be kept in different shelves (or *ClassTable* should save each record's class using `__class__`). Here's an example of a *Student* added in the GUI:

```
>>> import shelve
>>> db = shelve.open('folks')
>>> db['student'].info()
([('name', 'Sue'), ('id', 0), ('year', 3), ('age', 20)], [('job', 'cook'),
  ('pay', 6.25)])
```

Suggested exercises:

1. Add a print statement to the `__init__` constructor of the *Record* class, and load the *star* entry. It is called three times each time this one object is accessed (indexed). Why? (Hint: what does this object reference?)
2. As is, accessing a nonexistent field (attribute) raises an exception. Change the record classes to return *None* in this case instead, by adding a `__getattr__` method. Is this better than an exception?
3. Make up a new kind of record class (for example, to represent recipes from a cookbook), and create and browse persistent instances of the class with the tablebrowser GUI. Add a method to the class to implement some form of behavior. Classes subsume both record descriptions, and file processing programs (changing methods changes behavior); is there any kind of processing classes can't handle?

4. After you've made some *Person* objects, delete *person.py* and rerun the browser. It probably works, although the source file holding the *Person* class is missing. Why? (Hint: this is a "trick" question: do *ls person.** to see why).

5. Write a non-GUI program to process a shelve. For example, read through the *Person* instance shelve, and change names to uppercase letters. Then add a new attribute to all the instances in an *Actor* shelve; you won't need to update the *Actor* class for the new attribute. Why? In both cases is it easier to update stored instances, or modify the external class?

6. Add a formatted reporting method to *Record*, and use it to print already stored instances. The `%` operator and *string* module methods (*ljust*, *zfill*, etc.) can be used to format strings for printing in Python. How and where would you implement methods to perform cumulative operations over all the instances in a shelve? (Hint: you need a higher-level object).

7. In Chapter 2, our *Person* classes also had logic to compute a *tax* member on demand. We avoided it here: all attributes are real instance attributes. Why won't computed data members work in *FormGui*, with the current *ClassTable* wrappers? Is there a way around this limitation?

8. Study the *shelve* module's use of the pickler (currently, file *Lib/shelve.py*). It uses a *StringIO* class to intercept writes, and supply text for reads, imitating a true file. In effect, *StringIO* simulates files with in-memory strings; *shelve* stores the strings on the underlying dbm file. We'll see a similar internal file class in Appendix D. The *pickle* module is also a great advanced example.

9. Solve the circular reference problem: extend the *pickle/shelve* classes to map objects that appear in multiple slots, to unique shelve entries. You may need to generate object keys (identifiers).

10. Define a *mixin* class, *PersistentObject*, that provides persistence operations as methods. The current persistence system is external to the actual objects stored. Another way to implement persistence is with a superclass that provides the necessary interface methods. The class should define methods for saving, loading, deleting, and creating persistent instances. Does a *mixin* make sense here? How will it affect client programs? What state information does the class need to record and manage?

11. Consider adding latent loading support to the *mixin* class. At present, Python's persistence system loads an object as a whole—all its attribute's values are loaded at once. This could become expensive for large, linked objects. In principle, since we can intercept accesses to nested objects (using indexing, qualification, etc.), we could avoid loading nested objects until they are actually accessed. How would you propose implementing delayed loading? Would generated object keys (identifiers) help here?

# Summary

We have studied a fairly large but realistic system in this chapter: the *FormGui* browser class, and the table wrappers for mapping variants. We've also explored some *Tkinter* concepts, a few new Python language features, and object persistence along the way.

Like *Tkinter*, persistence is a popular Python extension, and the main emphasis here has been on how to use it. But as in Chapter 11, part of our goal has been to show another example of Python's extension tools in action. We'll see how *dbm* is integrated into Python in Chapter 14.

But first, Chapter 13 shifts gears, from extensions to language concepts. It explores advanced Python topics by developing new object types in Python. As we've seen in this chapter, the persistence system is based on both C extension types (*dbm*) and tools coded in Python (shelve and pickle). And a similar combination was used for *Tkinter* in the last chapter. Although C extensions are a central concept in Python development, extending the Python language in Python is just as important.

*In this chapter:*
- *"Roses are Red, Violets are Blue; Lists are Mutable, and So is Class Foo"*
- *Implementing Stacks*
- *Implementing Sets*
- *Classical Data Structures in Python*

# 13

# *Implementing Objects*

## *"Roses are Red, Violets are Blue; Lists are Mutable, and So is Class Foo"*

Data structures are a central theme in most programs. As we've seen, Python already provides a set of built-in types for dealing with structured data: lists, strings, tuples, dictionaries, etc. For simple systems, these types are usually enough. In fact, dictionaries make many of the classical searching algorithms unnecessary in Python, and lists replace much of the work you'd do to support collections in a language like C.

But for advanced applications, we may need to add more sophisticated types of our own, to handle extra requirements. In this chapter, we'll explore data structure implementations in Python. As we'll see, data structures take the form of new object types in Python, integrated into the language's type model. Objects we code in Python become full-fledged data types; they can act just like built-in lists, numbers, and dictionaries. Along the way we'll also study advanced features of Python modules and classes.

Although the examples in this chapter illustrate advanced programming techniques, they also underscore Python's support for writing reusable software. By coding object implementations with classes, modules, and other Python tools, they become generally useful components, which may be used in any program that imports them. In effect, we'll be building libraries of data structure classes, whether we plan for it or not.

This chapter also lays some groundwork for Chapter 14, *Extending Python*. In particular, pay special attention to the *stack* implementation here; we'll migrate it to C in Chapter 14 without impacting its clients. The discussion of Python object implementations won't really be complete, until we see how they can also be coded as C extension types in Chapter 14. But for many applications the Python-based implementations we'll study here are sufficient.

## Implementing Stacks

Stacks are a common yet straightforward data structure, used in a variety of applications: language processing, graph searches, etc. In short, stacks are a last-in-first-out collection of objects. Strictly speaking, the last item added to the collection is always the next one to be removed. Clients use stacks by:

- Pushing items onto the top
- Popping items off the top

Depending on client requirements, there may also be tools for testing if the stack is empty, fetching the top item without popping it, iterating over a stack's items, testing for item membership, etc. In Python, a simple list is often adequate for implementing a stack: because we can change lists in place, we can either add and delete items from the front (left) or end (right):

*Table 13-1: Stacks as lists*

| Operation | Top is end-of-list | Top is front-of-list | Top is front-of-list |
|---|---|---|---|
| *New* | *stack = ['a', 'b', 'c']* | *stack = ['c', 'b', 'a']* | *stack = ['c', 'b', 'a']* |
| *Push* | *stack.append('d')* | *stack.insert(0, 'd')* | *stack[0:0] = ['d']* |
| *Pop* | *x = stack[-1]; del stack[-1:]* | *x = stack[0]; del stack[:1]* | *x = stack[0]; stack[:1] = []* |

This list arrangement works, and will be relatively fast. But it also binds stack-based programs to the stack representation chosen: stack operations will all be hard-coded. If we later want to change how a stack is represented, or extend its basic operations, we're stuck: every stack-based program will have to be updated.

For instance, to add logic that monitors the number of stack operations a program performs, we'd have to add code around each hard-coded stack operation. In a large system, this operation may be non-trivial. As we'll see in the next chapter, we may also decide to move stacks to a C-based implementation, if they prove to be a performance bottleneck. As a rule, hard-coded operations on built-in data structures don't support future migrations as well as we'd sometimes like.

## *A Stack Module*

A better approach is to encapsulate stack implementations using Python's code reuse tools. Let's begin by implementing a stack as a module containing a Python list, plus functions to operate on it.

*Example 13-1: File: stack1.py*

```
stack = []                                     # on first import
error = 'stack1.error'                         # local exceptions

def push(obj):
    global stack                               # use 'global' to change
    stack = [obj] + stack                      # add item to the front

def pop():
    global stack
    if not stack:
        raise error, 'stack underflow'         # raise local error
    top, stack = stack[0], stack[1:]           # remove item at front
    return top

def top():
    if not stack:                              # raise local error
        raise error, 'stack underflow'         # or let IndexError occur
    return stack[0]

def empty():       return not stack            # is the stack []?
def member(obj):   return obj in stack         # item in stack?
def item(offset):  return stack[offset]        # index the stack
def length():      return len(stack)           # number entries
def dump():        print '<Stack:%s>' % stack
```

This module creates a list object (*stack*), and exports functions to manage access to it. The stack is declared global in functions that change it, but not in those that just reference it. The module also defines an error object ("error") that can be used to catch exceptions raised locally in this module. Some stack errors are built-in Python exceptions: method *item* triggers an *IndexError* for out-of-bounds indexes.

Most of the stack's functions just delegate the operation to the embedded list used to represent the stack. In fact, the module is really just a wrapper around a Python list. But this extra layer of interface logic makes clients independent of the actual implementation of the stack: we're able to change the stack later without impacting its clients.

### *Using the Stack module*

As usual, the best way to understand this code is to see it in action. Here's an interactive session that illustrates the module's interfaces.

```
% python
>>> import stack1
>>> stack1.dump()
<Stack:[]>
>>> stack1.length(), stack1.empty()
(0, 1)
>>> for i in range(5): stack1.push(i)
...
>>> stack1.dump()
<Stack:[4, 3, 2, 1, 0]>
>>> stack1.item(0), stack1.item(-1), stack1.length()
(4, 0, 5)
>>> stack1.pop(), stack1.top()
(4, 3)
>>> stack1.member(4), stack1.member(3)
(0, 1)
>>> for i in range(stack1.length()): print stack1.item(i),
...
3 2 1 0
>>> while not stack1.empty(): print stack1.pop(),
...
3 2 1 0
>>> stack1.top()
Traceback (innermost last):
  File "<stdin>", line 1, in ?
  File "./stack1.py", line 17, in top
    raise error, 'stack underflow'        # or let IndexError occur
stack1.error: stack underflow
>>> try:
...     stack1.pop()
... except stack1.error, message:
...     print message
...
stack underflow
>>>
```

All *stack* operations are module functions here. For instance, it's possible to iterate over the stack, but we need to use counter-loops and indexing methods (*item*). Printing requires a special method call too. There's nothing preventing clients from accessing (and changing) *stack1.stack* directly. As we've seen, modules encapsulate object behavior, but information-hiding is a convention: clients should normally use the stack through the module's function interfaces.

Notice how the *stack1.error* is trapped with a *try* statement in the session: the module's exception object is imported along with the module's functions. Of course, in more realistic programs this module would probably be imported by different modules, and used asynchronously:

*Example 13-2: File: client1.py*

```
from stack1 import *
push(123)                    # 'stack' module-name not needed
...
result = pop()
```

*Example 13-3: File: client2.py*

```
import stack1
if not stack1.empty():       # qualify by module name
    x = stack1.pop()
stack1.push(1.23)            # both clients share the same stack
```

The actual *stack* object in *stack1.py* is initialized to the empty list ("[]") once, when the module's first imported anywhere in a program (from any module); later imports don't rerun the module's code.

Suggested exercise: the module isn't very efficient, in that it uses slicing and concatenation to add and remove items from the stack's list, and both make new list copies. Change the *stack* module to use one of the in-place list modification schemes shown in Table 13-1: *append*, *insert*, etc. (Hint: see Chapter 2, *A Sneak Preview*).

## A Stack Class

Perhaps the biggest drawback of the module-based stack is that it only supports a single stack object. All clients of the *stack* module effectively share the same stack. Sometimes we want this: a stack can serve as a shared-memory object for multiple modules. But to implement a true stack datatype, we need to use classes.

Modules and classes both allow us to encapsulate data structure implementations behind interfaces, to simplify future migrations. But classes are Python's abstract data type tool. As we saw earlier, classes also support multiple instances, inheritance, and operator hooks, so they have some critical advantages over modules when implementing object behavior:

*Multi-instance*
: Classes support multiple copies of the objects they describe. Each instance gets a new attribute namespace (for per-instance data), and inherits the class's attributes.

*Customization*
: Classes allow for future extensions and specializations. Subclasses can augment, replace, or extend behavior defined by the original class, by using attribute inheritance rules.

*Operators*

Classes may define specially named methods to overload Python operators, and intercept class operations. Instances can be manipulated both by method calls and expressions.

To illustrate, let's define a full-featured stack class. The *Stack* class below defines a new datatype, with a variety of behavior. Like the module, the class uses a Python list to hold stacked objects. But this time, each instance gets its own list. The class defines both "real" methods, and specially named methods to implement operator and metaclass behavior. Comments in the code describe special methods.

*Example 13-4: File: stack2.py*

```
error = 'stack2.error'                       # when imported: local exception

class Stack:
    def __init__(self, start=[]):            # self is the instance object
        self.stack = []                      # start is any sequence: stack..
        for x in start: self.push(x)
        self.reverse()                       # undo push's order reversal

    def push(self, obj):                     # methods: like module + self
        self.stack = [obj] + self.stack      # top is front of list

    def pop(self):
        if not self.stack:
           raise error, 'stack underflow'
        top, self.stack = self.stack[0], self.stack[1:]
        return top

    def top(self):
        if not self.stack:
           raise error, 'stack underflow'
        return self.stack[0]

    def empty(self):
        return not self.stack                     # instance.empty()

    def __repr__(self):
        return '[Stack:%s]' % self.stack          # print, backquotes,..

    def __cmp__(self, other):
        return cmp(self.stack, other.stack)       # '==', '>, '<=', '!=',..

    def __len__(self):
        return len(self.stack)                    # len(instance), not instance
```

*Example 13-4: File: stack2.py (continued)*

```
    def __add__(self, other):
        return Stack(self.stack + other.stack)     # instance1 + instance2

    def __mul__(self, reps):
        return Stack(self.stack * reps)            # instance * reps

    def __getitem__(self, offset):
        return self.stack[offset]                  # intance[offset], in, for

    def __getslice__(self, low, high):
        return Stack(self.stack[low : high])       # instance[low:high]

    def __getattr__(self, name):
        return getattr(self.stack, name)           # instance.sort()/reverse()/..
```

### *Things to notice*

As usual, instances are created by calling the *Stack* class like a function. In most respects the *Stack* class implements operations exactly like the *stack* module above. But here, access to the stack is qualified by *self*, the subject instance object. Each instance has its own *stack* attribute, which refers to the instance's own list. Instance stacks are created and initialized in the `__init__` constructor method, not when the module is imported.

Some of *Stack*'s methods make new *Stack* instances: `__add__`, `__mul__`, and `__getslice__` return a new Stack holding the result. This imitates the normal sequence semantics for concatenation, repetition, and slicing. But this is arbitrary: we could instead use these methods to change the *self.stack* list in place, if we wanted the "+", "*", and "[:]" operations to have side effects (like C's "+=", "*=", and so on.).

In general, only a few methods have fixed result types: `__repr__` must return a string representation, and `__cmp__` should return an integer code (discussed below). Others must follow expected behavior to integrate with Python primitives: `__getitem__` should raise an *IndexError* for out-of-bounds indexes, to terminate *for* loops and *in* tests; other exceptions aren't treated as end-of-sequence signals.

### *Classes imitate built-in types*

Like lists and dictionaries, *Stack* defines both methods and operators for manipulating instances by attribute qualification and expressions. It also defines the `__getattr__` metaclass method to intercept references to attributes not defined in

### Initialization logic

The Stack's `__init__` constructor method accepts an optional argument to specify an initial value for the new *Stack* instance. The argument can be any sequence. More accurately, it can be any object that responds to *for* loop iteration: a built-in sequence (lists, tuples, strings), or an instance of a Python class or C extension type that provides iteration methods (`__getitem__` for classes). Since Stacks are sequences, the argument can also be another Stack instance: *Stack(instance)* copies a Stack.

The constructor reverses the stack's list after making it: pushing items from a sequence reverses their order (the last is on top), so we reverse to make the leftmost item the top. *self.reverse* invokes the built-in list reverse method: the call is routed through the Stack's `__getattr__` method. Since the instance-object has already been created by the time `__init__` runs, the constructor can call other Stack methods through *self*. Note that there's no `__del__`: the wrapped list is reclaimed (garbage-collected) when the *Stack* instance is.

the class, and route them to the wrapped list object (to support list methods: *sort*, *append*, *reverse*, etc.). Many of the module's operations become operators in the class:

*Table 13-2: Module/class operation comparison*

| Module Operations | Class Operations | Class Method |
|---|---|---|
| `module.empty()` | *not* instance | `__len__` |
| `module.member(x)` | *x* in instance | `__getitem__` |
| `module.item(i)` | *instance[i]* | `__getitem__` |
| `module.length()` | *len(instance)* | `__len__` |
| `module.dump()` | *print* instance | `__repr__` |
| `range() counter loops` | for *x* in instance | `__getitem__` |
| manual loop logic | *instance + instance*, ... | `__add__`, ... |
| `module.stack.reverse()` | *instance.reverse()* | `__getattr__` |
| `module.push/pop/top` | *instance.push/pop/top* | *push/pop/top* |

The class's real methods (*push/pop/top/empty*) work the same, but here the stack is an attribute of an object (*self*), not a global variable in the module. Together, Stack's methods integrate instances into Python's object model in a fairly seamless fashion. For instance, the "+" operator concatenates stacks, "==" tests for stack equality, and list-methods like *sort* can be applied to stacks as if they were lists.

In effect, classes let us extend Python's set of built-in types, with reusable types implemented in Python modules. Class-based types may be used just like built-in types: depending on which operation methods they define, classes can implement numbers, mappings, and sequences, and may be mutable or not. Class-based types may also fall somewhere in-between these categories.

For instance, *Stack* is a sequence that doesn't provide methods for assignment to indexes or slices (`__setitem__`, `__setslice__`). But stacks can be changed in-place, using the local push/pop methods, or list methods (intercepted by `__getattr__`). Even though it doesn't provide all the usual sequence modification operations, it's not quite immutable.

### *Using the Stack class*

Here's an interactive session showing how *Stack* class operations correspond to the module above. The *Stack* class is imported, and used to make a single instance object *obj*. Compare this session with the module session above: many of the module's functions becomes Python expressions and statements here.

There's extra functionality here too. We can use *Stack* objects in *print* statements, and convert them to strings with backquotes (both invoke the `__repr__` method). We can also *iterate* through stacks directly: when class-instances appear in *in* tests or *for* loops, Python calls the `__getitem__` method with successively higher indexes, until *IndexError* is raised. Counter-loops work but aren't required.

```
% python
>>> from stack2 import Stack
>>> obj = Stack()                              constructor: __init__
>>> print obj                                  printing: __repr__
[Stack:[]]
>>> `obj`                                      string conversion: __repr__
'[Stack:[]]'
>>> len(obj), not obj                          length: __len__
(0, 1)
>>> for i in range(5): obj.push(i)             push is a real method
...
>>> obj
[Stack:[4, 3, 2, 1, 0]]
>>> obj[0], obj[-1], len(obj)                  indexing: __getitem__
(4, 0, 5)
>>> obj.pop(), obj.top()
(4, 3)
>>> 4 in obj, 3 in obj                         membership: __getitem__
(0, 1)
>>> for i in range(len(obj)): print obj[i],
...
3 2 1 0
>>> for x in obj: print x,                     iteration: __getitem__
...
```

```
3 2 1 0
>>> while obj: print obj.pop(),                truth-testing: __len__
...
3 2 1 0
>>> obj.top()
Traceback (innermost last):
  File "<stdin>", line 1, in ?
  File "./stack2.py", line 20, in top
    raise error, 'stack underflow'
stack2.error: stack underflow
>>> import stack2
>>> try:
...     obj.pop()
... except stack2.error, message:
...     print message
...
stack underflow
>>>
```

### *Using advanced Stack class features*

Here's another interactive session that illustrates some of the extra utility provided by the class-based implementation. We're able to make multiple *Stack* instances, as expected.

We're also able to apply most sequence operations to *Stack* objects: slicing, indexing, repetition, the *len* function, and more. For instance, slicing a stack without limits (*instance[:]*) makes a new stack that's a copy of the operand. We can also copy a stack by multiplying it by 1 (*instance * 1*), adding it to a new empty stack (*Stack() + instance*), or passing in to the constructor (*Stack(instance)*).

*Stack* supports basic type operations too: for example, comparison operators (">", "= =", etc.) are routed to the `__cmp__` method. Like C's *strcmp* function, `__cmp__` methods return a result of -1, 0, or 1, to designate less-than, equal-to, or greater-than relationships, respectively. Python translates the integer result to the expression operator. The built-in *cmp()* function returns the integer flag directly: *Stack* uses it to delegate comparisons to the wrapped list objects.

Clients may also use list methods on stacks: they can be sorted, reversed, appended, etc. This might be dangerous (the effect of a stack *append* depends on which end is the top), but provides extra utility we don't need to implement in the *Stack* class. To disable selected list methods, we can test the attribute name in `__getattr__` and raise an *AttributeError* exception for methods not allowed:

```
def __getattr__(self, name):
    if name in ['append', 'insert', 'remove']:
        raise AttributeError, 'list method not supported by Stack'
    else:
        return getattr(self.stack, name)
```

```
% python
>>> from stack2 import *
>>> x = Stack("spam");  y = Stack([1,2,3])          __init__
>>> z = x + y                                       __add__
>>> z                                               __repr__
[Stack:['s', 'p', 'a', 'm', 1, 2, 3]]
>>> z.top(), z[0], z[-1], z[len(z)-1]               __getitem__, __len__
('s', 's', 3, 3)
>>> for n in x: print n,                            __getitem__
...
s p a m
>>> for i in range(len(z)): print z[i],
...
s p a m 1 2 3
>>> 's' in x, 'S' in x
(1, 0)
>>> x * 2                                           __mul__
[Stack:['s', 'p', 'a', 'm', 's', 'p', 'a', 'm']]
>>> x.reverse()                                     __getattr__
>>> x * 2                                           __mul__
[Stack:['m', 'a', 'p', 's', 'm', 'a', 'p', 's']]
>>> x[:-1], x[1:]                                   __getslice__
([Stack:['m', 'a', 'p']], [Stack:['a', 'p', 's']])
>>>
>>> (x[2:] + x[:2]) * 2                             getslice/add/mul
[Stack:['p', 's', 'm', 'a', 'p', 's', 'm', 'a']]
>>> while x: print x.pop(),
...
m a p s
>>> x.empty(), not x                                __len__
(1, 1)
>>> y
[Stack:[1, 2, 3]]
>>> z = y[:]                                        __getslice__
>>> z.pop()
1
>>> y, z                                            distinct stacks
([Stack:[1, 2, 3]], [Stack:[2, 3]])
>>> y > z, z > y                                    __cmp__
(0, 1)
>>> z.push(0)
>>> y > z, z > y                                    __cmp__
(1, 0)
```

### *Stack client modules*

As before, *Stack* would normally be imported in module files, in real programs:

*Example 13-5: File: client1.py*

```
from stack2 import Stack
x = Stack()
x.push(123)                         # qualify the instance name
...
result = x.pop()
```

*Example 13-6: File: client2.py*

```
import stack2
x = stack2.Stack()
...
if not x.empty():                  # this isn't client1's stack
    a = x.pop()
x.push(1.23)
```

This time the client modules won't share the same stack. But what if we really want a stack that's shared by multiple clients? We can still implement this with the class-based implementation: just make a single class instance in a shared module:

*Example 13-7: File: sharedstack.py*

```
from stack2 import Stack
stack = Stack()                         # make one instance, to be shared
```

*Example 13-8: File: client1.py*

```
from sharedstack import stack           # get shared instance, not class
stack.push(123)                         # qualify shared object's name
...
result = stack.pop()
```

*Example 13-9: File: client2.py*

```
import sharedstack
if not sharedstack.stack.empty():       # can qualify stack by module name
    x = sharedstack.stack.pop()         # both clients share the same stack
sharedstack.stack.push(1.23)
```

The only way this instance differs from a real module is that we need to qualify the shared object's name to get to the stack methods: there's no direct equivalent of *from** module function copies, so we can't call *pop*, *push*, etc., as unqualified names (though this could be simulated with bound methods).

Because classes can simulate modules using shared instances, they're usually a better way to implement objects: both shared objects, and true multiple-instance object datatypes. Classes are more powerful than modules when it comes to type operations. Modules are usually best used as packaging tools.

### *Customization: performance monitors*

So far we've seen how classes support multiple instances and integrate better with Python's object model by defining operator methods. One of the other main reasons for using classes is to allow for future extensions and customizations: by implementing stacks with a class we can later add subclasses that specialize the implementation for new demands.

### *"One class fits all"*

In the interactive sessions, *Stack* objects hold both numbers and strings. In general, *Stack* instances can hold objects of any type: numbers, lists, functions, modules, etc. Further, *Stack*s can hold arbitrary combinations of types: both numbers and strings, etc. We can even use *Stack* objects to implement stacks of stacks, by pushing and popping other *Stack* instances.

This conclusion follows from the fact that stacks are stored as lists: Python lists are heterogeneous and nestable. But it also stems from the lack of type/size declarations in Python: because Python is dynamically typed, a single data structure implementation is usually enough to support arbitrarily many component object types.

Unless different component types require special handling, there's no need for distinct collection classes for each base type. If you've used strongly typed languages like C++ or Pascal, you can probably appreciate the simplicity of this scheme.

In fact, classes provide for future expansion, even if we can't predict future requirements. As we saw earlier in the book, changes only need appear in the new subclasses: they don't always imply inline changes to the original class. For instance, suppose we've started using the Stack class above, but we start running into performance problems. One way to isolate bottlenecks is to instrument data structures with logic that keeps track of usage statistics, which we can analyze after running client applications.

Because *Stack* is a class, we can add such logic in a new subclass, without affecting the original stack module (or its clients). The following subclass extends *Stack*'s methods, to keep track of overall *push/pop* usage frequencies, and record the maximum size of each *Stack* instance.

*Example 13-10: File: stacklog.py*

```
from stack2 import Stack

class StackLog(Stack):                          # count pushes/pops, max-size
    pushes = pops = 0                           # shared/static class members
    def __init__(self, start=[]):               # could also be module vars
        self.maxlen = 0
        Stack.__init__(self, start)

    def push(self, object):
        Stack.push(self, object)                        # do real push
        StackLog.pushes = StackLog.pushes + 1           # overall stats
        self.maxlen = max(self.maxlen, len(self))       # per-instance stats
```

*Example 13-10: File: stacklog.py (continued)*

```
    def pop(self):
        StackLog.pops = StackLog.pops + 1                  # overall counts
        return Stack.pop(self)                             # not 'self.pops': instance

    def stats(self):
        return self.maxlen, self.pushes, self.pops # get counts from instance
```

***Using the extended stack subclass.*** This subclass works the same as the original *Stack*; it just adds monitoring logic. The new *stats* method is used to get a statistics tuple through an instance.

```
% python
>>> from stacklog import StackLog
>>> x = StackLog()
>>> x.stats()                                       (maxlen, pushes, pops)
(0, 0, 0)
>>> for i in range(3): x.push(i)
...
>>> x.pop(), x, x.stats()
(2, [Stack:[1, 0]], (3, 3, 1))
>>> y = StackLog("spam")
>>> y.pop(), y
('s', [Stack:['p', 'a', 'm']])
>>> y.stats(), x.stats()                            maxlen varies per instance
((4, 7, 2), (3, 7, 2))
>>> y.pop()
'p'
>>> y.stats(), x.stats()                            pushes/pops for all instances
((4, 7, 3), (3, 7, 3))
>>> for i in range(3): print x.pop(),
...
1 0
Traceback (innermost last):
  File "<stdin>", line 1, in ?
  File "./stacklog.py", line 16, in pop
    return Stack.pop(self)                          # not 'self.pops': instance
  File "./stack2.py", line 14, in pop
    raise error, 'stack underflow'
stack2.error: stack underflow
>>> y.stats(), x.stats()
((4, 7, 6), (3, 7, 6))
```

Notice that the exception raised on stack overflow is still *stack2.error*, even though we didn't import *stack2* directly here. *x* and *y* share the *push/pop* counts, but have their own length statistics.

### *Optimization: tuple tree stacks*

As you probably expect, there are a variety of ways to implement stacks, some more efficient than others. So far, our stacks have used slicing and concatenation to implement pushing and popping. This method is relatively inefficient: both

## *Static class data*

The subclass's *pushes* and *pops* counts are class attributes (*static* class data). Since they're shared by all instances, they can be used to keep track of overall *push* and *pop* calls among all *Stack* instances. The *maxlen* attribute is instance data: it keeps track of each instance's own maximum-length. More generally, any attribute-name that's assigned as an attribute of *self* becomes instance data: we need to go through the class-name *StackLog* to update the overall counters, but can access them through *self*. Chapter 9, *Moving Menus to Classes* discusses class and instance data in more detail.

operations make copies of the wrapped list object. For large stacks this practice can add a significant penalty.

Of course, we can avoid the copy penalty by rewriting *push* and *pop* to change the underlying list in-place, using one of the schemes suggested above. Since neither *push* nor *pop* create a new *Stack*, the side effects will probably be harmless. See the exercises above and ahead for details.

Another approach is to change the underlying data structure completely. For example, we can store the stacked objects in a binary tree of tuples: each item may be recorded as a pair: *(object, tree)*, where *object* is the stacked item, and *tree* is either another tuple pair giving the rest of the stack, or *None* to designate an empty stack. A stack with items *[1, 2, 3, 4]* might look like Figure 13-1.

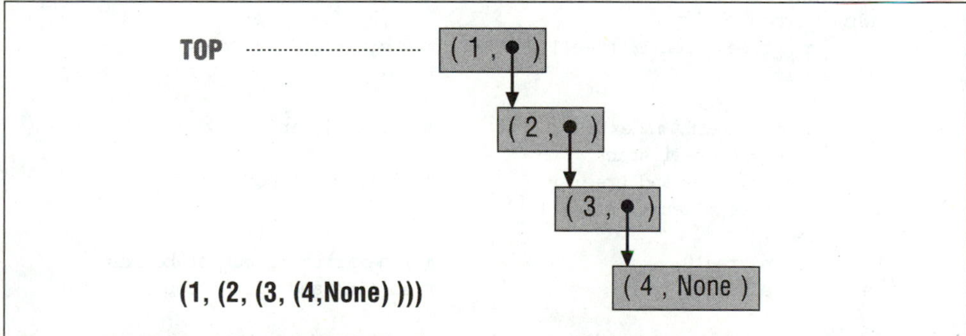


*Figure 13–1: A tuple-based stack representation*

This tuple-based representation is similar to the notion of "cons-cells" in Lisp-family languages: the object on the left is the *car*, and the rest of the tree on the right is the *cdr*. Because we only add or remove a top tuple to push and pop items, this structure avoids copying the entire stack. For large stacks, the benefit might be significant.

As a rule, Python lists are best thought of as variable-length arrays: if we need to change a collection's size frequently, we're sometimes better off using finer-grained representations like this.

Here's a class that implements these ideas.

*Example 13-11: File: faststack.py*

```
class FastStack:
    def __init__(self, start=[]):                # init from any sequence
        self.stack = None                        # even other (fast)stacks
        for i in range(-len(start), 0):
            self.push(start[-i - 1])             # push in reverse order

    def push(self, node):                        # grow tree 'up/left'
        self.stack = node, self.stack            # new root tuple: (node, tree)

    def pop(self):
        node, self.stack = self.stack            # remove root tuple
        return node                              # TypeError if empty

    def empty(self):
        return not self.stack                    # is it 'None'?

    def __len__(self):                           # on: len, not
        len, tree = 0, self.stack
        while tree:
            len, tree = len+1, tree[1]           # visit right subtrees
        return len

    def __getitem__(self, index):                # on: x[i], in, for
        len, tree = 0, self.stack
        while len < index and tree:              # visit/count nodes
            len, tree = len+1, tree[1]
        if tree:
            return tree[0]                       # IndexError if out-of-bounds
        else: raise IndexError                   # so 'in' and 'for' stop

    def __repr__(self): return '[FastStack:' + `self.stack` + ']'
```

The `__getitem__` method handles indexing, *in* tests, and *for* loop iteration as before, but this version has to traverse a tree to find a node by index. Notice that this isn't a subclass of the original *Stack* class. Since nearly every operation is implemented differently here, inheritance won't really help. But clients that restrict themselves to the operations that are common to both classes can still use them interchangeably: they just need to import a stack class from a different module to switch implementations.

***Using tuple-based stacks.*** Here's a session with this stack version; as long as we stick to pushing, popping, indexing, and iterating, this version is indistinguishable from the original.

```
>>> from faststack import FastStack
>>> x = FastStack()
>>> x.push(123)
>>> x
[FastStack:(123, None)]
>>> x.empty(), x.pop(), x.empty()
(0, 123, 1)
>>> x = FastStack()
>>> for i in range(10): x.push(i)
...
>>> x
[FastStack:(9, (8, (7, (6, (5, (4, (3, (2, (1, (0, None))))))))))]
>>> while x: print x.pop(),
...
9 8 7 6 5 4 3 2 1 0
>>> x
[FastStack:None]
>>> x = FastStack("spam")
>>> print x                                              __repr__
[FastStack:('s', ('p', ('a', ('m', None))))]
>>> z = FastStack()
>>> for n in x: z.push(n)                                __getitem__
...
>>> z
[FastStack:('m', ('a', ('p', ('s', None))))]
>>> y = FastStack(x)                                     __init__: copy
>>> y
[FastStack:('s', ('p', ('a', ('m', None))))]
>>>
>>> for n in x: print n,                                 __getitem__
...
s p a m
>>> y.pop(), y.pop(), y.push(3.1415)
('s', 'p', None)
>>> y
[FastStack:(3.1415, ('a', ('m', None)))]
>>> for i in range(len(y)): print y[i],                  __len__, __getitem__
...
3.1415 a m
>>> y[-1], y[0], y[len(y)-1]                             __getitem__, __len__
(3.1415, 3.1415, 'm')
```

***Timing the improvement.*** So how much of a performance improvement does this change buy us? The only way to really be sure is to time the two implementations. Let's first define a module for timing functions in Python: the built-in *time* module provides a *time* function that we can use to get the current time in seconds. The function *timer.test* runs a function *reps* times and returns the number of elapsed seconds.

*Example 13-12: File: timer.py*

```
def test(reps, func):
    import time
    start = time.time()            # current seconds
    for i in xrange(reps):
        x = func(i)                # call it 'reps' times
    return time.time() - start     # stop - start time
```

Next, we define a test driver script. It expects three command-line arguments: the number of pushes, pops, and indexing operations to perform (we'll vary these arguments to test different scenarios). When run at the top level, the script creates 20 instances of the original and tuple-based stack classes, and performs the specified number of operations. Pushes and pops change the stack; indexing just accesses it.

*Example 13-13: File: stacktim.py*

```
#!/usr/local/bin/python
import stack2            # list-based stacks: [x]+y
import faststack         # tuple-tree stacks: (x,y)
from timer import test

from sys import argv
pushes, pops, items = eval(argv[1]), eval(argv[2]), eval(argv[3])

def doit(stack_class, rep):
    x = stack_class('spam')
    for i in range(pushes): x.push(i)
    for i in range(items):  t = x[i]
    for i in range(pops):   x.pop()
    #print rep, x[0], len(x)

print test(20, lambda i: doit(stack2.Stack, i))         # test Stacks
print test(20, lambda i: doit(faststack.FastStack, i))  # test FastStacks
```

Here are some of the timings reported by the test driver script. Note that these results will vary widely depending on the hardware platform, but should be relatively similar. The results here were obtained on a slow PC-based machine.

```
% stacktim.py 10 10 10          FastStack loses: indexing trees is slower
3.2023639679
4.39087200165
% stacktim.py 50 0 50
9.84667301178
```

```
45.5347839594
% stacktim.py 20 0 20
4.25936794281
10.1393669844
% stacktim.py 20 20 20
5.75762796402
9.31342589855
% stacktim.py 100 10 10            FastStack wins: pushes and pops dominate
14.667247057
13.2526339293
% stacktim.py 100 0 0
13.1788409948
9.53274106979
% stacktim.py 50 50 0
11.3787109852
8.38151097298
% stacktim.py 100 50 0
18.0909260511
12.2539288998
```

As you may have expected, the results show that the tuple-based stack performs better when we do more pushing and popping, but worse if we do much indexing. Indexing lists is extremely fast (it's essentially just a direct index of a C array), but very slow for tuple trees: the Python class must traverse the tree manually.

Performance optimization is often more complex than expected, especially in dynamic languages like Python. Statistics are the only way to be sure. Here, it's probably safe to say that *FastStack* will be faster in normal situations where clients use push/pop operations more than anything else (these operations really define a stack in the first place). But if the stack will be indexed, iterated over, etc., the amount of the win isn't as clear.

---

*NOTE* The *time* built-in function returns wall clock time: real elapsed time, not CPU utilization time. Its results are influenced heavily by system load and other processes on a multitasking machine. For the tests here, there were no other active processes on the test machine. We'll see other ways to measure actual CPU time in Chapter 14.

---

### *Designing types with specially-named class methods*

The following table gives a complete listing of all the special methods available to classes. Some methods implement basic type operations, some overload expression operators, and some intercept class operations (metaclass protocols). We've seen most of these used before; all methods to which Python assigns a "special" interpretation begin and end with two underscores ("__") to distinguish them from user-defined attributes.

*Table 13-3: Special class methods*

| Method signature | Operation implemented | Description |
|---|---|---|
| All types | | |
| `__init__`*(self, args . . . )* | Instance constructor: *class(args . . . )* | Initialize the new instance, *self* |
| `__del__`*(self)* | Instance destructor | Clean-up when instance free'd |
| `__repr__`*(self)* | *`self`, print self, repr(self)* | Return a string representation |
| `__str__`*(self)* | *str(self), print self* (or `__repr__`) | Return a string representation |
| `__cmp__`*(self, other),* `__rcmp__` | *self > x, x = = self, cmp(self, x)* | All comparisons: return –1, 0, or 1 |
| `__hash__`*(self)* | *dictionary[self], hash(self)* | Return an integer hash-key |
| `__call__`*(self, *args)* | Calls: *self(args . . . )* | If instance is called like a function |
| `__getattr__`*(self, name)* | *self.name* | On undefined attribute access |
| `__setattr__`*(self, name, value)* | *self.name = value* | On all attribute assignments |
| `__delattr__`*(self, name)* | *del self.name* | On all attribute deletions |
| Collections | | |
| `__len__`*(self)* | *len(self), truth-value: if self* | Sequence/mapping collection size |
| `__getitem__`*(self, key)* | *self[key], x in self, for x in self* | Indexing, membership, iteration |
| `__setitem__`*(self, key, value)* | *self[key] = value* | Assignment to collection key/index |
| `__delitem__`*(self, key)* | *del self[key]* | Index/key component deletion |
| `__getslice__`*(self, low, high)* | *self[low:high]* | Sequence slicing |
| `__setslice__`*(self, low, high, seq)* | *self[low:high] = seq* | Sequence slice assignment |
| `__delslice__`*(self, low, high)* | *del self[low:high]* | Sequence slice deletion |
| Numbers | | |
| `__add__`*(self, other),* `__radd__` | *self + other, other + self* | Addition (sequence, number, etc.) |
| `__sub__`*(self, other),* `__rsub__` | *self - other, other - self* | Subtraction |

*Table 13-3: Special class methods (continued)*

| Method signature | Operation implemented | Description |
|---|---|---|
| `__mul__`*(self, other)*, `__rmul__` | *self * other, other * self* | Multiplication, sequence repetition |
| `__div__`*(self, other)*, `__rdiv__` | *self / other, other / self* | Division |
| `__mod__`*(self, other)*, `__rmod__` | *self % other, other % self* | Remainder of division |
| `__divmod__`*(self, other)* | *divmod(self, other)* | Division and remainder (tuple) |
| `__pow__`*(self, other)* | *pow(self, other)* | Raise number to an exponent |
| `__lshift__`*(self, other)*, `__rlshift__` | *self << other, other << self* | Bitwise left-shift (or other) |
| `__rshift__`*(self, other)*, `__rrshift__` | *self >> other, other >> self* | Bitwise right-shift |
| `__and__`*(self, other)*, `__rand__` | *self & other, other & self* | Bitwise "and" |
| `__xor__`*(self, other)*, `__rxor__` | *self ^ other, other ^ self* | Bitwise exclusive "or" |
| `__or__`*(self, other)*, `__ror__` | *self \| other, other \| self* | Bitwise "or" |
| `__neg__`*(self)* | *– self* | Unary negation |
| `__pos__`*(self)* | *+ self* | Unary positive |
| `__abs__`*(self)* | *abs(self)* | Absolute value |
| `__invert__`*(self)* | *~ self* | Bitwise complement |
| `__nonzero__`*(self)* | truth-value: if *self* | Or uses `__len__` if defined |
| `__coerce__`*(self, other)* | Mixed-type expression, *coerce()* | Return (self, other) converted |
| `__int__`*(self)* | *int(self)* | Convert to integer |
| `__long__`*(self)* | *long(self)* | Convert to long integer |
| `__float__`*(self)* | *float(self)* | Convert to floating-point number |
| `__oct__`*(self)* | *oct(self)* | Return octal string representation |
| `__hex__`*(self)* | *hex(self)* | Return hex string representation |

Normally, when an instance is used in an operation for which it doesn't define a method, an exception is raised. But `__repr__`, `__str__`, and `__cmp__` are exceptions: by default, Python prints generic representations, and compares by addresses. Python's language reference gives additional usage details we won't repeat here; refer to the manual for more information.

### *Some special cases*

Here are a few general considerations, when designing classes based on these operation hooks.

`__getitem__`
: As we've seen earlier, *for* iteration and *in* membership tests call the `__getitem__` method with successively-higher offsets, until an *IndexError* is raised.

`__coerce__`
: If `__coerce__` is defined, Python calls it before the real operator methods are tried (i.e., before `__add__`, etc.). It should return a tuple containing both the operands converted to a common type (or *None* if it can't convert). We'll see an example later in the book.

`__del__`
: The destructor method is called when the instance is about to be reclaimed, i.e., when its reference-count reaches zero. This isn't necessarily when a *del* deletion operation is used on the instance: more than one object might reference it. When an instance is reclaimed, all objects it owns (embeds) are reclaimed automatically, unless they've became referenced elsewhere. There's usually no need to *del* data structures managed by classes.

`__setattr__`
: If defined, this method is called for every attribute assignment, even assignments to *self* in methods. This can lead to loops if we're not careful: see the discussion in Chapter 12, *Persistent Information*. Conversely, `__getattr__` is called only for undefined attribute references.

`__len__`
: Since an empty sequence means *false* in Python, this method is also used for truth-value testing on the instance. If it returns zero, the instance is *false*, and is *true* otherwise. The `__nonzero__` method is the same, but is intended for non-collection types.

*str* and *repr*
: When printing objects, Python uses the *str* operation, but *str* defaults to *repr*. Because of this, we can define string conversion as `__str__` and/or `__repr__` methods. If there's no `__str__` method, the object prints as the result of `__repr__`. By providing both, we can implement different representations.

### *Right-side variants for binary operators*

All binary operator methods have a twin that starts with a *r* prefix: for example, `__add__` and `__radd__`. Right-side variants have the same argument signatures: "(self, other)", but "self" is on the right of the operator. The non-*r* form is called when the instance appears on the left of the operator; the *r* form is only called when the instance is on the right, and the left operand isn't an instance (see Chapter 10, *More Class Magic* for more details):

```
instance + non-instance  =>  __add__
instance + instance      =>  __add__
non-instance + instance  =>  __radd__
```

### *Operation conventions: imitate built-ins*

Interpretation of overloaded operators is up the class: arbitrary user-defined actions can be assigned to expression operators. But in general, classes should try to mimic built-in operator interpretations where possible. For instance, the "+" operator usually means concatenation for ordered collections (sequences), and returns a new instance of the type/class, rather than changing *self* in place. By convention, in-place changes are normally implemented as called methods (*append*, *insert*, etc.).

### *Operation type categories aren't absolute*

The table above groups operations by types, but some span categories: "+" and "*" are numeric addition and multiplication, but they're also used for sequence concatenation and repetition. Some methods are more specific to a type category. For example, the `__oct__` method returns a string representation of a numeric type's octal value (base 8). But as a rule, classes can mix and match operations from different type categories arbitrarily: they're not restricted to a subset of the available methods. For instance:

- The *Set* class we'll see in a moment uses the "&" operation to denote intersection, though "&" normally means bitwise conjunction for numeric types.
- In Chapter 11, *Graphical User Interfaces*, we saw how *Tkinter* allows linked variables to be fetched and set by calling them with and without parameters: *var()*, and *var(value)*. Internally, this is just the `__call__` method, with an optional argument.
- Even sequence operations don't have a fixed interpretation: the *mSQL* interface we saw briefly in Chapter 12, allows queries to be submitted using index operations: *database["sql-query"]*. The `__getitem__` method catches and executes the query.

Another common idiom in Python uses the `__getitem__` sequence method to iterate over external files as though they were lists. Here's an example class (inspired by a newsgroup post from Chris Hoffmann), which lets clients step through lines in a file, using *for* loops.

*Example 13-14: File: filescan.py*

```
class File:
    def __init__(self, filename):
        self.file = open(filename, 'r')      # open file; closed auto

    def __getitem__(self, i):
        line = self.file.readline()          # get next line
        if line:                             # sequential access only
            return line
        else:
            raise IndexError                 # end 'for' loops, 'in'

if __name__ == '__main__':
    print "\n"  in File("filescan.py")
    print "X\n" in File("filescan.py")       # file membership
    for line in File("filescan.py"):         # file iteration
        print '.', line,
```

We can achieve similar effects by using the *readlines* file method manually, but the class encapsulates file interface details; we'll be able to add special handling later by subclassing without changing *File* clients. Naturally, consistency goes a long way when designing new class-based types. But with a little creativity, operator overloading turns out to be useful for much more than data-structure implementation.

Suggested exercises:

1. Static class members. Add support for an overall maximum-length counter in class *StackLog* (i.e., the largest stack, among all instances). Also, return a dictionary from method *stats*, not a tuple; for example: *{'pushes': 30, 'maxlen': 20, 'pop': 15}*. What's the point of using dictionaries?

2. Sequence operations. Add other sequence operations to the *FastStack* class: slicing, concatenation, and repetition. Like indexing, they'll require tree traversals. Should stacks support item and slice assignment? How about attribute assignment? (Class instances support attribute assignment, by default.)

3. Side effect operators. Change the *Stack* class's binary operators to modify *self*, instead of returning a new class instance as the result. Here's the "+" operator change, to get you started; do you think this approach is generally a good idea?

   ```
   def __add__(self, other):                       # instance1 + instance2
       self.stack = self.stack + other.stack       # change myself directly
       return self                                 # I'm the result too
   ```

4. Type safety. As coded, the *Stack* class assumes both operands are *Stack* instances in the `__add__` and `__cmp__` methods: an *AttributeError* will be

raised if *other* doesn't have the *stack* member. Type testing won't help much here: all we could do is raise an error anyhow. But we could support more general concatenations, by iterating over *other* instead of qualifying and concatenating:

```
def __add__(self, other):
    result = self.stack[:]                    # copy my list
    for x in other: result.append(x)          # instance1 + instance2
    return Stack(result)
```

Since stacks are sequences too, we can still add stacks as before. Another approach is to provide the `__radd__` method we saw earlier in the book. This lets us add *other* to *self*'s list directly:

```
return self.stack + other
```

If *other* is a *Stack*, the "+" expression here triggers `__radd__`. Implement this scheme. Note that the `__coerce__` method could also help here (it allows us to convert operands up before the operator method is called); we'll see how in Chapter 15, *Embedding Python*.

5. In-place list changes. Apply the same optimizations to the *Stack* class as suggested for the module: replace slicing and concatenation with in-place changes on the list (*append*, *insert*, *del*). See Chapter 2 for one possible coding. To grow and shrink lists, in-place list operations use the *realloc* C function. *insert* is slightly slower than *append*, since Python must shift items in the list block to make room for the new node at the front. Use the timing script to compare in-place changes, to both the original *Stack* and the *FastStack* optimization. Which is faster? What conclusions can you draw regarding classes and built-in types?
6. Improved algorithms. Design a *FastStack* variant that performs well for both push/pop operations and random indexing. Normally, this sort of design might require some sort of frontend indexing tree. But consider Python-specific alternatives: what about storing references to stacked items in a dictionary, using the index as a key? Since assignment makes references, this scheme won't copy stacked objects: the tuple tree and dictionary will refer to the *same* stacked object. Should the variant replace *FastStack*, or be a subclass of it? Would this scheme make push/pop operations as slow as the original *Stack*?
7. *Stack* attributes. Experiment with the *dir* function on the *stack* module and classes. For example, *dir(stack1)* is the same as accessing the module's attribute dictionary, as we saw earlier in the book: *stack1.__dict__.keys()*. For

classes, we can inspect instance or class names: *dir(instance)* is the same as *instance.__dict__.keys()*, and *dir(instance.__class__)* gets class attributes. When we get to C types in Chapter 14, we'll see analogous mechanisms for inspecting members and methods.

### *Don't touch that dial . . .*

We'll revisit the stack implementations in Chapter 14, where we'll move them to C-based implementations. In fact, the stack implementations here might be considered prototypes for the C versions. Although they can be used as is, we'll see that they can be translated to C, without affecting well-behaved clients. We'll also see that the C versions use analogous implementation techniques: the special class methods we used here become fields in C type-descriptor *structs*. Given the relative speeds of C and Python, C migration is an important option, especially for frequently used tools.

# Implementing Sets

Another commonly-used data structure is the *set*: collections of objects that support operations like:

| | |
|---|---|
| Intersection | Make a new set with all items in common |
| Union | Make a new set with all items in either operand |
| Membership | Test if an item exists in a set |

and other operations, depending on the intended use. Python lists, tuples, and strings come close to the notion of a set: the *in* operator test membership, *for* iterates, etc. Here, we'd like to add operations not directly supported by Python sequences directly: intersection, union, and more. We're extending built-in types.

## Set Functions

As before, let's first start out with a function-based set manager. This time, instead of managing a shared set object in a module, let's define functions to implement set operations on Python sequences.

*Example 13-15: File: inter.py*

```
def intersect(list1, list2):
    res = []                         # start with an empty list
    for x in list1:                  # scan the first list
        if x in list2:
            res.append(x)            # add common items to the end
    return res
```

*Example 13-15: File: inter.py (continued)*

```
def union(list1, list2):
    res = map(None, list1)              # make a copy of list1
    for x in list2:                     # add new items in list2
        if not x in res:
            res.append(x)
    return res
```

Note the use of *map* in *union*: calling it with *None* as the function-argument converts any sequence object to a list. Using an empty slice (*list1[:]*) won't work, since we get back a copy of the same type as the object sliced. The *map* trick lets union work on any sequence: lists, strings, tuples, and class/type instances. (More on conversions at the end of this chapter.)

### *Testing the basic set functions*

These functions work on sequences as expected. Notice that we can use them on different sequence types (strings, lists, tuples, etc.), and even on mixed operand types: the last command below computes the union of a list and a tuple. Python's generic type operations let us mix and match similar types.

```
% python
>>> from inter import *
>>> s1 = "SPAM"
>>> s2 = "SCAM"
>>> intersect(s1, s2), union(s1, s2)
(['S', 'A', 'M'], ['S', 'P', 'A', 'M', 'C'])
>>> intersect([1,2,3], (1,4))
[1]
>>> union([1,2,3], (1,4))
[1, 2, 3, 4]
>>>
```

The result is always a list here, regardless of the type of sequences passed in. We could work around this by converting types, or using a class abstraction to bypass the issue (more on this later). But type conversions aren't clear cut, if the operands are mixed-type sequences (which type do we convert to?).

### *Supporting multiple operands*

If we're going to use the intersect and union functions as general tools, one useful extension is support for multiple arguments (more than two). The following functions use Python's variable-length argument lists feature to compute the intersection and union of arbitrarily many operands.

*Example 13-16: File: inter2.py*

```
def intersect(*args):
    res = []
    for x in args[0]:                   # scan the first list
        for other in args[1:]:          # for all other arguments
            if x not in other: break    # this item in each one?
        else:
            res.append(x)               # add common items to the end
    return res

def union(*args):
    res = []
    for seq in args:                    # for all sequence-arguments
        for x in seq:                   # for all nodes in argument
            if not x in res:
                res.append(x)           # add new items to result
    return res
```

### *Testing the enhanced set functions*

The multioperand functions work on sequences in the same way as the original functions, but support three or more operands. Notice that the last two examples in the following session work on lists with embedded compound objects: the *in* tests used by the intersect and union functions apply equality testing to sequence nodes recursively, as deep as necessary to determine collection comparison results.

```
% python
>>> from inter2 import *
>>> s1, s2, s3 = "SPAM", "SCAM", "SLAM"
>>> intersect(s1, s2), union(s1, s2)                 2 operands: same
(['S', 'A', 'M'], ['S', 'P', 'A', 'M', 'C'])
>>> intersect([1,2,3], (1,4))
[1]
>>> intersect(s1, s2, s3)                            3 operands
['S', 'A', 'M']
>>> union(s1, s2, s3)
['S', 'P', 'A', 'M', 'C', 'L']
>>> intersect([1,2,3], (1,4), range(-2,2))           list, tuple, list
[1]
>>> union([1,2,3], (1,4), range(-2,2))
[1, 2, 3, 4, -2, -1, 0]
>>>
>>> from stack2 import Stack
>>> x = Stack("eggs"); y = Stack("toast"); z = Stack("spam")
>>> x, y, z
([Stack:['e', 'g', 'g', 's']], [Stack:['t', 'o', 'a', 's', 't']],
 [Stack:['s', 'p', 'a', 'm']])
>>> intersect(x, y, z)
['s']
>>> union(x, y, z)
['e', 'g', 's', 't', 'o', 'a', 'p', 'm']
```

```
>>>
>>> l1 = [[1,2], "hello", (3.14, 0), 9]
>>> l2 = (9, (3.14, 1), "bye", [1,2], "mello")          compound nodes
>>> intersect(l1, l2)                                    equality is recursive
[[1, 2], 9]
>>> union(l1, l2)
[[1, 2], 'hello', (3.14, 0), 9, (3.14, 1), 'bye', 'mello']
```

## Set Classes

In the overview in Chapter 2, we briefly met a class that implements sets. We'll expand on the presentation here. The following class implements sets that can hold any type of objects; like the stack class above, it's essentially just a wrapper around a Python list which adds common set operations.

*Example 13-17: File: set.py*

```
class Set:
    def __init__(self, value = []):     # on object creation
        self.data = []                  # manages a local list
        self.concat(value)

    def intersect(self, other):         # other is any sequence type
        res = []                        # self is the instance subject
        for x in self.data:
            if x in other:
                res.append(x)
        return Set(res)                 # return a new Set

    def union(self, other):
        res = self.data[:]              # make a copy of my list
        for x in other:
            if not x in res:
                res.append(x)
        return Set(res)

    def concat(self, value):            # value: a list, string, Set...
        for x in value:                 # filters out duplicates
           if not x in self.data:
                self.data.append(x)

    def __len__(self):          return len(self.data)
    def __getitem__(self, key): return self.data[key]
    def __and__(self, other):   return self.intersect(other)
    def __or__(self, other):    return self.union(other)
    def __repr__(self):         return '<Set:' + `self.data` + '>'
```

### Testing the Set class

The *Set* class is used like the *Stack* class we saw earlier in this chapter: we make instances, and apply sequence operators plus unique set operations to them. Intersection and union can be called as methods, or by using the "&" and "|" operators (normally used for built-in integer objects). Because we can string operators in expressions ("x & y & y"), there isn't an obvious need to support multiple operands in intersect/union methods here.

```
% python
>>> from set import Set
>>> x = Set([1,2,3,4])                              __init__
>>> y = Set([3,4,5])
>>> x & y, x | y                                    __and__, __or__
(<Set:[3, 4]>, <Set:[1, 2, 3, 4, 5]>)
>>> y.concat(x)
>>> for n in y: print n,                            __getitem__
...
3 4 5 1 2
>>> y.concat(y)                                     no duplicates
>>> y
<Set:[3, 4, 5, 1, 2]>

>>> z = Set("hello")                                set of strings
>>> z & "mello", z | "mello"
(<Set:['e', 'l', 'o']>, <Set:['h', 'e', 'l', 'o', 'm']>)
>>> z
<Set:['h', 'e', 'l', 'o']>

>>> a = Set(range(-3, 3)); b = Set(range(-2, 2)); c = Set(range(-1, 3))
>>> a & b & c
<Set:[-1, 0, 1]>
>>> a | b | c                                       stringing operators
<Set:[-3, -2, -1, 0, 1, 2]>
>>> a | b | c | "spam"
<Set:[-3, -2, -1, 0, 1, 2, 's', 'p', 'a', 'm']>
>>> a & ( a | b | c | "spam")                       3 union + 1 intersect
<Set:[-3, -2, -1, 0, 1, 2]>
```

### *Profiling Set performance*

Once we start using the *Set* class, the first problem we might encounter is its performance: its nested *for* loops and *in* scans become exponentially slow. But how slow? Again, we need numbers to be sure. Here's a test script for timing the *Set* class's performance. Its *doit* function accepts a class object and a repetition counter again; as we've seen, classes are really first-class data objects in Python.

*Example 13-18: File: settime.py*

```
import set

def doit(Class, rep):
    a = Class(range(50))                    # a 50-integer set
    b = Class(range(20))                    # a 20-integer set
    c = Class(range(10))
    d = Class(range(5))
    for i in range(5):
```

*Example 13-18: File: settime.py (continued)*

```
        t = a & b & c & d              # 3 intersections
        t = a | b | c | d

if __name__ == '__main__':
    import timer, sys
    print 'start...'
    print timer.test(eval(sys.argv[1]), lambda i: doit(set.Set, i))
```

*timer* is the module used for stacks earlier. This script imports the *set.Set* class, and passes it to a function that exercises it. The *doit* function makes four sets and combines them with intersection and union operators five times. A command-line argument controls the number of times this process is repeated. More accurately, each call to the *doit* function makes 34 *Set* instances (4 + [5 * (3 + 3)]), and runs the *intersect* and *union* methods 15 times each (5 * 3) in the *for* loop's body. Here's this script's output.

```
% python settime.py 1
start...
7.95001333423
```

It reports an 8-second run-time. Although this was run on a very slow machine, it's probably not what we'd like in a general-purpose data type. But which parts should we spend time optimizing at this point? Again, to be sure, we need numbers. This time, we'll turn to the Python profiler tool for more details.

***Using the Python profiler.*** Python comes with a profiler module called *profile*, which provides a variety of interfaces for measuring code performance. It is structured and used much like the *pdb* debugger we saw earlier: the profiler is written in Python, using the interpreter's registration hooks to catch program control flow events.

Like *pdb*, we import the profiler module and call its functions to measure performance. The simplest profiling interface is its *profile.run(statement-string)* function, as in *pdb*. When invoked, the profiler runs the code string, collects statistics during the run, and issues a report on the screen when the statement completes. Here's how our set timing program is run under the profiler.

```
% python
>>> import set, settime
>>> import profile
>>> profile.run("settime.doit( set.Set, 0 )")
         5571 function calls (320 primitive calls) in 88.340 CPU seconds

   Ordered by: standard name
```

```
    ncalls  tottime  percall  cumtime  percall filename:lineno(function)
         0    0.000             0.000          profile:0(profiler)
         1    0.120    0.120   88.340   88.340 profile:0(settime.doit( set.Set,..
         1    0.000    0.000   88.220   88.220 python:0(190.C.1)
        15    1.730    0.115    6.460    0.431 set.py:13(union)
        34    0.540    0.016    4.770    0.140 set.py:2(__init__)
        34    4.230    0.124    4.230    0.124 set.py:20(concat)
  5440/231   58.820    0.011   86.080    0.373 set.py:26(__getitem__)
      15/1    0.150    0.010   87.690   87.690 set.py:27(__and__)
      15/1   11.570    0.771   74.060   74.060 set.py:28(__or__)
      15/1   11.130    0.742   87.680   87.680 set.py:6(intersect)
         1    0.050    0.050   88.220   88.220 settime.py:3(doit)
```

The report's format is straightforward; by default, we get the number of calls and times spent in each function invoked during the run. "Primitive" calls are non-recursive. Note that the set test took significantly longer: when the profiler is enabled, each interpreter event is routed to a Python handler. This gives us an accurate picture of performance but makes the program being profiled run slower than normal.

As you might have expected, the profile shows that the vast majority of the program's time is spent in the `__getitem__` index method, called by both *for* loops, and the nested *in* tests. In this case, the bottleneck is clear: we need a faster way to check set membership than nested list scans. Especially for large sets, the current algorithm becomes impractical.

At this point, we could either move the implementation to C (as we'll see in Chapter 14), or improve the algorithm and/or data-structures in Python. Since the profile shows our time is being spent in list scans, the algorithm is probably the best target here.

### *More on the Python profiler*

The profiler is a sophisticated and extensible system: it's packaged as a set of classes that can be subclassed to create specialized profilers. There are also facilities for sorting and customizing profiler reports, saving statistics to files for later reporting (using the *pstats* module), and more.

We won't go into all the profiler's interfaces here; see the Python library manual section on the accompanying CD-ROM that discusses the profiler for more information. Note that the profiler, like the debugger, doesn't work on C extensions called from Python code, but does profile nested Python code embedded in (called from) a C program (for example, *Tkinter* callbacks).

## *Optimization: Moving Sets to Dictionaries*

As suggested in Chapter 2, one way to optimize set performance is by changing the implementation to use dictionaries instead of lists, for storing sets internally. Because lookup time is constant and short for dictionaries, we can replace the *in* list scans of the original set with a direct dictionary fetch. In traditional terms, moving sets to dictionaries replaces linear search with fast hash tables.

The following class is a subclass of the original set: it redefines the methods that deal with the internal representation, but inherits others: the inherited "&" and "|" methods trigger the new intersect and union methods here, and the inherited *len* method works on dictionaries as is.

This extension is more seamless than the stack optimization we saw earlier. As long as *Set* clients aren't dependent on the order of items in a set, they can switch to this version directly by just changing the name of the module where *Set* is imported from; the class name is the same.

*Example 13-19: File: fastset.py*

```
import set
                                           # fastset.Set extends set.Set
class Set(set.Set):
    def __init__(self, value = []):
        self.data = {}                     # manages a local dictionary
        self.concat(value)                 # hashing: linear search times

    def intersect(self, other):
        res = {}
        for x in other:                    # other: a sequence or Set
            if self.data.has_key(x):       # use hash-table lookup
                res[x] = None
        return Set(res.keys())             # a new dictionary-based Set

    def union(self, other):
        res = {}                           # other: a sequence or Set
        for x in other:                    # scan each set just once
            res[x] = None
        for x in self.data.keys():         # '&' and '|' come back here
            res[x] = None                  # so they make new fastset's
        return Set(res.keys())

    def concat(self, value):
        for x in value: self.data[x] = None

    # inherit and, or, len
    def __getitem__(self, key):  return self.data.keys()[key]
    def __repr__(self):          return '<Set:' + `self.data.keys()` + '>'
```

The main functional difference in this version is the order of items in the set: because dictionaries are randomly ordered, this *Set*'s order will differ from the original (but sets are unordered by definition). For example, we can store compound objects in *fastset* sets, but the order of items varies:

```
>>> from fastset import Set
>>> a = Set([(1,2), (3,4), (5,6)])
>>> b = Set([(3,4), (7,8)])
>>> a & b
<Set:[(3, 4)]>
>>> a | b
<Set:[(7, 8), (3, 4), (1, 2), (5, 6)]>
>>> b | a
<Set:[(7, 8), (5, 6), (1, 2), (3, 4)]>
```

---

*NOTE* This version also can't be used to store unhashable objects. As we saw in Chapter 11, mutable objects can't usually be used as dictionary keys (lists, dictionaries, etc.). For instance: *Set([[1,2],[3,4]])* raises an exception. Tuples work here since they're immutable; Python computes a hash value and tests key equality internally.

---

### *Timing the results*

So how did we do? Here's a script we can use to compare our set class's performance. It reuses the *timer* module used to test stacks, and the *doit* function we saw earlier.

*Example 13-20: File: settime2.py*

```
from settime import doit
import set, fastset

import timer, sys
print 'start...'
print timer.test(eval(sys.argv[1]), lambda i: doit(set.Set, i))
print timer.test(eval(sys.argv[1]), lambda i: doit(fastset.Set, i))
```

This time, the performance improvement is more dramatic:

```
% python settime2.py 1
start...
8.06903800073
2.03199542621
```

At least for this test case, run-time goes from 8 to 2 seconds when we move to the dictionary-based set implementation. In fact, this fourfold speedup may be sufficient: a further migration to C might not help as much here. Python dictionaries are already optimized hash tables that we might be hard pressed to improve on. Unless we have evidence that dictionary-based sets are still too slow, our work here is probably done. For comparison, here's the profiler's output when run on the optimized *Set* class.

```
>>> import profile, settime
>>> import fastset
>>> profile.run("settime.doit( fastset.Set, 0 )")
         511 function calls (483 primitive calls) in 10.110 CPU seconds

   Ordered by: standard name

   ncalls  tottime  percall  cumtime  percall filename:lineno(function)
       15    1.520    0.101    5.170    0.345 fastset.py:15(union)
       34    1.510    0.044    1.510    0.044 fastset.py:23(concat)
      380    4.050    0.011    5.860    0.015 fastset.py:28(__getitem__)
       34    0.510    0.015    2.020    0.059 fastset.py:4(__init__)
       15    1.810    0.121    4.020    0.268 fastset.py:8(intersect)
        0    0.000             0.000          profile:0(profiler)
        1    0.120    0.120   10.110   10.110 profile:0(settime.doit( fastset..
        1    0.000    0.000    9.990    9.990 python:0(190.C.2)
     15/1    0.270    0.018    9.720    9.720 set.py:27(__and__)
     15/1    0.260    0.017    8.860    8.860 set.py:28(__or__)
        1    0.060    0.060    9.990    9.990 settime.py:3(doit)
```

Suggested exercises:

1. Study Jim Roskind's writeup on the profiler in the Python library reference manual. Among other things, it describes a profiler subclass that's faster than the standard interface shown here.

2. The original set functions aren't accurate mathematically: items might appear in the set redundantly (for instance, when intersecting with redundant items in left operand). The set classes fix this problem: their *concat* methods remove duplicates—how? Change the set functions to remove duplicates too.

3. Is there a workaround for the unhashable object limitation in *fastset*? Since some class instances can be put in dictionaries, how about providing a wrapper class? (See Chapter 11 for details.)

4. How does *fastset.Set* support iteration? Recall that *for* loops call `__getitem__` repeatedly with successively higher indexes, but dictionary keys aren't offsets. How does *fastset* get around this?

5. Add difference methods to both set classes: delete items in one set from the other. Two possible implementations appear below. Which do you think is faster? Install these methods in the classes, and time or profile to find out. Then add a `__sub__` operator overloading method for the "-" operator, which invokes the *diff* methods. Does this method need to appear in both classes? Do Python's operator precedence rules make sense for set expressions? (See Appendix C, *A Mini-Reference*, for details.)

```
def diff(self, other):                    # for list-based set
    list = self.data[:]                   # copy my list
    for obj in other:                     # delete other's nodes
        try:
```

```
            list.remove(obj)
        except:
            pass
    return Set(list)

def diff(self, other):                # for dictionary-based set
    dict = {}
    for obj in self.data.keys():      # copy my dictionary
        dict[obj] = None
    for obj in other:                 # delete other's keys
        if dict.has_key(obj):
            del dict[obj]
    return Set(dict.keys())
```

## *Optimizing fastset by Coding Techniques (Or Not)*

If you study *fastset* closely, you might notice a potential bottleneck. Each time we call a dictionary's *keys* method, Python makes a new list to hold the result. As is, `__getitem__` rebuilds the keys list each time we index a *fastset*. Since *for* iteration indexes a set repeatedly, this may be a factor in the intersect and union methods if *other* is a *fastset* too. Perhaps the class could be made faster by eliminating some *keys* calls. For instance, we could use lists to store items and temporary dictionaries in intersect/union:

*Example 13-21: File: fastset2.py*

```
import set
                                          # fastset2.Set extends set.Set
class Set(set.Set):
    def intersect(self, other):           # store as lists, use dicts
        res, tmp = {}, {}
        for x in self.data:               # convert self to dict
            tmp[x] = None
        for x in other:                   # other: a sequence or Set
            if tmp.has_key(x):            # use hash-table lookup
                res[x] = None
        return Set(res.keys())            # a new list-based set

    def union(self, other):
        res = {}                          # other: a sequence or Set
        for x in other:                   # scan each operand just once
            res[x] = None
        for x in self.data:
            res[x] = None
        return Set(res.keys())
```

In this version, sets are kept as lists internally, so we only need to override the original *Set*'s intersect and union methods. Since sets are lists, `__getitem__` is faster: we index the wrapped list directly. By intuition, this might seem to be faster than the dictionary-based *fastset* module. But as we've seen earlier, intuition about performance is almost always wrong in a dynamic language like Python:

*Example 13-22: File: settime3.py*

```
from settime import doit
import set, fastset, fastset2

import timer, sys
print 'start...'
print timer.test(eval(sys.argv[1]), lambda i: doit(set.Set, i))
print timer.test(eval(sys.argv[1]), lambda i: doit(fastset.Set, i))
print timer.test(eval(sys.argv[1]), lambda i: doit(fastset2.Set, i))
```

When we run this timing script with all three set variants, we find that there's no noticeable improvement for the *fastset2* version. To the contrary, it's slightly slower than the dictionary-based *fastset*:

```
C:\stuff>python settime3.py 10
start...
7.24100005627
1.62199997902
2.3029999733
C:\stuff>python settime3.py 20
start...
14.5609999895
3.26399993896
4.62700009346
```

This time, we ran the tests on a faster machine under MS-DOS. The relative performance of *set* and *fastset* are the same: *fastset* is still roughly four times faster. However, the *fastset2* optimization is slower than *fastset* (despite our best intentions). The gain from speeding indexing is offset by the need to convert the list to a dictionary for fast intersection. Next we might try to compensate for this with a different coding for intersection:

```
def intersect(self, other):
    res = {}
    for x in other:                    # store other's items
        res[x] = 1
    for x in self.data:
        if res.has_key(x):             # store mine, count=2
            res[x] = 2
    for x in res.keys():
        if res[x] == 1:                # scan dict, save 2's
            del res[x]
    return Set(res.keys())
```

But this method fails us too! The cost of the extra logic negates the elimination of the conversion step:

```
C:\stuff>python settime3.py 20
start...
14.7910000086
3.30499994755
4.68599998951
```

Despite apparent inefficiencies, there's no clear reward for optimizing code here; the initial algorithmic improvement was a much bigger win. Suggested exercise: Is there a better algorithm here? What about a hybrid approach, which stores the set as both a list and a dictionary?

### *Fix algorithms before tweaking code or migrating to C*

As this example demonstrates, sometimes the algorithm is the real culprit behind performance problems, not the coding style or implementation language. By removing the combinatorial list scanning algorithm of the original *Set* class, we made the Python implementation dramatically faster.

Although migration to C almost always optimizes performance, the algorithm should be checked first using profiling tools. Recoding in Python often gives us much more "bang for the buck." Moving the original set class to C without fixing the algorithm wouldn't address the real problem: a C translation would still be slow.

Moreover, coding tricks didn't help much here either. In Python, it's almost always best to code for readability first and optimize later if needed, based on profiling data. It would be hard to improve on the original *fastset*, despite its simplicity.

## *Case Study: Adding Relational Algebra to Sets*

Finally, here's an example that shows how far an extensible set class can take us. The *RSet* subclass defined in Example 13-23 below adds basic relational algebra operations for sets of dictionaries. It assumes the items in sets are mappings (*rows*), with one entry per column (*field*). *RSet* inherits all the original *Set* operations (iteration, intersection, union, "&" and "|" operators, uniqueness filtering, etc.), and adds new operations as methods:

- *Select*: Return a set of nodes that have a field equal to a given value.
- *Bagof*: Collect set nodes that satisfy an expression string.

- *Find*: Select tuples according to a comparison, field, and value.
- *Match*: Return nodes in two sets that have the same values for common fields.
- *Product*: Compute the Cartesian product, formed by concatenating tuples from two sets.
- *Join*: Collect and concatenate tuples from two sets that have the same value for a given field.
- *Project*: Extract named fields from the tuples in a table.
- *Difference*: Remove one set's tuples from another.

We won't go into many details on these operations here: see a database text for background information.

*Example 13-23: File: rset.py*

```
from set import Set

class RSet(Set):                                    # extends set.Set class
    def list(self):                                 # for sets of dictionaries
        print '\ntable =>'
        for x in self.data:
            for f in x.keys():
                print '['+f+']=' + `x[f]`,          # formatted table print
            print

    def select(self, field, value):
        result = []
        for x in self.data:                         # select tuples by field
            if x[field] == value:
                result.append(x)
        return RSet(result)                         # return RSet, not Set

    def bagof(self, expr):
        res = []
        for X in self.data:                         # run expr in my scope
            if eval(expr): res.append(X)            # 'X' is the loop var
        return RSet(res)                            #  use 'X' in expr string

    def find(self, field, cmp, value):
        return self.bagof('X['+ `field` +'] ' + cmp + ' ' + `value`)

    def match(self, other, field):
        result = []
        for x in self.data:
            for y in other:
                if y[field] == x[field]:            # 'other' is any sequence
                    result.append(x)                # 'x' is in self's list
        return RSet(result)

    def join(self, other, field):
        result = []                                 # match plus fields union
```

*Example 13-23: File: rset.py (continued)*

```
        for x in self.data:                                 # symbolic table links
            for y in other:
                if y[field] == x[field]:
                    compos = self.copy_tuple(x)
                    for k in y.keys():
                        if not x.has_key(k):
                            compos[k] = y[k]
                    result.append(compos)
        return RSet(result)

    def product(self, other):
        result = []                                         # permute tuples
        for x in self.data:                                 # between two tables
            for y in other:                                 # rename common fields
                compos = self.copy_tuple(x)
                for k in y.keys():
                    if not x.has_key(k):
                        compos[k] = y[k]
                    else:
                        i = 1
                        while x.has_key(k + '_' + `i`):
                            i = i+1
                        compos[k + '_' + `i`] = y[k]
                result.append(compos)
        return RSet(result)

    def project(self, fields):
        result = []
        for x in self.data:                                 # pick-out fields
            tuple = {}                                      # a 'vertical subset'
            for y in fields:
                if x.has_key(y):
                    tuple[y] = x[y]
            if tuple and not tuple in result:               # Set removes repeats too
                result.append(tuple)
        return RSet(result)

    def copy_tuple(self, tup):
        res = {}
        for field in tup.keys():
            res[field] = tup[field]                         # to copy dictionaries
        return res

    def input_tuple(self, fields):
        tup = {}
        for x in fields:
            valstr = raw_input(x + ' => ')                  # input tuple fields
            tup[x] = eval(valstr)                           # any type: parse it
        self.data.append(tup)

    def difference(self, other):
        res = []                                            # should be in Set?
```

*Example 13-23: File: rset.py (continued)*

```
        for x in self.data:                          # requires Rset(result)
            if x not in other: res.append(x)
        return RSet(res)
```

The following test program illustrates how these operations are used.

*Example 13-24: File: reltest.py*

```
from rset import RSet

def test():
    a = RSet(
            [{'name':'marv',   'job':'engineer'},
             {'name':'andy',   'job':'engineer'},
             {'name':'sam',    'job':'manager'},
             {'name':'mary',   'job':'prez'},
             {'name':'mira',   'job':'architect'},
             {'name':'john',   'job':'engineer'},
             {'name':'eddy',   'job':'administrator'}
            ])

    b = RSet(
            [{'job':'engineer',  'pay':(25000,60000)},
             {'job':'manager',   'pay':(50000,'XXX')},
             {'job':'architect','pay':None},
             {'job':'prez',      'pay':'see figure 1'}
            ])

    c = RSet(
            [{'name':'marv',   'job':'engineer'},
             {'name':'andy',   'job':'engineer'},
             {'name':'sam',    'job':'manager'},
             {'name':'julie', 'job':'engineer'},
             {'name':'steve', 'job':'manager'}
            ])

    a.list()
    a.select('job', 'engineer').list()
    a.join(b, 'job').list()

    a.project(['job']).list()
    a.select('job', 'engineer').project(['name']).list()

    a.find('job', '>', 'engineer').list()
    c.find('job', '!=', 'engineer').list()
    a.bagof("X['name'][0] == 'm'").list()
    a.bagof("X['job'] > 'engineer'").list()
    a.bagof("X['job'] > 'engineer' or X['name'] == 'eddy'").list()

    a.project(['job']).difference(b.project(['job'])).list()
    a.join(b, 'job').project(['name', 'pay']).list()
    a.select('name','sam').join(b,'job').project(['name', 'pay']).list()

test()
```

Here's this program's output. Notice that we can't use the table-browser GUI in Chapter 12 on the tables: they're collections at the top level, not mappings.

```
table =>
[job]='engineer' [name]='marv'
[job]='engineer' [name]='andy'
[job]='manager' [name]='sam'
[job]='prez' [name]='mary'
[job]='architect' [name]='mira'
[job]='engineer' [name]='john'
[job]='administrator' [name]='eddy'

table =>
[job]='engineer' [name]='marv'
[job]='engineer' [name]='andy'
[job]='engineer' [name]='john'

table =>
[pay]=(25000, 60000) [job]='engineer' [name]='marv'
[pay]=(25000, 60000) [job]='engineer' [name]='andy'
[pay]=(50000, 'XXX') [job]='manager' [name]='sam'
[pay]='see figure 1' [job]='prez' [name]='mary'
[pay]=None [job]='architect' [name]='mira'
[pay]=(25000, 60000) [job]='engineer' [name]='john'

table =>
[job]='engineer'
[job]='manager'
[job]='prez'
[job]='architect'
[job]='administrator'

table =>
[name]='marv'
[name]='andy'
[name]='john'

table =>
[job]='manager' [name]='sam'
[job]='prez' [name]='mary'

table =>
[job]='manager' [name]='sam'
[job]='manager' [name]='steve'

table =>
[job]='engineer' [name]='marv'
[job]='prez' [name]='mary'
[job]='architect' [name]='mira'

table =>
[job]='manager' [name]='sam'
[job]='prez' [name]='mary'
```

```
table =>
[job]='manager' [name]='sam'
[job]='prez' [name]='mary'
[job]='administrator' [name]='eddy'

table =>
[job]='administrator'

table =>
[pay]=(25000, 60000) [name]='marv'
[pay]=(25000, 60000) [name]='andy'
[pay]=(50000, 'XXX') [name]='sam'
[pay]='see figure 1' [name]='mary'
[pay]=None [name]='mira'
[pay]=(25000, 60000) [name]='john'

table =>
[pay]=(50000, 'XXX') [name]='sam'
```

Suggested exercises:

1. The difference method here should probably go in the original *Set* superclass (see prior exercise); but why might we want it in *RSet* instead? (Hint: what's the result type?)
2. Test the inherited "&", "|", and *in* operators, and define more operator methods for *RSet* methods. How can we handle methods with more than two arguments? (Hint: operands can be a tuple of values).
3. Persistent tables. The test program uses in-memory dictionary constants for tables, and the operations make new dictionaries for result tables. In Chapter 12 the table browser started as a dictionary tool and was extended to support file-based mappings. Use the same techniques here to design an extension of *RSet* that maps tables to external storage: either shelves, *dbm* files, or flat files. (Hint: recall that persistence can be used without *shelve*, and so without a top-level mapping.)
4. Functional programming. Experiment with alternative implementations for the *bagof* method. Python provides a built-in function *filter(function, list)*, which collects items in the list for which the function returns a "true" result.

   ```
   >>> filter(lambda x: x > 0, [1, -2, 3, 4, -1, -5])
   [1, 3, 4]
   ```

   Also consider adding Python's other functional-programming tools as set methods. We've seen *map* and *reduce* before (see Chapter 2 for an example of *reduce* usage, and see Appendix A, *...And Other Cool Stuff*, for an overview). Since *map* and *reduce* are already built in, is there any reason to make these methods of the class?

# Classical Data Structures in Python

In this section we'll take a brief look at ways to implement other traditional data structures in Python:

- Binary search trees
- Graph searching
- Reversing sequences
- Permuting sequences
- Generating programs
- Sorting sequences
- Converting sequences

Part of the goal here is to see Python's utility as a general-purpose language. But this topic also underscores some unique notions in Python programming; as we'll see, some of these are more useful than others.

## Binary Search Trees

Typically, binary trees are represented as a triple: *(Left-subtree, Node-value, Right-subtree)*. Binary trees impose an order on inserted nodes: items less than a node are stored in its left subtree, and items greater are inserted in the right. At the bottom, the subtrees are empty. For example, after inserting integer objects in this order: *[3, 1, 9, 2, 7]*, a binary tree might have the structure shown in Figure 13-2:

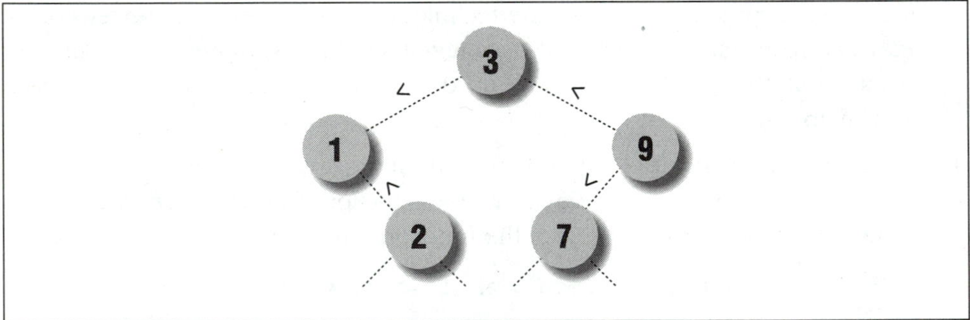


*Figure 13-2: A binary search tree*

Because of this structure, binary trees naturally support recursive traversals. There's fairly wide latitude in the tree implementations. Here we'll use a class-based approach:

- *BinaryTree* is a header object, which initializes and manages the actual tree.
- *EmptyNode* is the empty object, shared at all empty subtrees (at the bottom).
- *BinaryNode* objects are nonempty tree node triples, with a value and two subtrees.

Binary trees are constructed with smart objects (class instances) that know how to handle insert/lookup and printing requests and pass them to subtree objects. In fact, this is another example of the OOP composition relationship in action. A single empty class instance is shared by all empty subtrees in a binary tree. Inserts replace an *EmptyNode* with a *BinaryNode* at the bottom.

*Example 13-25: File: btree.py*

```
class BinaryTree:
    def __init__(self):        self.tree = EmptyNode()
    def __repr__(self):        return `self.tree`
    def lookup(self, value):   return self.tree.lookup(value)
    def insert(self, value):   self.tree = self.tree.insert(value)

class EmptyNode:
    def __repr__(self):
        return '*'
    def lookup(self, value):                      # fail at the bottom
        return 0
    def insert(self, value):
        return BinaryNode(self, value, self)      # add new node at bottom

class BinaryNode:
    def __init__(self, left, value, right):
        self.data, self.left, self.right  =  value, left, right

    def lookup(self, value):
        if self.data == value:
            return 1
        elif self.data > value:
            return self.left.lookup(value)              # look in left
        else:
            return self.right.lookup(value)             # look in right

    def insert(self, value):
        if self.data > value:
            self.left = self.left.insert(value)         # grow in left
        elif self.data < value:
            self.right = self.right.insert(value)       # grow in right
        return self

    def __repr__(self):
        return '( %s, %s, %s )' % (`self.left`, `self.data`, `self.right`)
```

As usual, *BinaryTree* can hold objects of any type that supports ">" and "<" comparisons; this includes class instances with the `__cmp__` method. To illustrate this module's interfaces, here's an example session.

```
% python
>>> from btree import BinaryTree
>>> x = BinaryTree()
>>> for i in [3,1,9,2,7]: x.insert(i)
...
>>> for i in range(10): print (i, x.lookup(i)),
...
(0, 0) (1, 1) (2, 1) (3, 1) (4, 0) (5, 0) (6, 0) (7, 1) (8, 0) (9, 1)
>>> y = BinaryTree()
>>> y
*
>>> for i in [3,1,9,2,7]:
...     y.insert(i); print y
...
( *, 3, * )
( ( *, 1, * ), 3, * )
( ( *, 1, * ), 3, ( *, 9, * ) )
( ( *, 1, ( *, 2, * ) ), 3, ( *, 9, * ) )
( ( *, 1, ( *, 2, * ) ), 3, ( ( *, 7, * ), 9, * ) )
>>> z = BinaryTree()
>>> for c in 'badce': z.insert(c)
...
>>> z
( ( *, 'a', * ), 'b', ( ( *, 'c', * ), 'd', ( *, 'e', * ) ) )
>>> z = BinaryTree()
>>> for c in 'abcde': z.insert(c)
...
>>> z
( *, 'a', ( *, 'b', ( *, 'c', ( *, 'd', ( *, 'e', * ) ) ) ) )
```

Suggested exercises:

1. The class here doesn't allow an initial value to be passed in and doesn't support deletions. It also doesn't distinguish the key from the stored data: the two are the same. Improve this.

2. In the last example, *abcde* becomes linear, since all left-subtrees are empty. Lookups won't benefit from the tree's partitioning of the search space. Explore tree balancing techniques.

3. Suggested exercise: Make *BinaryTrees* act like sequence objects by adding sequence operation methods. Here's a `__getitem__` implementation to get you started. Notice how exceptions are used to terminate recursion, when the item has been found; we'll revisit this idea in the next section.

*Example 13-26: File: btree2.py*

```
Found = 'Found'                           # jump to the 'found' handler

class BinaryTree:
    def __getitem__(self, i):             # index tree in sorted order
        try:
            self.tree.count(0, i)
        except Found, value:
            return value                  # value found: 'i' in range
        raise IndexError                  # no exception: 'i' out-of-bounds

class BinaryNode:
    def count(self, i, n):
        k = self.left.count(i, n)         # count items in left
        if k == n:
            raise Found, self.data        # at node N: exit recursion
        else:
            return self.right.count(k+1, n)  # count items in right

class EmptyNode:
    def count(self, i, n):  return i     # don't count empty's
```

This extension might be used like this:

```
x = BinaryTree()
for i in [3,1,9,2,7]:  x.insert(i)
for i in range(5):  print (i, x[i]),    # "(0, 1) (1, 2) (2, 3) (3, 7) (4, 9)"
x[5]                                    # raises "IndexError"
```

Install and test these methods, and add others: `__add__`, `__len__`, `__getslice__`, `__setitem__`, etc. Should you add in place or subclass? How useful are these extensions? What about their efficiency?

### *But dictionaries usually work just as well*

The binary tree classes illustrate general programming in Python, and certainly may be useful in some scenarios. But as coded and used here, they really don't buy us anything that we can't already get from built-in dictionaries:

```
>>> x = {}
>>> for i in [3,1,9,2,7]: x[i] = None                # insert
...
>>> x
{7: None, 1: None, 9: None, 3: None, 2: None}
>>> for i in range(10): print (i, x.has_key(i)),     # lookup
...
(0, 0) (1, 1) (2, 1) (3, 1) (4, 0) (5, 0) (6, 0) (7, 1) (8, 0) (9, 1)
```

Because dictionaries are built in to the language, they're easier to use, and will almost always be faster than Python-based data structure implementations. As we've seen earlier, they're coded in C, using expandable hash tables and optimized hashing algorithms.

The message here is: dictionaries and built-in sequences are usually the best tools for searching and collections. If we need to add extra search logic, we can use classes as we did here (or C types). But as a rule, if we base those classes on built-in datatypes like dictionaries and lists, performance is usually better. Suggested exercise: Time the performance difference between *BinaryTrees* and dictionaries.

## *Graph Searching*

Many problems can be represented as graphs: a set of states, with transitions (arcs) that lead from one state to another. Here's a Python program that searches through a directed, cyclic graph to find the paths between a start state and a goal. The graph is represented as a dictionary: each state is a dictionary key, with a list of nodes it leads to (its arcs). The search algorithm traverses the graph in a depth-first fashion and traps cycles in order to avoid looping. The test graph we'll use looks like Figure 13-3.

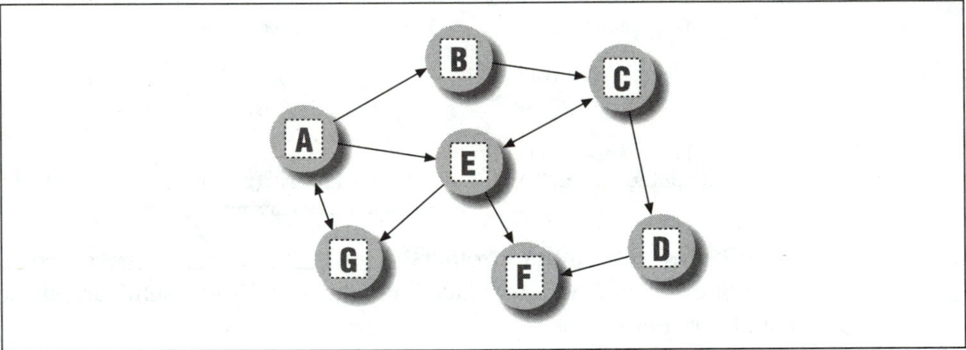


*Figure 13-3: A directed graph*

Arrows at the end of arcs indicate valid paths (*A* leads to *B*, *E*, and *G*). Let's first define a test-driver script, which imports and uses a searcher module by name. This file also builds the test graph.

*Example 13-27: File: gtest.py*

```
Graph = {'A':  ['B', 'E', 'G'],
         'B':  ['C'],                  # a directed, cyclic graph
         'C':  ['D', 'E'],             # stored as a dictionary
         'D':  ['F'],                  # 'key' leads-to [nodes]
         'E':  ['C', 'F', 'G'],
         'F':  [ ],
         'G':  ['A']  }

def batch(soln):
    if soln:  return 1                              # generate all paths
```

*Example 13-27: File: gtest.py (continued)*

```
def interactive(soln):
    if not soln:
        print 'No (more) solutions'                        # end of the search?
    else:
        print 'Solution:', soln, 'length:', len(soln)
        answer = raw_input('More? ')                       # after each solution
        return  answer in ['Y', 'y', 'yes', 'Yes']

if __name__ == '__main__':
    from sys import argv                        # script test routine
    exec "import " + argv[1]                    # load a searcher module
    gsearch = eval(argv[1])                     # aliase the module name
    gsearch.More  = interactive                 # change its continue function
    gsearch.search('A', 'G', Graph)
    gsearch.More = batch
    for x in ['AG', 'GF', 'BA', 'DA']:
        print x, gsearch.search(x[0], x[1], Graph)
```

The searcher module calls its *More* function after each solution, and when no more solutions can be found. Here, the *batch* version succeeds silently, causing all solutions to be generated; *interactive* asks the user if the search should continue or not: a zero return value stops the search.

Now let's add two modules that implement the actual search algorithms. The first search uses recursion and the second uses an explicit stack of paths to be expanded. Both keep track of nodes visited along a path, to avoid cycles: if an extension is already on the current path, it's a loop. The resulting solutions list is sorted by increasing lengths using the list *sort* method, and the built-in *cmp* function (discussed earlier).

*Example 13-28: File: gsearch1.py*

```
print 'gsearch1...'
More = lambda x: 1                              # continuation test: generate all

def search(start, goal, graph):
    solns = []
    if generate([start], goal, solns, graph):
        More([])
    solns.sort( lambda x, y: cmp(len(x), len(y)) )      # sort by path length
    return solns

def generate(path, goal, solns, graph):
    state = path[-1]
    if state == goal:
        solns.append(path)                              # change solns in-place
        return More(path)                               # resume at prior level?
    else:
        for arc in graph[state]:
            if arc in path:                             # cycle found: skip it
```

*Example 13-28: File: gsearch1.py (continued)*

```
                continue
            if not generate(path + [arc], goal, solns, graph):
                return 0
        return 1                                        # resume prior level

if __name__ == '__main__':
    import gtest
    print search('E', 'D', gtest.Graph)
```

*Example 13-29: File: gsearch2.py*

```
print 'gsearch2...'
More = lambda x: 1

def search(start, goal, graph):
    solns, stopped = generate( ([start], []), goal, graph)
    if not stopped:
        More([])
    solns.sort( lambda x, y: cmp(len(x), len(y)) )
    return solns

def generate(paths, goal, graph):                   # returns solns list
    solns = []                                      # use a tuple-stack
    while paths:
        front, paths = paths                        # pop the top path
        state = front[-1]
        if state == goal:
            solns.append(front)                     # goal on this path
            if not More(front):
                return solns, 1
        else:
            for arc in graph[state]:                # add all extensions
                if arc not in front:
                    paths = (front + [arc]), paths
    return solns, 0

if __name__ == '__main__':
    import gtest
    print search('E', 'D', gtest.Graph)
```

Here are some of the ways to interact with this system. The order of solutions may differ between the two searcher modules: the order of *gsearch2* depends on how extensions are added to the paths list.

```
% python gsearch1.py
gsearch1...
[['E', 'C', 'D'], ['E', 'G', 'A', 'B', 'C', 'D']]
% python
>>> import gtest, gsearch2
gsearch2...
>>> gsearch2.search('E', 'D', gtest.Graph)
[['E', 'C', 'D'], ['E', 'G', 'A', 'B', 'C', 'D']]
```

```
% python gtest.py gsearch1
gsearch1...
Solution: ['A', 'B', 'C', 'E', 'G'] length: 5
More? Y
Solution: ['A', 'E', 'G'] length: 3
More? Y
Solution: ['A', 'G'] length: 2
More? Y
No (more) solutions
AG [['A', 'G'], ['A', 'E', 'G'], ['A', 'B', 'C', 'E', 'G']]
GF [['G', 'A', 'E', 'F'], ['G', 'A', 'B', 'C', 'D', 'F'],
    ['G', 'A', 'B', 'C', 'E', 'F'], ['G', 'A', 'E', 'C', 'D', 'F']]
BA [['B', 'C', 'E', 'G', 'A']]
DA []
% python gtest.py gsearch2
gsearch2...
Solution: ['A', 'G'] length: 2
More? y
Solution: ['A', 'E', 'G'] length: 3
More? n
AG [['A', 'G'], ['A', 'E', 'G'], ['A', 'B', 'C', 'E', 'G']]
GF [['G', 'A', 'E', 'F'], ['G', 'A', 'E', 'C', 'D', 'F'],
    ['G', 'A', 'B', 'C', 'E', 'F'], ['G', 'A', 'B', 'C', 'D', 'F']]
BA [['B', 'C', 'E', 'G', 'A']]
DA []
```

## *Moving graphs to classes*

Using dictionaries to represent graphs is efficient: connected nodes are located by a fast hashing operation. But depending on the application, other representations might make more sense. For instance, classes can be used to model nodes in a network too, much like the binary tree example earlier. To illustrate, here's an alternative coding for our graph searcher; it uses a simpler single-module structure.

*Example 13-30: File: graph.py*

```
class Silent:
    def found(self, soln): return 1     # 1 means continue
    def final(self): pass

class Interact:
    def found(self, soln):
        print 'Solution:', soln, 'length:', len(soln)
        answer = raw_input('More? ')                    # after each solution
        return  answer in ['Y', 'y', 'yes', 'Yes']
    def final(self):
        print 'No (more) solutions'                     # end of the search?

silent   = Silent()
interact = Interact()     # make one instance

class Graph:
    mode = silent
```

*Example 13-30: File: graph.py (continued)*

```
    def __init__(self, label, extra=None):
        self.name = label
        self.data = extra
        self.arcs = []

    def __repr__(self):
        return self.name

    def search(self, goal):
        Graph.solns = []
        if self.generate([self], goal):
            self.mode.final()
        Graph.solns.sort(lambda x,y: cmp(len(x), len(y)))
        return Graph.solns

    def generate(self, path, goal):
        if self == goal:
            Graph.solns.append(path)
            return self.mode.found(path)
        else:
            for arc in self.arcs:
                if arc in path:
                    continue
                if not arc.generate(path + [arc], goal):
                    return 0
            return 1

if __name__ == '__main__':
    for name in "ABCDEFG":                          # make objects first
        exec "%s = Graph('%s')" % (name, name)      # label=variable-name

    A.arcs = [B, E, G]
    B.arcs = [C]                    # now configure their links:
    C.arcs = [D, E]                 # embedded class-instance list
    D.arcs = [F]
    E.arcs = [C, F, G]
    G.arcs = [A]

    Graph.mode = interact           # change continue behavior
    A.search(G)
    Graph.mode = silent
    for (start, stop) in [(A,G), (G,F), (B,A), (D,A)]:
        print start.search(stop)
```

In this version, graphs are represented as a network of embedded class instances. Each node in the graph contains a list of the nodes it leads to (*arcs*) which it knows how to search. The *generate* method walks through the objects in the graph. But this time, links are directly available on each node's *arcs* list; there's no need to index (or pass) a dictionary to find linked objects.

This version also provides a cleaner encapsulation of user interaction: rather than changing a *More* function in searcher modules, clients set a *mode* attribute of the searcher class to one of two exported class instances. The *Silent* and *Interact* classes implement two standard behaviors. Notice the use of *exec* in the self-test code: it executes dynamically constructed strings to do the work of seven assignment statements (*A=Graph('A')*, *B=Graph('B')*, etc.); we'll revisit *exec* later. Like *gsearch1*, this version implements a depth-first, left-to-right search through the graph:

```
C:\stuff\graph>python graph.py
Solution: [A, B, C, E, G] length: 5
More? y
Solution: [A, E, G] length: 3
More? y
Solution: [A, G] length: 2
More? y
No (more) solutions
[[A, G], [A, E, G], [A, B, C, E, G]]
[[G, A, E, F], [G, A, E, C, D, F], [G, A, B, C, E, F], [G, A, B, C, D, F]]
[[B, C, E, G, A]]
[]
```

### *Using exceptions to exit early*

One final improvement: instead of using return values to terminate recursive search levels, let's use Python's exception system to exit the search immediately. In the following variant, a *stopSearch* exception is raised by *Interact* when the user asks to end the search. When used properly, exceptions can often eliminate complex logic that handles rare special cases.

*Example 13-31: File: graph2.py*

```
class Silent:
    def found(self, soln): pass
    def final(self): pass

class Interact:
    def found(self, soln):
        print 'Solution:', soln, 'length:', len(soln)
        answer = raw_input('More? ')                  # after each solution
        if answer not in ['Y', 'y', 'yes', 'Yes']:
            raise stopSearch
    def final(self):
        print 'No (more) solutions'                   # end of the search?

silent     = Silent()
interact   = Interact()   # make one instance
stopSearch = ''           # exit search fast

class Graph:
    mode = silent
```

*Example 13-31: File: graph2.py (continued)*

```
    def __init__(self, label, extra=None):
        self.name = label
        self.data = extra
        self.arcs = []

    def __repr__(self):
        return self.name

    def search(self, goal):
        Graph.solns = []
        try:
            self.generate([self], goal)
        except stopSearch:
            pass
        else:
            self.mode.final()
        Graph.solns.sort(lambda x,y: cmp(len(x), len(y)))
        return Graph.solns

    def generate(self, path, goal):
        if self == goal:
            Graph.solns.append(path)
            self.mode.found(path)
        else:
            for arc in self.arcs:
                if arc not in path:
                    arc.generate(path + [arc], goal)
```

Suggested exercises:

1. Would *self.solns.append(path)* work in the *generate* methods above, instead of qualifying the *Graph* class? Why? (Hint: see the simpler version in Chapter 2; class members are inherited.)

2. Generalize the notion of goal matching. Add a *satisfies* method to replace the "==" test in *generate.* By default, it should still test equality. But by making the test a method, subclasses can provide other matching, possibly based on values of the optional *data* node member.

3. Explore ordered search strategies. For instance, some graph algorithms score arcs by various factors, and attempt paths by their relative score. Add an *order* method to perform scoring, and call it in the *generate* method before iterating over arcs. By default, it should return the *arcs* list intact.

4. Provide other user-interaction classes. For instance, when searching large graphs, we may want to report solutions as soon as they're found but without pausing for a user response. Add a *Logger* class that displays solutions to *stdout* (or if you feel ambitious, to a pop-up *Tkinter* text box).

5. If we add new paths to the end of the paths list in *gsearch2*, it performs a breadth-first search. This scheme tries shorter paths first. Code this change. Is this always a better approach? How would you make the graph classes implement a breadth-first search?

6. (Difficult) Write a Tkinter GUI program using the *Canvas* widget, which allows users to create nodes and arcs interactively. At the end of a layout session, generate graph construction code using either the dictionary or class-based representations earlier. Then define a user interaction class that highlights the arcs whenever a solution is found.

### *But is this the right tool for the job?*

In this section, we use built-in datatypes to represent the graph: first dictionaries, then lists. So far, so good. But there's another drawback in our approach here. Although these modules are certainly useful in many contexts, they're probably too slow to be used for searching very large graphs. If efficiency is important, Python may not be the best tool for delivery of graph-based algorithms.

Like all dynamic languages, Python is slower than compiled languages like C or C++. It's designed for flexibility, not for implementing CPU-intensive tasks like graph algorithms. Because of this property, it might be a good idea to classify the graph searchers here as prototypes, which we can later migrate to a C-based implementation if needed, once we've solidified the desired behavior in Python. We can use the timing and profiler techniques shown earlier to select components for C migration.

In fact, this is the approach commonly taken to program such demanding tasks as image processing and numerical programming in Python. Rather than implementing image processing algorithms in Python directly, Python programs make use of linked-in image processing libraries. Moreover, Python programs are often used to develop initial prototypes for objects to be reimplemented in C or FORTRAN.

Of course, performance isn't critical in every application; in many situations, the Python implementations here will suffice. But unless an optimizing Python compiler appears, a hybrid approach often works best: using Python for rapid development and C for performance-critical components. The lesson is to use the right tool for the task at hand. We'll learn how to mix in C modules in Chapter 14.

## *Reversing Sequences*

Reversal of collections is another typical operation. We can code it either recursively or iteratively in Python, as functions or class methods. Here's a first attempt at two simple reversal functions.

*Example 13-32: File: rev1.py*

```
def reverse(list):                  # recursive
    if list == []:
        return []
    else:
        return reverse(list[1:]) + list[:1]

def ireverse(list):                 # iterative
    res = []
    for x in list: res = [x] + res
    return res
```

Both reversal functions work correctly on lists. But if we try reversing nonlist sequences (strings, tuples, etc.) we're in trouble: the *ireverse* function always returns a list for the result regardless of the type of sequence passed:

```
>>> ireverse("spam")
['m', 'a', 'p', 's']
```

Much worse, the *reverse* recursive version won't work at all for nonlists: it gets stuck in an infinite loop! The reason is subtle: when *reverse* reaches the empty string (""), it's not equal to the empty list ([]), so the *else* clause is selected. But slicing an empty sequence returns another empty sequence (indexes are scaled): the *else* clause recurs again with an empty sequence, and without raising an exception. And so on (until we run out of memory).

The following versions fix both problems by using generic sequence handling techniques:

- *reverse* uses the *not* operator to detect the end of the sequence, and returns the empty sequence itself, rather than an empty list constant. Since the empty sequence is the type of the original argument, the "+" operation always builds the correct type sequence as the recursion unfolds.
- *ireverse* uses the fact that slicing a sequence returns a sequence of the same type. It first initializes the result to the slice "[:0]", a new, empty slice of the argument's type. Later, it uses slicing to extract one-node sequences to add to the result's front, instead of a list constant.

*Example 13-33: File: rev2.py*

```
def reverse(list):
    if not list:                             # empty? (not always [])
        return list                          # the same sequence type
    else:
        return reverse(list[1:]) + list[:1]  # add front item on the end

def ireverse(list):
    res = list[:0]                           # empty, of same type
    for i in range(len(list)):
```

*Example 13-33: File: rev2.py (continued)*

```
        res = list[i:i+1] + res                        # add each item to front
    return res
```

These functions work on any sequence, and return a new sequence of the same type as the sequence passed in: if we pass in a string, we get a new string as the result. In fact, they reverse any sequence object that responds to slicing, concatenation, and *len*—even instances of user-defined Python classes and C types.

```
% python
>>> from rev2 import *
>>> reverse([1,2,3]), ireverse([1,2,3])
([3, 2, 1], [3, 2, 1])
>>> reverse("spam"), ireverse("spam")
('maps', 'maps')
>>> reverse((1.2, 2.3, 3.4)), ireverse((1.2, 2.3, 3.4))
((3.4, 2.3, 1.2), (3.4, 2.3, 1.2))
```

### *But we get reversal for free in Python*

Here again, these functions probably aren't very useful: as we've seen, Python provides a built-in reverse method for lists, which reverses the subject list in place. Although there is no equivalent for tuples and strings (and user-defined sequences), we can convert other sequences to lists to reverse and convert the result back to the original type. Since the built-in reverse method is coded in C, it's probably faster than the reverse functions above, even if we need to convert first.

```
>>> L = ['a', 'b', 'c', 'd']
>>> L.reverse()
>>> L
['d', 'c', 'b', 'a']
>>> L = map(None, "spam")                    convert to list
>>> L.reverse()
>>> L
['m', 'a', 'p', 's']
```

If the reversed sequence doesn't need to be retained, we can also use *range* to process the sequence's items in reverse order, without explicitly reversing, converting, or copying:

```
>>> S = "SPAM"
>>> for i in range(len(S)-1, -1, -1): print i, S[i]
...
3 M
2 A
1 P
0 S
```

The *range* (and *xrange*) built-in functions accept an optional third argument, giving the increment between each item in the result. The third argument defaults to

1. It also allows negative ranges when the first argument is greater than the second. Here, we use a negative step to make a list of decreasing integers: indexes from right to left.

We could have used this technique in the stack class constructors we saw earlier. To push items from a four-node sequence *start* in reverse order, we can visit them with decreasing indexes in a variety of ways:

```
for i in range(len(start)-1, -1, -1):      #  3,  2,  1,  0  -->
    self.push(start[i])                    #  3,  2,  1,  0

for i in range(-len(start), 0):            # -4, -3, -2, -1  -->
    self.push(start[-i - 1])               #  3,  2,  1,  0

for i in range(-1, -(len(start)+1), -1):   # -1, -2, -3, -4  -->
    self.push(start[i])                    #  3,  2,  1,  0
```

Suggested exercise: Write a program to compare the performance of the reverse functions and the built-in techniques discussed here.

## Permuting Sequences

Here's a more useful sequence operation that's not supported by Python's built-in tools: collection permutations. The following functions shuffle sequences in a number of ways:

- *permute* constructs a list with all valid permutations of the original sequence.
- *subset* constructs a list with all valid permutations of a specific length.
- *combo* works like *subset*, but order doesn't matter: permutations of the same items are filtered out.

These results are useful in a variety of algorithms: searches, statistical analysis, etc. All three functions make use of the generic sequence slicing tricks of the reversal functions above, so that the result list contains sequences of the same type as the one passed in: when we permute a string, we get back a list of strings.

*Example 13-34: File: permcomb.py*

```
def permute(list):
    if not list:                                    # shuffle any sequence
        return [list]                               # empty sequence
    else:
        res = []
        for i in range(len(list)):
            rest = list[:i] + list[i+1:]            # delete current node
            for x in permute(rest):                 # permute the others
                res.append(list[i:i+1] + x)         # add node at front
        return res
```

*Example 13-34: File: permcomb.py (continued)*

```
def subset(list, size):
    if size == 0 or not list:                     # order matters here
        return [list[:0]]                         # an empty sequence
    else:
        result = []
        for i in range(len(list)):
            pick = list[i:i+1]                    # sequence slice
            rest = list[:i] + list[i+1:]          # keep [:i] part
            for x in subset(rest, size-1):
                result.append(pick + x)
        return result


def combo(list, size):
    if size == 0 or not list:                     # order doesn't matter
        return [list[:0]]                         # xyz == yzx
    else:
        result = []
        for i in range(0, (len(list) - size) + 1):  # iff enough left
            pick = list[i:i+1]
            rest = list[i+1:]                     # drop [:i] part
            for x in combo(rest, size - 1):
                result.append(pick + x)
        return result
```

As in the reversal function, all three of these work on any sequence object that supports *len*, slicing, and concatenation operations. For instance, we can use *permute* on instances of the *stack.Stack* class defined at the start of this chapter; we'll get back a list of *Stack* instances with shuffled nodes.

### Testing sequence permutations

Here are our sequence shufflers in action. Permuting a list enables us to find all the ways the items can be arranged. Order matters: *[1, 2, 3]* is not the same as *[1, 3, 2]* so both appear in the result.

```
% python
>>> from permcomb import *
>>> permute([1,2,3])
[[1, 2, 3], [1, 3, 2], [2, 1, 3], [2, 3, 1], [3, 1, 2], [3, 2, 1]]
>>> permute('abc')
['abc', 'acb', 'bac', 'bca', 'cab', 'cba']
>>> permute('help')
['help', 'hepl', 'hlep', 'hlpe', 'hpel', 'hple', 'ehlp', 'ehpl', 'elhp', 'elph',
 'ephl', 'eplh', 'lhep', 'lhpe', 'lehp', 'leph', 'lphe', 'lpeh', 'phel', 'phle',
 'pehl', 'pelh', 'plhe', 'pleh']
```

Combinations are related to permutations, but we put a fixed-length constraint on the result, and order doesn't matter here: *abc* is the same as *acb*, so only one is added to the result set.

```
>>> combo([1,2,3], 3)
[[1, 2, 3]]
>>> combo('abc', 3)
['abc']
>>> combo('abc', 2)
['ab', 'ac', 'bc']
>>> combo('abc', 4)
[]
>>> combo((1, 2, 3, 4), 3)
[(1, 2, 3), (1, 2, 4), (1, 3, 4), (2, 3, 4)]
>>> for i in range(0, 6): print i, combo("help", i)
...
0 ['']
1 ['h', 'e', 'l', 'p']
2 ['he', 'hl', 'hp', 'el', 'ep', 'lp']
3 ['hel', 'hep', 'hlp', 'elp']
4 ['help']
5 []
```

Finally, subsets are just fixed-length permutations; order matters, so the result is bigger than for combinations. In fact, calling *subset* with the length of the sequence is identical to *permute*.

```
>>> subset([1,2,3], 3)
[[1, 2, 3], [1, 3, 2], [2, 1, 3], [2, 3, 1], [3, 1, 2], [3, 2, 1]]
>>> subset('abc', 3)
['abc', 'acb', 'bac', 'bca', 'cab', 'cba']
>>> for i in range(0, 6): print i, subset("help", i)
...
0 ['']
1 ['h', 'e', 'l', 'p']
2 ['he', 'hl', 'hp', 'eh', 'el', 'ep', 'lh', 'le', 'lp', 'ph', 'pe', 'pl']
3 ['hel', 'hep', 'hle', 'hlp', 'hpe', 'hpl', 'ehl', 'ehp', 'elh', 'elp', 'eph',
   'epl', 'lhe', 'lhp', 'leh', 'lep', 'lph', 'lpe', 'phe', 'phl', 'peh', 'pel',
   'plh', 'ple']
4 ['help', 'hepl', 'hlep', 'hlpe', 'hpel', 'hple', 'ehlp', 'ehpl', 'elhp',
   'elph', 'ephl', 'eplh', 'lhep', 'lhpe', 'lehp', 'leph', 'lphe', 'lpeh',
   'phel', 'phle', 'pehl', 'pelh', 'plhe', 'pleh']
5 ['help', 'hepl', 'hlep', 'hlpe', 'hpel', 'hple', 'ehlp', 'ehpl', 'elhp',
   'elph', 'ephl', 'eplh', 'lhep', 'lhpe', 'lehp', 'leph', 'lphe', 'lpeh',
   'phel', 'phle', 'pehl', 'pelh', 'plhe', 'pleh']
```

Suggested exercise: make these three functions methods of the *Set* class defined earlier.

## Generating Programs

For the sake of illustration, let's pretend Python didn't have its *map* and *lambda* built-in tools, but we wanted to generate functions dynamically and apply them to lists. We can always generate code at run-time using the *exec* statement and *eval* built-in.

We used *eval* earlier to:

- Convert strings to numbers (*sys.argv* command-line arguments)
- Evaluate names (import-by-name in the graph searcher above, after an import statement *exec*)
- Run expressions (in the *RSet* extension's *bagof* method).

Here's an *exec* example that runs a *def* string to make a new function object.

*Example 13-35: File: genfunc.py*

```
def genfunc(args, expr):
        exec 'def temp(%s): return %s' % (args, expr)       # def temp(args):..
        return temp                                          # sets local var

def imap(func, list):
        res = []
        for x in list: res.append(func(x))                  # run func on nodes
        return res

if __name__ == "__main__":
    def square(x): return x * x
    print imap(square, [1, 2, 3, 4])                         # [1, 4, 9, 16]
    print imap(genfunc('x', 'x * x'), [1, 2, 3, 4])          # [1, 4, 9, 16]
    print map(lambda x: x * x, [1, 2, 3, 4])                 # [1, 4, 9, 16]
```

We'll explore these built-ins in more detail later, but in brief:

- *exec* runs a string containing a Python statement and returns nothing
- *eval* runs a string containing a Python expression and returns its result

Without arguments, both run the code-string in the namespace of the call to the built-in. Here, it's as though the *def* string was inserted into the text of the *genfunc* function. But these built-ins allow us to construct Python code dynamically, by building strings at run-time.

In fact, Python's compiler is always available when Python programs are run: there's really no distinction between the Python development environment (where programs are written) and the execution environment (where they run). As we'll see later, these built-ins are more general than shown so far.

---

*NOTE* We could use *eval* to fetch *temp* in the *genfunc* function, but it's not required: because *temp* isn't declared global, Python uses the usual local/global/built-in lookup path when it's referenced in the function. When the *def* string runs, it executes in the function's local namespace, and assigns/creates the name *temp*. When the return statement later references *temp*, it's found in the local namespace, bound to a new function object.

---

### *"Been there, done that"*

Okay; you can probably guess where this example is headed. As the last *print* statement shows, *map* and *lambda* do the job better than what we coded here. But there are other contexts where dynamic code construction still comes in handy. We'll expand on this in more detail later in the book.

## *Sorting Sequences*

Another staple of many systems is sorting: ordering items in a collection according to some constraint. Here's a simple sort routine in Python, which orders a list of objects on a field. Because Python indexing is generic, the field can be an index or key: we can sort lists of sequences or mappings with this function.

*Example 13-36: File: sort1.py*

```
def sort(list, field):
    res = []                                      # always returns a list
    for x in list:
        i = 0
        for y in res:
            if x[field] <= y[field]: break        # list node goes here?
            i = i+1
        res[i:i] = [x]                            # insert in result slot
    return res

if __name__ == '__main__':
    table = [ {'name':'john', 'age':25}, {'name':'doe', 'age':32} ]
    print sort(table, 'name')
    print sort(table, 'age')

    table = [ ('john', 25), ('doe', 32) ]
    print sort(table, 0)
    print sort(table, 1)
```

```
% python sort1.py
[{'name':'doe', 'age':32}, {'name':'john', 'age':25}]
[{'name':'john', 'age':25}, {'name':'doe', 'age':32}]
[('doe', 32), ('john', 25)]
[('john', 25), ('doe', 32)]
```

### *Adding comparison functions*

Since functions can be passed in like any other object, we can allow for an optional comparison function. In the next version, the third argument takes a function that should return *true* if the first argument should be placed before the second. A *lambda* is used to provide an ascending-order test by default. We also return a new sequence that's the same type as the *list* passed in, by applying the slicing techniques used above: if we sort a tuple of nodes, we get back a tuple.

*Example 13-37: File: sort2.py*

```
def sort(list, field, func = lambda x,y: x <= y):          # default: ascending
    res = list[:0]                                          # return operand type
    for j in range(len(list)):
        i = 0
        for y in res:
            if func( list[j][field], y[field] ): break
            i = i+1
        res = res[:i] + list[j:j+1] + res[i:]               # list can be immutable
    return res

if __name__ == '__main__':
    table = ( {'name':'doe'}, {'name':'john'})
    print sort(table, 'name', lambda x,y: x > y)
    print sort(table, 'name', lambda x,y: x < y)
```

```
% python sort2.py
( {'name':'john'}, {'name':'doe'})
( {'name':'doe'}, {'name':'john'})
```

## Generalizing comparisons

Finally, we can dispense with the notion of a field altogether, and let the passed-in function handle indexing, if needed. Here's a more general sorter.

*Example 13-38: File: sort3.py*

```
def sort(list, func = lambda x,y: x <= y):
    res = list[:0]
    for j in range(len(list)):
        i = 0
        for y in res:
            if func(list[j], y): break
            i = i+1
        res = res[:i] + list[j:j+1] + res[i:]
    return res

if __name__ == '__main__':
    table = ( {'name':'doe'}, {'name':'john'})
    print sort(table, lambda x, y: x['name'] > y['name'])
    print sort(table, lambda x, y: x['name'] <= y['name'])
```

Running this module as a top-level program produces the same output as *sort2* above. Since the *field* argument is gone, this version is much more general; for instance, it's also useful for sorting strings.

### *"One of these things just doesn't belong here"*

But this time we're really making extra work for ourselves. Fast sorting is already built-in to the language: as we've seen, Python lists have a *sort* method, which orders lists in place (instead of making a new list). By default, *sort* orders the list by increasing values. We can also pass in a Python function to compare operands during the sort: it should return –1, 0, or 1 to designate before, same, or after positioning in the result, respectively. This corresponds to the result of the built-in *cmp* function.

```
>>> L = [{'n':3}, {'n':20}, {'n':0}, {'n':9}]
>>> def cmpn(x, y):
...     return cmp(x['n'], y['n'])
...
>>> L.sort(cmpn)
>>> L
[{'n': 0}, {'n': 3}, {'n': 9}, {'n': 20}]

>>> L = [{'n':3}, {'n':20}, {'n':0}, {'n':9}]
>>> L.sort( lambda x, y: cmp(x['n'], y['n']) )
>>> L
[{'n': 0}, {'n': 3}, {'n': 9}, {'n': 20}]
```

Passing in a comparison function makes the sort slower. But regardless, the built-in *sort* method will usually be faster than anything we can write in Python: it calls the fast *qsort* function in the standard C library to order the list. In fact, it might be faster to convert a nonlist sequence to a list first using the *map(None, x)* trick, so it can be ordered with the built-in method:

```
list = map(None, sequence-object)
list.sort()
<convert list back to other sequence-type>
```

The built-in *tuple(list)* converts lists back to tuples, and *string.joinfields(list, '')* is one way to convert back to strings. Since we can pass application-specific comparison functions to *sort*, there's usually no reason to write custom sort routines in Python.

Suggested exercise: Write an *OrderedSequence* wrapper class that orders an embedded object by sorting on insertions (i.e., after each *append*, "+", etc.). Is this way faster than calling the "sort" method on demand?

## *Converting Sequences*

Speaking of conversions, are there any general ways to convert between built-in types? Here's a final example that implements conversions between the various built-in sequence types. Subclasses define what it means to be a list, tuple, or string, and the superclass handles sequences generically.

*Example 13-39: File: seqcon1.py*

```
class sequence:                               # don't make sequence() directly
    def __init__(self, value=[]):
        self.data = self.empty()              # empty is virtual
        self.concat(value)

    def convert(self, Maker):
        new = Maker()
        new.concat(self.data)
        return new

    def concat(self, items):                  # "in" is generic
        for x in items: self.add(x)           # add is virtual

    def to_string(self): return String(self.data)
    def to_list(self):   return List(self.data)
    def to_tuple(self):  return Tuple(self.data)

    def __repr__(self): return `self.data`

class List(sequence):
    def empty(self):     return []
    def add(self, item): self.data.append(item)

class String(sequence):
    def empty(self):     return ''
    def add(self, item): self.data = self.data + item

class Tuple(sequence):
    def empty(self):     return ()
    def add(self, item): self.data = self.data + (item,)

if __name__ == "__main__":
    x = List("spam")
    print x, x.convert(String), x.to_tuple()
    y = String("eggs")
    print y, y.convert(Tuple),  y.to_list()
```

### *But use built-in sequence conversions*

As is, these classes only handle conversions; to make this a complete sequence wrapper, we'd also need to add sequence-operator methods, as shown earlier (`__add__`, `__getitem__`, etc.). Here's a test:

```
% python seqcon1.py
['s', 'p', 'a', 'm'] 'spam' ('s', 'p', 'a', 'm')
'eggs' ('e', 'g', 'g', 's') ['e', 'g', 'g', 's']
```

But again, we've implemented something that Python already provides. There are a variety of ways to convert objects to other types in Python, both sequences and others. Table 13-4, Table 13-5, and Table 13-6 summarize Python's built-in tools for converting from one kind of sequence object to another.

*Table 13-4: Sequence converters*

| Converter | Converts to | Converts from |
|---|---|---|
| *map(None, X)* | Lists | Strings, tuples, user-defined sequences |
| *tuple(X)* | Tuples | Strings, lists, user-defined sequences |
| *string.joinfields(X, '')* | Strings | Lists and tuples of strings |

All three converters in Table 13-4 are implemented in C, so they're likely to be faster than scanning sequences manually in *for* loops to convert types. User-defined sequences (class and type instances) must implement indexing and *len* operations to be used in *map* and *tuple* converters. The *joinfields* call requires an empty string as the second argument.

Table 13-5 shows how these operations can be applied; the *constructor* call in the last column assumes that the user-defined sequence allows an initial-value sequence to be passed in. The table also shows an empty slice for conversion to the same type of sequence (i.e., a copy); *map* and *tuple* also accept lists and tuples. Multiplying by one and adding to an *empty* may make copies too (depending on the type).

*Table 13-5: Sequence conversions*

| From/To | String | Tuple | List | User-defined |
|---|---|---|---|---|
| **String** | *X[:]* | *tuple(X)* | *map(None, X)* | *constructor(X)* |
| **Tuple** | *joinfields(X, '')* | *X[:]* | *map(None, X)* | *constructor(X)* |
| **List** | *joinfields(X, '')* | *tuple(X)* | *X[:]* | *constructor(X)* |
| **User-defined** | *joinfields(tuple(X), '')* | *tuple(X)* | *map(None, X)* | *X[:]* |

If we want to automate conversion, it's straightforward: the following function accepts a sequence, and an empty constant of the target type; it doesn't support the *constructor* conversion scheme.

*Example 13-40: File: seqcon2.py*

```
from string import joinfields

def seqcon(seq, to):
    if to == '':
        if type(seq) in map(type, ['', [], ()]):
            return joinfields(seq, '')
        else:
            return joinfields(tuple(seq), '')
    if to == []:
        return map(None, seq)
```

*Example 13-40: File: seqcon2.py (continued)*

```
    if to == ():
        return tuple(seq)
    raise TypeError

if __name__ == '__main__':
    print seqcon('spam', []), seqcon((1, 2, 3), [])
    print seqcon('eggs', ()), seqcon([4, 5, 6], ())
    print seqcon(['a', 'b'], ''), seqcon(('c', 'd'), '')

    class Test:
        def __init__(self, val):  self.data = val
        def __len__(self):        return len(self.data)
        def __getitem__(self, i): return self.data[i]

    print seqcon(Test("ab"),[]), seqcon(Test("cd"),()), seqcon(Test(['a']),'')
```

The module's self-test code shows how it is used.

```
% python seqcon2.py
['s', 'p', 'a', 'm'] [1, 2, 3]
('e', 'g', 'g', 's') (4, 5, 6)
ab cd
['a', 'b'] ('c', 'd') a
```

### *Other built-in conversions*

Dictionaries have methods for converting themselves to lists. We've already seen most in action: *keys* and *values* return a dictionary's components as lists, and the *item* method returns a tuple list with both:

```
>>> D = {'s': 1, 'p': 2, 'a': 3, 'm': 4}
>>> D.items()
[('p', 2), ('m', 4), ('a', 3), ('s', 1)]
>>> D.keys()
['p', 'm', 'a', 's']
>>> D.values()
[2, 4, 3, 1]
```

Strings can be converted to numbers with either the *eval* built-in function or the *string* module's functions: *atoi*, *atof*, and *atol* convert to integer, floating-point, and long integers, respectively. To convert numbers to strings, we can either use backquotes or the "%" formatting operator.

```
>>> fstr = "3.14159"
>>> istr = "1234"
>>> eval(fstr), eval(istr)
(3.14159, 1234)
>>> import string
>>> string.atof(fstr), string.atoi(istr)
(3.14159, 1234)
>>> s1 = "%d" % 1234
```

```
>>> s2 = '3.14159'
>>> s1, s2
('1234', '3.14159')
```

As a rule, *eval* is usually slower than the *string* functions, since it's a much more general (and complex) parser. Also note that the *atol* function isn't quite the same as the *atol* function in C: you get a *Python* long, which is an arbitrary-precision integer (and considerably slower to use).

*Table 13-6: String/object conversions*

| Converter | Converts from | Converts to |
|---|---|---|
| *eval* | Strings | Any object with a syntax |
| *string.atoi, atof, atol* | Strings | Integer, float, long |
| backquotes | Any Python object | Strings |
| "%" string operator | Objects with format codes | Strings |

## *The Moral of the Story*

As we've seen in this section, Python has the right tools for implementing data structure libraries: modules, classes, and a rich set of built-in types and operations. Many of these examples illustrate techniques that are useful in most applications. Indeed, data structure support is one of Python's strongest points: when we need to extend the set of built-in types, classes provide a tight integration with Python's object model.

But as we've also seen, "hand-rolled" class implementations aren't always the best approach. Often, built-in Python tools accomplish the same goals much faster. In fact, this is one of the main ways Python speeds development: common data structures are built in to the language. Because of this, data structure libraries aren't always as critical in Python as they are in lower-level languages like C and C++.

Perhaps more importantly, we've also seen that C-based implementations will often do better than Python classes. Even though Python is easy to use, it's not always the best tool for the job at hand. And this is one of the kernel ideas behind Python: developers should be able to mix and match tools as appropriate for a given system. Chapter 14 takes up Python/C integration and mixed-language programming.

*In this chapter:*
- *"I Am Lost at C"*
- *Examples We've Already Seen*
- *Moving Stacks to a C Extension Module*
- *Moving Stacks to a C Extension Type*
- *Now, Forget Most of the Details*

# 14
# *Extending Python*

## *"I Am Lost at C"*

So far, we've been using Python as it comes out of the box. We've used interfaces to services outside Python, and coded extensions as Python modules. But we haven't added any external services beyond the built-in set. For many users, this makes perfect sense: standalone programming is one of the main ways people apply Python. It already has interfaces to filesystems, GUIs, system services, and much more.

But in many systems, Python's ability to integrate with C-compatible modules becomes a critical feature. In fact, Python's role as an extension and interface tool for larger systems is one of the main reasons for its popularity. Its design supports mixed-language, hybrid systems. Often a static language like C isn't enough by itself; integrating Python yields more flexible systems and dramatically faster development modes. Moreover, moving components of a Python program to C can optimize performance.

In this chapter and Chapter 15, *Embedding Python*, we'll explore Python's tools for interfacing to the outside world: both its ability to be used as an embedded language in other systems and the interfaces for extending Python with new modules and types implemented in C-compatible languages. There are two distinct integration APIs:

- The *extending interface*: tools for calling C extensions from Python programs
- The *embedding interface*: tools for calling embedded Python code from C modules

Either Python or C can be on top. Some systems use one scheme or the other, and some systems use both schemes. For instance, embedded Python code can also use application-specific C extensions. As we'll see, Python has well-defined C interfaces and a remarkably open architecture that lets us mix languages arbitrarily.

### This Chapter's Scope

Python/C integration is a big topic: this chapter deals with C extensions, and the next discusses embedding. In principle, the entire set of *extern* C functions in the Python system makes up its run-time interface. But here we'll concentrate on those that are commonly used to implement integration with external modules.

Also, we won't try to document every integration technique here; in fact, some are evolving as this book is being written. Instead we'll look at how tools we've already used are integrated for use in Python and explore some typical integration strategies. For instance, to illustrate extension techniques, we'll migrate the last chapter's stack implementations to C to optimize their performance. Some common integration topics (tools, C++ integration) appear at the end of Chapter 15.

---

*NOTE* Because some form of C integration is at the core of most Python domains, we need to address it in this book. Still, if you don't plan to extend or embed Python in C, you can skip or skim the next two chapters without missing anything critical.

Extending and embedding tools are often considered "wizard-level" topics. In some cases, advanced programmers add C extensions and embedding interfaces, and others use them by programming exclusively in Python. But Python's integration interfaces really only require a basic knowledge of C programming.

Although this is advanced material, if you know enough about programming to recognize a need for an extension language, you probably already have the required background knowledge for this chapter. We assume that the reader has a basic knowledge of C development.

---

## Examples We've Already Seen

Although it might not have always been obvious, we've already used Python's extension interfaces earlier in the book. Some of the tools we've used illustrate basic extension concepts.

*Files*
: External files are integrated as an extension type: we make a new file object by calling the *open* function, and call the created object's methods to manipulate it. File object method calls are mapped to functions in the standard C library.

*Shell tools*

The *os* module is an extension module that maps directly onto POSIX functions on UNIX systems. The *os* module just registers POSIX functions so they can be called from Python programs and handles converting arguments and results to and from C data format. For instance, the *os.popen* and *os.fork* functions are just wrappers over standard C library functions. Similarly, the *regex* module is a wrapper over a regular expression library.

*GUIs*

Tkinter integrates a flat GUI API, and makes it look like an object-oriented framework. As we've seen earlier in this book, *Tkinter* is composed of both a C extension module and a Python library module. Because *Tkinter* wraps the C extension module in classes, we can extend widgets and build up GUIs by subclassing basic widget classes. *Tk* becomes object-oriented in Python, because Python is an object-oriented language. *Tkinter* also uses Python's embedding interfaces: when a GUI event occurs, the C layer catches it first and dispatches the call to a registered Python object.

*Persistence*

*dbm* and persistent-object shelve files are integrated as mappings: we were able to use both as though they were normal dictionary objects. Instead of using the low-level *dbm* file access API, we're presented with a higher-level interface that allows indexing, method calls, etc. The integration was even seamless enough to let us use *dbm* files and shelves in programs written for dictionaries (the table browser); there's no need for special API interfacing code for each kind of mapping file system.

## And Everything Else

Every time we use a built-in or intrinsic datatype, we're using Python's C extension type interfaces. Lists, numbers, strings, dictionaries, functions, classes, etc. are all implemented using the same extension tools we use to add C extensions of our own. The only difference is that intrinsic types don't have to be imported, and usually have special syntax for making instances (instead of constructor functions).

In fact, every kind of object a Python program uses makes use of extension module or type interfaces in some fashion. As we've seen, even intrinsic functions (*len, range*) exist in a predefined extension module called `__builtin__`, and class instance objects are implemented internally by a C extension type. Whether we add extensions on our own or not, Python's C integration interface is a core component of the system.

Since Python's intrinsic types are implemented with the same integration tools exposed for our use, the C extensions we add can do anything a built-in type can do. For instance, Python lists respond to method calls (*append*, *sort*), and operators ("+", "*"); extension types we add can do the same. We were able to overload operators earlier with classes by defining specially named methods; for extension types we fill in function pointer slots in type descriptors instead, but the end result is the same.

> ### *Use the source, Luke!*
>
> Python's internal use of extension module/type interfaces can be studied in the system's source code (currently, in the *Modules* and *Objects* directories of the Python source tree). They're a great source of supplemental examples for extension writers.

# *Moving Stacks to a C Extension Module*

Since Python objects can be implemented in either Python or C, some of this chapter is really a continuation of Chapter 13, *Implementing Objects*: Python's data-structure support includes its C extension tools. To illustrate, we'll optimize the stacks we coded in Python in Chapter 13, by migrating them to C here. But the techniques we'll study in this section apply to integrating any kind of external component (flat C libraries, etc.).

Let's first introduce some general extension ideas. There are two ways to extend Python with services coded in C (or C-compatible languages): by writing C extension modules, and by writing C extension types.

- *C modules* correspond exactly to Python modules. But C modules manually register methods using C function pointers when initialized (when first imported). C module functions are responsible for converting arguments passed from Python to C form, and converting results from C to Python. They're also responsible for communicating errors back to Python.
- *C types* are similar to Python classes: they define a constructor function for making instances, plus methods and operators to apply to instances. The main difference is that C types register the constructor, instance methods, and operation handlers using C function pointers. A type descriptor replaces special method names. But as we'll see, C types aren't really classes: there's no notion of inheritance or subclassing unless we add Python wrapper classes.

C types usually also define a C module, to export the constructor function. Clients import the module and call the constructor to make instances of the C type. As we'll see, both C modules and types are either bound in to Python libraries and executables or loaded dynamically when first imported. Dynamic loading works just like Python modules: C extensions are added when imported, without rebuilding Python.

## C Modules and Types Work Like Python Modules and Classes

Other than the distinctions noted above, C modules and types correspond closely to Python modules and classes. In fact, this is a crucial parallel to note: C modules and types serve the same roles as modules and classes written in Python:

- C modules are used to implement flat function libraries and shared data structures.
- C types are used when we need to support multiple copies of an object.

They're also implemented in very similar ways. In this chapter, we'll study C module and type-based implementations of the stack data structure we saw in Chapter 13. The C type-based implementation will use the same stack processing algorithms as the C module.

But the stack becomes C static data in the module, and a C *struct* in the type. Each C stack type instance gets a new copy of the stack *struct*, much like a new class instance attribute dictionary. And the stack type functions use a *self* object pointer to process the subject instance, exactly like Python class methods. Moreover, the stack type is able to overload Python operators like a class.

## A C String Stack Module

Since they're somewhat simpler, let's begin by studying C extension modules. Instead of getting into more details right way, we'll look at a real C module first. The C source code in Example 14-1 implements a stack of character strings. It starts out empty, grows in response to *push* calls, and shrinks when *pop* is called.

This C module behaves identically to the Python stack module we saw in the last chapter; it implements a stack that can be shared by more than one client (importer), but there can only be one copy of its stack. In fact, there's a direct correspondence between the methods in this C module and the ones in the Python module we saw earlier in the book. But there are two notable differences:

*Strings only*
: The stack here is dramatically limited compared to the Python implementation: it can only contain Python strings. Because Python is dynamically typed, the

Python version can hold objects of any type: strings, lists, classes, etc. We could push and pop generic Python objects (*PyObject**s) in C too, but C's stronger typing requires a distinct implementation for each kind of stack, if we want a more direct (and efficient) structure.

*Fixed length*

To keep things simple, the stacks here also have an arbitrary fixed-length limit. We could improve this by using a different algorithm and C linked lists. Still, coding in C or C++ is a sure way to gain an appreciation for the flexibility we get for free from Python's dynamic typing and variable-length, nestable data structures.

The stack module appears on the next few pages. Most of its code is straightforward if you're familiar with C. As shown in Figure 14-1, stacks are represented as an array of pointers (*stack*) into an array of characters (*strings*). This same structure will be used for the C type later, but each instance gets its own copy of the data structures.

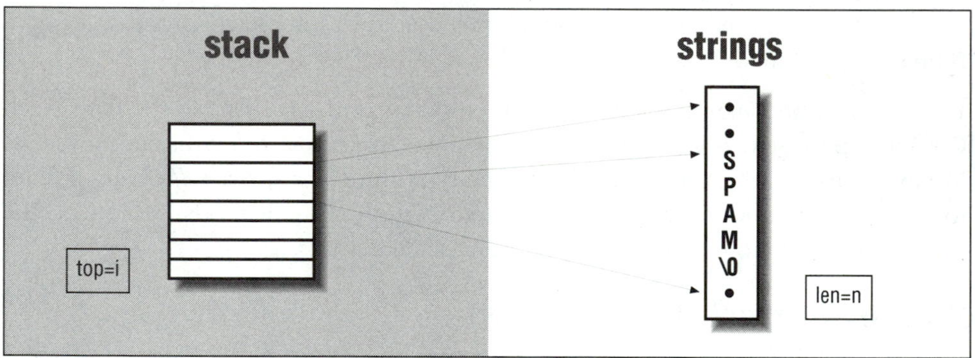


*Figure 14-1: C string-stack implementation*

As you study C examples be sure to read the comments but ignore non-Python code. These listings are fairly long; C code gets big quickly (at least compared to Python programs!). Showing smaller, artificial examples would take less space but would also teach less. Instead the examples here are simple but are realistically scaled. If you want to start with a smaller extension example, see the *getenv/putenv* integration in Chapter 2, *A Sneak Preview*.

Of course, you have to know something about C to get the most out of these examples. But the extension concepts should be accessible to other readers too. For instance, Python API names all start with *Py* or *PY*; the rest of the code can generally be ignored. Most of the C examples in this book use ANSI function-headers; they may need to be converted for older C compilers. C programs, in general, aren't as portable as Python programs; other platform issues are pointed out along the way.

*Example 14-1: File: stackmod.c*

```
/******************************************************
 * stackmod.c: a shared stack of character-strings;
 * a C extension module for use in Python programs;
 * linked into python libraries or loaded on import;
 ******************************************************/

#include "Python.h"               /* Python header files */
#include <stdio.h>                /* C header files */
#include <string.h>

static PyObject *ErrorObject;    /* locally-raised exception */

#define onError(message) \
       { PyErr_SetString(ErrorObject, message); return NULL; }


/*****************************************************************************
* LOCAL LOGIC/DATA (THE STACK)
*****************************************************************************/

#define MAXCHARS 2048
#define MAXSTACK MAXCHARS

static int  top = 0;                /* index into 'stack' */
static int  len = 0;                /* size of 'strings' */
static char *stack[MAXSTACK];       /* pointers into 'strings' */
static char strings[MAXCHARS];      /* string-storage area */


/*****************************************************************************
* EXPORTED MODULE METHOD-FUNCTIONS
*
* Define 1 static (local) C function per module method. Each method-function
* gets 2 'PyObject*' Python-object arguments when called:
* 'self'-- only used for C extension data-types (not here)
* 'args'-- a 'tuple' holding the argument objects passed from Python code.
* Each returns a Python object: a result, None, or NULL to raise an exception.
*****************************************************************************/

static PyObject *
stack_push(PyObject *self, PyObject *args)        /* args: (string) */
{
    char *pstr;
    if (!PyArg_ParseTuple(args, "s", &pstr))      /* convert args: Python->C */
        return NULL;                              /* NULL triggers exception */
    if (top == MAXSTACK)                          /* python sets arg-error msg */
        onError("stack overflow")                 /* iff maxstack < maxchars */
    if (len + strlen(pstr) + 1 >= MAXCHARS)
        onError("string-space overflow")
```

*Example 14-1: File: stackmod.c (continued)*

```
    else {
        strcpy(strings + len, pstr);                /* store in string-space */
        stack[top++] = &(strings[len]);             /* push start address */
        len += (strlen(pstr) + 1);                  /* new string-space size */
        Py_INCREF(Py_None);                         /* a 'procedure' call */
        return Py_None;                             /* None: no errors */
    }
}

static PyObject *
stack_pop(PyObject *self, PyObject *args)
{                                                   /* no arguments for pop */
    PyObject *pstr;
    if (!PyArg_ParseTuple(args, ""))                /* verify no args passed */
        return NULL;
    if (top == 0)
        onError("stack underflow")                  /* return NULL = raise */
    else {
        pstr = Py_BuildValue("s", stack[--top]);  /* convert result: C->Py */
        len -= (strlen(stack[top]) + 1);
        return pstr;                                /* return new python string */
    }                                               /* pstr ref-count++ already */
}

static PyObject *
stack_top(PyObject *self, PyObject *args)           /* almost same as item(-1) */
{                                                   /* but different errors */
    PyObject *result = stack_pop(self, args);       /* get top string */
    if (result != NULL)
        len += (strlen(stack[top++]) + 1);          /* undo pop */
    return result;                                  /* NULL or string object */
}

static PyObject *
stack_empty(PyObject *self, PyObject *args)         /* no args: '()' */
{
    if (!PyArg_ParseTuple(args, ""))                /* or PyArg_NoArgs */
        return NULL;
    return Py_BuildValue("i", top == 0);            /* boolean: a python int */
}

static PyObject *
stack_member(PyObject *self, PyObject *args)
{
    int i;
    char *pstr;
    if (!PyArg_ParseTuple(args, "s", &pstr))
        return NULL;
    for (i = 0; i < top; i++)                   /* find arg in stack */
        if (strcmp(pstr, stack[i]) == 0)
            return PyInt_FromLong(1);           /* send back a python int */
    return PyInt_FromLong(0);                   /* same as Py_BuildValue("i" */
```

*Example 14-1: File: stackmod.c (continued)*

```
}

static PyObject *
stack_item(PyObject *self, PyObject *args)    /* return Python string or NULL */
{                                             /* inputs = (index): Python int */
    int index;
    if (!PyArg_ParseTuple(args, "i", &index))     /* convert args to C */
        return NULL;                              /* bad type or arg count? */
    if (index < 0)
        index = top + index;                      /* negative: offset from end */
    if (index < 0 || index >= top)
        onError("index out-of-bounds")            /* return NULL = 'raise' */
    else
        return Py_BuildValue("s", stack[index]); /* convert result to Python */
}                                                 /* no need to INCREF new obj */

static PyObject *
stack_len(PyObject *self, PyObject *args)     /* return a Python int or NULL */
{                                             /* no inputs */
    if (!PyArg_ParseTuple(args, ""))
        return NULL;
    return PyInt_FromLong(top);               /* wrap in python object */
}

static PyObject *
stack_dump(PyObject *self, PyObject *args)    /* not "print": reserved word */
{
    int i;
    if (!PyArg_ParseTuple(args, ""))
        return NULL;
    printf("[Stack:\n");
    for (i=top-1; i >= 0; i--)                    /* formatted output */
        printf("%d: '%s'\n", i, stack[i]);
    printf("]\n");
    Py_INCREF(Py_None);
    return Py_None;
}


/******************************************************************************
* METHOD REGISTRATION TABLE: NAME-STRING -> FUNCTION-POINTER
*
* List of functions defined in the module. A name->address method map, used
* to build-up the module's dictionary in "Py_InitModule". Once imported, this
* module acts just like it's coded in Python. The method functions handle
* converting data from/to python objects, and linkage to other C functions.
******************************************************************************/


static struct PyMethodDef stack_methods[] = {
 { "push",       stack_push,     1 },             /* name, address */
 { "pop",        stack_pop,      1 },             /* '1': tuple arg-lists */
```

*Example 14-1: File: stackmod.c (continued)*

```
 { "top",        stack_top,       1 },
 { "empty",      stack_empty,     1 },
 { "member",     stack_member,    1 },
 { "item",       stack_item,      1 },
 { "len",        stack_len,       1 },
 { "dump",       stack_dump,      1 },
 { NULL,         NULL }                          /* end, for initmodule */
};


/******************************************************************************
* INITIALIZATION FUNCTION (IMPORT-TIME)
*
* Initialization function for the module. Called on first "import stackmod" in
* a Python program. The function is usually called "initstackmod": this name's
* added to the built-in module table in config.c statically (if added to file
* Module/Setup), or called when the module's loaded dynamically as a shareable
* object-file found on PYTHONPATH. File and function names matter if dynamic.
******************************************************************************/

void
initstackmod()
{
    PyObject *m, *d;

    /* create the module and add the functions */
    m = Py_InitModule("stackmod", stack_methods);        /* registration hook */

    /* add symbolic constants to the module */
    d = PyModule_GetDict(m);
    ErrorObject = Py_BuildValue("s", "stackmod.error");  /* export exception */
    PyDict_SetItemString(d, "error", ErrorObject);       /* add more if need */

    /* check for errors */
    if (PyErr_Occurred())
        Py_FatalError("can't initialize module stackmod");
}
```

## Anatomy of a C Extension Module

Example 14-1 illustrates the structure common to all C modules. Although some of this structure can vary depending on your application and coding style, the sections of this file are fairly typical:

*Python header files*
: It first includes the standard *Python.h* header file (from the installed Python *Include* directory). This file defines almost all exported Python API services. Later we'll see other special-purpose header files.

*Local data/logic*

In this module, we need to declare data structures for representing the string stack. Python doesn't know anything about these components. For modules that just wrap an existing C library for Python use, there may be no local data at all.

*Method functions*

The file next defines a set of functions that are called from Python in response to calls in Python programs. These are the exported functions of our module. They each get two Python objects as input, and send a Python object back to Python as the result (or *NULL* to trigger an exception). Method functions are responsible for converting objects to or from C datatypes. They're all C "static" (local to this file): Python calls them using function-pointers, not by name.

*Registration table*

Near the end, we provide an initialized table (array) which maps function names to function pointers (addresses). The names in the table become attribute names that Python code uses to call the C functions. The function pointers are used by Python to dispatch attribute calls to the C functions in this file. In effect, the table "registers" attributes in the module. A *NULL* entry terminates the table. Registration tables are the hook from Python calls to C functions.

*Initialization function*

Finally we provide an initialization function, which Python calls the first time this module is imported in a program. This function calls the API function *Py_InitModule* to build up the new module's dictionary from the entries in the registration table. It also adds an entry in its dictionary for a locally raised exception; as we'll see later, this allows Python *try* statements to catch it by name.

## *Using the Python Run-time API*

The stack module interfaces with Python using a set of functions known as the Python API. It includes tools for converting data, calling embedded code, setting exceptions, and more. Throughout this chapter, we'll introduce API functions used in the examples. They all have names that start with a *Py* prefix.

### *Python objects in C*

The most common Python API component used in C is the Python object datatype, called *PyObject**. Python objects never have a more specific type-signature in C (though the API has functions for testing a *PyObject**'s type). For instance, method functions get pointers to two objects, and return another.

```
static PyObject *
stack_push(PyObject *self, PyObject *args)
```

Here, *stack_push* uses the input objects passed from the Python interpreter:

*args*
: A tuple holding the arguments passed from the Python call.

*self*
: Is ignored: it's only useful for extension-types (discussed later)

It returns a Python object to the Python caller, or *NULL*.

*result*
: A Python object, *PyObject**, as the result (new, or *incref*d: see below).

*None*
: The Python *None* object, *Py_None*, if there is no result (for *procedures*).

*NULL*
: Or a C *NULL* pointer to flag an error and raise a Python exception.

## Python/C Linkage Details

There are two different components to the binding between Python and C extensions. On one level, the Python interpreter must be able to route calls in Python code to registered C functions. On a more basic level, C modules must be linked into the same executable as Python to be called at all.

### How Python routes calls to C functions

A C module's registration table is the key to call routing. Here's how the links are created:

- Python automatically calls the module's initialization function the first time it's imported (by an *import* or *from* statement).
- When the initialization function calls the *Py_InitModule* API function, Python uses the entries in the passed-in registration table to build up the module's attribute dictionary.
- Python saves the associated C function-pointers in the module's dictionary as the values of the function name entries. *Py_InitModule* also adds the new module to the *sys.modules* dictionary.

Once initialized, references to the module's attributes (*stackmod.push*) use normal qualification mechanisms to fetch the C function pointer from the C module's dictionary. After the module's attribute is fetched by hashing in the module's dictionary, the C function call is direct (by address).

For instance, a call in a Python program *stackmod.push('hello')* is routed to the C *stack_push* function, with the string-object *hello* in the *args* tuple passed in, as shown in Figure 14-2.

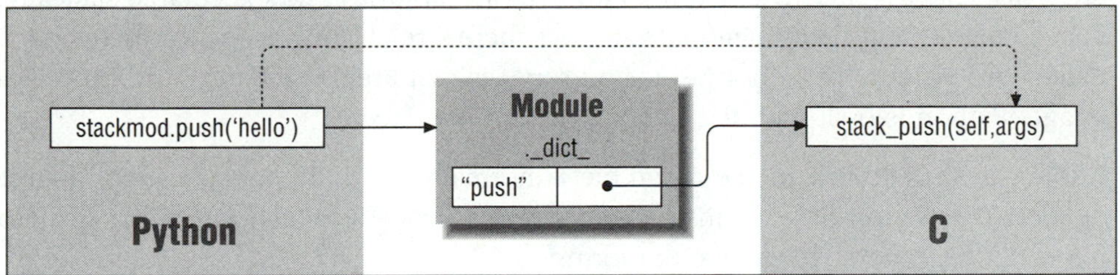


*Figure 14-2: C function-call dispatching*

> ## *C functions are first-class objects too*
>
> C functions are another object type. Like everything else in Python, functions (and type methods) implemented in a C extension module are first-class objects. They can be used just like functions and class methods coded in Python. For instance, given a C extension module M with a registered function F, `x=M.F` fetches the C function object; it can later be called anonymously, with `x( . . . )`.

### *How the C code gets linked with Python*

But how does C code we write get added to the Python system in the first place? There are two different ways to bind C extensions with Python: statically (when Python is built) or dynamically (while the program is running). Since method functions are called by function pointer, their names don't need to be linked with Python. But because Python calls module initialization functions (*initstackmod*) by name, these references must be resolved by the C linker.

***Static binding.*** Under static binding, extensions are added to Python permanently. But the process is surprisingly simple; to add the *stackmod.c* C extension statically:

1. Put (or make a link to) *stackmod.c* in the *Modules* directory of the Python source tree.
2. Add a line to the *Modules/Setup* file to declare the new module:

```
stackmod stackmod.c
```

3. Run a *make* command in the top level of the Python source tree to rebuild Python.

Python's build system takes care of updating built-in tables, changing makefiles, etc. This strategy binds the module into Python's libraries and executable statically; it becomes a new built-in module. In fact there's really no distinction between C extensions written by Python users and services that are a standard part of the language; Python is built with the same extension interfaces.

Adding the single line in the *Setup* file is normally the only configuration change needed. The Setup file has instructions on this process, which we won't go into here. But, in general, lines take the form:

```
<module> ... [<sourcefile> ...] [<cpparg> ...] [<library> ...]
```

The *<cpparg>* and *<library>* parts are added to Python makefiles if used. For instance, when the following line is adding in the *Setup* file:

```
stackmod stackmod.c
```

Python extends its *<module-name>/<initialization-function>* built-in table in the generated *config.c* file, which is usually compiled each time you rebuild *python*:

```
...
{ "stackmod", initstackmod },          /* becomes a new builtin module */
```

It also extends *Modules/Makefile*, so *stackmod* is linked into the Modules library file:

```
...
stackmod.o: $(srcdir)/stackmod.c; $(CC) $(CFLAGS)  -c $(srcdir)/stackmod.c
```

When *stackmod* is imported, its name is found in the generated table and its code is already linked into Python's libraries. Already compiled *.o* object files can also be put in the Modules directory (instead of the *.c* source); the Setup entry would then be: *stackmod stackmod.o.*

Note that the name of the module's initialization function must match the name used in the *Setup* file, or you'll get linker errors when you rebuild Python. The name of the source or object file doesn't have to match the module name: the *config.c* table uses the leftmost name in Setup, and Makefiles get the rest.

***Dynamic binding.*** The alternative dynamic loading approach is actually simpler, provided you're on a system that supports dynamic loading of C object modules. (Most systems do.) To add the *stackmod.c* extension at run-time, follow these simple steps.

1. Compile *stackmod.c* into a shareable object file (a *.so* or *.sl* file on some UNIX platforms)
2. Put the object file in a directory on Python's module search path (shell variable *PYTHONPATH*)

If we take this route, the module is loaded and initialized at run-time, when first imported by a Python program. Where it is possible, this can be a much more flexible approach:

- Because there's no need to rebuild Python to add extensions, C modules can be added even if you don't have access to Python's source code. For example, on-site extensions may be coded in either Python or C.
- Because dynamically loaded extensions aren't added to Python's libraries, Python's size does not increase; extensions are added to the Python process only if used.

Unfortunately, some of the details of dynamic loading are extremely platform dependent and are prone to change. For instance, the formats of both the module file and initialization function names vary from platform to platform. Given a module <*X*>, the Sun UNIX port searches for an object file called <*X*>*.so* or <*X*>*module.so*, and tries to call an initialization function named *init*<*X*> in the object file.

But on other platforms, the object file might be expected to have a suffix of *.o*, *.sl*, *.slb*, or *.pyd*, and Python may expect to find an initialization function called *init*<*X*> or *_init*<*X*>. Naming conventions depend on the platform's notion of a dynamically-loadable object file. Check the Python extension manual for up-to-date details or consult the *import*.c* files in the *Python* directory of Python's source tree. Compilation requirements for generating shareables vary widely too; check your C compiler's documentation.

***Python module search path order.*** Dynamic loading adds a fourth way that Python can resolve a module import:

- By loading a *.py* source code file
- By loading a *.pyc* compiled code file
- By initializing a statically bound extension module
- By loading and initializing a dynamically bound extension module

Python finds external modules by checking each directory on the module search path in turn and finds statically bound modules by checking the *config.c* table. As a rule, you should avoid using the same name for modules that exist in different forms (*stack.py* and *stack.so*, for example). Python's search for an imported module can roughly be described in pseudocode:

```
initialize "sys.path" from $PYTHONPATH plus installation-defaults

def import(module):
    if "module" was imported before:
        return the existing module object

    if there's a statically-bound "module" in the config table:
       initialize it and return

    for each directory on sys.path:
        1. look for a dynamically-loadable C module: "module.so", "module.sl"...
        2. look for a "module.py" source-code module second
        3. look for a "module.pyc" compiled-code module last
        if any was found: break

    if we found a ".py" source-file:
        see if there's a ".pyc" compiled-code module file in the same
        directory, that's not older than the ".py" file we found.
        if there is:
            use the ".pyc" instead
```

In other words, dynamically linked C extensions have priority over same-named Python modules, and statically linked modules have priority over all other module types. But again, you shouldn't depend on the order of searching, especially within the same directory: use different directories or module names to make modules distinct.

---

*NOTE* Python uses the *sys.path* list to search for modules; because it's available to Python programs too, it can be extended or changed from inside a Python application as needed.

---

## *Converting Python Data To/From C Form*

C modules that interact with Python are responsible for converting Python objects to and from C formats. For instance, arguments are passed in to extension functions as a Python *tuple* of objects; an API function handles conversion to C. Similarly, C extension functions return Python objects: API functions build Python objects from C data.

There are distinct API tools for handling input conversions (Python to C), and output conversions (C to Python). In both cases, type conversion is left to C extension functions; Python doesn't know anything about the type signatures of C extension functions it calls. Instead, Python uses standard call patterns.

### *Why file suffixes aren't used in imports*

When we wrote and used Python source code modules, we saw that *import* and *from* statements always omit the *.py* filename suffix from the module name. For example, if we write a module *spam.py*, we import it with *import spam*, not *import spam.py*.

Besides the fact that an *import* statement assigns to a variable name too, it's usually impossible for a client module to know what a module's suffix will really be. It may be *.py* (a Python source-file), *.pyc* (a compiled Python module), *.so* (a shareable-library C extension on some UNIX systems), *.dll* (a shareable on Microsoft Windows), or even have no extension at all (a statically bound extension module).

But even if a module could guess at an extension, it would be a bad idea to try: part of the point behind Python's seamless extension structure is to make C modules look just like Python modules. If we hard-coded a *.py* suffix, we wouldn't be able to move modules to C without affecting all their clients.

### *Python to C: using Python argument lists*

In C extension module functions, the arguments passed from a Python program are sent from Python in the second parameter (*args*). When the C function is entered, the arguments are a Python tuple object; the API function *PyArg_ParseTuple* is the simplest way to extract its components and convert them to C form.

*PyArg_ParseTuple* takes a Python object, a format string, and a variable-length list of C target addresses. It converts the items in the tuple to C datatype values according to the format string and stores the results in the C variables whose addresses are passed in. The effect is much like C's *scanf* function. For example, the stack module converts a passed-in Python string argument to a C *char** using the *s* convert code:

```
PyArg_ParseTuple(args, "s", &pstr)
```

and converts integer arguments to C with the *i* code. If there are multiple arguments, we just string format codes together, and include corresponding C targets. For instance, to convert an argument list holding a string, an integer, and another string to C:

```
PyArg_ParseTuple(args, "sis", &stringarg1, &intarg, &stringarg2)
```

And to verify that no arguments were passed, we use an empty format string:

```
PyArg_ParseTuple(args, "")
```

*PyArg_ParseTuple* checks that the number and types of the arguments passed from Python matches the format string in the call. If there's a mismatch, it sets an exception and returns zero to C (see below).

### *C to Python: returning values to Python*

There are two ways to convert C data to Python objects: using type-specific API functions or the general object-builder function *Py_BuildValue*. *Py_BuildValue* is essentially the inverse of *PyArg_ParseTuple*: it converts C data to Python objects according to a format string. For instance, to make a Python string object from a C *char**, the stack module uses an *s* convert code:

```
pstr = Py_BuildValue("s", stack[--top])
```

As before, the *i* code converts C integers to Python integer objects. But we can also use more specific object constructors:

```
Py_BuildValue("i", top == 0)        generic object builder
PyInt_FromLong(1)                   type-specific builder
```

Both calls make a Python integer object from a C integer value. *Py_BuildValue* is slower than more specific converters (it has to parse the format string), but it is convenient: there's just one function name to remember for most object types. *Py_BuildValue* also has extended features for building Python lists, tuples, and dictionaries (discussed below); it takes more work to make these with type-specific builders.

### *Python to C: using Python return values*

When Python is being run as an embedded language (discussed in Chapter 15), API functions may also return Python objects to C. This case is almost the same as passed-in Python arguments in C extension functions, except that Python return values aren't always a tuple.

To convert returned Python objects to C form, we can use the *PyArg_Parse* API function. This function works just like *PyArg_ParseTuple*: it takes an object, a format string, and C targets. But *PyArg_Parse* doesn't expect the Python object to be a tuple. We need to supply *(..)* pairs (discussed below) in the format string to extract parts of returned tuples: *(sis)*.

## *Old-style calling conventions*

If you look back at the extension example in Chapter 2, you'll notice that it uses *PyArg_Parse* to convert argument lists, instead of *PyArg_ParseTuple*. The former is also backward compatible with an older conversion variant (*getargs*).

If the third column in a module's name/function registration table is zero (or absent), Python passes argument lists using old-style *getargs* conventions: the argument list might not be a tuple, so *PyArg_Parse* is used to extract values. But normally the third column in a module's name/function registration task tables should be *1*, and *PyArg_ParseTuple* should be used for argument list conversions. We will see more on this subject later in this chapter.

### *Common conversion codes*

With a few exceptions, *PyArg_Parse(Tuple)* and *Py_BuildValue* use the same conversion codes in format strings. A list of all supported conversion codes appears in Python's extension manual. The most commonly used codes appear in Table 14-1; tuple, list, and dictionary formats can be nested.

*Table 14-1: Common Python/C data conversion codes*

| Format-string code | C datatype | Python object type |
|---|---|---|
| *s* | *char** | String |
| *s#* | *char*, int* | String, length |
| *i* | *int* | Integer |
| *l* | *long int* | Integer |
| *c* | *char* (or *int* for build) | String |
| *f* | *float* | Floating-point |
| *d* | *double* | Floating-point |
| *O* | *PyObject** | Raw (unconverted) object |
| *O&* | *&converter, void** | Converted object (calls converter) |
| *(items)* | Targets or values | Nested tuple |
| *[items]* | Series of arguments/values | List |
| {items} | Series of *key,value* arguments | Dictionary |

*Notes:*

- We pass in the address of a *char** for *s* codes when converting to C, not the address of a *char* array: Python copies out the address of an existing string. C strings usually must be null-terminated.

- The *O* code is useful if we need a raw Python object (as we'll see later, this can be useful if we need to access object attributes by name later, or pass them to other API functions).
- The *O&* code lets us pass in C converter functions for custom conversions. This comes in handy if we need to do special processing to map an object to a C datatype not directly supported by conversion codes (for instance, to or from an entire C struct or C++ class-instance).
- The last two entries (*[si..]* and *{ds..}*) are currently only supported by *Py_BuildValue*: we can construct lists and tuples with format strings, but can't unpack them. Instead the API includes type-specific routines for accessing sequence and mapping components.

*PyArg_ParseTuple* supports some extra codes, which must not be nested in tuple formats (*(..)*):

|
: The remaining arguments are all optional (*varargs*). The C targets are unchanged if arguments are missing in the Python tuple. For instance: "ab|cd" requires two arguments, but allows up to four.

:
: The function name follows, for use in error-messages set by the call (argument mismatches). Normally Python sets the error message to a generic string.

;
: A full error message follows, running to the end of the format string.

This format code list isn't exhaustive, and the set of convert codes may expand over time; refer to Python's extension manual for further details.

---

*NOTE* We pass in pointers to targets for *PyArg_ParseTuple*, but actual values for *Py_BuildValue*. If you want to remember this rule, think of Python's data converters as though they were C's input/output converters:

```
Input (Python-to-C):
    Python: PyArg_ParseTuple(object, format, pointers..)
    C:      sscanf(string, format, pointers..)

Output (C-to-Python):
    Python: Py_BuildValue(format, values..)
    C:      printf(format, values..)
```

---

## *Handling Exceptions*

Errors are communicated both to and from Python, using traditional C return values. C extensions raise Python exceptions by returning error-values, and Python exceptions are caught by C as bad API-call return values. Python itself keeps track of exceptions, to be raised when Python callers are resumed.

### *Raising Python exceptions in C*

C extension code is responsible for telling Python about errors it detects. In short, extension-module functions return a C *NULL* value (for the result object) to flag an error. When control returns to Python, the *NULL* result triggers a normal Python exception in the Python code that called the C function.

C code can also set the names (object) and messages ("extra data") of exceptions it raises by returning NULL. The stack module uses the *PyErr_SetString* API function to set the exception object to a locally-defined Python object *ErrorObject*, and set the exception's extra data to a character string:

```
static PyObject *ErrorObject;    /* locally-raised exception */
#define onError(message) \
       { PyErr_SetString(ErrorObject, message); return NULL; }
```

Python translates the message string to a Python string object internally. *ErrorObject* is assigned a new Python string object in the initialization function. To clients of this module, the exception object can be referenced as *stackmod.error*, since it is stored in the module's dictionary under this name. (The string object's value is *stackmod.error* too; this is a common convention.)

*PyErr_SetString* has relatives for setting the exception object and data in a variety of flavors. C modules may also set a built-in Python exception; for instance:

```
PyErr_SetString(PyExc_IndexError, "index out-of-bounds")
```

raises a Python *IndexError* exception, with the message string data. We'll use this technique later in the book.

### *Detecting errors that occur in Python*

The inverse case matters too: Python also communicates errors back to enclosing C code. Python API functions may be called from C extensions, or an enclosing C layer when Python is embedded (as we'll see later). Python to C error communication works the same way for both.

To detect errors raised in Python API functions, C callers check the return value. For pointer result functions, Python returns *NULL* pointers on errors. For integer result functions, Python generally returns a status code of –1 to flag an error and a 0 or positive value on success (*PyArg_ParseTuple* is an exception to this rule: it returns 0 when it detects an error).

*Propagating Python errors.* When an error is raised inside a Python API function, both the exception object, and its associated "extra data" are automatically set by Python: there's no need to set it again in the calling C function. For instance, when an argument-passing error is detected in the *PyArg_ParseTuple* function (a bad return status), the stack module just returns *NULL* to propagate the exception to the enclosing Python layer, instead of setting its own message. Later, we'll see that embedded call layers usually handle Python errors locally.

Finally, if we just want check if an error has been set in Python but hasn't yet been raised, *PyErr_Occurred* can be used. For instance, the initialization function in our C module uses this after calling a set of API functions, instead of checking each one's result individually. Another API function, *PyErr_Clear* can be used to clear an error set in Python, if it's to be handled locally in the extension module, instead of propagated to the enclosing Python level.

## Handling Reference Counts

Earlier in this book, we mentioned that Python uses a reference-count scheme to implement garbage collection. Each Python object carries a count of the number of objects that reference it. When the count reaches zero, Python reclaims the object's memory space automatically, since it's no longer needed. Normally, Python manages the reference counts for objects in our programs behind the scenes; Python programs simply make and use objects, without concern for managing their storage space.

But when extending or embedding Python, integrated C code is also responsible for managing the reference counts of the Python objects it uses. The degree to which this becomes important depends on how many raw Python objects a C module processes and which Python API functions it calls. In simple cases it's a minor concern; when the API is used extensively, it can become a significant issue.

The *stack* module only uses reference count management in one way, to return the Python *None* object from a function (procedure), and designate success:

```
Py_INCREF(Py_None);                   /* a 'procedure' result */
return Py_None;                       /* None: no errors */
```

C module functions are expected to return either an object with an incremented reference count, or *NULL* to signal an error. The Python *None* object is available to C as *Py_None*. But since it's an object, we need to add a reference to it before passing it to Python. The Python macro *Py_INCREF* increments any object's reference count. It has three relatives:

*Py_INCREF*
: Increments an object's reference count

*Py_DECREF*
: Decrements an object's reference count (reclaim if zero)

*Py_XINCREF*
: Like *Py_INCREF*, but ignores a *NULL* object pointer

*Py_XDECREF*
: Like *Py_DECREF*, but ignores a *NULL* object pointer

As a general rule, API functions that create new objects increment their reference counts for us; unless a new object is to be passed back to Python, the C program that creates them should eventually decrement its count. Since the other macros aren't used in this example, we'll postpone further details until later.

---

*NOTE* Python will never reclaim a Python object held by C as long as C increments the object's reference count. Although it requires counter management, Python's garbage collector scheme is better suited to C integration than some.

---

## Other API Functions Used

We've used a few other API services that we should introduce here:

*PyModule_GetDict*
: Fetches a module object's attribute dictionary (`__dict__`)

*PyDict_SetItemString*
: Assigns a dictionary's key, passed in as a *char** (*dict['key'] = value*)

*PyMethodDef*
: The C type of entries in registration tables (a *struct*)

*Py_FatalError*
: Signals a fatal error to Python; the process exits after Python cleanup

## Summary: What C Modules Are Expected to Do

We've covered a lot of details here. Linking language systems is unavoidably complex, especially if one is a low-level language like C. But in typical Python-based development, most of our work is usually done in Python itself. C interfaces only

### *The "Great Renaming"*

Exposed symbols in Python's libraries have names that start with *Py* or *PY* (most are *Py*). This helps distinguish Python API functions in your code, and avoids name clashes with global symbols in your own C libraries. Unlike Python, C has a single global scope, which includes all *extern* names *#included* or referenced from every file seen during a compile. In Python terms, it's as if C has the *from** statement, but not the *import* statement.

As this book was being written, the *Py* naming convention was a recent addition. In the past, Python's C interface used more generic names (*object*, *initmodule*, *call_object*, etc.). To support code written before the renaming, Python includes a header file, *rename2.h*, which maps old names to new ones, using *#defines*:

```
#define object PyObject
#define initmodule Py_InitModule
#define call_object PyEval_CallObject
...
```

By including this header, code using old-style names can still be compiled and linked. If you do nothing to old code, it should compile as is: the *rename2* header is pulled in by old Python include files. If you move to the newer *Python.h* header file, the C compiler should flag all old names as errors. You might also see a *rename1.h* file in old Python installations; this file mapped new names to old ones, and is now obsolete.

If you encounter code with the old-style API names, the "rename2" header file can be used to translate to "Py" names. "rename2.h" can also be used as a (nearly) exhaustive list of Python API services. As of this writing the name conversion isn't 100% complete: some code in the Python system still uses the old names. But by the time you read this book, old-style names should be gone from Python itself completely.

come into play when migrating prototypes or adding external libraries. To summarize what we've seen so far, C extension modules are responsible for a number activities:

*Conversions*
: Converting Python data to and from C form.

*Exceptions*
: Reporting, detecting, and propagating errors.

*References*
: Managing object reference counts as needed

*Registration*
: Registering operations to be called from Python

*Initialization*
: Defining an initialization function that calls *Py_InitModule*

*Binding*
: Linking with Python libraries, statically or dynamically

They perform most of these tasks by calling Python API functions. As we'll see in a moment, C types perform the same duties, but the registration task becomes more complex.

And as we'll see in Chapter 15, C programs that use embedded Python code perform many of the same activities. But since C calls Python in this mode, there's no notion of registration or initialization, and there's an extra task: initializing Python itself.

## Testing the Extension Module

Let's step through some interaction with this module. Since it's been linked in to the Python libraries and executable, it acts just like a built-in module: we simply import it and call its function attributes. Python handles initialization and routes method-calls to the registered C functions. The C functions handle input and output data conversions.

### Basic usage

In fact, this listing is really just a "proof of concept": the interaction is exactly like what we saw for the Python-coded stack module. There's no difference from the Python client's viewpoint. We import the module and call its methods as though it were a Python-coded module. Also like modules, there's no way to make new stacks: the module is a flat function library, which manages a shared stack object.

There's no notion of operators here either, only attributes (just like the Python module). Indexing, membership, and printing are supported, but only as module method calls. We can iterate over a stack with *range*, using its *len* and *item* methods, but it's an indirect process. Most stack module attributes are callable functions, but some are data members (the exception object is used without calling it).

```
% python
>>> import stackmod                 import the C module
>>> stackmod.push('new')            call its registered methods
>>> stackmod.dump()                 C function: stack_dump
[Stack:
```

```
0: 'new'
]
>>> for c in "SPAM": stackmod.push(c)
...
>>> stackmod.dump()             print by calling a function
[Stack:
4: 'M'
3: 'A'
2: 'P'
1: 'S'
0: 'new'
]
>>> stackmod.len(), stackmod.top()
(5, 'M')
>>> x = stackmod.pop()          C function: stack_pop
>>> x
'M'
>>> stackmod.dump()
[Stack:
3: 'A'
2: 'P'
1: 'S'
0: 'new'
]
>>> stackmod.member('P'), stackmod.member('Q')
(1, 0)
>>> stackmod.len(), stackmod.item(1), stackmod.item(-1)
(4, 'S', 'A')
>>> for i in range(stackmod.len()): print "%d=%s" % (i, stackmod.item(i)),
...
0=new 1=S 2=P 3=A
```

### *Raising exceptions*

Some errors are set by Python itself. For instance, argument-list errors are detected by Python when we call *PyArg_ParseTuple*; if it returns an error status, our module just propagates the exception to the enclosing Python layer by returning *NULL*. There's no need to set an error message locally. Similarly, attribute error descriptions are set by Python internally, when a name is used that's not in the module's dictionary (initialized from the registration table).

Other errors (overflow, underflow, etc.) are detected by our C module. For these errors, we set the error name (the exception object) and the error message (the extra data of the exception), by calling *PyErr_SetString* in the *onError* macro. We still return *NULL* from the module method functions to tell Python an error has occurred. Python clients of the module can trap the module's local errors by using an *except try* statement clause with the *stack.error* exception (a Python object in the C module's dictionary). Notice that out-of-bounds indexes are trapped and reported, using the local exception object.

```
>>> stackmod.push()
Traceback (innermost last):
  File "<stdin>", line 1, in ?
TypeError: function requires exactly 1 argument; 0 given

>>> stackmod.push('a', 1)
Traceback (innermost last):
  File "<stdin>", line 1, in ?
TypeError: function requires exactly 1 argument; 2 given

>>> stackmod.push(99)
Traceback (innermost last):
  File "<stdin>", line 1, in ?
TypeError: argument 1: expected string, int found

>>> stackmod.length()
Traceback (innermost last):
  File "<stdin>", line 1, in ?
AttributeError: length

>>> dir(stackmod)
['__doc__', '__name__', 'dump', 'empty', 'error', 'item', 'len', 'member',
'pop', 'push', 'top']

>>> stackmod.empty()
0
>>> while 1: print stackmod.pop(),
...
A P S new
Traceback (innermost last):
  File "<stdin>", line 1, in ?
stackmod.error: stack underflow

>>> stackmod.top()
Traceback (innermost last):
  File "<stdin>", line 1, in ?
stackmod.error: stack underflow
>>> stackmod.empty()
1

>>> for i in range(1000): stackmod.push('hello' + `i`)
...
Traceback (innermost last):
  File "<stdin>", line 1, in ?
stackmod.error: string-space overflow

>>> stackmod.len()
239
>>> stackmod.item(0), stackmod.item(-1), stackmod.item(238)
('hello0', 'hello238', 'hello238')

>>> stackmod.item(239)
Traceback (innermost last):
  File "<stdin>", line 1, in ?
```

```
stackmod.error: index out-of-bounds

>>> n = 0
>>> for i in range(stackmod.len()): n = n + len(stackmod.item(i)) + 1
...
>>> n
2041                                              # calc the string-array size

>>> try:
...     stackmod.push('hello239')
... except stackmod.error, message:               catch stack-module errors
...     print message
...
string-space overflow
```

Suggested exercises:

1. Install this module in your Python system and remake Python's libraries and executable (static binding). If you're on a system with dynamic loading, compile the C file as a shareable object module, and load it dynamically from Python. Which technique is more convenient?
2. Add a *clear* method to the stack module to make the stack empty. Can you think of any other way to reuse the stack without clearing it first?
3. Pick a C-compatible library you're familiar with and write a Python interface for it by wrapping its functions in an extension module. Is there any way this could be done automatically?

# Moving Stacks to a C Extension Type

The C stack module works well if we only need a single stack, shared among all the module's clients; if we need more than one stack, we're out of luck. But C types can be used to implement multiple-instance objects. Just as we saw how Python classes let us make multiple copies of a stack, C types let us make multiple stacks implemented in C. Each instance gets its own copy of the C data used to represent a stack.

As noted earlier, C types usually provide a C module to export a constructor function, plus methods and operators for working with generated instances. In fact, C types really just build on the concepts we saw in the C module: they register function pointers, do type conversions, and communicate errors to Python.

Like modules, types are linked into Python libraries and executables. They're either added statically by rebuilding Python or loaded dynamically when first imported. The main addition for types is the use of type descriptors: C programs define Python type templates, and fill in relevant slots with C function pointers to register operation handlers. Type instances are allocated C *structs*, with pointers to type descriptors.

### *"Ooh, baby! Call me now and help me finish what I started on my own . . ."*

So began a recent post that found its way onto the Python Internet newsgroup (among others). I doubt that the poster had this in mind at the time (ahem), but the phrase illustrates the concept behind Python module initialization protocol well.

Both Python and C modules may specify arbitrary startup actions: as top-level statements in Python modules, and as initializer functions in C modules. Python automatically runs a module's startup logic when it's imported the first time in a program. Startup actions are the right place to configure the module, initialize exported data structures, etc.

Once initialized this way, future imports just fetch the already loaded module, rather than running the initialization actions again. After the import time initialization, clients can use a module's exports at will, by accessing its attributes.

As for the rest of this news post, the relationship to Python is less clear. (I've seen some great Python extension modules, but this may be taking the paradigm a bit too far :-)

## *A C String Stack Type*

Let's look at a real example again, before discussing specifics. The following C file defines a C extension type, which implements stacks of character strings. The stacks here work exactly like the C module's stack; in fact the algorithms and data structures are identical.

The main difference is that we allow for multiple copies now: C functions use the *self* argument to access the subject instance, exactly like Python classes. Further, many of the methods in the module become operators in the type; indexing, membership, and iteration are all handled by an index operation method.

In fact, this type is almost like the Python stack class we saw earlier. It implements the same methods and operators, and the constructor function is called *Stack* as before. For comparison, most of the methods defined in a C type have direct counterparts in classes (`__init__`, `__getitem__`, `__cmp__`, etc.).

But just as in the C module, the stacks created by the C type can only hold character strings, not arbitrary Python objects. Further, there's no notion of inheritance here: when information is fetched from the *self* type instance, it usually comes from a flat C *struct*, not an inheritance hierarchy.

*Example 14-2: File: stacktyp.c*

```
/*****************************************************
 * stacktyp.c: a character-string stack data-type;
 * a C extension type, for use in Python programs;
 * stacktype module clients can make multiple stacks;
 * similar to stackmod, but 'self' is the instance,
 * and we can overload sequence operators here;
 *****************************************************/

#include "Python.h"

static PyObject *ErrorObject;      /* local exception */
#define onError(message) \
       { PyErr_SetString(ErrorObject, message); return NULL; }


/******************************************************************************
 * STACK-TYPE INFORMATION
 ******************************************************************************/

#define MAXCHARS 2048
#define MAXSTACK MAXCHARS

typedef struct {                    /* stack instance object */
    PyObject_HEAD                   /* python header: ref-count + &typeobject */
    int top, len;
    char *stack[MAXSTACK];          /* per-instance state info */
    char strings[MAXCHARS];         /* same as stackmod, but multiple copies */
} stackobject;

staticforward PyTypeObject Stacktype;     /* shared type-descriptor */

#define is_stackobject(v)  ((v)->ob_type == &Stacktype)


/******************************************************************************
 * INSTANCE METHODS
 ******************************************************************************/

static PyObject *              /* on "instance.push(arg)" */
stack_push(self, args)         /* 'self' is the stack instance object */
    stackobject *self;         /* 'args' are args passed to self.push method */
    PyObject    *args;
{
    char *pstr;
    if (!PyArg_ParseTuple(args, "s", &pstr))      /* convert args: Python->C */
        return NULL;                              /* NULL raises exception,  */
    if (self->top == MAXSTACK)                    /* with arg-error message  */
        onError("stack overflow")
    if (self->len + strlen(pstr) + 1 >= MAXCHARS)
        onError("string-space overflow")
    else {
        strcpy(self->strings + self->len, pstr);
```

*Example 14-2: File: stacktyp.c (continued)*

```
        self->stack[self->top++] = &(self->strings[self->len]);
        self->len += (strlen(pstr) + 1);
        Py_INCREF(Py_None);
        return Py_None;                           /* return None: no errors */
    }
}

static PyObject *
stack_pop(self, args)
    stackobject *self;
    PyObject    *args;                            /* on "instance.pop()" */
{
    PyObject *pstr;
    if (!PyArg_ParseTuple(args, ""))              /* verify no args passed */
        return NULL;
    if (self->top == 0)
        onError("stack underflow")                /* return NULL = raise */
    else {
        pstr = Py_BuildValue("s", self->stack[--self->top]);
        self->len -= (strlen(self->stack[self->top]) + 1);
        return pstr;
    }
}

static PyObject *
stack_top(self, args)
    stackobject *self;
    PyObject    *args;
{
    PyObject *result = stack_pop(self, args);     /* pop and undo */
    if (result != NULL)
        self->len += (strlen(self->stack[self->top++]) + 1);
    return result;
}

static PyObject *
stack_empty(self, args)
    stackobject *self;
    PyObject    *args;
{
    if (!PyArg_ParseTuple(args, ""))
        return NULL;
    return Py_BuildValue("i", self->top == 0);    /* boolean: a python int */
}

static struct PyMethodDef stack_methods[] = {     /* instance methods */
 { "push",       stack_push,     1 },             /* name/address table */
 { "pop",        stack_pop,      1 },             /* like list append, sort */
 { "top",        stack_top,      1 },
 { "empty",      stack_empty,    1 },             /* extra ops besides optrs */
 { NULL,         NULL }                           /* end, for getattr here */
};
```

*Example 14-2: File: stacktyp.c (continued)*

```
/*****************************************************************************
 * BASIC TYPE-OPERATIONS
 *****************************************************************************/

static stackobject *                /* on "x = stacktype.Stack()" */
newstackobject()                    /* instance constructor function */
{                                   /* these don't get an 'args' input */
    stackobject *self;
    self = PyObject_NEW(stackobject, &Stacktype);  /* malloc, init, incref */
    if (self == NULL)
        return NULL;               /* raise exception */
    self->top = 0;                 /* extra constructor logic here */
    self->len = 0;
    return self;                   /* a new type-instance object */
}

static void                        /* instance destructor function */
stack_dealloc(self)                /* when reference-count reaches zero */
    stackobject *self;
{                                  /* do cleanup activity */
    PyMem_DEL(self);               /* same as 'free(self)' */
}

static int
stack_print(self, fp, flags)
    stackobject *self;
    FILE *fp;
    int flags;                         /* print self to file */
{                                      /* or repr or str */
    int i;
    fprintf(fp, "[Stack:\n");
    for (i=self->top - 1; i >= 0; i--)
        fprintf(fp, "%d: '%s'\n", i, self->stack[i]);
    fprintf(fp, "]\n");
    return 0;                          /* return status, not object */
}

static PyObject *
stack_getattr(self, name)              /* on "instance.attr" reference  */
    stackobject *self;                 /* make a bound-method or member */
    char *name;
{                                                     /* exposed data-members */
    if (strcmp(name, "len") == 0)                     /* really C struct fields */
        return Py_BuildValue("i", self->len);
    if (strcmp(name, "__members__") == 0)             /* __methods__ is free */
        return Py_BuildValue("[s]", "len");           /* make a list of 1 string */
    else
        return Py_FindMethod(stack_methods, (PyObject *)self, name);
}

static int
stack_compare(v, w)
```

*Example 14-2: File: stacktyp.c (continued)*

```
    stackobject *v, *w;
{
    int i, test;                /* compare objects and return -1, 0 or 1 */
    if (v->top < w->top)        /* check stack-size, then stacked strings */
        return -1;
    if (v->top > w->top)
        return 1;
    else
        for (i=0; i < v->top; i++)
            if ((test = strcmp(v->stack[i], w->stack[i])) != 0)
                return test;
    return 0;
}


/*****************************************************************************
 * SEQUENCE TYPE-OPERATIONS
 *****************************************************************************/

static int
stack_length(self)
    stackobject *self;              /* called on "len(instance)" */
{
    return self->top;               /* don't wrap in a python object */
}

static PyObject *
stack_concat(self, other)
    stackobject *self;                          /* on "instance + other" */
    PyObject    *other;                         /* 'self' is the instance */
{
    int i, len, top;
    stackobject *new, *right;
    if (! is_stackobject(other))
        onError("'+' requires two stacks")      /* no mixed types */
    right = (stackobject *)other;
    if (self->top + right->top > MAXSTACK)
        onError("stack overflow")               /* will the sum fit? */
    if (self->len + right->len > MAXCHARS)
        onError("string-space overflow")
    else {                                      /* '+' makes new stack object */
        new = newstackobject();                 /* instead of in-place change */
        len = top = 0;
        for (i=0; i < self->top; i++) {
            new->stack[top++] = &(new->strings[len]);
            strcpy(new->strings + len, self->stack[i]);       /* copy self */
            len += (strlen(self->stack[i]) + 1);
        }
        for (i=0; i < right->top; i++) {
            new->stack[top++] = &(new->strings[len]);
            strcpy(new->strings + len, right->stack[i]);      /* copy right */
            len += (strlen(right->stack[i]) + 1);
```

*Example 14-2: File: stacktyp.c (continued)*

```
        }
        new->top = top; new->len = len;
        return (PyObject *)new;
    }
}

static PyObject *
stack_repeat(self, n)                   /* on "instance * N" */
    stackobject *self;                  /* new stack = repeat self n times */
    int n;                              /* XXXX very inefficient! improve me */
{
    int i;
    stackobject *next, *temp;           /* copy self N times */
    temp = newstackobject();            /* start with new, empty stack */
    for (i=0; i < n; i++) {
        next = (stackobject *)stack_concat(temp, self);
        if (next == NULL) {
            Py_XDECREF(temp);                   /* delete result so-far */
            return NULL;                        /* propogate exception */
        }
        else {
            Py_XDECREF(temp);                   /* delete result-so-far */
            temp = next;                        /* set new result */
        }
    }
    return (PyObject *)temp;
}

static PyObject *
stack_item(self, index)                         /* on "instance[offset]", "in/for" */
    stackobject *self;                          /* return the i-th item of self */
    int index;                                  /* negative index pre-adjusted */
{
    if (index < 0 || index >= self->top) {
        PyErr_SetString(PyExc_IndexError, "index out-of-bounds");
        return NULL;                                        /* not local error: */
    }                                                       /* else 'in' whines */
    else
        return Py_BuildValue("s", self->stack[index]);      /* convert output */
}

static PyObject *
stack_slice(self, ilow, ihigh)
    stackobject *self;                          /* on "instance[ilow:ihigh]" */
    int ilow, ihigh;                            /* negative-adjusted, not scaled */
{
    /* XXXX return the ilow..ihigh slice of self in a new object */
    onError("slicing not yet implemented")
}
```

*Example 14-2: File: stacktyp.c (continued)*

```
/******************************************************************************
 * TYPE DESCRIPTORS
 ******************************************************************************/

static PySequenceMethods stack_as_sequence = { /* sequence supplement     */
      (inquiry)       stack_length,           /* sq_length    "len(x)"   */
      (binaryfunc)    stack_concat,           /* sq_concat    "x + y"    */
      (intargfunc)    stack_repeat,           /* sq_repeat    "x * n"    */
      (intargfunc)    stack_item,             /* sq_item      "x[i], in" */
      (intintargfunc) stack_slice,            /* sq_slice     "x[i:j]"   */
      (intobjargproc)     0,                  /* sq_ass_item  "x[i] = v" */
      (intintobjargproc)  0,                  /* sq_ass_slice "x[i:j]=v" */
};

static PyTypeObject Stacktype = {      /* main python type-descriptor */
  /* type header */                    /* shared by all instances */
      PyObject_HEAD_INIT(&PyType_Type)
      0,                               /* ob_size */
      "stack",                         /* tp_name */
      sizeof(stackobject),             /* tp_basicsize */
      0,                               /* tp_itemsize */

  /* standard methods */
      (destructor)  stack_dealloc,   /* tp_dealloc  ref-count==0  */
      (printfunc)   stack_print,     /* tp_print    "print x"     */
      (getattrfunc) stack_getattr,   /* tp_getattr  "x.attr"      */
      (setattrfunc) 0,               /* tp_setattr  "x.attr=v"    */
      (cmpfunc)     stack_compare,   /* tp_compare  "x > y"       */
      (reprfunc)    0,               /* tp_repr     `x`, print x  */

  /* type categories */
      0,                             /* tp_as_number   +,-,*,/,%,&,>>,pow...*/
      &stack_as_sequence,            /* tp_as_sequence +,[i],[i:j],len, ...*/
      0,                             /* tp_as_mapping  [key], len, ...*/

  /* more methods */
      (hashfunc)   0,                /* tp_hash    "dict[x]" */
      (binaryfunc) 0,                /* tp_call    "x()"     */
      (reprfunc)   0,                /* tp_str     "str(x)"  */

};  /* plus others: see Include/object.h */


/******************************************************************************
 * MODULE LOGIC
 ******************************************************************************/

static PyObject *
stacktype_new(self, args)                  /* on "x = stacktype.Stack()" */
    PyObject *self;                        /* self not used */
    PyObject *args;                        /* constructor args */
{
```

*Example 14-2: File: stacktyp.c (continued)*

```
    if (!PyArg_ParseTuple(args, ""))      /* Module-method function */
        return NULL;
    return (PyObject *)newstackobject();  /* make a new type-instance object */
}                                         /* the hook from module to type... */

static struct PyMethodDef stacktype_methods[] = {
    { "Stack",  stacktype_new,  1 },             /* one function: make a stack */
    { NULL,     NULL }                           /* end marker, for initmodule */
};

void
initstacktype()                    /* on first "import stacktype" */
{
    PyObject *m, *d;
    m = Py_InitModule("stacktype", stacktype_methods);   /* make the module, */
    d = PyModule_GetDict(m);                             /* with 'Stack' func */
    ErrorObject = Py_BuildValue("s", "stacktype.error");
    PyDict_SetItemString(d, "error", ErrorObject);       /* export exception */
    if (PyErr_Occurred())
        Py_FatalError("can't initialize module stacktype");
}
```

## Anatomy of a C Extension Type

Many of the concepts in this code are the same as in extension modules. As before, everything in this file is *static* (local), except the module initialization function. The most obvious difference here is the structure of the file. There are two registration tables now: one for type instance methods, and one for the constructor function module. There's also a new section for a type descriptor, which registers operation handlers as slots (members) in a C *struct*, instead of a name/function table. Here's a brief description of the components of this file; study the code for more details.

*Python header files*

As in the module, we include *Python.h* so we can use Python API tools.

*Local data/logic*

In this version, the stack becomes a C *struct*, so we can allocate multiple copies. The *struct* includes the same information that the module used to represent the stack, and begins with a *PyObject_HEAD*. This macro puts Python-managed information at the front of each instance's allocated memory block: a reference count, plus a pointer to the associated type descriptor, *Stacktype*. We also define a type testing macro, *is_stackobject*, which tests an instance's type descriptor.

*Instance methods*

Like the module file, a set of method-functions follows next. But here, the functions process an implied instance-object: the *self* parameter is passed a pointer to the Python object which was qualified, and the instance methods use *self* to access stack data. This works exactly like the *self* argument in class methods. *args* is a tuple of the arguments passed as before. There's also a *registration table* for instance methods here: they're looked up in the *stack_getattr* function each time an instance is qualified, instead of being resolved at import time.

*Basic type operations*

Next, the file defines functions to handle basic operations common to all types. There are functions for creating new instances and deleting existing instances when their reference counts reach zero (similar to the `__init__` and `__del__` methods of classes). It also provides functions for instance printing, attribute qualification, and comparisons, which all have class method counterparts too. The comparison function returns –1, 0, or 1, to designate a <, ==, or > relationship. Notice that they no longer get *self* and *args* arguments, and the return-value isn't always a *Pyobject**: type operations have more specific signatures.

*Sequence operations*

Functions for handling sequence type operations come next. Stacks respond to most sequence operators: *len*, +, *, and *[i]*. Note that the indexing handler, *stack_item* handles indexing, *in* membership tests, and *for* iterator loops. For the last two items, Python calls the indexing handler repeatedly, with successively higher index values (just like a class's `__getitem__`). To designate the end of the sequence, *stack_item* raises the built-in *IndexError* (*PyExc_IndexError*), not the local error; Python only catches *IndexError* when iterating.

*Type descriptors*

The type descriptors section has two initialized C *structs*: one for registering the basic type operations, and one for registering sequence operations. In fact, the type descriptors give access to all the C functions we coded in the prior three sections. Basic type operations and sequence operations are dispatched directly, through the function pointers stored in the descriptors. Instance method calls are routed indirectly, using the registered *getattr* type operation handler. Because this is a central concept, we'll discuss it further later in this chapter.

*Constructor module*

Finally, at the bottom we define a one-function module, to export the constructor function *stacktype.Stack*. This is the interface clients use to make instances of the type. Everything else in this file is only accessible through an *instance*. As before, we define a static function, a registration-table which gives the function's name and address, and an initialization-function to be called when the stack-type module is first imported.

## Using Type Descriptors

The type descriptor is the Python to C linkage mechanism: it's used to register type operation handler functions. All instances get a pointer to the type descriptor *struct* for dispatching operations at run-time. In effect, it serves the same purpose as a class's attribute dictionary.

The type descriptors section has two intialized C structs: one for basic type operations (*Stacktype*), and one for sequence operations (*stack_as_sequence*). Both are templates, with slots for registering operation handlers as function pointers. In both, a *zero* (*NULL*) pointer means an operation isn't defined for the type. Only the deallocaton method is required to be present.

### Type categories: template supplements

The *stack_as_sequence struct* is a supplement to the main *Stacktype* template; *Stacktype* has a pointer to the supplemental struct. The main type descriptor has slots for up to three supplemental structs: for number, mapping, and sequence-type operations. In fact, the three type category slots determine which operators a type supports, and which category it falls under (see the number and mapping type examples later in this chapter).

For instance, if we want to overload number operators like `^` or `%`, we use the number category slot, and fill in a number supplement struct. This is one way types differ from classes: in classes, we can pick and choose which operators we want to overload, by supplying specially named methods; classes aren't limited to the operators in a category. Types can use more than one category supplement, but it's more complex.

### Mutability: assignment operation slots

The slots for setting components and attributes also determine whether a type is mutable or not. Our stack type leaves the item, slice, and attribute assignment slots zero, since it doesn't support changing stacks below the top, and has no writable attributes. Stack instances are immutable sequences, except for the *push* and *pop* methods. This is analogous to the assignment methods in classes (`__setitem__`, etc.); like types, the class is mutable only if it's defined.

## *How Python Routes Calls to C Type-Handler Functions*

C method calls and operators are dispatched much like C module function calls. But for types, the module only serves to export a constructor function, and (usually) an exception object. The type descriptor is central to everything that happens with type instance objects.

For type instances, methods are looked up in the separate instance method registration table each time they're called. Operators are dispatched by fetching function pointers from the type descriptors, not a registration table. Instance method calls are dispatched in two steps:

- Python first fetches a pointer to the *getattr* handler function from the type descriptor (*stack_getattr*).
- The *getattr* handler calls the API function *Py_FindMethod* to make a bound method object from the instance method registration table, which Python calls.

The *getattr* handler can do whatever it wants with the qualification. For example, *stack_getattr* intercepts `__members__` qualifications, and returns a list with the name of a C data member of the internal implementation. The *getattr* handler works much like the `__getattr__` special method in classes.

### *The life and times of a type instance object*

Here's a more concrete example of the sort of processing that occurs to typical type instance objects.

*Creation.* When a Python client program executes the call:

```
X = stacktype.Stack()
```

the call is routed to the bound-in module's function, and *X* is assigned a new instance of the C stack-type. The constructor function *newstackobject* calls an API function to make a new type-instance object:

```
PyObject_NEW(stackobject, &Stacktype);
```

*PyObject_NEW* allocates a new block of memory to hold an instance's *struct* (*stackobject*), a reference counter, and a pointer to the instance's main type descriptor (*&Stacktype*). It initializes the object's reference count to 1, sets its type pointer, and a new Python object is born (cigars for everyone! :-).

***Method calls.*** Once the type instance object is created, Python programs use its attributes as usual. A method call:

```
X.push('spam')
```

is routed first to the C *stack_gettattr* function, which in turn calls *Py_FindMethod* to look up the name *push* in the instance method registration table. Finally, Python calls the fetched C *stack_push* function, passing the string object *spam* in the *args* argument, and a pointer to the instance-object *X* in *self.*

***Member access.*** Data member references in Python clients:

```
X.__members__
```

are routed to *stack_gettattr* too. But this time, the C function handles the request itself, instead of asking Python to look up a method name. A new Python object is created and returned (a list for `__members__`). If a method is accessed without being called (*X.push*), *Py_FindMethod* makes a bound method object.

***Expressions.*** When *X* is used in an addition expression:

```
X + Y
```

Python fetches a C function pointer from the concatenation handler slot in the sequence supplement of *X*'s type descriptor. The operation is dispatched to the C *stack_concat* function.

***Deallocation.*** Finally, when the instance object's reference count falls to zero, Python calls the registered destructor function, *stack_dealloc*, to perform cleanup actions and free the memory block with *PyMem_DEL*. At this point, we can assume the object has had a full and productive life and we may close any data associated with it. Figure 14-3 illustrates most of the steps we just described.

The type descriptor is used every time we process a type instance, much like a class's attribute dictionary. By following its links, Python finds registered stack functionality in a variety of forms:

*Table 14-2: Operations supported by the C stack type*

| Methods | Basic operations | Sequence operations | Data members |
|---|---|---|---|
| *push* | new | Length: *len(x)* | `__methods__` |
| *pop* | dealloc | Concatenation: + | `__members__` |
| *top* | Print: *print x* | Repeat: * | *len* (C *struct* information) |
| *empty* | Getattr: *x.attr* | Item: *[i], in, for* | |
| | Compare: *cmp*, <, == | Slice: *[i:j]* (not coded) | |

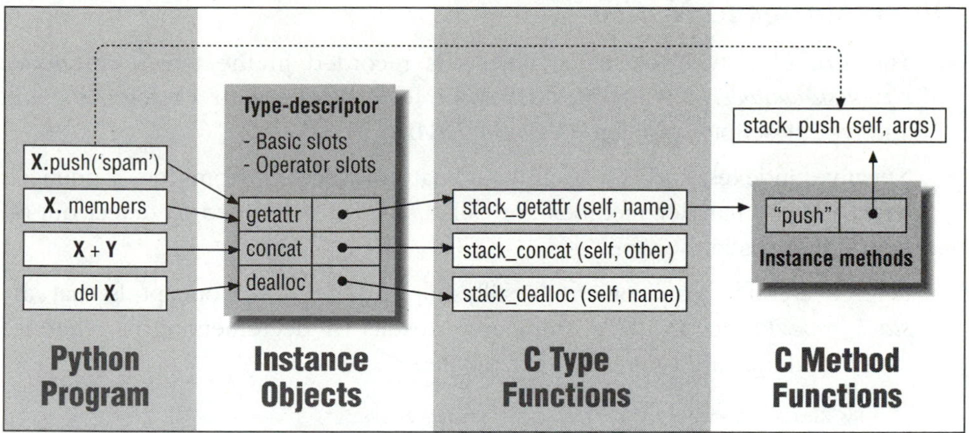


*Figure 14-3: C type operation dispatching*

*Notes:*

- Methods are found indirectly, using the *getattr* handler and the instance registration table
- Basic and sequence type operations come from type descriptors directly
- Data members come from the *getattr* handler function's logic
- The *new* operation is exported by a module, and `__methods__` is automatically defined

## *How C Type Code Gets Linked into Python*

Just like extension modules, types are added to Python by either static binding or dynamic binding.

*Static binding*
: Add a line to *Modules/Setup* like *stacktype stacktyp.c*, put the source file (or a link to it) in the *Modules* directory, and re-make Python.

*Dynamic binding*
: Compile the source file into a dynamically loadable object file and put it in a directory named in the *PYTHONPATH* environment variable.

Under either scheme, the module containing the *Stack* constructor function becomes available for import in Python programs. The Python run-time system handles the routing of calls to registered C functions.

## Other Things to Notice

- The size of a type's instance objects is recorded in the type's descriptor: *sizeof(stackobject)* already includes space for a header with a reference count and type descriptor pointer (*PyObject_HEAD*).
- Negative indexes and slices are automatically scaled from the sequence's length before handler methods are called. But we still need to detect out-of-bound indexes in the type.
- Reference-count management is still simple. One new concept is that the *stack_repeat* function deletes temporary results by decrementing its reference count (making sure to ignore *NULL* pointers):

```
Py_XDECREF(temp);        /* delete result so-far */
```

- When printing type instances, three operation slots are tried: *print*, *repr*, or *str*. If none is defined, a default format is used (< . . . >). Object-to-string conversions (backquotes, *repr* and *str* built-ins) skip the *print* operation slot. The stack type only defines *print*.
- As mentioned earlier in relation to classes, deletion of C sequence and mapping type components is detected as an assignment of a *NULL* value. See Chapter 12, *Persistent Information*, for more details.
- Usually, the *dealloc* operation handler must be defined. In all other cases, Python checks for *NULL* pointers and does something reasonable. For instance, a default output format is used if there's no registered *print* (or string conversion) operation, and an exception is raised when an object that doesn't register an *item* handler is indexed (*X[i]*).
- For the stack type, the filename (*stacktyp.c*) isn't the same as the module name (*stacktype*). When binding modules statically, the initialization function name (*initstacktype*) should match the module name coded in the *Modules/Setup* entry shown above; the filename is irrelevant at run-time. File and initialization-function names vary when binding dynamically.

Suggested exercises:

1. Given a stack type instance *X*, what's the difference between *X.len* and *len(X)*? How is each resolved internally by the C stack type implementation?
2. Code the empty slicing operation method; scale out-of-bounds slice indexes instead of raising exceptions (like built-in lists). Add a *repr* function and register it by adding it to the type descriptor. (*repr* is called to create the string representation of a type; it's like *print*, but returns the text instead of printing it.)

3. Allow *MAXSTACK* and *MAXCHARS* to vary per instance. Pass them in to the *Stack* constructor function, and make separate memory blocks for the pointer and character arrays.
4. Change the stack implementation to be more dynamic. As is, it uses the same fixed-length arrays for stack and string storage arrays that the module used. This example was used for illustration, but it's not consistent with other dynamic data structures in Python. It would be better to use linked lists and *malloc* each string added to a stack; this is slower but allows for variable-length stacks. Code this change. Where and when would you delete the *malloc*'d stack data of an instance?
5. Implement stacks of arbitrary Python objects: push *PyObject** pointers, *INCREF* when pushed and *DECREF* when popped. Do you think your stack type is faster than Python's built-in lists? Bind the new extension into Python and time the two versions to find out.
6. Study extension modules and types in the Python source tree. At present, *Modules/dbmmodule.c* is a mapping type, *Objects/intobject.c* is a numeric type, and *Objects/listobject.c* is another sequence type. Number descriptors are bigger than sequences, and mappings are smaller (also see the discussion and examples below).

   To improve performance, the *intobject* type caches and reuses small integer value objects. This minimizes heap allocations; it only works because numbers are immutable (it doesn't matter if two numbers share the same *struct*). Notice that the integer and list types don't have a module interface: They're not imported and constructed with a function call, because they have special constructor syntax (`24`, `[1, 2, 3]`). As a rule, things in the *Objects* directory are intrinsic types, without modules.
7. The C stack type doesn't export a function for creating instances from C: we can only make instances by calling the *stacktype.Stack* constructor function from Python code. In fact, everything in the C file is static (local to the file), except for the module initialization function (*initstacktype*). How would you make stack instances in C, using this interface? (Hint: you could either export the *newstackobject* function, or run an embedded Python type-constructor call from C; see Chapter 15).

## Testing the Extension Type

Now let's interact with the C stack type to show how its features are used. There are both a C module here (to export the *Stack* constructor function) and a C type that defines instance methods, members, and operators. Most of the C logic is devoted to type instance operations.

### *Basic usage*

Just like the simple module, the stack type's module is bound in to the Python executable; we import it like a normal built-in module, and call its *Stack* function to create instances of the datatype. We can make as many instances as we need: each gets its own local stack, which is manipulated by calling the methods and operators implemented by the C type, and accessing data members (*len*). Stack instance attributes are accessed by qualifying an instance, just like instances of Python classes and built-in types (files, etc.).

Here again, the interaction will probably seem familiar: it's exactly as if we're importing a Python-coded class, making instances, and calling their methods. As long as we only make instances and call methods through instances, there's no real distinction to clients. Python handles initialization and routes method calls to C functions; the C functions handle type conversions. It's only when we try to subclass C types or access unbound methods that the differences become apparent.

```
% python
>>> import stacktype                          load the type's module
>>> x = stacktype.Stack()                     make a type-instance
>>> x.push('new')                             call type-instance methods
>>> x                                         call the type's print function
[Stack:
0: 'new'
]
```

### *Using stack operators*

Many of the stack module's methods become operators in the type. Once we've made an instance we can process it with both method calls, and operators defined by the stack type, exactly like built-in types (for instance, *append* and + for lists). It's up to the C type to determine which operator categories (sequence, mapping, or number) apply, and to fill in appropriate operator slots in the type descriptors.

Here, the stack is a sequence: it supports indexing (*[1]*), slicing (*[0:1]*), concatenation (+), and more. We can also step through a stack's items in a *for* loop: the registered *stack_item* method is used for indexing, *in* membership tests, and *for* loops. For *in* and *for*, Python calls *stack_item* repeatedly until an *IndexError* is raised (signaling the end of the sequence); as for classes, the registered *stack_length* method isn't used for *in*. For this method to work, *stack_item* has to set the exception object to *PyExc_IndexError* (*IndexError* in Python), not the local exception object *ErrorObject*.

```
>>> x[0]                                      C function: stack_item
'new'
>>> x[1]                                      raise IndexError, not stacktype.error
Traceback (innermost last):
  File "<stdin>", line 1, in ?
```

```
IndexError: index out-of-bounds
>>>
>>> x[0:1]                                      stack_slice
Traceback (innermost last):
  File "<stdin>", line 1, in ?
stacktype.error: slicing not yet implemented
>>>
>>> x = x + 'd'                                 stack_concat
Traceback (innermost last):
  File "<stdin>", line 1, in ?
stacktype.error: '+' requires two stacks
>>>
>>> y = stacktype.Stack()                       stacktype_new -> newstackobject
>>> for c in 'SPAM': y.push(c)                  stack_getattr -> stack_push
...
>>> y
[Stack:
3: 'M'
2: 'A'
1: 'P'
0: 'S'
]

>>> z = x + y                                   stack concatenation: stack_concat
>>> z
[Stack:
4: 'M'
3: 'A'
2: 'P'
1: 'S'
0: 'new'
]

>>> len(z), z[0], z[-1]                         len, item, negative indexes
(5, 'new', 'M')
>>> x
[Stack:
0: 'new'
]
```

### *Inspecting stack instances*

All types get the built-in __methods__ member for free: it returns a list of the method-function names defined for instances (in the C name/function registration table). __members__ is defined by the stack type itself by testing attribute names when a qualification is being resolved (in *stack_getattr*). It returns data members of the C representation that we want to expose to Python (*len*, the size of the string array). Printing a stack calls the *stack_print* method, but backquotes, and *str* and *repr* built-ins make a default string representation; we'd have to provide *repr* or *str* methods in the C type to improve this situation.

```
>>> x.__methods__                               built-in attribute
['empty', 'pop', 'push', 'top']
>>> x.__members__                               stack_getattr
['len']
>>> x.len, z.len                                stack_getattr
(4, 12)
>>> len(x)                                      stack_length
1
>>> x * 4                                       stack repetition: stack_repeat
[Stack:
3: 'new'
2: 'new'
1: 'new'
0: 'new'
]

>>> for s in z: print s,                        stack iteration: stack_item
...
new S P A M
>>> 'S' in z, 'Q' in z                          stack membership: stack_item
(1, 0)
>>>
>>> dir(stacktype)
['Stack', '__doc__', '__name__', 'error']
>>> print y
[Stack:
3: 'M'
2: 'A'
1: 'P'
0: 'S'
]

>>> `y`
'<stack object at cb000>'
>>> str(y), repr(y)
('<stack object at cb000>', '<stack object at cb000>')
>>>
```

### *Using stack comparisons*

Like C's *strcmp*, class and type comparisons return –1, 0, or 1, for "less than," "equal," or "greater than" results; the C type's *stack_compare* is registered to handle all comparison requests. The built-in *cmp* function returns the comparison result directly, but Python uses the result to evaluate comparison operators (>, ==. etc.). Python's *is* operator tests for object identity (i.e., whether the objects reference the same memory address), instead of calling the *stack_compare* method.

Notice that there are three ways to copy a stack, even without defining slicing or constructor arguments: by manually copying items over or by using the `+` or `*` operators, as shown here. The same techniques can be used to copy built-in sequences without slicing: lists, strings, and tuples (`[] + list`, `list * 1`).

```
>>> t = stacktype.Stack()
>>> for s in y: t.push(s)                  1 of 3 ways to copy...
...
>>> t                                       stack_print
[Stack:
3: 'M'
2: 'A'
1: 'P'
0: 'S'
]
>>> t == y, t is y, t > y, t >= y           stack_compare
(1, 0, 0, 1)
>>> y.pop()                                 stack_getattr -> stack_pop
'M'
>>> t == y, t is y, t > y, t >= y
(0, 0, 1, 1)
>>> y < y, y < t
(0, 1)
>>> t = y                                   '=' makes shared references as usual
>>> t.pop()
'A'
>>> y
[Stack:
1: 'P'
0: 'S'
]

>>> t = stacktype.Stack() + y               copy method 2...
>>> t.pop();  t.push('Q')
'P'
>>> t
[Stack:
1: 'Q'
0: 'S'
]

>>> y
[Stack:
1: 'P'
0: 'S'
]

>>> t == y, t is y, t <> y, t < y, t > y
(0, 0, 1, 0, 1)
>>> cmp(t, y), cmp(y, t)                    stack_compare
(1, -1)
>>>
>>> t = y * 1                               copy method 3... (y[:] not supported)
>>> t is y, t == y                          address test, stack_compare
(0, 1)
>>> t
[Stack:
1: 'P'
0: 'S'
]
```

### *More exceptions*

The type handles errors in the same way as the module we saw earlier. Notice that the *len* instance method isn't the same as calling the *len()* built-in function with a stack instance. The former returns the instance's *len* data member (the size of the internal character-array), and the latter calls the registered *stack_length* function to fetch the number of items in the stack.

```
>>> for i in range(1000): y.push('hello' + `i`)        stack_push
...
Traceback (innermost last):
  File "<stdin>", line 1, in ?
stacktype.error: string-space overflow
>>>
>>> y.len, y[-2], len(y), y.top()
(2045, 'hello237', 241, 'hello238')
>>> t.top()
'p'
>>> try:
...     y = y + y                                        stack_concat
... except stacktype.error, message:                     catch stack-type exception
...     print message
...
string-space overflow
>>> y.len
2045
```

## *How Much Faster are the C Module and Type?*

Let's compare the performance of the C-based stack implementations to the Python module and class we discussed in Chapter 13. After all, performance was a primary reason for migration to C here.

### *The timer module*

First, we need a way to measure elapsed time. We can reuse the timer module discussed in Chapter 13.

*Example 14-3: File: timer.py*

```
def test(reps, func):
    import time
    start = time.time()             # current seconds
    for i in xrange(reps):
        x = func(i)                 # call it 'reps' times
    return time.time() - start      # stop - start time
```

### *The test driver*

Next, we write a test driver script that exercises the Python and C stack implementations.

*Example 14-4: File: exttim.py*

```
#!/usr/local/bin/python
from timer import test                  # second counter (time.time)
import stack1, stack2, faststack        # python stacks: module, classes
import stackmod, stacktype              # c extension stacks: module, type

from sys import argv
from string import atoi                   # versus eval()
rep, pushes, pops, items = 50, 50, 50, 50  # defaults
try:
    [rep, pushes, pops, items] = map(atoi, argv[1:])
except: pass
print rep, pushes, pops, items

def doit_module(mod):
    for i in range(pushes): mod.push('hello')    # strings only for C
    for i in range(items):  t = mod.item(i)
    for i in range(pops):   mod.pop()

def doit_object(Maker):                          # type has no init args
    x = Maker()                                  # type or class instance
    for i in range(pushes): x.push('hello')      # strings only for C
    for i in range(items):  t = x[i]
    for i in range(pops):   x.pop()

# test modules: python/c
print "Python module:", test(rep, lambda i: doit_module(stack1))
print "C ext module: ", test(rep, lambda i: doit_module(stackmod)), '\n'

# test objects: class/type
print "Python Stack:    ", test(rep, lambda i: doit_object(stack2.Stack))
print "Python FastStack:", test(rep, lambda i: doit_object(faststack.FastStack))
print "C Stack exttype: ", test(rep, lambda i: doit_object(stacktype.Stack))
```

### *The results are in*

Finally, the output reported by this script appears below. There are three conclusions we can draw:

- The C module is roughly three times faster than the equivalent Python module.
- The C type is about four times faster than the original Python *Stack* class
- The C type is at least three times faster than the optimized Python *FastStack* class.

Of course, these claims must be qualified by the fact that different test scenarios will behave differently and by pragmatic factors such as the quality of the C compiler, whether the extensions were compiled with optimizations or not, and the accuracy of the timing functions. But in general, the speedup is substantial.

Further, the C implementations aren't influenced by operation mixtures like the optimized Python *FastStack* is. The C type is consistently four times better than *Stack* and often much more than three times better than *FastStack*. For string stacks at least, the C type is a clear winner over the optimized Python class. In fact, C implementations can sometimes beat improved Python algorithms.

```
% exttim.py
50 50 50 50
Python module: 27.5023419857
C ext module:  10.410284996

Python Stack:      37.6321159601
Python FastStack: 93.4225100279
C Stack exttype:  8.73115205765

% exttim.py 100 20 20 10
100 20 20 10
Python module: 17.9466160536
C ext module:  7.32388603687

Python Stack:      26.4153330326
Python FastStack: 25.7986600399
C Stack exttype:  7.29558992386

% exttim.py 50 20 20 0
50 20 20 0
Python module: 8.22448396683
C ext module:  3.17821490765

Python Stack:      11.93866992
Python FastStack: 8.62700295448
C Stack exttype:  3.20586705208

% exttim.py 5 50 50 20
5 50 50 20
Python module: 2.66598296165
C ext module:  1.13262403011

Python Stack:      4.15749597549
Python FastStack: 3.7459230423
C Stack exttype:  1.06879794598
```

### *Size isn't everything*

As before, these results will differ among machines, but should be relatively similar. These tests were run on a slow PC-based machine, with no other processes active at test time. But the test machine's hardware details are far too embarrassing to reveal here :-).

### *Performance measurement in multiprocess environments*

As mentioned in Chapter 13, the *time.time* function returns the wall-time in seconds; we subtract start and stop times to get total elapsed seconds. But this doesn't work well if the processor is also serving other tasks while the test is being run: results are influenced strongly by the system's load during tests.

To compensate, we've used *time.time*, and run tests without any other activity going on in parallel on the test machine. But there are at least four ways to perform timing tests in Python:

*time.time()*
: The wall-clock seconds function we've been using.

*time.clock()*
: The processor (CPU) time used by the process, in seconds.

*os.times()*
: A tuple of four values: (user CPU time, system CPU time, child user time, child system time).

*% time <cmd>*
: A command-line program that reports user, system, etc. CPU times for a shell command.

The last three of these methods can be used to measure the CPU time used by a process, instead of actual elapsed time. On a multiprocessing system like UNIX, this is usually more accurate. The *time.clock* function is the same as the standard C library *clock* function, but it divides the result by the *clocks per second* constant automatically, to yield a result in seconds.

Unfortunately, the last three techniques aren't universally portable, which is why we've been using *time.time* so far. Further, the results for *time.time* and *time.clock* are virtually identical if there's no other activity on the machine while a test is being run. But where applicable, the *clock* function is often better.

***An improved timer module.*** Here's a new timer module which returns both wall-time and actual CPU time for running a function.

*Example 14-5: File: timer2.py*

```
def test(reps, func):
    import time
    start_wall = time.time()                    # current real seconds
    start_cpu  = time.clock()                   # current processor secs
    for i in xrange(reps):                      # call it 'reps' times
        x = func(i)
    cpu_time  = time.clock() - start_cpu
    wall_time = time.time()  - start_wall       # total = stop - start time
    return { 'cpu': cpu_time, 'wall': wall_time }
```

***Results with no competition.*** If we replace the *timer* import in our time scripts with *timer2*, we get similar results for wall and CPU elapsed time if no other processes are at work.

```
% python exttim.py
50 50 50 50
Python module: { 'cpu': 16.48, 'wall': 16.6019810438 }
C ext module:  { 'cpu': 6.44, 'wall': 7.15087091923 }

Python Stack:     { 'cpu': 23.81, 'wall': 24.8268470764 }
Python FastStack: { 'cpu': 52.72, 'wall': 53.1106050014 }
C Stack exttype:  { 'cpu': 5.34, 'wall': 5.73373091221 }

% python settime2.py 1
start...
{ 'cpu': 19.19, 'wall': 19.2964919806 }
{ 'cpu': 4.24, 'wall': 4.65165698528 }

% python stacktim.py 50 50 10
{ 'cpu': 12.49, 'wall': 12.501363039 }
{ 'cpu': 10.3, 'wall': 10.3846340179 }
```

***Results vary by system load.*** But when there's other activity, the wall-time results are inaccurate. Note that these results were run on a different machine, but are proportional to the earlier tests. They also vary significantly, due to the precision of the timing functions on the host machine. Performance measurement is an inexact science!

```
% python stacktim.py 50 50 10
{ 'cpu': 14.35, 'wall': 24.0419069529 }        wall-time too big, but proportional
{ 'cpu': 11.11, 'wall': 22.6884750128 }

% python stacktim.py 50 50 10
{ 'cpu': 12.55, 'wall': 16.1622509956 }        optimized stack loses by wall-time
{ 'cpu': 8.76, 'wall': 18.1656130552 }

% python stacktim.py 50 50 10
{ 'cpu': 12.67, 'wall': 29.3420358896 }        optimized stack wins too big here
```

```
{ 'cpu': 10.27, 'wall': 17.6955940723 }

% python stacktim.py 50 50 10
{ 'cpu': 9.58, 'wall': 13.4472529888 }        optimized stack loses by wall-time
{ 'cpu': 8.7, 'wall': 15.6518740654 }
```

### *Comparing apples and oranges?*

To some extent, the comparison here isn't completely fair: the C stacks have limited lengths and only support Python string objects; the Python stacks are much more general.

C's performance would probably be about the same if it supported arbitrary object stacks (we'd just stack *PyObject**s instead of characters). But arbitrary-length stacks may slow the C version significantly: we'd have to call *malloc* and *free* to push and pop items, and this is usually the biggest bottleneck in Python itself. (On the other hand, we wouldn't need to copy strings onto the stack.)

Nevertheless, the results here are roughly indicative of C migration effects: it's almost always a major win. In fact, for some applications such as numeric processing, the speed gain for moving to C or FORTRAN can be far more dramatic than the improvement we achieved here.

## *Implementing Mapping and Number Types*

The stack extension type illustrates how to implement sequence objects: collections that respond to operations like indexing, concatenation, and iteration. As mentioned earlier, C types can also take the form of mappings and numbers, and respond to all the operations used for built-in dictionaries and number types. We just need to link an appropriate supplemental type descriptor to the main type *struct*, in the type category slots. Here we'll take a brief look at how these other types are implemented.

### *A mapping type: Python dictionaries*

To illustrate, the switching logic used to implement Python's dictionary type appears below. It's taken from file *Objects/mappingobject.c* in the Python build tree written by Python's inventor, Guido van Rossum. We won't show the entire implementation here: see the source code for more details. The listings give the signatures for new C functions, and comments give the context in which each type slot's method is applied.

*Example 14-6: File: mapping.txt*

```
typedef struct {
    PyObject_HEAD
    ...etc.              /* a dictionary instance */
} mappingobject;

static int mapping_length(mappingobject *mp);
static PyObject *mapping_subscript(mappingobject *mp, PyObject *key);
static int mapping_ass_sub(mappingobject *mp, PyObject *key, PyObject *value);


static PyMappingMethods mapping_as_mapping = {  /* mapping type supplement */
        (inquiry)       mapping_length,         /* mp_length        'len(x)'  */
        (binaryfunc)    mapping_subscript,      /* mp_subscript     'x[k]'    */
        (objobjargproc) mapping_ass_sub,        /* mp_ass_subscript 'x[k] = v'*/
};

static struct PyMethodDef mapp_methods[] = {      /* dictionary methods */
        { "has_key",      mapping_has_key },      /* 'dict.has_key(k)'  */
        { "items",        mapping_items },        /* 'dict.items()'     */
        { "keys",         mapping_keys },         /* 'dict.keys()'      */
        { "values",       mapping_values },       /* 'dict.values()'    */
        { NULL,           NULL }
};

static PyObject *mapping_getattr(mappingobject *mp, char *name)
{
        return Py_FindMethod(mapp_methods, (PyObject *)mp, name);
}

PyTypeObject Mappingtype = {                  /* dictionary type-descriptor */
        PyObject_HEAD_INIT(&PyType_Type)      /* shared by all instances    */
        0,
        "dictionary",
        sizeof(mappingobject),
        0,
        (destructor)mapping_dealloc,      /* tp_dealloc */
        (printfunc)mapping_print,         /* tp_print */
        (getattrfunc)mapping_getattr,     /* tp_getattr: search method table */
        0,                                /* tp_setattr: no mutable attributes */
        (cmpfunc)mapping_compare,         /* tp_compare */
        (reprfunc)mapping_repr,           /* tp_repr */
        0,                                /* tp_as_number */
        0,                                /* tp_as_sequence */
        &mapping_as_mapping,              /* tp_as_mapping: the operator link */
};                                        /* the rest are all zero (unused) */
```

As we've seen, dictionaries provide both methods and operators:

*Methods*

To resolve method references (i.e., attributes), the main type descriptor installs the *mapping_getattr* function: as in the stack type, *Py_FindMethod* looks up the method by name in the type's registration table.

*Operators*

For operators, the main type descriptor contains a link to the *mapping_as_mapping* supplement in the mapping category slot. When a dictionary appears in an expression (*len*, indexing), Python follows the link to a handler function.

In fact, this type descriptor routes operations just like the stack type seen earlier in this chapter. The only difference is that this type uses the mapping slot and configures a different supplemental descriptor; it's not a sequence.

### A number type: Python integers

To implement a C type that responds to numeric operators (+, *, etc.) we define a different type supplement descriptor. This descriptor is much larger than mapping or sequence descriptors: there are more operators to overload. To illustrate, we again turn to a built-in type: Python integers. The following logic comes from the file *Objects/intobject.c*, written by Guido van Rossum. Here too, we'll just show the configuration tables; for more details, refer to the source file.

*Example 14-7: File: integer.txt*

```
typedef struct {
        PyObject_HEAD     /* an integer instance object */
        long ob_ival;     /* shared/reused when possible */
} intobject;

static int int_nonzero(intobject *v);                              /*inquiry*/
static PyObject *int_neg(intobject *v);                            /*unary*/
static PyObject *int_add(intobject *v, intobject *w);              /*binary*/
static PyObject *int_pow(intobject *v, intobject *w, intobject *z); /*ternary*/


static PyNumberMethods int_as_number = {  /* number type supplement */
        (binaryfunc)  int_add,            /* nb_add       'x + y'          */
        (binaryfunc)  int_sub,            /* nb_subtract  'x - y'          */
        (binaryfunc)  int_mul,            /* nb_multiply  'x * y'          */
        (binaryfunc)  int_div,            /* nb_divide    'x / y'          */
        (binaryfunc)  int_mod,            /* nb_remainder 'x % y'          */
        (binaryfunc)  int_divmod,         /* nb_divmod    'divmod(x, y)'   */
        (ternaryfunc) int_pow,            /* nb_power     'pow(x, y)'      */
        (unaryfunc)   int_neg,            /* nb_negative  '-x'             */
        (unaryfunc)   int_pos,            /* nb_positive  '+x'             */
        (unaryfunc)   int_abs,            /* nb_absolute  'abs(x)'         */
        (inquiry)     int_nonzero,        /* nb_nonzero   'if x'           */
        (unaryfunc)   int_invert,         /* nb_invert    '~x'             */
        (binaryfunc)  int_lshift,         /* nb_lshift    'x << y'         */
        (binaryfunc)  int_rshift,         /* nb_rshift    'x >> y'         */
        (binaryfunc)  int_and,            /* nb_and       'x & y'          */
        (binaryfunc)  int_xor,            /* nb_xor       'x ^ y'          */
        (binaryfunc)  int_or,             /* nb_or        'x | y'          */
        0,                                /* nb_coerce    (n/a)            */
```

*Example 14-7: File: integer.txt (continued)*

```
        (unaryfunc)   int_int,              /* nb_int      'int(x)'      */
        (unaryfunc)   int_long,             /* nb_long     'long(x)'     */
        (unaryfunc)   int_float,            /* nb_float    'float(x)'    */
        (unaryfunc)   int_oct,              /* nb_oct      'oct(x)'      */
        (unaryfunc)   int_hex,              /* nb_hex      'hex(x)'      */
};

PyTypeObject Inttype = {
        PyObject_HEAD_INIT(&PyType_Type)
        0,
        "int",
        sizeof(intobject),
        0,
        (destructor)int_dealloc,   /* tp_dealloc */
        (printfunc)int_print,      /* tp_print */
        0,                         /* tp_getattr */
        0,                         /* tp_setattr */
        (cmpfunc)int_compare,      /* tp_compare */
        (reprfunc)int_repr,        /* tp_repr */
        &int_as_number,            /* tp_as_number: the link */
        0,                         /* tp_as_sequence */
        0,                         /* tp_as_mapping */
        (hashfunc)int_hash,        /* tp_hash */
};                                 /* rest are zero */
```

Since integers are a central datatype, most of the number operation slots are filled in. In user-defined numeric types, we can pick and choose operators to respond to. In Python 1.5 (and later), use NULL pointers in unimplemented operation slots. Python releases 1.4 and earlier might not detect NULL pointers; instead, provide pointers to dummy functions for unimplemented operations.

Integers don't define the *coerce* operation, since Python converts numbers up in other types (floats, longs): because integers are the most primitive type, there's no upward conversion to implement. Other types use the coerce slot to convert up, in mixed-type expressions (see the float type's implementation for details). As mentioned earlier, the integer type reuses instance heap blocks where possible, to minimize heap allocations and deallocations.

### *Other possibilities*

The stack type demonstrates most of the common sequence type methods. The only common operations it doesn't implement are assignment to indexes, slices, and attributes (stacks are roughly immutable). To add these, we just define functions and add them to the type descriptor or supplement slots:

```
/* list[index] = value */
static int list_ass_item(listobject *list, int index, PyObject *value);

/* list[low:high] = value */
```

```
static int list_ass_slice(listobject *list, int low, int high, PyObject *value);

/* object.attribute = value */
static int mytype_setattr(mytype *x, char *name, PyObject *value);
```

It's also possible to implement types that don't fall into any category: if we leave all three category slots blank in the descriptor, types can still implement objects' attributes (members, methods). Although such types won't respond to operators, attributes are enough in some contexts (Python file objects, for example).

Finally, to mix operators from different type categories we can provide more than one linked category supplement (in fact, this is how class-instance objects are implemented). But the order in which Python resolves operations in this case isn't intuitive. For instance, if we provide both mapping and sequence supplements, an expression *object[index]* can be resolved as a either a sequence or mapping index. Since the choice is ambiguous, extensions shouldn't depend on which type's methods are selected first.

### *Python is extensible to the core*

Notice how Python itself is built with the same extension tools exported for use by Python programmers. Every built-in type is really a C extension type. This is one reason that integration is so straightforward in Python: it's a core component of the system itself.

Although these examples implement Python types, we can implement mappings and numbers of our own by imitating the configuration logic here and linking in the extension. For instance, the *dbm* extension implements mapping operations in the same way as built-in dictionaries. It's just a matter of filling in the slots with your own functions.

## *Getting Keyword Argument Values in C Functions and Methods*

Since C extension functions have argument names that Python doesn't know about, keywords in calls aren't passed to C extensions by default. As we've seen, they get the *self* object pointer (for use by types), plus the argument tuple. The argument tuple only contains nonkeyword arguments in the call.

But C extensions can support keyword arguments too by setting special flags. In the name/address *PyMethodDef* registration table of a module or type, the third entry is an integer flag. So far we've used values 0 and 1 to get different argument tuple behavior (1 means the arguments are always in a tuple).

If the third value in a registration table's entry is 2, Python will also pass a dictionary holding the keyword values to the C function as a third argument. The value has a symbolic name *METH_KEYWORDS* in the method object include file. Here's an abstract example:

```
static PyObject *
function(PyObject *self, PyObject *args, PyObject *keywordDict)
{ ... }

static struct PyMethodDef methods[] = {
    { "name", function, METH_KEYWORDS },      /* flag=2: pass keywords */
}
```

In fact, the third argument works just like the ***name* catch-all for keywords in Python functions. But here, it always gets *all* keyword arguments, since Python doesn't know how to match them to C variable names. Within the C function, keyword values can be fetched using the dictionary-access API functions we'll use in Chapter 15. For instance, given a key passed as a C character string, *PyDict_GetItemString(pdict, cstring)* fetches a dictionary value.

Note that this approach works for both C functions, and C type methods because both implement callable attributes as *PyMethodDef* registration tables. Also notice that this technique assumes that clients know about the keyword names supported by the C extension function; they may or may not have a relation to the original C source file's names. The current definition of *PyMethodDef* actually allows for up to four slots:

*Table 14-3: Registration table slots*

| Field | Type | Role |
|---|---|---|
| Name | *char** | Attribute name in Python |
| Function | Function pointer | C function to call |
| Flags | Integer | Argument passing mode |
| Doc-string | *char** | Documentation string |

The *doc-string* entry becomes the method's `__doc__` attribute if present (documentation strings are covered in Appendix A, *...And Other Cool Stuff*). The *flags* entry uses the values in the following table.

*Table 14-4: Registration table argument-passing flags*

| Value | Name | Meaning |
|---|---|---|
| 0 | <no constant> | Don't tuple arguments: use *PyArg_Parse* |
| 1 | *METH_VARARGS* | Always tuple arguments: use *PyArg_ParseTuple* |
| 2 | *METH_KEYWORDS* | Pass keyword dictionary argument too |

As usual in C, *PyMethodDef* fields default to zero (*NULL*) if omitted. Most of these details are prone to change; see include file *methodobject.h* and/or the Python extension manual for up-to-date details. Like methods, documentation strings can be associated with C modules too, by calling a special version of the module initialization routine, with extra arguments. See *modsupport.h* for more details.

## *Making C Types More Object Oriented: Wrapper Classes*

As we've seen, C extension types serve the same roles as Python classes, and are implemented in similar ways. But there's no inheritance in types: type instance attributes come straight from C *structs*, flat registration tables, or program logic. Because of this, C types can't inherit attributes from each other, or from Python classes. There's also no notion of unbound methods for C types, unlike classes.

Further, Python classes can't inherit from C types either: types don't have an attribute dictionary. But we can work around this limitation: by adding Python *stub* wrapper classes as interfaces to types, Python classes can subclass C types to specialize them. For instance, here's a wrapper class for the C stack type:

*Example 14-8: File: oopstack.py*

```
import stacktype                                    # get the C type/module
class Stack:
    def __init__(self, start=None):                 # make/wrap a C type-instance
        self._base = start or stacktype.Stack()     # deleted when class-instance is
    def __getattr__(self, name):
        return getattr(self._base, name)            # methods/members: type-instance
    def __cmp__(self, other):
        return cmp(self._base, other)
    def __repr__(self):                             # 'print' is not really repr
        print self._base,; return ''
    def __add__(self, other):                       # operators: special methods
        return Stack(self._base + other._base)      # operators are not attributes
    def __mul__(self, n):
        return Stack(self._base * n)                # wrap result in a new Stack
    def __getitem__(self, i):
        return self._base[i]                        # 'item': index, in, for
    def __len__(self):
        return len(self._base)
```

Class *Stack* makes a new stack type instance, or wraps an existing one passed in. The type instance is embedded in the class instance, as member *_base*. If something is passed in to the *Stack* constructor, it's assumed to be a type instance (this should probably be verified at run-time by the class).

Such stub classes are mostly empty shells: they wrap a type instance using class-based operator overloading and metaclass protocols we saw earlier. For instance, the `__getattr__` method handles all named type attributes (methods, members).

Python clients can use the class as though it was the original C type. But more importantly, Python clients can extend and override the type's operations by subclassing:

*Example 14-9: File: substack.py*

```
from oopstack import Stack              # get the 'stub' class (C-type wrapper)

class Substack(Stack):
    def __init__(self, start=[]):       # extend the 'new' operation
        Stack.__init__(self)            # initialize stack from any sequence
        for str in start:               # start can be another stack too
            self.push(str)
    def morestuff(self):                # add a new method
        print 'more stack stuff'
    def __getitem__(self, i):           # extend 'item' to trace accesses
        print 'accessing cell', i
        return Stack.__getitem__(self, i)
```

Here's how these classes may be used; most operations are passed to the embedded C type instance.

```
% python
>>> import oopstack, substack
>>> x = oopstack.Stack()                          make a wrapper-class instance
>>> x.push('class')                               __getattr__ -> type getattr
>>> x * 2                                         __mul__ -> type mul
[Stack:
1: 'class'
0: 'class'
]

>>> y = oopstack.Stack()                          make class + type objects
>>> for c in "SPAM": y.push(c)
...
>>> y[2]                                          __getitem__ -> type indexing
'A'
>>> z = x + y                                     __add__ -> type add
>>> for s in z: print s,                          use new class/type instance
...
class S P A M
>>> len(z)
5
>>> z.__methods__, z.__members__, z.pop()         __getattr__ -> type
(['empty', 'pop', 'push', 'top'], ['len'], 'M')
>>> type(z), type(z._base)
(<type 'instance'>, <type 'stack'>)
>>>
>>> a = substack.Substack(x + y)                  make subclass instance
>>> a
[Stack:
4: 'M'
3: 'A'
```

```
2: 'P'
1: 'S'
0: 'class'
]

>>> a[3]                                            extended __getitem__
accessing cell 3                                    subclass -> class -> type
'A'
>>> a.morestuff()                                   an added method
more stack stuff
>>> b = substack.Substack("C" + "++")
>>> b
[Stack:
2: '+'
1: '+'
0: 'C'
]

>>> b.pop(), b.pop()                                inherited __getattr__ -> type
('+', '+')
>>> c = b + substack.Substack(['-', '-'])           inherited __add__ makes a Stack
>>> for s in c: print s,                            Stack.__getitem__ -> type
...
C - -
```

For the most part, the *Stack* class works exactly like the C type; *Substack* adds initialization from sequences, and more. Both illustrate some differences between types and classes, and class design issues:

- The type *print* function isn't really the same as `__repr__`. We fake the type's *print* operation by printing the type instance and returning an empty string for `__repr__` in the class.
- Stack's `+` and `*` operators return a new *Stack* class instance, but this is arbitrary; we could instead return a raw type instance, and make clients wrap it in a *Stack* class instance manually:

  ```
  result = Stack(instance1 + instance2)          # wrap raw C type-instance
  ```

- When we subclass *Stack* in *Substack*, the automatic conversion in *Stack*'s `+` and `*` methods probably isn't what we want: to make Substack's `+` and `*` return a new *Substack* instead, we have to wrap it manually, much like a C/C++ *cast*:

  ```
  result  = instance1 + instance2                # a Stack
  result  = Substack(instance1 + instance2)      # a Substack
  ```

  *Substack*'s constructor allows arbitrary sequences: we can pass a C type instance, a *Stack* class-instance, or a simple sequence (list, string, etc.). We could also redefine `__add__` and `__mul__` locally in *Substack*, to wrap the result in a *Substack* instance. As usual, hierarchy design is flexible; we can either put operators that make new instances in lower classes, or use manual class calls.

### *Wrappers are a partial but powerful solution*

The wrapper class technique doesn't make C types completely object oriented: there's still no easy way for C extension types to inherit from other types or classes. If extensions are coded in C++, they can use inheritance outside Python, but there's no support in Python itself for inheritance among extension types.

Some of this behavior can be simulated by using type wrapper classes in larger hierarchies. For instance, a *stub* class could both wrap a C type and inherit from other Python classes (and other *stub* classes) to combine services. In the example above, *oopstack.Stack* could also inherit from other *stub* classes. But there's no notion of inheritance or subclassing in types without wrapper classes.

Still, wrapper classes are usually sufficient: they let us use OOP to specialize types, as though they were root level superclasses. C extension types (and modules) are really meant for writing interfaces to flat services coded in C. For existing services, adding inheritance to the service itself isn't really practical. But Python wrapper classes can usually add as much of an OOP flavor as Python clients need.

For example, the *Tkinter* module uses the wrapper class technique to add an object-oriented interface to a flat C extension. We're able to specialize, extend, and embed *Tk* widgets because they're wrapped in Python classes. There's no practical reason for making *Tk* itself an object-oriented API; adding a front end object-oriented interface is usually enough.

Suggested exercise: Code wrapper classes for some of Python's built-in types: lists, dictionaries, files, etc. Some of these already exist in Python's source tree: see the *Lib* and *Demo* directories.

## *Special Methods Map to Type Descriptor Slots*

In closing, the following table shows the correspondence between the specially-named class methods we studied in Chapter 13, and the type descriptor slots we've studied in this chapter. The type slot entries here are Python's internal names for the type descriptor *struct* fields; refer to the code listings above for layout details and see the table in Chapter 13 for more details on the overloaded operations.

There's usually a one-to-one mapping from methods to type slots, though some methods apply to more than one type-category supplement. For instance, `__getitem__` may be sequence or mapping indexing, and `__add__` corresponds to both addition and concatenation.

But the main point to notice here is that the techniques are virtually the same. Python and Python-based systems naturally support extensions coded in either Python or C. Both languages may provide modules of services. And both can implement new object types that integrate closely with Python's built-in type model.

*Table 14-5: Class method/type descriptor slot equivalence*

| Python class method | C type slot | Operation implemented |
|---|---|---|
| All types | | |
| `__init__`*(self, args . . . )* | (Module function) | Instance constructor |
| `__del__`*(self)* | *tp_dealloc* | Instance destructor |
| `__repr__`*(self)* | *tp_repr, tp_print* | *'self', print self, repr(self)* |
| `__str__`*(self)* | *tp_str* | *str(self), print self* |
| `__cmp__`*(self, other)* | *tp_compare* | *self > x, x == self, cmp(self, x)* |
| `__hash__`*(self)* | *tp_hash* | *dictionary[self], hash(self)* |
| `__call__`*(self, *args)* | *tp_call* | *self(args . . . )* |
| `__getattr__`*(self, name)* | *tp_getattr* | *self.name* |
| `__setattr__`*(self, name, value)* | *tp_setattr* | *self.name = value* |
| `__delattr__`*(self, name)* | *tp_getattr(NULL)* | *del self.name* |
| Collections | | |
| `__len__`*(self)* | *sq_length*<br>*mp_length* | *len(self), truth-value: if self* |
| `__getitem__`*(self, key)* | *sq_item*<br>*mp_subscript* | *self[key], x in self, for x in self* |
| `__setitem__`*(self, key, value)* | *sq_ass_item*<br>*mp_ass_subscript* | *self[key] = value* |
| `__delitem__`*(self, key)* | *sq_ass_item(NULL)*<br>*mp_ass_subscript(NULL)* | *del self[key]* |
| `__getslice__`*(self, low, high)* | *sq_slice* | *self[low:high]* |
| `__setslice__`*(self, low, high, seq)* | *sq_ass_slice* | *self[low:high] = seq* |
| `__delslice__`*(self, low, high)* | *sq_ass_slice(NULL)* | *del self[low:high]* |
| Numbers | | |
| `__add__`*(self, other)* | *nb_add*<br>*sq_concat* | *self + other* |
| `__sub__`*(self, other)* | *nb_subtract* | *self - other* |
| `__mul__`*(self, other)* | *nb_multiply* | *self * other* |

*Table 14-5: Class method/type descriptor slot equivalence (continued)*

| Python class method | C type slot | Operation implemented |
|---|---|---|
| | *sq_repeat* | |
| `__div__`*(self, other)* | *nb_divide* | *self / other* |
| `__mod__`*(self, other)* | *nb_remainder* | *self % other* |
| `__divmod__`*(self, other)* | *nb_divmod* | *divmod(self, other)* |
| `__pow__`*(self, other)* | *nb_power* | *pow(self, other)* |
| `__lshift__`*(self, other)* | *nb_lshift* | *self << other* |
| `__rshift__`*(self, other)* | *nb_rshift* | *self >> other* |
| `__and__`*(self, other)* | *nb_and* | *self & other* |
| `__xor__`*(self, other)* | *nb_xor* | *self ^ other* |
| `__or__`*(self, other)* | *nb_or* | *self \| other* |
| `__neg__`*(self)* | *nb_neg* | *– self* |
| `__pos__`*(self)* | *nb_pos* | *+ self* |
| `__abs__`*(self)* | *nb_abs* | *abs(self)* |
| `__invert__`*(self)* | *nb_invert* | *~ self* |
| `__nonzero__`*(self)* | *nb_nonzero* | truth-value: *if self* |
| `__coerce__`*(self, other)* | *nb_coerce* | mixed-type expression, *coerce()* |
| `__int__`*(self)* | *nb_int* | *int(self)* |
| `__long__`*(self)* | *nb_long* | *long(self)* |
| `__float__`*(self)* | *nb_float* | *float(self)* |
| `__oct__`*(self)* | *nb_oct* | *oct(self)* |
| `__hex__`*(self)* | *nb_hex* | *hex(self)* |

Notice that there are no right-side versions of type descriptor slots, as there are for class methods (for instance, `__add__` and `__radd__`). Instead, types provide conversions in either the registered *coerce* handler, or the *operator* handler itself. In mixed-type expressions, Python calls the registered coerce handler (if one is registered) before the actual operator handler.

For instance, the Python *float* object type provides a *coerce* method that converts a nonfloat right operand to a float object first, if necessary. Its binary operator methods can then assume both operands are valid float objects. More generally, user-defined C extension types can implement any of the data conversions that built-in types perform, including the automatic upward conversions in mixed-type arithmetic expressions. See *Objects/floatobject.c* in the Python source tree for more details.

# *Now, Forget Most of the Details*

That's the end of our discussion on C extensions for the present; a few related topics appear later in the book, and we'll revisit the subject from an abstract perspective at the conclusion of this book. Chapter 15 explores a symmetric topic: embedding Python in C. Before we move on, here are a few general remarks on the extension process.

As mentioned earlier, there's a lot of inevitable complexity, when linking a low-level language like C to Python. Usually, it's a relatively rare activity; in typical Python-based systems, most of our time is spent writing Python code. And by comparison, Python's integration system is remarkably straightforward to use. But still it's not quite the same as writing Python modules and classes!

Fortunately, we don't normally need to write extension modules and types from scratch. Python also provides tools to automate much of the coding task. For example, the *modulator* tool (discussed in Chapter 15) generates skeleton extension source files automatically; we just fill in the function bodies with conversion code and application logic. Other tools go even further.

Some manual intervention is required by most extension tools, and it helps to understand the underlying structures. But while we can't usually ignore all the details we've seen in this chapter, extension tools eliminate much of the low-level coding work.

## *But Remember the "Why": Extensions as Packaging Tools*

This chapter's examples stress the idea of using extensions as a way to optimize Python programs. But there's another important role for the tools we've studied in this chapter. Extension modules, types, and wrapper classes are often used as packaging tools for existing libraries and systems.

When we write a Python extension module for a system's API, the system automatically becomes easier to use. It inherits the rapid turnaround and high-level programming tools of the Python language. In fact, Python integrations can be an attractive delivery medium for application-level APIs; they complement traditional C-based interfaces.

For instance, we've seen how Python lets us graft an object-oriented model onto a flat system without changing the system itself. And as we'll see later in the book, it also makes interfacing with classes implemented in C++ straightforward; the same wrapper class techniques we used for C extension types here will apply.

By packaging an API in a dynamic, high-level language like Python, it becomes accessible to both developers and technically naive end users. Python is arguably simple enough for nonprogrammers to pick up, yet powerful enough for substantial development efforts.

*In this chapter:*

- *Python's Embedded Call API*
- *Basic Embedding Strategies*
- *An Embedded Call API Client*
- *Case Study: Embedding User-Coded Validations*
- *Other Approaches: Registering Callable Objects*
- *Automated Integration Techniques*
- *Summary: Python/C Integration Techniques*

# 15

# *Embedding Python*

## *"Add Python. Mix Well. Repeat."*

In Chapter 14, *Extending Python*, we saw only half of the Python/C integration picture: calling C services from Python. This mode lets us speed up operations by moving them to C, package libraries by wrapping them in C extension modules and types, etc. But the inverse can be just as useful—calling Python from C.

In fact, Python's role as an embedded language is critical to application scripting work and end user customization. By delegating selected components of an application to Python code, we can open them up to on-site changes without having to ship the system's C code. And by providing embedded-code hooks into an application, we can make systems more flexible.

This chapter is really a continuation of the prior one; it presents the other half of the Python/C integration story. In practice, there isn't always a clear distinction between extending and embedding. For instance, embedded Python code can use application-specific extensions to interface with the enclosing C system. Similarly, Python code that uses C extensions might register objects to be run as embedded code from C.

Because of this it's best to consider Python's integration support as a whole and choose parts that are appropriate for a given task. A system's structure usually determines an appropriate approach: C extension wrappers, embedded code calls, or both. At the end of this chapter, we'll also discuss some topics that span integration strategies: both embedding and extending.

# *Python's Embedded Call API*

In Python, the embedded-call API is more flexible than the extension interfaces. This is largely due to the fact that the goal isn't as clear-cut. When extending Python, there is a distinct separation for Python and C responsibilities and a clear structure for the integration. C modules and types are required to fit the Python module/type model by conforming to standard extension structures. This makes the integration seamless for Python clients: C extensions look like Python objects and handle most of the work.

But when Python is embedded the structure isn't as clear: because C is the enclosing level there's no way to know what model the embedded Python code should fit. Instead Python provides a collection of general embedding interface tools, which we use and structure according to our embedding goals. As we'll see later in this chapter, they all correspond to tools available to Python programs. Embedded Python code can take a variety of forms:

*Table 15-1: Common embedding strategies*

| Code medium | Description | Python equivalent |
|---|---|---|
| Character strings | Running code: expressions/statements | *eval("expr"), exec "stmt"* |
| Callable objects | Calling functions, classes, and methods | *apply(object, args)* |
| Module file references | Using objects defined in modules by name | *import, reload, getattr, setattr* |
| Object attributes | Using object methods/members by name | *getattr, setattr*, etc. |
| Modules and scripts | Running a whole file of Python code | *import, os.system/popen* |

As this table shows, there's usually a one-to-one mapping from C-embedded API functions to Python built-ins. In fact, Python code can be embedded either in C or Python (we'll expand on this idea in Chapter 16, *Processing Language and Text*). But embedding Python in C requires some creativity on our part to structure the integration. As we'll see later, we can combine embedding strategies to build up arbitrary higher-level interfaces.

For instance, to use callable objects, or access object attributes by name, we first have to get a Python object from somewhere: it has to be registered to C or fetched from a module file first. If C is on top, registration may require running embedded Python code to call back to the enclosing C layer through a C extension; if Python is on top, registration is simpler. And for other applications, registration doesn't make sense at all. The embedding API is flexible enough to handle a variety of application structures.

> ### *Running code files and scripts*
>
> This chapter discusses all but the last of the entries in Table 15-1; Python scripts are run from C just like any other executable program (using C's standard *system*, *popen*, *fork*, etc.); modules with top-level actions are run by importing them. Here are a few details.
>
> The API function *PyRun_SimpleFile(FILE *file, char *filename)* runs a file of Python code in the `__main__` module's namespace, exactly like passing it to the interpreter on the command line (*% python filename*). The file's name is only used for reporting errors. A lower-level function, *PyRun_File*, also allows a parse mode and global/local namespace dictionary objects to be passed in, much like the *PyRun_String* interface we'll see shortly.
>
> Scripts and code module files provide a looser integration binding but aren't as direct or powerful as the other techniques (strings, objects, etc.) we'll explore here. They also may require an extra administration tasks to manage the external files, but this varies per application.

## *Common Embedded API Functions*

Since we've already discussed basic Python/C interfaces in Chapter 14, we'll focus on some larger examples here. Before we jump into the code, let's preview some of the Python API functions we'll see along the way. Python provides functions for running character strings, calling objects, loading modules, accessing object attributes, and more. Here's a sampling; some were introduced in Chapter 14.

### *Administrative*

*Python.h*
: This is the standard Python API header file. We'll use a few more of these files here.

*Py_Initialize*
: Initializes embedded Python libraries the first time it is called.

### *Error handling*

*PyErr_SetString*
: Sets the current exception: the object, plus a string-object as extra data.

*PyExc_IndexError*
: Python's built-in *IndexError* exception object in C.

*PyErr_Fetch*
: Fetch the object and extra data of the last exception set.

*PyErr_Occurred*
: Has an error been raised in the Python API itself?

*PyErr_Print*
: Print the last exception, with a stack trace giving the source code context.

### *Object access*

*PyObject*
: A generic Python object in C.

*Py_None*
: The Python *None* object.

*PyString_Check*
: Is the object a Python string? (Check its type descriptor.)

*PyModule_Check*
: Is the object a Python module?

*PyObject_Print*
: Print any Python object.

*PyObject_GetAttrString*
: Fetch an object's attribute, given a C *char** attribute name.

*PyObject_SetAttrString*
: Assign an object's attribute, given a C *char** attribute name.

### *Object ownership*

*Py_INCREF*
: Add a reference/owner (increment the header's reference count).

*Py_DECREF*
: Remove a reference; if no longer referenced, call the object's destructor.

*Py_XINCREF*
: Add a reference; do nothing if the object pointer is *NULL*.

*Py_XDECREF*
: Remove a reference; do nothing on *NULL* pointers.

### *Type-specific utilities*

*PyDict_New*
: Make a new (empty) dictionary object.

*PyDict_SetItemString*
: Assign to a dictionary object's key, given a C *char** key.

*PyDict_GetItemString*
: Fetch the value associated with a key from a dictionary object.

*PyModule_GetDict*
: Get the attribute dictionary associated with a Python module object.

*PyTuple_Size*
: Return the number of items in a Python tuple object.

*PyTuple_SetItem*
: Store an object in a tuple, at a given offset (for filling in new tuples).

*_PyTuple_Resize*
: Expand or compact a tuple object (versus making a new one).

### *Module interfaces*

*PyImport_GetModuleDict*
: Get the *sys.modules* loaded module dictionary object.

*PyImport_AddModule*
: Find an already-loaded module, or make a new one, but don't load the file.

*PyImport_ImportModule*
: Find or load a module (same as Python's *import*).

*PyImport_ReloadModule*
: Reload an already-loaded module object (same as Python's *reload()*).

### *Running embedded code*

*PyEval_CallObject*
: Call a Python callable object: function, class, bound method, built-in, etc.

*PyRun_SimpleFile*
: Run a script (file of Python code) in the namespace of module `__main__`.

*PyRun_SimpleString*
: Run a Python statement string in the namespace of module `__main__`.

*PyRun_String*
: Run a Python expression or statement string in any namespace.

*PyRun_InteractiveLoop*
: Run the Python interactive command line (in the *stdin/stdout* window).

*PyEval_EvalCode*
: Run a Python compiled code object (low level).

*Py_CompileString*
: Compile a string into a Python code object.

### Data conversion

*PyInt_FromLong*
: Make a Python integer object from a C *long*.

*PyString_FromString*
: Build a Python string object from a C *char** (null-terminated).

*PyString_AsString*
: Return a C *char** pointing to the text of a Python string object.

*Py_BuildValue*
: Convert C value(s) to Python objects, according to a format string.

*Py_VaBuildValue*
: Same, but allow the C values to be an explicitly passed *varargs* list.

*PyArg_Parse*
: Convert Python object(s) to C values/targets, according to a format string.

*PyArgs_VaParse*
: Same, but allow the C targets to be an explicitly passed *varargs* list.

*PyArg_ParseTuple*
: Convert a tuple of Python objects to C values/targets.

### Extension tools

*PyMethodDef*
: A C function in name/address registration tables of extension modules.

*PySequenceMethods*
: The sequence supplement type descriptor in C extension types.

*PyTypeObject*
A type descriptor, for C extension types.

*PyObject_HEAD*
The Python header in type instances (reference count, type pointer).

*PyObject_NEW*
Make a type instance: *malloc* the header plus type *struct*, set header fields.

*PyMem_DEL*
Delete a type instance when reference count reaches zero (calls C *free*).

This list is nowhere near exhaustive: as mentioned earlier, Python's API really includes all its *extern* functions, and everything in the *rename2.h* header file. But it's representative of the sorts of activities integrated C code needs to do. (See Python's extension manual for more details.)

# *Basic Embedding Strategies*

The API functions can do much all by themselves, but they're fairly low level. In practice it's sometimes more convenient to build higher-level interfaces to the API. But to get started, let's explore some simple examples of typical ways that the API functions are used:

- Running simple statement strings
- Running strings with results and namespaces
- Calling Python objects in modules directly
- Running strings without modules

The middle two examples make use of Python module-file and object-attribute interfaces. And all but the last perform the same simple task: accessing variables and functions in the Python *string* module. They print *string.uppercase* (a string of the uppercase letters), and call the *string.lower* function to change the uppercase string to lowercase. The last example is more specialized.

## *Running Simple Statement Strings*

C programs can run code to do things in the Python environment using strings: *PyRun_SimpleString* runs code strings in the namespace of module `__main__`. This is the most straightforward embedding interface, but it's limited: all code runs in the same namespace, and the code-strings must be Python statements. There's no expression result, just a status code: –1 denotes an error (syntax, names, etc.).

### Detecting API call errors

These programs really work, but they're deliberately artificial to illustrate basic embedding concepts. We'll see more realistic C programs and makefiles later. Some error checking has been omitted to keep these short, too: as a rule, the return value should be checked after every Python API call.

As in the prior chapter, a *NULL* or –1 return value usually designates an error detected and raised in Python (the *PyArg_Parse** functions return zero on errors). Alternatively, we can call *PyErr_Occurred* after a series of API calls, as described in the last chapter. C programs can call *PyErr_Print* to display the error on *stdout*, or fetch errors using *PyErr_Fetch*: *PyErr_Fetch(PyObject **obj, PyObject **msg, PyObject **traceback)*. See API documentation for more information.

*Example 15-1: File: basic1.c*

```
#include <Python.h>
char *getprogramname() { return "basic1"; }

main() {
    printf("%s\n", getprogramname());
    Py_Initialize();
    PyRun_SimpleString("import string");
    PyRun_SimpleString("print string.uppercase");
    PyRun_SimpleString("x = string.uppercase");
    PyRun_SimpleString("print string.lower(x)");
}
```

Under this scheme, there's no easy way to get Python results or set Python data. Still it's a simple way to access Python services from C. For instance, some Python tools might be easier to invoke with embedded Python code, if there's no C API. When Python's embedded, *Py_Initialize* should always be called before using other API functions; it initializes Python libraries the first time its called, and does nothing on later calls. The *getprogramname* function here has to be defined only if you have certain extensions enabled; if you can link without it, it's not required.

To build a standalone executable from this C file, we need to link in Python's libraries (currently four). We also must link Python's *config.o* and *getpath.o* object files, and any external extension libraries bound to Python statically. The *main* function comes from our C file. Assuming no extension libraries are needed, here's a minimal *makefile* for building a C program that embeds Python. Directory names will vary, and build details differ on some platforms; we'll see a more sophisticated *makefile* later in this chapter.

*Example 15-2: File: makefile.1*

```
PY = /home/mark/python-1.3/Python-1.3

PLIBS = $(PY)/Modules/libModules.a \
        $(PY)/Python/libPython.a \
        $(PY)/Objects/libObjects.a \
        $(PY)/Parser/libParser.a

POBJS = $(PY)/Modules/config.o $(PY)/Modules/getpath.o

basic1: basic1.o
        cc -g basic1.o $(POBJS) $(PLIBS) -lm -o basic1

basic1.o: basic1.c
        cc basic1.c -c -g -I$(PY)/Include -I$(PY)/.
```

Finally, here's the C program's output; the first three examples in this section produce these same results. Using simple strings, all activity and output happens in the Python system; the C program acts like a programmer typing at Python's interactive command line. There's no way to set inputs to Python code, short of building up legal program strings in C. And there's no way to get Python program results unless we intercept and parse *stdout* text written by the program.

```
% basic1
basic1
ABCDEFGHIJKLMNOPQRSTUVWXYZ
abcdefghijklmnopqrstuvwxyz
```

## Running Strings with Results and Namespaces

If we need to get results of Python expressions, we can do it with strings and conversions: the API function *PyRun_String* runs a code string too, but we get back a Python object for expression results, and can pass in dictionary objects to be used as global and local namespaces for variables the string uses.

This lets us communicate with embedded Python code, and partition namespaces as needed for an application. As we'll see later in this chapter, using code strings also lets us store embedded Python code in a persistent database instead of in separate module files. Under this scheme, we typically combine five API functions:

*PyImport_ImportModule*
: Load or make a module (or fetch an already-loaded module).

*PyModule_GetDict*
: Fetch the module's attribute dictionary, to use as a namespace.

*PyRun_String*
    Run the string in the namespace, as an expression or statement.

*PyArg_Parse*
    If it's an expression, a Python object result is returned; convert to C.

*Py_DECREF*
    Release ownership of the module and result (it's *None* for statements).

Here's the *string* module example again, using this string-based approach.

*Example 15-3: File: basic2.c*

```
#include <Python.h>          /* standard API defs  */
#include <import.h>          /* PyImport functions */
#include <graminit.h>        /* parse-mode flags   */
#include <pythonrun.h>       /* PyRun interfaces   */

char *getprogramname() { return "basic2"; }

main() {
    char *cstr;
    PyObject *pstr, *pmod, *pdict;
    printf("%s\n", getprogramname());
    Py_Initialize();

    /* get string.uppercase */
    pmod  = PyImport_ImportModule("string");
    pdict = PyModule_GetDict(pmod);
    pstr  = PyRun_String("uppercase", eval_input, pdict, pdict);

    /* convert to C */
    PyArg_Parse(pstr, "s", &cstr);
    printf("%s\n", cstr);

    /* assign string.X */
    PyObject_SetAttrString(pmod, "X", pstr);

    /* print string.lower */
    (void) PyRun_String("print lower(X)", file_input, pdict, pdict);
    Py_DECREF(pmod);
    Py_DECREF(pstr);
}
```

Notice that we use three special Python header files here to define module interface and string execution tools. To grab a namespace dictionary for running strings, we usually need to first get a module, and then fetch its dictionary. *PyImport_ImportModule* loads a module, or fetches one that's already loaded. Once we have the module, *PyModule_GetDict* gets its dictionary; we pass it to the *global* and *local* namespace parameters of *PyRun_String*. To run strings that don't exist in a module file, we can also make *new* dictionaries with *PyDict_New*, for each namespace, instead of using modules (see Example 15-5).

When we use *PyRun_String*, we're also responsible for passing in a parse mode flag: here, either *eval_input* or *file_input*, to parse an expression or statement, respectively. If we run a statement, we get back the Python *None* object as a result; it should normally be *DECREF*d too.

If we're using specific modules, there's no reason to run in `__main__`: here, we go straight to module *string* to get variables and run functions. In this example, the function *PyObject_SetAttrString* is used to set a variable in the *string* module (*X*): this is one way to send data from C to Python when strings are used. We're able to get output as the results of expressions here; in other contexts, we might instead fetch variables set by code-strings from modules, using *PyObject_GetAttrString*.

### *More on module access*

*PyImport_AddModule* fetches a module if it's already been imported (i.e., if it's in *sys.modules*), but *PyImport_AddModule* doesn't load the module if it has not been imported previously. This method works well for accessing prebuilt modules like `__main__`. But *PyImport_AddModule* will return an empty module object if the module's not already loaded. As a rule, always use the function *PyImport_ImportModule* to access Python modules from C.

## *Calling Python Objects in Modules Directly*

Strings are adequate for many embedding applications. But sometimes a more direct approach works better. For instance, *PyEval_CallObject* calls a known Python object; where applicable, it can save the parsing step required when running code strings. Of course, to call a Python object we have a pointer to it. We might run code strings to import an object's module, execute Python code to register it, or fetch it by module/attribute-name. The last approach typically involves (at least) five API functions:

*PyImport_ImportModule*
: Load the module file (or find an already-loaded module object).

*PyObject_GetAttrString*
: Fetch the callable object by name, from the module object.

*Py_BuildValue*
: Build a Python argument list tuple to pass to the function.

*PyEval_CallObject*
: Call the fetched Python object, with the arguments tuple.

*PyArg_Parse*
Convert the return value (a Python object) to a C value.

plus reference count management (*Py_INCREF/DECREF*), error handling (*PyErr_Print*), etc. Here's an example that fetches a *string* module method and calls it directly. Where appropriate, calling specific objects like this can be a more direct embedding structure. Moreover, namespaces are associated with callable objects automatically; they're not passed in with the call here.

*Example 15-4: File: basic3.c*

```
#include <Python.h>
#include <import.h>
char *getprogramname() { return "basic3"; }

main() {
    char *cstr;
    PyObject *pstr, *pmod, *pfunc, *pargs;
    printf("%s\n", getprogramname());
    Py_Initialize();

    /* get string.uppercase */
    pmod = PyImport_ImportModule("string");
    pstr = PyObject_GetAttrString(pmod, "uppercase");

    /* convert string to C */
    PyArg_Parse(pstr, "s", &cstr);
    printf("%s\n", cstr);
    Py_DECREF(pstr);

    /* call string.lower(string.uppercase) */
    pfunc = PyObject_GetAttrString(pmod, "lower");
    pargs = Py_BuildValue("(s)", cstr);
    pstr  = PyEval_CallObject(pfunc, pargs);
    PyArg_Parse(pstr, "s", &cstr);
    printf("%s\n", cstr);

    /* free owned objects */
    Py_DECREF(pmod);
    Py_DECREF(pstr);
    Py_DECREF(pfunc);
    Py_DECREF(pargs);
}
```

We get the Python module with *PyImport_ImportModule* as before. But here, we fetch variable *string.uppercase* by attribute name using *PyObject_GetAttrString*, not by running a code string expression. To call the *string.lower* function, we fetch the function object itself, build an argument tuple with *Py_BuildValue*, and call the function directly with *PyEval_CallObject*. The function's return value comes back as a Python object, which we then convert to C with *PyArg_Parse* (discussed in Chapter 14).

## *Running Strings Without Modules*

Finally, for code strings that aren't associated with a module file, we can avoid modules completely, by making new dictionaries to serve as namespaces. Here's a simple example that uses *PyDict_New* to make namespaces, dictionary *get/set* functions to manage them, and *PyRun_String* to execute code.

*Example 15-5: File: basic4.c*

```
#include <Python.h>
#include <graminit.h>
#include <pythonrun.h>
char *getprogramname() { return "basic4"; }

main() {
    int cval;
    PyObject *pdict, *pval;
    Py_Initialize();

    /* make a new namespace */
    pdict = PyDict_New();
    PyDict_SetItemString(pdict, "__builtins__", PyEval_GetBuiltins());

    PyDict_SetItemString(pdict, "Y", PyInt_FromLong(2));   /* dict['Y'] = 2   */
    PyRun_String("X = 99",  file_input, pdict, pdict);     /* run statements  */
    PyRun_String("X = X+Y", file_input, pdict, pdict);     /* same X and Y    */
    pval = PyDict_GetItemString(pdict, "X");               /* fetch dict['X'] */

    PyArg_Parse(pval, "i", &cval);                         /* convert to C */
    printf("%d\n", cval);                                  /* result=101 */
    Py_DECREF(pdict);
}
```

Under this scheme, variable names used in the code string are looked up (or created) in the passed-in dictionaries. We can make a new dictionary for each namespace an application needs: variables used by strings run in one namespace won't clash with names in another namespace.

In effect, dictionaries take the place of Python modules. Later in this chapter, we'll build "dummy modules" which achieve the same effect and associate names with namespaces. And in Chapter 16, we'll see that this form is exactly the same as Python *eval* and *exec* built-ins.

## *Other Possibilities*

As we'll discuss later in this chapter, it's also possible for Python code to register callable objects to C ahead of time. This model works much like *basic3* above, but the enclosing C layer doesn't need to access a Python module to get an object; instead, it runs Python code to specify objects to be called from C. We'll compare this scheme to string and module-based approaches later.

### *What's the __builtins__ entry for?*

Notice that we need to initialize a `__builtins__` key in the new namespace dictionary. To support a restricted execution mode, Python requires that all namespaces include the built-in dictionary explicitly. This requirement allows applications to tailor the set of built-ins to prohibit some operations. Restricted execution mode can be important when running programs across a network, in a web browser, etc. See Appendix A, *...And Other Cool Stuff*, for more details.

Normally you don't need to care about `__builtins__`: Python manages the entry in most other cases. *eval* and *exec* add `__builtins__` for you, and dictionaries fetched from modules already include it. The *dummy modules* interface in the extended API we'll see later encapsulates namespace creation details.

As you may expect, most of the techniques shown here can be combined arbitrarily. For instance, function *PyRun_String* can be used to fetch the *string.lower* function with a string expression, instead of getting it by attribute name with *PyObject_GetAttrString*:

```
pmod  = PyImport_ImportModule("string");
pfunc = PyObject_GetAttrString(pmod, "lower");    /* getattr(string,"lower") */
```

is the same as:

```
PyObject *pdict;
pmod  = PyImport_ImportModule("string");          /* run code-string in module */
pdict = PyModule_GetDict(pmod);
pfunc = PyRun_String("lower", eval_input, pdict, pdict);
```

Alternatively, we can fetch *lower* by *key* from the module's dictionary using *PyDict_GetItemString*. Module dictionaries are the same as the `__dict__` module attribute in Python:

```
PyObject *pdict;
pmod  = PyImport_ImportModule("string");          /* import string */
pdict = PyModule_GetDict(pmod);                   /* string.__dict__['lower'] */
pfunc = PyDict_GetItemString(pdict, "lower");     /* but don't decref pfunc */
```

We can also import *string* into `__main__` using *PyRun_SimpleString*, and fetch it from the `__main__` module's dictionary using module *getattr* functions. In general, the embedding API is almost as flexible as the Python language, since it exports many of the same operations to C.

### *More on reference count management*

In the examples above, *Py_DECREF* releases ownership of Python objects held by C. For instance, every *PyObject** result in *basic3* has an incremented reference count when it's sent to C from the API. The enclosing C layer is responsible for decrementing the count when the object's no longer needed.

But there are no absolute rules on which API functions add references to results and which ones don't. For instance, the *PyDict_GetItemString* function returns a dictionary entry without incrementing its count. There's no guarantee that the object will still exist in the future after Python API functions are called. If we need to hold on to it in C, we need to use *Py_INCREF* to assume ownership manually. If not, we need to avoid using *DECREF* on the object in C.

As a rule, API functions that make new Python objects transfer ownership of the result to C; they must be *DECREF*d. For instance, function return values and string expression results are all new objects. But some areas are more gray: fetching modules with *import* functions gives us ownership but may not make a new module object because we might share an existing one.

See Python's extension manual for more details; it includes an good overview of the object ownership concept in Python. For details on a particular API function, see later examples here or Python API documentation. The table below gives a sampling of some API result ownership rules. It shows the old (Python 1.2) names, reference-count behavior, and Python equivalents for some of the API functions discussed above. Details for other functions appear in later examples.

*Table 15-2: Common API function behavior*

| New name | Old name (1.2) | INCREF's Result? | Python equivalent |
|---|---|---|---|
| *PyImport_AddModule* | *add_module* | No | n/a[a] |
| *PyImport_ImportModule* | *import_module* | Yes | *import module* |
| *PyImport_ReloadModule* | *reload_module* | Yes | *reload(module)* |
| *PyImport_GetModuleDict* | *get_modules* | No | *sys.modules* |
| *PyModule_GetDict* | *getmoduledict* | No | *module.*`__dict__` |
| *PyDict_GetItemString* | *dictlookup* | No | *dict[key]* |
| *PyDict_SetItemString* | *dictinsert* | n/a | *dict[key]=val* |
| *PyObject_GetAttrString* | *getattr* | Yes | *getattr(obj, attr)* |
| *PyObject_SetAttrString* | *setattr* | n/a | *setattr(obj, attr, val)* |
| *PyArg_ParseTuple* | *newgetargs* | n/a | n/a |
| *Py_BuildValue* | *mkvalue* | Yes | n/a |
| *PyEval_CallObject* | *call_object* | Yes | *apply(func, argtuple)* |
| *PyRun_String* | *run_string* | Yes | *eval(expr), exec stmt* |

*Table 15-2: Common API function behavior (continued)*

| New name | Old name (1.2) | INCREF's Result? | Python equivalent |
|---|---|---|---|
| *PyErr_Print* | *print_error* | n/a | *traceback.print_exc* |
| *PyDict_New* | *newdictobject* | Yes | {} |

[a] n/a = not applicable

## *Building Higher-Level Embedding Interfaces*

All the strategies above are fairly flexible. But regardless of the approach taken, you can probably tell by now that there is a lot of manual code involved: we need to manage modules, attributes, and results, do data conversions, handle reference counts, etc. Naturally, one way to simplify these tasks is to build higher-level embedded call interfaces on top of the built-in API.

In the next section, we'll look at an extended C API that adds simpler interfaces for common embedded operations. It also illustrates ways to combine the built-in API functions.

For instance, a single C function call can run a function in an external module file: module access, data conversion, and object ownership details are automated. Both inputs and outputs are converted using Python format strings.

This API and its clients are big programs, but they show how the built-in API can be used in realistic embedding scenarios. As a preview, here's what we'll be looking at in the remainder of this discussion:

- A higher-level API for embedded Python calls: a header file plus five C files
- A client program: the main C file, *makefile*, and Python support files
- A purchase order validations case study: code string and module function versions
- An overview of object registration techniques

We'll first study an extended API for running embedded code; it's just a wrapper around Python's API functions that makes them more convenient. Then we'll show how the API can be used in client programs. We'll also see how to build an executable that embeds Python with extension libraries. Most of the code listings here are heavily commented. As usual, we'll point out new ideas along the way, but the listings provide additional information: API function type signatures, reference count rules, etc.

### *API portability issues*

Some of the examples below use the *stdarg.h* C include file to support a variable-length arguments list (for inputs, etc.). Unfortunately this method isn't universally portable. If you have trouble compiling, consult the manpage on *varargs*, or study one of the files in the Python source tree that uses *stdarg* (for example, *Python/modsupport.c*). It's possible to use *#ifdef* to write portable *varargs* code in C but this obscures the code.

# *A Higher-Level Embedded Call API*

In this section, we'll develop a higher-level interface to Python's embedded API tools. Before we get into the code, here's an overview. The API demonstrates one way to make use of built-in interfaces. It adds support for common embedding approaches: code strings, module references, and Python objects, as Figure 15-1 illustrates.

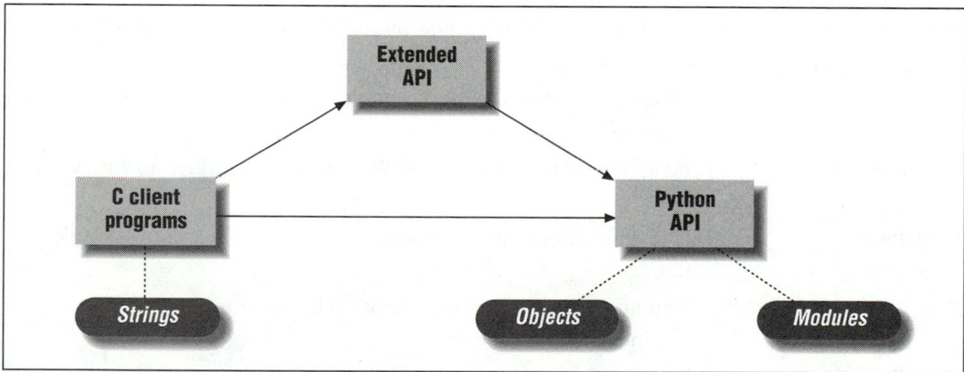


*Figure 15-1: Embedded-call API structure*

In this figure, solid lines represent calls, and dashed lines represent management responsibilities. C programs can call both the extended API functions and the lower-level API functions built-in to Python. The extended API is implemented on top of the built-in API. Code strings and modules usually exist independently of both Python and C, and objects are created by Python on demand:

*Strings*
: Typically managed by C. They may be loaded from files or databases, fetched from user interfaces, etc. Code strings are passed to Python but are separate from it.

*Modules*

Managed by Python, even if they are accessed or created by C. In the extended API, clients pass module and object names to the API but don't process the modules directly.

*Objects*

Created by Python, and are found in its address space. But Python objects can be exported to (and owned by) C programs too; C can pass objects to the API.

In the extended API, data sent to and from Python are converted automatically, using Python format strings and passed-in C values and pointers. Here are the main tools the extended API introduces.

*Table 15-3: Embedded call API tools*

| Export | Description |
|---|---|
| *PY_RELOAD* | If true, reload modules whenever their attributes are referenced. |
| *PY_DEBUG* | If true, run embedded strings, functions, and methods in the *pdb* debugger. |
| *Make_Dummy_Module* | Create a named fileless module, to be used as a namespace for strings. |
| *Load_Module* | Load (or reload) a module by name, and return the module object (internal). |
| *Load_Attribute* | Fetch a raw object from a module, given the module and object names. |
| *Get_Global* | Fetch a variable from a module, given the module and variable name. |
| *Set_Global* | Assign a variable in a module, given the module and variable names. |
| *Run_Codestr* | Run an expression or statement code string in a named module's namespace. |
| *Run_Function* | Run a function (or class) in a module, given the module and function names. |
| *Run_Method* | Run a method of a known object, given the method name. |
| *Get_Member* | Fetch a data member (attribute) from a known object by name. |
| *Set_Member* | Assign a data member of a known object by name. |
| *Run_Command_Line* | Start the Python interactive command line in the *stdin/stdout* window. |

Code listings for the extended API are presented on the following pages. First, let's define a C header file that declares all the wrapper functions we'll provide. The file's comments describe general features of the API, and the prototypes give function type signatures.

*Example 15-6: File: pyembed.h*

```
/***********************************************************************
 * AN ENHANCED PYTHON EMBEDDED-CALL INTERFACE
 * Wraps Python's run-time embedding API functions for easy use.
 * Most (except Run_Method) assume the call's qualified by a module
 * (namespace). The module can be a file-name reference or a dummy module
 * created to provide a namespace for file-less strings. These routines
 * provide debugging, module (re)loading, input/output conversions, etc.
 *
 * Python is automatically initialized when the first call occurs.
 * Input/output conversions use the standard conversion format-codes.
 * Errors are flagged as either a -1 int, or a NULL pointer result.
 * Exported names use upper-case to minimize clashes [but this scheme
 * isn't fool-proof: there's no "import" in C, just "from*"]. Also
 * note that the varargs code here may not be portable to all
 * varieties of C.
 ***********************************************************************/

#ifndef PYEMBED_H
#define PYEMBED_H

#include <stdio.h>
#include <Python.h>
#include <import.h>
#include <pythonrun.h>
#include <graminit.h>

/* from Python/modsupport.c: does input-conversion */
/* but not debugging, reloading, output-conversion */

extern
PyObject* PyEval_CallFunction(PyObject *obj, char *format, ...);
extern
PyObject* PyEval_CallMethod(PyObject *obj, char *methodname, char *format, ...);


extern int PY_RELOAD;     /* reload modules when attributes are referenced? */
extern int PY_DEBUG;      /* start debugger when string/function/member run? */

typedef enum {
     PY_EXPRESSION,       /* what is a code-string? */
     PY_STATEMENT         /* expr's and statements differ */
} StringModes;


/** PYEMBED0.C: MODULES **/
extern char      *Init(char *modname);
extern int        Make_Dummy_Module(char *modname);
extern PyObject *Load_Module(char *modname);
extern PyObject *Load_Attribute(char *modname, char *attrname);
extern int        Run_Command_Line(char *prompt);
```

*Example 15-6: File: pyembed.h (continued)*

```
/** PYEMBED1.C: MODULE-VARIABLES **/
extern int
    Convert_Result(PyObject *presult, char *resFormat, void *resTarget);
extern int
    Get_Global(char *modname, char *varname, char *resfmt, void *cresult);
extern int
    Set_Global(char *modname, char *varname, char *valfmt, ... /*val*/);


/** PYEMBED2.C: CODE-STRINGS **/
extern PyObject*
    Debug_Codestr(StringModes mode,
                  char *codestring, PyObject *moddict);
extern int
    Run_Codestr(StringModes mode,                  /* expr or stmt? */
                char *code,   char *modname,       /* code, module  */
                char *resfmt, void *cresult);      /* output result */


/** PYEMBED3.C: FUNCTIONS/CLASSES **/
extern PyObject*
    Debug_Function(PyObject *func, PyObject *args);
extern int
    Run_Function(char *modname, char *funcname,          /* or classname */
                 char *resfmt,  void *cresult,           /* output */
                 char *argfmt,  ... /* arg, arg... */ ); /* input args */


/** PYEMBED4.C: OBJECT-METHODS/MEMBERS **/
extern int
    Run_Method(PyObject *pobject, char *method,       /* uses Debug_Function */
                   char *resfmt,  void *cresult,             /* output */
                   char *argfmt,  ... /* arg, arg... */ );   /* inputs */
extern int
    Get_Member(PyObject *pobject, char *attrname,
                   char *resfmt,  void *cresult);            /* output */
extern int
    Set_Member(PyObject *pobject, char *attrname,
                   char *valfmt,  ... /* val, val... */ );   /* input */

#endif (!PYEMBED_H)
```

## Using Python Modules in C

The first thing we may want to do is load modules and fetch objects they define by name. As we saw earlier, Python provides API functions to accomplish these tasks; here *Load_Attribute* adds a higher-level interface. The extended *Load_Module* function also provides for automatic module reloads: if the

*PY_RELOAD* flag is set, a module is reloaded each time it, or one of its attributes, is referenced from C (for instance, each time we call one of its functions). Here are some things to notice:

*Importing modules*
: Importing a module with *PyImport_ImportModule* is almost the same as a Python *import* statement, but not quite. It loads a module file and puts it in *sys.modules*, but it doesn't bring the module name into any other module's namespace.

*Reloading modules*
: As we saw in Chapter 7, *Adding a Simple User Interface*, dynamic reloading lets us change module files without stopping a program that uses them. Reloading a module reexecutes its new code, in the same module namespace dictionary. Normally, this replaces its functions, classes, and variables with the new versions. In this API, reloading occurs on module references.

*Dummy modules*
: The *Make_Dummy_Module* function creates a module object with no associated file; this comes in handy for creating multiple namespaces when running code strings. For instance, we can make a new namespace for each component of a C system that runs embedded code strings. Dummy modules are marked by setting a `__dummy__` module attribute to *None* (to avoid reloading these later: there's no file).

*Recursive calls*
: Module imports may set off recursive Python invocations: the module's code is executed before the import call returns. The module's code might use C extensions, etc. In general, the Python interpreter and API can be called with arbitrarily deep recursion. Embedded code may call extensions, which call embedded code, and so on.

*Example 15-7: File: pyembed0.c*

```
/*****************************************************************************
 * MODULE INTERFACE
 * make/import/reload a python module by name
 *****************************************************************************/

#include "pyembed.h"

int PY_RELOAD = 0;     /* reload modules dynamically? */
int PY_DEBUG  = 0;     /* debug embedded code with pdb? */

char *Init(char *modname) {
    Py_Initialize();                                  /* init python if needed */
    return modname == NULL? "__main__" : modname;    /* default to '__main__' */
}
```

*Example 15-7: File: pyembed0.c (continued)*

```
int
Make_Dummy_Module(char *modname)      /* namespace for strings: if no file */
{                                     /* instead of sharing __main__ for all */
    PyObject *module, *dict;          /* note: __main__ is created in py_init */
    Py_Initialize();
    module = PyImport_AddModule(modname);     /* fetch or make, no load */
    if (module == NULL)                       /* module not incref'd */
        return -1;
    else {                                           /* module.__dict__ */
        dict = PyModule_GetDict(module);             /* ['__dummy__'] = None */
        PyDict_SetItemString(dict, "__dummy__", Py_None);
        PyDict_SetItemString(dict, "__builtins__", PyEval_GetBuiltins());
        return 0;
    }
}


PyObject *
Load_Module(char *modname)             /* returns module object */
{
    /* 4 cases...
     * 1) module "__main__" has no file, and not prebuilt: fetch or make
     * 2) dummy modules have no files: don't try to reload them
     * 3) reload set and already loaded (on sys.modules): "reload()" before use
     * 4) not loaded yet, or loaded but reload off: "import" to fetch or load */

    PyObject *module, *result;
    modname = Init(modname);                       /* default to __main__ */
    module  = PyDict_GetItemString(                /* in sys.modules dict? */
                  PyImport_GetModuleDict(), modname);

    if (strcmp(modname, "__main__") == 0)           /* no file */
        return PyImport_AddModule(modname);        /* not incref'd */
    else
    if (module != NULL &&                                /* dummy: no file */
        PyDict_GetItemString(PyModule_GetDict(module), "__dummy__"))
        return module;                                   /* not incref'd */
    else
    if (PY_RELOAD && module != NULL && PyModule_Check(module)) {
        module = PyImport_ReloadModule(module);    /* reload-file/run-code */
        Py_XDECREF(module);                        /* still on sys.modules */
        return module;                             /* not incref'd */
    }
    else {
        module = PyImport_ImportModule(modname);   /* fetch or load module */
        Py_XDECREF(module);                        /* still on sys.modules */
        return module;                             /* not incref'd */
    }
}
```

*Example 15-7: File: pyembed0.c (continued)*

```
PyObject *
Load_Attribute(char *modname, char *attrname)
{
    PyObject *module;                          /* fetch "module.attr" */
    modname = Init(modname);                   /* use before PyEval_CallObject */
    module  = Load_Module(modname);            /* not incref'd, may reload */
    if (module == NULL)
        return NULL;
    return PyObject_GetAttrString(module, attrname);  /* func, class, var,.. */
}                                                     /* caller must xdecref */


/* extra ops */
int
Run_Command_Line(char *prompt)
{
    int res;                 /* interact with python, in "__main__" */
    Py_Initialize();         /* in the program's "stdio" window     */
    if (prompt != NULL)
        printf("[%s <ctrl-d exits>]\n", prompt);
    res = PyRun_InteractiveLoop(stdin, "<stdin>");
    return res;
}
```

## Using Python Module Variables in C

Next let's define interfaces for fetching and changing Python module level (global) variables from C. When we run code strings, this can be a convenient way to communicate without argument-passing or imported APIs: C sets global variables to provide input data, and fetches global variables set by the embedded code as the result. We'll see an example of this technique in a moment.

The *Get_Global* function fetches a variable's value (after loading or reloading its module if needed) and converts it from Python to C form, according to a passed-in Python format string. *Set_Global* converts C values to Python form before assigning them to Python variables.

*Example 15-8: File: pyembed1.c*

```
/*****************************************************************************
 * GET/SET MODULE-LEVEL (GLOBAL) PYTHON VARIABLES BY NAME
 * handles module (re)loading, input/output conversions;
 * useful for passing data to/from codestrings: no arguments
 * ex: make/load module + set-inputs + run-codestring + get-outputs
 *****************************************************************************/

#include "pyembed.h"
#include <stdarg.h>
```

*Example 15-8: File: pyembed1.c (continued)*

```
int
Convert_Result(PyObject *presult, char *resFormat, void *resTarget)
{
    if (presult == NULL)                /* error when run? */
        return -1;
    if (resTarget == NULL) {            /* NULL: ignore result */
        Py_DECREF(presult);             /* procedures return None */
        return 0;
    }
    if (! PyArg_Parse(presult, resFormat, resTarget)) { /* convert Python->C */
        Py_DECREF(presult);                             /* may not be a tuple */
        return -1;                                      /* error in convert? */
    }
    if (strcmp(resFormat, "O") != 0)       /* free object unless passed-out */
        Py_DECREF(presult);
    return 0;                              /* 0=success, -1=failure */
}                                          /* if 0: result in *resTarget  */


int
Get_Global(char *modname, char *varname, char *resfmt, void *cresult)
{
    PyObject *var;                                  /* "x = modname.varname" */
    var =  Load_Attribute(modname, varname);        /* var is incref'd */
    return Convert_Result(var, resfmt, cresult);    /* convert output to C form */
}


int
Set_Global(char *modname, char *varname, char *valfmt, ... /* cval(s) */)
{
    int result;
    PyObject *module, *val;                         /* "modname.varname = val" */
    va_list cvals;
    va_start(cvals, valfmt);                        /* C args after valfmt */

    module = Load_Module(modname);                  /* get/load module */
    if (module == NULL)
        return -1;
    val = Py_VaBuildValue(valfmt, cvals);           /* convert input to Python */
    va_end(cvals);
    if (val == NULL)
        return -1;
    result = PyObject_SetAttrString(module, varname, val);
    Py_DECREF(val);                                 /* set global module var */
    return result;                                  /* decref val: var owns it */
}                                                   /* 0=success, varname set */
```

## *Running Embedded Code Strings*

The next file adds support for running and debugging embedded Python code represented as C character strings. The string can contain a Python expression or statement: Python's parser handles the two differently and returns no result for statements. For expressions, we get back a Python object, which is converted to C form according to a passed-in format string.

If embedded debugging is enabled (*PY_DEBUG*), embedded strings are routed to Python's *pdb* debugger (see Chapter 11, *Graphical User Interfaces*) instead of being run directly. The program stops immediately when the embedded call is made; we can step through the embedded code, set breakpoints, etc. by interacting with *pdb* in the C program's *stdin* window. Expression results are always returned to C, even while debugging.

---

*NOTE* Python's standard input/output/error streams are the same as those in C: Python's *print* statement sends text to the enclosing C program's *stdout* file stream. The situation isn't as clear when Python's embedded in a C++ program: Python's *stdout* might not be the same as C++'s *cout*. Buffering differences may make the two interleave unexpectedly; we can work around this with explicit files, manual *stdout* flushing, etc.

---

*Example 15-9: File: pyembed2.c*

```
/**************************************************************************
 * RUN EMBEDDED CODE-STRINGS
 * handles debugging, module (re)loading, namespaces, output conversions;
 * pbd.runeval returns a value: "eval(expr + '\n', globals, locals)";
 * pdb.run is just a statement: "exec cmd + '\n' in globals, locals"
 **************************************************************************/

#include "pyembed.h"

PyObject *
Debug_Codestr(StringModes mode, char *codestring, PyObject *moddict)
{
    PyObject *pdbfunc, *presult;
    char *pdbname = (mode == PY_EXPRESSION ? "runeval" : "run");

    pdbfunc = Load_Attribute("pdb", pdbname);    /* "pdb.run(stmt, d, d)" */
    if (pdbfunc == NULL)                         /* get func from pdb.py  */
        return NULL;                             /* and call it with args */
    else {
        presult =
            PyEval_CallFunction(pdbfunc, "(sOO)", codestring, moddict, moddict);
```

*Example 15-9: File: pyembed2.c (continued)*

```
        Py_DECREF(pdbfunc);
        return presult;                        /* or use Run_Function.. */
    }
}


int
Run_Codestr(StringModes mode, char *code,     /* expr or stmt string */
            char *modname,                    /* loads module if needed */
            char *resfmt, void *cresult)      /* converts expr result to C */
{
    int parse_mode;                           /* "eval(code, d, d)", or */
    PyObject *module, *dict, *presult;        /* "exec code in d, d" */

    module = Load_Module(modname);            /* get module, init python */
    if (module == NULL)                       /* not incref'd */
        return -1;
    dict = PyModule_GetDict(module);          /* get dict namespace */
    if (dict == NULL)                         /* not incref'd */
        return -1;

    parse_mode = (mode == PY_EXPRESSION ? eval_input : file_input);
    if (PY_DEBUG)
        presult = Debug_Codestr(mode, code, dict);          /* run in pdb */
    else
        presult = PyRun_String(code, parse_mode, dict, dict); /* eval direct */
                                                            /* increfs res */
    if (mode == PY_STATEMENT) {
        int result = (presult == NULL? -1 : 0);         /* stmt: 'None' */
        Py_XDECREF(presult);                            /* ignore result */
        return result;
    }
    return Convert_Result(presult, resfmt, cresult);    /* expr val to C */
}
```

## Running Functions and Classes in Module Files

Another way to embed Python is by calling functions (and classes) defined at the top level of external module files. This technique can be more powerful than raw code strings: users have more control over the embedded code's structure. There's also a more direct way to send input from C and get output from Python as argument lists and return values, respectively. But it may require special handling for the external Python files.

*Run_Function* calls a function (or class) in a module file, given the names of the module and function. Module interfacing is automated. Results are converted to C form according to a format string. Here, we also convert inputs (the argument list) to Python form, using an additional format-string.

There is also support for routing embedded function calls to the debugger when *PY_DEBUG* is set: control stops before the function is entered. Note that we can use *Run_Function* to call a class in a module too; we get back a class instance object if we use the "O" output conversion code.

*Example 15-10: File: pyembed3.c*

```
/**************************************************************************
 * RUN EMBEDDED MODULE-FUNCTIONS
 * handles module (re)import, debugging, input/output conversions;
 * note: also useful for calling classes at the top-level of a module
 * to make Python instances: use class-name and 'O' result convert-code;
 * use argfmt="()" for no args, cresult='NULL' for no result (procedure);
 **************************************************************************/

#include "pyembed.h"
#include <stdarg.h>

PyObject *
Debug_Function(PyObject *func, PyObject *args)
{
    int oops, res;
    PyObject *presult;

    /* much magic: expand tuple at front */
    oops = _PyTuple_Resize(&args, (1 + PyTuple_Size(args)), 1);
    oops |= PyTuple_SetItem(args, 0, func);
    if (oops)
        return NULL;                        /* "args = (funcobj,) + (arg,..)" */

    res = Run_Function(                     /* "pdb.runcall(funcobj, arg,..)" */
             "pdb",  "runcall",             /* recursive run_function */
             "O",    &presult,
             "O",     args);                /* args already is a tuple */
    return (res != 0) ? NULL : presult;     /* errors in run_function? */
}                                           /* presult not yet decref'd */


int
Run_Function(char *modname, char *funcname,          /* load from module */
             char *resfmt,  void *cresult,            /* convert to c/c++ */
             char *argfmt,  ... /* arg, arg... */ )   /* convert to python */
{
    PyObject *func, *args, *presult;
    va_list argslist;
    va_start(argslist, argfmt);                  /* "modname.funcname(args)" */

    func = Load_Attribute(modname, funcname);    /* reload?; incref'd */
    if (func == NULL)                            /* func may be a class */
        return -1;
    args = Py_VaBuildValue(argfmt, argslist);    /* convert args to python */
    if (args == NULL) {                          /* args incref'd */
        Py_DECREF(func);
```

*Example 15-10: File: pyembed3.c (continued)*

```
        return -1;
    }
    if (PY_DEBUG && strcmp(modname, "pdb") != 0)    /* debug this call? */
        presult = Debug_Function(func, args);       /* run in pdb; incref'd */
    else
        presult = PyEval_CallObject(func, args);    /* run function; incref'd */

    Py_DECREF(func);
    Py_DECREF(args);                                  /* result may be None */
    return Convert_Result(presult, resfmt, cresult);  /* convert result to C */
}
```

## Using Object Attributes: Methods and Members

Finally, the next file provides interfaces for calling, fetching, and setting an object's attributes by name. There's no module here; instead, we pass in an object obtained from other API interfaces. For instance, an object from calling:

- *Load_Attribute* to get an object from a module directly
- *Run_Codestr* to get an object from a module with an expression
- *Run_Function* with output format *O*, to get an unconverted function or class call result
- Other: *Get_Global*, registered objects, lower-level API tools like *PyRun_String*, and so on

The tools here can also be used to process objects passed to C *extension* functions from Python. The object can be anything with named attributes: a class, class instance, type instance, module, etc. In fact, the get/set functions here are almost identical to the module-variable interfaces above, but there is no module-fetch logic. If debug mode is enabled, method calls are routed to the function debugging interface.

*Example 15-11: File: pyembed4.c*

```
/*****************************************************************************
 * RUN EMBEDDED OBJECT-METHODS, ACCESS OBJECT-ATTRIBUTES
 * handles debugging, input/output conversions; no module to reload here
 *****************************************************************************/

#include "pyembed.h"
#include <stdarg.h>

int
Run_Method(PyObject *pobject,  char *method,
               char *resfmt,   void *cresult,            /* convert to c/c++ */
               char *argfmt,   ... /* arg, arg... */ )  /* convert to python */
{
```

*Example 15-11: File: pyembed4.c (continued)*

```
    PyObject *pmeth, *pargs, *presult;
    va_list argslist;                           /* "pobject.method(args)" */
    va_start(argslist, argfmt);

    Py_Initialize();                            /* init if first time */
    pmeth = PyObject_GetAttrString(pobject, method);
    if (pmeth == NULL)                          /* get callable object */
        return -1;                              /* bound method? has self */
    pargs = Py_VaBuildValue(argfmt, argslist);  /* args: c->python */
    if (pargs == NULL) {
        Py_DECREF(pmeth);
        return -1;
    }
    if (PY_DEBUG)                               /* debug it too? */
        presult = Debug_Function(pmeth, pargs);
    else
        presult = PyEval_CallObject(pmeth, pargs);   /* run interpreter */

    Py_DECREF(pmeth);
    Py_DECREF(pargs);
    return Convert_Result(presult, resfmt, cresult);
}


int
Get_Member(PyObject *pobject, char *attrname,
           char *resfmt,  void *cresult)              /* convert to c/c++ */
{
    PyObject *pmemb;                                  /* "pobject.attrname" */
    Py_Initialize();
    pmemb = PyObject_GetAttrString(pobject, attrname);  /* incref'd */
    return Convert_Result(pmemb, resfmt, cresult);      /* do getargs, decref */
}


int
Set_Member(PyObject *pobject, char *attrname,
           char *argfmt,  ... /* arg, arg... */ ) /* convert to python */
{
    int result;
    PyObject *pval;
    va_list argslist;                          /* "pobject.attrname = v" */
    va_start(argslist, argfmt);
    Py_Initialize();                           /* init if first time */
    pval = Py_VaBuildValue(argfmt, argslist);  /* input: C->Python */
    if (pval == NULL)
        return -1;
    result = PyObject_SetAttrString(pobject, attrname, pval);     /* setattr */
    Py_DECREF(pval);
    return result;
}
```

## *Comparing API Modes*

As you may expect, we can mix this API's functions with the lower-level built-in API functions arbitrarily. For example, the *Debug_Codestr* function in *pyembed2.c* uses built-in tools to run *pdb* functions:

```
PyObject *
Debug_Codestr(StringModes mode, char *codestring, PyObject *moddict)
{
    PyObject *pdbfunc, *presult;
    char *pdbname = (mode == PY_EXPRESSION ? "runeval" : "run");

    pdbfunc = Load_Attribute("pdb", pdbname);    /* "pdb.run(stmt, d, d)" */
    if (pdbfunc == NULL)                         /* get func from pdb.py  */
        return NULL;                             /* and call it with args */
    else {
        presult =
            PyEval_CallFunction(pdbfunc, "(sOO)", codestring, moddict, moddict);
        Py_DECREF(pdbfunc);
        return presult;                          /* or use Run_Function.. */
    }
}
```

The built-in *PyEval_CallFunction* (and its relative, *PyEval_CallMethod*) automatically builds an input argument list from a format string. But the extended *Run_Function* interface also:

- Handles module/attribute references
- Supports embedded code reloading and debugging
- Converts output data (the return value) to C

These additions aren't all useful for predefined modules like *pdb*, but to compare the two interfaces, here's how we could achieve the same effect by calling *Run_Function*:

```
PyObject *
Debug_Codestr(StringModes mode, char *codestring, PyObject *moddict)
{
    int stat;
    PyObject *presult;
    char *pdbname = (mode == PY_EXPRESSION ? "runeval" : "run");
    stat = Run_Function(
                 "pdb",    pdbname,          /* pdb.runeval(str, d, d) */
                 "O",      &presult,
                 "(sOO)",  codestring, moddict, moddict);
    return (stat != 0) ? NULL : presult;     /* presult not yet decref'd */
}
```

# An Embedded Call API Client

Now that we've seen the basic API and added some higher-level functions, let's put them to work. The following file defines a C *main* program that illustrates most embedded call techniques: both native Python API function calls and use of the extended API we just saw. We'll see its output shortly.

## The C main Program

*Example 15-12: File: main.c*

```
/**********************************************************************
* test-file for simple embedded-calls.
* this includes a "main" function: C is 'on top' in the program.
**********************************************************************/

#include "pyembed.h"
#define TRACE(msg) printf("\n%s\n", msg);
char *getprogramname() { return "test"; }    /* not always needed */


main(argc, argv)
int argc;
char **argv;
{
    printf("Hello from C.\n");
    Py_Initialize();                /* initialize embedded python libraries */
    PySys_SetArgv(argc, argv);      /* optional: export command args to python */
    BASIC_EMBEDDING();
    EMBEDDED_CALL_API();
    printf("Bye from C.\n");
    Py_Exit(0);                     /* optional: runs sys.exitfunc handler */
}


BASIC_EMBEDDING()          /* test low-level interfaces */
{
    PyObject *module, *dict, *pstack;

    /*****************************************************************
     * run code-strings in default namespace (module '__main__');
     * uses embedding + extending: os/sys use C extension modules;
     * can call PyRun_SimpleString, PyRun_String, PyEval_CallObject..
     *****************************************************************/

    TRACE("SIMPLE STRINGS")
    PyRun_SimpleString("import sys, os");
    PyRun_SimpleString("print 'Hello,', os.environ['USER'] + '.'");
    PyRun_SimpleString("print 'Args: ', sys.argv");
    PyRun_SimpleString("print 'Path: ', sys.path[0:2], '...'");
```

*Example 15-12: File: main.c (continued)*

```
    /*****************************************************************
     * use the stack-type extension in embedded code; PyRun_String uses
     * explicit namespaces and parse-modes; the PyRun_String results
     * are None, but they should really be DECREF'd  and return values
     * should be checked for NULL (a python error/exception occurred);
     *****************************************************************/

    TRACE("STACK EXTENSION")
    module = PyImport_AddModule("__main__");             /* fetch a module */
    dict   = PyModule_GetDict(module);                   /* get its __dict__ */
    PyRun_String("from stacktype import *", file_input, dict, dict);
    PyRun_String("x = Stack()", file_input, dict, dict);
    PyRun_String("for c in 'SPAM':\n"                        /* multi-line */
                 "\tx.push(c)\n", file_input, dict, dict);   /* stmts okay */
    PyRun_String("print x, len(x)", file_input, dict, dict);

    /* make a new instance */
    pstack = PyRun_String("Stack()", eval_input, dict, dict);
    PyObject_Print(pstack, stdout, 0);
    Py_DECREF(pstack);
}


EMBEDDED_CALL_API()                     /* test enhanced wrappers */
{
    int i, status, result;
    char *strres;                       /* actual text is stored in python */
    PyObject *pobject1, *pobject2;      /* raw python objects: 'O' output codes */

    /*****************************************************************
     * use the run_codestr wrapper like PyRun_SimpleString:
     * run string in __main__ (NULL 1), with no result (NULL 2);
     * see order1.c (ahead) for dummy-module creation/use;
     *****************************************************************/

    Run_Codestr(PY_STATEMENT, "print 'Hello api world'", NULL, "", NULL);

    /*****************************************************************
     * turn on dynamic reload-on-call mode, and call a function in a
     * module file; the file can be changed between the five calls here;
     * calls "main.func(4, 8)": see mainc.py for equivalent Python code;
     *****************************************************************/

    TRACE("DYNAMIC RELOADING")
    PY_RELOAD = 1;
    for (i=0; i < 5; i++) {
        status = Run_Function("main", "func", "i", &result, "(ii)", 4, 8);
        if (status == -1) {
            printf("Error running func\n");
            PyErr_Print();                          /* python stack dump */
        }
        else
```

*Example 15-12: File: main.c (continued)*

```
        printf("result => %d\n", result);
    if (i < 4) {
        printf("change main.py now...");      /* edit in another window */
        getchar();                             /* wait for a keypress */
    }
}

/*********************************************************************
 * turn on dynamic debugging, and run a string and a function;
 * pdb stops execution as soon as the embedded code starts: set
 * breakponts, step through code, etc.; both run "main.func(4, 8)";
 *********************************************************************/

TRACE("DYNAMIC DEBUGGING")
PY_RELOAD = 0;
PY_DEBUG  = 1;         /* could do both at once */

status = Run_Codestr(PY_EXPRESSION, "func(4, 8)", "main", "i", &result);
printf("%d, %d\n\n", status, result);

status = Run_Function("main", "func", "i", &result, "(ii)", 4, 8);
printf("%d, %d\n", status, result);
PY_DEBUG = 0;

/*********************************************************************
 * a few attribute tests: sys module, already imported in __main__;
 * in general, return values should be checked for errors too;
 *********************************************************************/

TRACE("OBJECT ATTRIBUTES")
Run_Command_Line("check sys");                              /* in __main__ */
Run_Codestr(PY_EXPRESSION, "sys", NULL, "O", &pobject1);   /* __main__.sys */
Get_Member(pobject1, "version", "s", &strres);              /* sys.version */
printf("version => %s...\n", strres);

Set_Member(pobject1, "version", "s", "1.4 1996?");          /* change it */
Run_Codestr(PY_STATEMENT, "print sys.version", NULL, "", NULL);

Get_Member(pobject1, "modules", "O", &pobject2);            /* sys.modules */
Run_Method(pobject2, "has_key", "i", &result, "(s)", "main"); /* .has_key*/
printf("result => %d\n", result);
Py_XDECREF(pobject2);

Get_Member(pobject1, "stdout", "O", &pobject2);             /* sys.stdout */
Run_Method(pobject2, "write", "", NULL, "(s)", "right...\n");  /* .write*/

Py_XDECREF(pobject1);    /* need to free raw python objects */
Py_XDECREF(pobject2);    /* passed out with "O" format code */
}
```

## Building Programs that Embed Python

Here's a more complex embedded *makefile*. When Python's embedded in a C program, we need to link in Python's libraries, plus configuration files and installed extension libraries. The following file shows how we might build an executable from the *main.c* source file in Example 15-2 above. It assumes the *Tkinter* GUI and *dbm* database extensions have been enabled in the *Modules/Setup* file and includes the extended API modules we wrote earlier. Of course, makefile syntax varies widely, and build details may vary on some platforms (Python is usually a single DLL on Microsoft Windows). This example is meant for illustration only.

*Example 15-13: File: makefile*

```
###########################################################################
# A minimal makefile for programs that embed Python, with the
# Tkinter and dbm extensions enabled. In general, link:
#
#    - Python's libraries (currently 4)
#    - Python's config.o and getpath.o (configuration files)
#    - Libraries for extensions outside Python's build-tree
#    - Your "main" function, plus any application modules and libraries.
#
# Here, we need Tk and dbm libraries (since these extensions were
# enabled in Modules/Setup), plus the "pyembed" wrapper modules.
#
# To see which extension libraries must be linked, check the Makefile
# generated in the "Modules" directory of the Python tree. Your file
# paths will vary, and there are more general ways to code this.
###########################################################################


TK = /home/mark/python-1.3
PY = /home/mark/python-1.3/Python-1.3

PLIBS = $(PY)/Modules/libModules.a \
        $(PY)/Python/libPython.a \
        $(PY)/Objects/libObjects.a \
        $(PY)/Parser/libParser.a

POBJS = $(PY)/Modules/config.o $(PY)/Modules/getpath.o

CLIBS = -L/usr/lib \
        -L$(TK)/tcl7.4 \
        -L$(TK)/tk4.0 \
        -L$/usr/X11/lib \
        -ldbm -ltk -ltcl -lX11 -lm

APIMODS = pyembed0.o pyembed1.o pyembed2.o pyembed3.o pyembed4.o

main: main.o $(APIMODS)
        cc -g main.o $(APIMODS) $(POBJS) $(PLIBS) $(CLIBS) -o main
```

*Example 15-13: File: makefile (continued)*

```
main.o: main.c pyembed.h
	cc main.c -c -g -I$(PY)/Include -I$(PY)/.

pyembed0.o: pyembed0.c pyembed.h
	cc pyembed0.c -g -c -I$(PY)/Include -I$(PY)/.
pyembed1.o: pyembed1.c pyembed.h
	cc pyembed1.c -g -c -I$(PY)/Include -I$(PY)/.
pyembed2.o: pyembed2.c pyembed.h
	cc pyembed2.c -g -c -I$(PY)/Include -I$(PY)/.
pyembed3.o: pyembed3.c pyembed.h
	cc pyembed3.c -g -c -I$(PY)/Include -I$(PY)/.
pyembed4.o: pyembed4.c pyembed.h
	cc pyembed4.c -g -c -I$(PY)/Include -I$(PY)/.

clean:
	rm *.o *.pyc
```

## An External Module Function

To illustrate reload mode, the C program runs a Python module function *main.func* repeatedly, pausing before each call, to allow the file to be modified. Here's the file that is referenced by C; it's embedded Python code, but it actually exists in a file that's external to the C program.

*Example 15-14: File: main.py*

```
######################################################
# change this file between calls: auto-reload mode
# gets the new version each time 'func' is called;
# for the test, the last line was changed to:
#     return x + y
#     return x * y
#     return x \y      - syntax error
#     return x / 0      - zero-divide error
#     return pow(x, y)
######################################################

def func(x, y):
    return x + y              # change me
```

### Reloading in Python

Finally, here's a Python program used to test *main.func* reloading before it was written in C. It shows how to code (or prototype) the corresponding operations in Python. The C API *PyErr_Print* function is similar to the Python *traceback.print_exc*; both display the current exception.

*Example 15-15: File: mainc.py*

```
import main, traceback
for i in range(5):
    try:
        reload(main)
        res = main.func(4, 8)
    except:
        print 'error'
        traceback.print_exc()
    else: print res
    if i < 4: raw_input('change main.py now...')
```

## *Running the C Program*

Here's the output we get from running the standalone executable created from the C program. It's mostly straightforward, but here are some highlights:

- The result of the module function call is different each time while reload mode is turned on.
- Control stops in the Python debugger for all string and function calls while debug mode is enabled.
- The stack-extension section uses the *Stack* C extension type we implemented in Chapter 14.
- The interactive command line is spawned from C: it runs in the namespace of module `__main__`.

Study the C program for more details on each of the test outputs here.

```
% main
Hello from C.

SIMPLE STRINGS
Hello, mark.
Args: ['main']
Path: ['.', '/home/mark/python-1.3/Python-1.3/Lib'] ...

STACK EXTENSION
[Stack:
3: 'M'
2: 'A'
1: 'P'
0: 'S'
]
 4
[Stack:
]
Hello api world

DYNAMIC RELOADING
```

```
result => 12
change main.py now...
result => 32
change main.py now...
Error running func
  File "./main.py", line 13
    return x \y              # change me
                                      ^
SyntaxError: invalid token
change main.py now...
Error running func
Traceback (innermost last):
  File "./main.py", line 13, in func
    return x / 0              # change me
ZeroDivisionError: integer division or modulo
change main.py now...
result => 65536

DYNAMIC DEBUGGING
> <string>(0)?()
(Pdb) s
> ./main.py(12)func()
-> def func(x, y):
(Pdb) s
> ./main.py(13)func()
-> return pow(x, y)          # change me
(Pdb) w
  <string>(0)?()
> ./main.py(13)func()
-> return pow(x, y)          # change me
(Pdb) p x
4
(Pdb) s
--Return--
> ./main.py(13)func()->65536
-> return pow(x, y)          # change me
(Pdb) s
--Return--
> <string>(0)?()->65536
(Pdb) c
0, 65536

> ./main.py(12)func()
-> def func(x, y):
(Pdb) s
> ./main.py(13)func()
-> return pow(x, y)          # change me
(Pdb) c
--Return--
> ./main.py(13)func()->65536
-> return pow(x, y)          # change me
(Pdb) c
0, 65536
```

```
OBJECT ATTRIBUTES
[check sys <ctrl-d exits>]
>>> sys
<module 'sys'>
>>> sys.version
'1.3 (Feb  7 1996)  [GCC 2.5.8]'
>>> dir()
['Stack', '__builtins__', '__doc__', '__name__', 'c', 'error', 'os', 'sys', 'x']
>>>
version => 1.3 (Feb  7 1996)  [GCC 2.5.8]...
1.4 1996?
result => 1
right...
Bye from C.
```

Suggested exercises:

1. Add selective module reloading. Instead of reloading all modules when reload mode is set, reload a module when it is referenced if and only if its name has been registered for reloading. You may also implement reloading by module/function name pairs, but this won't apply to code strings. Why?
2. Add selective debugging. Route embedded calls to *pdb* only if they match registered module names (and possibly function and method names, if you want to be more accurate). What about strings?
3. Add a *\n* to the end of code strings before executing them. Compound statements may need an extra newline if they end on an indented line. This isn't an issue if the string is debugged: *pdb* adds a *\n*.
4. Add more specific error messages. Instead of relying on the messages set in Python when something has not been found, add *module/attribute not found* messages locally.
5. Can *Get_Global/Set_Global* be implemented in terms of the *Get_Member/Set_Member* functions? They're almost the same, except for the module fetch (module variables are really object attributes).
6. *Get_Global* assumes a single target for the result. This function fails for compound objects. Extend it so that it handles multiple output targets, instead of requiring "O" output codes and a separate *PyArg_Parse* step. Apply the same fix to other API functions with outputs. Does this make the function-calls too complex?
7. *Run_Codestr*'s last two arguments are ignored when running statements. It may be better to write a separate function for statements. Consider the tradeoffs for this design.

8. Run embedded code strings to pop up *Tkinter* GUI widgets, access shelves, etc. Would it cause problems if *Tkinter* windows appeared in a non-*Tkinter* GUI enclosing application?
9. Study *Tkinter*'s callable object registration system (see *Tkinter.py* and *tkinter.c* in Python's source tree). When callbacks are registered as *command* or *bind* events, the *self._register* method is the link to the C *tkinter* module (in the current implementation). It saves the callable object passed in as client data for a C callback handler. On an event, the C module runs the saved action using *PyEval_CallObject*. We'll discuss this strategy more later in this chapter.
10. Experiment with passing lists, tuples, and dictionaries in and out of embedded code. So far, we've showed only input/output conversions for simple types (integers, strings, etc.). For compound inputs, *Py_BuildValue* supports the extended format-codes we saw in Chapter 14. For outputs, we can get unconverted objects with the "O" format code and access components with API functions.

# *Case Study: Embedding User-Coded Validations*

Here's a more realistic example of Python embedding at work. Suppose we've written a C-based system that manages orders submitted against an inventory of products. Now, let's further suppose that we've decided that we're going to ship binaries only (libraries and/or executables), not source code. But we'd still like to make some of the system's validations configurable on-site, by our customers.

It may be that we can't predict the structure of some tests ahead of time. Or maybe we just want to open up parts of our the system for customization, without requiring end-users to know about the internals of our C implementation. Whatever the reason, what we need are hooks in our system, where we can delegate validations to customizable code. In other words, we want an embedded scripting-language like Python.

By using Python as an embedded extension language, users get a powerful language that's simple to learn and use. In fact, users need learn only one language because Python can be applied across all our systems. And because Python supports extending, we can also expose selected parts of our system as extension modules and types, for use in user-customizable embedded code.

Let's look at a concrete example of how embedding can help us here. The following two examples illustrate embedded Python validations: first as code strings and then as module functions.

## Running Validations as Embedded Code Strings

Code strings are often the easiest way to represent embedded Python code. There are no external module files to manage, and code can be stored in a database. But data communication requires extra protocols.

### The inventory prototype

First let's define a Python module to simulate an inventory database interface. It's used by both embedding examples we'll see. It defines interfaces for inventory and buyer data stores, which are used by the validation code (and the enclosing C program). Normally this information would be fetched from a file, shelve, or other database storage medium, and might be implemented in C.

This file is an example of both how embedded Python code can also use application-specific extensions, and how Python prototyping can be used in typical development. It lets us test the system before real data have been entered. (Note: this module file name is really *inventor.py* for older "8.3" PC systems.)

*Example 15-16: File: inventory.py*

```
# simulate inventory/buyer databases while prototyping

Inventory = { 111: 10,               # "sku (product) : quantity"
              121: 1,                # would usually be a file or shelve:
              131: 100,              # the operations below could work on
              222: 5 }               # an open shelve (or dbm file) too...

Skus = Inventory.keys()              # cache keys if they won't change

def skus():             return Skus
def stock(sku):         return Inventory[sku]
def reduce(sku, qty):  Inventory[sku] = Inventory[sku] - qty

Buyers = ['ISpam', 'USpam', 'ATest']   # or keys() of a shelve/dbm file

def buyers():           return Buyers
def add_buyer(buyer):  Buyers.append(buyer)

def print_files():
    print Inventory, Buyers     # check updates effect
```

### The validations code string

Next, here's the code string that runs as embedded Python code. The enclosing program loads the file's contents as a single character string and passes it to Python to be executed all at once. Because it's normal Python code, it can set variables, define functions and classes, and even import modules and C extensions defined onsite. In fact, it has access to all Python services (GUIs, databases, shell tools, etc.) and extensions added by the application. It runs in the module namespace specified by the enclosing C program.

As is, this string exists in a flat text file which users can edit onsite. In practice, we might use environment variables to find it, link it to an HTML page, or store it in a database, where users can edit it with GUI data entry tools. However it's stored, it allows users to change the validation's logic without rebuilding the enclosing C system. Also note that it imports the *inventory* prototype module above; when *inventory* is later changed to use a real database, the code here won't need to be updated (even if *inventory* is moved to a C extension module).

*Example 15-17: File: order1.py*

```
# input vars:  PRODUCT, QUANTITY, BUYER
# output vars: ERRORS, WARNINGS

import string               # all python tools are available to embedded code
import inventory            # plus C extensions, Python modules, classes,..
msgs, errs = [], []         # warning, error message lists

def validate_order():
    if PRODUCT not in inventory.skus():       # this function could be imported
        errs.append('bad-product')            # from a user-defined module too
    elif QUANTITY > inventory.stock(PRODUCT):
        errs.append('check-quantity')
    else:
        inventory.reduce(PRODUCT, QUANTITY)
        if inventory.stock(PRODUCT) / QUANTITY < 2:
            msgs.append('reorder-soon:' + 'PRODUCT')

first, last = BUYER[0], BUYER[1:]             # code is changeable on-site:
if first not in string.uppercase:             # this file is run as one long
    errs.append('buyer-name:' + first)        # code-string, with input and
if BUYER not in inventory.buyers():           # output vars used by the C app
    msgs.append('new-buyer-added')
    inventory.add_buyer(BUYER)
validate_order()

ERRORS   = string.join(errs)      # add a space between messages
WARNINGS = string.join(msgs)      # pass out as strings: "" == none
```

### *The enclosing C program*

Now here's the C program that runs the Python validation above. It loads the file into a character array, and calls the *Run_Codestr* extended API function to execute the Python code. An order entry file is simulated as an array of C *structs* here; normally, this would be a real external file.

The C program makes its own Python namespace (module) for running the embedded strings, using *Make_Dummy_Module*. To communicate with the Python code string, the C program sets variables in the new namespace to the components of an order entry using *Set_Global*. Results are fetched from the *ERRORS* and *WARNINGS* variables using *Get_Global*. The Python code is expected to set these to a string of messages, separated by blanks (or the empty string if no errors are found).

We also call an *inventory* module function to display the simulated database contents after each validation: some validations not only check conditions but change the database as a side effect. This may not be appropriate for some applications; to prevent changes from Python, we would just omit interfaces in the *inventory* module.

*Example 15-18: File: order1.c*

```
/* run embedded code-string validations */

#include <stdio.h>
#include <string.h>
#include "pyembed.h"

struct {
    int product;            /* or use a string if key is structured: */
    int quantity;           /* python code san spilt it up as needed */
    char *buyer;            /* first-initial/last */
} orders[] = {
    { 111, 2, "ISpam" },      /* this would usually be an orders file */
    { 222, 5, "ATest" },      /* which the python code could read too */
    { 141, 3, "USpam" },
    { 222, 1, "4More" },
    { 222, 0, "Stuff" },      /* the script might live in a database too */
    { 131, 9, "NMore" }
};
int numorders = 6;

run_user_validation()
{                                   /* python's initialized automaticaly */
    int i, status;                  /* XXXX should check status everywhere */
    char script[4096];              /* XXXX should malloc a big-enough block */
    char *errors, *warnings;
    FILE *file;

    file = fopen("order1.py", "r");          /* customizable validations */
    fread(script, 1, 4096, file);
    status = Make_Dummy_Module("orders");    /* application's own namespace */
    for (i=0; i < numorders; i++) {
        printf("\n%d (%d, %d, '%s')\n",
            i, orders[i].product, orders[i].quantity, orders[i].buyer);

        Set_Global("orders", "PRODUCT",  "i", orders[i].product);   /* int */
```

*Example 15-18: File: order1.c (continued)*

```
        Set_Global("orders", "QUANTITY", "i", orders[i].quantity);  /* int */
        Set_Global("orders", "BUYER",    "s", orders[i].buyer);     /* string */

        status = Run_Codestr(PY_STATEMENT, script, "orders", "", NULL);
        if (status == -1) {
            printf("Python error during validation.\n");
            PyErr_Print();  /* show traceback */
            continue;
        }

        Get_Global("orders", "ERRORS",   "s", &errors);          /* can split */
        Get_Global("orders", "WARNINGS", "s", &warnings);        /* on blanks */

        printf("errors:   %s\n", strlen(errors)? errors : "none");
        printf("warnings: %s\n", strlen(warnings)? warnings : "none");
        Run_Function("inventory", "print_files", "", NULL, "()");
    }
}

main(int argc, char **argv)         /* C's on-top, Python's embedded */
{                                   /* but Python uses C extensions too */
    run_user_validation();          /* don't need argv in embedded code */
}

char *getprogramname() { return "order1"; } /* or save argv[0] */
```

### *Testing the validation string in Python*

Because the validation code is written in Python, we can also test it from a Python script. This can be a useful strategy if the C program hasn't been developed yet. The C program may also take a long time to start up or to reach the embedded call; the following Python script tests the validation string by simulating the enclosing C program. In effect, we're prototyping the C layer. *exec* runs embedded Python code in Python; we'll revisit it again in Chapter 16.

*Example 15-19: File order1c.py*

```
#!/usr/local/bin/python
# to test the embedded-code script, without the enclosing C app

import inventory                    # inventory, buyers
import sys, traceback               # stack dump on errors

orders = [(111, 2, 'ISpam'),        # (product, quant, buyer)
          (222, 5, 'ATest'),
          (141, 3, 'USpam'),
          (222, 1, '4More'),
          (222, 0, 'Stuff'),
          (131, 9, 'NMore')]
```

*Example 15-19: File order1c.py (continued)*

```
names  = {}                                    # namespace dict
script = open('order1.py', 'r').read()         # load code-string
for order in orders:
    print '\n', orders.index(order), order
    names['PRODUCT'], names['QUANTITY'], names['BUYER'] = order
    try:
        exec script in names, names
    except:
        print 'error in embedded code:', sys.exc_type, sys.exc_value
        traceback.print_exc()
        continue
    print 'errors:   ', names['ERRORS']   or 'none'
    print 'warnings:', names['WARNINGS'] or 'none'
    inventory.print_files()
```

### Running the validation program

Finally, here's the output of running the validations code. The output came from running the standalone C executable generated from *order1.c*. We'll omit makefile details for this example: the makefile is the same as the *main* makefile shown earlier (Example 15-13), except that *order1.c* is the C file.

```
% order1

0 (111, 2, 'ISpam')
errors:   none
warnings: none
{222: 5, 121: 1, 131: 100, 111: 8} ['ISpam', 'USpam', 'ATest']

1 (222, 5, 'ATest')
errors:   none
warnings: reorder-soon:222
{222: 0, 121: 1, 131: 100, 111: 8} ['ISpam', 'USpam', 'ATest']

2 (141, 3, 'USpam')
errors:   bad-product
warnings: none
{222: 0, 121: 1, 131: 100, 111: 8} ['ISpam', 'USpam', 'ATest']

3 (222, 1, '4More')
errors:   buyer-name:4 check-quantity
warnings: new-buyer-added
{222: 0, 121: 1, 131: 100, 111: 8} ['ISpam', 'USpam', 'ATest', '4More']

4 (222, 0, 'Stuff')
Python error during validation.
Traceback (innermost last):
  File "<string>", line 24, in ?
  File "<string>", line 15, in validate_order
ZeroDivisionError: integer division or modulo
```

```
5 (131, 9, 'NMore')
errors:  none
warnings: new-buyer-added
{222: 0, 121: 1, 131: 91, 111: 8} ['ISpam', 'USpam', 'ATest', '4More', 'Stuff',
'NMore']
```

Running the Python simulation/prototype version *order1c.py* produces identical output, except that the stack frame on the divide-by-zero error includes the *exec* line in the Python module. Python code strings can be embedded in both C and Python programs:

```
% order1c.py
.
.
.
4 (222, 0, 'Stuff')
error in embedded code: ZeroDivisionError integer division or modulo
Traceback (innermost last):
  File "order1c.py", line 20, in ?
    exec script in names, names
  File "<string>", line 24, in ?
  File "<string>", line 15, in validate_order
ZeroDivisionError: integer division or modulo

5 (131, 9, 'NMore')
errors:  none
warnings: new-buyer-added
{222: 0, 121: 1, 131: 91, 111: 8} ['ISpam', 'USpam', 'ATest', '4More', 'Stuff',
'NMore']
```

## Running Validations in External Module Files

Representing embedded code actions as functions in module files is a somewhat more powerful strategy than strings; it eliminates the global variables set/get steps. Further, it avoids recompiling embedded code each time it's run. But writing functions is more complex, and the external files must be administered. The extra code complexity is minor but may matter, depending on the skill level of the embedded code programmer.

### The validations code file

Here's the file that holds the functions that C calls. It can be changed arbitrarily, both during development and onsite after the C system has been shipped. As before, end users don't need to rebuild the C program to change the validations. And as usual, this file is located on Python's module search path when it's imported (from Python or C). The *PYTHONPATH* environment variable should include the directory where this file is located; in a real system, this variable would probably be configured when the system's installed.

Because this is a Python module file, it has access to all Python services just like the string version, and can import other modules defined onsite. But when we use module functions the input/output mapping is more direct: it takes the form of function arguments and return values. Moreover, this code is compiled only once, when it is first imported; if the function is called frequently this approach can be faster than running uncompiled strings.

*Example 15-20: File: order2.py*

```
# input = args, output = return value tuple

import string
import inventory

def validate(product, quantity, buyer):          # function called by name
    msgs, errs = [], []                          # via mod/func name strings
    first, last = buyer[0], buyer[1:]
    if first not in string.uppercase:
        errs.append('buyer-name:' + first)
    if buyer not in inventory.buyers():
        msgs.append('new-buyer-added')
        inventory.add_buyer(buyer)
    validate_order(product, quantity, errs, msgs)     # mutable list args
    return string.join(msgs), string.join(errs)       # use "(ss)" format

def validate_order(product, quantity, errs, msgs):
    if product not in inventory.skus():
        errs.append('bad-product')
    elif quantity > inventory.stock(product):
        errs.append('check-quantity')
    else:
        inventory.reduce(product, quantity)
        if inventory.stock(product) / quantity < 2:
            msgs.append('reorder-soon:' + `product`)
```

### *The enclosing C program*

The C client uses the *Run_Function* interface in the extended API. Since the Python function returns two values (as a Python tuple), the C module uses the "O" output conversion code to get the result as a raw Python object. The *PyArg_Parse* function is used to extract the tuple's components manually before deleting it.

*Example 15-21: File: order2.c*

```
/* run embedded module-function validations */

#include <stdio.h>
#include <string.h>
#include "pyembed.h"

struct {                          /* same as order1 */
    int product;
```

*Example 15-21: File: order2.c (continued)*

```
    int quantity;
    char *buyer;
}orders[] = {
    {111, 2, "ISpam"},
    {222, 5, "ATest"},
    {141, 3, "USpam"},
    {222, 1, "4More"},
    {222, 0, "Stuff"},
    {131, 9, "NMore"}
};
int numorders = 6;

run_user_validation()
{
    int i, status;                  /* should check status everywhere */
    char *errors, *warnings;        /* no file/string or namespace here */
    PyObject *results;

    for (i=0; i < numorders; i++) {
        printf("\n%d (%d, %d, '%s')\n",
            i, orders[i].product, orders[i].quantity, orders[i].buyer);

        status = Run_Function(
                      "order2", "validate",       /* order2.validate(p,q,b) */
                      "O",      &results,
                      "(iis)",   orders[i].product,
                                 orders[i].quantity, orders[i].buyer);
        if (status == -1) {
            printf("Python error during validation.\n");
            PyErr_Print();  /* show traceback */
            continue;
        }
        PyArg_Parse(results, "(ss)", &warnings, &errors);
        Py_DECREF(results);
        printf("errors:   %s\n", strlen(errors)? errors : "none");
        printf("warnings: %s\n", strlen(warnings)? warnings : "none");
        Run_Function("inventory", "print_files", "", NULL, "()");
    }
}

main(int argc, char **argv)
{
    run_user_validation();
}

char *getprogramname() { return "order2"; }
```

### Testing the validation file in Python

As before, it may help to call the validations from Python first if the C program doesn't yet exist. Because we're running a function in a normal Python module here, we just import and call it using *apply* to pass a tuple of arguments; there's no need to use *exec* to run an embedded code string.

*Example 15-22: File order2c.py*

```
#!/usr/local/bin/python
# to test the embedded-code script, without the enclosing C app

import order2                         # get validation function
import inventory                      # inventory, buyers
import sys, traceback                 # stack dump on errors

orders = [(111, 2, 'ISpam'),          # (product, quant, buyer)
          (222, 5, 'ATest'),
          (141, 3, 'USpam'),
          (222, 1, '4More'),
          (222, 0, 'Stuff'),
          (131, 9, 'NMore')]
                                                       # no namespace or script
for order in orders:
    print '\n', orders.index(order), order
    try:
        (warnings, errors) = apply(order2.validate, order)
    except:
        print 'error in embedded function:', sys.exc_type, sys.exc_value
        traceback.print_exc()
        continue
    print 'errors:  ', errors   or 'none'
    print 'warnings:', warnings or 'none'
    inventory.print_files()
```

### Running the validation program

And finally, here's the output from the C standalone program made from *order2.c*. The output here is also almost the same as the code string validations output seen earlier, but the exception information is different: there are extra Python call levels for the functions in the validations module.

```
% order2
0 (111, 2, 'ISpam')
errors:  none
warnings: none
{222: 5, 121: 1, 131: 100, 111: 8} ['ISpam', 'USpam', 'ATest']

1 (222, 5, 'ATest')
errors:  none
warnings: reorder-soon:222
{222: 0, 121: 1, 131: 100, 111: 8} ['ISpam', 'USpam', 'ATest']
```

```
2 (141, 3, 'USpam')
errors:  bad-product
warnings: none
{222: 0, 121: 1, 131: 100, 111: 8} ['ISpam', 'USpam', 'ATest']

3 (222, 1, '4More')
errors:  buyer-name:4 check-quantity
warnings: new-buyer-added
{222: 0, 121: 1, 131: 100, 111: 8} ['ISpam', 'USpam', 'ATest', '4More']

4 (222, 0, 'Stuff')
Python error during validation.
Traceback (innermost last):
  File "./order2.py", line 14, in validate
    validate_order(product, quantity, errs, msgs)     # mutable list args
  File "./order2.py", line 24, in validate_order
    if inventory.stock(product) / quantity < 2:
ZeroDivisionError: integer division or modulo

5 (131, 9, 'NMore')
errors:  none
warnings: new-buyer-added
{222: 0, 121: 1, 131: 91, 111: 8} ['ISpam', 'USpam', 'ATest', '4More', 'Stuff',
'NMore']
```

The Python version's output is identical but there's an extra stack frame on errors:

```
% order2c.py
.
.
.
4 (222, 0, 'Stuff')
error in embedded function: ZeroDivisionError integer division or modulo
Traceback (innermost last):
  File "order2c.py", line 18, in ?
    (warnings, errors) = apply(order2.validate, order)
  File "./order2.py", line 14, in validate
    validate_order(product, quantity, errs, msgs)     # mutable list args
  File "./order2.py", line 24, in validate_order
    if inventory.stock(product) / quantity < 2:
ZeroDivisionError: integer division or modulo
```

Suggested exercises:

1. Expand the programs to use real persistent shelves (or other files) for orders, inventory, and buyers. Store the embedded code string in a shelve too. Would the table browser we wrote in Chapter 12, *Persistent Information*, be useful for browsing or editing here?

2. Experiment with passing lists or dictionaries in/out of the validation code in these examples. Passing in is easy: use the extended *Py_BuildValue* format codes discussed in Chapter 14. Passing out requires an "O" code.
3. The single output target for results scheme fails here: we have to use the "O" code to get the result tuple, and split it up with *PyArg_Parse*. Consider allowing multiple output targets.
4. Experiment with turning embedded call debug and reload modes on; set the flags in the *.c* files before running code. For strings, where are you when control stops? How about function calls? Does reload mode help for strings? (Hint: strings and variables can be associated with real or dummy modules.)
5. Build C executables with the *main* files here and run them. You'll need Python's libraries to link and will need to add the path to the validation module to *PYTHONPATH*. Would it make any sense to package the extended API functions in a Python extension module too? (Hint: Python code can be embedded in Python programs too, but most API operations have one-line Python counterparts.)
6. Consider other designs. For example, we might get by with extending techniques alone. If the C system was wrapped in a C extension module, precoded Python scripts could be on top when the system runs. These scripts could be modified on site or could call other modules that could be modified or written on site. The core of the C system would still be hidden (behind an extension module), but users could still tailor the parts we code in Python and ship them in source code form. Would this method work in the current example (embedded validations)?

# Other Approaches: Registering Callable Objects

With a little creativity, there are a variety of ways we might embed Python-coded logic. For instance, some applications may be able to run Python code to register callable objects (functions, bound methods, etc.) ahead of time by passing them to a C extension function. The C layer saves the passed in object. Later the object can be called directly using the saved pointer and the *PyEval_CallObject* API function.

This method is more direct but more complex. For example, where does the registering Python code get executed? If Python is on top, this might be trivial; as we saw earlier, *Tkinter* programs register a Python object to handle callbacks, by passing the object to a C extension. This architecture uses both extending and embedding: Python encloses the C layer, and the C layer calls registered Python objects on events.

### *The times they are a-changin': embedded linking rules*

This book uses the 1.3 linking scheme. In Python 1.2, programs embedding Python had to recompile a *config.c* source file, with a *-DNO_MAIN* compile switch to suppress Python's *main* function. The Python 1.3 scheme is simpler: we need only link in the already compiled *config.o*, plus other objects shown in makefiles earlier. The *main* function is defined by the enclosing application, not by Python.

However, as a rule, extension interfaces are more prone to change than other parts of the system; the makefile details discussed in this chapter are likely to evolve over time. Moreover, some platforms have unique linkage procedures. For instance, Python is probably a *DLL* file if you're embedding Python on a Microsoft Windows platform.

For up-to-date information, consult Python's extension manual or platform-specific documentation. The *Makefile* generated in Python's *Modules* directory also gives the command used to build the *python* executable; your linkage rules will be similar.

But if C is on top, object registration isn't as straightforward. For the order validation system, we need to run extra embedded Python code that creates and registers callable objects. For example, we might define a registration function in a bound-in C extension module called *cmodule*:

```
static PyObject *  handler = NULL;      /* keep Python object in C */

static PyObject *
Register_Handler(PyObject *self, PyObject *args)
{
    Py_XDECREF(handler);                /* called before? */
    Py_XINCREF(args);                   /* add a reference */
    handler = args;                     /* save Python callable object */
    Py_INCREF(Py_None);                 /* return 'None': success */
    return Py_None;
}
```

In practice we'd probably store the object under some context or key, to map it to a particular event. Later, the function object can be called directly from C:

```
Catch_Event(char *info, int code)
{
    PyObject *args, *pres;
    args = Py_BuildValue("(si)", info, code);      /* make arg-list */
    pres = PyEval_CallObject(handler, args);       /* apply: run a call */
    Py_DECREF(args);
```

```
    if (pres != NULL)
        ...use and decref 'pres' result; PyArg_Parse converts it to C
}
```

This structure is typical for callback-based systems: a C layer catches an event and passes it to a Python object registered by Python code. The registering Python code that calls the C registration function might be a string or module reference, or it could be a predefined configuration startup file with an expected pathname:

```
def function(info, code):
    ...handle an event, return a result (or None)

import cmodule
cmodule.Register_Handler(function)
```

In more realistic systems, the registration call might take other forms. For instance, we saw that *Tkinter* callbacks are registered in *command* options or *bind* calls. We could build in some flexibility here too; for example, environment variables can give the startup Python filename. Under this scheme, the only thing hard-coded in the system is an environment-variable name.

But, at least for examples we've seen in this chapter, it's probably easier to run code in strings or modules. Object registration adds an extra step for end users: they need to write Python embedded code to implement validations, plus code to import modules and register their functions manually. The techniques we saw earlier make the registration step unnecessary.

Still, an appropriate embedding structure depends on the application and the level of skill of the embedded programmers. In *Tkinter*, for example, we need to associate callback actions with objects; there's no notion of external modules for widgets, and strings might be inconvenient (unlike strings, registered objects come with their own namespaces). Like other embedded actions, callbacks can be routed to:

- Code strings
- Module file objects
- Registered objects and their methods
- Code files and scripts

and any other scheme that can be implemented with Python's embedded call API. Results may come back as function or expression results, global variables, mutable objects, *stdout* text, or exported API calls. Python's integration tools let us combine embedding and extending techniques, according to each system's requirements.

## *"And the winner is . . . "*

Calling functions in modules is usually faster than running code strings: calling functions avoids reparsing/recompiling the embedded code each time it runs. The difference may be significant for large code strings that are run repeatedly:

```
% time order1c.py > /dev/null
6.580u 0.490s 0:07.31 ...        7 seconds
% time order2c.py > /dev/null
3.110u 0.580s 0:03.93 ...        4 seconds
```

Calling registered objects may be faster than calling module functions but probably not significantly faster once the module has been loaded. Further, calling module functions allows for dynamic reloading, as we saw earlier. But it's possible to precompile strings into code objects and run code objects instead. For instance, the API function:

```
PyCodeObject *Py_CompileString(char *string, char *filename, int parsemode)
```

compiles a string into a Python code object. The *filename* is only used for error reporting, and the *parsemode* is the expression/statement flag discussed earlier in this chapter. Once we have a code object, we can pass it to the *PyEval_EvalCode* API function to execute it later. See Python's API (and the *Python/ceval.c* file) for more details. The built-in *compile* function allows Python programs to precompile strings too; code objects are run by passing them to *eval* and *exec* dynamic execution built-ins (see Chapter 16 for more details on *compile*).

Of course speed isn't the only consideration when structuring an embedded code interface; the application's structure and the role of the embedded code are important too. Managing external module files may not be an option, and object registration requires an extra end user task. Further, functions are a more direct model, but simple expression strings may be easier for some end users to code.

As a rule, we should be careful about reading too much into any timing results in Python. In extension work, flexibility and simplicity often matter more than raw speed. Selecting an extension tool or technique based on its speed alone is a little like picking a director of engineering based on her assembler coding skills :-) .

# *Other Integration Topics*

## *Using Python with C++*

All Python header files are already configured for use with C++ compilers: they automatically define the required *extern "C" {. . .}* wrappers for exposed symbols when they're included in C++ files. There's no need to recompile Python itself with C++, to use its embedding or extending API tools.

Extension modules (and types) can be written in C++ too. But if Python is compiled as a C system, all C++ functions called by Python usually have to be declared *extern "C"* (though some compilers get by without the declarations). This restriction includes module initialization functions, and registered method and type operation functions in extension modules coded in C++.

## *Strategies for Sharing Classes Between Languages*

Since Python is an object-oriented language, it would seem natural to share class definitions with languages like C++. It's fairly straightforward to use instances of classes defined in one language in the other, but sharing classes in general is a harder problem (for example, inheritance hierarchies that span languages are complex). We don't have time to study this topic in depth but here are some general ideas.

### *Making Python class instances outside Python*

C and C++ programs can make instances of Python classes by calling Python class objects. As we've seen earlier in this book, class instances in Python are made by calling a class like a function. If a class is defined in a module file, C can make an instance by using the *Run_Function* interface described earlier in this chapter (or similar logic), passing it module and class names and constructor arguments. A class instance is returned (a *PyObject**), which can be processed with the object attribute interfaces in *pyembed4.c* (calling methods, fetching members, etc.).

### *Making C++ class instances in Python*

To Python, C++ classes are just another kind of external C service. To export them for use in Python programs, we just need to wrap them in a C extension module or type. For instance, for a class *CxxClass*, we might define a C (or C++) extension module which registers functions for creating, using, and destroying instances. Here's an abstract example:

*Example 15-23: File: CxxClassWrapper.cc*

```
#include <Python.h>              /* Python header file */
#include <CxxClass.h>            /* C++ class's header */

static PyObject *
new_CxxClass(self, args)
```
   - *return a pointer to a 'new CxxClass' instance, as a Python long or integer*

```
static PyObject *
method_CxxClass(self, args)
```
   - *call instance->method(), using the instance object passed-in (in args)*

```
static PyObject *
del_CxxClass(self, args)
```
   - *use 'delete' to free the class-instance pointer passed-in (in args)*

- *registration table*
- *initialization function (extern "C")*

The method and initialization functions here should usually be declared *extern "C"* if this is compiled by C++. Such a module handles all the details of C++ interfacing; Python clients are ignorant of the C++ details. In fact, Python doesn't know anything about the layout or structure of the C++ class object: it gets a C++ pointer (as a Python integer) and manipulates it by passing the pointer to functions in the class wrapper extension module:

```
from CxxClassWrapper import *
object = new_CxxClass()              # object is an integer object
method_CxxClass(object, arg)         # but it's really a C++ pointer
del_CxxClass(object)
```

Better yet, we could also structure the wrapper as a C extension type instead of a module, to hide the C++ instance pointer and allow method calls by attribute name qualification in Python:

```
object = CxxClassWrapper.new()       # make a C++ object: a type-instance
object.method(arg)                   # it looks like a Python type-instance
del object                           # also deleted if object is reassigned
```

But whether we use a C module or type to wrap the C++ class, we lose the object-oriented nature of the C++ class. As we did for other C extension types in Chapter 14, we can wrap the C++ extension in a Python *stub-class*, to make the integration more seamless:

*Example 15-24: File: cxxclass.py*

```
from CxxClassWrapper import *              # get the C++ interface module

class CxxClass:                            # define a Python stub-class
    def __init__(self):
        self._base = new_CxxClass()        # make/save C++ object pointer
```

*Example 15-24: File: cxxclass.py (continued)*

```
    def method(self, arg):
        method_CxxClass(self._base, arg)      # send methods to extension
    def __del__(self):
        del_CxxClass(self._base)              # delete the wrapped C++ object
```

Such a *stub-class* wrapper not only makes flat modules act like types, but it also lets us subclass exposed C++ classes inside Python: Python class semantics is applied up to the *stub* superclass (where the class transfers control to the C++ interface). The *stub-class* might even be automatically generated, given a description of the C++ class. However it's created, the wrapper makes the C++ class act like a normal Python class:

```
from cxxclass import CxxClass              # get the stub-class

object = CxxClass()                        # make a C++ class instance in Python
object.method(arg)
del object

class CxxSub(CxxClass):                    # subclass the C++ class in Python
    def method(self, arg):
    - redefine or extend a C++ method here...
```

We've really only scratched the surface of C++ class integration here. Some creativity is required to support some of C++'s more esoteric features in Python. For instance, it's also possible to route C++ virtual method calls back down to methods in Python subclasses, but it may require a *stub-class* on the C++ side of the interface too (this topic involves more details than we have time to get into here).

Suggested exercises:

1. If you're familiar with C++, pick a C++ class, and integrate it for use in Python by defining an extension module (or type) plus a Python *stub-class*. The *stub-class* should make and delete the C++ instance and route method calls to methods in the C extension. How would you propose routing C++ virtual method calls to methods in subclasses defined in Python?
2. Then, pick a Python class, and write a *stub-class* for it in C++. The class constructor should make and store an instance of the Python class, methods should call attributes of the stored Python instance, and the destructor should free (*DECREF*) the Python instance. How about virtuals here?
3. The solutions to the last two exercises are fairly symmetric; can you generalize the two techniques? Is there a common representation you could map classes to? What about object ownership issues?

4. Would the `__getattr__` metaclass trick help in the *CxxClass* wrapper class? In principle, one `__getattr__` method might handle all methods in a C++ object instead of coding (or generating) one Python wrapper method for each. In fact, a single Python wrapper class could handle all C++ objects. But how would you route method calls to C++ given a string name for a method (or member)?
5. Wrapping C++ class instances in a module, type, and/or wrapper-class essentially seals off inheritance at the language boundaries: Python knows nothing of the inheritance hierarchy of the C++ class whose instances are passed into Python. Similarly, C++ doesn't notice Python's inheritance rules. How would you improve on this? Does it matter (i.e., is inheritance important at integration points)? What about an external hierarchy description or Python classes to combine wrapped C++ instances?

### *Making wrapped objects look like Python objects*

The technique outlined above only addresses instance creation, deletion, and attribute access. But this is only part of the picture when integrating objects in Python. As we've seen earlier in this book, both Python classes and C extension types can overload operators (+, *[i]*), and intercept meta-operations (*object.attribute*, *print*). By adding these metaobject hooks to wrapper classes and extension types, instances become full-fledged Python objects that are able to participate in arbitrary expressions.

For example, we wrote a wrapper class at the end of Chapter 14, which made a C type act like a Python class, able to support subclassing and inheritance. Given a sufficiently complete wrapper class, we can do the same for wrapped external objects. With appropriate support code, clients could use wrapped C++ class instances in Python expressions, instead of being limited to method calls. We only need define all the specially named methods in the *CxxClass* stub class above.

But to make this work, we also need to implement a conversion protocol to allow wrapped and built-in objects to be mixed in expressions. Let's consider the "+" expression case. When a wrapped object and a built-in appear together in an expression, there are two basic approaches to handling conversions: the wrapper class's `__add__` method can either:

*Convert down*
: Convert wrapped C++ objects to native Python objects, each time one appears in a + expression. Python performs the + operation after class's conversion.

*Convert up*
: Convert native Python operand objects to C++ objects, before the operation. The wrapper class asks C++ to perform the + operation after conversion.

Either way, Python programs usually won't be able to tell that the object is really a wrapped C++ item if conversions are handled well. Let's take a quick, abstract look at examples of both techniques.

***Converting wrapped objects down.*** The following stub class converts wrapped objects down to Python objects, when they appear in expressions. The *interface* module is assumed to be an extension which handles C++ handshaking and knows how to handle C++ objects generically. To keep this example short, this class only handles conversions in + expressions, qualifications, and indexing; a more complete class would define all specially named methods.

*Example 15-25: File: coerce1.py*

```
import interface                                # C++ handshaking module
class Stub:
    def __init__(self, object):
        self.wrapped = object
    def __add__(self, other):                   # 'Stub + other', 'Stub + Stub'
        return self.toPython() + other
    def __radd__(self, other):                  # 'other + Stub'
        return other + self.toPython()
    def __getattr__(self, name):
        if name == "__coerce__":                # coerce tried before add/radd
            raise AttributeError, name          # fail: convert in add methods
        try:
            return Stub(interface.getField(self.wrapped, name))
        except:
            raise AttributeError, name
    def __getitem__(self, index):
        try:
            return Stub(interface.getIndex(self.wrapped, index))
        except:
            raise IndexError    # end for-loops, in-tests
    def __repr__(self):
        return "(" + `self.toPython()` + ")"
    def toPython(self):
        return interface.convertDown(self.wrapped)     # a native Python object
```

We saw the __add__ and __radd__ methods earlier; __radd__ handles cases where *self* is on the right of the + operator, and a noninstance is on the left. When Python notices a class instance in an expression, it first tries to call a __coerce__ method for the instance, if one can be found, before trying the __add__ or __radd__ operator methods. Since we're not using *coerce* here, we need to fail when the request comes to __getattr__ (*getattr* catches *all* undefined attribute references, both from programs and Python itself).

When *Stub* instances are added, the add methods can interact in subtle ways. For example, when two Stub instances are added, Python first calls __add__, which converts the left operand down and readds. This in turn triggers the `__radd__` method which converts the right operand down. Finally, the + operator is applied to two built-in Python objects. Here's how + expressions are converted down:

```
"Stub + 99"   =>  __add__   =>  native + 99
"99 + Stub"   =>  __radd__  =>  99 + native
"Stub + Stub" =>  __add__   =>  native + Stub  =>  __radd__  =>  native + native
```

The end result is that expressions with *Stub* instances are translated into operations on built-in types. When a *Stub* is indexed or qualified (`__getitem__`, `__getattr__`), a new wrapper class instance is returned instead, which can later appear in other expressions.

***Converting native objects up.*** Depending on the application, it may make more sense to convert Python operands up to the wrapped object's type in mixed-type expressions. The following simple classes show two ways to convert up: we either define a `__coerce__` method to convert before the add/radd methods are called, or do type testing and conversion within the add/radd methods themselves. When defined, `__coerce__` is called before add/radd, and should return a tuple with *self* and the *other* argument converted to a common type.

*Example 15-26: File: coerce2.py*

```
def sameclass(self, other):
    return (type(other) == type(self) and          # InstanceType?
            other.__class__ == self.__class__)     # from same class?

class Stub2:
    def __init__(self, value):
        self.data = value
    def __coerce__(self, other):
        if sameclass(self, other):             # called before add methods
            return self, other                 # convert other up if needed
        else:
            return self, Stub2(other)
    def __add__(self, other):                  # 'stub + other', 'stub + stub'
        return self.data + other.data          # other converted: add Stub2's
    __radd__ = __add__                         # 'other + stub': transitive

class Stub3:
    def __init__(self, value):
        self.data = value
    def __add__(self, other):
        if sameclass(self, other):
            return self.data + other.data          # add Stub3 instances
        else:
            return self + Stub3(other)             # coerce other up and re-add
    __radd__ = __add__
```

Both classes allow their instances to be on the left or right of a + operator, and allow these instances to be added to Python built-in objects or other *Stub* instances. Converting Python objects up may be less useful when emulating built-in types (that is, it may require creation of an external object), but this will vary per application.

Whether we handle mixed-type expressions by converting wrapped objects down or Python objects up, these techniques make wrapped objects compatible with Python's built-in object types. Clients normally won't notice the difference.

In general, Python's metaobject protocol lets us make just about anything act like a built-in Python object type. Naturally the amount and complexity of integration logic depends on how we want our wrapped objects to behave. Conversion protocols are usually required only if we want to mimic built-in types in expressions; for many applications, methods and members are sufficient.

Suggested exercises:

1. Add *print* statements to the operator methods in these examples, create instances, and trace the control flow of + expressions. Alternatively, you can monitor execution by running under the debugger. You'll need to prototype the *interface* module for *coerce1*.
2. Study the examples in the *Demo/classes* directory of the Python install tree. Most of these illustrate conversion protocols shown here in more detail.
3. What sort of support code would be necessary to implement the generic object handling assumed to exist in the *interface* module? Could it be generated automatically from C++ class headers?

# *Automated Integration Techniques*

Since the structure of C extension modules and types is well defined, there are a number of attempts underway to automate extension writing. Some may evolve further by the time you read this book; see the Python FAQ for up-to-date information. Here's a brief look at the most prominent approaches.

## *Modulator: a Boilerplate Code Generator Tool*

Writing extension modules and types is fairly straightforward. The hard part is usually remembering the names of all the Python interface components we need. This becomes especially challenging (if not tedious) for types: not only do we need to know the type signatures of standard methods, but we have to remember all the slots in the type descriptor structures and link all the fields properly by hand.

## *Metaobject protocol limitations*

As we've seen, adding special methods to wrapper classes can make external objects behave like normal built-in types. Or almost: there are a few cases where Python expects real built-in (native) objects, not class or type instances masquerading as such.

For example, sequence indexes and slices currently expect subscripts to be real Python integers. If we use class instances *X* and *Y* in these contexts:

```
listobject[X]       # We want X to simulate a Python integer
listobject[X:Y]     # X and Y are wrapper's around C++ numbers
```

it won't work, even if their classes provide `__int__` or `__coerce__` methods. Because Python doesn't automatically convert the arguments, we'll get an exception. We can work around this constraint by manually calling converter methods or by using the *int* built-in to convert (provided the class defines an `__int__` method), but it's less than 100% seamless:

```
listobject[X.toPython()]
listobject[int(X):int(Y)]
```

Manual conversions are only required in a few contexts, and for most applications the holes are irrelevant. For instance, the *range* function accepts and converts instances of classes that define an `__int__` method. More automatic conversions may be added in the future; for the present, the forgery isn't complete when simulating Python object semantics.

For most of us, memorization isn't really an option! Normally, we'd resort to cut-and-paste editing or copy an existing extension and modify it for our needs. This works if the extension is close to what we're trying to write; if it's radically different, we'll have a big editing job ahead (using a mapping type as a template for a number type won't help much because the operator methods are different).

The *modulator* tool, written by Jack Jansen, provides a better solution. Given a GUI-based description of a module and/or type, it automatically generates boilerplate code. We get a complete skeleton C file, with most of the integration details already coded (method functions, type descriptors, etc.). We just need to fill in the empty functions with application-specific code. For library wrappers this usually takes only a few lines of code per generated function to convert data and call the wrapped C function.

### Using modulator

Here's what *modulator*'s screens look like. It's a *Tkinter* GUI program (there's a non-GUI interface, but it's not as convenient). It currently resides in the *Tools* directory, which is part of the Python distribution tree. When we run the *Tools/modulator/modulator.py* script, the main screen lets us define a C module, and add methods we want the module to register (export to Python) by typing in the *Add method* field:

```
% python modulator.py
```

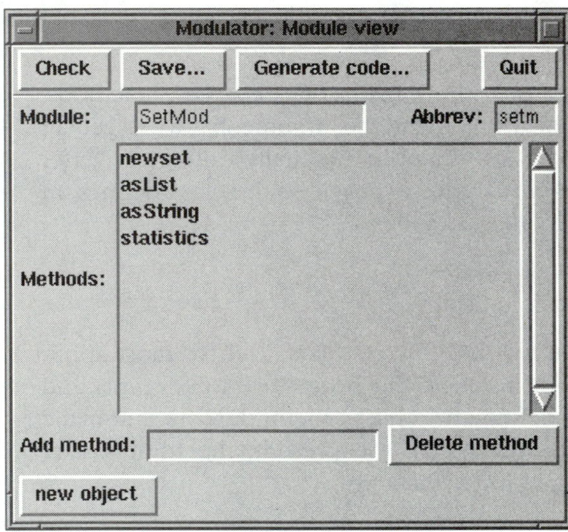


*Figure 15-2: Modulator: module window*

The window shown in Figure 15-2 pops up. To generate code for a C type too, press the *new object* button: another window pops up with check boxes for type categories (for operator supplement descriptors), and the standard type operation functions. It looks like Figure 15-3. There's also a field for entry of type instance methods.

When all the forms have been filled out, we press the *Generate code . . .* button to generate the skeleton C file; the window shown in Figure 15-4 comes up to ask us what we'd like to call the generated C file.

And that's it: if we've filled out everything properly, we'll have a skeleton C extension file, ready for editing. If not, we can try again: code generation usually takes only a few seconds (or less). In fact, this process is so convenient that it's a standard first step for many extension writers. For instance, the extension examples in this book were started by generating code with *modulator*.

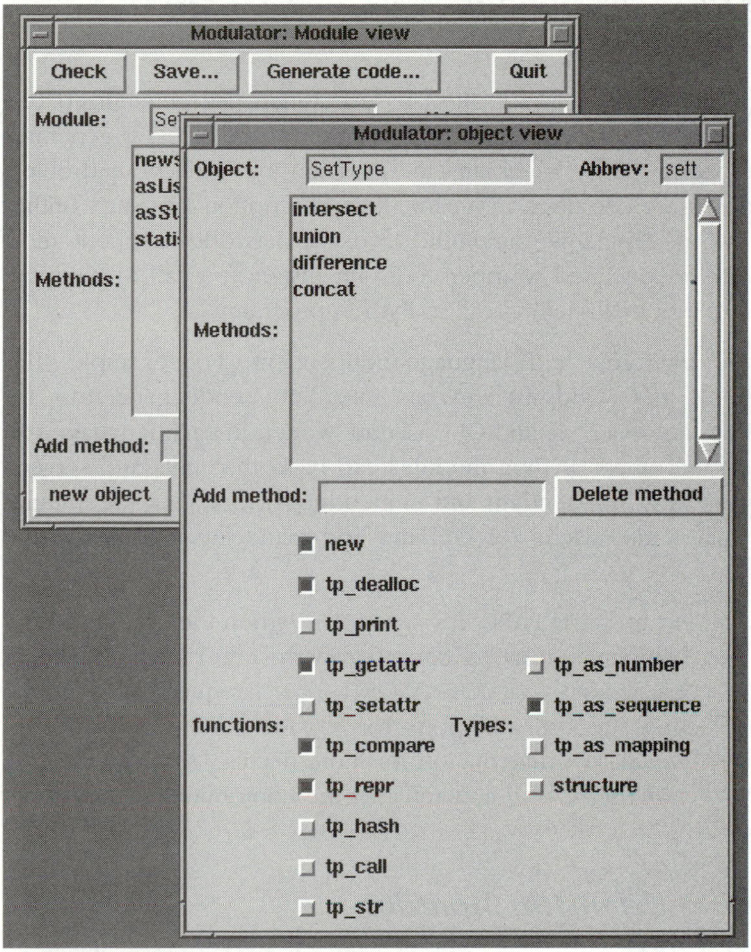

*Figure 15-3: Modulator: object/type window*

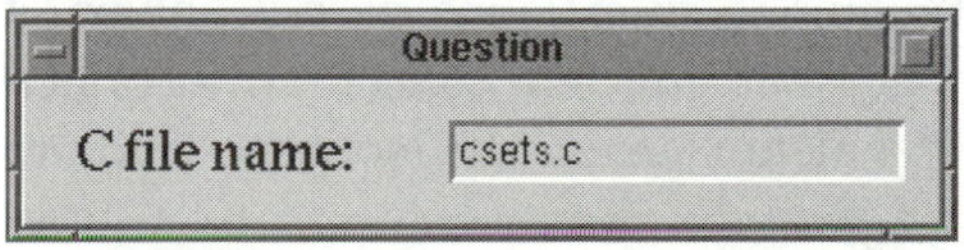

*Figure 15-4: Modulator: output file window*

*Modulator* won't write the entire extension for us (that would be quite a trick!), but it does enough to get us started. Unless we're developing interfaces for objects to be distributed across a network, *modulator* is probably the most practical tool for extension writers today.

## ILU: Creating Client/Server Integrations from an Interface Description

The public domain ILU package is a CORBA-based system, for generalized distributed programming. Given a description of a program's interfaces, it generates all the required wrapper code for integrating the program into a distributed object environment. Interfaces are described in an interface description language (either OMG IDL or ILU's ISL). Programs communicate using network calls, but most details are hidden in the generated wrapper code: for instance, a call to a remote server object becomes a normal method call in Python programs.

ILU integrations are platform- and language-independent. For example, ILU already runs on UNIX and Windows and has integration code generators for Python, Common Lisp, Modula 3, C, and C++. Clients written in each language can use servers coded in the others. Python modules can be both clients and servers, which roughly corresponds to extending and embedding Python, but the integration isn't as tight. ILU is also useful for defining and managing modules in the same address space.

At present, ILU is a project at Xerox PARC. It's a popular Python tool, but it's also a large system and too complex for us to cover properly here. For instance, it includes the IDL/ISL code generator, a CORBA ORB (object request broker), distributed garbage collection support, and ports for a wide variety of platforms. Refer to the Python FAQ or ILU documentation for more details. (Also see the URL *ftp://ftp.parc.xerox.com/pub/ilu/ilu.html* and refer to the contributed ILU example in Appendix A.)

## bgen: Generating Extension Modules from C Header Files

Guido van Rossum's *bgen* system attempts to generate C extension module wrappers for libraries of C functions. Instead of requiring an extra interface definition, it scans the library's header files to get the necessary function signatures. In principle, this is enough information to create complete C extension modules, ready to be compiled and linked with Python.

Because of the nature of C header files, this isn't a completely automatic process; some manipulation of the output may be necessary. Since *bgen* is still experimental, we won't go into further details here. See the *Tools* directory in the Python source tree for more information.

## *SWIG: a C Extension Code Generator*

The SWIG system was announced too late to cover in this book, but it promises to be an important tool for extension writers. SWIG stands for "Simplified Wrapper and Interface Generator". Roughly, it uses ANSI C/C++ type-signatures given in an interface description file, to generate the wrapper code needed to call external C functions from Python.

Because SWIG has access to type-signatures, it can emit complete C extension code, with data conversion logic, etc. This is a step beyond the skeleton code generated by the "modulator" tool (see above). At this writing, SWIG supports four languages: Python, Perl, Tcl, and Guile. It can be found on this book's CD-ROM.

## *Object-Oriented Extension Types*

As we've seen, C extension types aren't quite the same as Python classes. There's work underway to bridge the gap, by integrating C++ classes into Python's object model, and/or providing for extension-type inheritance within Python itself. If this work is successful, C types might become full-fledged members of Python's inheritance model: there'd be no need for the *stub* wrapper classes we studied. But this work is too experimental to discuss further here.

## *The New Abstract Object Access API*

With Python 1.3, there's also a new run-time interface for using Python objects from C, designed by Jim Fulton. Essentially, this new API allows Python objects to be processed in C using a set of generic interface functions, instead of navigating through type descriptors. It provides a consistent interface for accessing object attributes. Unfortunately, the API was released after this part of the book was written so we don't have time to do it justice here. But we can make some general remarks.

In some sense, the abstract object access API adds another dimension to embedding Python in C. Besides calling Python code, C programs can use exported Python objects in the same way that Python programs do. Objects fetched from modules, returned by embedded calls, or passed to extensions can be manipulated in C to communicate with Python programs.

For instance, C programs can use the API to process collections passed from Python (lists, strings, etc.). Operations such as attribute access, concatenation, and slicing are available as C function calls, given Python object pointers. The object access API can also simplify the construction of objects passed to Python, and may provide a convenient route for translating Python programs to C. The API is defined in the *abstract.h* include file in Python 1.3. See the include file and Python 1.3 documentation for more details.

Suggested exercises:

1. Experiment with generating code for modules and types under *modulator*. Create a *Set* C type to mimic the Python set classes of the Chapter 13, *Implementing Objects*, and link it with Python.
2. If you are using Python release 1.3 or later, study the new abstract object API. What other tools does it supersede or improve on? Then apply its functions to make the C stack type from Chapter 14 more polymorphic. How would the API help in this system?
3. Bill Janssen has written a tutorial introduction to using ILU with Python. Get the tutorial and study the ILU system further. For more information, there's also an ILU manual, available from the same sources. ILU is currently at *ftp://ftp.parc.xerox.com/pub/ilu/ilu.html*, and is available on this book's CD-ROM, but see Python's FAQ for up-to-date sources.

# Summary: Python/C Integration Techniques

This chapter concludes our discussion of C integration topics. We've covered a lot of territory; in closing, Figure 15-5 gives a summary of some of the techniques we have presented.

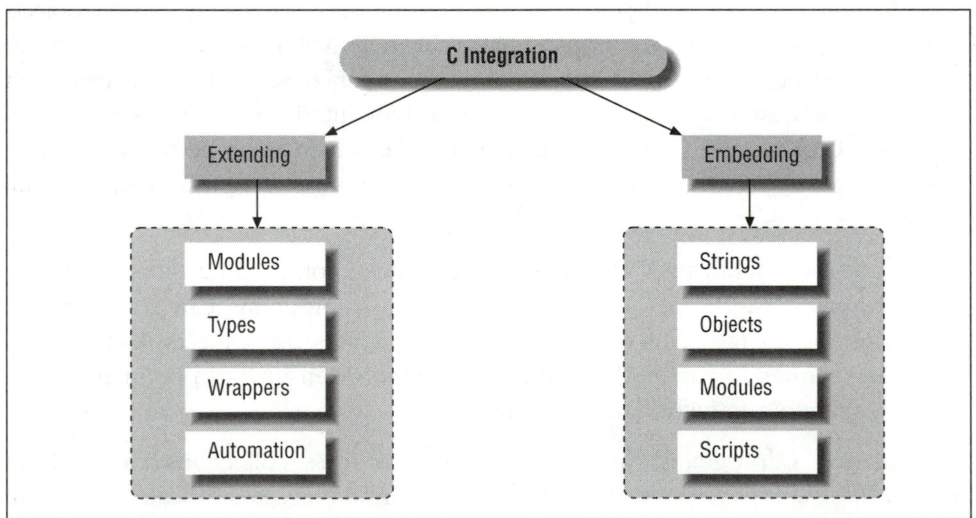


*Figure 15-5: Integration strategies*

C extensions can be implemented as modules or types (which usually exist in a module), with an optional wrapper class layer on top. Tools like *modulator* automate some of the extension writing process. Embedded Python code can take any of the forms shown here.

As mentioned earlier, this set is by no means carved in stone. In fact, new techniques are likely to appear over time. For instance, the ILU system mentioned above subsumes in-process extending and embedding in the context of a distributed object programming model. But for many applications, Python's basic C interfaces provide the glue needed to apply Python as an extension tool in larger systems and applications.

## Integration is a Two-Way Street

As we have also noted earlier, it's important to view this set as a whole, since different applications call for different approaches. For example, C libraries can be packaged as extension modules or types. But at the same time, a C library might provides hooks for user-defined components by executing embedded Python code. As we've seen, the *Tkinter* GUI extension calls registered, embedded objects; as Figure 15-6 illustrates, it works both ways.

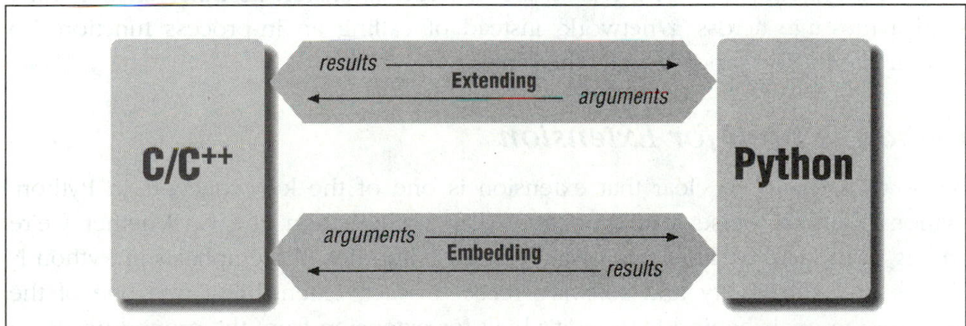


*Figure 15-6: Integration data flows*

We've seen how to bind the Python and C systems, how to invoke procedures in one language from the other, and how to implement data conversions at each of the four data paths in the following table (Table 15-4).

This table isn't complete; for instance, there are a variety of ways to convert data, and C interfaces must also handle exceptions and reference counts. But it's representative of the kinds of activities we perform to link Python and C functionality.

*Table 15-4: Integration tools*

| | Binding | Invoking | Arguments | Results |
|---|---|---|---|---|
| **Extending** | Dynamic/static linking | Registered functions | *PyArg_ParseTuple* | *Py_BuildValue* |
| **Embedding** | Makefiles, libraries | Python API functions | *Py_BuildValue* | *PyArg_Parse* |

## A General Integration Model

Python's integration system is based on a simple yet general function call model. As we've seen, it's remarkably seamless: to Python code, C services look just like more Python code. Because of this, it's possible to migrate services from Python to C without affecting their clients. In effect, even the implementation language is encapsulated in Python. As we'll discuss in the conclusion to this book, this language independence fosters prototyping-based development.

Moreover, Python's integration model isn't limited to simple function calls. When higher-level integration is needed, Python's basic tools can be used to construct more complex systems. For instance, if we need to implement a distributed programming system, there's no reason a registered extension module function can't send a message across a network, instead of calling an in-process function. To Python clients, the process looks the same.

## Python is Built for Extension

By now it should be clear that extension is one of the key concepts in Python. Python's built-in toolset can be extended in both Python and C. Whether we're coding in the Python language or integrating C libraries, the emphasis in Python is always on extensibility and software reuse. In fact, extensibility was one of the main design goals behind Python: it's built for extension from the ground up.

For some applications, extending Python in Python is enough. Python's language tools, such as classes, modules, and built-in types, provide all the extensibility many systems need. But when we need to implement multilanguage systems, Python's integration tools and open architecture provide general support.

To some extent, Python borrows both from languages that incorporate high-level types (Lisp) and those that depend on external libraries (C++). Python's approach is layered: it provides both extension tools and built-in tools for cases where we don't want to write a new data structure library to get started:

*Table 15-5: Python tool-set layers*

| Tool set | Components | Purpose |
|---|---|---|
| Built-ins | Lists, dictionaries, strings, etc. | High-level tools for simple, fast programming |
| Python extensions | Functions, classes, modules | Adding extra features and new object types |
| C/C++ extensions | C modules, C types | Integrating external systems, optimizing components |

In Chapter 13, we saw that built-in data structures take us far, without coding any extensions at all. In fact, built-in tools are sometimes a better choice than our own implementations. But once we start dealing with more complex systems, Python's extension tools become indispensable features.

# 16

# *Processing Language and Text*

*In this chapter:*


- *"See Jack Hack. Hack, Jack, Hack"*
- *Strategies for Parsing Text in Python*
- *Case Study: A Calculator GUI*
- *The "Big Finish": A Real Calculator GUI*


## *"See Jack Hack. Hack, Jack, Hack"*

In one form or another, processing text-based information is one of the more common tasks applications need to perform. This can include anything from scanning a text file by columns to parsing statements in a language defined by a formal grammar. In this chapter, we'll explore ways to handle language and text-based information and summarize some Python development concepts.

Some of this material is advanced but the examples are small. For example, recursive descent parsing is a compiler writer's tool, but we'll use a simple example to illustrate how it can be implemented in Python. We'll also see that it's often unnecessary to write custom parsers for each language processing task in Python. They can usually be replaced by exporting APIs for use in Python programs, and sometimes by a single built-in function call. Finally, we'll close with a fun example of Python at work.

## *Strategies for Parsing Text in Python*

There are a variety of ways to handle text processing in Python:

- String module utilities
- Regular expression matching
- Parser-generator integrations: *yacc*, *bison*, etc.
- Hand-coded parsers
- Running Python code with the *eval* and *exec* built-ins

For simpler tasks, Python's built-in *string* object is often all we really need. As we've seen, strings can be indexed, concatenated, sliced, and processed with built-in functions and the *string* module. But our emphasis in this chapter is on higher-level tools and techniques for analyzing textual information. Let's briefly explore each of the approaches above, and some representative examples.

## String Module Utilities

Python's *string* module includes utilities we can use to split and join strings around tokens:

*string.split*
: Split a string into substrings, using white space as delimiters (tabs, spaces, newlines).

*string.splitfields*
: Split a string into substrings, using a passed-in string as the delimiter.

*string.join*
: Concatenate a list or tuple of strings, adding a space between each.

*string.joinfields*
: Concatenate a list or tuple of strings, adding a passed-in string between each.

*split* functions chop a string into a list of substrings, and *join* functions put them back together. Despite their simplicity, they can handle surprisingly complex text parsing tasks. Moreover, the *string* module is very fast because it has been migrated to C. Here are three short examples to illustrate how to use the interfaces:

- Summing columns in a file
- Parsing and unparsing rule strings
- Searching C source files for constants

---

*NOTE* This section concentrates on the *string* module's split and join utilities. See Appendix C for other text-processing exports in *string*. Among other things, it provides a "find" substring search function, and many of C's standard string utilities. Also see the *tparse* package in the CD-ROM (and Python Internet site) contributions directory; it implements a REXX-like parsing scheme based on templates.

---

### Summing columns in a file

Scanning files by columns is a fairly common task. For instance, suppose we have a file containing columns of numbers, output by another system, and need to sum each column's numbers. In Python, string splitting does the job. As an added bonus, it's easy to make the solution a reusable tool in Python.

*Example 16-1: File: summer.py*

```
#!/usr/local/bin/python
import string

def summer(numCols, fileName):
    sums = [0] * numCols                               # make list of zeros
    for line in open(fileName, 'r').readlines():       # scan file's lines
        cols = string.split(line)                      # split up columns
        for i in range(numCols):                       # around blanks/tabs
            sums[i] = sums[i] + eval(cols[i])          # add numbers to sums
    return sums

if __name__ == '__main__':
    import sys
    print summer(eval(sys.argv[1]), sys.argv[2])       # '% summer.py cols file'
```

We can both *import* this module and call its function, and *run* it as a shell tool from the command-line. The summer calls *split* to make a list of strings representing the line's columns, and *eval* to convert column strings to numbers. Here's an input file that uses both blanks and tabs to separate columns:

```
% cat table.txt
1       5       10   2   1.0
2       10      20   4   2.0
3       15      30   8    3
4       20      40  16   4.0

% summer.py 5 table.txt
[10, 50, 100, 30, 10.0]
```

Suggested exercise: Since the script uses *eval* to convert strings from the file into Python numbers, we could also store arbitrary expressions in columns; see Chapter 2, *A Sneak Preview*, for an example. Can you think of a way this would be useful? What if the expressions could assign and reference Python variables? What happens if we try to sum columns of strings?

Suggested exercise: As is, the function isn't very flexible. It fails if the number of columns in a line is less than *numCols*; an uncaught *IndexError* is raised. Change the function to allow differing column lengths (hint: the range might use the *len* of the split line). Then change the function to determine the number of columns automatically by inspecting the first line's split result. *numCols* could still be passed in as an optional argument to override this feature (in case line lengths vary). Would classes be useful here?

### *Parsing and unparsing rule strings*

Here's one way splitting and joining strings can be used to parse sentences in a simple language. It's taken from a rule-based expert-system shell (*holmes*) written in Python, and mentioned briefly in Appendix A, *...And Other Cool Stuff.* Rule strings in *holmes* take the form:

```
"rule <id> if <test1>, <test2>... then <conclusion1>, <conclusion2>..."
```

Tests and conclusions are conjunctions of terms ("," means "and"). Each term is a list of words or variables separated by spaces; variables start with a "?". To use a rule, we translate it to an internal form—a dictionary with nested lists. To display a rule, we translate back to the string form. For instance, given a call:

```
rules.internal_rule('rule x if a ?x, b then c, d ?x')
```

The conversion in function *internal_rule* below proceeds as follows:

```
string = 'rule x if a ?x, b then c, d ?x'
i = ['rule x', 'a ?x, b then c, d ?x']
t = ['a ?x, b', 'c, d ?x']
r = ['', 'x']
result = {'rule':'x', 'if':[['a','?x'], ['b']], 'then':[['c'], ['d','?x']]}
```

It first splits around the *if*, then around the *then*, and finally around *rule*. The result is the three substrings that were separated by the keywords. Test and conclusion substrings are split around "," and spaces last, and *join* is used to convert back (unparse) to the original string for display.

*Example 16-2: File: rules.py*

```
from string import *

def internal_rule(string):
    i = splitfields(string, ' if ')
    t = splitfields(i[1],   ' then ')
    r = splitfields(i[0],   'rule ')
    return {'rule':strip(r[1]), 'if':internal(t[0]), 'then':internal(t[1])}

def external_rule(rule):
    return ('rule '    + rule['rule']           +
            ' if '     + external(rule['if'])   +
            ' then '   + external(rule['then']) + '.')

def internal(conjunct):
    res = []                                     # 'a b, c d'
    for clause in splitfields(conjunct, ','):    # -> ['a b', ' c d']
        res.append(split(clause))                # -> [['a','b'], ['c','d']]
    return res

def external(conjunct):
    strs = []
    for clause in conjunct:                      # [['a','b'], ['c','d']]
        strs.append(join(clause))                # -> ['a b', 'c d']
    return joinfields(strs, ', ')                # -> 'a b, c d'
```

As usual, we can test components of this module interactively:

```
>>> import rules
>>> rules.internal('a ?x, b')
[['a', '?x'], ['b']]

>>> r = rules.internal_rule('rule x if a ?x, b then c, d ?x')
>>> rules.external_rule(r)
'rule x if a ?x, b then c, d ?x.'
```

Parsing by splitting strings around tokens only takes us so far: there's no direct support for recursive nesting of components, and syntax errors aren't handled very gracefully. But for simple language tasks like this, string splitting might be enough, at least for prototyping the system. We can always add a more robust rule parser later or reimplement rules as embedded Python code or classes.

Suggested exercise: What happens when there's a syntax error in a rule? Could a program detect errors by traversing the result after a parse?

Suggested exercise: The following rule class saves the original string to avoid unparsing steps:

```
class Rule:
    def __init__(self, string=None):
        if string != None:
            self.internal = internal_rule(string)     # parse on creation
            self.external = string                    # for user displays
```

Create a knowledge base by storing *Rule* objects (or lists of rules) in a persistent shelve called *kbase* (see Chapter 12, *Persistent Information*). Rules ids may be used as keys if they're stored one per slot. Then write a rule browser GUI with *Tkinter* that lets users browse and edit rules in the shelve (see Chapter 11, *Graphical User Interfaces*). Would the *FormGui* browser from Chapter 12 help here? How about using a table wrapper class to reparse after string edits?

### *Searching C source files for constants*

In Chapter 2, we saw a script that searches for files that use any of the *#define* constants in a C header file. To search files, the *grep* command was run on all the C source files in a directory. As coded there, it was very slow for header files with many constants because it ran *grep* on each file repeatedly.

I promised to show a better solution: the secret really has more to do with *grep* itself than with Python. If we pass a multiline search pattern to *grep* (using its *-F* flag) it searches each line in the file for a match on any line in the pattern. The solution is to collect constants first and call *grep* on each file just once:

*Example 16-3: File: finder2.py*

```
#!/usr/local/bin/python
import string, glob, os, sys
try:
    srcdir = sys.argv[1]           # optional arg = directory | '-'
except:                            # scan C header, grep for constants
    srcdir = '.'
header = '/usr/local/include/Py/rename2.h'

oldnames = []
for line in open(header, 'r').readlines():         # scan by lines
    if line[:7] == '#define':                      # starts with '#define'?
        oldnames.append(string.split(line)[1])     # get word after #define

if srcdir == '-':                                  # "finder2.py -": dump names
    oldnames.sort()
    print string.joinfields(oldnames,'\n')
else:
    oldnames = string.joinfields(oldnames, '\n')       # put newlines between
    for source in glob.glob(srcdir + '/*.[ch]'):       # all ".c"/".h" files
        print source
        print os.popen('grep -w -n -F "%s" %s' % (oldnames, source)).read()
print 'done.'
```

This script searches for occurrences of renamed symbols in the Python *rename2* header file (described in Chapter 14, *Extending Python*). We could let the compiler find the old names too, but this script may be a beginning effort at an automated name converter. If we pass in a directory name of "-" this version dumps the header's constants to *stdout*. *joinfields* is used to put end-of-line separators between entries in the *oldnames* list.

Suggested exercise: Change *finder2* to use the built-in *grep* library module rather than spawning a shell command with *os.popen*. What effect does the change have on the speed of running the program?

## *Regular Expression Matching*

Splitting and joining strings is a simple way to process text, as long as it follows the format you expect. For example, the *finder* script above works for typical *#define* lines, but fails if there are any spaces between the "#" and *define*. For more general text analysis tasks, Python provides regular expression matching utilities commonly found in UNIX tools, in the form of two standard modules:

*regex*
: Implements UNIX-style regular expression matching for strings.

*regsub*
: Provides regular expression matching with replacement (substitutions).

NOW re module

---

*NOTE* Both *regex* and *regsub* are modules that must be imported, with functions that must be called. Regular expressions aren't part of the syntax of the Python language itself. In practice, modules aren't much different from embedded syntax, and have a few advantages. Since patterns are strings, they can be constructed at run-time. And since the utilities are structured as extensions, patterns may be precompiled into type-instance objects.

---

### *regex: finding patterns in strings*

The *regex* module has two main search functions, plus utilities for precompiling, etc. In all of these, *string* is the string to be searched and *pattern* is a string containing a regular expression pattern:

*regex.match(pattern, string)*
: Returns the length of the substring at the start of *string* matching *pattern.*

*regex.search(pattern, string)*
: Returns the first position in string where the pattern is matched (or –1).

*regex.compile(pattern)*
: Compiles a pattern into a regular expression object for later matching.

*regex.set_syntax(mode)*
: Select a syntax for patterns (see later in the chapter).

Objects returned by *compile* calls support matching by methods. If *object* is a compiled regular expression pattern, then it can be processed with a number of attributes:

*object.match(string [,from])*
: Like *regex.match*, but pattern is implied; if used, *from* is a start index.

*object.search(string [,from])*
: Like *regex.search*, but pattern is implied; *from* works the same here.

*object.group(index, index, . . . )*
: Return substrings matched by grouped subexpressions in the pattern.

*object.regs[index]*
: Stop/start index tuples for substrings matched by grouped subexpressions.

Compiling patterns ahead of time speeds matching programs that use multiple patterns repeatedly. Since Python automatically caches the last pattern passed to *search* or *match*, programs that just use a single pattern don't need to compile it first.

The two statements:

```
object = regex.compile(pattern)
length = object.match(string)
```

are equivalent to *length = regex.match(pattern, string)*. The regular expression examples we'll see shortly illustrate the module's interfaces in more detail.

### *regsub: regex plus substitution*

The *regsub* module builds on *regex* functionality, to add substitution of matched substrings:

*regsub.sub(pattern, replacement, string)*
: Replace the first occurrence of a pattern in a string.

*regsub.gsub(pattern, replacement, string)*
: Replace all the occurrences of a pattern in a string.

*regsub.split(string, pattern)*
: Split a strings into substrings, using pattern as delimiter.

> ## *How regular expressions are integrated into Python*
>
> These two modules illustrate typical extension strategies. As currently implemented, the *regex* module is coded in C, and *regsub* is written in Python (with implications we'll see in a moment). *regsub* imports *regex*, and adds logic to replace a matched substring, found by calling *regex.search*. *regex* is a normal C extension module, which serves as a wrapper for a public-domain package written in C. But *regex* is both an extension module and an extension type: its *compile* function makes a new type instance object. Suggested exercise: Study the implementation of the *regex/regsub* modules.

### *Using regular expression patterns*

The *regex* module supports regular expression syntaxes used in a number of common UNIX utilities. Programs can select an expression syntax by calling *regex.set_syntax(mode)*, where *mode* is an integer bitmask. The library module *regex_syntax.py* defines mode settings and provides constants for *awk*, *egrep*, *grep*, and *emacs*-style expressions:

- *RE_SYNTAX_AWK*
- *RE_SYNTAX_EGREP*

- *RE_SYNTAX_GREP*
- *RE_SYNTAX_EMACS*

*Emacs*-style syntax is the default. Syntax varies slightly in each syntax mode, and we won't document each flavor in detail here. But as an overview, regular expressions are built up by concatenating single-character regular expression forms in the following table. The longest-matching string is always matched by each form. In the table, *Re* means any regular expression form, *C* is a character, and *N* denotes a digit.

*Table 16-1: Common regular expression operators*

| Form | Match | Description |
|---|---|---|
| . | Any | Matches any single character except *newline* |
| *C* | Literal | An ordinary character (not an operator) matches itself |
| *[abc]* | Selection | Matches any single character in the bracketed list |
| *[a-z]* | Range | Matches any single character in the range, inclusive |
| *[^abc]* | Negation | Matches any single character not in the list (and/or range) |
| *C* | Escape | A backslash escape makes a special character ordinary |
| *t* | Tab | Normal escape characters like tab, backspace, and return |
| ^*Re* | From start | Anchors the match to the leftmost portion of a string |
| *Re$* | To end | Anchors the match to the rightmost portion of a string |
| ^*Re$* | Entire line | Constrains the *Re* to match the entire string (line) |
| *ReRe* | Concatenation | Adjacent *Re*'s match adjacent substrings |
| *Re** | Repetition | Matches zero or more occurrences of the *Re* |
| *Re+* | Repetition | Matches one or more occurrences of the *Re* |
| *Re?* | Optional | Matches zero or one occurrences of the *Re* |
| \\(*Re*\\) | Grouping | Matches *Re*, but saves the matched substring in a register |
| *N* | Backreference | Matches the contents of the *N*th substring register |
| *Re*\\ \| *Re* | Selection | Matches one of the *Re*'s |
| \\<*Re* | Start word | Constrains *Re* to match at the beginning of a word |
| *Re*\\> | End word | Constrains *Re* to match something at the end of a word |

Ranges and selections can be combined. For instance, *[a-zA-Z0-9_]+* matches the longest possible string of one or more letters, digits, or underscores. Special characters can be escaped as usual in Python strings: *[\t ]** matches zero or more tabs and spaces (i.e., skips whitespace).

The grouping construct, \\(*Re*\\), lets us extract matched substrings after a successful match. The portion of the string matched by the expression in parentheses is retained in a numbered register. It's available through either the *group* method, or the *regs* member of a compiled regex object (see the following examples).

The table gives the default *emacs* quoting rules. Some operators are syntax specific; they may or may not require a preceding backslash depending on the syntax used, and operator precedence may vary. Also, there are additional operators and features not shown here. For instance, symbolic names may be associated with a group's matched substring by using the *symcomp* method instead of *compile*.

The Python library manual gives additional details. But to demonstrate how the *regex* and *regsub* interfaces are typically used we'll turn to some short examples:

- Basic patterns
- Scanning C header files for patterns
- A file searching utility (*grep*)
- Replacing tabs in files

### Basic patterns

Let's start with a file that matches simple pattern forms, to illustrate how operators can be combined. All the *print* statements show a result of 2, except the last (which fails, and prints a return code of –1). For *search*, 2 means the pattern was matched at the third character; for *match*, a two-character string was matched. Check the table earlier to see which operators are applied in these patterns.

*Example 16-4: File: patterns.py*

```
import regex

# literals, sets, ranges
print regex.search("A.C.", "xxABCDxx")
print regex.search(" *A.C[DE][D-F][^G-ZE]G\t+ ?", "..ABCDEFG\t..")

# line boundaries
print regex.search("[\t ]+A.CDE[^G-ZA-E]G\t+ ?$", "..  ABCDEFG\t ")

# alternatives
print regex.search("A\|XB\|YC\|ZD", "..AYCD..")

# word boundaries
print regex.search("\<ABCD", "..ABCD ")
print regex.search("ABCD\>", "..ABCD ")

# groups
x = regex.compile("A\(.\)B\(.\)C\(.\)")      # saves 3 substrings
x.match("A0B1C2")
print x.group(3)

# backreferences
x = regex.compile("\(.\)\\1")                 # repeat prior character
print x.match("AA")
print x.match("AB")     # fails: -1
```

### *Scanning C header files for patterns*

Chapter 2 presented a script that used regular expressions to find *#define* and *#include* lines in C header files. Here's an expanded version which also handles both defines with one argument (C macros), and continuation lines (following a backslash). Unlike *finder* above, unusual lines are handled by the generality of the patterns. Continuation lines are concatenated and grouping is used to extract matched substrings.

*Example 16-5: File: cheader.py*

```
#! /usr/local/bin/python
import sys, regex, string

# patt_define  matches:  "#define name ..."
# patt_macro   matches:  "#define name(arg) ..."
# patt_include matches:  "#include (<|")name/name/name.name..."

patt_define = regex.compile(
  '^#[\t ]*define[\t ]+\([a-zA-Z0-9_]+\)[\t ]*')

patt_macro = regex.compile(
  '^#[\t ]*define[\t ]+\([a-zA-Z0-9_]+\)(\([_a-zA-Z][_a-zA-Z0-9]*\))[\t ]+')

patt_include = regex.compile(
  '^#[\t ]*include[\t ]+[<"]\([a-zA-Z0-9_/\.]+\)')

def scan(file):
    lineno = 0
    while 1:                            # scan input file line-by-line
        line = file.readline()
        if not line: break
        lineno = lineno + 1
        n = patt_macro.match(line)
        if n >= 0:
            line, lineno = cont(file, line, lineno)
            name, arg = patt_macro.group(1, 2)      # two matched substrings
            body = line[n:]
            print '%d) %s[%s] = %s' % (lineno, name, arg, string.strip(body))
            continue

        n = patt_define.match(line)                 # save length-of-match
        if n >= 0:
            line, lineno = cont(file, line, lineno)
            name = patt_define.group(1)             # substring for \(...\)
            body = line[n:]
            print '%d) %s = %s' % (lineno, name, string.strip(body) or None)
            continue

        if patt_include.match(line) >= 0:
            regs = patt_include.regs                # start/stop indexes
            a, b = regs[1]                          # for nested patterns
            filename = line[a:b]                    # slice out of line
```

Just for a moment, let's consider the situation carefully. By and large, the root of the complexity in developing software isn't related to the role it's supposed to perform: usually this is a well-defined real-world process. Rather, it stems from the mapping of real-world tasks onto computer-executable models. And this mapping is performed in the context of programming languages and tools.

The path toward easing the software bottleneck must therefore lie, at least partially, in optimizing the act of programming itself by deploying the right tools. Given this realistic scope, there's much that can be done now: there are a number of purely artificial overheads inherent in our current tools.

## *The Static Language Build Cycle*

Using traditional static languages, there is an unavoidable overhead in moving from coded programs to working systems: compile and link steps add a built-in delay to the development process. In some environments it's common to spend many hours each week just waiting for a static language application's build cycle to finish. Given that modern development practice involves an iterative process of building, testing, and rebuilding, such delays can be expensive and demoralizing (if not physically painful! :-) .

Of course, this varies from shop to shop, and in some domains the demand for performance justifies build cycle delays. But I've worked in C++ environments, where programmers joked about having to "go to lunch" whenever they recompiled their systems. Except they weren't really joking.

## *Artificial Complexities*

With many traditional programming tools, you can easily lose the forest for the trees: the act of programming becomes so complex that the real-world goal of the program becomes obscured. Traditional languages divert valuable attention to syntactic issues and development of bookkeeping code. Obviously, complexity isn't an end in itself: it must be clearly warranted. Yet some of our current tools are often so complex that the language itself makes the task harder and lengthens the development process.

## *One Language Does Not Fit All*

Many traditional languages implicitly encourage homogeneous, single-language systems. By making integration complex, they impede the use of multiple language tools. Instead of being able to select the right tool for the task at hand, developers are often compelled to use the same language for every component of an application. Since no language is good at everything, this constraint inevitably sacrifices both product functionality and programmer productivity.

Until our machines are as clever at taking directions as we are (arguably, not the most rational of goals :-), the programming task won't go away. But for the time being, we can still make substantial progress by making the mechanics of that task easier. And this topic is what I want to talk about now.

## *Enter Python . . .*

If this book has achieved its goals, by now you should have a good understanding of why Python has been called a "next generation scripting language." Compared with similar tools, it has some critical distinctions which we're finally in a position to summarize.

### *Your mileage may vary*

But before doing that, let me stress that all the languages below are useful tools, for a variety of applications. Language comparison is a perilous endeavor (at best! :-), and I don't mean to be rude to users of other tools here. But since the contrasts underscore some of the main reasons for using Python, a few words are probably in order. But just a few.

*Tcl*

Like Tcl, Python can be used as an embedded extension language. Unlike Tcl, Python is also a full-featured programming language. For many, Python's data structure tools and support for programming-in-the-large make it useful in more domains. Tcl demonstrated the utility of integrating interpreted languages with C modules. Python provides similar functionality plus a powerful, object-oriented language; it's not just a command string processor.

*Perl*

Like Perl, Python can be used for writing shell tools: it makes it easy to use system services. Unlike Perl, Python has a simple, readable syntax and a remarkably coherent design. To some, this makes Python easier to use and a better choice for programs that must be reused or maintained by others. Without question, Perl is a powerful system administration tool. But once we move beyond processing text and files, Python's features become attractive.

*Scheme*

Like Scheme (and Lisp), Python supports dynamic typing, incremental development, and metaprogramming: it exposes the interpreter's state and supports run-time program construction. Unlike Lisp, Python has a procedural syntax, familiar to users of mainstream languages like C and Pascal. If extensions are to be coded by end users this can be a major advantage.

*Smalltalk*

Like Smalltalk, Python supports object-oriented programming (OOP) in the context of a highly dynamic language. Unlike Smalltalk, Python doesn't extend the object system to include fundamental program control flow constructs. Users need not come to grips with the concept of *if* statements being message receiving objects to use Python. Python is more conventional.

*Icon*

Like Icon, Python supports a variety of high-level data types and operations, such as lists, dictionaries, and slicing. Unlike Icon, Python is fundamentally simple. Programmers (and end users) don't need to master such esoteric concepts as backtracking just to get started.

*BASIC*

Like modern structured BASIC dialects, Python has an interpretive/interactive nature. Unlike most BASICs, Python includes standard support for advanced programming features such as classes, modules, exceptions, high-level data types, and general C integration.

Naturally, there are other factors to consider when comparing language tools. For instance, Python's "no strings attached" copyright can also be a distinct advantage. Unlike some languages, Python requires no special handling or fees when shipped with commercial products; it's *true* freeware.

To be fair, all of these languages (and others) have merit and unique strengths of their own. In fact, Python borrowed most of its features from languages such as these. It's not Python's goal to replace every other language: different tasks require different tools, and mixed-language development is one of Python's main ideas. But Python's blend of advanced programming constructs and integration tools make it a natural choice for the problem domains we've mentioned in this book.

# But What About That Bottleneck?

Back to our original question: How can the act of writing software be made easier? At some level, Python is really "just another computer language." It's certainly true that Python the language doesn't represent much that's radically new from a theoretical point of view. So why should we be excited about Python when so many languages have been tried already?

What does make Python of interest, and what may be its larger contribution to the development world, is not its syntax or semantics, but its worldview: Python's combination of tools makes rapid development a realistic goal. In a nutshell, Python fosters rapid development, by providing the following features.

- Fast build-cycle turnaround
- A very-high-level, object-oriented language
- Integration facilities to enable mixed-language development

Specifically, Python attacks the software development bottleneck on four fronts.

## *Python Provides Immediate Feedback During Development*

Python's development cycle is dramatically shorter than that of traditional tools. In Python there are no compile or link steps. Python programs simply import modules at run-time and use the objects they contain. Because of this, Python programs run immediately after changes are made. And in cases where dynamic module reloading can be used, it's even possible to change and reload parts of a running program without stopping it at all. Figure 1 shows Python's impact on the development cycle.

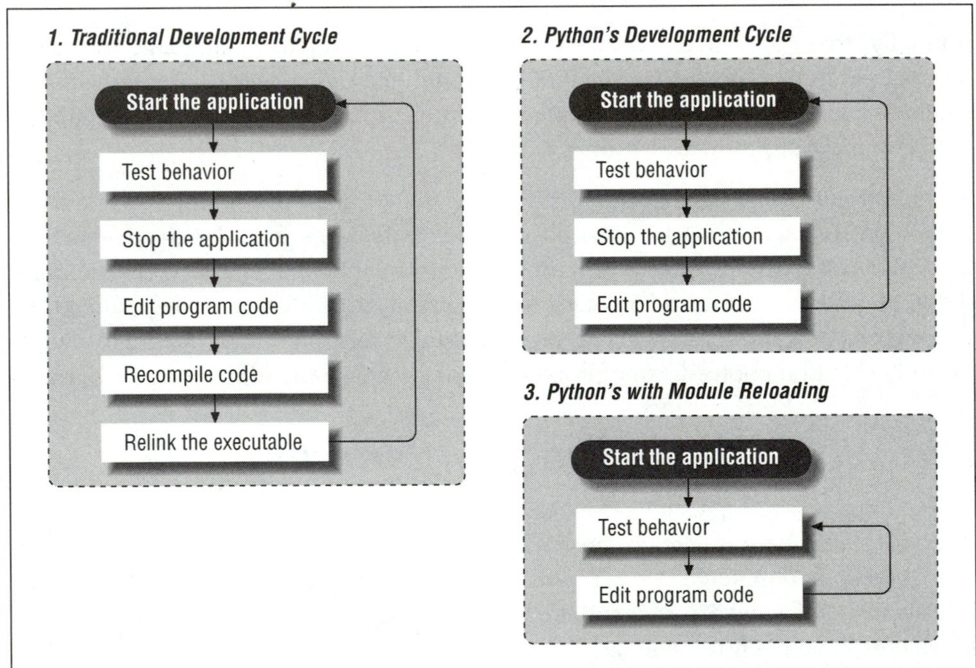


*Figure 1: Development cycles*

Because Python is interpreted, there's a rapid turnaround after program changes. And because Python's parser is embedded in Python-based systems, it's easy to

## *Python versus Java: Round 1?*

Because the *Grail* WWW browser uses Python in the same way that Sun's Java language is typically employed, there's been interest in comparing the two. Roughly, Java is a dialect of C++. As this book is being written, Java is still relatively new, so comparisons are probably premature. But some of the distinctions between the two languages illustrate key Python concepts.

Like Java, Python supports OOP, compilation to byte code, portability, and use as an applet programming language. (See Appendix A, *...And Other Cool Stuff*; at present, Python can be used for applet coding in Grail, and in Netscape as a plug-in). But compared to Java, Python is:

- *Higher level.* Python's first-class object model, dynamic typing, and built-in data types make it an arguably simpler language. Since Java is based on C++, it inherits much of that language's complexity. In contrast, Python has a simple core, with dynamic OOP thrown in as an option.
- *Completely free.* Python comes with complete source code, which you can use any way you like. In fact, you could sell the source code if you were so inclined (though it probably won't make you rich overnight :-) .
- *General purpose.* Nothing about Python is web-specific; even its safe execution mode is an option. As its library of extensions attests, Python is used in a wide variety of domains. Other Java roles aren't yet clear.
- *More dynamic.* Python and C programs can execute arbitrary strings of embedded code at run-time. Users of Python can code extensions onsite because the development and run-time environments are the same.

Most of these distinctions reflect different intended roles. Some would call Python and Java "apples and oranges"; others would call them entirely different food groups! Java is designed for use across a network; because of that, some operations are restricted. And true to its C++ heritage, Java's design emphasizes efficiency at the expense of flexibility.

On the other hand, Python is geared more toward scripting, prototyping, and rapid development. For example, it has a deliberately open design, supports run-time program construction, and usually provides unlimited access to system services. Such utility is useful in Python applications but would be a cardinal sin in Java's current domains.

Some would argue that a higher-level language like Python makes more sense for scripting work, and that applet programming falls in this domain. We won't resolve the debate here; there's clearly room for more than one language in a developer's toolbox.

modify programs at run-time. For example, in Chapter 11, *Graphical User Interfaces,* we saw how GUI programs developed with Python allow developers to change the code that handles a button press while the GUI remains active; the effect of the code change may be observed immediately when the button is pressed again. There's no need to stop and rebuild.

More generally, in Python the entire development process becomes an exercise in rapid prototyping. Python lends itself to experimental, interactive program development. Python also encourages developing systems incrementally, by testing components in isolation and putting them together later. In fact, we've seen that we can switch from testing components (unit tests) to testing whole systems (integration tests) arbitrarily, as illustrated in Figure 2.

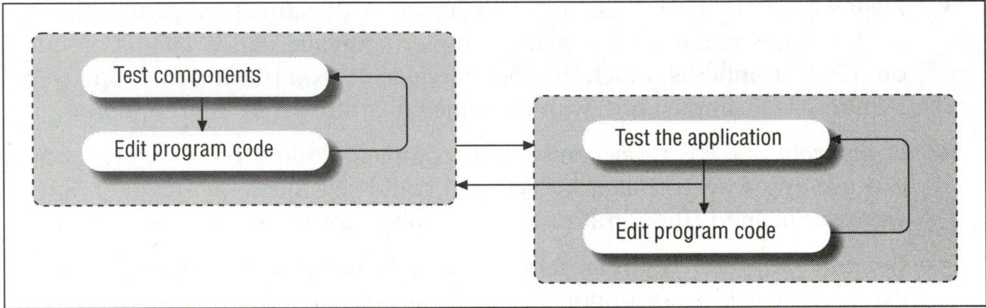


*Figure 2: Incremental development*

## *Python Is "Executable Pseudocode"*

Python's very-high-level nature means there's less for us to program and manage. Lack of compile and link steps isn't really enough by itself. For instance, a C or C++ interpreter might provide fast turnaround but it still would be almost useless for rapid development: the language is too complex and low-level.

But because Python is also a simple language, coding is dramatically faster too. For example, its dynamic typing, built-in objects, and garbage-collection eliminate much of the manual bookkeeping code required in lower-level languages like C and C++. Since things like:

- Type declarations
- Memory management
- Block and line delimiters
- Common data structure implementations

are all conspicuously absent, Python programs are typically a fraction of the size of their C or C++ equivalents; there's less to write and read, and less opportunity for coding errors.

Because most bookkeeping code is missing, Python programs are clearer to understand and more closely reflect the actual problem they're intended to address. And Python's high-level nature not only allows algorithms to be realized more quickly, it also makes it easier to learn the language.

## *Python Is OOP "Done Right"*

For OOP to be useful, it must be easy to apply. Python makes OOP a flexible tool by delivering it in a dynamic language. More importantly, its class mechanism is a simplified subset of C++'s, and it's this simplification that makes OOP useful in the context of a rapid development tool. For instance, when we looked at data structure classes in Chapter 13, *Implementing Objects*, we saw that Python's dynamic typing let us apply a single class to a variety of object types; we didn't need to write variants for each supported type.

In fact, Python's OOP is so easy to use that there's really no reason not to apply OOP in most parts of an application. Python's class model has features that are powerful enough for complex programs:

- Multiple inheritance
- Virtual methods and data
- Constructors and destructors
- Operator overloading and metaclass protocols
- First-class instances, classes, and methods

Yet because they're provided in simple ways, they don't interfere with the problem we're trying to solve.

## *Python Fosters Hybrid Applications*

As we've seen earlier in this book, its extending and embedding support makes it useful in mixed-language systems. Without good integration facilities, even the best rapid development language is a "closed box" and not generally useful in modern development environments. But Python's integration tools make it usable in hybrid, multi component applications. As one consequence, systems can simultaneously utilize the strengths of Python for rapid development, and traditional languages such as C for execution efficiency.

While it's possible to use Python as a standalone tool, it doesn't impose this mode. Instead, Python encourages an integrated approach to application development. By supporting arbitrary mixtures of Python and traditional languages, Python really fosters a spectrum of development paradigms, ranging from pure prototyping to pure efficiency. Figure 3 shows the abstract case.

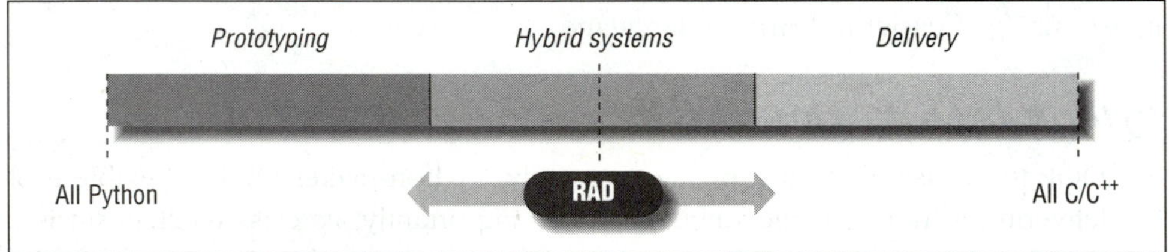


*Figure 3: The development mode "slider"*

As we move to the left extreme of the spectrum, we optimize speed of development. Moving to the right side optimizes speed of execution. And somewhere in between is an optimum mix for any given project. With Python, not only can we pick the proper mix for our project, but we can also later move the RAD slider in the picture arbitrarily as our needs change:

*Going to the right*
: Projects can be started on the left end of the scale in Python and can be moved toward the right gradually, module by module, as needed to optimize performance for delivery.

*Going to the left*
: Similarly, we can move strategic parts of existing C or C++ applications on the right end of the scale to Python, to support end-user programming and customization on the left end of the scale.

This flexibility of development modes is crucial in realistic environments. Python is optimized for speed of development but that alone isn't enough. By themselves, neither C nor Python is adequate to address the development bottleneck; together, they can do much more. As shown in Figure 4 for instance, apart from standalone use, one of Python's most common roles splits systems into:

- *Frontend* components that can benefit from Python's ease-of use
- *Backend* modules that require the efficiency of static languages like C, C++, or FORTRAN

Whether we add Python frontend interfaces to existing systems, or design them in early on, such a division of labor can open up a system to its users without exposing its internals.

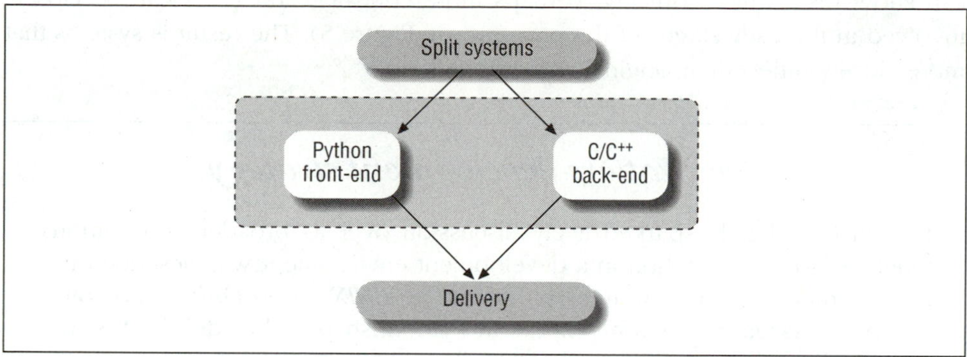


*Figure 4: Hybrid designs*

When developing new systems, we also have the option of writing entirely in Python at first and optimizing as needed for delivery by moving performance-critical components to compiled languages. As we saw in Chapter 14, *Extending Python*, because Python and C modules look the same to clients, migration to compiled extensions is transparent.

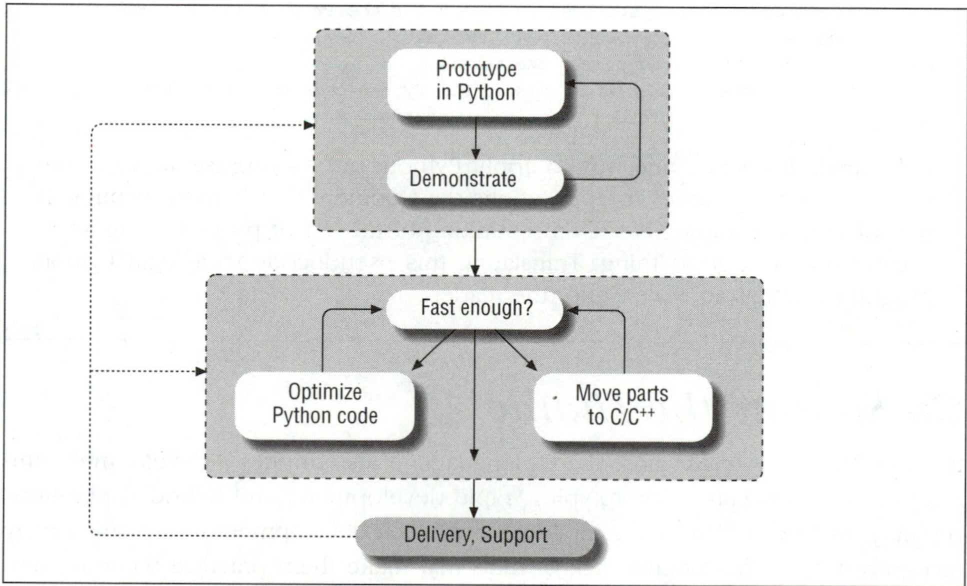


*Figure 5: Prototyping with Python*

Prototyping doesn't make sense in every scenario. Sometimes splitting a system into a Python frontend and a C/C++ backend up front works best. And prototyping doesn't help much when enhancing existing systems. But where it can be applied, early prototyping can be a major asset. By prototyping in Python first, we can show results more quickly. Perhaps more critically, end users can be closely involved in the early stages of the process (see Figure 5). The result is systems that more closely reflect their original requirements.

### *The Watters development strategy*

Python has already sparked lively discussion over its broader ramifications. One way to utilize Python in a development environment was described in a recent article by Aaron Watters, published by *UNIX World Online* (See Bibliography). Aaron presents his model in Python-ish pseudocode; the first half roughly corresponds to the prototyping figure above:

```
def Develop(vague_inaccurate_requirements):
    Product = a simple implementation of the requirements in Python.
    while the customers don't like the Product:
        Product = what the customers claim to want.
    while the Product is too slow:
        Identify a bottleneck in the Product by profiling.
        Optimize the bottleneck in Python.
        if it's still a bottleneck:
            Reimplement the bottleneck as a compiled extension module.
    Develop an acceptance test in Python for the Product (in Python!).
    while the Product doesn't pass the test:
        debug the Product (or the test!).
    Deliver the Product with some or all Python code byte-compiled
            to protect proprietary source.
```

Of course, this is just one way to apply Python, but it's representative of the sort of fresh approaches to applications development that Python inspires. If part of Python's impact is such a rethinking of the act of programming itself, it can only be a good thing. Translating this pseudocode to a legal Python program is left as an exercise for the reader :-) .

## *On Sinking the Titanic*

In short, Python is really more than a language; it also implies a development philosophy. The concepts of prototyping, rapid development, and hybrid applications certainly aren't new. But while the benefits of such development modes are widely recognized, there has been a lack of tools that make them practical without sacrificing programming power. This is one of the main gaps that Python's design fills:

*Python provides a simple but powerful rapid development language, along with the integration tools needed to apply it in realistic development environments.*

This combination makes Python arguably unique among similar tools. For instance, Tcl is a good integration tool but not a full-blown language; Perl is a powerful system administration language but a weak integration tool. But Python's marriage of a powerful dynamic language and integration opens the door to fundamentally faster development modes. With Python, it's no longer necessary to choose between fast development and fast execution.

By now it should be clear that a single programming language can't satisfy all our development goals. In fact, our needs are sometimes contradictory: the goals of efficiency and flexibility will probably always clash. Given the high cost of making software, the choice between development and execution speed is crucial. Although machine cycles are cheaper than programmers, we can't yet ignore efficiency completely.

But with a tool like Python, we don't need to decide between the two goals at all. Just as a carpenter wouldn't drive a nail with a chainsaw, software engineers are empowered to use the right tool for the task at hand: Python when speed of development matters, compiled languages when efficiency dominates, and combinations of the two when our goals are not absolute.

Moreover, we don't have to sacrifice code reuse or rewrite exhaustively for delivery when applying rapid development with Python. We can have our rapid development cake and eat it too:

*Reusability*
: Because Python is a high-level, object-oriented language, it encourages writing reusable software and well-designed systems.

*Deliverability*
: Because Python is designed for use in mixed-language systems, we don't have to move to more efficient languages all at once.

In typical Python-oriented development, a system's frontend and infrastructure may be written in Python for ease of development and modification, but the kernel is still written in C or C++ for efficiency. Python has been called the tip of the iceberg in such systems—the part made visible to end users of a package (see Figure 6).

Such an architecture uses the best of both worlds. It can be extended by adding more Python code or writing C extension modules, depending on performance requirements. But this is just one of many mixed-language development scenarios:

*System interfaces*
: Packaging systems as Python extension modules makes them more accessible

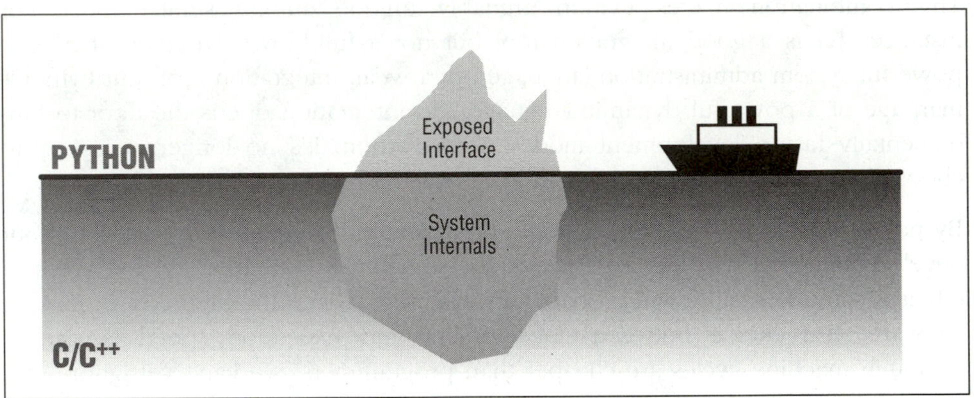


*Figure 6: "Sinking the Titanic" with mixed-language systems*

*End-user customization*
: Delegating components to embedded Python code provides for on-site changes

*Pure prototyping*
: Python prototypes can be moved to C all at once for delivery, or piecemeal

*Legacy code migration*
: Moving existing code from C to Python makes it simpler and more flexible

*Standalone use*
: Of course, using Python all by itself leverages its existing library of tools

Python's open design lets us apply it in whatever way makes sense for each new project.

## So What's Python: The Sequel

As we've seen in this book, Python is a multifaceted tool, useful in a wide variety of domains. What can we say about Python to sum up here? In terms of some of its best attributes, Python is a:

- General-purpose
- Object-oriented
- Interpreted
- Very-high-level
- Openly designed

- Freely available
- And refreshingly coherent

language, useful for both extension work and standalone development. But a better answer is really up to you, the reader. Since Python is a general-purpose tool, what it "is" depends on how you choose to use it.

Python's certainly far from perfect (if the term has any meaning at all, in a domain as subjective as programming language design!). But its combination of language and integration features seems to be a perfect fit for today's development environments, and a natural match for paradigms that could dramatically improve the way we do the business of software development. Philosophically speaking, Python is about nothing less than quality of craft. On the other hand, it can also be a lot of fun to use :-) .

## *In the Final Analysis . . .*

I hope this book has taught you something about Python, both the language, and its roles. Beyond this text, there's really no substitute for doing some original Python programming. The appendixes give summary details, and Chapter 3, *Getting Started*, lists sources of additional information to help you on your way.

The task of programming computers will probably always be hard. Perhaps happily, there will continue to be a need for intelligent software engineers, skilled at translating real-world tasks into computer-executable form, for at least the foreseeable future. After all, if it were too easy, none of us would get paid! :-)

But current development practice and tools make that task unnecessarily difficult: many of the obstacles faced by software developers are purely artificial. We have come far in our quest to improve the speed of computers. The time has come to focus our attentions on improving the speed of development.

Python, as a mixed-paradigm tool, has the potential to foster development modes that simultaneously leverage the benefits of rapid development and traditional languages. While Python won't solve all the problems of the software industry, it offers hope for making programming simpler, faster, and at least a little more enjoyable.

It may not get us off that island altogether, but it sure beats bananas and coconuts.

## "Roll the Closing Credits"

Just for fun, here's a script that plays the Monty Python theme song. It uses the *ftplib* library module to download an audio file, and the POSIX *os.popen* function to send it to an audio filter command. It's extremely nonportable, and probably won't work on your machine without some tweaking (see the comments and help string). If needed, you can always download the file by hand or find it on the CD-ROM and do the right thing.

*Example 1: File: sousa.py*

```
#!/usr/local/bin/python

#################################################
# Usage: % sousa.py
# Fetch and play the Monty Python theme song.
# Inspired by an idea from Jeff Bauer.
#
# This may not work on your system as is: it
# requires a machine with ftp access, and uses
# Sun audio filters. Configure as needed.
#################################################

import os, sys
from ftplib import FTP                          # socket-based ftp tools
from posixpath import exists                    # file existence test

sample = 'sousa.au'
filter = { 'sunos5': '/usr/bin/audioplay',
           'linux1': '<unknown>',
           'sunos4': '/usr/demo/SOUND/play' }

helpmsg = """
Sorry: can't find an audio filter for your system!
Add an entry to the script's "filter" dictionary for
your system's audio command, or run the ftp code and
use the ".au" file. Also see module: Lib/audiodev.py.
"""

# check the filter
if filter.has_key(sys.platform) and exists(filter[sys.platform]):
    print 'Working...'
else:
    print helpmsg
    sys.exit(1)

# ftp the audio file
if not exists(sample):
    theme = open(sample, 'w')
    ftp = FTP('ftp.python.org')                 # connect to ftp site
    ftp.login()                                 # use anonymous login
    ftp.cwd('pub/python/misc')
```

*Example 1: File: sousa.py (continued)*

```
        ftp.retrbinary('RETR ' + sample, theme.write, 1024)
        ftp.quit()
        theme.close()

    # send it to audio device
    theme = open(sample, 'r')
    audio = os.popen(filter[sys.platform], 'w')    # spawn shell tool
    audio.write(theme.read())                       # send to stdin
```

# IV

# *Appendixes*

- Appendix A, *. . . And Other Cool Stuff*
- Appendix B, *Futurisms*
- Appendix C, *A Mini-Reference*
- Appendix D, *An Application Framework*
- Appendix E, *A Python Tutorial*
- Appendix F, *Python Classes for C++ Programmers*
- Bibliography
- Glossary
- Index

The appendixes provide common reference material, and give some general information about Python.

- Appendix A takes a short look at other Python application areas that we couldn't cover in this book because of space and/or complexity. It includes overviews and contributed examples from common Python domains.
- Appendix B lists possible Python extensions.
- Appendix C provides some critical reference sources.
- Appendix D gives source code listings for an application framework example that you can study on your own.
- Appendix E is optional reading; it can be used as a first step for beginners or as a language feature summary.
- Appendix F summarizes some Python/C++ differences.

- The Bibliography points to additional sources of information.
- The Glossary contains terms used throughout the book.

Appendix C covers only common topics; we won't duplicate Python's reference manuals here. As noted in the Preface, this book isn't an exhaustive Python reference or a replacement for Python's manuals. Since Python is evolving, this book really can't fill such a role. Covering every Python language and extension detail could easily fill another book (the standard reference manuals are hundreds of pages long!). Once you've learned how to use Python, this book can be supplemented with the reference manuals that come with Python, as needed.

### *Other reading*

The standard reference manuals are probably the next stop after you've read this book. They can be found on the accompanying CD-ROM. Beyond that, there have also been a number of articles written about Python, and other domain-specific Python books are already in the works. See Bibliography, and the Python Frequently Asked Questions (FAQ) resource for details.

Papers and proceedings from Python workshops are also a good source of information; they're kept on the Python WWW site. Chapter 3, *Getting Started*, tells where to find the WWW page and lists other electronic sources of information.

Beyond all of these sources of information, studying Python programs that come with the system is a great way to learn more: see the *Demo* and *Lib* directories in the Python build directory for Python examples, and the *Modules* and *Objects* directory for C extensions. Note: these directory names may change over time; check your Python installation tree. You can find these files on the CD-ROM, too.

# *. . . And Other Cool Stuff*

*In this appendix:*

- *Grail: A Python-Based WWW Browser*
- *PythonWin: Python as a PC/Windows Tool*
- *The freeze Tool: Packaging Python Executables*
- *The pindent Script: Block Delimiters (If You Insist!)*
- *Distributed Programming Tools*
- *Built-in Internet/WWW Tools*
- *Python on the Macintosh*
- *Python as a Netscape Web Browser Plug-in*
- *Other Contributions on the CD-ROM*
- *Recent Extensions*

## *"So Many Applications, So Little Time"*

Because Python is a general-purpose language, we've emphasized concepts that span domains in this book. Most of the ideas we've looked at will apply to any Python application you'll encounter. For instance, extension techniques are at the core of many Python-based systems.

Still, applications are as much responsible for Python's popularity as the language itself. Unfortunately, we don't have time or space to really do justice to more advanced Python domains here; for example, Common Object Request Broker Architecture (CORBA) and WWW scripting are large topics, which are addressed by more specific texts.

But just to hint at other work going on in the Python world today, this appendix briefly introduces a handful of applications and tools not covered earlier. Most of the examples are just "teasers," intended to point you toward other topics to study on your own. Sources of additional information are given along the way.

From a Python perspective, most of these systems are really just instances of Python's integration tools at work. Although we won't discuss domain-specific background details here, some of the systems below are testimonies to just how far a modular, extensible scripting language like Python can take us.

## *Grail: A Python-Based WWW Browser*

Python's inventor has also created an extensible browser for the WWW, called Grail, in conjunction with a research effort at CNRI. Grail release 0.3 was put out as this appendix was being written; it's currently available at the URL *http://monty.cnri.reston.va.us/grail/*, and can be found on this book's CD-ROM.

Grail is an exciting application but is too advanced for us to cover in depth here. But for a quick overview, here's a quote from Guido's release statement:

> Grail is an extensible Internet browser. It supports the protocols and file formats commonly found on the World-Wide Web, such as HTTP, FTP, and HTML, but, unlike other browsers, it is easily extended to support other protocols or file formats, such as CNRI's handle protocol. Grail is distributed by CNRI free of charge for non-commercial purposes.
>
> Grail is written and extensible in Python, a free object-oriented programming language (see *http://www.python.org*). It also uses Tk, a free UI toolkit by John Ousterhout.
>
> Grail lets you download fragments of Python code that execute inside the browser on your local machine. These little Python applications ("applets") can do things like display animations, interact with the user in new ways, even create additional menus that pop up dialogs if you like. Applets run in a restricted execution environment, so that broken or malicious applets ("Trojan Horses") can't erase your files or crash your computer.
>
> Grail is still a prototype. However, it already supports full HTML 2.0, including images, forms and imagemaps, uses asynchronous document transfer, supports printing and saving documents, searching, bookmarks, history, and more.
>
> Apart from running applets, Grail is extensible in other areas, such as:
>
> - New protocols (e.g. CNRI's handle protocol)
> - New file formats (e.g. for handling JPEG or sound directly)
> - New HTML tags (e.g. tables)
> - New user interface features (e.g. bookmarks or annotations) (not yet in this release)
>
> There's a mailing list for Grail users and developers. Send email to *grail-request@python.org* with (just) the word "subscribe" in the body to subscribe yourself. To reach the Grail development team at CNRI, send email to *grail-feedback@python.org*.

## *A Simple Applet Example*

Writing Grail applets is remarkably straightforward. In fact, applets are really just *Tkinter* programs; with a few exceptions, they don't need to "know" about Grail at all. Here's a short example taken from Grail's homepage. The code listed below adds a button to the browser, which changes its appearance each time it's pressed (its bitmap is reconfigured in the button callback handler). There are two components to this page definition: an HTML file, plus the Python applet code it references.

*HTML file*

As usual, the *test.html* HTML file which follows describes how to format the web page when the HTML's URL address is selected in a browser. But here the *APP* tag also specifies a Python applet (class) to be run by the browser. By default, the Python module is assumed to have the same name as the class and must be stored in the same location (URL directory) as the HTML file that references it. Additional *APP* tag options can override the applet's default location.

*Applet file*

The applet adds widgets to the *Tkinter*-based Grail browser. Applets are simply classes in Python modules. When the *APP* tag is encountered in the HTML, the Grail browser downloads the *Question.py* source-code module below, and makes an instance of its *Question* class, passing in the browser widget as the *master* (parent). The *master* is the hook that lets applets attach new widgets to the browser itself: applets extend the GUI constructed by the HTML. Nothing in this class is Grail-specific; in fact, it can be run (and tested) standalone as a Python/*Tkinter* program.

*Example A-1: File: test.html*

```
<HEAD>
<TITLE>Grail Applet Test Page</TITLE>
</HEAD>

<BODY>
<H1>Test an Applet Here!</H1>
Click this button!
<APP CLASS=Question>
</BODY>
```

*Example A-2: File: Question.py*

```
# file: Question.py
# in the same location (URL) as the html file
# that references it; adds widgets to browser;

from Tkinter import *
```

*Example A-2: File: Question.py (continued)*

```
class Question:                                         # run by grail?
    def __init__(self, master):                         # master=browser
        self.button = Button(master,                    # add a new button
                             bitmap='question',
                             command=self.action)       # callback handler
        self.button.pack()

    def action(self):
        if self.button['bitmap'] == 'question':         # toggle image
            self.button.config(bitmap='questhead')      # on each press
        else:
            self.button.config(bitmap='question')

if __name__ == '__main__':
    root = Tk()                                  # run stand-alone?
    button = Question(root)                      # master=Tk: default top-level
    root.mainloop()
```

In effect, Grail applets are simply Python modules that are linked into HTML pages by using the *APP* tag. The Grail browser downloads the sourcecode identified by an *APP* tag and runs it locally.

Applets interact with the user by creating one or more arbitrary *Tk* widgets. Naturally, the example above is artificial; but notice that the button's callback handler could do anything we can program in Python: updating persistent information, popping up new user interaction dialogs, calling C extensions, etc.

## *Other Bells and Whistles*

By default, the applet module file has the same name as the class (from the *CLASS* tag option) and resides at the same URL address as the HTML file. In general, *APP* tags can specify a number of options:

```
<APP CLASS=name
     SRC=url
     MENU=name
     additional attributes ...>
```

*CLASS*

The class to be instantiated for the applet. If it has the form *module.class*, the class is presumed to be defined by a module named *module*. Otherwise the module name is presumed to be the same as the class name (*class.class*).

*SRC*

The URL of a directory containing the applet module file (named *module.py*). The URL defaults to the directory containing the HTML file that invoked the applet.

*MENU*

If present, instead of a frame inside the viewer's text, the widget's master is a menu in the browser's menu bar with the name given. The applet is expected to add entries to this menu that provide new commands, using the menu methods we saw in Chapter 11, *Graphical User Interfaces.*

Any additional attributes are passed as keyword arguments to the constructor of the applet class, with their names converted to lowercase. Grail applets may also access special Grail objects through special attributes of the *master* argument passed to every applet constructor. These objects include the HTML parser that instantiates the applet, the viewer object containing the applet, and the browser itself.

Grail has other features we won't mention here, and it's likely to evolve over time. Python also supports a trusted ("safe") execution mode for restricting access to operations that might be dangerous on the client machine. For more information, see the distribution's URL (also the WWW tools section later in this appendix).

Finally, Figure A-1 shows a screen shot of Grail in action (contributed by Michael McLay) to hint at what's possible. It shows the animated "game of life" demo. Everything you see here is implemented using Python and the *Tkinter* GUI interface. To run the demo, you need to install Python with the *Tk* extension (see Chapter 3, *Getting Started*), and download the Grail browser to run locally on your machine or copy it off the CD. Point the browser at the URL shown in the example. You can view this example's source code and other Grail examples, at the demo URL.

## *Grail portability*

Since Grail is based on Python and *Tk*, it can be run on any platform both these tools support. By the time you read this, the Grail browser should be available on the UNIX (X Windows), Microsoft Windows, and Macintosh platforms.

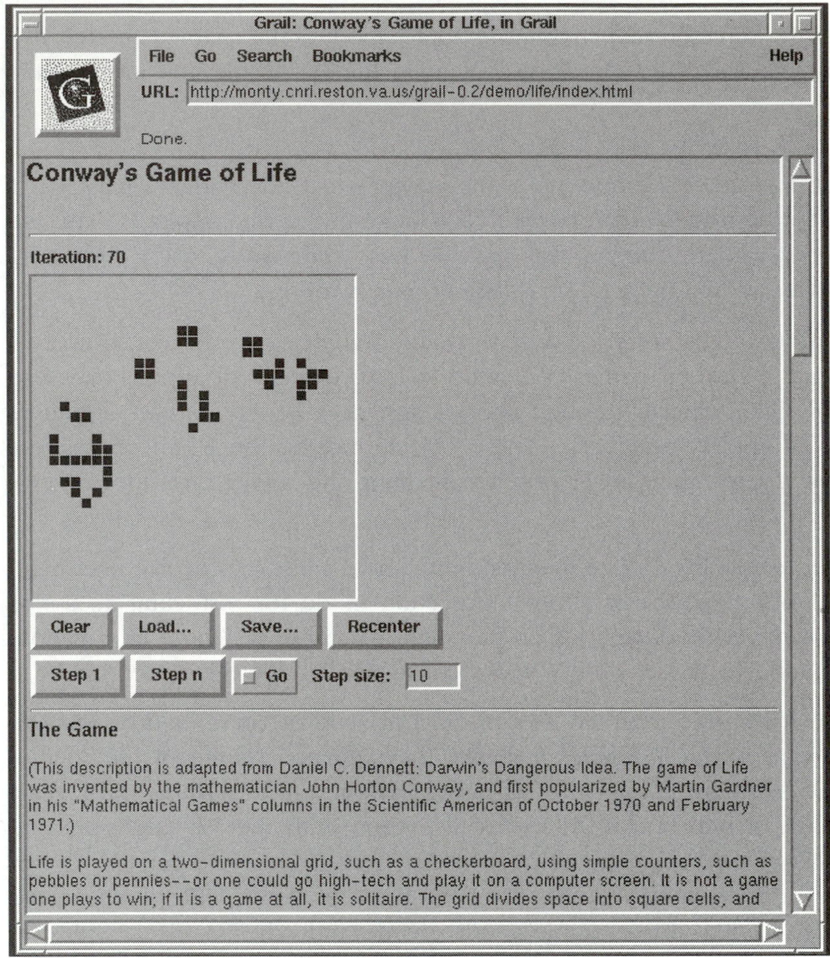


*Figure A-1: The Grail Web browser*

## *PythonWin: Python as a PC/Windows Tool*

Mark Hammond has developed ports of Python for Microsoft Windows platforms. They run on the NT, Windows 95, and Windows 3.1x (for both win32 and win16 APIs). All required components are on the accompanying CD-ROM and are FTP'able from *ftp.python.org*, in directory *pub/python/pythonwin* (but see Python's FAQ for up-to-date locations).

The CD-ROM and the FTP directory include both console (text) and GUI-based versions of the port. Besides letting us run Python programs on Windows machines, the ports also provide:

- Socket interfaces
- Dynamic loading of DLLs
- A simple GUI development environment: an MDI with editing, interaction, etc.
- A class-based interface to the MFC class library
- A class-based OLE interface that lets Python programs act as both clients and servers

The MFC and OLE interfaces make it possible to use Python both as a Windows GUI development tool and as a scripting language for Windows applications. For instance, it's possible to use Python as a scripting tool for products such as Microsoft Word and Access, much like Visual Basic.

## An OLE Integration Example

To illustrate the OLE interface, here are a few examples contributed by Mark Hammond. With the OLE extension, any Python class can be turned into a fully functional OLE2 automation server with just one line of code (to specify a base class). This means that almost any other OLE2 application can call a Python script without knowing anything about Python itself. For example, the file that follows allows a programmer to execute Python code from Visual Basic by coding:

```
Python = CreateObject("Python.Interpreter")
num    = Python.Eval("1+1")
```

The OLE integration details are handled automatically by the superclass (and the MFC framework it uses): an application is spawned, the appropriate method is called, and the result (if any) is returned correctly.

*Example A-3: File: ole1.py*

```
# Expose the Python interpreter to OLE.
# Called whenever an OLE object called
# "Python.Interpreter" is invoked.

class OLEInterpreter(OleDocServer):
    def __init__(self):
        dispids={1: ("Eval", self.Eval), 2: ("Exec", self.Exec)}
        OleDocServer.__init__(self,
              "{30BD3490-2632-11cf-AD5B-524153480001}", dispids)

    def Eval(self, exp):
        if type(exp)<>type(''):
            raise oleautsv.exc_type_mismatch, (1, "Argument must be a string")
```

*Example A-3: File: ole1.py (continued)*

```
        return eval(exp)

    def Exec(self, exp):
        if type(exp)<>type(''):
            raise oleautsv.exc_type_mismatch, (1, "Argument must be a string")
        exec exp
```

It's just as easy to use Python as an OLE client. At this writing, the OLE client interface comes in two flavors. Module *oleauto* exposes the OLE API without giving it Python-like semantics. Module *ole* attempts to make OLE calls as transparent as possible. For example, using *oleauto* directly, a call to the interface may look like:

```
ob = oleauto.connect('Word.Basic')
ob.Invoke('FileNew','normal.dot')
```

Using *ole*, the call parameters become methods (using the `__getattr__` metaclass protocol):

```
ob = ole.WordBasic()
ob.FileNew('Normal.dot')
```

The OLE client interface provides functions for connecting to existing (running) OLE objects, making new OLE objects from the registry, creating new identifiers etc. Object identifiers can be a *ProgID* (*Word.Basic*) or an OLE *CLSID* (*{88DEE000-2E3C-11CE-8B22-00001D0B96CA}*).

In Python, OLE objects are wrapped in class-instance objects. These OLE wrapper objects have methods for fetching and setting property values of the wrapped OLE object, calling its methods (by name or *DISPID*), etc. All of these concepts are far too OLE-specific for us to describe further here. See the port's documentation for more details.

## The Development GUI

*PythonWin* is the GUI version of the port; Figure A-2 shows what its development interface looks like. We get an MDI with an interaction window (roughly like the standard Python command line), plus any number of text editor windows for browsing and changing source modules. Menu options run scripts, import modules, etc. There's also a Python object browser and other features we won't mention here.

In addition to OLE support, *PythonWin* also has an interface to the MFC class library for Windows GUI development. For a quick demonstration of some of the available classes, type *import guidemo* at the *Interactive Window* prompt. In Figure A-2, we see the fonts demo that comes with the system, displaying an editorial comment from the demo's developer :-).

*NOTE* The *PythonWin* system is likely to evolve over time. In particular, the OLE interfaces outlined above will be solidified further, before you read this. Check the current release of the package at Python's FTP site for up-to-date information. Also see *WPY*, discussed later in this appendix.

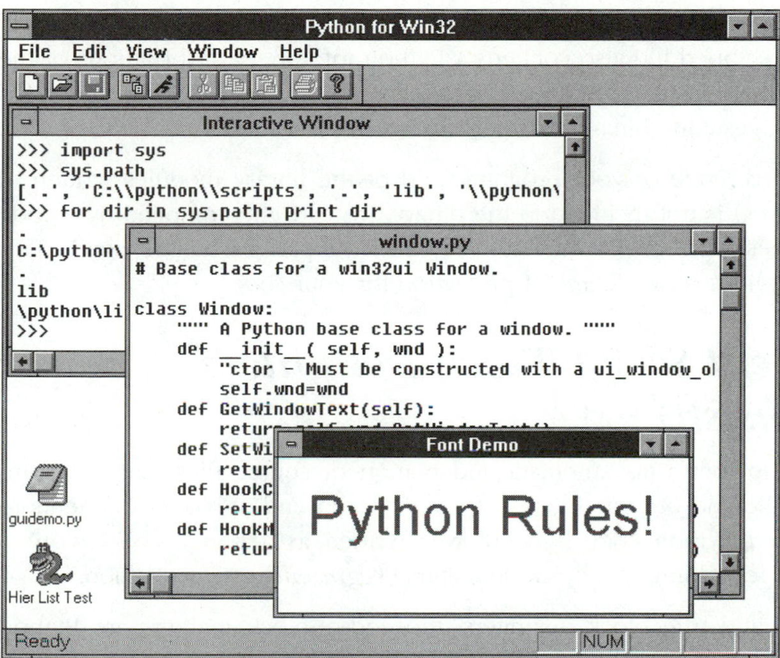

*Figure A-2: The PythonWin system*

# *The freeze Tool: Packaging Python Executables*

The *freeze* script generates C files that package Python modules for compilation. The resulting compiled form allows Python programs to be shipped without source code and without the overhead of importing *.pyc* compiled Python module files. Further, recipients of *frozen* Python programs don't need to have Python installed at their site. The *freeze* tool is found in the *Tools* directory of the Python build tree. Here are a few notes on its operation, paraphrased from the *README* file.

The *freeze* tool is invoked with a command like: *python freeze.py hello.py*, where *hello.py* is your program. It transitively collects all modules your code references. There's some "magic" in this process that we won't get into here; see the documentation in the *freeze* directory. *freeze* creates three files: *frozen.c*, *config.c* and *Makefile*. To produce the frozen (binary) version of your program, you simply type **make**.

The binary file is an executable, so this works only if your platform is compatible with that on the receiving end (i.e., the same major operating system revision and CPU type). The shipped file also contains a Python interpreter and portions of the Python run-time system. *freeze* takes some measures to avoid linking unneeded modules, but the resulting binary is usually not small.

The Python source code of your program (and of the library modules written in Python that it uses) is not included in the binary; instead, the compiled byte code (the instruction stream used internally by the interpreter) is packaged. This arrangement provides some degree of protection for your code.

## The pindent Script: Block Delimiters (If You Insist!)

The *pindent* script performs automatic indentation of source files that use comments to mark the end of code blocks. It can also add end-of-block comments to properly indented Python code. Pindent was written as a partial concession to those that argue for adding real block delimiters (*begin/end*, etc.) to Python.

*pindent* doesn't add true block delimiters: the end-of-block markers are Python comments. But this is often enough to satisfy exceptional constraints. In Python 1.3, the *pindent.py* script lives in the Python *Tools/scripts* directory. The *pindent* script has options and limitations we won't discuss in this book. But here are a few general remarks based on the most recent documentation.

*pindent* works in two modes. When called as *pindent -c*, it takes a valid Python program as input and outputs a version augmented with block-closing comments. When called as *pindent -r* it assumes its input is a Python program with block-closing comments but with improper indentation, and outputs a correctly indented version.

A block-closing comment is a comment of the form *# end <keyword>*, where *<keyword>* is the keyword that opened the block. If the opening keyword is *def* or *class*, the function or class name may be repeated in the block-closing comment optionally. For example:

```
def foobar(a, b):
    if a == b:
        a = a+1
    elif a < b:
        b = b-1
    else:
        print 'oops!'
    # end if
# end def foobar
```

Naturally, using *pindent* defeats much of the purpose and elegance of Python's syntax: you'll be making extra work for yourself (and wear out your keyboard considerably faster!). But if you run into a case that requires an end-of-block marker or makes proper indentation inconvenient, *pindent* may help.

# Distributed Programming Tools

For multitasking systems, Python provides modules for using:

- *RPC* calls (with *xdr* support)
- Signals
- Sockets
- Threads
- Pipes
- Process forking
- Spawning shell commands

Additionally, the *ILU* extension provides higher-level client/server support, implementing a system- and language-independent distributed objects model.

Signals, sockets, and threads are C extension modules in Python's *Modules* directory. The *RPC* and *xdr* modules currently reside in the *Demo* directory. Pipes, forking, and shell command functions are discussed earlier in the book; they're part of the built-in *os* module (*os.pipe*, *os.fork*, *os.system*, *os.popen*). The *ILU* extension is described briefly at the end of Chapter 15, *Embedding Python*. See the library reference manual, and Appendix C, *A Mini-Reference*.

## Using Sockets in Python

Since sockets are a pervasive tool, let's briefly explore some basic concepts here. Python's built-in *socket* module is a thin wrapper over the *BSD* socket interface. It works much like Python's file objects (which wrap C's *stdio* file system). The *socket* function returns a new socket object, which has methods that implement socket system calls. Like file *read* and *write* methods, parameters to socket methods are somewhat higher level than in the C socket API. As usual, all socket errors raise Python exceptions.

To illustrate, here are two very minimal example programs using the TCP/IP protocol, taken from Guido van Rossum's library reference: a server that echoes all data that it receives back (servicing only one client), and a client using the server.

*Server*
: The server must perform the method call sequence: *socket, bind, listen, accept,* and may repeat the *accept* to service more than one client.

*Client*
: The client only needs to execute the sequence: *socket, connect.*

Also note that the server does not *send/recv* on the socket it is listening on; instead, it uses the new socket returned by *accept.* Socket codes (*AF_INET,* etc.) are defined as variables exported by the socket module.

*Example A-4: File: sockserver.py*

```
# Echo server program
from socket import *
HOST = ''                          # symbolic name meaning the local host
PORT = 50007                       # arbitrary non-privileged server
s = socket(AF_INET, SOCK_STREAM)
s.bind(HOST, PORT)
s.listen(1)
conn, addr = s.accept()
print 'Connected by', addr
while 1:
    data = conn.recv(1024)
    if not data: break
    conn.send(data)
conn.close()
```

*Example A-5: File: sockclient.py*

```
# Echo client program
from socket import *
HOST = 'daring.cwi.nl'             # the remote host
PORT = 50007                       # the same port as used by the server
s = socket(AF_INET, SOCK_STREAM)
s.connect(HOST, PORT)
s.send('Hello, world')
data = s.recv(1024)
s.close()
print 'Received', `data`
```

Sockets aren't really a Python-specific concept so we won't discuss further details in this code here. The examples above are simply meant to show how to access sockets from a Python program; sockets are really just another instance of Python's integration tools at work (they're a C extension type in Python).

For more information, consult the Python library reference manual. For socket usage, see a good UNIX text or refer to the socket manpages on your system. For additional socket examples, consult the *Demo/sockets* directory in the Python source tree, or *grep* (search) for *socket* references in the Python library module directory; most of the Internet library utilities make use of the socket module. See also library module *SocketServer.py*.

### *Socket portability*

The *socket* module is available on all systems that support BSD-style socket interfaces; this includes most platforms that Python runs on (including Microsoft Windows). At present the socket module only supports the *AF_UNIX* and *AF_INET* address families.

## *Bidirectional IPC in Python*

Process communication works the same in Python as in C because Python's IPC tools are interfaces to standard C tools. We saw how to use *os.system*, *os.popen*, *os.fork*, and *os.execv* earlier in this book. I also promised to show how to use explicit pipes.

To give an idea of what's possible, here's a function that spawns a process and connects the parent and child by linking their *stdin/stdout* streams. Writing to *stdout* sends data to the other process, and reading from *stdin* gets data from the other process. In effect, doing this implements bidirectional communication between the parent and child processes (see Figure A-3). This is really a UNIX trick: see a UNIX text for more details.

*Example A-6: File: ipc.py*

```
import os

def spawn(prog, args):
    pipe1 = os.pipe()                   # parent stdin, child stdout:  (in, out)
    pipe2 = os.pipe()                   # child stdin,  parent stdout: (in, out)
    pid = os.fork()                     # make a copy of this process
    if pid:
        os.close(pipe1[1])              # in parent process after fork
        os.close(pipe2[0])              # close child ends
        os.dup2(pipe1[0], 0)            # sys.stdin  = pipe1[0]
        os.dup2(pipe2[1], 1)            # sys.stdout = pipe2[1]
    else:
        os.close(pipe1[0])              # in child process after fork
```

*Example A-6: File: ipc.py (continued)*

```
        os.close(pipe2[1])              # close parent ends
        os.dup2(pipe2[0], 0)            # sys.stdin  = pipe2[0]
        os.dup2(pipe1[1], 1)            # sys.stdout = pipe1[1]
        args = (prog,) + args
        os.execv(prog, args)            # new program in this process:
                                        # never returns here
```

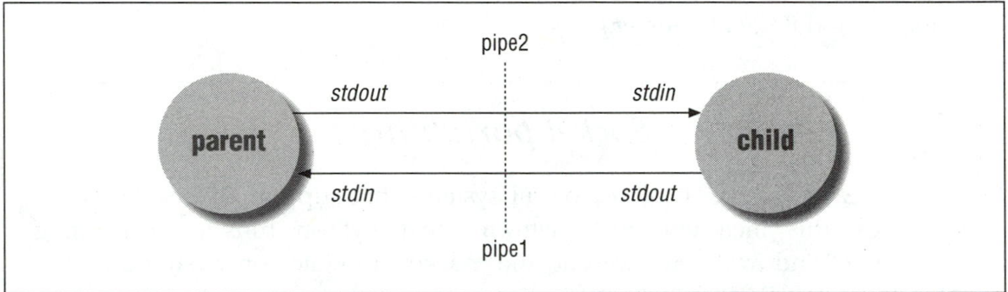


*Figure A-3: Bidirectional pipe IPC*

## A Simple ILU Example

ILU is a large system which we won't cover here. But to hint at the nature of the ILU/Python integration, here's a short example donated by Bill Janssen. It implements a single consumer object that accepts messages from a number of producer processes. Such a consumer object can collect and organize the feedback from multiple producers. There are three components here:

*ILU ISL file*
: The interface description for the consumer object.

*Python consumer script*
: Defines the shared object and forks producers.

*Python producer script*
: Sends messages to the consumer by calling its method.

Each producer process calls an asynchronous method of the consumer object implemented by the consumer process. To make this example work, you need the ILU/Python extension. Run the ILU *python-stubber* program against *pythonExPC.isl*:

```
% python-stubber pythonExPC
client stubs for interface "pythonExPC" to pythonExPC.py ...
server stubs for interface "pythonExPC" to pythonExPC__skel.py ...
%
```

The stubber generates Python stub files for both clients and severs according to the ISL declarations. To run the system, type the command *python consumer.py* (or *ilupython consumer.py*, if you don't have dynamic loading of object code), and watch it run. The producer processes call the consumer object's *fromProducer* method periodically, sending their names and the current time.

But notice that the *fromProducer* method isn't implemented in the same address space as the producer: it's implemented by the class *realConsumer*, in the consumer process. Parameters passed by producers are automatically passed to the consumer process; the *fromProducer* method can use them arbitrarily. ILU generates all the code needed to map the producer's method calls to process communication primitives.

There's much more to ILU than this example shows. For instance, it also accepts CORBA IDL (in place of the ILU ISL shown here). ILU is typically used to implement objects shared across network and language boundaries. For more information, see ILU's FTP site, currently *ftp://ftp.parc.xerox.com/pub/ilu/ilu.html.* ILU is also available on this book's CD-ROM.

*Example A-7: File: pythonExPC.isl*

```
INTERFACE pythonExPC;

TYPE consumer = OBJECT
  METHODS
    ASYNCHRONOUS fromProducer (producerID : ilu.CString, data : ilu.CString)
  END;
```

*Example A-8: File: consumer.py*

```
import pythonExPC__skel, os, ilu

class realConsumer(pythonExPC__skel.consumer):
    def fromProducer(self, producerID, something):
        print 'producer', producerID, 'says: ', something

def main():
    # make a consumer object for producer processes to report to
    m = realConsumer()
    sbh = m.IluSBH()

    # fork off producer processes
    os.system("python producer.py producer1 7  '" + sbh + "'&");
    os.system("python producer.py producer2 10 '" + sbh + "'&");
    os.system("python producer.py producer3 23 '" + sbh + "'&");

    # now sit back in the ILU loop and wait for reports
    ilu.RunMainLoop()

main()
```

*Example A-9: File: producer.py*

```
import pythonExPC, ilu, time, sys, string

def do_work(m, id, period):
    while 1:
        time.sleep(period)                          # every N seconds
        m.fromProducer(id, str(time.time()))        # to consumer process...

def main(argv):
    producer_id = argv[1]
    period      = string.atoi(argv[2])
    consumer    = ilu.ObjectOfSBH(pythonExPC.consumer, argv[3])
    do_work(consumer, producer_id, period)

if len(sys.argv) < 4:
    print "Usage: python producer.py ",
    print "PRODUCER-ID PERIOD-IN-SECONDS CONSUMER-SBH &"
    sys.exit(1)
else:
    main(sys.argv)
```

## Python as an AI language: The holmes Expert System Shell

*holmes* is an expert system shell written completely in Python. It implements both forward and backward chaining inference and uses a simplified unification algorithm to match rule patterns and bind variables (nested subterms aren't allowed). The backward chainer implements backtracking-based search, and explanations for deductions and questions are available. A simple interactive interface allows rules and queries to be entered; rules may also be loaded from files.

*holmes* comes in two versions; the second adds an index tree class to store rules for fast match detection instead of performing linear list scans. Example rule bases are provided (see the parsing case study in Chapter 16, *Processing Language and Text*, for an example *holmes* rule). Since *holmes* is a large system and requires an artificial intelligence (AI) background to be understood, we won't go into further details here. For more information, see the *holmes* entry in the *ftp.python.org/contrib/Misc* directory, on the accompanying CD-ROM.

## Built-in Internet/WWW Tools

Python comes with a collection of modules that simplify Internet and WWW protocol interfacing. These modules make it possible to use Python as a scripting language for Internet-based systems. Here's the current module list, taken from the library reference; some of these modules require Python's *sockets* module.

*cgi*
: Common Gateway Interface, used in server-side scripts.

*urllib*
: Open an arbitrary object given by its URL address (sockets).

*httplib*
: HTTP protocol client (sockets).

*ftplib*
: FTP protocol client (sockets).

*gopherlib*
: Gopher protocol client (sockets).

*nntplib*
: NNTP protocol client (sockets).

*urlparse*
: Parse a URL string into a tuple.

*htmllib*
: HTML file parser: WWW hypertext markup language.

*sgmllib*
: As much of an SGML parser as needed to parse HTML.

*rfc822*
: Parse RFC 822-style mail headers.

*mimetools*
: Tools for parsing MIME-style message bodies.

So what do all these acronyms mean? Most of these protocols are just ways to interpret information sent between a server and a client over the Internet. A client may be a WWW browser, an FTP interface, etc. For example, Figure A-4 illustrates typical data transfers during a web browser session:

*HTTP*
: The hypertext transfer protocol is used to send web-related information between clients and servers. The server runs an HTTP server to intercept incoming requests from the network.

*HTML*
: When a user points a WWW browser at a URL (Internet address), the request is sent to the HTTP server on the remote machine. If the URL refers to an HTML file, the HTML code at that location is downloaded over the Internet to the client machine, where it is used to build a page in the browser. HTML code is the web's page description language.

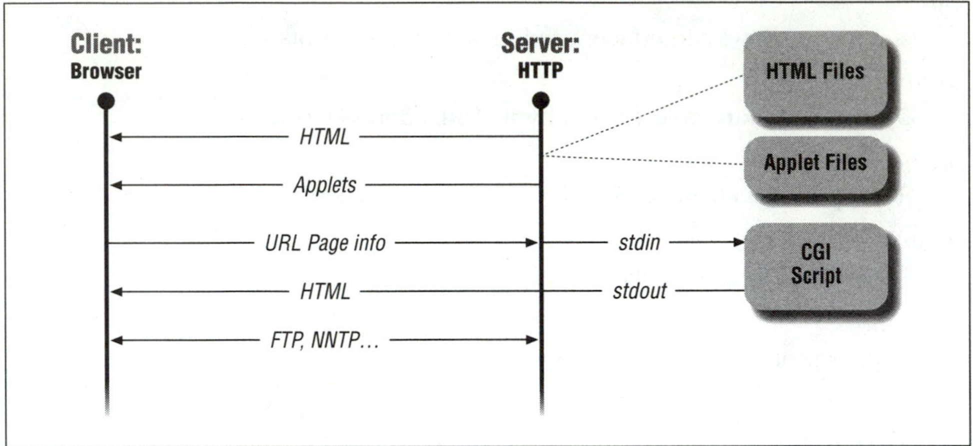


*Figure A-4: Common Internet data streams*

*CGI*
: If the file referenced by a URL is a CGI script, the HTTP server instead spawns the CGI script to run on the server, after setting environment variables to pass in context. The CGI script's *stdin* and *stdout* streams are tied to the input from and output to the client. Typically a CGI script gets page input information from *stdin* and writes HTML to *stdout* to create a new page in the client browser.

*Applets*
: As we saw earlier, when the client is the Grail browser the *APP* tag in a downloaded HTML file causes Grail to download the applet's source code over the Internet and instantiate the Python class it defines. Grail downloads Python source code and runs it locally; unlike CGI scripts, the applet code runs on the client, not the server.

*Other*
: The FTP and NNTP protocols define other ways to transfer data over the Internet; they're typically used for file transfer and news readers. Python's interfaces provide the handshaking logic needed to interpret the data streams sent under these protocols. Other tools interpret standard protocols for mail headers, etc.

Grail uses most of Python's Internet modules. It's really a separate system from Python but we've included applets in the diagram above to show how they fit in with Python's other Internet tools. Grail applets simply provide another way to interact with a server which offloads processing to the client machine. Naturally, Python's Internet modules are useful on their own, whether Grail is the client or not. For instance, CGI scripts can often provide sufficient user interaction.

This is a somewhat simplified discussion, and we won't elaborate further here; for more background information, see a book on WWW protocols. For details on Python's WWW tools, see Python's library reference. It includes useful examples for most of the modules listed earlier in this section. Also see the use of the *ftplib* module in the *sousa.py* program at the end of the Conclusion for an FTP client example.

## A Simple Python CGI Example

Here's a Python CGI script, contributed by Timothy O'Malley. It requires an understanding of HTML, but the basic functionality is straightforward: the script gets information from a page using the *cgi* module's interface and writes HTML to *stdout* to create new pages on the web client (browser).

The example acts like a *mailto* HTML tag; it interacts with a user to construct a mail message. To use the script below, place it in your server's CGI directory (here, */cgi-bin*). Create a URL link in an HTML page like:

```
http://machine.at.com/cgi-bin/cgimail?python-list@cwi.nl
```

where *cgimail* is the Python script file below, and the address after the "?" is where you want the mail to be sent. The script is invoked twice:

1. When the URL above is selected in a web browser, the script is run on the server, with one command-line argument: *python-list@cwi.nl*, the mail recipient. *ShowMailForm* prints HTML to put up a *FORM* in the browser that requests the text of the mail message.
2. When the user clicks on the *Submit* button of the created form, the script is run again, with no arguments. This time, *SendMail* extracts the mail details from the *stdin* stream using the *cgi* module interface, and the mail is sent to the recipient by spawning the *sendmail* program.

If errors occur, another page is generated by the *SendError* function. Notice that the *FormContent* class imported from the *cgi* module gives us a dictionary-like interface to page information sent from the browser. Python's *cgi* module parses the *stdin* stream to extract information behind the scenes. The *cgi* module itself is coded in Python; see the Python library manual for more details on the interface.

*Example A-10: File: cgimail*

```
#!/usr/local/bin/python

import os, string, sys
from cgi import *

# The trailing space is required!
sendmail_cmd = "/usr/lib/sendmail -oi "
```

*Example A-10: File: cgimail (continued)*

```
def SendError(str):
    errmsg = escape(str)
    print "Content-type: text/html\n\n"
    print "<HEADER>\n<TITLE> CGI Error </TITLE>\n</HEADER>\n"
    print "<BODY>\n"
    print "<H1>CGI Error</H1>\n"
    print "<H3><STRONG>" + errmsg + "</STRONG></H3>\n"
    print "</BODY>"
    sys.exit(0)


def ShowMailForm(to):
    recipient = escape(to)
    title = "Mail to " + recipient
    print "Content-type: text/html\n\n"
    print "<HEADER>\n<TITLE>" + title + "</TITLE>\n</HEADER>\n"
    print "<BODY>\n"
    print "<H1>" + title + "</H1>\n"
    print '<FORM ACTION="/cgi-bin/cgimail" METHOD=POST>'
    print '<INPUT TYPE="hidden" NAME="to" VALUE="' + recipient + '"> <P>'
    print '<P ALIGN=center><TABLE BORDER CELLPADDING=2>'
    print '<TR><TD>Your Email:</TD><TD><INPUT name="from" size=40></TD>'
    print '<TR><TD>Subject:</TD><TD><INPUT name="subj" size=40></TD>'
    print '</TABLE></P>'
    print '<P><TEXTAREA name="msg" ROWS=12 COLS=48>Your Comments'
    print '</TEXTAREA> </P>'
    print '<P><INPUT TYPE="submit" VALUE="Submit Form"> or'
    print '<INPUT TYPE="reset"  VALUE="Reset Form"> </P>'
    print "</FORM>"
    #print_environ()
    print "</BODY>"


def SendMail():
    form = FormContent()     # handles stdin parsing

    # Required Items
    if not form.has_key("to"):   SendError("No Recipient Specified")
    if not form.has_key("from"): SendError("No Sender Specified")
    if not form.has_key("msg"):  SendError("No Message Specified")
    real_to   = form["to"][0]
    real_from = form["from"][0]
    real_msg  = form["msg"][0]

    # Non-required Items
    real_name = "UNKNOWN SENDER"
    real_subj = ""
    if form.has_key("name"): real_name = form["name"][0]
    if form.has_key("subj"): real_subj = form["subj"][0]

    # Send the mail.
    try: mfd = os.popen(sendmail_cmd + real_to, "w")
```

*Example A-10: File: cgimail (continued)*

```
    except: SendError("Unable to send mail")

    mfd.write("To:    " + real_to + "\n")
    mfd.write("From: " + real_from + "\n")
    mfd.write("Subject:  " + real_subj + "\n")
    mfd.write("X-Sender: " + real_name + "\n")
    mfd.write("X-Warning: This mail was sent from an HTTPD server. No\n")
    mfd.write("X-Warning: attempt was made to verify the sender's identity.\n")
    mfd.write("\n" + real_msg + "\n")
    mfd.close()

    # Output Resulting HTML page.
    # When writing HTML, we must be careful to escape any special
    # characters.  The escape() routine handles the translation
    # for us.
    #
    real_to   = escape( real_to )
    real_from = escape( real_from )
    real_name = escape( real_name )
    real_msg  = escape( real_msg )

    print "Content-type: text/html\n\n"
    print "<HEADER>\n<TITLE> Mail Sent to " + real_to + "</TITLE>\n</HEADER>\n"
    print "<BODY>\n"
    print "<H1>Successfully sent mail to " + real_to + "</H1>\n"
    print "Here's what was sent:<P><HR><PRE>"
    print "To:    " + real_to
    print "From: " + real_from
    print "Subject: " + real_subj
    print "X-Sender: " + real_name
    print "X-Warning: This mail was sent from an HTTPD server. No"
    print "X-Warning: attempt was made to verify the sender's identity."
    print "\n" + real_msg
    print "</PRE><HR>"
    print "</BODY>"


def Main():
    if len(sys.argv) == 1:
        SendMail()
    elif len(sys.argv) == 2:
        ShowMailForm(sys.argv[1])
    else:
        SendError("Too Many Arguments on Command Line")

Main()
```

# *Other GUI Interfaces: WPY and wxPython*

As mentioned in Chapter 11, there are a handful of GUI APIs for Python besides *Tkinter.* The *WPY* system is a portable GUI framework for Python based on the MFC model. The *wxPython* GUI interface is also a portable GUI solution. Both systems are still maturing as this book is being written, but are useful in their current forms; here are a few details on each system.

*WPY*
: An object-oriented GUI system based on the MFC model. Programs written *WPY* run unchanged and with native look and feel on NT (Win32), Microsoft Windows 3.1, and UNIX (using *Tk*). *WPY* also runs on OS/2 machines with Windows 3.1 support. Source and binaries for NT and Linux are currently available on the accompanying CD-ROM and in the */pub/python/wpy* directory at *ftp.python.org*. Jim Ahlstrom is currently the main developer.

*wxPython*
: An interface to *wxWindows*, *wxPython* is a portable GUI class library written in C++. It supports XView, Motif, and Microsoft Windows. There's also some support for the Macintosh and CURSES. *wxWindows* preserves the look and feel of the underlying graphics toolkit. Harri Pasanen is the main contact at present. *wxPython* is also at *ftp.python.org*. Also see *wxPython*'s WWW page, currently at *http://www.aiai.ed.ac.uk/~jacs/wx/wxpython/wxpython.html.*

Python also includes an interface to Guido van Rossum's *STDWIN* portable GUI system; see the Python library manual for further details (*STDWIN* is deprecated, but is still used).

## *A WPY Example*

Let's take a quick look at the *WPY* interface at work. The following description, source code, and screen shot were contributed by *WPY*'s inventor, Jim Ahlstrom:

> This is a Python version of the Scribble program which comes with Microsoft Visual C++. It is written in Python using WPY. WPY is a Python module which provides a class library, a message system and other tools for writing portable graphical user interface (GUI) code. WPY is based on the Microsoft Foundation Classes, so the Python version of Scribble looks much like the C++ version.
>
> Python programs written with WPY will run unchanged on UNIX systems as well as on PC's. The UNIX version of WPY uses Tk. WPY supports native look and feel on all supported platforms.

Python is ideally suited to GUI development since it is a fast object-oriented scripting language with advanced data types such as lists and dictionaries.

WPY is free software written by Jim Ahlstrom and published with the same licensing restrictions as Python itself (hardly any). It comes with 2000 lines of documentation and seven small demo programs. To get WPY, follow the links from http://www.python.org.

*Example A-11: File: demo5.py*

```
#! /usr/local/bin/python
from wpy import *
import string

class CScribDoc(CDocument):
    def __init__(self, templ):
        CDocument.__init__(self, templ)
        self.pen = self.thin_pen = CPen(2, (200, 0, 0)).Create()
        self.thick_pen = CPen(5, (0, 200, 0)).Create()
        self.m_strokeList = []
    def NewStroke(self):
        s = CStroke(self.pen)
        self.m_strokeList.append(s)
        self.SetModifiedFlag()
        return s
    def OnCloseDocument(self):
        CDocument.OnCloseDocument(self)
        self.pen = None
    def DeleteContents(self):
        self.m_strokeList = []
    def Serialize(self, is_storing):
        print "Nothing happens"
    def OnMenuPenThinpen(self, control):
        if string.find(control.wpyText, "Thick") >= 0:
            self.pen = self.thick_pen
        else:
            self.pen = self.thin_pen

class ScribFrameMenu(CMenu):
    def __init__(self):
        CMenu.__init__(self)
        file        = MenuFile(self)
        edit        = MenuEdit(self)
        pen         = CMenuButton(self, "Pen")
        view        = MenuView(self)
        window      = MenuWindow(self)
        help        = MenuHelp(self)

        # file items:
        new         = MenuFileNew(file)
        close       = MenuFileClose(file)
        CMenuLine(file)
        exit        = MenuFileExit(file)
```

*Example A-11: File: demo5.py (continued)*

```
        # edit items

        # pen items:
        thin              = CMenuRadio(pen, "Thin pen", None)
        thin.wpyMessage   = "Toggles the line thickness between thin and thick"
        thick             = CMenuRadio(pen, "Thick pen", thin)
        thick.wpyMessage = thin.wpyMessage
        thick.wpyHandler = thin.wpyHandler

        # view items
        status            = MenuViewStatusbar(view)
        status.wpyCheckValue = 0
        status.EnableMenuItem(0)

        # window items
        new          = MenuWindowNewwindow(window)
        cascade      = MenuWindowCascade(window)
        tileh        = MenuWindowTilehorz(window)
        tilev        = MenuWindowTilevert(window)
        arrange      = MenuWindowArrangeicons(window)

        # help items
        about        = MenuHelpAbout(help)

class ScribMainFrameMenu(CMenu):
    def __init__(self):
        CMenu.__init__(self)
        file         = MenuFile(self)
        view         = MenuView(self)
        help         = MenuHelp(self)

        # file items:
        new          = MenuFileNew(file)
        CMenuLine(file)
        exit         = MenuFileExit(file)

        # view items
        status       = MenuViewStatusbar(view)

        # help items
        about        = MenuHelpAbout(help)

class CStroke:
    def __init__(self, pen):
        self.pen = pen
        self.m_pointArray = []
    def DrawStroke(self, DC):
        DC.SelectObject(self.pen)
        i = self.m_pointArray[0]
        DC.MoveTo(i[0], i[1])
        for i in self.m_pointArray[1:]:
            DC.LineTo(i[0], i[1])
```

*Example A-11: File: demo5.py (continued)*

```
class CScribView(CScrollView):
    def OnCreate(self, event):
        self.m_pStrokeCur = None
        self.m_ptPrev = None
    def OnDraw(self, DC):
        for stroke in self.wpyDocument.m_strokeList:
            stroke.DrawStroke(DC)
    def OnLButtonDown(self, x, y, flags):
        point = (x, y)
        self.m_pStrokeCur = self.wpyDocument.NewStroke()
        self.m_pStrokeCur.m_pointArray.append(point)
        self.SetCapture()
        self.m_ptPrev = point
        DC = self.GetDC()
        DC.SelectObject(self.wpyDocument.pen)
        self.ReleaseDC(DC)
        return 0
    def OnLButtonUp(self, x, y, flags):
        if GetCapture() != self:
            return
        point = (x, y)
        DC = self.GetDC()
        DC.MoveTo(self.m_ptPrev[0], self.m_ptPrev[1])
        DC.LineTo(x, y)
        self.ReleaseDC(DC)
        self.m_pStrokeCur.m_pointArray.append(point)
        ReleaseCapture()
        self.wpyDocument.UpdateAllViews(self, None)
        self.wpyDocument.SetModifiedFlag(0)
        return 0
    def OnMouseMove(self, x, y, flags):
        if GetCapture() != self:
            return
        point = (x, y)
        self.m_pStrokeCur.m_pointArray.append(point)
        DC = self.GetDC()
        DC.MoveTo(self.m_ptPrev[0], self.m_ptPrev[1])
        DC.LineTo(x, y)
        self.ReleaseDC(DC)
        self.m_ptPrev = point
        return 0

class MyApp(CWinApp):
    def InitInstance(self):
        templ = CMultiDocTemplate(CScribDoc,
                                  CMDIChildWnd,
                                  CScribView,
                                  ScribFrameMenu)
        templ.wpyText = "Python Scribble"
        self.AddDocTemplate(templ)
        main_frame = CMDIFrameWnd()
        main_frame.wpyStatusLine = CStatusBar(self, "")
```

*Example A-11: File: demo5.py (continued)*

```
        # Menu when there are no frames
        main_frame.wpyMenu = ScribMainFrameMenu()
        main_frame.Create()
        self.FileNew()

# Start the application, respond to events.
app = MyApp()
```

Naturally this program example's structure depends heavily on the MFC framework, which we won't attempt to describe here; see a book or reference on MFC programming for more details. Finally, Figure A-5 shows the scene when this script is run, if you've bound in the *WPY* extension to your Python system. We get a drawing canvas, which Jim has used to express his programming-language preference :-).

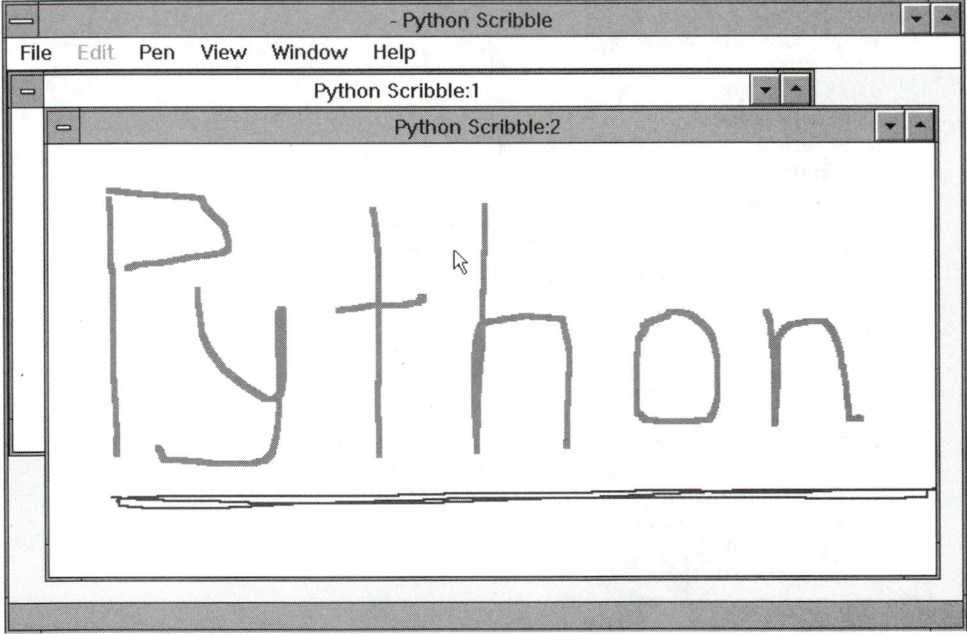


*Figure A-5: The WPY system on Microsoft Windows*

## Python on the Macintosh

Python has also been ported for use on Macintosh systems. The ports include support for a variety of native Macintosh utilities: AppleEvents, Toolboxes, etc., and run on both 68k and PowerPC platforms. See the CD-ROM, the FAQ, and the *pub/python/mac* directory at *ftp.python.org* for more information.

### *WPY versus PythonWin and Tkinter*

There's some overlap and cross-fertilization between the *PythonWin* ports mentioned above and *WPY*. *PythonWin* and *WPY* both expose the MFC framework and work on PCs. But they address different problems: *WPY*'s emphasis is on GUI portability, and *PythonWin* provides more Windows-specific tools for Python (OLE scripting, etc.).

*WPY* and *Tkinter* both aim to provide portable GUI frameworks, but they take opposite approaches. *WPY* takes an API developed for Microsoft Windows (MFC) and implements it on UNIX systems. Conversely, *Tkinter* is based on an API originally developed for UNIX/X-Windows (*Tk*), which has been ported to Microsoft Windows and the Macintosh (the Windows and Macintosh *Tk* ports are being polished as this book is being written). The MFC and *Tk* API's are both widely used, though substantially different.

## *Python as a Netscape Web Browser Plug-in*

As this book was being finished, Tyler Brook and Jon Smirl announced a system that integrates Python into Netscape WWW browsers using Netscape's plug-in system. Roughly, the integration allows Python to serve as an embedded scripting language for the Netscape browser. The concept is somewhat similar to the notion of applets in Grail (discussed earlier in this appendix).

The plug-in integration uses a DLL-based version of Python and the WPY GUI framework (mentioned earlier), on Microsoft Windows machines. A new version is being implemented by Jim Ahlstrom at this writing. For more information, see Python sites or the URL: *http://www.halcyon.com/radical3/*.

### *Stop the presses: new Netscape plug-ins*

As of this book's release, there are now two Netscape plug-ins for Python: one in the WPY package and one in PythonWin. Both of these packages are described earlier in this appendix; they can be found on this book's CD-ROM (and at Python's Internet sites).

# *Python Functional Programming Topics*

This section looks at topics of interest to programmers familiar with functional languages such as Scheme.

## *Functional Programming Tools*

We used most of Python's built-in functional programming tools earlier in the book. Here's a summary:

*apply(function, args)*
: Call a function (or other callable object) with the list of arguments passed-in as a tuple.

*lambda <arg>, <arg>, . . . : <expression>*
: Generate an anonymous function object. *<arg>* can be any formal argument: names, default argument assignments, etc. Lambda is much like a *def* statement, except that it can appear in places that syntactically require expressions (not statements). Further, the lambda's body is limited to an expression (not one or more statements).

*map(function, sequence, . . . )*
: Apply *function* to every item of *sequence*, and return the list of results. If more than one sequence is passed, *function* should take as many arguments as there are sequences, and is applied to items of the sequences in parallel (shorter sequences are padded with *None*s). If *function* is *None*, identity is used: *map* returns a list of the items in sequence, or a list of tuples of parallel nodes if multiple sequences are passed in (transpose).

*filter(function, sequence)*
: Construct a sequence with the elements in *sequence* for which *function* returns *true*. If *function* is *None*, the identity function is used: all *false* elements in *sequence* are removed.

*reduce(function, sequence, initializer?)*
: Apply the two-argument *function* to the items in *sequence* to reduce it to a single value. The optional *initializer* is essentially prepended to the sequence, so empty sequences work properly. For instance, *reduce(lambda x,y: x * y, mylist, 1)* returns the product of all the items in *mylist*.

## *Implementing Symbols*

In the current implementation, Python doesn't always map lexically equivalent strings to the same string object. But it's simple to define symbol tables that do: Python dictionaries map equivalent keys to the same entry. Usually dictionaries are sufficient for implementing arbitrary symbol tables.

If we also want to associate information with symbol table entries, we simply store data structures or class instances in the dictionary. Here's an example that emulates Lisp *atoms* with property-lists. The *intern* function maps multiple occurrences of a name to the same entry using a dictionary. Symbols are represented as class instances in the dictionary; instance attribute dictionaries serve as property lists.

*Example A-12: File: symbol.py*

```
class Symbol:
    def __init__(self, name):              # symbol = named class instance
        self.name = name
    def __repr__(self):                    # prints as name
        return self.name
    def props(self):                       # property-list = attributes
        return self.__dict__
    def getprop(self, name):               # or just: symbol.prop
        return getattr(self, name)
    def putprop(self, name, value):        # or just: symbol.prop = value
        setattr(self, name, value)

table = {}

def intern(name):
    try:
        return table[name]                 # return existing entry?
    except KeyError:
        table[name] = Symbol(name)         # else store and return new symbol
        return table[name]
```

And here's how this module might be used:

```
% python
>>> from symbol import intern
>>> x = intern('spam')
>>> y = intern('spam')
>>> x.putprop('type', 'pork')
>>> y.getprop('type')
'pork'
>>> x.type
'pork'
>>> y.props()
{'type': 'pork', 'name': 'spam'}
>>> z = intern('SPAM')
>>> z.props()
{'name': 'SPAM'}
>>> import symbol
>>> symbol.table
{'spam': spam, 'SPAM': SPAM}
```

## *Implementing Closures in Python*

Another common question raised by programmers with a *Scheme* background is how to implement *closures*: callable objects that retain information from the scope in which they are created. The following suggestions are based on a recent discussion on the Python newsgroup.

As we've seen, nested functions in Python don't have access to the names in the function enclosing them (recall the local/global/builtin three-scope search rule). But closure like behavior can by implemented by setting default arguments to values in the enclosing scope:

```
def outer():
    x = 'hello'
    def inner(x=x):        # save the enclosing function's "x"
        print x
    return inner

func = outer()
func()
```

Notice that other definitions for *inner* won't work:

*def inner()*
: Without the default argument in *inner*, we get a *NameError* when we try to print *x*: it is found in the outer function's scope, which goes away after the call to *outer* returns.

*def inner(x)*
: Without the default value assignment, the call to *func* fails: the nested function will expect a real parameter to be passed.

But the default argument assignment saves *outer*'s *x* in the inner function object. As we've seen earlier in this book, Python's *lambda* can be used in place of *def* when we're generating anonymous functions:

```
def outer(x):
    return (lambda a, b=x: a + b)   # add to original "x"

func = outer('world')
func('hello')
func('bye')
```

In fact, we used *lambda* in our GUI examples in Chapter 11 to implement closure behavior:

```
def make_widgets(self):
    Button(self, command = lambda x=self: x.action())
```

*Example 16-5: File: cheader.py (continued)*

```
            print '%d) include %s' % (lineno, filename)

def cont(file, line, lineno):
    while line[-2:] == '\\\n':
        next = file.readline()       # merge continuation lines
        if not next: break
        line, lineno = line[:-2]+next, lineno+1
    return line, lineno

if len(sys.argv) == 1:
    scan(sys.stdin)                  # no args: read stdin
else:
    scan(open(sys.argv[1], 'r'))     # arg: input file name
```

Let's run this script on the following text file; line numbers have been added to correlate with the results.

*Example 16-6: File: test.h*

```
 1  #ifndef TEST_H
 2  #define TEST_H
 3
 4  #include <stdio.h>
 5  #include <lib/spam.h>
 6  #  include   "Python.h"
 7
 8  #define DEBUG
 9  #define HELLO 'hello regex world'
10  #  define SPAM  1234
11
12  #define EGGS sunny +\
13  side + up
14
15  #define  ADDER(arg) 123 + arg
16  # define  ADDER_PLUS_PLUS(arg)  123 \
17           + arg
18  #endif
```

```
% cheader.py test.h
2) TEST_H = None
4) include stdio.h
5) include lib/spam.h
6) include Python.h
8) DEBUG = None
9) HELLO = 'hello regex world'
10) SPAM = 1234
13) EGGS = sunny +side + up
15) ADDER[arg] = 123 + arg
17) ADDER_PLUS_PLUS[arg] = 123           + arg
```

Suggested exercises:

1. When continuations are present, this script reports the last continuation line's line number. Change it to report the number of the first line instead.
2. This example was inspired by Guido van Rossum's *h2py* C header to Python translator. Study the *Tools/scripts/h2py.py* script for a more complete solution to this problem. It also handles comments and scans included files recursively.
3. Add support for multiple arguments to *#define* macros. Can you do it by extending the regular expression pattern, or will this require logic that calls *match* repeatedly?
4. Write a tool which runs a Python program and automatically starts a text editor on uncaught exceptions, positioned at the offending line in the source file(s). Use *regex* to extract filename and line number information from Python error messages. *os.popen*, *os.system*, or *os.fork/pipe* may be used to spawn programs and capture output. Will this tool catch syntax errors in a module file?
5. Write a Python name cross-referencer script. Scan a module file, matching identifier patterns, but skipping string constants. Keep a list of line numbers for each symbol in a dictionary and filter out keywords. For the more ambitious: follow nested imports, and group symbols by their scope (function, class, module, etc.). Since there are no declarations in Python, can you tell where symbols are defined?

### *A file searching (grep) utility*

Here's a script that searches for patterns in a set of files, much like the *grep* command-line program. The patterns are assumed to be stored as lines in a text file, and the files to be searched are specified by a passed-in pattern for Python's *glob.glob* filename expansion tool. The search files pattern should be quoted in most shells; with no arguments, the script prompts the user to enter parameters interactively.

*Example 16-7: File: pygrep1.py*

```
#!/usr/local/bin/python
import sys, regex, glob

help_string = """
Usage options.
interactive:  % pygrep1.py
command line: % pygrep1.py pattern-file search-files-pattern
"""

def handle_args():
    if len(sys.argv) == 1:
        return raw_input("patterns? >"), raw_input("files? >")
```

*Example 16-7: File: pygrep1.py (continued)*

```
    else:
        try:
            return sys.argv[1], sys.argv[2]
        except:
            print help_string
            sys.exit(1)

def compile_patterns(pattfile):
    res = []
    for pattstr in open(pattfile, 'r').readlines():
        try:
            res.append(regex.compile(pattstr[:-1]))    # make regex object
        except:                                        # strip end-of-line
            print 'pattern ignored:', pattstr          # or use regex.match
    return res

def searcher(pattfile, srchfiles):
    patts = compile_patterns(pattfile)                # compile for speed
    for file in glob.glob(srchfiles):                 # all matching files
        lineno = 1                                    # glob uses regex too
        print '\n[%s]' % file
        for line in open(file, 'r').readlines():        # all lines in file
            for patt in patts:
                if patt.search(line) >= 0:              # try all patterns
                    print '%04d)' % lineno, line,       # report line match
                    break
            lineno = lineno+1

if __name__ == '__main__':
    from regex_syntax import *
    regex.set_syntax(RE_SYNTAX_EGREP)      # emacs is the default
    apply(searcher, handle_args())
```

The regular expression syntax is set to *egrep* mode initially (or else we'll get the default *emacs* style). Notice the use of a triple-quoted string; it's a convenient way to code blocks of text. Here's what a typical run of this script might look like. Patterns are put in a file called *patts*, and all Python files matching **.py* are searched; Python's *glob.glob* filename expander uses *regex* internally too.

```
% pygrep1.py -h

Usage options.
interactive:  % pygrep1.py
command line: % pygrep1.py pattern-file search-files-pattern

% cat patts
import
for

% pygrep1.py patts "*.py"
```

```
[pygrep1.py]
0002) import sys, regex, glob
0022)     for pattstr in open(pattfile, 'r').readlines():
0030)     patts = compile_patterns(pattfile)              # compile for speed
0031)     for file in glob.glob(srchfiles):              # all matching files
0034)         for line in open(file, 'r').readlines():      # all lines in fi
0035)             for patt in patts:
0042)     from regex_syntax import *

[filescan.py]
0010)             raise IndexError            # end 'for' loops, 'in'
0015)     for line in File("filescan.py"): print '.', line,

% pygrep1.py
patterns? >patts
files? >*.c
```

Suggested exercise: Experiment with this script on your system. Add a command-line mode that accepts a pattern directly (without requiring a pattern file). Then add support for specifying the regular expression syntax on the command line (*awk*, *emacs*, etc.).

Suggested exercise: Study the *grep.py* and *glob.py* modules' use of *regex* in the Python library directory. Both are available as shell commands (*os.system/popen*) and built-in Python modules.

### *Replacing tabs with periods*

Finally, here's a simple but typical file "massaging" task: suppose we want to replace all tabs in a text file with four "`.`" characters. Perhaps we want to highlight their occurrence or align indented text in a standard way. Or maybe we want to see how much space is saved by using tabs instead of spaces. Whatever the motivation, let's use this example to demonstrate some differences between string utilities and regular expression substitutions, by writing and timing some alternative solutions.

Here are five short scripts that perform the mapping; they're all shell filters—they read input from *stdin*, and write the result to *stdout*. The first script manually checks for tabs and reads the file character by character. The next two scripts use *regsub*; one reads line by line with *readline* and the other loads the file all at once with *read*. The last two scripts are the same but use *string* utilities instead: they split on tabs and join with periods. Can you guess which script is faster by just looking at the source code? (Please, no wagering.)

*Example 16-8: File: filter1*

```
#!/usr/local/bin/python
from sys import *
while 1:
      c = stdin.read(1)              # read one character at a time
      if c == '':                    # change all tabs to 4 '.'s
            break
      elif c == '\t':
            stdout.write('.'*4)
      else:
            stdout.write(c)
```

*Example 16-9: File: filter2*

```
#!/usr/local/bin/python
import sys, regsub                   # use regex/regsub
line = sys.stdin.readline()          # read line-by-line
while line:
    sys.stdout.write( regsub.gsub('\t', '.'*4, line) )
    line = sys.stdin.readline()
```

*Example 16-10: File: filter3*

```
#!/usr/local/bin/python
import sys, regsub
sys.stdout.write( regsub.gsub('\t', '.'*4, sys.stdin.read()) )
```

*Example 16-11: File: filter4*

```
#!/usr/local/bin/python
from string import *                 # use spilt/joinfields
import sys                           # read a line at a time,
line = sys.stdin.readline()          # in case stdin is a pipe
while line:
    sys.stdout.write( joinfields( splitfields(line, '\t'), '.'*4) )
    line = sys.stdin.readline()
```

*Example 16-12: File: filter5*

```
#!/usr/local/bin/python
from sys import *                    # use splitfields, read input all at once
from string import *
stdout.write( joinfields( splitfields(stdin.read(), '\t'), '.'*4) )
```

All five versions produce identical output. But the results of timing these programs in the UNIX shell may be surprising. Timings for a 850-line, 19K input text file with numerous tabs follow; the scripts create a 24K output file with periods.

```
% time filter1 < input.txt > filter.out
61.090u  0.350s  1:03.04       manual, read char-by-char

% time filter2 < input.txt > filter.out
73.820u  0.380s  1:14.57       regsub, read line-by-line
```

```
% time filter3 < input.txt > filter.out
64.590u  2.830s  1:07.79        regsub, read all-at-once

% time filter4 < input.txt > filter.out
7.020u  0.340s   0:07.77        string, read line-by-line

% time filter5 < input.txt > filter.out
1.770u  0.390s   0:02.43        string, read all-at-once
```

The timings are given as user time/system time/total time triples, in elapsed seconds. The tests were run on a relatively slow PC machine; your results may vary radically but relative performance should be similar. The usual caveats about timing on a UNIX system apply: results depend on load, page faults, etc. We're also using the UNIX shell's *time* command here, instead of Python's *time* function shown earlier.

***File processing differences.*** As you might expect, the character-by-character version is very slow, and line-by-line versions are slightly slower than reading a file all at once. In both case, we transfer processing from Python tools coded in C to manual logic coded in Python. Using *readlines* and *for* loops would help some here but not much.

As mentioned earlier, moving towards finer granularity in your Python code usually translates to slower performance. Of course, there are exceptions, and the extra overhead may be insignificant: the best approach to Python programming is to code for clarity first and optimize later only if needed.

***Substitution differences.*** What you may not have expected is that the *regsub* versions are dramatically slower than the equivalent *string* utility versions. In the best cases, using *regsub* takes 1 minute and 7 seconds; using *string* takes just 2.4 seconds. At least in this example, the string utilities make the program faster by roughly a factor of 30. In fact, *regsub* isn't any better (and can be worse) than using character by character input.

These results don't reflect the underlying *regex* C extension module's performance. But the fact that *regsub* is coded in Python makes it significantly slower.

## Parser Generators

Of course, regular expressions and string splitting aren't powerful enough to handle complex grammars. For more sophisticated language analysis tasks, we sometimes need a full-blown parser. Since Python is built for integrating C tools, we can write integrations to traditional parser generator systems such as *yacc* and *bison*. Better yet, we could use an integration that already exists.

> ### *Python development lesson 1: Prototype and migrate*
>
> The *string* module's functions are much faster, simply because they've been moved to a C language implementation; *regsub* (at present) is implemented in Python. When you import *string*, it's replaced by the *strop* C extension module internally; *strop*'s methods are reportedly 100–1000 times faster than their Python-coded equivalents.
>
> In fact, the *string* module was originally written in Python too but demands for string efficiency prompted recoding it in C. The result was dramatically faster performance for string client programs without impacting the interface. String module clients became instantly faster without having to be modified for the new C-based module.
>
> Which is a great lesson about how to develop in Python: modules can be prototyped in Python at first and translated to C later for speed and efficiency. Because the interface to Python and C extension modules is identical (both are imported), C translations of modules are backward compatible with their Python prototypes. The only impact of the translation of such modules on clients is an improvement in performance.
>
> In fact there's usually no need to move every module to C for delivery of an application: we can pick and choose performance-critical modules (like *string*) for translation, and leave others in Python. Ideally we use the profiler or timing information to isolate which modules will give the most improvement when translated to C. As we saw in Chapter 13, *Implementing Objects*, bottlenecks are sometimes obvious, but profiling is the best way to be sure.

There's also a Python-specific parsing system available on Python's FTP site: the *kwParsing* system, developed by Aaron Watters, is a parser generator written in Python (see Appendix A for access information). Since these are all complex tools, we won't cover their interfaces here. Check the sources listed in Chapter 3, *Getting Started*, for information on available parser generator tools for Python.

## *Hand-Coded Parsers*

Since Python is a general purpose programming language, it's also reasonable to consider writing a hand-coded parser. For instance, recursive descent parsing is a fairly well-known technique for analyzing language based information. Since Python is a very high-level language, writing the parser itself is usually easier than it would be in a traditional language like C or C++.

### *Python development lesson 2: Don't reinvent the wheel*

Parser generators bring up another point about Python work: to use these tools in Python programs, you'll need an extension module that integrates them. The first step in such scenarios should always be to see if the extension already exists in the public domain. Especially for common tools like these, chances are that someone else has already written an integration which you can use off the shelf instead of writing one from scratch.

Of course, not everyone can donate all their extension modules to the public domain, but there's a growing library of available components that you can pick up for free and a community of experts to query. As this book was being written, the Python Software Activity (PSA) started a *locator* service, to help people find extension modules that have already been written. See URL *http://www.python.org*. This will probably become a first stop when shopping for an extension you plan to use.

### *Case study: an expression parser/evaluator*

Here's an example of a custom parser for a simple grammar: it parses and evaluates arithmetic expression strings. This example shows the utility of Python as a general-purpose programming language. Although Python is often used as a front end or rapid development language, it's also useful for the kinds of things we'd normally write in a systems development language like C or C++.

***The expression grammar.*** The grammar our parser will recognize can be described as follows:

```
goal -> <expr> END                       [number, variable, ( ]
goal -> <assign> END                     [set]

assign -> 'set' <variable> <expr>        [set]

expr -> <factor> <expr-tail>             [number, variable, ( ]

expr-tail -> ^                           [END, ) ]
expr-tail -> '+' <factor> <expr-tail>    [+]
expr-tail -> '-' <factor> <expr-tail>    [-]

factor -> <term> <factor-tail>           [number, variable, ( ]

factor-tail -> ^                         [+, -, END, ) ]
factor-tail -> '*' <term> <factor-tail>  [*]
factor-tail -> '/' <term> <factor-tail>  [/]
```

```
term -> <number>                        [number]
term -> <variable>                      [variable]
term -> '(' <expr> ')'                  [(]

tokens: (, ), num, var, -, +, /, *, set, end
```

This is a fairly typical grammar for a simple expression language; example expressions appear at the end of the module listing below. Strings to be parsed are either an expression or an assignment to a variable-name ("*set*"). Expressions involve numbers, variables, and the operators `+`, `-`, `*`, and `/`. Because *factor* is nested in *expr*, `*` and `/` have higher precedence (i.e., bind tighter) than `+` and `-`. Expressions can be enclosed in parentheses to override precedence, and all operators are left associative: "`1-2-3`" is the same as "`(1-2)-3`".

Tokens are just the most primitive components of the expression language. Each grammar rule above is followed in square brackets by a list of tokens used to select it. In recursive descent parsing we determine the set of tokens that can possibly start a rule's substring, and use that information to predict which rule will work ahead of time. For rules that iterate (the *-tail* rules), we use the set of possibly following tokens to know when to stop. Typically, tokens are recognized by a string processor (a "scanner"), and a higher-level processor uses the token stream to predict and step through grammar rules and substrings (a "parser").

***The parser code.*** The system is structured as two modules, holding two classes:

*Scanner*
: Handles low-level character-by-character analysis.

*Parser*
: Embeds a *Scanner* instance and handles higher-level grammar analysis.

The *Parser* is also responsible for computing the expression's value, and testing the system. In this version, the *Parser* evaluates the expression while it's being parsed. To use the system, we create a *Parser* with an input string and call its *parse* method. We can also call *parse* again later with a new expression string.

There's a deliberate division of labor here. The *Scanner* extracts tokens from the string, but knows nothing about the grammar. The *Parser* handles the grammar, but is naive about the string itself. This modular structure keeps the code relatively simple. And it's another example of the OOP composition relationship at work.

*Example 16-13: File: scanner.py*

```
####################################################
# the scanner (lexical analyser)
####################################################
```

*Example 16-13: File: scanner.py (continued)*

```
import string
SyntaxError    = 'SyntaxError'          # local errors
LexicalError   = 'LexicalError'

class Scanner:
    def __init__(self, text):
        self.next = 0
        self.text = text + '\0'

    def newtext(self, text):
        Scanner.__init__(self, text)

    def showerror(self):
        print '=> ', self.text
        print '=> ', (' ' * self.start) + '^'

    def match(self, token):
        if self.token != token:
            raise SyntaxError, [token]
        else:
            value = self.value
            if self.token != '\0':
                self.scan()                 # next token/value
            return value                    # return prior value

    def scan(self):
        self.value = None
        ix = self.next
        while self.text[ix] in string.whitespace:
            ix = ix+1
        self.start = ix

        if self.text[ix] in ['(', ')', '-', '+', '/', '*', '\0']:
            self.token = self.text[ix]
            ix = ix+1

        elif self.text[ix] in string.digits:
            str = ''
            while self.text[ix] in string.digits:
               str = str + self.text[ix]
               ix = ix+1
            if self.text[ix] == '.':
                str = str + '.'
                ix = ix+1
                while self.text[ix] in string.digits:
                   str = str + self.text[ix]
                   ix = ix+1
                self.token = 'num'
                self.value = string.atof(str)
            else:
                self.token = 'num'
                self.value = string.atol(str)
```

*Example 16-13: File: scanner.py (continued)*

```
        elif self.text[ix] in string.letters:
            str = ''
            while self.text[ix] in (string.digits + string.letters):
                str = str + self.text[ix]
                ix = ix+1
            if string.lower(str) == 'set':
                self.token = 'set'
            else:
                self.token = 'var'
                self.value = str

        else:
            raise LexicalError
        self.next = ix
```

*Example 16-14: File: parser1.py*

```
#####################################################
# the parser (syntax analyser, embeds interpreter)
#####################################################

UndefinedError = 'UndefinedError'
from scanner import Scanner, LexicalError, SyntaxError

class Parser:
    def __init__(self, text=''):
        self.lex  = Scanner(text)               # embed a scanner
        self.vars = {'pi':3.14159}              # add a variable

    def parse(self, *text):
        if text:                                # main entry-point
            self.lex.newtext(text[0])           # reuse this parser?
        try:
            self.lex.scan()                     # get first token
            self.Goal()                         # parse a sentence
        except SyntaxError:
            print 'Syntax Error at column:', self.lex.start
            self.lex.showerror()
        except LexicalError:
            print 'Lexical Error at column:', self.lex.start
            self.lex.showerror()
        except UndefinedError, name:
            print "'%s' is undefined at column:" % name, self.lex.start
            self.lex.showerror()

    def Goal(self):
        if self.lex.token in ['num', 'var', '(']:
            val = self.Expr()
            self.lex.match('\0')                    # expression?
            print val
        elif self.lex.token == 'set':               # set command?
            self.Assign()
```

*Example 16-14: File: parser1.py (continued)*

```
            self.lex.match('\0')
        else:
            raise SyntaxError

    def Assign(self):
        self.lex.match('set')
        var = self.lex.match('var')
        val = self.Expr()
        self.vars[var] = val            # assign name in dict

    def Expr(self):
        left = self.Factor()
        while 1:
            if self.lex.token in ['\0', ')']:
                return left
            elif self.lex.token == '+':
                self.lex.scan()
                left = left + self.Factor()
            elif self.lex.token == '-':
                self.lex.scan()
                left = left - self.Factor()
            else:
                raise SyntaxError

    def Factor(self):
        left = self.Term()
        while 1:
            if self.lex.token in ['+', '-', '\0', ')']:
                return left
            elif self.lex.token == '*':
                self.lex.scan()
                left = left * self.Term()
            elif self.lex.token == '/':
                self.lex.scan()
                left = left / self.Term()
            else:
                raise SyntaxError

    def Term(self):
        if self.lex.token == 'num':
            val = self.lex.match('num')               # numbers
            return val
        elif self.lex.token == 'var':
            if self.vars.has_key(self.lex.value):
                val = self.vars[self.lex.value]       # lookup name's value
                self.lex.scan()
                return val
            else:
                raise UndefinedError, self.lex.value
        elif self.lex.token == '(':
            self.lex.scan()
            val = self.Expr()                         # sub-expression
```

*Example 16-14: File: parser1.py (continued)*

```
            self.lex.match(')')
            return val
        else:
            raise SyntaxError


####################################################
# self-test code
####################################################

def test(ParserClass):
    x = ParserClass('4 / 2 + 3')     # allow different Parser's
    x.parse()

    x.parse('3 + 4 / 2')             # like eval('3 + 4 / 2')...
    x.parse('(3 + 4) / 2')
    x.parse('4 / (2 + 3)')
    x.parse('4.0 / (2 + 3)')
    x.parse('4 / (2.0 + 3)')
    x.parse('4.0 / 2 * 3')
    x.parse('(4.0 / 2) * 3')
    x.parse('4.0 / (2 * 3)')
    x.parse('(((3))) + 1')

    y = ParserClass()
    y.parse('set a 4 / 2 + 1')
    y.parse('a * 3')
    y.parse('set b 12 / a')
    y.parse('b')

    z = ParserClass()
    z.parse('set a 99')
    z.parse('set a a + 1')
    z.parse('a')

    z = ParserClass()
    z.parse('pi')
    z.parse('2 * pi')
    z.parse('1.234 + 2.1')

if __name__ == '__main__':
    print 'parser1...'
    test(Parser)                     # test local Parser

def interact(parser=Parser):         # command-line entry
    x = parser()
    while 1:
        cmd = raw_input('Enter=> ')
        if cmd == 'stop':
            break
        x.parse(cmd)
```

***Things to notice.*** The parser keeps a dictionary (*self.vars*) to manage variable names: they're stored in the dictionary on a *set* command and fetched from it when they appear in an expression.

Tokens are represented as strings, with an optional associated value (a numeric value for numbers and a string for variable names).

The Parser uses iteration (*while* loops) instead of recursion, for the *expr-tail* and *factor-tail* rules. Other than this optimization, the rules of the grammar map directly onto Parser methods: tokens become calls to the *Scanner*, and nested rule references become calls to other methods.

***Running the parser.*** When file *parser1.py* is run as a top-level program, its self-test code is executed. Note that all integer math uses Python long integers (unlimited precision integers), because the scanner converts numbers to strings with *string.atol*. Also notice that mixed integer/floating-point operations cast up to floating point since Python operators are used to do the actual calculations.

```
% python parser1.py
parser1...
5L
5L
3L
0L
0.8
0.8
6.0
6.0
0.666666666667
4L
9L
4L
100L
3.14159
6.28318
3.334
```

As usual, we can also test and use the system interactively.

```
% python
>>> import parser1
>>> x = parser1.Parser()
>>> x.parse('1 + 2')
3L
```

Error cases are trapped and reported:

```
>>> x.parse('1 + a')
'a' is undefined at column: 4
=>  1 + a
=>      ^
>>> x.parse('1+a+2')
```

```
'a' is undefined at column: 2
=> 1+a+2
=>   ^
>>> x.parse('1 * 2 $')
Lexical Error at column: 6
=>  1 * 2 $
=>        ^
>>> x.parse('1 * - 1')
Syntax Error at column: 4
=> 1 * - 1
=>     ^
>>> x.parse('1 * (9')
Syntax Error at column: 6
=>  1 * (9
=>        ^
```

Pathologically big numbers are handled well:

```
>>> x.parse('888888888888888888888888888888888888888888888.9999999')
8.88888888889e+44
>>> x.parse('999999999999999999999999999999999999999999 + 2')
1000000000000000000000000000000000000000001L
>>> x.parse('999999999999999999999999999999.8888888888 + 1.1')
1e+30
```

There's also an interactive loop interface:

```
>>> parser1.interact()
Enter=> 4 * 3 + 5
17L
Enter=> 5 + 4 * 3
17L
Enter=> (5 + 4) * 3
27L
Enter=> set a 99
Enter=> set b 66
Enter=> a + b
165L
Enter=> # + 1
Lexical Error at column: 0
=>  # + 1
=>  ^
Enter=> a * b + c
'c' is undefined at column: 8
=>  a * b + c
=>          ^
Enter=> a * b * + c
Syntax Error at column: 8
=>  a * b * + c
=>          ^
Enter=> a
99L
Enter=> a * a * a
970299L
Enter=> stop
>>>
```

## *Python development lesson 3: Divide and conquer*

As the parser system demonstrates, modular program design is almost always a major win. By using Python's program structuring tools (functions, modules, classes, etc.) big tasks can be broken down into small, manageable parts which can be coded and tested independently.

For instance, the *Scanner* can be tested without the *Parser*, by making an instance with an input string and calling its *scan* or *match* methods repeatedly. We can even test it like this interactively, from Python's command line. By separating programs into logical components, they become easier to understand and modify. Imagine what the *Parser* would look like if the *Scanner*'s logic was embedded, rather than called.

### *Adding a parse tree interpreter*

One weakness in the *parser1* program is that it embeds expression evaluation logic in the parsing logic: the result is computed while the string is being parsed. This makes evaluation quick but it can also make it difficult to modify the code, especially in larger systems. To simplify, we could restructure the program to keep expression parsing and evaluation separate. Instead of evaluating the string, the parser can build up an intermediate representation of it that can be evaluated later.

Here's a variant of *parser1* that implements this idea. The parser analyzes the string, and builds up a parse tree, that is, a tree of class instances that represents the expression, and may be evaluated in a separate step. The parse tree is built from classes that "know" how to evaluate themselves: to compute the expression, we just ask the tree to evaluate itself. Root nodes in the tree ask their children to evaluate themselves and then combine the results. In effect, evaluation is just a recursive traversal of a tree of embedded class instances.

*Example 16-15: File: parser2.py*

```
TraceDefault    = 0
UndefinedError = "UndefinedError"
from scanner import Scanner, SyntaxError, LexicalError


####################################################
# the interpreter (a smart objects tree)
####################################################

class TreeNode:
    def validate(self, dict):           # default error check
        pass
    def apply(self, dict):              # default evaluator
        pass
```

*Example 16-15: File: parser2.py (continued)*

```
    def trace(self, level):                  # default unparser
        print '.'*level + '<empty>'

# ROOTS

class BinaryNode(TreeNode):
    def __init__(self, left, right):             # inherited methods
        self.left, self.right = left, right      # left/right branches
    def validate(self, dict):
        self.left.validate(dict)                 # recurse down branches
        self.right.validate(dict)
    def trace(self, level):
        print '.'*level + '[' + self.label + ']'
        self.left.trace(level+3)
        self.right.trace(level+3)

class TimesNode(BinaryNode):
    label = '*'
    def apply(self, dict):
        return self.left.apply(dict) * self.right.apply(dict)

class DivideNode(BinaryNode):
    label = '/'
    def apply(self, dict):
        return self.left.apply(dict) / self.right.apply(dict)

class PlusNode(BinaryNode):
    label = '+'
    def apply(self, dict):
        return self.left.apply(dict) + self.right.apply(dict)

class MinusNode(BinaryNode):
    label = '-'
    def apply(self, dict):
        return self.left.apply(dict) - self.right.apply(dict)

# LEAVES

class NumNode(TreeNode):
    def __init__(self, num):
        self.num = num                    # already numeric
    def apply(self, dict):                # use default validate
        return self.num
    def trace(self, level):
        print '.'*level + `self.num`

class VarNode(TreeNode):
    def __init__(self, text, start):
        self.name   = text                       # variable name
        self.column = start                      # column for errors
    def validate(self, dict):
        if not dict.has_key(self.name):
```

*Example 16-15: File: parser2.py (continued)*

```
            raise UndefinedError, (self.name, self.column)
    def apply(self, dict):
        return dict[self.name]                  # validate before apply
    def assign(self, value, dict):
        dict[self.name] = value                 # local extension
    def trace(self, level):
        print '.'*level + self.name

# COMPOSITES

class AssignNode(TreeNode):
    def __init__(self, var, val):
        self.var, self.val = var, val
    def validate(self, dict):
        self.val.validate(dict)                 # don't validate var
    def apply(self, dict):
        self.var.assign( self.val.apply(dict), dict )
    def trace(self, level):
        print '.'*level + 'set '
        self.var.trace(level + 3)
        self.val.trace(level + 3)


####################################################
# the parser (syntax analyser, tree builder)
####################################################

class Parser:
    def __init__(self, text=''):
        self.lex     = Scanner(text)             # make a scanner
        self.vars    = {'pi':3.14159}            # add constants
        self.traceme = TraceDefault

    def parse(self, *text):                      # external interface
        if text:
            self.lex.newtext(text[0])            # reuse with new text
        tree = self.analyse()                    # parse string
        if tree:
            if self.traceme:                     # dump parse-tree?
                print; tree.trace(0)
            if self.errorCheck(tree):            # check names
                self.interpret(tree)             # evaluate tree

    def analyse(self):
        try:
            self.lex.scan()                      # get first token
            return self.Goal()                   # build a parse-tree
        except SyntaxError:
            print 'Syntax Error at column:', self.lex.start
            self.lex.showerror()
        except LexicalError:
            print 'Lexical Error at column:', self.lex.start
```

*Example 16-15: File: parser2.py (continued)*

```
            self.lex.showerror()

    def errorCheck(self, tree):
        try:
            tree.validate(self.vars)          # error checker
            return 'ok'
        except UndefinedError, varinfo:
            print "'%s' is undefined at column: %d" % varinfo
            self.lex.start = varinfo[1]
            self.lex.showerror()              # returns None

    def interpret(self, tree):
        result = tree.apply(self.vars)        # tree evals itself
        if result != None:                    # ignore 'set' result
            print result

    def Goal(self):
        if self.lex.token in ['num', 'var', '(']:
            tree = self.Expr()
            self.lex.match('\0')
            return tree
        elif self.lex.token == 'set':
            tree = self.Assign()
            self.lex.match('\0')
            return tree
        else:
            raise SyntaxError

    def Assign(self):
        self.lex.match('set')
        vartree = VarNode(self.lex.value, self.lex.start)
        self.lex.match('var')
        valtree = self.Expr()
        return AssignNode(vartree, valtree)              # two subtrees

    def Expr(self):
        left = self.Factor()                             # left subtree
        while 1:
            if self.lex.token in ['\0', ')']:
                return left
            elif self.lex.token == '+':
                self.lex.scan()
                left = PlusNode(left, self.Factor())     # add root-node
            elif self.lex.token == '-':
                self.lex.scan()
                left = MinusNode(left, self.Factor())    # grows up/right
            else:
                raise SyntaxError

    def Factor(self):
        left = self.Term()
        while 1:
```

*Example 16-15: File: parser2.py (continued)*

```
            if self.lex.token in ['+', '-', '\0', ')']:
                return left
            elif self.lex.token == '*':
                self.lex.scan()
                left = TimesNode(left, self.Term())
            elif self.lex.token == '/':
                self.lex.scan()
                left = DivideNode(left, self.Term())
            else:
                raise SyntaxError

    def Term(self):
        if self.lex.token == 'num':
            leaf = NumNode(self.lex.match('num'))
            return leaf
        elif self.lex.token == 'var':
            leaf = VarNode(self.lex.value, self.lex.start)
            self.lex.scan()
            return leaf
        elif self.lex.token == '(':
            self.lex.scan()
            tree = self.Expr()
            self.lex.match(')')
            return tree
        else:
            raise SyntaxError


####################################################
# self-test code: use my parser, parser1's tester
####################################################

if __name__ == '__main__':
    print 'parser2...'
    import parser1
    parser1.test(Parser)        #  run parser1.test with Parser here
```

***Running the new parser.*** When *parser2.py* is run as a top-level program, we get the same test code output as for *parser1*. In fact, it reuses the same test code: both parsers pass in their *Parser* class object to *parser1.test*. We could reset *parser1.Parser* instead, but passing in parameters is always better than changing modules from the outside. And since classes are objects, we can also pass this version of the *Parser* to *parser1*'s interactive loop: *parser1.interact(parser2.Parser)*. The new parser's external behavior is identical to that of the original.

Notice that the new parser reuses the same *Scanner* module too. To catch errors raised by *Scanner*, it also imports the specific strings that identify the *Scanner*'s exceptions.

***Parse tree structure.*** The intermediate representation of an expression is a tree of class instances, whose shape reflects the order of operator evaluation. This parser also has logic to print an indented listing of the constructed parse tree if the *traceme* attribute is set. Indentation gives the nesting of subtrees, and binary operators list left subtrees first. For example:

```
% python
>>> import parser2
>>> p = parser2.Parser()
>>> p.traceme = 1
>>> p.parse('5 + 4 * 2')

[+]
...5L
...[*]
......4L
......2L
13L
```

When this tree is evaluated, the *apply* method recursively evaluates subtrees and applies root operators to their results. Here, * is evaluated before +, since it's lower in the tree: the *Factor* method consumes the * substring before returning a right subtree to *Expr*.

```
>>> p.parse('5 * 4 - 2')

[-]
...[*]
......5L
......4L
...2L
18L
```

In this example, the * is evaluated before the -: the *Factor* method loops though a substring of * and / expressions before returning the resulting left subtree to *Expr*.

```
>>> p.parse('1 + 3 * (2 * 3 + 4)')

[+]
...1L
...[*]
......3L
......[+]
.........[*]
............2L
............3L
.........4L
31L
```

Trees are made of nested class instances. This last expression's tree looks like Figure 16-1 internally. From an OOP perspective, it's another way to use composition.

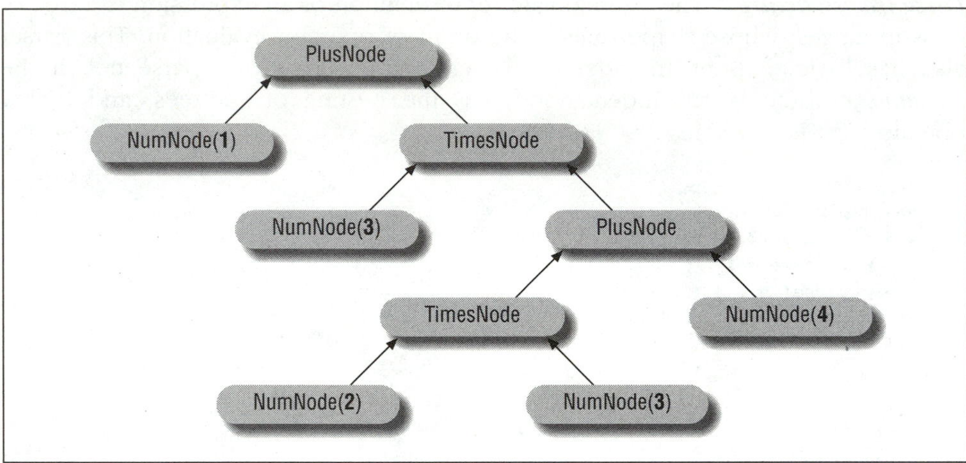


*Figure 16-1: Parse tree built for "1 + 3 * (2 * 3 + 4)"*

Since tree nodes are just class instances, this tree could be created and evaluated manually too:

```
PlusNode( NumNode(1),
          TimesNode( NumNode(3),
                     PlusNode( TimesNode(NumNode(2), NumNode(3)),
                               NumNode(4) ))).apply({})
```

but we might as well let the parser build it for us (Python's not Lisp! :-).

Suggested exercise: Add logic to trace the parser's methods as they're called. Is this easier than stepping through a parse interactively with the debugger? What kind of changes would you make to display the token that was expected when a *SyntaxError* is raised?

***Generalizing the apply method.*** Since *BinaryNode* subclasses already record their operator string (the *label* class attribute) for tree traces, we could build up code strings for subexpressions instead of running Python operators. We might be tempted to define a general *apply* at the *BinaryNode* level, to replace the *apply* methods in its subclasses.

```
class BinaryNode(TreeNode):
    def apply(self, dict):
       return eval('self.left.apply(dict)' +
                    self.label             +
                   'self.right.apply(dict)')
```

This example uses the *eval* built-in which we'll expand on shortly. This saves some code, but Python has to reparse the expression that we've just parsed.

Because of that it's noticeably slower. Suggested exercise: Make this change, and time or profile the result. How much of a slowdown is there? Is it significant, given the nature of this program?

***Handling errors.*** The *Scanner* and *Parser* can both raise exceptions on errors (lexical errors, syntax errors, and undefined name errors). They're caught at the top level of the *parser*, and end the current parse. There's no need to set and check status flags to terminate the recursion.

Since math is done using long integers, floating-point, and Python's operators, there's usually no need to trap numeric overflow or underflow errors. But as is, the Parser doesn't handle errors like division by zero: they make the parser system exit with a Python stack dump:

```
% python
>>> import parser2
>>> parser2.Parser('2 / 0').parse()
Traceback (innermost last):
  File "<stdin>", line 1, in ?
  File "./parser2.py", line 108, in parse
    self.interpret(tree)            # evaluate tree
  File "./parser2.py", line 131, in interpret
    result = tree.apply(self.vars)          # tree evals itself
  File "./parser2.py", line 39, in apply
    return self.left.apply(dict) / self.right.apply(dict)
ZeroDivisionError: long division or modulo

>>> parser2.Parser().parse('2.0 / 0.0')
[same stack-trace]
```

And here's a debugging session that triggers the division by zero exception in *Parser2*; note that we can call a class instance's methods when the program is stopped in a method.

```
% python
>>> import pdb, parser1, parser2
>>> pdb.run('parser1.interact(parser2.Parser)')
> <string>(0)?()
(Pdb) c
> <string>(1)?()
(Pdb) c
Enter=> 1 / 0
ZeroDivisionError: 'long division or modulo'
> <string>(1)?()
(Pdb) w
> <string>(1)?()
  ./parser1.py(138)interact()
-> x.parse(cmd)
  ./parser2.py(108)parse()
-> self.interpret(tree)             # evaluate tree
  ./parser2.py(131)interpret()
-> result = tree.apply(self.vars)           # tree evals itself
```

```
  ./parser2.py(39)apply()
-> return self.left.apply(dict) / self.right.apply(dict)

[plus three 'd' commands]

(Pdb) d
> ./parser2.py(39)apply()
-> return self.left.apply(dict) / self.right.apply(dict)
(Pdb) p self
<DivideNode instance at b0500>
(Pdb) p self.right
<NumNode instance at b0480>
(Pdb) p self.right.apply(dict)
0L
(Pdb) p self.left.apply(dict)
1L
```

Suggested exercise: Add exception-handling logic to the system to trap numeric errors like this. Where's the best place for it to be added? What kind of error reporting should be done?

## *What's Wrong with This Picture?*

The hand-coded parser programs shown earlier illustrate some interesting concepts, and underscore the power of Python for general-purpose programming. Depending on your job description, they may also be typical of the sort of thing you'd write regularly in a traditional language like C. Parsers are an important component in a wide variety of applications, but in many cases, they're not as necessary as you might think. Let me explain why.

So far, we started with an expression parser and added a parse tree interpreter here, to make the code easier to modify. As is, the parser works, but it will be slow compared to a C implementation. If the parser is used frequently, we could speed it up by moving parts to C extension modules. For instance, the scanner might be moved to C initially, since it's often called from the parser. Ultimately we might add components to the grammar to allow expressions to access application-specific variables and functions.

## *Running Embedded Python Code: eval and exec*

All the things mentioned in the previous paragraph constitute good engineering. But depending on your application this approach may not be the best one in Python. The easiest way to evaluate input expressions in Python is to let Python do it, by calling the *eval* built-in function. In fact, we can replace the entire expression evaluation program with one function call. The next example will demonstrate how this is done.

More important, the following example underscores one of the basic ideas behind the language: if you already have an extensible, embeddable, high-level language system, why invent another? More often than not Python itself can satisfy our language based component needs.

# *Case Study: A Calculator GUI*

A next logical extension for the expression evaluator is a GUI interface. In this section we'll study a Python calculator program that provides a graphical interface, similar to the calculator programs available under most window managers. Let's first look at the code and discuss some of the concepts it illustrates.

The *CalcGui* class in this module uses the *guitools* module we wrote for use with the table browser GUI in Chapter 12—yet another example of code reuse at work. *CalcGui* is a subclass of *Frame* directly; there's no menu or toolbar. Instead, the GUI contains an *Entry* field at the top (to display and change the expression), and six rows (nested *Frames*) of buttons for entering numbers, variables names, and operations.

*Example 16-16: File: calcgui1.py*

```
#!/usr/local/bin/python

from Tkinter  import *                                     # widgets, constants
from guitools import frame, button, entry                  # widget builders

class CalcGui(Frame):
    def __init__(self):                                    # an extended frame
        Frame.__init__(self)                               # on default top-level
        self.pack(expand=YES, fill=BOTH)                   # all parts expandable
        self.master.title('Python Calculator 0.1')         # 6 frames plus entry
        self.master.iconname("pcalc1")

        self.names = {}                                    # namespace for variables
        text = StringVar()
        entry(self, TOP, text)

        rows = ["abcd", "0123", "4567", "89()"]
        for row in rows:
            frm = frame(self, TOP)
            for char in row: button(frm, LEFT, char,
                                lambda x=text, y=char: x.set(x.get() + y))

        frm = frame(self, TOP)
        for char in "+-*/=": button(frm, LEFT, char,
                                lambda x=text, y=char: x.set(x.get()+' '+y+' '))

        frm = frame(self, BOTTOM)
        button(frm, LEFT, 'eval',  lambda x=self, y=text: x.eval(y) )
        button(frm, LEFT, 'clear', lambda x=text: x.set('') )
```

*Example 16-16: File: calcgui1.py (continued)*

```
    def eval(self, text):
        try:
            text.set('eval(text.get(), self.names, self.names)')
        except SyntaxError:
            try:
                exec(text.get(), self.names, self.names)
            except:
                text.set("ERROR")          # bad as statement too?
            else:
                text.set('')               # worked as a statement
        except:
            text.set("ERROR")              # other eval expression errors

if __name__ == '__main__': CalcGui().mainloop()
```

## Running Code Strings

The module shown in Example 16-16 implements a GUI calculator in 44 lines! But of course, it cheats: expression evaluation is delegated to Python. It calls the built-in *eval* and *exec* functions to do most of the work:

*eval*
: Parses, evaluates, and returns the result of a Python expression represented as a string.

*exec*
: Runs an arbitrary Python statement represented as a string; there's no return value.

*exec* is also a statement in Python (the statement works the same as the function). Both accept optional dictionaries to be used as global and local namespaces for assigning and evaluating names used in the code strings. In effect, *self.names* becomes a symbol table for running calculator expressions.

By default a code string's namespace defaults to the caller's namespaces. If we didn't pass in dictionaries here, the strings would run in the *eval* method's namespace. Since the method's local namespace goes away after the method call returns, there would be no way to retain names assigned in the string.

### Optimizing dynamically constructed code

In the last chapter, we mentioned that code strings can be precompiled before being executed, to save time. Since we've started to use *eval* and *exec* in earnest, here are a few more details.

### *Python development lesson 4: Embedding beats parsers*

The calculator uses *eval* and *exec* to call Python's parser/interpreter at runtime instead of analyzing and evaluating expressions manually. In effect, the calculator runs embedded Python code, from a Python program; *eval* and *exec* are similar to the C embedded call functions we saw earlier.

Python's development environment (the parser and byte-code compiler) is always a part of systems that use Python, regardless of whether Python is on top or embedded. Because there's no difference between the development and delivery environments, Python's parser can be used by Python programs.

But calling this *cheating* is too harsh: we've replaced the entire expression evaluator with a single call to *eval.* Since Python's parser is always available, we can often use it directly, instead of hand-coding language processors. In effect, the Python language itself can replace many small custom languages. Besides saving development time, clients have to learn just one language, one that's simple enough for end-user coding.

Further, Python can take on the *flavor* of any application. If a language interface requires application-specific extensions, we just add Python classes, or export an API for use in embedded Python code as a C extension module or type. By evaluating Python code that uses application-specific extensions, parsers become almost completely unnecessary.

There's also a critical added benefit to this approach: embedded Python code has access to all the tools and features of a powerful, full-blown programming language. It can use lists, functions, classes, external modules, even Python extensions like the *Tkinter* GUI module and persistent object shelves. You'd probably spend years trying to provide similar functionality in a custom language parser. Just ask Guido :-).

Although it's simple to execute code at runtime using *eval* and *exec*, some applications require optimal performance. In such cases, the built-in *compile* function can be used to convert raw strings to byte-code objects. When strings are executed repeatedly, precompiling with *compile* can speed programs substantially; there's no need for Python to reparse the code each time it is run.

Here's a simple example. As we've seen, we can create arbitrary code strings at runtime, embed them in data-structures if desired, and execute them with the eval and exec built-ins:

```
% python
>>> prog = ["x = 99", "y = 1", "x = x + y"]     a list of statements
>>> ns = {}                                     a namespace to run them in
```

```
>>> for stmt in prog:
...     exec stmt in ns, ns
...
>>> eval("x", ns, ns)                         an expression string
100
>>> print ns['x'], ns['y']
100 1
```

This example creates a list of code strings, and executes them in a new namespace dictionary (it acts much like a simple interpreter). But if these strings are to be executed more than once, it's to our advantage to compile them to "code" objects, and execute the compiled objects instead of the strings:

```
% python
>>> prog = ["x = 99", "y = 1", "x = x + y"]          string list
>>> code = []
>>> for stmt in prog:                                precompile
...     code.append(compile(stmt, "(string)", "exec"))  to byte-code
...
>>> result = "x"
>>> rcode  = compile(result, "(string)", "eval")      "eval": expr
>>>
>>> ns = {}                        namespace for code objects to run in
>>> for stmt in code:              execute precompiled code objects in list
...     exec stmt in ns, ns
...
>>> print eval(rcode, ns, ns)      execute precompiled expr code object
100
>>> print ns['x'], ns['y']
100 1
```

Here, we still use the same *exec* and *eval* to run the code. But this time, we're running objects returned by *compile*; they're not parsed when run.

The compile built-in takes three arguments: the code string to compile, a filename label for runtime error reporting (here, *(string)*), and a parser mode string. The parser mode can be *eval* for expressions, *exec* for statements, or *single* for a single interactive statement (which prints the result if it's not "None").

*compile* returns an executable object, which is essentially a container for the byte-code produced by running the string through the Python compiler. The byte-code object may be executed later, by calling eval or exec.

---

*NOTE* Don't be fooled by the similarity between the *compile* built-in function, and the *regex.compile* function we saw earlier in this chapter. Both allow us to avoid reparsing strings. But here, *compile* acts on arbitrary Python code; *regex.compile* handles regular expressions only. Also see Chapter 15 for information on the *Py_CompileString* C API function; it's equivalent to the *compile* function here, but is used to precompile Python code embedded in (run from) C.

---

## *Building the Interface*

In *CalcGui* the constructor, buttons are represented as lists of strings; each string represents a row and each character in the string represents a button. Lambdas with default argument values are used to set callback data for each button. The callback function for each button saves the button's character and the linked text entry variable; a button press just adds the character to the end of the entry widget's current string.

The *eval* callback saves *self* and the text entry variable; when pressed, it dispatches expressions to the local *eval* method to evaluate the current expression in the entry field and display the result. Notice the use of nested exception handlers in *eval.*

- We first assume the string is an expression and try *eval.*
- If that fails due to a syntax error, we try evaluating the string as a statement using *exec.*
- Finally, if both methods fail, we report an error in the string (a syntax error, undefined name, etc.).

Statements and bad expressions might be parsed twice, but the overhead doesn't really matter here. We don't have to know whether the string is an expression or a statement.

## *Buttons as Classes*

Note that button presses don't trigger a *CalcGui* method: the lambda functions call the linked variable's get/set methods directly. Since there are no *CalcGui* methods involved, buttons could also be implemented as a separate class. For instance, we could use a class for operand buttons, but this strategy takes more code:

```
class OperandButton(Button):
    def __init__(self, parent, text, char):
        self.text = text
        self.char = char
        Button.__init__(self, parent, text=char, command=self.press)
        self.pack(side=LEFT, expand=YES, fill=BOTH)
    def press(self):
        self.text.set( self.text.get() + self.char )      # show my char

...
for char in row: OperandButton(frm, text, char)    # in CalcGui
```

*OperandButton* has the same effect as the lambda. It subclasses *Button* to save the entry variable and character. It's also considerably more work: unless we plan to extend or reuse operator buttons, there's really no compelling reason to replace the lambdas with class instances in this example.

### *Classes as closures*

Readers with a background in functional languages might recognize *OperandButton* as closure-like behavior. The *press* method retains the *text* and *char* values when it's later called. A more complete discussion of closures in Python appears in Appendix A.

## *Running the GUI*

When *calcgui1.py* is run as a top-level program, the window shown in Figure 16-2 comes up with buttons for entry of numbers, variable names, and operators. The GUI is built by attaching buttons to frames: each row of buttons is a nested *Frame*. The GUI itself is a *Frame* subclass, with an attached *Entry* and six embedded row *Frames*. Since this version just builds up a code string to pass to the Python interpreter all at once, we can type any Python expression or statement in the entry field; the buttons are really just a convenience.

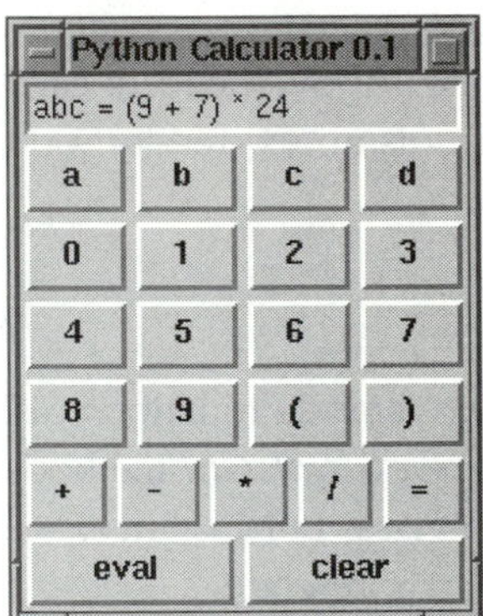


*Figure 16-2: CalcGui1 window*

In fact, the entry field isn't much more than a command line: we can type in arbitrary statements: *import*, assignments, etc. Typing *import sys* and *dir(sys)* displays *sys* attributes in the calculator's entry field.

Note that variable names can be combinations of letters "abcd" (or anything we type in manually). They're assigned and evaluated in dictionaries used to represent the calculator's namespace. Figure 16-3 gives the picture after we expanded the calculator window interactively, and pressed *eval*. The calculator's frame, entry field, and buttons are made expandable in the *guitools* utility module functions.

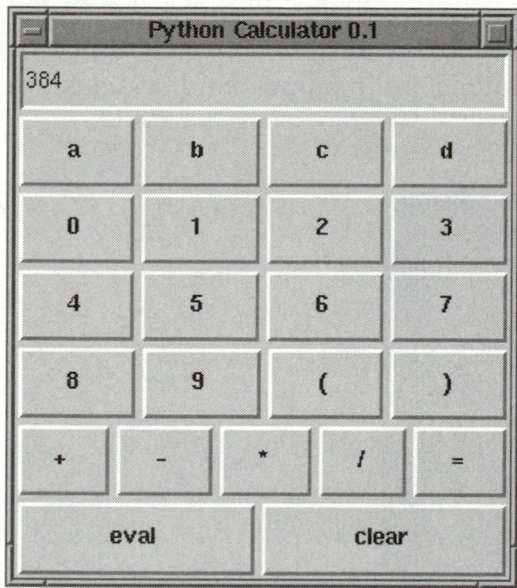


*Figure 16–3: Resizing the calculator*

## *Alternative Layouts*

The calculator layout is controlled by packing options (sides), as well as the order in which buttons are added (created). Figure 16-4 shows some alternative constructions and the layouts they produce:

*calcalt1*
: Attaches operand frames to the top first, attaches the operator frame to the right second, and attaches the *eval/clear* frame to the bottom last. Operand buttons are attached to the left inside their frame, and operators to the top in all these layouts.

*calcalt2*
: Attaches the *eval/clear* frame to the bottom first, attaches the operator frame on the right second, and attaches the operand frames to the top last.

*calcalt3*
: Attaches the operator frame to the right first, adds operand frames on top next, and adds the *eval/clear* frame on bottom last.

Even for a simple layout like this, we can arrange the widgets in a wide variety of configurations. By varying the order and attachment options of the nested frames, and of the buttons inside them, we can come up with almost any layout we want (though some layouts may be more reasonable than others).

*Tk* follows an algorithm to pack widgets in a way that makes the best use of the window's real estate, given the order of creation and packing options. Roughly, frames get whatever space is left over after adding prior frames, and widgets are expanded to fill available space.

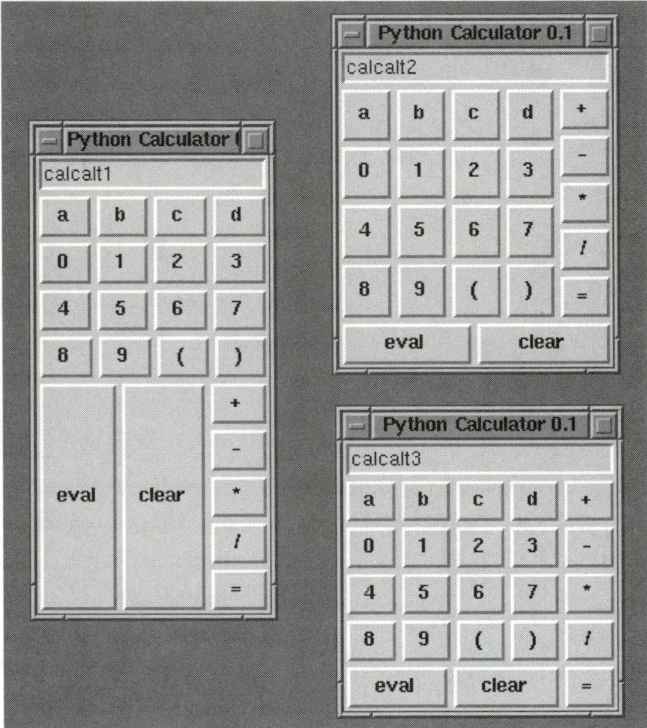


*Figure 16-4: Layout alternatives*

For more information, see *Tk*'s manpage on the packer, or other *Tk* documentation. You can also learn a lot just by trying out alternative orders of creation and packing sides in this example. Since Python provides rapid turnaround for GUI changes, it's possible to answer layout questions fast, by experimenting with the system interactively.

Suggested exercise: Play!

## *Attaching Calculators to Other Windows*

As is, *CalcGui* is designed to be run as a separate window. But since it's a *Frame* subclass, it could also be attached to a larger frame, if we add a parent parameter to the constructor. For instance, we could add a calculator in the corner of another window by attaching and packing a *CalcGui* instance. (In fact, this is exactly how applet widgets are added to the Grail Web browser; see Appendix A.)

To support attachment, we also have to change the *master* calls in the constructor: *master* won't be a *Toplevel* window if there are enclosing *Frames*. To get a GUI's *Toplevel* window regardless of a widget's nesting, we can call the *_root* method, instead of *master*. But here it probably makes more sense to delete the master calls if we plan on embedding *CalcGui* instances: nested widgets shouldn't set window or icon titles for the whole GUI. If we change the start of the constructor in *calcgui1* to the following:

```
class CalcGui(Frame):
    def __init__(self, parent=None):                    # an extended frame
        Frame.__init__(self, parent)                    # in top-level or other
        self.pack(expand=YES, fill=BOTH)                # still expandable
```

then the class in the following module can reuse the *CalcGui* frame by attaching an instance to itself:

*Example 16-17: File: calcplus.py*

```
from Tkinter  import *
from calcgui1 import CalcGui                        # add parent arg
                                                    # no master calls

class Outer(Frame):
    def __init__(self):
        Frame.__init__(self)
        self.pack()
        Label(self, text='Calc Attachment').pack()          # side=top
        CalcGui(self)                                       # add calc frame
        Button(self, text='Quit', command=self.quit).pack()

Outer().mainloop()
```

Note that the *Outer* instance contains a *CalcGui* instance; this isn't a subclass relationship, it's composition again. This is one way to extend *CalcGui* without modifying its code or subclassing. Figure 16-5 shows the resulting interface; we've added a label at the top and a *Quit* button at the bottom, by attaching *CalcGui* to a container *Frame*.

## *Extending Calculators by Subclassing*

We can achieve similar effects by subclassing *CalcGui* instead of attaching it. Here's a module that extends *calcgui1*, without requiring the changes we had to make to *CalcGui*'s constructor for attaching:

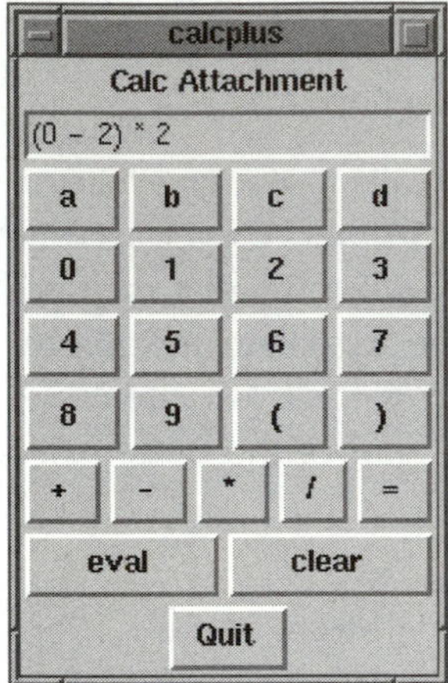


*Figure 16-5: Attaching calculators—middle*

*Example 16-18: File: calcsub.py*

```
from Tkinter  import *
from calcgui1 import CalcGui

class Inner(CalcGui):
    def __init__(self):
        CalcGui.__init__(self)
        Label(self,  text='Calc Subclass').pack()                # add after
        Button(self, text='Quit', command=self.quit).pack()      # top implied

Inner().mainloop()
```

If we run this file as a top-level program (*% python calcsub.py*), we'll get the window shown in Figure 16-6; note that the label and new button are arranged after items *CalcGui*'s constructor adds.

# *The "Big Finish": A Real Calculator GUI*

Of course, real calculators don't usually work by building up expression strings and evaluating them all at once. Traditionally expressions are evaluated as they're entered and temporary results are displayed as they're computed. Implementing this behavior is a bit more work for us: we need to evaluate expressions manually instead of calling the *eval* function only once. But this example demonstrates some advanced programming techniques and provides an interesting final example for this book.

The *calcgui2* module below implements a traditional calculator in Python. Its *CalcGui* class is similar to the prior version, but it adds another row of buttons, and

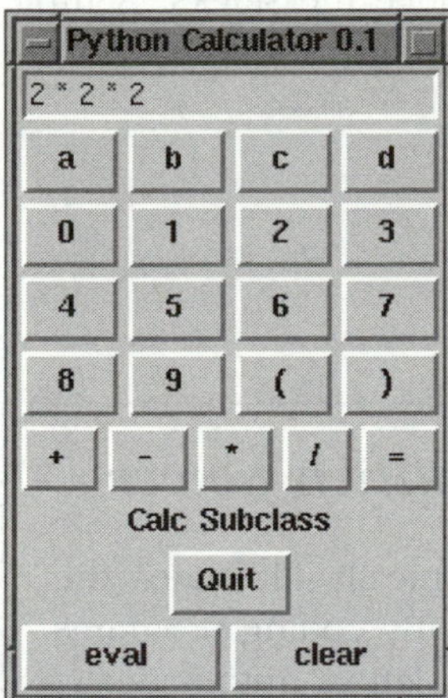


*Figure 16-6: Extending calculators by subclassing*

inherits some common methods from the *GuiMixin* class we discussed in Chapter 11. Since the new version uses the entry field for expressions, there's a new *cmd* button which pops up a dialog box for entry of arbitrary Python expressions and statements.

## Expression Stacks

Most of the changes in this version involve managing the expression display and evaluating expressions. *CalcGui* embeds an instance of the *Evaluator* class to manage two stacks: one records pending operators, and one records pending operands. *CalcGui* manages the GUI itself, controls the entry/display field at the top, and sends operators and operands to *Evaluator*; *Evaluator* manages the expression evaluation stacks.

Roughly, when a new operator is seen (i.e., when an operator button is pressed), the prior operand in the entry field is pushed onto the operands stack. The operator is then added to the operators stack after all pending operators of higher precedence have been popped and applied to pending operands. When *eval* is pressed, all remaining operators are popped and applied and the result is the last remaining value on the operands stack; it's displayed in the calculator's entry field, ready for use in another operation.

The evaluation algorithm is probably best described by working through some examples. Let's step through entry of some expressions and watch the evaluation stacks grow. Stack tracing is enabled with the *debugme* flag in the module; if a value of *true* is assigned, the operator and operand stacks are displayed each time the *Evaluator* class is about to apply an operator and reduce the stacks. A tuple holding the stack lists, *([<operators>], [<operands>])*, is printed to *stdout* on each reduction.

```
1) Entered keys: "5 * 3 + 4 <eval>" [result = 19]

(['*'], ['5', '3'])       [on '+' press: displays "15"]
(['+'], ['15', '4'])      [on 'eval' press: displays "19"]
```

### *Python development lesson 5: Reusability is power*

Attaching and subclassing the calculator like this graphically illustrates the power of Python as a tool for writing reusable software. By coding programs with modules and classes, components written in isolation automatically become general-purpose tools. Python's program organization features promote reusable code.

In fact, code reuse is one of Python's major strengths and has been one of the main themes of this book. Of course, we've also seen that object-oriented design takes some forethought, and the benefits of code reuse aren't apparent immediately. And as we saw in Part 2, *Language Fundamentals*, sometimes we're interested in a quick fix rather than a future use for the code.

But coding with some reusability in mind can save development time in the long run. For instance, the hand-coded parsers shared a *Scanner*, the calculator GUI uses the *guitools* module we discussed earlier, and the next example will reuse the *GuiMixin* class again. Sometimes we're able to finish part of a job before we start.

Note that the pending (stacked) `*` subexpression is evaluated when the `+` is pressed: `*` operators bind tighter than `+`, so the code is evaluated immediately before the `+` operator is pushed. When the `+` button is pressed, the entry field contains *3*. In general, the entry field always holds the prior operand when an operator button is pressed. Since the text entry's value is pushed onto the operands stack before the operator is applied, we have to pop results before displaying them after *eval* or `)` is pressed (otherwise the results are pushed onto the stack twice).

```
2) "5 + 3 * 4 <eval>" [result = 17]

(['+', '*'], ['5', '3', '4'])    [on 'eval' press]
(['+'], ['5', '12'])             [displays "17"]
```

Here, the pending + isn't evaluated when the * button is pressed: since * binds tighter we need to postpone the + until the * can be evaluated. The * operator isn't popped until its right operand has been seen; on the *eval* press there are two operators to pop and apply to operand stack entries.

```
3) "5 + 3 + 4 <eval>" [result = 12]

(['+'], ['5', '3'])       [on the second '+']
(['+'], ['8', '4'])       [on 'eval']
```

For strings of same-precedence operators, we pop and evaluate immediately, instead of postponing evaluation. This results in a left-associative evaluation, in the absence of parentheses: 5+3+4 is evaluated as ((5+3)+4). Order doesn't matter for + and * operations.

```
4) "1 + 3 * ( 1 + 3 * 4 ) <eval>" [result = 40]

(['+', '*', '(', '+', '*'], ['1', '3', '1', '3', '4'])    [on ')']
(['+', '*', '(', '+'], ['1', '3', '1', '12'])             [displays "13"]
(['+', '*'], ['1', '3', '13'])                            [on 'eval']
(['+'], ['1', '39'])
```

In this case, all the operators and operands are stacked (postponed) until we press the ) button at the end. When the ) button is pressed, the parenthesized subexpression is popped and evaluated, and *13* is displayed in the entry-field. On pressing *eval*, the rest is evaluated, and the final result (*40*) is shown. Note that we can use the result as the left operand of another operator. In fact any temporary result can be used again: if we keep pressing an operator button without typing new operands, it's reapplied to the result of the prior press. Figure 16-7 shows how the two stacks look at their highest level. The top operator is applied to the top two operands and the result is pushed back for the operator below.

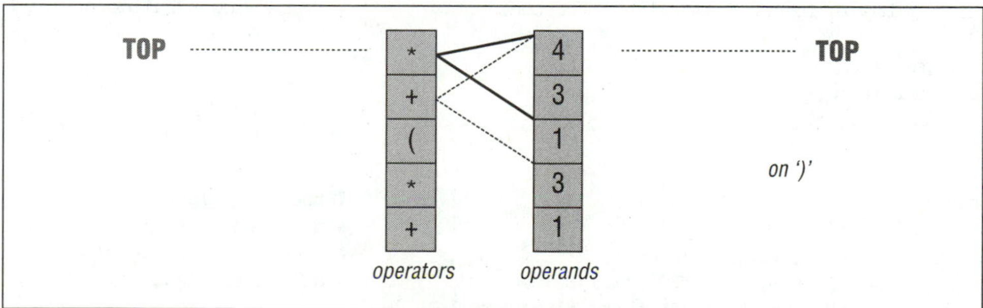


*Figure 16–7: Evaluation stacks: 1 + 3 * (1 + 3 * 4)*

```
5) "1 + 3 * ( 1 + 3 * 4 <eval>" [result = *ERROR*]

([’+’, ’*’, ’(’, ’+’, ’*’], [’1’, ’3’, ’1’, ’3’, ’4’])      [on eval]
([’+’, ’*’, ’(’, ’+’], [’1’, ’3’, ’1’, ’12’])
([’+’, ’*’, ’(’], [’1’, ’3’, ’13’])
([’+’, ’*’], [’1’, ’*ERROR*’])
([’+’], [’*ERROR*’])
([’+’], [’*ERROR*’, ’*ERROR*’])
```

We're fairly loose about error handling in this version too. Many errors are made impossible by the algorithm itself, but things like unmatched parentheses still trip up the evaluator. But instead of trying to detect all possible error cases explicitly, we use a general *try* statement in the *reduce* method to catch them all: expression errors, undefined name errors, syntax errors, etc.

Operands and temporary results are always stacked as strings, and operators are applied by calling *eval*. When an error occurs inside an expression, a result operand of **ERROR** is pushed, which makes all remaining operators fail in *eval* too. **ERROR** percolates to the top of the expression; at the end, it's the last operand and is displayed in the text entry field.

## The Calculator's Code

Finally, here's our new module and some screen shots of the GUI interfaces. As usual, there's no substitute for interacting with the program if you have access to a Python system with *Tkinter* installed (see the CD-ROM).

*Example 16-19: File: calcgui2.py*

```
#!/usr/local/bin/python

from Tkinter  import *                               # widgets, constants
from guimixin import GuiMixin                        # quit, help methods
from guitools import frame, label, button, entry     # reuse widget builders

debugme = 1
def trace(*args):
    if debugme: print args


class CalcGui(GuiMixin, Frame):                      # the main class
    def __init__(self):                              # an extended frame
        Frame.__init__(self)                         # on default top-level
        self.pack(expand=YES, fill=BOTH)             # all parts expandable
        self.master.title('Python Calculator 0.2')
        self.master.iconname("pcalc2")

        self.eval = Evaluator()                 # embed a stack handler
        self.text = StringVar()                 # make a linked variable
        self.text.set("0")
        self.erase = 1                          # clear "0" text next
```

*Example 16-19: File: calcgui2.py (continued)*

```
        self.makeWidgets()                          # build the gui itself

    def makeWidgets(self):                          # 7 frames plus text-entry
        entry(self, TOP, self.text)
        rows = ["abcd", "0123", "4567", "89()"]
        for row in rows:
            frm = frame(self, TOP)
            for char in row: button(frm, LEFT, char,
                                 lambda x=self, y=char: x.onOperand(y))

        frm = frame(self, TOP)
        for char in "+-*/=": button(frm, LEFT, char,
                                 lambda x=self, y=char: x.onOperator(y))

        frm = frame(self, TOP)
        button(frm, LEFT, 'cmd',  self.onMakeCommand)
        button(frm, LEFT, 'dot',  lambda x=self: x.onOperand('.'))
        button(frm, LEFT, 'help', self.help)
        button(frm, LEFT, 'quit', self.quit)       # from guimixin

        frm = frame(self, BOTTOM)
        button(frm, LEFT, 'eval',  self.onEval)
        button(frm, LEFT, 'clear', self.onClear)

    def onClear(self):
        self.eval.clear()
        self.text.set('0')
        self.erase = 1

    def onEval(self):
        self.eval.shiftOpnd(self.text.get())       # last or only opnd
        self.eval.closeall()                       # apply all optrs left
        self.text.set(self.eval.popOpnd())         # need to pop: optr next?
        self.erase = 1

    def onOperand(self, char):
        if char == '(':
            self.eval.open()
            self.text.set('(')                     # clear text next
            self.erase = 1
        elif char == ')':
            self.eval.shiftOpnd(self.text.get())   # last or only nested opnd
            self.eval.close()                      # pop here too: optr next?
            self.text.set(self.eval.popOpnd())
            self.erase = 1
        else:
            if self.erase:
                self.text.set(char)                    # clears last value
            else:
                self.text.set(self.text.get() + char)  # else append to opnd
            self.erase = 0
```

*Example 16-19: File: calcgui2.py (continued)*

```
    def onOperator(self, char):
        self.eval.shiftOpnd(self.text.get())  # push opnd on left
        self.eval.shiftOptr(char)             # eval exprs to left?
        self.text.set(self.eval.topOpnd())    # push optr, show opnd|result
        self.erase = 1                        # erased on next opnd|'('

    def onMakeCommand(self):
        new = Toplevel()                      # a new top-level window
        new.title('Enter Python command')     # arbitrary python code
        frm = frame(new, TOP)
        label(frm, LEFT, '>>>')
        ent = StringVar()
        entry(frm, LEFT, ent)
        button(frm, RIGHT, 'Run', lambda s=self, e=ent: s.onCommand(e))

    def onCommand(self, entry):
        try:
            value = self.eval.runstring(entry.get())
            entry.set('OKAY')
            if value != None:                 # run in eval namespace dict
                self.text.set(value)          # expression or statement
                self.erase = 1
        except:                               # result in calc field
            entry.set('ERROR')                # code in popup field


class Evaluator:
    def __init__(self):                       # expression evaluator
        self.names = {}                       # a names-space for vars
        self.opnd, self.optr = [], []         # two empty stacks
        self.runstring("from math import *")  # preimport math modules
        self.runstring("from random import *")# into calc's namespace

    def clear(self):
        self.opnd, self.optr = [], []         # leave names intact

    def popOpnd(self):
        value = self.opnd[-1]                 # pop/return top|last opnd
        self.opnd[-1:] = []                   # to display and shift next
        return value

    def topOpnd(self):
        return self.opnd[-1]                  # top operand (end of list)

    def open(self):
        self.optr.append('(')                 # treat '(' like an operator

    def close(self):                          # on ')' pop downto highest '('
        self.shiftOptr(')')                   # ok if empty: stays empty
        self.optr[-2:] = []                   # pop, or added again by optr

    def closeall(self):
```

*Example 16-19: File: calcgui2.py (continued)*

```
        while self.optr:                           # force rest on 'eval'
            self.reduce()                          # last may be a var name
        try:
            self.opnd[0] = self.runstring(self.opnd[0])
        except:
            self.opnd[0] = '*ERROR*'               # pop else added again next:
                                                    # optrs assume next opnd erases
    def reduce(self):
        trace(self.optr, self.opnd)
        try:                                       # collapse the top expr
            operator       = self.optr[-1]         # pop top optr (at end)
            [left, right]  = self.opnd[-2:]        # pop top 2 opnds (at end)
            self.optr[-1:] = []                    # delete slice in-place
            self.opnd[-2:] = []
            result = self.runstring(left + operator + right)
            if result == None:
                result = left                      # assignment? key var name
            self.opnd.append(result)               # push result string back
        except:
            self.opnd.append('*ERROR*')            # stack/number/name error

    beatsMe = {'*': ['+', '-', '(', '='],          # class member
               '/': ['+', '-', '(', '='],          # optrs to not pop for key
               '+': ['(', '='],                    # if prior optr is this: push
               '-': ['(', '='],                    # else: pop/eval prior optr
               ')': ['(', '='],                    # all left-associative as is
               '=': ['('] }

    def shiftOpnd(self, newopnd):                  # push opnd at optr, ')', eval
        self.opnd.append(newopnd)

    def shiftOptr(self, newoptr):                  # apply ops with <= priority
        while (self.optr and
               not self.optr[-1] in self.beatsMe[newoptr]):
            self.reduce()
        self.optr.append(newoptr)                  # push this op above result

    def runstring(self, code):
        try:
            return `eval(code, self.names, self.names)`    # try expr: string
        except:
            exec code in self.names, self.names            # try stmt: None


if __name__ == '__main__': CalcGui().mainloop()
```

This version preimports the *math* and *rand* modules into the evaluation namespace; things like *pi*, *sin*, and *floor* can be typed manually in the entry field or the command pop-ups. We're also using lists to record the stacks. Note the use of assignment of empty lists to slices to delete nodes: *self.opnd[-2:]=[]*, and the use of list assignment to extract list components: *[left, right] = self.opnd[-2:]*.

Suggested exercises:

1. Change the *Evaluator* class to use embedded instances of the *Stack* class we wrote in Chapter 13, for the operator and operand stacks. What are the benefits and drawbacks of this approach, compared to using lists directly? Note that speed isn't critical in GUI programs since most of the time is spent waiting for the user to trigger an event (but long-running callbacks are a bad idea in any language). Would the C string stack extension type from Chapter 14 work here as well?

2. Alternate object models. As is, the object model here is fairly *flat*: buttons are widget-class instances, but button presses call back to methods in the top-level *CalcGui* class. Consider the tradeoffs of making buttons classes in this version. For instance, buttons would need to access state information in the *CalcGui* class. How would this impact the design?

## *Running the New Calculator*

*calcgui2.py* is a UNIX script. When we run it as a top-level program, a calculator window comes up, as we see in Figure 16-8. It's similar to the prior version, but there's an extra row of buttons that pop up a command-line entry box (*cmd*), add a . to the current number to make it floating-point (*dot*), and get help or quit the program. *quit* invokes the inherited *GuiMixin* verification dialog we saw earlier in this book.

*Figure 16–8: CalcGui2 main window*

Figure 16-9 shows the picture after popping up a command-line box with *cmd*, and typing **pi** in it. A statement or expression entered in the command box is submitted by pressing the *Run* button. The result of a command box expression is displayed in the calculator's entry field (so it can be used in a larger expression) and the status of the command is displayed in the command box.

Note the use of **pi** here: *CalcGui* preimports things in the *math* and *rand* modules into the namespace where expressions are evaluated. We could have typed **pi** in the calculator's entry field too; operands are evaluated as strings with *eval*.

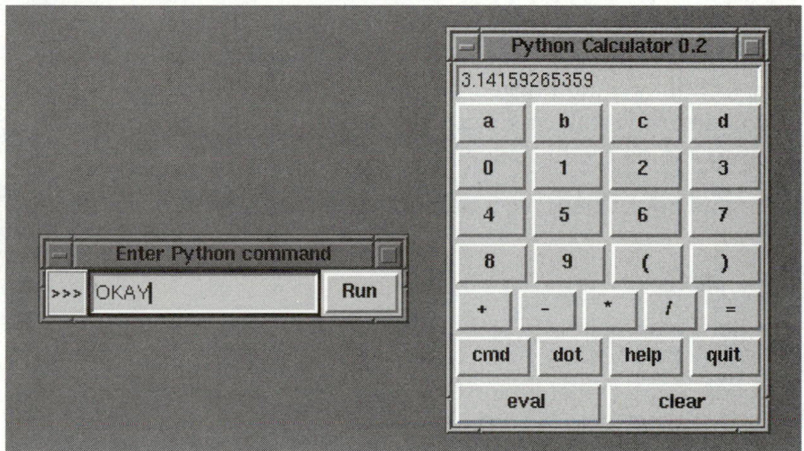


*Figure 16-9: Pop-up command-line entry form— "pi"*

In Figure 16-10, we pressed (, *0*, –, and *2*, typed *L* after *2* to make it a long integer, and pressed ) to get *-2L*. After that, we pressed + repeatedly. When operator buttons are pressed repeatedly like this, the left operand is taken from the entry field. In effect, we add a number to itself each time + is pressed, and compute successive negative powers of two: -2, -4, -8, . . . .

The calculator supports long integers (unlimited precision), negatives, and floating-point, just because Python does: operands and expressions are evaluated with the *eval* built-in, which calls the Python parser/interpreter at run-time.

And finally, Figure 16-11 shows a screen shot after stretching the calculator box, pressing *cmd* twice, and pressing *help*. The calculator's window is resizable by default, and it gets embedded widget resizability from the *guitools* functions. Pressing *help* triggers the help method inherited from *GuiMixin*.

Command box dialogs are new, nonmodal *Toplevel* windows. We can pop up as many as we like, without blocking the calculator or other command boxes. Here we type an *import* statement in one to load custom math functions from a user-defined module, and then use them in an expression in another box.

## *Python development lesson 6: Have fun*

In closing, here's a less tangible but important aspect of Python programming. A common remark among new users is that it's easy to say what you mean in Python without getting bogged down in complex syntax or obscure rules. It's a programmer-friendly language. In fact, it's not too uncommon for Python programs to run on the first attempt.

As we've seen in this book, there are a number of factors behind this distinction, including:

- Lack of declarations
- A clear, simple syntax
- No compile steps
- High-level object types

Python is specifically designed to optimize speed of development (we'll expand on this idea in the Conclusion). For many users, the end result is a remarkably expressive and responsive language, which can actually be fun.

For instance, the calculator programs shown earlier were thrown together in one afternoon, starting from vague, incomplete goals. There was no analysis phase, no need for a formal design, and no official coding stage. I typed up some ideas and they worked. Moreover, Python's interactive nature allowed me to experiment with new ideas and get immediate feedback.

Naturally, this "seat of the pants" programming mode doesn't work for every project. Sometimes more up-front design is warranted. For more demanding tasks, Python has modular constructs and fosters systems that can be extended in either Python or C.

Of course, a simple calculator GUI may not be what we would normally call "serious" software development. But maybe that's part of the point.

As usual, the module imported from the GUI might be a Python file, or a C extension module bound in statically, or loaded dynamically when imported. We can also type arbitrary expressions in the calculator's entry field; in fact, any Python code that can be evaluated in the calculator's namespace dictionaries can be entered in the GUI.

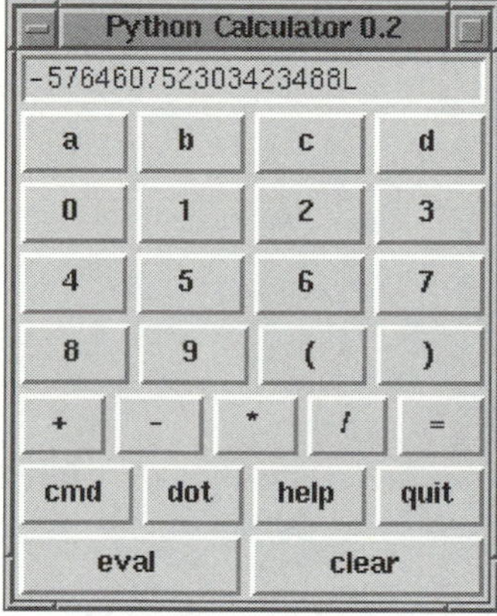


*Figure 16-10: Powers of 2—long integers*

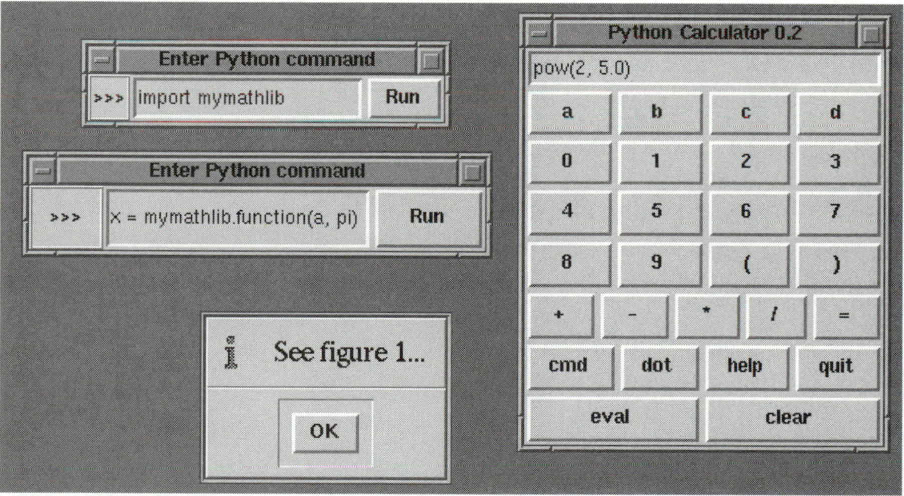


*Figure 16-11: Pop-ups, modules, and help*

# Conclusion: Python and the Development Cycle

## "That's the End of the Book, Now Here's the Meaning of Life"

Well, the meaning of Python, at least. At the start of this book I promised that we'd return to the issue of Python's roles after seeing how it's used in practice. In closing, here are some of my own opinions on the broader implications of the language. In particular, Python's role as a prototyping tool can profoundly affect the development cycle. It fosters a new paradigm, usually called RAD (Rapid Application Development).

## "Something's Wrong with the Way We Program Computers!"

This has to be one of the most overused lines in the business. Still, given time to ponder the big picture, most of us would probably agree that we're not quite there yet. Over the last few decades the computer software industry has made significant progress on streamlining the development task (anyone remember dropping punch cards?). But at the same time, the cost of developing potentially useful custom applications is still often high enough to make them impractical.

Moreover, systems built using modern tools and paradigms are often delivered far behind schedule. Software engineering remains largely defiant of the sort of quantitative measurements employed in other engineering fields. In the software world, it's not uncommon to take one's best time estimate for a new project and multiply by a factor of two or three to account for unforeseen overheads in the development task. This situation is clearly unsatisfactory for software managers, developers, and end users.

# *The "Gilligan Factor"*

It has been suggested (tongue in cheek :-) that if there were to be a patron saint of software engineers, that honor would fall on none other than Gilligan, the character in the pervasively popular American television show of the 1960s, *Gilligan's Island.* Gilligan is the enigmatic, sneaker-clad first mate, widely held to be responsible for the shipwreck that stranded the island's residents.

To be sure, Gilligan's situation seems oddly familiar. Stranded on a desert island without all but the most meager of modern technological comforts, Gilligan and his cohorts must resort to scratching out a living using the resources naturally available. In episode after episode, we observe the Professor developing exquisitely intricate tools for doing the business of life on their remote island, only to be foiled in the implementation phase by the ever-bungling Gilligan.

But clearly it was never poor Gilligan's fault! How could one possibly be expected to implement designs for such sophisticated applications as home appliances and telecommunications devices, given the rudimentary technologies available in such an environment? He simply lacked the proper tools. For all we know, Gilligan may have had the capacity for engineering on the grandest level. But you can't get there with bananas and coconuts.

And pathologically, time after time, Gilligan wound up inadvertently sabotaging the best of the Professor's plans; misusing, abusing, and eventually destroying his inventions. If he could just pedal his makeshift stationary cycle faster and faster (he was led to believe), all would be well. But in the end, inevitably, the coconuts were sent hurling into the air, the palm branches came crashing down around his head, and poor Gilligan was blamed for the failure of the technology.

Dramatic though this image may be :-) , some observers would consider it a striking metaphor for the software industry. Like Gilligan, software engineers are often asked to perform tasks with arguably inappropriate tools. Like Gilligan, our intentions are sound, but technology can hold us back. And like poor Gilligan, we inevitably must bear the brunt of management's wrath, when our systems are delivered behind schedule. You can't get there with bananas and coconuts . . . .

# *Doing the Right Thing*

Of course, this is a exaggeration, added for comic effect. But few of us would argue that the bottleneck between ideas and working systems has disappeared completely. Even today, the cost of developing software far exceeds the cost of computer hardware. Why must programming be so complex?

The nested *lambda* generates an anonymous callback function, which retains information (callback data) from the enclosing scope, to be used when the event occurs. *self.action* is called later, after the name *self* goes out-of-scope. Default arguments work, but they can be subverted if we pass in a real argument:

```
func = outer('world')
func('hello', 'spam')      # overwrites saved value (default)
```

This wasn't a problem for GUI callbacks (the system always passes no arguments). But there are other ways to implement closures safely, using classes and bound methods. For instance, bound methods retain state:

```
class counter:
    def __init__(self, start):
        self.start = start
    def close(self):
        self.start = self.start + 1
        return self.start

c1 = counter(10).close           # bound-method objects retain 'self'
c2 = counter(24).close           # 'self' retains the original values
print c1(), c2(), c1(), c2()     # 11, 25, 12, 26
```

We made use of this technique earlier in this book too, as an implementation for calculator buttons in Chapter 16. But since Python allows class instance objects that inherit a `__call__` method to be called like functions, we can also use class instances as closures:

```
class counter:
    def __init__(self, start):
        self.start = start
    def __call__(self):
        self.start = self.start+1
        return self.start

c1 = counter(10)                 # callable class-instance objects
c2 = counter(24)                 # 'self' retains original values
print c1(), c2(), c1(), c2()     # 11, 25, 12, 26
```

Of course, we're just using the fact that class objects retain state here; it's almost the same as lexical closures, but we need to explicitly specify values to be retained. Whether this is better or worse than retaining everything from an enclosing scope is, well, beyond our scope.

---

*NOTE* As of Python release 1.2, *Tkinter* didn't allow class-instance objects with a `__call__` method to be registered as callback handlers. If you need to associate callback data with an action, use lambdas with defaults, or bound methods of classes with attributes.

---

# *Other Contributions on the CD-ROM*

Here's a sampling of some other contributed Python sources on the accompanying CD-ROM and the *ftp.python.org* FTP site, in directory *pub/python/contrib* (some sources are shipped with Python in the *Contrib* directory in release 1.2). This set is constantly growing and changing, so check the FTP site for up-to-date details.

*Table A–1: A sample of contributed software*

| System/directory | Description |
|---|---|
| *py-apache.tar.gz* | Embedding Python in the *Apache* HTTP server |
| *PyGres95-1.0b.tgz* | Interface to the *Postgres95* database system |
| *vpApp.tar.gz* | A GUI application framework using Motif |
| *PymSQL.tar.gz* | Mini-SQL interface (see Chapter 12, *Persistent Information*) |
| *kjbuckets.tar.gz* | Aaron Watters's C extension for hash table-based datatypes |
| *kwParsing.tar.gz* | Aaron Watters's parser generator written in Python |
| *expy-0.4a.tar.gz* | Interface to Don Libes's *expect* library for automating interactive tasks |
| *subproc.py* | Ken Manheimer's subprocess manager |
| *soundex.tar.gz* | Soundex module by David Wayne Williams |
| *surd.py* | Rational numbers by Nick Seidenman |
| *tk4buttons.shar* | *triButton.c* and *studButton.c* for *Tk* 4.0b3 |
| *memmon* | Python and C++ code to monitor memory management |
| *sybasemodule.c* | John Redford's SYBASE interface (seee also: Oracle module in the */Lib*) |
| *vms.tar.gz* | Limited port of Python 1.2 to VMS |
| *dbhash.tar.gz* | BSD hash (*db*) keyed-file interface (in Python release 1.3 as the *bsddb module*) |
| *xfreeze.tar.gz* | Produce executable, without overwriting current directory (with optimization) |
| *zlib.tar.gz* | Data compression using GNU *zlib* (by Andrew Kuchling) |
| *forth/* | A Forth interpreter written in Python by Nick Seidenman |
| *lutz/* | More demos by Mark Lutz, including an enhanced Python shell (*psh*) |
| *popmail/* | POP and SMTP mail clients by *jkute@mcs.com* |
| *rsa/* | RSA public key cryptosystem by Jan-Hein Buhrman and Niels Ferguson |
| *stoffel/* | Games by Stoffel Erasmus |
| *tkdialogs/* | *Tk* dialogs by Ken Howard |
| *turing/* | Turing machine emulator by Amrit Prem |

# *Recent Extensions*

Here's a peek at some useful Python extensions that have been contributed to the Python archives recently. Most are available in the *pub/python/contrib* directory, at *ftp.python.org* (or check the FAQ).

## *Python and expect*

As shown in the table above, an interface to Don Libes's *expect* tool also exists for Python. This is the other major tool (besides *Tk*) Python borrows from the Tcl language. Roughly, *expect* supports automation of interactive tasks. See Appendix C, Bibliography, and the interface module itself for more information. The *expect* interface is currently available as the file *expy-0.4a.tar.gz* in the *contrib* FTP directory.

## *The bsddb Module: Keyed Files and B-Trees*

A new keyed-access database interface appeared around the time that release 1.3 came out. It's an integration of the BSD *db* library. The *bsddb* module also supports BSD *B-Tree* files. See the *contrib* directory or release 1.3 for more details.

## *A Portable dbm Module*

Release 1.3 also adds a *dumbdbm* library module, which is a portable implementation of *dbm* keyed-access files. Since it's written in Python, it's slower than a true *dbm* library integration. However, *dumbdbm* may be useful on platforms that don't support *dbm* directly. Release 1.3 also adds an *anydbm* module, which provides a portable interface to whatever *dbm* variant is installed: *dbm, gdbm, bsddb,* or *dumbdbm.*

## *The PyGres Database Extension*

An interface to the *Postgres95* relational database system for Python was contributed after the release of Python 1.3. It provides a full-featured SQL database system for use in Python programs. *Postgres95* is a freely distributable database system, which conforms to (most of) ANSI SQL and provides a number of interesting extensions. The *PyGres95* Python extension module wraps the *Postgres95* interface for easy use in Python. For instance, table values are converted to and from Python lists.

## *Python and Tix: Extended Widgets for Tkinter*

Another recently contributed extension adds the *Tix* extended widget library to the *Tkinter* interface. In short, *Python-Tix* is a patch to *Tkinter* that allows the *Tix* widget set to be used from Python in the same way as the basic *Tk* toolkit. The *Tix* extension adds roughly twenty new widgets to *Tk*, including *Notebook*, *FileSelectBox*, and form widgets. *Python-Tix* works with *tcl* 7.4, *tk* 4.0, Python 1.3, and *Tix* 4.0b4, but it should also work on higher-level compatible versions. It runs on any platform that supports all four systems.

## *Python and Rivet: Tk Without Tcl*

*Rivet* is a "*Tcl*-less" *Tk*: a library that implements the *Tk* GUI API without requiring the *Tcl* language to be linked in. A Python extension for *Rivet* allows programs to make use of the *Tk* API, without creating any *Tcl* dependencies, or exposing *Tcl* details. The Python *Rivet* interface is nearly identical to *Tkinter*.

## *Pregex: POSIX-style Regular Expressions*

The *pregex* extension is an interface to POSIX-compliant regular expression libraries. It's an alternative to the built-in Python *regex* module. Among other things, *pregex* provides a thread-safe interface.

## *Kjbuckets: A Hash Table-based Extension Type Module*

Aaron Watters contributed a data structure extension that supports a variety of advanced object types: sets, mappings, and graphs. Because it's written in C, the types it implements are more efficient than Python-based counterparts. For more details, see the contributions directory on the accompanying CD-ROM or the Python FTP or Web sites.

## *A Tkinter-based Debugger GUI*

A beta version of a debugger GUI for Python was contributed to the public domain just before this book was finished. It's written using the *Tkinter* API; for more details, check the contributions sites.

# *Recent Language Additions*

Since Python 1.3 was released late in this book's development, some of its new tools aren't mentioned in the text. Here's a peek at some things we skipped.

## *Support for deep Object Copies*

Python 1.2 added the ability to make deep (rather than top-level) copies of objects. For instance, making a list copy with an empty slice (*list[:]*) only copies the top-level object-reference array by default. Using the new *copy* module, entire object trees may be copied without manually visiting nested objects.

The *copy* library module implements deep copies with a recursive traversal that handles circular data structures and repeated appearances. The basic interface is straightforward:

```
import copy
x = copy.copy(y)          # make a shallow copy of object y (like y[:])
x = copy.deepcopy(y)      # make a deep copy of object y (an entire tree)
```

*copy* supports some of the same special-method protocols for classes as the *pickle* module; there are also some limitations on which object types may be copied. See Python's library reference manual.

## *Package Imports*

This extension is new in release 1.3. Python now allows module names in imports to take the form of arbitrarily long directory paths. In effect, the module name in Python reflects the filesystem hierarchy. Packages depend on extensions developed by Ken Manheimer and import hooks implemented in Python.

Two new library modules implement package interfaces: *ni.py*, and *ihooks.py* (in the *Lib* directory). Roughly, a *package* is a module that contains other modules and nested packages. Package nesting reflects hierarchical package paths. To enable package imports, the statements:

```
import ni; ni.ni()
```

should appear at the top of the program file (module). The *ni* module uses import hooks to install the package system. Later, an import of the form:

```
import P.Q.M
```

imports the file in directory path *P/Q/M.py*, located on the *sys.path* module search path (by default). Packages can be imported directly, but this method is less useful than importing the module files they lead to. There's also support for altering package search paths dynamically at each level. See Python 1.3 release notes (*Misc/NEWS*), and the *Lib/ni.py* module file's internal documentation for more details.

## *Documentation Strings*

These strings appeared by release 1.2 but weren't used in this book. Roughly, modules, functions, classes, and methods may include a string constant before any statements. The string is taken to be documentation for the object, accessible through the object's __doc__ attribute. For instance:

*Example A-13: File: docstr.py*

```
"module documentation: docstr.__doc__"

class spam:
    "class documentation: spam.__doc__, docstr.spam.__doc__"
    def method(self, arg):
        "method documentation: spam.method.__doc__, self.method.__doc__"
        code...

def func(args):
    "function documentation: docstr.func.__doc__"
    code...
```

The advantage of using strings over simple comments is that the string may be fetched from an object at run-time (for instance, as information in a browser). See also Chapter 14, *Extending Python*: C extensions may have doc-strings too. However, at this writing doc-strings are not universally used.

## *The New Object Access API*

The object access API is new with release 1.3. We mentioned this development at the end of Chapter 15. Jim Fulton's abstract object API allows for uniform, high-level, generic access to Python objects from C without manual navigation of type descriptors. In effect, type operations such as attribute access, addition, and slicing are available as C function calls, given Python object pointers. See the *Include/abstract.h* file in the 1.3 release (or 1.3 release notes).

## *Trusted Execution*

Python now has the hooks needed to implement "trusted" execution of code. This is a critical feature for WWW scripts since they're downloaded and run locally, when activated (see the section called "Built-in Internet/WWW Tools""). The Python *rexec.py* library module provides an interface to the restricted execution system. Roughly, trusted execution replaces the normal built-in functions with a customized subset. For more details, see recent Python release notes.

### *Interpreter Optimizations*

Ongoing work is being done to optimize the Python interpreter and run-time engine. With release 1.3, function call optimizations have been incorporated.

### *A Third Argument for raise and apply*

In Python 1.3, the *raise* statement supports an optional third argument (after the exception object and extra data). If present, it's assumed to be a *traceback* object, to be used in the stack trace report. It's intended for tools like debuggers, that need to *fake* an exception's context. The *apply* built-in also accepts an optional third parameter for a dictionary of keyword arguments (see Chapter 8, *Adding Text-Based Menus*).

## *And Even More Cool Stuff*

It's impossible to mention all the exciting work being done, and I apologize to those I've missed here. Some systems were mentioned earlier in the book; for instance, the *modulator* tool, *bgen*, SWIG, the *mSQL* database interface, and others. See the list of works in progress in Appendix B, *Futurisms*, and refer to sources mentioned in Chapter 3 for recent developments in the Python world.

Suggested exercise: Pick some of the topics above, and study them further on your own. Most applications mentioned in this appendix are available on the accompanying CD-ROM, are shipped with Python, or are accessible over the Internet. Refer to Chapter 3 for sources of more information. The Python FAQ file is usually the first place to look.

# B

*In this appendix:*
- *"The Bleeding Edge"*
- *Likely Extensions*
- *Longer-Term Possibilities*

# *Futurisms*

## *"The Bleeding Edge"*

This appendix mentions probable future extensions to Python. As this book was being written, there were a number of initiatives underway that seemed likely to become part of future versions of Python. In fact, some of these may already be a part of Python by the time this book is printed.

Although Python's core feature set has stabilized, Python is still an evolving language. Like every language, new features are bound to creep in to Python over time. Because new Python releases are always backward compatible with earlier ones, the examples in this book should work as described on any version of Python, release 1.3 or later. But newer releases will include additional tools not covered here.

Because it's impossible to predict what features will show up in Python in the future, we won't cover these proposed extensions in greater detail here. Python's standard manuals, and the *HISTORY* and *NEWS* files in the distribution tree, can always be consulted for information on recent growth in the language.

## *Likely Extensions*

These initiatives are likely to become a part of Python soon.

### *Tkinter on Microsoft Windows and the Macintosh*

Ports for the *Tkinter* GUI system used in this book for both of these popular platforms were nearing completion as this book was being written; both are already available in beta form. Check the Python FTP or WWW sites or read recent release notes for more information.

## *Numerical Extensions: A Matrix Object, Complex Numbers*

A special interest group of the PSA is implementing a matrix object for Python. The extension will support efficient numerical processing, with performance comparable to optimized C code. Plans include support for a *matrix* C extension-type, *matlib*-style matrix operations, complex numbers, and standard libraries such as *LAPACK* and *FFTPACK* (among others). Jim Fulton's *FDL* (pronounced "fiddle") tool is being employed to automate FORTRAN numeric library integrations. Due to the level of interest in numeric Python work, this enhancement seems certain.

## *Image Processing Extensions*

A special interest group (SIG) of the PSA is exploring ways to implement image processing extensions for Python. Some of this work is based on the proposed numeric extensions (above). Also see the *PIL* package on the CD-ROM.

## *More Interpreter Optimizations*

Optimizing Python is an ongoing process, and a number of suggestions are on the table. For example, the efficiency of the underlying C *malloc* procedure has a significant impact on Python's performance; alternatives are being explored.

## *Python as an OLE Scripting Tool*

The current state of this effort was discussed in Appendix A, *...And Other Cool Stuff*. There's been some interest in making Python an OLE scripting language, using the generic scripting interface to be released initially in the Microsoft Internet Explorer. Roughly, this would allow Python to be used in any product that implements Microsoft's scripting interface. This might eventually include most Windows applications. A similar integration for AppleScript on Macintosh platforms might surface as well.

## *Portable Database Interfaces*

Another PSA SIG is discussing a common database API for Python. If successful, the API will work on a variety of underlying database systems.

## *Simplified Object Reference Management*

There have also been proposals for making temporary management in C extensions simpler. If successful, some reference count management code (*Py_INCREF*, *Py_DECREF*) might become unnecessary. One suggestion involves keeping a temporary pool of objects, reclaimed at regular intervals.

## *Possible Changes in Python 1.4*

Release 1.4 might be out before this book. It will be a minor enhancement, and as usual will be backward compatible with the 1.3 release used in this text. Here are some of the things Guido van Rossum (Python's creator) has considered introducing; of course this is extremely tentative, and subject to change.

*Tkinter*
: New methods to support new functionality in *Tk*

*Tkinter*
: Support for *Tk* 4.1 and *Tcl* 7.5, plus Macintosh and Microsoft Windows ports

*Complex numbers*
: *1j* and *1J* constants, and a *cmath* numeric library

*Exponent syntax*
: *X**Y* may work the same as the current *pow(X, Y)*

*Mapping syntax*
: (Uncertain) *X[1,2,3]* may be the same as *X[(1,2,3)]*: an index, not a slice

And whatever else Guido decides to throw in there :-).

### *Late-breaking news: Python 1.4 beta on the CD-ROM*

The beta 2 release of Python 1.4 was announced just weeks before this book was printed. The source-code package is available on the CD-ROM that accompanies this book.

Since there isn't much new in Python 1.4, the 1.3 executables on the CD should suffice for most purposes. But if you have a C compiler, you can also build a Python 1.4 executable from the source code on the CD (see Chapter 3, *Getting Started*, for build details). And as always, the latest Python 1.4 (and beyond) releases can be found at the Python Internet sites; see Chapter 3 for the URLs.

# *Longer-Term Possibilities*

A number of possible developments have been discussed in the Python forums. Some are more realistic than others, and a few are really just waiting for a developer's attention.

## *bgen Extensions*

The *bgen* tool referred to in Chapter 15, *Embedding Python*, is a work in progress. But the concept of extension module generation from header files is sound and has been used in other extension systems.

## *Persistence Optimizations*

As noted in Chapter 12, *Persistent Information*, the Python 1.2 persistence system is coded in Python, and is really a prototype for a more efficient version. Some discussion is under way.

## *Tighter C++ Interfaces*

Chapter 15, also hinted at the concept of object oriented extension types and automated C++ class interfaces. A variety of work is being done in this area.

## *Visual Python*

There's wide interest in a visual development tool based on Python. The exact details are unclear, but this might include a development IDE (editor, debugger, project manager, etc.) and some sort of GUI layout tool, based on one of the popular GUI API's for Python. Other features (a class browser, etc.) are more open-ended. A preliminary feature wish list has already been drafted; it seems likely that a tool like this will appear, though perhaps as a commercial product.

## *A Python Compiler or Python-to-C Translator*

There's been a good amount of discussion in the Python forums on crafting a Python compiler to optimize performance. Although Python's inventor is doubtful about the performance gains (due to Python's dynamic type system), some work seems likely in this area. One technique discussed would add optional type declarations, to allow a compiler to generate better code. A Python-to-C translator is also an option to a full-blown compiler and may be more attractive to prototype developers. At least one translator is known to be under development at the time this book is being written.

## *A Standard Python GUI*

There's also been interest in selecting a standard Python GUI interface. Another PSA SIG is currently addressing this issue. It recently chose to promote *Tkinter* and *WPY* as portable Python GUI APIs. However, the market (if the freeware world is really a market!) seems to decide these issues on its own. At present, the *Tk* interface is a de facto standard, and now runs on Microsoft Windows and Macintosh platforms, in addition to X Windows. But it's unclear whether any one GUI tool will (or should) dominate.

## A Full-Blown Python OODB System

Object-oriented databases (OODBs) can be constructed with Python's persistence tools but it requires substantial support logic (to manage object identifiers, support latent loading of linked objects, etc.). There's been some talk about how this system might be implemented.

## Got Any Other Ideas?

Again, predicting the future like this is dubious at best. Nearly every week enhancements are discussed in the Python on-line forums. Like most public domain tools, Python development is driven both by its inventor and its users' requirements. Undoubtedly, this is one reason for its popularity.

# A Mini-Reference

*In this appendix:*

- *Python Statements*
- *Built-In Object Types*
- *Syntax Definition*
- *Character String Formatting Codes*
- *Built-In Functions*
- *The sys Module's Contents*
- *Special Attribute Names for Types*
- *Functions in the string Module*
- *Operations by Type Categories*
- *POSIX System-Level Functions*
- *Math Module Functions*

This appendix summarizes prominent language features in Python. Some of the information here was derived from either Guido van Rossum's Python reference manuals or the Python *Quick Reference* prepared originally by Ken Manheimer and expanded by Chris Hoffmann and Anthony Baxter. The *Quick Reference* is available in ASCII, Postscript, and HTML form; it's an excellent supplement, once you've mastered basic concepts. The manuals provide additional details. See the Bibliography for sources. The manuals and quick reference documents are also available on the enclosed CD-ROM.

## Python Statements

The following table and examples summarize Python's statements. A formal syntax definition appears later.

*Table C-1: Common Python statements*

| Statement | Examples |
|---|---|
| Assignment | `curly, moe, larry = 'good', 'bad', 'ugly'` |
| Function/method calls | `stdout.write("spam, ham, toast\n")` |
| Print | `print 1, "spam", 4, 'u',` |
| If/elif/else | `if "python" in text: mail(poster, spam)` |
| For/else | `for peteSake in spam: print peteSake` |
| While/else | `while 1: print 'spam',i;  i=i+1` |
| Break, Continue, Pass | `while 1: pass` |
| Try/except/else, Try/finally | `try: spam() except: print 'spam error'` |
| Raise | `raise overWorked, cause` |
| Import, From | `import chips; from refrigerator import beer` |
| Def, Return | `def f(a, b, c=1, *d): return a+b+c+d[0]` |
| Class | `class subclass(superclass): staticData = []` |
| Global | `def function(): global x, y; x = 'new'` |
| Del | `del spam[k]; del spam[i:j]; del spam.attr` |
| Exec | `exec "import " + moduleName in ldict, gdict` |

## Assignment

```
spam = 'SPAM'                   basic form
spam, ham = 'yum', 'YUM'        same as: spam = 'yum'; ham = 'YUM'
[spam, ham] = ['yum', 'YUM']    same as: spam = 'yum'; ham = 'YUM'
spam = ham = 'lunch'            same as: ham = 'lunch'; spam = ham
```

## Expressions

```
spam(eggs, ham)                 call a function (procedure)
spam.ham(eggs)                  call an object's attribute (method)
spam                            print a value at the command-line
spam < ham and ham != eggs      compound expressions
spam < ham < eggs               chained comparisons (range tests)
```

## Print

```
print spam, ham                 print 2 values separated by a space
print spam, ham,                do the same, but don't add a line-feed
```

## *if* Selections

```
if spam > 10:
    <statements1>               do this if spam is greater than 10
elif ham:
    <statements2>               do this if ham is non-zero or non-empty
```

```
else:
    <statementsN>                        do this if all tests fail
```

## *for Loops*

```
for <variable(s)> in <sequence>:        assign items to variables
    <statements>                        execute the body for each

for spam in breakfast_objects:
    <statements>
    if ham: break
    if eggs: continue
else:
    print 'ham not found'
```

## *while Loops*

```
while <test>:                           loop header test
    <statements>                        loop body, to be repeated

while spam > 0:
    <statements>
    if test: break                      "break" jumps out of a loop early
    if test: continue                   "continue" goes back to the top
else:
    print 'ham not found'               if we didn't run into a "break"
```

## *try and raise*

```
try:
    <statements>                        run code, catch errors here
except <error>, <details>:
    <statements>                        run if error is raised
else:
    <statements>                        else run if no errors raised

raise SpamError                         trigger an exception manually
raise SpamError, details                trigger an exception with data

try:
    <statements>                        execute this, catch errors here
finally:
    <statements>                        run whether there's an exception or not
```

## *import, from*

```
import spamMod                          import a module itself (spamMod.ham)
from spamMod import ham, bacon          copy objects out of a module (ham)
from spamMod import *                   copy everything out of a module (ham)
```

### def and return

```
def <name>(<argument>, <argument>=default, ..., *<vararg>, **<kwarg>):
    <statements>
    return <object/value>                     each call is a new local scope
```

### class

```
class <name> (<superclass>, ...):            classes to inherit attributes from
    <statements>                             the class is a new local scope
    def method(self, <argument>, ...):       methods- functions called through self
        <statements>
```

# Built-In Object Types

Figure C-1 shows how Python's built-in (intrinsic) types are related. Notice that functions, methods, instances, and modules may all be implemented in Python or a C-compatible language. Internally, only functions have a distinct type for C implementations; bound methods reference a function, and C extension modules and types use the same mechanisms as Python.

## Constants and Operations

The following tables and examples summarize common built-in types. Types are categorized according to whether they may be changed in place or not and the operation categories they support.

*Table C-2: Major built-in datatypes*

| Type | Constants | Category | Changes | Typical operations |
|---|---|---|---|---|
| Numbers | 123, 3.14, 0177, 0xFFA, 99L, .2e-5 | Number | Immutable | n + m, n % m, pow(n, m), n & m, n and m, n >> m |
| Strings | '', '123', `x`, "it's", """...""" | Sequence | Immutable | s + s, s[i], s[i:j], s * n, s >= s, s % f, if s: |
| Lists | [], [1, [2, 3]], ["x", (y, z)] | Sequence | Mutable | l+l, l[i], l[i:j], l.sort() l.append(v), l[i]=v, len(l) |
| Tuples | (), (1,), (1,2), ([1, 2], (3, 4)) | Sequence | Immutable | t+t, t[i], t[i:j], o in t, not t, t < t, apply(func,t) |

*Table C-2: Major built-in datatypes (continued)*

| Type | Constants | Category | Changes | Typical operations |
|---|---|---|---|---|
| Dictionaries | `{}`, `{'a':1,'b':2}`, `{1:[], type(x):0}` | Mapping | Mutable | `d['k']`, `d['k'] = v`, `len(d)`, `d.keys()`, `d.items()` |
| Extensions | `constructor call:` file = open(...) | (Any) | (Any) | `operators, methods, members: file.read(), file.close()` |

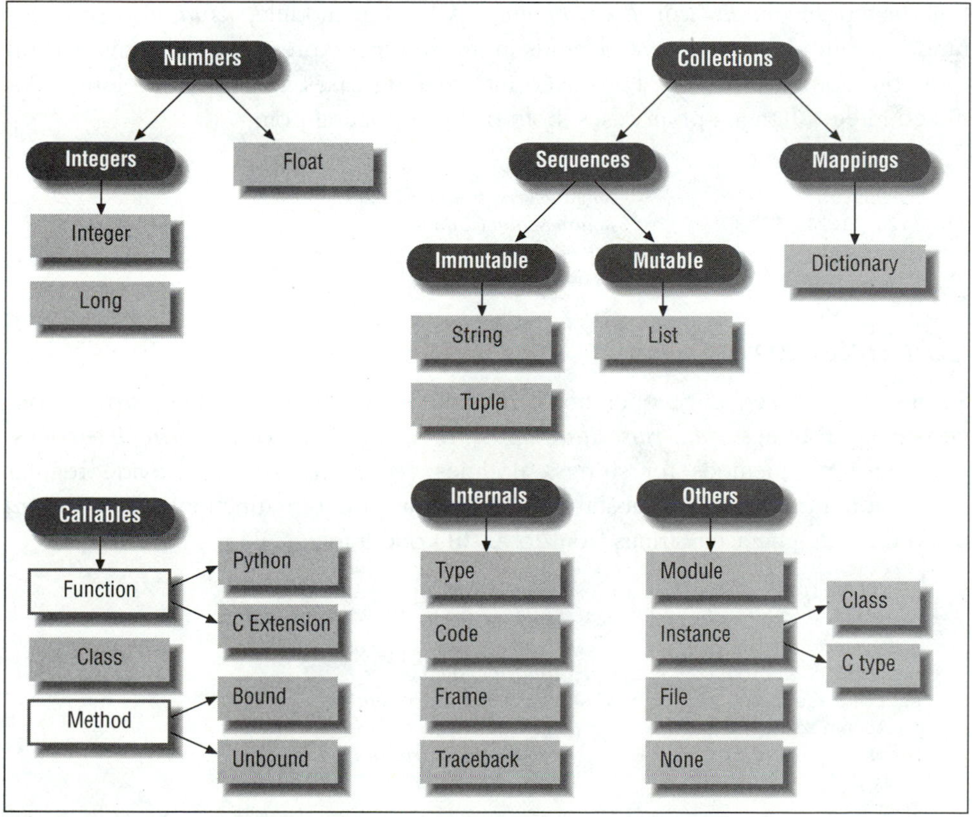


*Figure C-1: Python's type hierarchy*

*Table C-3: Built-in types by categories*

| | Mutable | Immutable |
|---|---|---|
| Number | (None) | Integer, long, float |
| Sequence | List | String, tuple |
| Mapping | Dictionary | (None) |

## Numbers

Python supports all the usual mathematical expression operators ("+", "*", etc.), along with built-in mathematical functions (*abs*, *max*, *pow*), and services in the built-in module *math* (*tan*, *floor*, *pi*, etc.). A built-in module, *rand*, also provides random number generation. Operands in mixed-type expressions are converted up to a common type as in C. For mixed integer/long cases, both become longs. For mixed integer/floating-point cases, both become floating-point.

```
1234                        normal integers (C longs)
99999999L                   long integers (unlimited size)
1.23, 3.14e-10              floating-point (C doubles)
0177                        octal constants
0x9ff                       hexidecimal constants
```

## Character Strings

Strings support sequence operations. An additional built-in module, *string*, contains utility routines: *split*, *rjust*, *find*, *upper*, *atoi*, and many of C's *string.h* services. There are no methods for strings. Modules *regex* and *regsub* provide regular expression matching and substitution for strings. Built-in functions *chr* and *ord* convert single-character strings from/to ASCII code integers.

```
''                               empty strings
s1 = 'spam'                      single quotes
s2 = "spam's"                    double quotes (same as single)
string[i], string[i:j]           indexing, slicing
sstring + string, string * 3     concatenation, repetition
"a %s parrot" % 'dead'           string formatting
block = """Warning:              triple-quotes surround blocks of text
spam
Spam
SPAM!
"""
```

## Lists

Python lists are roughly variable-sized object-reference arrays: they grow and shrink on demand, can be changed in place, support nesting, and can contain any kinds of objects.

| | |
|---|---|
| `[]` | *an empty list* |
| `[0]` | *single-item list* |
| `[0, 1, 2, 3]` | *4-item list: indexes 0..3* |
| `range(4) xrange(0, 4)` | *range() and xrange() make integer lists/tuples* |
| `x in list` | *membership, iteration* |
| `['abc', ['def', 'ghi']]` | *nested sublists* |
| `list[i], list[i:j]` | *indexing, slicing* |
| `list + list, list * 3` | *concatenation, repetition* |
| `list.append(newvalue)` | *growing, methods* |
| `del list[k], list[i:j] = []` | *shrinking* |
| `list[i:j] = [1,2,3]` | *inserting, changing slices* |

## Tuples

Tuples are heterogeneous sequences like lists, but they can't be changed in place.

| | |
|---|---|
| `()` | *an empty tuple* |
| `(0,)` | *a one-item tuple* |
| `(0, 1, 2, 3)` | *4-item tuple* |
| `('abc', ('def', 'ghi'))` | *nested tuples* |
| `tuple[i], tuple[i:j]` | *indexing, slicing* |
| `tuple + tuple, tuple * 3` | *concatenation, repetition* |

## Dictionaries

Dictionaries are Python's associative arrays: objects are stored and fetched by key. In Python, almost any datatype object can be used as a dictionary key (not just strings).

| | |
|---|---|
| `{}` | *an empty dictionary* |
| `{'spam': 2, 'ham': 1, 'eggs': 3}` | *3-item dictionary* |
| `{'pork': {'ham': 'fry', 'brats': 'grill'}}` | *nested dictionaries* |
| `dict['eggs'], dict['pork']['ham']` | *indexing* |
| `dict.has_key('eggs'), dict.keys()` | *dictionary methods* |

## Files

In Python, files are an extension datatype, that's really just a thin integration to C's *stdio* file system.

| | |
|---|---|
| `o = open("/tmp/spam", 'w')` | *create an output file* |
| `i = open('data', 'r')` | *create an input file* |
| `i.read(), i.readline(), i.read(1)` | *read input file, line, or character* |
| `o.write(s), o.writelines(l)` | *write output string or lines* |
| `o.close()` | |

## Others

Extension datatypes are built in but must be imported to be used (for example, arrays, and the *dbm* interface). Python's library manual documents all the extra types (and modules) available.

### Memory management

Python uses a reference count garbage collection strategy to reclaim objects automatically when they're no longer needed (no longer referenced anywhere). This strategy usually works well and avoids pausing programs to collect all at once (some older language implementations reclaim memory only when all space is already exhausted).

However, reference count garbage collectors don't handle circular data structures well (when two objects reference each other); in rare cases, objects must be forcibly deleted using the *del* statement. As we've seen, the burden of managing reference counts also falls on C extensions that receive ownership of Python objects from the Python API. But Python's scheme ensures that objects exported to C are not deleted too soon.

## Built-In Type Methods

Python types respond to operators and/or method calls. Some have dedicated processing modules. Here's a summary for major built-in types with callable methods.

### Lists

List methods are mostly used to implement in-place changes (though assignment to indexes and slices often achieves similar effects). Some methods provide fast, C-coded implementations of common operations.

*Table C-4: List methods*

| Method | Description |
|---|---|
| *list.append(x)* | Insert object *x* at the end of the list |
| *list.sort(test?)* | Sort list in place, in ascending order (or per a passed-in compare function: –1, 0, 1) |
| *list.reverse()* | Reverse items in list in place |
| *list.index(x)* | Return the offset of the first occurrence of object *x* in list (exception if not found) |
| *list.insert(i, x)* | Insert object *x* into list, at offset i (*like list[i:i] = [x]*) |

*Table C-4: List methods (continued)*

| Method | Description |
|---|---|
| *list.count(x)* | Return the number of occurrences of *x* in list |
| *list.remove(x)* | Delete the first occurrence of object *x* from list (exception if not found) |

## *Dictionaries*

Dictionary methods convert dictionary entries to lists and provide key membership testing (the *in* sequence membership test operator doesn't work, because dictionaries are unordered).

*Table C-5: Dictionary methods*

| Method | Description |
|---|---|
| *dict.has_key(k)* | Return *true* if dict has a key *k*, or false otherwise |
| *dict.keys()* | A new list holding all of *dict*'s keys |
| *dict.values()* | A new list holding all of the stored values in *dict* |
| *dict.items()* | A new list of tuple pairs: *(key, value)*, one for each entry in *dict* |

## *Files*

File objects are created with the *open(name, mode)* built-in function; there's no special syntax for objects. File methods provide the usual input/output operations plus a few peripheral actions. Data transfer uses Python strings: the *read* methods all return a string object with the characters read (or an empty string at EOF), and the *write* methods write the characters in a passed-in string object.

If the file is opened in binary mode (*b*), the strings may contain nonprintable character codes. All file access is based on method calls, not expression operators (though wrapper classes can add this). Files are a preimported C extension type. *IOError* is raised on all file-related errors.

*Table C-6: File methods*

| Method | Description |
|---|---|
| *file.read(size?)* | Read at most *size* characters from file, or all upto EOF if bytes is absent |
| *file.readline()* | Read the next complete line, up to and including the *\n* marker |
| *file.readlines()* | Read all (remaining) lines all at once, into a list of strings |
| *file.write(string)* | Write the string to the external file exactly as is |

*Table C-6: File methods (continued)*

| Method | Description |
|---|---|
| *file.writelines(list)* | Write all string in the list to the file, without adding *\n* separators |
| *file.close()* | Close the file, in the operating system (the Python file object endures) |
| *file.tell()* | Return the file's current position (like C's *ftell*) |
| *file.seek(offset, whence)* | Set the current file position for random access (C's *fseek*: see Chapter 12, *Persistent Information*) |
| *file.isatty()* | Return *true* if the file is connected to a *tty*-like device (interactive device) |
| *file.flush()* | Flush the file's *stdio* buffer (C's *fflush*); sometimes needed for *pipes* |

# Syntax Definition

The following BNF-like definition of Python's syntax was derived from the file *Grammar/Grammar*, in the Python source tree directory. It's used as input to Python's parser generator system.

## Grammar Conventions

The grammar rules below use the following symbol/operator forms.

xxx: . . .
: The definition of nonprimitive production rule *xxx*.

xxx
: A reference to a nonprimitive (i.e., a nested component).

'xxx'
: A literal occurrence of characters *xxx* (shown in boldface).

xxx*
: Means *xxx* repeated zero or more times.

xxx+
: Means repeat *xxx* one or more times (not optional).

[xxx]
: Means *xxx* is optional.

xxx | yyy
: Means a selection of *xxx* or *yyy* (concatenation is the default, and binds tighter).

(xxx)
: Groups a series of symbols.

## *Primitive Tokens*

The following symbols are analyzed by the character scanner.

NAME
: Variable name (see Chapter 4, *Writing Basic Shell Tools*, for rules).

NUMBER
: Numeric constant.

STRING
: Character string constant.

NEWLINE
: The end of a line ("\n").

ENDMARKER
: The end of a file (or string).

INDENT
: Indentation (handled by the character scanner).

DEDENT
: Stop indentation (also in the character scanner).

## *Top-Level ("start") Symbols*

Python parses any of the following three constructs, depending on the code's context.

single_input
: A single interactive statement (in the *python* command line).

file_input
: A module or sequence of commands read from an input file (or embedded statements).

eval_input
: The input for the *eval()* and *input()* functions (or embedded expression code).

## Grammar Rules

The following rules define the Python language. Syntax errors raise a *SyntaxError* exception when the offending code is read (imported, typed interactively, or run embedded). Some expressions are legal syntactically but not semantically and are disqualified by the interpreter after the parse. For instance:

- In assignments, additional restrictions are enforced by the interpreter.
- The compiler also checks that the default (empty) *except* clause is last in a *try*.
- *access_stmt* isn't implemented; along with *accesstype*, it's officially "deprecated."
- *argument* is really interpreted to mean: `[keyword '='] test`.

### Top level

```
single_input:  NEWLINE | simple_stmt | compound_stmt NEWLINE

file_input:    (NEWLINE | stmt)* ENDMARKER

eval_input:    testlist NEWLINE* ENDMARKER
```

### Statements

```
stmt:           simple_stmt | compound_stmt

simple_stmt:    small_stmt (';' small_stmt)* [';'] NEWLINE

small_stmt:     expr_stmt | print_stmt  | del_stmt    | pass_stmt    |
                flow_stmt | import_stmt | global_stmt | access_stmt  | exec_stmt

compound_stmt:  if_stmt | while_stmt | for_stmt | try_stmt | funcdef | classdef
```

#### Simple statements.

```
expr_stmt:       testlist ('=' testlist)*

print_stmt:      'print' (test ',')* [test]

del_stmt:        'del' exprlist

pass_stmt:       'pass'

flow_stmt:       break_stmt | continue_stmt | return_stmt | raise_stmt

break_stmt:      'break'
```

```
continue_stmt:   'continue'

return_stmt:     'return' [testlist]

raise_stmt:      'raise' test [',' test [',' test]]

import_stmt:     'import' dotted_name (',' dotted_name)* |
                 'from' dotted_name 'import' ('*' | NAME (',' NAME)*)

dotted_name:     NAME ('.' NAME)*

global_stmt:     'global' NAME (',' NAME)*

access_stmt:     'access' ('*' | NAME (',' NAME)*) ':' accesstype  (',' accesstype)*

accesstype:      NAME+

exec_stmt:       'exec' expr ['in' test [',' test]]
```

*Compound statements.*

```
if_stmt:         'if' test ':' suite ('elif' test ':' suite)* ['else' ':' suite]

while_stmt:      'while' test ':' suite ['else' ':' suite]

for_stmt:        'for' exprlist 'in' testlist ':' suite ['else' ':' suite]

try_stmt:        'try' ':' suite (except_clause ':' suite)+ ['else' ':' suite] |
                 'try' ':' suite 'finally' ':' suite

except_clause:   'except' [test [',' test]]

classdef:        'class' NAME ['(' testlist ')'] ':' suite

funcdef:         'def' NAME parameters ':' suite

parameters:      '(' [varargslist] ')'

varargslist:     (fpdef ['=' test] ',')*
                 ('*' NAME [',' '*' '*' NAME] | '*' '*' NAME) |
                 fpdef ['=' test] (',' fpdef ['=' test])* [',']

fpdef:           NAME | '(' fplist ')'

fplist:          fpdef (',' fpdef)* [',']

suite:           simple_stmt | NEWLINE INDENT stmt+ DEDENT
```

## *Expressions*

```
test:            and_test ('or' and_test)* | lambdef

and_test:        not_test ('and' not_test)*
```

```
not_test:        'not' not_test | comparison

comparison:      expr (comp_op expr)*

comp_op:         '<' | '>' | '==' | '>=' | '<=' | '<>' | '!=' |
                 'in' | 'not' 'in' | 'is' | 'is' 'not'

expr:            xor_expr ('|' xor_expr)*

xor_expr:        and_expr ('^' and_expr)*

and_expr:        shift_expr ('&' shift_expr)*

shift_expr:      arith_expr (('<<' | '>>') arith_expr)*

arith_expr:      term (('+' | '-') term)*

term:            factor (('*' | '/' | '%') factor)*

factor:          ('+' | '-' | '~') factor |  atom trailer*
```

*Basic components.*

```
atom:            '(' [testlist] ')' | '[' [testlist] ']' | '{' [dictmaker] '}' | '`'
                 testlist '`' | NAME | NUMBER | STRING+

trailer:         '(' [arglist] ')' | '[' subscript ']' | '.' NAME

arglist:         argument (',' argument)* [',']

argument:        [test '='] test

subscript:       test | [test] ':' [test]

exprlist:        expr (',' expr)* [',']

testlist:        test (',' test)* [',']

dictmaker:       test ':' test (',' test ':' test)* [',']

lambdef:         'lambda' [varargslist] ':' test
```

# Name/Scope Rules

*Assignment*

Creates a new variable if it doesn't yet exist, and considers names in functions and classes to be local variables unless they're declared in *global* statements.

*Reference*

Raises an exception if the variable hasn't been assigned yet and uses the closest occurrence found by searching at most three scopes: local, global, and then built-in.

*Qualification*

Attribute qualification (*object.attr, getattr(object, attr)*) only searches the namespace of the qualified object (plus higher classes, if the object is a class or class-instance). Attribute assignment (*object.attr = value, setattr(object, attr, value)*) creates the attribute in the object's own namespace if it doesn't yet exist.

See Part 2, *Language Fundamentals*, for more details.

## Reserved Words

Python reserves the following words. They can't be used as variable names in your programs, and must be typed as shown (lowercase).

*Table C-7: Reserved words*

| | | | |
|---|---|---|---|
| *access* | *and* | *break* | *class* |
| *continue* | *def* | *del* | *elif* |
| *else* | *except* | *exec* | *finally* |
| *for* | *from* | *global* | *if* |
| *import* | *in* | *is* | *lambda* |
| *not* | *or* | *pass* | *print* |
| *raise* | *return* | *try* | *while* |

## Operator Precedence

Operator binding is implied by the grammar rules above: operators lower in the rule call chain bind tighter. In the following table, precedence increases (operators bind stronger) moving down. Within a precedence level, operators group left to right (but comparisons group right to left). As usual, parentheses override the default binding rules. The same precedence is used if you overload operators in classes and extension types; as in C++, we can't add new operators, only intercept those already built in to the language.

*Table C-8: Operator precedence*

| Operators | Description |
|---|---|
| *x or y, lambda* | Logical "or" (*y* is only evaluated if *x* is false) |
| *x and y* | Logical "and" (*y* is only evaluated if *x* is true) |
| *not x* | Logical negation |
| <, <=, >, >=, = =, <>, !=, *is, is not, in, not in* | Comparison operators, sequence membership |
| *x \| y* | Bitwise "or" |
| *x ^ y* | Bitwise "exclusive or" |
| *x & y* | Bitwise "and" |
| *x << y, x >> y* | Shift *x* left or right by *y* bits |
| *x + y, x - y* | Addition/concatenation, subtraction |
| *x * y, x / y, x % y* | Multiply/repetition, divide, remainder/format |
| *-x, +x, ~x* | Unary negation, identity, bitwise compliment |
| *x[i], x[i:j], x.y, x(. . .)* | Indexing, slicing, qualification, function calls |
| (. . .), [. . .], {. . .}, ` . . . ` | Tuple, list, dictionary, string conversion |

# *Character String Escape Codes*

The following backslash escape codes can be used to embed special characters in Python character string constants. The octal/hex escapes provide for arbitrary character codes. Note: the null character ("\0") is not used to terminate Python strings; Python records a string's end internally. Null can be embedded in Python strings, but they're not as important as in C.

*Table C-9: Character escapes*

| | | | |
|---|---|---|---|
| *newline* | Ignored (continuation) | *n* | Linefeed (LF) |
| \\ | Backslash (\) | *v* | Vertical tab (VT) |
| \' | Single quote (') | *t* | Horizontal tab (TAB) |
| \" | Double quote (") | *r* | Carriage return (CR) |
| *a* | Bell (BEL) | *f* | Formfeed (FF) |
| *b* | Backspace (BS) | *0XX* | Octal value |
| *e* | Escape (ESC) | *xXX* | Hex value |
| \0 | null (not end-of-string) | *other* | Any other char |

# *Character String Formatting Codes*

The format string on the right of a "%" string operator can contain the following "%" conversion codes:

*Table C-10: String format codes*

| | | | |
|---|---|---|---|
| s | String/object | X | Hex int (upper) |
| c | Character | e | Floating-point-1 |
| d | Decimal (int) | E | Floating-point-2 |
| i | Integer | f | Floating-point-3 |
| u | Unsigned (int) | g | Floating-point-4 |
| o | Octal integer | G | Floating-point-5 |
| x | Hex integer | % | Literal "%" |

A `%` in the format string introduces an object-to-string conversion code in this table. For instance:

```
"the %s" % 'Guido'
```

creates a string object "the Guido". When more than one conversion code appears, Python accepts a *tuple* of arguments on the right: `%s %s % (spam, eggs)`. Python also allows values in a dictionary to be named in the format string before the convert code:

```
"%(lang)s has %(num)03d quotes" % {'num':4, 'lang':'Python'}
```

makes the string "Python has 004 quotes". The `%s` code actually accepts any Python object, and converts it to a string using the *str()* built-in (provided the type implements *str* operations).

Python understands the usual width and precision arguments; both may be `*`, to refer to an integer in the arguments tuple. Standard flag prefix characters are also understood: `-` (left-justify), `+` (numeric sign), `0` (zero-fill), blank, and `#`. The full conversion code specification looks something like this; parts in braces are optional:

```
"%[flags][(name)][<width>][.<precision>]<code>"
```

Roughly, Python's `%` works like C's *sprintf* function. For more details on all these conversions, check the manpage for *printf* on your system or see a C text (or try these interactively in Python). Some C conversions don't map directly to Python; for instance *c* converts a one-character string (not a C *char*), and there's only one floating-point type (C's *double*). ANSI directives `%p` and `%n` are not supported.

## *Built-In Exceptions*

Python raises the following exception types in response to various events. They may be caught in *try* statements or allowed to pass (and eventually abort the program, with an error trace). All these names are built in: they don't need to be imported. To see an up-to-date listing, run a *dir(__builtin__)* call.

*Table C-11: Built-in exceptions*

| Name | Description |
|---|---|
| *AttributeError* | Attribute reference or assignment failure |
| *EOFError* | Immediate end-of-file hit by *input()* or *raw_input()* |
| *IOError* | I/O or file-related operation failure |
| *ImportError* | Failure of *import* to find module or attribute |
| *IndexError* | Out-of-range sequence subscript |
| *KeyError* | Reference to a nonexistent mapping (dictionary) key |
| *KeyboardInterrupt* | User entry of the interrupt key (often *Control-C*) |
| *MemoryError* | Recoverable memory exhaustion |
| *NameError* | Failure to find a local or global (unqualified) name |
| *OverflowError* | Excessively large arithmetic operation |
| *RuntimeError* | Obsolete catch-all; define a suitable error instead |
| *SyntaxError* | Parser encountering a syntax error |
| *SystemError* | Nonfatal interpreter error/bug (report it) |
| *SystemExit* | On *sys.exit()* call (exit may be aborted) |
| *TypeError* | Passing inappropriate type to operation or function |
| *ValueError* | Argument error not covered by *TypeError* or other |
| *ZeroDivisionError* | Division or modulus operation with zero as right operand |

## *Built-In Functions*

The following table lists the functions that are always available in Python, without imports. They all reside in the `__builtin__` module, which is always searched last under Python's scoping rules (which is like being preimported into every module). Python uses built-in functions for general operations (*raw_input*); operators and methods are used for type-specific operations (*list + list*, *list.append*). See the Python library reference or *Quick Reference* for more details on particular functions.

*Table C-12: Built-in functions*

| Function | Description |
|---|---|
| *abs(x)* | Return the absolute value of a number |
| *apply(func, args, kwdict?)* | Call function with argument tuple, keyword dictionary; *result=func(args . . .)* |
| *callable(x)* | Return 1 if *x* is callable; otherwise, return 0 |
| *chr(i)* | Return a one-character string holding the ASCII code *i* |
| *cmp(x, y)* | Return negative, zero, or positive: *x* is less than, equal, or greater than *y* |
| *coerce(x, y)* | Return a tuple with *x* and *y* converted to a common type |
| *compile(string, label, kind)* | Compile string into a code object; `kind=eval` or `exec`; `label=message` |
| *delattr(object, name)* | Delete named attribute from object (like: *del object.name*) |
| *dir(object?)* | Return a list of the attribute names in object, or the caller's local scope |
| *divmod(a, b)* | Return a tuple: *(a / b, a % b)* |
| *eval(code, global?, local?)* | Evaluate expression (string or code) in caller's scope, or passed dictionaries |
| *exec(code, global?, local?)* | Run statements (string, code, or file object); no result; also is a statement |
| *execfile(file, global?, local?)* | Run a named file of code in the caller's scope, or the passed-in dictionaries |
| *filter(func, list)* | Return list of items in *list* for which the call *func(item)* returns true |
| *float(x)* | Convert to floating-point |
| *getattr(object, name)* | Get a named attribute's value from object (name can be computed) |
| *globals()* | Return enclosing module's namespace dictionary |
| *hasattr(object, name)* | True if object has an attribute called name |
| *hash(object)* | Return the hash value of the object (if any) |
| *hex(x)* | Convert *x* to a hexadecimal string representation (a new string) |
| *id(object)* | Return the unique identity integer for the object (its address in memory) |
| *input(prompt?)* | Read and evaluate *stdin* input (show prompt first, if passed) |
| *int(x)* | Convert to an integer object |
| *len(x)* | The number of items in a collection (sequence, mapping, user-defined) |
| *locals( )* | Return local-scope dictionary |

*Table C–12: Built-in functions (continued)*

| Function | Description |
|---|---|
| *long(x)* | Convert to a long (unlimited precision) integer |
| *map(function, list,..)* | Return a list of results, of calling function (or None) on each item in list(s) |
| *max(s)* | Return the maximum value in a sequence |
| *min(s)* | Return the minimum value in a sequence |
| *oct(x)* | Convert to an octal string representation |
| *open(name, mode?, bufsz?)* | Make/connect a file object; mode defaults to *r*, *bufsz* is optional |
| *ord(c)* | Return ASCII integer code for a one-character string |
| *pow(x, y, z?)* | Raise *x* to the power *y*; if *z* passed, the result is *pow(x, y) % z*, quickly |
| *range(start?, end, step?)* | Make a list of consecutive integers up to end; start/step default to 0/+1 |
| *raw_input(prompt?)* | Read a string (line) from stdin input, stripping the *n* at the end |
| *reduce(func, list, init?)* | Apply func to successive pairs of list items; result starts as init if passed |
| *reload(module)* | Reimport a previously imported module file, replacing prior attributes |
| *repr(x)* | String representation of an object; same as backquotes: 'x' |
| *round(x, n?)* | Round floating-point *x* to *n* digits after the decimal point; *n* defaults to 0 |
| *setattr(object, name, value)* | Assign an attribute in object by name (like: object.name = value) |
| *str(x)* | Specially formatted printable string representation of object |
| *tuple(sequence)* | Convert a sequence to a tuple (see Chapter 13, *Implementing Objects*) |
| *type(object)* | The type of object (object's associated type object) |
| *vars(object?)* | Caller's local scope dictionary, or the namespace dictionary of object |
| *xrange(start, end, step)* | Like range, but generated integers (instead of making a list all at once) |

# *Built-In Modules*

Python comes with many precoded modules. Functionally they provide services that aren't intrinsic to the language itself (i.e., beyond intrinsic types, and built-in functions). Some modules are written in Python (in the *Lib* directory), some are C extension modules and/or types, and some are Python/C combinations.

The next table summarizes the most commonly-used built-in modules. In the table, *standard* means a module implemented in Python, and *built-in* denotes a C module (though this is prone to change). As the table shows, some modules are specific to a platform or extension.

### *On shooting at a moving target*

This set varies frequently and can even be changed at each site when Python's installed. For instance, some modules currently classified as demos, contributions, or extensions will almost certainly become standard modules shipped with Python in the future (*rpc*, *xdr*, the *wpy* GUI, etc.). Others may arise from special interest groups (a "matrix" type).

Because of that, this list should be taken as a "snapshot" of 1.3 modules. For up-to-date information, see the library reference manual. The manual and quick-reference list the contents of each module, which we won't document here. Some are illustrated elsewhere in this text; see the index. And technically, every module file in Python's *Lib*, *Tools*, and *Demo* directories is a standard Python module; see your Python install tree.

*Table C–13: Major built-in modules*

| **Module** | **Kind** | **Description** |
|---|---|---|
| Basics | | |
| *sys* | Built-in | Interpreter parameters and functions (see table below) |
| *types* | Standard | Constants for all built-in types (names type( ) results) |
| *traceback* | Standard | Print or fetch stack traceback objects |
| *pickle* | Standard | Convert Python objects to/from byte streams |
| *shelve* | Standard | Python persistent object stores (uses *pickle*) |
| *copy* | Standard | Shallow and deep copy operations (uses *pickle*) |
| *marshal* | Built-in | Convert Python objects to/from byte streams (constrained) |
| *imp* | Built-in | Access to import implementation |
| `__builtin__` | Built-in | Access to all built-in python identifiers |
| `__main__` | Built-in | Namespace of the top-level module: interpreter, script |

*Table C-13: Major built-in modules (continued)*

| Module | Kind | Description |
|---|---|---|
| Strings | | |
| *string* | Standard | More string operations and constants (uses built-in C *strop* module) |
| *regex* | Built-in | Regular expression matching operations |
| *regsub* | Standard | Regular expression substitution and splitting functions |
| *struct* | Built-in | Interpret strings as packed binary data (C *structs*) |
| *strop* | Built-in | The hidden C implementation of *string* module operations (use string) |
| Various | | |
| *math* | Built-in | Mathematical functions, defined by C standard: *sin, floor, sqrt, pi,* etc. |
| *rand* | Standard | Integer pseudo-random integer generator, like C *rand()* |
| *whrandom* | Standard | Wichmann-Hill floating-point pseudo-random number generator |
| *array* | Built-in | Type to efficiently representing arrays of uniform numeric-type values |
| Generic OS tools | | |
| *os* | Standard | Portable interface to OS dependent functionality |
| *time* | Built-in | Time-related functions (standard C library functions: time, sleep, etc.) |
| *getopt* | Standard | Parse command-line arguments in sys.argv; (like: UNIX *getopt*) |
| *tempfile* | Standard | Generate a temporary file name |
| Optional OS tools | | |
| *signal* | Built-in | Set handlers for asynchronous events (IPC: process signals) |
| *socket* | Built-in | Access to BSD socket interface (IPC: low-level networking) |
| *select* | Built-in | Access to UNIX select multiplex file synchronization (IPC) |
| *thread* | Built-in | Low-level primitives for working with process threads |
| UNIX OS tools | | |
| *posix* | Built-in | Standardized POSIX UNIX system calls (use *os* earlier) |
| *posixpath* | Standard | POSIX pathname functions (use *os* above) |
| *pwd* | Built-in | Access to the UNIX password database |
| *grp* | Built-in | Interface to UNIX group database |
| *dbm* | Built-in | Dictionary/file-like interface to UNIX *ndbm* database library |

*Table C-13: Major built-in modules (continued)*

| Module | Kind | Description |
|---|---|---|
| *gdbm* | Built-in | Dictionary/file-like interface to GNU's *dbm*-like database library |
| *anydbm* | Standard | Generic interface to *dbm* extensions (uses installed variant) |
| *bsddb* | Built-in | Interface to the BSD *db* keyed-access file library |
| *curses* | Built-in | Interface to the *ncurses* library, for character-based interfaces |
| *termios* | Built-in | POSIX-style tty control |
| *fcntl* | Built-in | *fcntl()* and *ioctl()* system calls |
| *posixfile* | Standard | Filelike object with support for locking |
| Other tools | | |
| *pdb* | Standard | Text-oriented (command-line) debugger |
| *wdb* | Standard | Window-oriented debugger (requires *STDWIN API*) |
| *profile* | Standard | Python source code profiler |
| *pstats* | Standard | Python code profiler utility for viewing statistics files |
| *dis* | Standard | Python byte-code disassembler |
| *glob* | Standard | Filename globbing (like: UNIX shell filename expansion) |
| *grep* | Standard | File string search (like: UNIX *grep* shell command) |
| *util* | Standard | Miscellaneous functions that don't belong elsewhere |
| Internet tools | | |
| *cgi* | Standard | Interpret WWW forms in server-side scripts |
| *urllib* | Standard | Open an arbitrary object given its URL (requires sockets) |
| *httplib* | Standard | HTTP protocol clients (requires sockets) |
| *ftplib* | Standard | FTP protocol client (requires sockets) |
| *gopherlib* | Standard | Gopher protocol clients (requires sockets) |
| *nntplib* | Standard | NNTP protocol clients (requires sockets) |
| *urlparse* | Standard | Parse a URL string into a tuple |
| *htmllib* | Standard | A parser for HTML files (WWW hypertext markup language) |
| *sgmllib* | Standard | As much of a SGML parser as needed to parse HTML |
| *rfc822* | Standard | A parser for RFC 822-style mail headers |
| *mimetools* | Standard | Tools for parsing MIME-style message headers |
| Multimedia tools | | |
| *audioop* | Built-in | Useful operations on sound fragments |
| *imageop* | Built-in | Useful operations on images |
| *aifc* | Standard | Access to audio files in AIFF or AIFC format |
| *jpeg* | Built-in | Access to JPEG image compressor and decompressor |

*Table C-13: Major built-in modules (continued)*

| Module | Kind | Description |
|---|---|---|
| *rgbimg* | Built-in | Access SGI RGB image files (not SGI specific) |
| Cryptography | | |
| *md5* | Built-in | Interface to RSA's MD5 message digest algorithm |
| *mpz* | Built-in | Interface to integer part of GNU multiple precision library |
| *rotor* | Built-in | Implementation of a rotor-based (Enigma) encryption algorithm |
| GUI interfaces | | |
| *Tkinter* | Standard | Python class-based interface to the *Tk* GUI API (uses *tkinter* module) |
| *tkinter* | Built-in | The hidden C extension module used by *Tkinter* (not for import) |
| *stdwin* | Built-in | Guido's *STDWIN* standard window system interface |
| *stdwinevents* | Standard | STDWIN event, command, and selection constants |
| *rect* | Standard | *STDWIN* rectangle manipulation operations |
| Other | | |
| SGI IRIX | n/a[a] | See the library manual |
| Macintosh | n/a | See the library manual |
| Windows/MFC | n/a | See the win32 extensions/port documentation |
| Linux | n/a | Most UNIX tools work, but see the Lib/Linux directory too |
| sunaudiodev | n/a | Access to sun (SunOS) audio interface |

[a] n/a = not applicable

# *The sys Module's Contents*

Since the built-in *sys* module is pervasive, the following table describes its exports.

*Table C-14: sys module exports*

| Attribute | Description |
|---|---|
| *argv* | List of: *[command, arguments . . . ]* passed to a Python script |
| *builtin_module_names* | List of names of modules compiled in Python |
| *exc_type* | Type of exception being handled (when an exception has been raised) |
| *exc_value* | Exception's parameter (raise's second argument: *extra data*) |
| *exc_traceback* | Exception's traceback object |
| *exit(status)* | Exit from Python process with status, by raising *SystemExit* |

*Table C-14: sys module exports (continued)*

| Attribute | Description |
|---|---|
| *exitfunc* | Assign a function to register an action to be called on exit (no args) |
| *getrefcount(object)* | Returns object's current reference count |
| *last_type* | Type of last unhandled exception |
| *last_value* | Value of last unhandled exception |
| *last_traceback* | Traceback object for last unhandled exception |
| *modules* | Dictionary of modules already loaded; writeable (to force reload) |
| *path* | List of strings specifying module load search path; writeable |
| *platform* | String identifying the system Python runs on: *sunos5*, *linux1*, etc. |
| *ps1* | String specifying primary prompt, if interactive; defaults to >>> |
| *ps2* | String specifying secondary prompt, if interactive; defaults to . . . |
| *setcheckinterval(reps)* | Set how often the interpreter checks for periodic tasks |
| *settrace(func)* | Set the system trace function: the hook used by debuggers, etc. |
| *setprofile(func)* | Set the system profile function: the profiler's hook (not each line) |
| *stdin* | Standard input file object; changeable; interpreter input |
| *stdout* | Standard output file object; changeable; some prompts, print |
| *stderr* | Standard error file object; changeable; interpreter prompts/errors |
| *tracebacklimit* | Maximum number of traceback levels to print; defaults to 1000 (!) |

## *Special Attribute Names for Types*

The next table summarizes some of the special built-in attributes of various built-in types. Note that these are different from the special method-names used in classes (see below), though they use the same double-underscore naming convention. Attributes of internal object types (code, frames, tracebacks) aren't shown; consult the language reference manual.

*Table C-15: Special type members*

| Attribute | Type(s) | Description |
|---|---|---|
| *object*.`__name__` | Module, class | The string name of module and class objects |
| *object*.`__dict__` | Module, class, instance | Dictionary used to store an object's writeable attributes |
| *object*.`__methods__` | Type instance | List of object's methods (name-strings) |
| *object*.`__members__` | Some type instances | List of object's data members (name-strings) |
| *object*.`__class__` | Class instance | Class object from which an instance was created |
| *object*.`__bases__` | Class | Tuple of object's base classes (immediate superclasses) |
| *func.func_code* | Function/method | Code object representing compiled function body |
| *func.func_globals* | Function/method | Global namespace dictionary (of enclosing module) |
| *method.im_self* | Instance methods | Implied instance object of a bound method |
| *method.im_func* | Instance methods | Associated function object for the method |

# *Functions in the string Module*

Another commonly used module is *string*: the extra string operations module. Since strings are immutable, all functions that modify the string return a new string object. Here's a summary of the callable functions it exports (it also exports string constants not shown here).

*Table C-16: String module functions*

| Function | Description |
|---|---|
| *atof(s)* | Convert string to floating-point |
| *atoi(s, base?)* | Convert string to integer, of given base (default 10) |
| *atol(s, base?)* | Convert string to a Python long integer (unlimited precision) |
| *expandtabs(s, tabsize)* | Replace tabs by one or more spaces |
| *find(s, sub, start?)* | Find the first occurrence of string *sub* in *s*, starting at *start* (default 0) |
| *rfind(s, sub, start?)* | Like *find*, but scan from the end (right to left, higher to lower indices) |

*Table C-16: String module functions (continued)*

| Function | Description |
|---|---|
| *index(s, sub, start?)* | Like find, but raise *ValueError* if not found, instead of returning –1 |
| *rindex(s, sub, start?)* | Like rfind, but raise *ValueError* if not found, instead of returning –1 |
| *count(s, sub, start?)* | Count the number of non-overlapping occurrences of *sub* in *s* |
| *split(s)* | Return a list of the whitespace-delimited words in *s* |
| *splitfields(s, sep)* | Return a list if the words in *s* separated by string *sep* occurrences |
| *join(x)* | Concatenate a list or tuple of strings, adding spaces between |
| *joinfields(x, sep)* | Like *join*, but add *sep* strings between the joined words in *x* |
| *strip(s)* | Remove leading and trailing whitespace from *s* |
| *swapcase(s)* | Convert lowercase to uppercase, and vice versa |
| *upper(s)* | Convert letters to uppercase |
| *lower(s)* | Convert letters to lowercase |
| *ljust(s, width)* | Left-justify the string in a field of the given width, pad with spaces (or: `%`) |
| *rjust(s, width)* | Right-justify the string in a field of the given width, pad with spaces (or: `%`) |
| *center(s, width)* | Center the string in a field of the given width, pad with spaces (or: `%`) |
| *zfill(s, width)* | Pad s on the left with zero digits, until it's of the desired width (or: `%`) |

# Operations by Type Categories

The following tables list the operations common to types of various categories. They omit boolean (`and`, `or`) and comparison (`!=`, `>`) operators because they work on every type. Note that some of these are specific to built-in types only. For instance, the *append* method is implemented for lists, but there's no requirement that user-defined mutable sequence types must implement such a method.

Also notice that these tables only list instance methods and operators. A more complete operation summary would also include type-specific modules (*math*, *string*, *regex*), and unique operations for each type (`%` string formatting, `x` string conversions, etc.). See other tables in this appendix for relevant methods and functions.

Special class methods are shown only for operators and most relevant built-in functions (not for type-specific methods). There are more specially named class methods than shown in these tables: see Chapter 13. All the class methods here also have C extension type descriptor slot counterparts; see Chapter 14, *Extending Python*.

*Table C-17: Operations for numbers—integer, long, float*

| Operations | Description | Class methods |
|---|---|---|
| *x + y, x - y* | Add, subtract | `__add__`, `__sub__` |
| *x * y, x / y, x % y* | Multiply, divide, remainder | `__mul__`, `__div__`, `__mod__` |
| *-x , +x* | Negative, identity | `__neg__`, `__pos__` |
| *abs(x)* | Absolute value | `__abs__` |
| *int(x)* | Convert to integer | `__int__` |
| *long(x)* | Convert to long integer | `__long__` |
| *float(x)* | Convert to float | `__float__` |
| *divmod(x)* | Divide/remainder tuple | `__divmod__` |
| *pow(x, y)* | Raise to a power | `__pow__` |
| $x \mid y$, *x ^ y, x & y* | Bitwise or, and, exclusive-or (integers) | `__or__`, `__xor__`, `__and__` |
| *x << n, x >> n* | Bitwise leftshift, rightshift (integers) | `__lshift__`, `__rshift__` |
| *~x* | Bitwise invert (integers) | `__invert__` |

*Table C-18: Operations for mappings—dictionary*

| Operations | Description | Class method |
|---|---|---|
| *len(d)* | Length: number stored items | `__len__` |
| *d[k]* | Index by key | `__getitem__` |
| *d[k] = x* | Change (or create) key entry | `__setitem__` |
| *del d[k]* | Delete item by key | `__delitem__` |
| *d.items()* | (key, value) list | n/a[a] |
| *d.keys()* | Keys list | n/a |
| *d.values()* | Values list | n/a |
| *d.has_key(x)* | Key membership test | n/a |

[a] n/a = not applicable

*Table C-19: Operations for all sequences—list, tuple, string*

| Operations | Description | Class method |
|---|---|---|
| *x in s, x not in s* | Membership tests | `__getitem__` |
| *for n in x:* | Iteration | `__getitem__` |
| *s + s* | Concatenation | `__add__` |
| *s * n, n * s* | Repetition | `__mul__` |
| *s[i]* | Index by offset | `__getitem__` |
| *s[i:j]* | Slicing | `__getslice__` |
| *len(s)* | Length | `__len__` |
| *min(s)* | Minimum | n/a[a] |
| *max(s)* | Maximum | n/a |

[a] n/a = not applicable

*Table C-20: Extra operations for mutable sequences—list*

| Operations | Description | Class method |
|---|---|---|
| *s[i] = x* | Index assignment | `__setitem__` |
| *s[i:j] = x* | Slice assignment | `__setslice__` |
| *del s[i]* | Index deletion | `__delitem__` |
| *del s[i:j]* | Slice deletion | `__delslice__` |
| *s.append(x)* | Add node at end | n/a[a] |
| *s.count(x)* | Count occurrences | n/a |
| *s.index(x)* | Find occurrence | n/a |
| *s.insert(i, x)* | Insert x at index i | n/a |
| *s.remove(x)* | Remove first occurrence | n/a |
| *s.reverse()* | Reversal | n/a |
| *s.sort(cmp?)* | Sorting | n/a |

[a] n/a = not applicable

# *POSIX System-Level Functions*

The *posix* module provides most standard POSIX functions for use on UNIX systems. Some aren't applicable to nonmultitasking systems like DOS. The *posix* module isn't intended to be imported directly: use these functions by importing the *os* module instead (*os* is a generic interface to platform-specific modules like *posix*). A supplemental module, *posixpath* provides additional path-related services (file existence tests, etc.), and *os* also provides a few exports of its own (*exec* variants, and so on).

*Table C-21: posix module services*

| Export | Description |
|---|---|
| *environ* | The shell environment variable dictionary: {variable:value, . . . } |
| *error* | POSIX-related errors |
| *chdir(path)* | Change the current working directory for this process |
| *chmod(path, mode)* | Change file modes |
| *chown(path, uid, gid)* | Change file ownership |
| *close(fd)* | Close file descriptor (not a *stdio* file object) |
| *dup(fd)* | Duplicate a file descriptor |
| *dup2(fd, fd2)* | Copy file descriptor *fd* to *fd2* |
| *execv(path, args)* | Execute file *path* with argument list *args*, replacing the current program |
| *execve(path, args, env)* | Like *execv*, but the *env* dictionary replaces the variable environment |
| *_exit(n)* | Exit process with status *n*, without performing cleanup (but use *sys.exit*) |
| *fdopen(fd, mode?, bufsize?)* | Return a file object (*stdio*) connected to the file descriptor *fd* |
| *fork()* | Spawn a child process: return 0 in the child, the child's process id in parent |
| *fstat()* | Return status for file descriptor *fd* (like *stat*) |
| *getcwd()* | Return the current working directory name as a string |
| *getegid()* | Return process's effective group id (also: *geteuid*, *getgid*, *getuid*) |
| *getpid()* | Return the current process's id |
| *getppid()* | Return the parent process's id |
| *kill(pid, sig)* | Kill the process *pid* by sending signal *sig* |
| *link(src, dst)* | Create a link to file *src*, named *dst* |
| *listdir(path)* | Make a list of names of the entries in directory *path* |
| *lseek(fd, pos, how)* | Set the current position of file descriptor *fd* (random access) |
| *lstat(path)* | Like *stat*, but don't follow symbolic links |
| *mkdir(path, mode)* | Make a directory called *path*, with the given *mode* |
| *nice(increment)* | Add increment to process's "niceness" (i.e., lower its CPU priority) |
| *open(file, flags, mode)* | Open a file descriptor-based file, return the file descriptor (not a file object) |
| *pipe()* | Return a pair of file descriptors (*r*, *w*), for reading and writing a new pipe |

*Table C-21: posix module services (continued)*

| Export | Description |
|---|---|
| *popen(cmd, mode, bufsize)* | Open a pipe to or from shell command *cmd* (to capture or send data) |
| *read(fd, n)* | Read *n* bytes from a file descriptor (low level; use file objects normally) |
| *readlink(path)* | Return the path referenced by a link |
| *rename(src, dst)* | Rename (move) file *src* to name *dst* |
| *rmdir(path)* | Remove (delete) a directory |
| *setgid(id)* | Set the current process's group id (also: *setuid* for user ids) |
| *stat(path)* | Run stat system call, return a tuple of integers with file information (*stat.py*) |
| *symlink(src, dst)* | Create a symbolic link to file *src*, called *dst* |
| *system(cmd)* | Execute a command string in a subshell process |
| *times()* | Elapsed user, system, child user, and child system CPU seconds (tuple) |
| *umask(mask)* | Set the numeric umask |
| *uname()* | Return OS name tuple: (system, node, release, version, machine) |
| *unlink(path)* | Unlink (delete) the file named by path |
| *utime(path, (atime, mtime))* | Set file's access and modification times |
| *wait()* | Wait for completion of a child process (return its id and status) |
| *waitpid(pid, options)* | Wait for child process with id *pid* to complete (see also: *time.sleep*) |
| *write(fd, str)* | Write string *str* to the file descriptor *fd* (low-level: use file objects normally) |

# *emacs Bindings for Python*

For users of the *emacs* text editor, a Python-specific binding originally written by Tim Peters comes with the system. See *Misc/python-mode.el* for basic Python interactions. There's also an *imenu* browsing interface in *Misc/pyimenu.el*. The *Quick-Ref* document gives a list of control key bindings.

# Unused Characters

The characters `@`, `$`, and `?` are not currently used in the Python language (except in string constants and comments). They can be used for preprocessor tools, but check Python's language reference first because there's no guarantee they won't be used by Python in the future. Of course, because Python is not a compiled language, normal Python extension techniques can often replace preprocessors used in languages like C.

# Math Module Functions

The *math* module provides functions defined as standard in C. Because they're standard, we won't describe them here (see C documentation). But for reference, here's a quick list of the functions available in the math module; it also defines constants *pi* and *e*.

| | | | |
|---|---|---|---|
| *acos(x)* | *cosh(x)* | *hypot(x, y)* | *sin(x)* |
| *asin(x)* | *exp(x)* | *ldexp(x, y)* | *sinh(x)* |
| *atan(x)* | *fabs(x)* | *log(x)* | *sqrt(x)* |
| *atan2(x, y)* | *floor(x)* | *log10(x)* | *tan(x)* |
| *ceil(x)* | *fmod(x, y)* | *modf(x)* | *tanh(x)* |
| *cos(x)* | *frexp(x)* | *pow(x, y)* | |

# Topics Summarized Elsewhere

Finally the Index at the end of this book provides access to other topics. For reference, here's a list of major topics that were summarized earlier in the book.

*Table C-22: Other summaries*

| Topic | Reference |
|---|---|
| Specially named class methods | See the table in Chapter 13 |
| Type descriptor slots for C types | See the table and code listings in Chapter 14 |
| Local/global namespace contexts | See the tables and discussion in Chapter 6, *Adding a Functional Interface*, and Chapter 9, *Moving Menus to Classes* |
| Variable naming rules | See Chapter 4 |
| Run-time API functions | See Chapter 14, and Chapter 15, *Embedding Python* |
| Python/C data conversion codes | See the table and discussion in Chapter 14 |
| Debugger (*pdb*) commands | See the table and examples in Chapter 11, *Graphical User Interfaces* |

*Table C-22: Other summaries (continued)*

| Topic | Reference |
|---|---|
| Using the Python profiler | See Chapter 13 |
| Python functionality sources | See the summary at the end of Chapter 10, *More Class Magic* |
| Special environment variables | See Chapter 3, *Getting Started* |
| Python language concepts | See the summary following Chapter 10 |
| Built-in type operations | See the summary in Chapter 8, *Adding Text-Based Menus* |
| Regular expressions overview | See Chapter 16, *Processing Language and Text* |
| Type conversions | See the tables at the end of Chapter 13 |
| Functional programming tools | See the discussion in Appendix A, *...And Other Cool Stuff* |
| *Tkinter* GUI classes, *Tk* mappings | See the tables at the end of Chapter 11 |
| *dbm* and *Shelve* file operations | See the table in Chapter 12 |

# D

# *An Application Framework*

*In this appendix:*

- *A File Packer Client: packapp.py*
- *A File Unpacker Client: unpkapp.py*
- *The Application Root Class: app.py*
- *Adding Stream Redirection: redirect.py*
- *Adding User Interaction and Menus: interact.py*
- *Adding File Simulation with Strings: internal.py*
- *A Utility and Self-Test Module: apptools.py*
- *A Limited Mail Message Extraction Script: mtool.py*

## *"What's File Packing Really, in the Grand Scheme of Things?"*

This appendix contains source listings for the application framework mentioned earlier in the book. At the end of Part 2, *Language Fundamentals*, we had moved our "quick and dirty" file packing scripts to menu classes. Still, we didn't do much about wrapping system-level components, automating stream redirection, etc. The classes here implement such an encapsulation: they provide a simplified and standardized system interface.

But rather than going through all the code here, studying the framework is left as a suggested learning exercise for the reader. *This is optional reading.* It's a comprehensive example and illustrates advanced OOP design in Python but doesn't introduce any concepts we haven't discussed earlier.

The framework consists of a general superclass, with subclasses that redirect input/output streams, map streams to internal strings, and handle user interaction. The source files in this listing include:

*packapp.py*
: The file packing script as an application instance (client).

*unpkapp.py*
: The file unpacking script, also as an application instance.

*app.py*
: The top-level *App* superclass.

*redirect.py*
: An *App* subclass that adds basic stream redirection.

*interact.py*
: An *App* subclass that adds user interaction and text-based menus.

*internal.py*
: An *App* subclass that adds internal (string-based) file objects and redirection.

*apptools.py*
: Extra top-level entry points for *App* classes, plus some self-test code (with output).

*mtool.py*
: A simple mail file scanner script.

*mtoolapp.py*
: The mail-file scanner, as an *App* instance, to show another client.

Our file packing scripts from Part 2, appear again, brought back to life as subclasses of the framework. Another script (a limited mail file scanner) is shown to contrast simple scripts and subclasses.

The classes here are much grander solutions to some of the issues raised in Part 2. For instance, user interaction and menus are extensions of a more generic application class. They subsume the simpler interaction classes developed earlier.

### *Complexity warning!*

This example is probably extreme in terms of class hierarchy complexity. As we've seen earlier in this book, Python classes are typically employed in much simpler ways. But when we need to build advanced OOP structures like this, Python has the right kinds of tools.

# A File Packer Client: packapp.py

```
#!/usr/local/bin/python

###########################################
# % packapp.py -v -o target src src...
# % packapp.py *.txt -o packed1
# >>> app.appRun('packapp.py', args...)
# >>> app.appCall(PackApp, args...)
###########################################

from apptools import StreamApp
from textpack import marker

class PackApp(StreamApp):
    def start(self):
        if not self.args:
            self.exit('packapp.py [-o target]? src src...')

    def run(self):
        for name in self.restargs():
            try:
                self.message('packing: ' + name)
                self.pack_file(name)
            except:
                self.exit('error processing: ' + name)

    def pack_file(self, name):
        self.setInput(name)
        self.write(marker + name + '\n')
        while 1:
            line = self.readline()
            if not line: break
            self.write(line)

if __name__ == '__main__':  PackApp().main()
```

# A File Unpacker Client: unpkapp.py

```
#!/usr/local/bin/python

#########################################
# % unpkapp.py -i packed1 -v
# app.appRun('unpkapp.py', args...)
# app.appCall(UnpackApp, args...)
#########################################

import string
from apptools import StreamApp
from textpack import marker
```

```
class UnpackApp(StreamApp):
    def start(self):
        self.endargs()           # ignore more -o's, etc.

    def run(self):
        mlen = len(marker)
        while 1:
            line = self.readline()
            if not line:
                break
            elif line[:mlen] != marker:
                self.write(line)
            else:
                name = string.strip(line[mlen:])
                self.message('creating: ' + name)
                self.setOutput(name)

if __name__ == '__main__':  UnpackApp().main()
```

# The Application Root Class: app.py

```
################################################################################
# an application class hierarchy, for handling top-level components;
# App is the root class of the App hierarchy, extended in other files;
################################################################################

import sys, os, traceback
AppError = 'App class error'                                 # errors raised here

class App:                                                   # the root class
    def __init__(self, name=None):
        self.name    = name or self.__class__.__name__   # the lowest class
        self.args    = sys.argv[1:]
        self.env     = os.environ
        self.verbose = self.getopt('-v') or self.getenv('VERBOSE')
        self.input   = sys.stdin
        self.output  = sys.stdout
        self.error   = sys.stderr                        # stdout may be piped

    def closeApp(self):                                  # not __del__: ref's?
        pass                                             # nothing at this level

    def help(self):
        print self.name, 'command-line arguments:'      # extend in subclass
        print '-v (verbose)'

    ####################################################
    # environmental services...
    ####################################################
```

```
def getopt(self, tag):
    try:                                          # test "-x" command arg
        self.args.remove(tag)                     # not real argv: > 1 App?
        return 1
    except:
        return 0

def getarg(self, tag, default=None):
    try:                                          # get "-x val" command arg
        pos = self.args.index(tag)
        val = self.args[pos+1]
        self.args[pos:pos+2] = []
        return val
    except:
        return default                            # None: missing, no default

def getenv(self, name, default=''):
    try:                                          # get "$x" environment var
        return self.env[name]
    except KeyError:
        return default

def endargs(self):
    if self.args:
        self.message('extra arguments ignored: ' + `self.args`)
        self.args = []

def restargs(self):
    res, self.args = self.args, []                # no more args/options
    return res

def message(self, text):
    self.error.write(text + '\n')                 # stdout may be redirected

def exception(self):
    return (sys.exc_type, sys.exc_value)          # the last exception

def exit(self, message='', status=1):
    if message:
        self.message(message)
    sys.exit(status)

def shell(self, command, fork=0, inp=''):
    if self.verbose:
        self.message(command)                               # how about ipc?
    if not fork:
        os.system(command)                                  # run a shell cmd
    elif fork == 1:
        return os.popen(command, 'r').read()                # get its output
    else:                                                   # readlines too?
        pipe = os.popen(command, 'w')
        pipe.write(inp)                                     # send it input
        pipe.close()
```

```
    ###################################################
    # input/output-stream methods for the app itself;
    # redefine in subclasses if not using files, or
    # set self.input/output to file-like objects;
    ###################################################

    def read(self, *size):
        return apply(self.input.read, size)

    def readline(self):
        return self.input.readline()

    def readlines(self):
        return self.input.readlines()

    def write(self, text):
        self.output.write(text)

    def writelines(self, text):
        self.output.writelines(text)

    ###################################################
    # to run the app...
    # main() is the start/run/stop execution protocol;
    ###################################################

    def main(self):
        res = None
        try:
            self.start()
            self.run()
            res = self.stop()                # optional return val
        except SystemExit:                   # ignore if from exit()
            pass
        except:
            self.message('uncaught: ' + `self.exception()`)
            traceback.print_exc()
        self.closeApp()
        return res

    def start(self):
        if self.verbose: self.message(self.name + ' start.')

    def stop(self):
        if self.verbose: self.message(self.name + ' done.')

    def run(self):  raise AppError, 'run must be redefined!'
```

# Adding Stream Redirection: redirect.py

```
################################################################################
# App subclasses for redirecting standard streams to files
################################################################################

import sys
from app import App

################################################################################
# an app with input/output stream redirection
################################################################################

class StreamApp(App):
    def __init__(self, ifile='-', ofile='-'):
        App.__init__(self)                              # call superclass init
        self.setInput( ifile or self.name + '.in')      # default i/o file names
        self.setOutput(ofile or self.name + '.out')     # unless '-i', '-o' args

    def closeApp(self):                                 # not __del__
        try:
            if self.input != sys.stdin:                 # may be redirected
                self.input.close()                      # iff still open
        except: pass
        try:
            if self.output != sys.stdout:               # don't close stdout!
                self.output.close()                     # input/output exist?
        except: pass

    def help(self):
        App.help(self)
        print '-i <input-file |"-">  (default: stdin  or per app)'
        print '-o <output-file|"-">  (default: stdout or per app)'

    def setInput(self, default=None):
        file = self.getarg('-i') or default or '-'
        if file == '-':
            self.input = sys.stdin
            self.input_name = '<stdin>'
        else:
            self.input = open(file, 'r')            # cmdarg | funcarg | stdin
            self.input_name = file                  # cmdarg '-i -' works too

    def setOutput(self, default=None):
        file = self.getarg('-o') or default or '-'
        if file == '-':
            self.output = sys.stdout
            self.output_name = '<stdout>'
        else:
            self.output = open(file, 'w')           # error caught in main()
            self.output_name = file                 # make backups too?

class RedirectApp(StreamApp):
    def __init__(self, ifile=None, ofile=None):
```

```
        StreamApp.__init__(self, ifile, ofile)
        self.streams = sys.stdin, sys.stdout
        sys.stdin    = self.input                  # for raw_input, stdin
        sys.stdout   = self.output                 # for print, stdout

    def closeApp(self):                            # not __del__
        StreamApp.closeApp(self)                   # close files?
        sys.stdin, sys.stdout = self.streams       # reset sys files


############################################################
# to add as a mix-in (or use multiple-inheritance...)
############################################################

class RedirectAnyApp:
    def __init__(self, superclass, *args):
        apply(superclass.__init__, (self,) + args)
        self.super   = superclass
        self.streams = sys.stdin, sys.stdout
        sys.stdin    = self.input                  # for raw_input, stdin
        sys.stdout   = self.output                 # for print, stdout

    def closeApp(self):
        self.super.closeApp(self)                  # do the right thing
        sys.stdin, sys.stdout = self.streams       # reset sys files
```

# *Adding User Interaction and Menus: interact.py*

```
##############################################################################
# App subclasses for handling simple character-based user-interaction
##############################################################################

import string
from app import App, AppError

##############################################################################
# an app with a read-eval-print loop
##############################################################################

class InteractiveApp(App):
    def run(self):                             # define App.run here
        while 1:
            command = self.readCommand()
            if not command:
                break
            result = self.evalCommand(command)
            if result == 0:
                break
            self.printResult(result)
```

```
    def readCommand(self, prompt='?'):       # subclass hooks + App.start,stop
        try:
            return raw_input(prompt)         # or self.input.readline()[:-1]
        except:
            return None

    def printResult(self, res):
        if res not in [1, None]:
            print res                        # or self.output.write('res'+'\n')

    def evalCommand(self, command):
        raise AppError, 'evalCommand must be redefined!'


###############################################################################
# an interactive app with a menu
# alternative ways to handle different menu types (dict, list, class)...
###############################################################################

class MenuApp(InteractiveApp):
    def readCommand(self):                        # print menu items first
        print '\n\tMENU...'                       # or: self.output.write('--\n')
        self.showOptions()                        # or: self.write(...)
        return InteractiveApp.readCommand(self, '==>')

    def evalCommand(self, cmd):
        try:
            return self.runOption(cmd)            # catch bad key or index, etc.
        except:
            print 'what? "%s"?\ntry again...' % cmd

    def showOptions(self):  raise AppError, 'showOptions undefined!'
    def runOptions(self):   raise AppError, 'runOptions undefined!'


class MenuDictApp(MenuApp):
    def showOptions(self):
        options = self.menu.keys()                # menu = dictionary/mapping
        options.sort()
        for cmd in options: print '\t\t' + cmd

    def runOption(self, cmd):
        return self.menu[cmd]()                   # bound method or function

class MenuListApp(MenuApp):                       # menu = list/sequence
    def showOptions(self):
        for i in range(len(self.menu)):
            print '\t\t%d) %s' % (i, self.menu[i][0])

    def runOption(self, cmd):
        return self.menu[string.atoi(cmd)][1]()
```

```
class MenuClassApp(MenuApp):
    def readCommand(self):
        return self.menu.readCommand()          # pass off to menu object
```

# *Adding File Simulation with Strings: internal.py*

```
################################################################################
# App subclasses that map input/output to internal strings
################################################################################

import sys, string
from app import App

################################################################################
# an App that redirects input/output streams to internal files (strings)
################################################################################

class InternalApp(App):
    def __init__(self, text=''):
        App.__init__(self)                  # i/o reset to classes
        self.input  = Input(text)           # use internal string i/o
        self.output = Output()
        self.input_name  = '<internal>'
        self.output_name = '<internal>'

    def stop(self):
        App.stop(self)
        return self.output.text             # result = saved output

class RedirectInternalApp(InternalApp):
    def __init__(self, input=''):
        InternalApp.__init__(self, input)          # streams reset to strings
        self.streams = sys.stdin, sys.stdout
        sys.stdin    = self.input                  # for raw_input, stdin
        sys.stdout   = self.output                 # for print, stdout

    def closeApp(self):                            # not __del__
        sys.stdin, sys.stdout = self.streams       # may be redirected


################################################################################
# redirect i/o to classes
# instances of these classes can be used anywhere a file object is expected;
# Note: we could reset/restore streams here instead of in App, but these
# classes are useful outside App, and are independant of App streams;
# there's probably more efficient representations for the file strings;
################################################################################

class FakeStream:
    def close(self):                        # to do: seek(), tell()...
        pass                                # as is: can't back up in file
```

```
    def flush(self):
        pass                              # pass: returns None
    def isatty(self):
        return 0

class Input(FakeStream):
    def __init__(self, input):            # input: any sliceable object,
        self.text = input                 # but find/getargs want real strings

    def read(self, *size):
        if not size:
            res, self.text = self.text, ''
        else:
            res, self.text = self.text[:size[0]], self.text[size[0]:]
        return res

    def readline(self):
        eoln = string.find(self.text, '\n')
        if eoln == -1:
            res, self.text = self.text, ''
        else:
            res, self.text = self.text[:eoln+1], self.text[eoln+1:]
        return res

    def readlines(self):
        res = []
        while 1:
            line = self.readline()
            if not line: break
            res.append(line)
        return res

class Output(FakeStream):
    def __init__(self):                             # output in self.output.text
        self.text = ''
    def write(self, string):
        self.text = self.text + string              # to do: handle errors here
    def writelines(self, lines):
        for line in lines: self.write(line)         # or use joinfields
```

# A Utility and Self-Test Module: apptools.py

```
#!/usr/local/bin/python

################################################################################
# extra entry-points, test-code, etc., for App class tree
################################################################################

import sys, os, string
from app import *                   # use this file to get everything
from internal import *              # or import from more specific module
```

```
from interact import *
from redirect import *


################################################################################
# Mix-in class examples: __init__ taken from RedirectInternalApp.
# The result (stdout output string) is returned from App.main() call.
#
# Multiple-inheritance name resolution is depth-first, l-top-r.
# We need InteractiveApp's run(), and RedirectInternalApp's __init__(),
# so there's a problem with either:
#
# class TestInteractiveApp(RedirectInternalApp, InteractiveApp):
#     pass      # wrong run!
#
# class TestInteractiveApp(InteractiveApp, RedirectInternalApp):
#     pass      # wrong __init__!
#
# Two solutions are illustrated in the 2 mix-in classes here.
# Note: this subclassing technique can be used to test any class
# derived from App (pack, mtool..): inherit from the tested class
# plus RedirectInternalApp, and resolve conflicts manually (or use
# FuncTestApp below, on the top-level entry-point in the tree).
# The "run =" is like "def run(self): InteractiveApp.run(self)"
################################################################################


class TestInteractiveApp(RedirectInternalApp, InteractiveApp):
    run = InteractiveApp.run

class TestMenuApp(MenuDictApp, RedirectInternalApp):
    __init__ = RedirectInternalApp.__init__
    stop     = RedirectInternalApp.stop              # resolve conflicts
    closeApp = RedirectInternalApp.closeApp          # by manual assignment


################################################################################
# Top-level external entry points (non-oop)
#
# import app
# from mtool2 import MtoolApp
# app.appCall(MtoolApp, '-x', '-i', '/home/lutz/mbox', '-t', 'steve')
#
# import app
# app.appRun('mtool2.py', '-i', '/home/lutz/mbox', '-f', 'andy', '-o', '-')
# app.appRun('mtool2.py', '-i /home/lutz/mbox', '-f andy -o -')
#
# _buildArgs() flattens the arguments passed in, splits multi-arg
# strings, and converts non-strings to strings.  List/tuple trees
# can be constructed and passed in-- flattened into a list of strings,
# and/or args can be passed in as args to appCall (varargs);
################################################################################
```

```
def _buildArgs(args):
    res = []
    for arg in args:
        if type(arg) in [type([]), type(())]:
            res = res + _buildArgs(arg)          # ['a', '-b', (1, 2)]
        elif type(arg) != type(''):
            res.append(`arg`)                    # 1 2.2
        else:
            res = res + string.split(arg)        # "f1 f2 f3"
    return res

def appCall(appClass, *args):                    # call an App like a function
    save_argv = sys.argv
    sys.argv  = [appClass.__name__] + _buildArgs(args)
    result    = appClass().main()
    sys.argv  = save_argv
    return result

def appRun(script, *args):                       # run as a new process
    arglist = _buildArgs(args)                   # or: ScriptOutput(s,a).read()
    cmdline = script + ' ' + string.join(arglist)
    return os.popen(cmdline, 'r').read()


################################################################################
# Treat an App run like a file.
# Here, read/write mean the view outside an app, instead of the app itself
# (not it's i/o streams).  ScriptPipe.write() sends data to the app, and
# ScriptPipe.read() gets the app's output.
################################################################################

class ScriptPipe:
    def __init__(self, cmdline, mode):
        self.pipe = os.popen(cmdline, mode)    # closed on deletion

    def __getattr__(self, name):
        return getattr(self.pipe, name)        # delegate to pipe file

    def cmdline(self, script, args):
        return script + ' ' + string.join(_buildArgs(args))

class ScriptOutput(ScriptPipe):                # use .read, .readline(),...
    def __init__(self, script, *args):
        ScriptPipe.__init__(self.cmdline(script, args) + " -o -", 'r')

class ScriptInput(ScriptPipe):                 # use .write(), .writelines(),...
    def __init__(self, script, *args):
        ScriptPipe.__init__(self.cmdline(script, args) + " -i -", 'w')
```

```
###############################################################################
# Simple i/o redirection
# Note: we can't rely on App.__del__ to restore streams when App.main()
# returns: __del__ won't run if any ref's to the App instance remain.
# (Example: if any get*() call fails, there's a traceback object with
# a reference).  Without App.closeApp, we'd have to call __del__ here.
###############################################################################

def _redirected1(input, function, args):              # the hard way...
    save_streams = sys.stdin, sys.stdout
    sys.stdin    = Input(input)
    sys.stdout   = Output()
    try:
        apply(function, args)
    except:
        sys.stderr.write('error in function! ')
        sys.stderr.write(`sys.exc_type` + ',' + `sys.exc_value` + '\n')
    result = sys.stdout.text
    sys.stdin, sys.stdout = save_streams
    return result


class FuncTestApp(RedirectInternalApp):               # the way of tao...
    def __init__(self, input, func, args):
        RedirectInternalApp.__init__(self, input)
        self.call = func, args
    def run(self):
        try:
            apply(apply, self.call)
        except:
            self.message('error in function!' + `self.exception()`)

def redirected(input, function, args):
    return FuncTestApp(input, function, args).main()


###############################################################################
# Test i/o redirection apps: 4 class levels, with i/o classes embedded.
# also: see Lib/StringIO.py for other string i/o (seek, tell..)
# also: see mtoolapp.py, packapp.py, unpkapp.py for other clients
###############################################################################

def _self_test():
    print raw_input('here we go => ')

    def testfunc(N):
        ans = raw_input('Enter? ')                  # from an Input instance
        for i in range(N):
            print ans                               # to an Output instance
        sys.stdout.write(sys.stdin.readline())      # from Input, to Output
        print "Ni!" * N

    input  = 'Spam!\nA shrubbery...'
    output = redirected(input, testfunc, (5,))      # make/run a FuncTestApp
```

```
        ans = raw_input('welcome back => ')
        print 'got it =>', ans                          # stdin, stdout reset?
        print 'testfunc output =>\n', output

        def tee():
            sys.stdout.writelines(sys.stdin.readlines())

        def tee2():
            text = sys.stdin.readlines()
            print text
            for line in text:
                sys.stdout.write('> ')
                print line,

        # more FuncTestApp's
        print 'tee output =>\n',  redirected("spam\nSpam\nSPAM!\n", tee,  ())
        print 'tee2 output =>\n', redirected("spam\nSpam\nSPAM!",   tee2, ())

        # more subclasses
        class EchoApp(TestInteractiveApp):
            def evalCommand(self, command):
                return 'got this -> ' + string.upper(command)

        output = EchoApp("guido\nis\ngod\n").main()
        print 'EchoApp output =>\n', output

        class DemoApp(TestMenuApp):
            menu = {
                'hello' : lambda: 'Hello world!',
                'play'  : lambda: 'Ni' * 4,
                'bye'   : lambda: 0,
            }

        output = DemoApp("hello\nspam\nplay\nbye").main()
        print 'DemoApp output =>\n', output

    if __name__ == '__main__': _self_test()        # when run at top-level
```

## Expected Output of apptools Self-Test Code

```
% python apptools.py
here we go => 111
111
welcome back => 222
got it => 222
testfunc output =>
Enter? Spam!
```

```
Spam!
Spam!
Spam!
Spam!
A shrubbery...Ni!Ni!Ni!Ni!Ni!

tee output =>
spam
Spam
SPAM!

tee2 output =>
['spam\012', 'Spam\012', 'SPAM!']
> spam
> Spam
> SPAM!
EchoApp output =>
?got this -> GUIDO
?got this -> IS
?got this -> GOD
?
DemoApp output =>

        MENU...
                bye
                hello
                play
==>Hello world!

        MENU...
                bye
                hello
                play
==>what? "spam"?
try again...

        MENU...
                bye
                hello
                play
==>NiNiNiNi

        MENU...
                bye
                hello
                play
==>
%
```

# A Limited Mail Message Extraction Script: mtool.py

```
#!/usr/local/bin/python/python
# mail-tool, version 1
# to do: handle continued lines, etc.
# see the mail-header tools in the standard library

import sys, os
sep = '#'*80 + '\n'

if len(sys.argv) < 3:
    print 'use: ?python mtool.py <from>|* <to>|* ?<input> ?<output>'
    sys.exit(1)

From = sys.argv[1]
To   = sys.argv[2]

if len(sys.argv) > 3:
    mfile = sys.argv[3]
    if len(sys.argv) > 4:
        ofile = sys.argv[4]
    else:
        ofile = 'mtool.out'
else:
    mfile = '/usr/spool/mail/' + os.environ['USER']
    ofile = 'mtool.out'

In  = open(mfile, 'r')
Out = open(ofile, 'w')

line = In.readline()
while line:
    if line[:5] == 'From ' and (From == '*' or line[5:5+len(From)] == From):
        prefix = [sep, line]
        while line:
            line = In.readline()
            if line == '\n':
                break
            if line[:4] == 'To: ' and (To == '*' or line[4:4+len(To)] == To):
                Out.writelines(prefix)
                while line:
                    Out.write(line)
                    line = In.readline()
                    if line[:5] == 'From ': break
                break
            prefix.append(line)
    else:
        line = In.readline()

Out.close()
print 'mtool finished: see "' + ofile + '".'
```

# *The Mail Tool as an App Subclass: mtoolapp.py*

```
#!/usr/local/bin/python

################################################################################
# mail-tool, version 2
# extract mail message by header matches
# to do: MMDH format (startMessage():'\1\1\1\1\n')
# to do: header-line continuations (first = whitespace)
#
# example use:
# mtool.py \* andy ~/mbox
# mtool.py steveo mlutz ~/mbox msgs
#
# mtoolapp.py -i ~/mbox -t andy
# mtoolapp.py -a -f steveo -t lutz -i ~/mbox -o msgs
#
# mtoolapp.py -t andy -i ~/mbox -o -
# mtoolapp.py -i ~/mbox -t andy -o - | diff - mtool.out
# cat ~/mbox | mtoolapp.py -i - -t andy -o - | diff - mtool.out
#
# from mtoolapp import *
# mtoolViewer('/home/lutz/mbox', 'steveo', 'lutz')
#
# from app import *
# appCall(MtoolApp, '-x', '-i', '/home/lutz/mbox', '-t', 'steveo')
# appRun('mtoolapp.py', '-i', '/home/lutz/mbox', '-f', 'andy', '-o', '-')
# ScriptOutput(...).read()
################################################################################

import string
from apptools import StreamApp, appCall, Output

class MtoolApp(StreamApp):
    mpath = '/usr/spool/mail/'
    sepln = 'MtoolApp' + ('#' * 64) + 'MtoolApp\n'

    def help(self):
        StreamApp.help(self)
        for arg in [
            '-f <from-pattern>',
            '-t <to-pattern>',
            '-c <cc-pattern>',
            '-s <subject-pattern>',
            '-x (function mode: overrides -o)',
            '-a (and mode: default=or)']: print arg

    def internalOutput(self):
        self.output = Output()
        self.output_name = '<internal>'

    def start(self):
```

```
        if not self.args:
            self.help()
            self.exit()
        else:
            self.selects = [
                ('From ',     self.getarg('-f')),
                ('To: ',      self.getarg('-t')),
                ('Cc: ',      self.getarg('-c')),
                ('Subject: ', self.getarg('-s'))
            ]
            self.andMode  = self.getopt('-a')
            self.funcMode = self.getopt('-x')
            self.setInput(self.mpath + self.getenv('USER'))
            if self.funcMode:
                self.internalOutput()
            else:
                self.setOutput('mtool.out')
            self.endargs()

    def eliminates(self, line):
        if self.andMode:
            for (start, patt) in self.selects:
                if (patt and
                    line[:len(start)] == start and
                    string.find(line, patt, len(start)) < 0):    # or regex
                       return 1                                  # patt !found

    def qualifies(self, line):
        if not self.andMode:
            for (start, patt) in self.selects:
                if (patt and
                    line[:len(start)] == start and
                    string.find(line, patt, len(start)) >= 0):   # or regex
                       return 1                                  # patt found

    def run(self):
        line = self.readline()
        while line:
            if line[:5] == 'From ':
                prefix = [self.sepln]
                match  = self.andMode
                while line:
                    if self.qualifies(line):
                        match = 1
                        break
                    if self.eliminates(line):
                        match = 0
                        break
                    if line == '\n':
                        break
                    prefix.append(line)
                    line = self.readline()
                if match:
                    self.writelines(prefix)
```

```
                    while line:
                        self.write(line)
                        line = self.readline()
                        if line[:5] == 'From ': break
                    continue
                line = self.readline()

        def stop(self):
            if not self.funcMode:
                self.message('mtool finished: see "%s".' % self.output_name)
            else:
                return string.splitfields(self.output.text, self.sepln)[1:]


##############################################################################
# to run from another program (gui...)
# mtoolViewer('/home/lutz/mbox', 'steveo', 'lutz', 0, 0, 1)
# pdb.run("mtoolCall('~/mbox', 'andy', 'lutz')")
# ...b MtoolApp.start;  c;  p self.args;  s;...
##############################################################################

def mtoolCall(Mfile, From, To, Cc='', Subj='', And=1, Mtype=MtoolApp):
    cmdargs = [
        ('-i', Mfile),
        ('-f', From ),
        ('-t', To   ),
        ('-c', Cc   ),
        ('-s', Subj )]
    cmdopts = [('-a', And)]

    args = ['-x']                               # function mode
    for (opt, arg) in cmdargs:
        if arg: args.append((opt, arg))         # add passed args
    for (opt, arg) in cmdopts:
        if arg: args.append(opt)                # add passed flags
    return appCall(Mtype, args)                 # use internal output

def mtoolViewer(*args):
    msgs = apply(mtoolCall, args)               # list of messages
    for msg in msgs:
        print msg; t = raw_input()              # pause between each


##############################################################################
# run mtool as a script
##############################################################################

if __name__ == '__main__':
    MtoolApp().main()
```

Suggested exercises:

1. Test the file packer/unpacker scripts here. They are used in the same way as those in Part 2 of the book, but command-line options follow the *App* class's conventions. Add file backup to the unpacker, by extending the *setOutput* method to call *os.rename* (see *unpkapp2* in the examples directory).

2. Study these code listings. Notice the use of multiple inheritance and manual conflict resolution in the *apptools* module. The Python library directory includes a *StringIO* module that implements string-based (internal) files in a slightly different way than the *internal* module here; compare the implementations.

3. Enhance the mail tool subclass to handle *continuation lines* in headers; in UNIX mailboxes they start with a whitespace character. Also add support for other mailbox formats (MMDH). Hint: if you have access to the example directories for this book (see the CD-ROM), a suggested solution appears in file *mtool3.py*; also study the mail file library modules in the Python library directories.

4. Add regular expression matching to the mail file tool: allow the match string for each header line type to be passed in as a regular expression. Use *regex.search* instead of *string.find* to detect matches.

5. Add a GUI-based interface for the mail file tool using *Tkinter*. Allow the user to select header types to match, and enter patterns. Would it make sense to add a GUI application subclass to the framework? What would the GUI subclass get from the *App* tree?

# A Python Tutorial

*In this appendix:*
- *Welcome to Python 101*
- *The Python hello world Program*
- *Interacting with Python*
- *Some Useful Statements*
- *Using Built-In Data Structures*
- *Using Functions*
- *Using Modules*
- *Using Classes*
- *Exception Handling*
- *Conclusion*

## Welcome to Python 101

So you've decided to learn Python but find yourself puzzled by concepts like nested module namespaces, dynamic variable typing, and slicing heterogeneous multi-dimensional lists. Not to worry! In this appendix, we'll see a "kinder, gentler" introduction to the language, based on simple interpreter interaction. After reading this appendix, you'll be able to tackle Python concepts and examples like a pro.

The presentation here is organized by language features instead of example roles. Its goal is to give a bottom-up introduction to Python, for those new to programming or dynamic language concepts in general. This appendix should also help if you find yourself frustrated by material in the main body of the book: we'll cover the essentials from a more basic perspective in this section.

We'll also take a simpler look at programming concepts, such as object-oriented programming (OOP), and exception handling. In order to illustrate fundamental concepts, the examples we'll see will be deliberately small and artificial; once you've mastered the material here, the main body of the book presents more realistic examples and provides more details. Part 2, *Language Fundamentals*, picks up where we leave off here.

# *The Python hello world Program*

The customary way to introduce a new language is to show how to display the character string *hello world* on the computer screen. In Python, this benchmark is arguably silly:

```
print 'Hello world!'
```

which consists of a print statement and a python string. This really doesn't tell us very much about Python! But let's use it as our point of departure to illustrate some of Python's features.

Before we get started, make sure you've got access to an installed version of Python. You'll probably find it helpful to enter some of the examples directly and see their results. There's nothing like interacting with a new language when first learning it, and Python's interactive interpreter makes this easy.

See Chapter 3, *Getting Started*, for details on how to configure and use the Python interpreter. If you need more help, your local Python guru or system administrator can help get you set up. Minimally, you need to be able to run the interpreter. You may also need to set the Python module search path in your environment. We'll see why these search paths are important in a moment.

# *Interacting with Python*

There are a number of ways to use the Python system. In the simplest mode, Python code can be entered and executed at the interactive command-line prompt. For example:

```
% python
>>> print 'Hello world!'
Hello world!
>>>
```

On the first line we start up the Python command-line interpreter from the operating system's command line, by typing **python**. On most UNIX systems, typing **python** causes the interpreter to be located according to the setting of the *PATH* environment variable. Check your installation for more details.

Once Python starts, it prints version information, and presents its own command-line prompt. By default, this is >>>. This prompt can be changed, but we'll use >>> in our examples. Our *hello world* program is typed in next, and as you might expect the message is printed. Python then prompts for more commands; we can type an end-of-file character to stop (usually *control+d*) or enter some more Python code.

At the >>> prompt, you can enter any Python command. Results of expressions (which are just Python data objects) are echoed back to the screen so there's no real reason to use the *print* statement in interactive mode. For instance, we can use Python like a calculator:

```
>>> 12 * 2
24
```

which probably isn't the best use of the language but proves the point. Or (and this is really the simplest *hello world* program in Python, but it's almost too trivial to mention):

```
>>> 'Hello world!'
'Hello world!'
```

We can also assign values to variables, which are added to the interactive namespace (more on this later in this appendix). Variable names in Python follow C's rules—roughly, any string of letters, digits, and underscores is a variable name:

```
>>> x = 12 * 2
>>> x + 1
25
```

Here, *x* received the value 24, so it wasn't printed. Note that x wasn't declared anywhere: in Python, all variables come into existence just by using them, and can be assigned values of any data type. More formally, assignment to a new variable creates it, but referencing an unassigned variable raises an error. As you might expect, Python includes most common arithmetic operators, grouping by parentheses, etc.:

```
>>> a = 3
>>> b = 4
>>> b / 2 + a
5
```

And just as in C, the type of an arithmetic expression is determined by the types of its operands: if any operand is floating-point, all are converted to floating-point automatically.

```
>>> b / (2 + a)                  integer division: (4 / 5) ⇒ integer
0
>>> b / (2.0 + a)                floating-point division: (4 / 5.0) ⇒ floating-point
0.8
```

Python also supports unlimited precision integers, if we ask it to; by adding an *L* suffix to a number, Python lets it become as big as we need:

```
>>> 9999999999999999999999999999 + 1
OverflowError: integer literal too large
>>> 9999999999999999999999999999L + 1
10000000000000000000000000000L
```

Like floating-point numbers, if any number in an expression is a long integer, all the other integers will be converted to long integers too. In passing, keep in mind that numbers are really just Python objects, and variables are just named object references; you'll see why this matters later in this appendix, when we talk about assignment.

# Some Useful Statements

Now let's introduce a few of Python's statements, so we can use them in later examples. As usual in all procedural languages, program execution flows sequentially, from one statement to the next, unless control flow altering statements are used. We've already met the assignment and print statements:

```
>>> x = 1
>>> y = 'Spam!'
>>> print x, y
1 Spam!
```

Assignment can be somewhat more complex. For example, Python allows multiple targets and multiple values (using tuples, to be discussed shortly), and allows multiple variables to be set to the same object:

```
a = b = c = 0
```

Python also allows multiple simple statements to appear on the same line separated by semicolons and recognizes comments introduced by a # and continuing to the end of the line; comments are just ignored:

```
a = 1;  b = 2;  c = 3;  print a, b, c         # a comment goes here
```

## *if* Statements

Beyond simple sequence, Python also supports the structured programming tools of selection and iteration. The *if* statement is the basic selection construct. Here's an example of its most complex form:

```
x = 2
if x == 1:
    print 'Hello Dolly!'
elif x == 2:
    print 'Hello world!'
else:
    print 'Hello jello!'
```

which prints our *Hello world!* motto. In an *if* statement, the *if* and *elif* parts all test an expression for a *true* result: Python executes the body of the first *if* or *elif* part that's *true*, and then exits the whole *if* statement completely. If none of them are *true*, it execute the *else* part's body (if present).

Like C, nonzero and zero are taken to be *true* and *false*, respectively. Python includes the usual Boolean and relational operators for building up complex tests. Comparisons return integer 1 or 0 (true or false):

```
>>> a = 3 < 4
>>> a
1
```

Like Lisp, Python also allows empty data structure objects (like lists, strings, and tuples—we'll meet these objects shortly) to represent *false*. In an *if*, the bodies of all parts are indented *blocks* of one or more statements. There may be more than one *elif* clause, and both the *elif* and *else* parts are optional. As usual, *if* statements can appear in other *ifs*; all Python compound statements can be nested arbitrarily deep.

## *Syntax Rules*

This is probably a good time to introduce Python's indentation-based syntax. Note that there were no *begin* or *end* markers around the bodies of the *if* statement ({ and } for C programmers). Instead, Python uses the actual indentation of the body's code to detect its start and finish. Python is clever enough to figure out when a block stops without having to be told explicitly.

The amount of indentation used isn't important, so long as it's consistent for all statements in a block; it can consist of any number and combination of tabs or blanks. Python also doesn't require us to type a ; at the end of each statement as in C. The end-of-line terminates most statements.

All compound statements follow the same pattern: a header on a new line, terminated with a colon (:), and a body of one or more statements indented under it (or some simple statements on the same line). At the interactive prompt, the Python command-line interpreter knows when the line just entered is the start of a compound statement, requiring a body. It prints ... prompts when it's expecting the rest of a statement to be entered and indented (pressing ENTER ends the statement). For example, at the interactive prompt, an *if* might be entered like this:

```
>>> x = 'killer rabbit'
>>> if x == 'bunny':
...     print 'hello little bunny'
... else:
...     print 'Run away! Run away!...'
...
Run away! Run away!...
```

(a poignant scene from the Monty Python film *The Holy Grail*), but we'll omit the prompting details of the command-line interpreter in some of our examples, since they won't apply when we move on to module files (stay tuned). In its simplest form, an *if* is just a single line:

```
if 1: print 'Hello world!'
```

In general, Python allows a compound statement's body to be on the same line as its header, if the body is a noncompound statement (or more than one noncompound statement, separated by semicolons). A note for C programmers: in Python, the Boolean operations are written out as *and*, *or*, and *not*:

```
if not 5 == 5 or (1 < 2 and 3 != 4):  print 'Hello world!'
```

which prints our string. Python comparisons can be strung together:

```
if 1 < 2 < 3:  print 'Hello world!'
```

which is really just shorthand for:

```
if 1 < 2 and 2 < 3:  print 'Hello world!'
```

## Looping Statements

Python's iteration support includes two looping statements: *while* and *for*. Python also includes some other implicit iteration constructs, such as the *map* built-in function; we'll ignore these constructs for now. The *while* loop is fairly standard:

```
i = 0
while i < 5:
      print 'Hello world!'
      i = i+1
```

which just prints our *Hello world!* slogan five times (for *i* values 0 through 4). The body of the *while* loop is executed repeatedly until the test at the top is no longer *true*. Here's another way to code this loop, which uses the fact that zero is *false* and moves the body to the header line:

```
i = 5
while i:  print 'Hello world!';  i = i-1                # i = 5, 4, 3, 2, 1
```

Like C, Python includes a *break* statement to exit a loop immediately; we could have written this example in a more roundabout fashion as follows:

```
i = 0
while 1:
    if i == 5:
        break
    else:
        print 'Hello world!'
        i = i+1
```

The previous forms are probably better because they make the loop's exit condition clearer. Breaks are useful in conjunction with *else* clauses on Python's looping statements: loop *else*s are executed when the loop exits normally (i.e., not by a break). This method sometimes saves checking exit conditions explicitly. Here's an example that checks if some positive integer *y* is prime, using a simplistic algorithm:

```
x = y / 2
while x > 1:
    if y % x == 0:                          # remainder is zero?
        print y, 'has factor', x
        break                               # skip the loop's 'else'
    x = x-1
else:                                       # exited normally: no factor found
    print y, 'is prime'
```

Note that the *else*'s indentation matches that of *while*, not the *if*. In the worst case, this code iterates from *(y/2)* down to *1*, which can be slow for big prime numbers (improvement on this form is left as an exercise for the reader). There's also a *pass* statement, which does nothing at all. A statement that does nothing can be useful too; it's mostly used as a place-holder in compound statements, though not necessarily like this:

```
>>> while 1: pass
```

which keeps going and going in an infinite loop. The *control-c* key combination usually breaks out of loops at the command line (unless it's caught by an exception-handler; to be discussed later in this appendix).

The *for* loop statement is a generic iterator over sequences. For example,

```
for X in <sequence data object>:
    <do something with X>
```

Our loop example would probably be simpler with a *for* loop:

```
>>> for i in range(5): print 'A shrubbery!'
...
A shrubbery!
A shrubbery!
A shrubbery!
A shrubbery!
A shrubbery!
```

But to understand the *for* loop, we really need to have a look at sequence data types first, which, coincidentally, brings us to our next section.

# Using Built-In Data Structures

As you might expect, Python programs deal with more than just numbers and strings. There are three other data types that are built-in to the language itself: lists, dictionaries, and tuples are central to most Python programming. Python also supports user-defined data types, through modules, classes, and C extensions, to be discussed later.

## Lists

Lists are written as zero or more items separated by commas, in square brackets:

```
>>> x = ['Spam!']
>>> x[0]
'Spam!'
```

This example creates a one-item list containing a string, and fetches its first item by indexing it. Like C, Python indexes start at 0 and can be any integer expression. Note that we didn't declare *x* or allocate space for the list itself: all Python data objects come into being just by writing them down and are reclaimed automatically when no longer referenced. Let's define a longer list and iterate over it:

```
>>> L = ['spam', 'Spam', 'SPAM!']
>>> for x in L:
...         print x,
...
spam Spam SPAM!
```

Here, we've made a three-item list and used the *for* statement to step through its items. *x* is assigned each of the items in *L* one-by-one, and the body of the *for* statement is executed for each in turn. The *print* statement ends with a comma here, so it doesn't start a new line; it adds a blank space instead.

The *for* statement is a generic iterator; it can step through any sequence data object, including strings:

```
>>> for x in 'Hello world!':
...         print x,
...
H e l l o   w o r l d !
```

The word *in* can be used both in a *for* loop and as a Boolean membership test:

```
>>> x = 'Hello';  y = 'world!'
>>> L = [x, y]
>>> 'Hello' in L
1
>>> 'Bye' in L
0
```

The *in* membership test is really an implied iteration; we could simulate it using a *for* loop:

```
>>> L = [2, 3, 4]
>>> 3 in L
1
```

and it can be imitated by:

```
for x in L:
    if x == 3: result = 1; break
else:
    result = 0
```

but there's no real compelling reason to do so (unless you're writing a tutorial). Iteration and membership can be combined as needed:

```
>>> L = ['H', 'o', 'w', 'd', 'y', '!']
>>> for x in 'Hello world!':
...     if x in L:
...         print x,
...
H o w o d !
```

## Range

Okay. We can't put off defining *range* any longer! The *range* built-in function simply builds an ordered list of integers, which we can step through in a *for* loop, like any other list:

```
>>> range(1,3)
[1, 2]
```

Like C *for* loops, Python ranges stop at 1 less than their upper limit. There's also an *xrange* that doesn't actually build the list of integers (to save space). Range limits can be positive or negative, and the lower limit can be omitted; it defaults to zero:

```
>>> range(5)
[0, 1, 2, 3, 4]
```

Ranges can be created manually, but it's much slower than using the built-in (we'll discuss *append* later):

```
r = []
while low < high:
    r.append(low); low = low+1
```

## Dictionaries

As mentioned earlier, Python includes a set of built-in high-level data types, which are ready to use. Let's introduce dictionaries next:

```
>>> d = {'spam': 'Hello world!'}
>>> d['spam']
'Hello world!'
```

Python dictionaries are associative arrays: data objects are stored and fetched by key instead of relative position. In this example, our string becomes associated with the string *spam*. Dictionaries are written as a comma-separated set of zero or more *key:value* pairs, in curly braces. Square brackets are used to index all data types, whether by position or by key. Dictionaries allow almost any data object to be used as a key. For instance:

```
>>> d = {2: 'world!', 1: 'Hello'}
>>> for x in range(1,3):
...             print d[x],
...
Hello world!
```

Here, we've used integers to store parts of our string away in a dictionary. We then access them using the integer keys 1 and 2 to get them back in the order we want. An important distinction: in this example, we used integers as keys, not as positions; equivalent list-based code might look like:

```
l = ['Hello', 'world!']
for x in range(0,2):
      print l[x],
```

Dictionaries come in handy any time you need a key/value mapping. This covers a lot of cases that need to be manually coded in other languages: symbol tables, records, property lists, etc. Internally, dictionaries are really just hash tables, which start small and grow on demand. One way to understand dictionaries is to note their similarity to *if* statements; indexing a dictionary:

```
table ={ 'Perl':     'Larry Wall',
         'Tcl':      'John Ousterhout',
         'Python':   'Guido van Rossum' }

creator = table[language]
```

is something like an *if* statement, but dictionaries are faster, more flexible, and can be changed at run-time:

```
if   language == 'Perl':     creator = 'Larry Wall'
elif language == 'Tcl':      creator = 'John Ousterhout'
elif language == 'Python':   creator = 'Guido van Rossum'
```

## *Tuples*

Let's move on to our third structured data type, the tuple. Tuples work much like lists, but their implementation is more efficient because their items can't be changed in place (this is a subject called mutability, which we'll look at shortly):

```
>>> d = ('Hello', 'brave', 'new', 'world!')
>>> for x in d:
...     print x,
...
Hello brave new world!
```

Tuples are written as a comma-separated list of items, in parentheses. The parentheses are sometimes optional, when there's more than one item in a tuple, and it's not syntactically ambiguous:

```
>>> x = 1, 2, 3
>>> x
(1, 2, 3)
```

Here, the value *1, 2, 3* is really a tuple without parentheses; it's packed into a tuple internally. Tuples can also be unpacked automatically, which lets us combine assignments:

```
>>> a, b, c = 1, 2, 3
>>> a, b, c
(1, 2, 3)
```

In this example, the tuple *1, 2, 3* is assigned to the variables in the tuple *a, b, c* by unpacking it into its parts. This method works for lists too (except that square brackets are required on both sides of the =). Unpacking can also occur in the parameters of a function heading (as we'll see shortly). Apart from the syntactic conciseness, tuple assignment allows swapping values without temporaries:

```
x, y = y, x                    # same as: "t = x; x = y; y = t"
```

Tuples are handy for associating multiple items as a set. For instance, Python functions can return multiple values by separating them with commas (which really just returns a tuple). In general, Python lists act like variable-sized arrays; Python tuples are intended for simple groupings. They can be used interchangeably, except that a tuple's contents can't be reset but a list's can. Because of this, tuples provide some integrity constraints. For instance:

```
L = [1, 2, 3]
T = (1, 2, 3)
L[1] = 'x'                     # allowed: L is [1, 'x', 3]
T[1] = 'x'                     # an error!
```

We'll see how to get around this constraint shortly.

## Conversions

Lists and tuples can be mapped back and forth arbitrarily:

```
>>> L = ['s', 'p', 'a', 'm']
>>> T = None
>>> for x in L:
...     T = x, T
...
>>> T
('m', ('a', ('p', ('s', None))))
>>> while T:
...     x, T = T
...     print x,
...
m a p s
```

Here we make a list of four strings, and an empty object represented by *None*, a special data object that is something like a C *null* pointer (any empty object would work here). The *for* loop then builds a tuple tree (really a binary tree), by tacking items of *L* onto the front of the current tuple *T*. Finally, *T* is traversed from left to right, giving the items in *L* reversed. We can convert dictionaries to lists too:

```
>>> D = {'a':1, 'b':2, 'c':3, 'd':4}
>>> D.items()
[('b', 2), ('c', 3), ('d', 4), ('a', 1)]
>>> L = []
>>> for (key, value) in D.items(): L.append(value)
...
>>> L
[2, 3, 4, 1]
```

Here, we make a four-item dictionary *D*. The built-in dictionary method *items* returns a list of *(key,value)* tuples, giving the dictionary's contents. We iterate over that in the *for* loop (using tuple unpacking), and tack items onto the end of list *L* with the list *append* method. Methods are extra operations (in addition to operators) unique to a data type, invoked by name qualification; more on this later.

Note that the values returned by *items* are no longer in the order in which we inserted them: dictionaries are unordered keyed collections (since they use hash tables to store data internally); lists, strings, tuples, and some user-defined types are ordered collections, also called sequences.

## General Properties

Now that we've seen lists, dictionaries, and tuples, let's look at some general properties of Python's data structures. Python structured data types are heterogeneous (they can hold objects of any data type), and support arbitrary nesting. Embedded sequence objects are referenced by a series of index operators (again, zero-based). Here's a list with nested sequences (sublists, tuples, and strings):

```
L = ['abc', [(1,2), ([3], 4)], 5]
```

*L* is really a tree of Python objects; picturing it as such may make it easier to understand the indexing. Figure E-1 shows what *L* looks like internally.

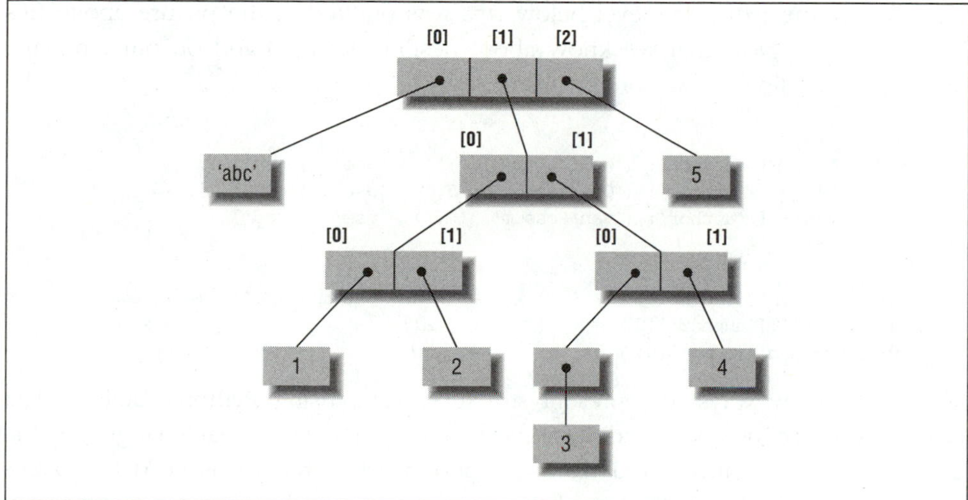


*Figure E-1: Tree of Python objects*

The objects embedded in *L* are accessed using consecutive index operations:

```
>>> L = ['abc', [(1,2), ([3], 4)], 5]
>>> L[0]
'abc'
>>> L[0][1]
'b'
>>> L[1][1]
([3], 4)
>>> L[1][0][1]
2
>>> L[1][1][0][0]
3
>>> L[2]
5
```

In Python, strings are really sequence objects too; but their components are all one-character strings again. Because of this, they're a special case: they're not really heterogeneous and don't support nesting. In the example, the string *abc* is really a three-item sequence; each of the three items is a one-item sequence again. Because indexing a string always returns a string, we can index the first item repeatedly:

```
>>> S = 'abc'
>>> S[0]
'a'
>>> S[0][0][0][0][0][0]
'a'
```

This is why the extra tree level below *abc* was omitted in the picture above (it's really a cycle). Now that we know about nesting, let's expand on our language table again, adding a few more details:

```
table = {
   'Perl':    { 'author': ('Wall', 'L.'),        'use': ['sys'] },
   'Tcl':     { 'author': ('Ousterhout', 'J.'), 'use': ['glue'] },
   'Python': { 'author': ('van Rossum', 'G.'), 'use': ['rad'] }
}

table['Python']['author']              # ('van Rossum', 'G.')
table['Perl']['author'][0]             # 'Wall'
table['Python']['use'][0]              # 'rad'
```

There are many ways to represent structured data using Python's built-in data types. Here we use a nested dictionary to record data on each language; the author's name is a tuple, and we use a nested list to record usage data, so this field can be extended with *append*. We could also use a class instance to represent each language's data items (as we'll see later), or a list or tuple, as long as we use indexes consistently:

```
table = { 'Perl': (('Wall', 'L.'), ['sys']), 'Tcl': (...etc.  }
```

As hinted at earlier, in Python all assignments just create object references; new objects are only created when constants (*[1,2,3]*) are evaluated, or as the result of an expression operator or built-in operation (*list1* + *list2*). Python accommodates object sharing by having two equality operators: "==" does a value comparison (recursively, for structured objects), and *is* tests if two items share the exact same object:

```
>>> x = 9
>>> y = 9                         numbers are (sometimes) mapped to the same object
>>> x == y
1
>>> x is y
1
>>> x = [1, 2]
>>> y = [1, 2]                    lists are always new, unique objects
>>> x == y
1
```

```
>>> x is y
0
```

This characteristic of Python has some interesting consequences for the data types we've looked at: it's possible that changing the value of a structured data object may change the value of other variables that share the same object:

```
>>> L = ['Hello', 'world']
>>> M = L                          M refers to the same object as L
>>> L.append('!')                  changing L changes M too!
>>> L
['Hello', 'world', '!']
>>> M
['Hello', 'world', '!']
```

This applies to shared dictionaries and nested objects too:

```
>>> x = [1, 2]
>>> y = ['a', x, 'c']
>>> z = {'a':x, 'b':2}
>>> x[0] = 3                       change an item inside y and z!
>>> y
['a', [3, 2], 'c']
>>> z
{'a': [3, 2], 'b': 2}
```

Here, *x* is the same as *y[1]* and *z['a']*. This object sharing turns out to be useful in practice. For example, large data structures are passed around a program as shared objects, instead of making frequent copies. References to shared objects also serve as a high-level analog to pointers in lower-level languages. Making true copies is sometimes necessary, but rare. (Incidentally, setting *x[0]* to *y* or *z* here creates a circular object, which causes the printer to loop forever! Don't try this at home.)

Python's data types share common generic operations. Let's look at some operations that work on sequences (lists, strings, and tuples). We've already seen indexing, membership (*in*), and equality. Comparisons are applied recursively to structured objects (even dictionaries), just like equality:

```
>>> x, y = [1, ('a', 3)], [1, ('a', 2)];  print (x > y,  x <= y)
(1 0)
```

Concatenation joins two sequences using the "+" operator. It always returns a new object, rather than changing either operand. Concatenation works on all sequence types but requires both operands to be the same sequence type:

```
>>> [1, 2, 3] + [4, 5, 6]
[1, 2, 3, 4, 5, 6]
>>> 'abc' + 'def'
'abcdef'
>>> (1, 2) + (3, 4) + (5, 6)
(1, 2, 3, 4, 5, 6)
>>> ['a', 2, 'c'] + 'def'      an error!
```

Repetition is just a shorthand: multiplying a sequence object by *N* is exactly like concatenating it *N* times:

```
>>> 'Ni!' * 4                    same as: 'Ni!' + 'Ni!' + 'Ni!' + 'Ni!'
'Ni!Ni!Ni!Ni!'
>>> ['Ni!'] * 4                  same as: ['Ni!'] + ['Ni!'] + ['Ni!'] + ['Ni!']
['Ni!', 'Ni!', 'Ni!', 'Ni!']
```

Slicing is more interesting: slices extract sections of lists, strings and tuples. Slicing doesn't work for dictionaries because they're unordered collections (there's no notion of a contiguous section in a dictionary). Slice expressions return a new object, of the same type as the object sliced. Here are some first examples:

```
>>> L = [3.14159, 'another', [7, 8, 9], 'string']
>>> L[1:]
['another', [7, 8, 9], 'string']
>>> L[:1]
[3.14159]
>>> L[1:] + L[:1]
['another', [7, 8, 9], 'string', 3.14159]
```

The first expression, `L[1:]` means: "create the list that contains items numbered [1] and beyond," which just returns the rest of the list, after the first item. The second expression, `L[:1]`, means: "create the list that contains my items up to but not including item number [1],"which builds a list containing the first item. We then concatenate the first item onto the end of the rest of the list, using the + operator. Slices turn out to be powerful and general operations: for a slicing operation on an ordered sequence object, *Object[LowerBound : UpperBound]*:

- If *LowerBound* is missing, the slicing operation defaults to 0.
- If *UpperBound* is missing, it defaults to the length of the object.
- If *LowerBound* is positive, it's the offset from the front, to the start of the slice.
- If *UpperBound* is positive, it's the offset from the front, to the item just past the end of the slice.
- If *LowerBound* is negative, it's the offset from the end, to the start of the slice.
- If *UpperBound* is negative, it's the offset from the end, to the item just past the end of the slice.
- If either bound exceeds the maximum limit, it's scaled (truncated) to the limit.

Here are some more examples of slices in action on lists:

```
>>> L = [1, 2, 3, 4]
>>> L[2:3]                       items 2..2 (2..(3-1))
[3]
>>> L[2:4]                       items 2..3
[3, 4]
>>> L[2:2]                       items 2..1 (empty)
```

```
[]
>>> L[1:len(L)]                    items 1..3  (len(L) is 4)
[2, 3, 4]
>>> L[-1:]                         items 3..3  (4-1..4-1)
[4]
>>> L[-2:]                         items 2..3
[3, 4]
>>> L[1:-1]                        items 1..2
[2, 3]
>>> L[:-2]                         items 0..1
[1, 2]
>>> L[:]                           items 0..3  (a new, unshared copy of L)
[1, 2, 3, 4]
```

Both indexes and slices can be negative: they simply name the offset from the end (right) instead of the front; again, the end is offset zero. It's actually as easy to access sequences from the end, as from the front. Negative slices extract a left-to-right section, not right-to-left (negative slices don't reverse the section); technically, Python just adds the length of the sequence to a negative index or slice before applying it:

```
>>> S = 'abcd'
>>> S[-1]                          same as: s[len(s)-1]
'd'
>>> S[-2]
'c'
>>> S[-3:-1]                       same as: s[len(s)-3, len(s)-1]  ⇒  s[1:3]
'bc'
>>> S[-1:-3]                       an empty slice: s[3:1],  low > high
''
>>> S[:-1]
'abc'
```

Slices can also be assigned to, which is one way to insert, delete, and overwrite parts of a sequence:

```
>>> L = ['Hello', 'world!']
>>> L[1:1] = ['blue']              insert item, between items 1 and 2
>>> L
['Hello', 'blue', 'world!']
>>> L[2:] = ['and', 'white']       insert 2 items, overwriting items 2..2
>>> L
['Hello', 'blue', 'and', 'white']
>>> L[len(L):] = ['world!']        insert an item at the end, like L.append()
>>> L
['Hello', 'blue', 'and', 'white', 'world!']
>>> L[1:4] = []                    delete items 1 through 3
>>> L
['Hello', 'world!']
```

The *len* function we've been using returns the length of a list (actually, it returns the length of any data structure that defines a length method, as we'll see later). The last slice rule above probably merits an example of its own: out-of-bound indexes are reported for indexing, but corrected for slicing.

```
>>> L
['Hello', 'world!']
>>> L[3]
IndexError: list index out of range
>>> L[0:3]
['Hello', 'world!']
>>> L[-1000:1000]
['Hello', 'world!']
```

Note that slices are not indexing: `L[:1]` is not really the same as `L[0]`, which returns the first item itself, not a list containing the first item. This distinction matters because the + concatenation operator expects two list operands, but the *append* list method expects an item. Slice expressions always return a new sequence object (more accurately, slices return a new object that contains references to items in the old list; the prior discussion about shared nested objects applies to slice results too).

As you can see, slices are flexible. But don't be alarmed by their complexity: they're not essential to all Python programming but are just another handy tool to have around. For instance, lists define methods for inserting and deleting, so slices are really optional in many cases.

One more bit of theory: most of Python's data types are variable in size (they can grow or shrink on demand), but only lists and dictionaries can change in size without making a new object. Here's the case for lists:

```
>>> L = [1, 'shrubbery', 3.14159]
>>> L
[1, 'shrubbery', 3.14159]
>>> L = L + ['another']
>>> L
[1, 'shrubbery', 3.14159, 'another']
>>> del L[0]
>>> L
['shrubbery', 3.14159, 'another']
>>> L.append([7,8,9])
>>> L
['shrubbery', 3.14159, 'another', [7, 8, 9]]
>>> L[1] = (1,2)
>>> L
['shrubbery', (1, 2), 'another', [7, 8, 9]]
```

Here, *L* starts with an integer, a string, and a floating-point number. We tack on another string by concatenating a one-item list with the + operator. Next, the first item `L[0]` is removed using the *del* statement (another generic operation). We then append a list (*[7, 8, 9]*), creating a nested sublist. We finally change the second item to a nested tuple (*(1,2)*). Dictionaries can similarly be grown by assigning to new keys and shrunk using *del* on an indexed item.

This example illustrates the distinction between changing an object in place and creating a new object altogether. In the first two commands (initial assignment and + concatenation), we're creating a new list object, and assigning it to the variable named *L*. But in the last three commands (*del*, *append*, assignment to an index), we're really changing the value of the list *L* refers to, not making a new list. (This is one reason *append* is usually faster than +.)

Unlike lists and dictionaries, strings and tuples can't be changed in place: they're called immutable sequence types. This policy has some benefits we won't discuss here. To modify a string or tuple, a new object must be created using slicing and concatenation:

```
>>> S = 'abc'
>>> S = S + 'xyz'                  bind S to a new object
>>> S
'abcxyz'
>>> S = S[3:]
>>> S
'xyz'
>>> del S[1]                       an error!
>>> S[1] = 'n'                     an error!
>>> S = S[0] + 'n' + S[2:]         ok: makes a new string object
>>> S
'xnz'
```

Although we can't change which items are in a tuple, we can change the items themselves if they are mutable (changeable). For instance,

```
>>> T = ([1, 2], 3)
>>> T[0] = 4
TypeError: can't assign to this subscripted object
>>> T[0][0] = 4
>>> T
([4, 2], 3)
```

Here, we're not allowed to change which item occupies *T[0]*, but we're able to change the value of that item itself because it's a list. This case doesn't apply to strings because the items in strings are all one-character strings, which by definition are immutable themselves.

This rule about mutability (changing data structures in place) seems complex but isn't a big concern in practice. Tuples are not used in contexts where in-place change is desired, and new versions can always be constructed by slicing and concatenating. Since Python lists and dictionaries have no restrictions on in-place changes, they are the tool of choice for modifiable data structures (along with classes, to be described later).

## Operations

Types share operation sets, according to the sequence/mapping/mutable categories. For instance, *in* membership tests work on all sequences: lists, tuples, and strings, but not on dictionaries. Most types also have operations unique to themselves. For example, strings have a special formatting operator that works much like the *sprintf* function in C, but is more general:

```
>>> 'That is %d %s bird!' % (1, 'dead')
That is 1 dead bird!
```

Similarly, lists have a set of methods that work only on lists; we've already seen an example of this earlier: the *append* list method. There are also list methods for sorting, reversing, etc. Because lists are changeable sequences, users of lists can select from all the operators that work on changeable sequences plus the methods that are unique to lists.

Before we move on, it should be pointed out that all the generic operators that work on numbers, strings, lists, tuples, and dictionaries can also be applied to user-defined data types, implemented as classes, or externally in C (extension types). Class instances can be indexed, sliced, concatenated, iterated over in *for* loops, etc. by providing operator overload methods. They can also define unique methods, like lists. C extension types can do the same (but by using different mechanisms).

This pattern of generic operators plus extra methods will hold true for both classes and C extension types. In fact, Python's built-in types are really just predefined C extension types, which provide functions for selected operators and tables of unique method names. We'll see how all this works later. For now, let's move on to some program organization structures: functions, modules, and classes.

# Using Functions

Rather quickly, you'll want to write code that can be used more than once. As in other languages, Python functions are one way to package the implementation of a given task: they allow a program to refer to a section of code by name. Since functions are by now a well-known language construct, let's jump right in to a simple example:

```
>>> def firstFunction(item):
...     print item
...
>>> firstFunction('Hello world!')
Hello world!
```

After defining the function, we call it, passing in the string *Hello world!*. As usual, a function is called by typing its name, followed by parentheses enclosing any data it will use. Here, the function's parameter *item* is assigned the value passed in at the call (our string), and the body of the function is executed . A function call runs the statements indented under the function's header after passed data is assigned to the function's parameters. A function's statements are run only when it is called.

## *Interactive programming*

A note about interactive coding: at the prompt, you can enter any Python statement. When you work interactively, you're really entering statements in a predefined module called `__main__` (modules are discussed next). Because of this fact, we can define new functions at the interactive prompt. In the example, we define a simple function that just prints whatever is passed in; the *def* statement is really a command that creates a function object and adds its name to the current namespace, module `__main__`. When called, the function's name is found in the namespace of the call itself (here, also `__main__`).

Note the absence of type-declarations in *firstFunction*: *item* is an untyped variable. At run-time, callers can pass in strings, integers, floating-point numbers, classes, even another function: *firstFunction* can be used to print any type of Python object. Python is smart enough to know what sort of object is being used, and prints it accordingly. Types originate from object creation: when a value is read in or created by a built-in operation, Python creates an object that carries its type along with it:

```
>>> firstFunction(24)
24
>>> firstFunction(['eggs', 'and', 'spam'])
['eggs', 'and', 'spam']
```

Let's turn to a slightly bigger example:

```
def count(string, chars):
    total = 0
    for x in string:
        if x in chars:
            total = total+1
    return total                    # return the object 'total' refers to
```

This function introduces local variables: the names *total* and *x* (and *string*, *chars*) are untyped variables that exist only while the function runs (more on this topic in a moment). We've also introduced the *return* statement: it simply passes back an object (or a set of objects as a list, tuple, or dictionary) to the caller, which becomes the value of the function call itself. As in C, the *return* statement is optional; if it's absent, a function is a procedure and is called as a statement instead of an expression.

Function *count* is supposed to return the number of characters in *string* that appear in *chars*:

```
>>> x = count('Hello world!', 'l');  x
3
>>> count('Hello world!', 'tutorial hell')
8
```

But because of Python's generic sequence operations, the *count* function can be used for more than we planned:

```
>>> count([1, 2, 3], [2, 4])
1
>>> count(['H', 'a', 'l'], 'Hello world!')
2
```

This sort of generic behavior is typical in Python code. Like everything else in Python, functions can also be used anonymously. The name *firstFunction* is really just a variable in __main__ that is bound to the function object created by *def*. We can use the function indirectly, without the name. Some examples:

```
x = firstFunction
x('Hello world!')

def indirect(func, arg): func(arg)
indirect(firstFunction, 'Hello world!')

schedule = [ (firstFunction, ('Hello world!',)), (count, ([1,2,3], [2,4])) ]
for (func, args) in schedule:
    apply(func, args)
```

Functions are just another type of Python object (just like numbers and lists). In the last example here, we also used the built-in *apply* function, which calls a function object using a tuple of arguments; *apply* is useful when we can't know what sort of argument list will be needed ahead of time.

### *Anonymous functions*

Python also supports anonymous functions with its *exec* and *lambda* tools. *exec* lets us build functions with strings (we'll see how in the body of this book). Here's a simple example of *lambda* at work:

```
>>> t = lambda x, y: x * y      like- def t(x, y): return x * y
>>> t(2,3)
6
```

Here, the lambda is an expression that creates a function that takes two arguments and returns their product. Lambdas are useful in conjunction with Python's functional programming tools (*map*, *reduce*, etc.) discussed later. Lambdas can become arbitrarily complex when nested but we'll ignore this for now.

Python functions have some handy features, such as *optional* and *default arguments*. Optional arguments are analogous to C's *varargs*, and defaults are similar to the same feature in C++. For example:

```
def optional(real, *rest):
    for arg in rest: print arg,       # rest is a tuple of arguments

def default(real, a=1, b=2):
    print a, b

>>> optional(1, 2, 3)
2 3
>>> optional(1)                       nothing gets printed: rest is '()'

>>> default(1, 2, 3)
2 3
>>> default(1)
1 2
```

Arguments are passed to Python functions using a pass-by-object-reference semantics, which is somewhere between C's pass-by-value and Pascal's *var* parameters. We'll look at this in detail later in the book, but it's actually simpler than it sounds: arguments are assigned to parameters in a function header exactly as though they were assigned with the "=" operator. In other words, the parameter in the function is just a reference to a shared object in the caller. So the earlier discussions about tuple unpacking, object sharing, and object mutability apply to argument passing too. For instance:

```
def argumentMagic(a, b, (c, d, e)):
    a = 'xyz'
    b[1] = 9
    e = c + d

>>> l = 'abc'
>>> m = [1, 2, 3]
>>> n = 1.1, 2.2, 0.0
>>> argumentMagic(l, m, n)
>>> l, m, n
('abc', [1, 9, 3], (1.1, 2.2, 0.0))
```

In this function, the assignment to *a* doesn't change *l*: it just creates a new object. The assignment to *b[1]* does change *m* because they share the same mutable object. And the tuple *n* gets unpacked on entry to the function, just like an assignment statement (nothing magic here!), but *n* is not changed. Object references allow functions to send back results both in the *return* statement and by changing structured mutable objects passed in (they can also set global variables, as we'll see in a moment).

As in most languages since Lisp, Python functions can be called recursively:

```
def countDown(N):
    if N == 0:                  # stop the call chain
        print 'Hello world!'
    else:
        print N; countDown(N-1)   # call myself again: N, N-1, N-2,...0
```

In this example, recursion is roughly just an implicit loop: *countDown* keeps calling itself until the exit condition (*N == 0*) is reached. This is exactly like enclosing the function body in a loop:

```
while 1:
    if N == 0:
        print 'Hello world!'; break
    else:
        print N; N = N-1
```

More accurately: a function is recursive if it's called again anywhere (not just from itself) before an earlier call exits. Recursion is a handy tool, especially when traversing big data structures whose size and shape isn't known ahead of time.

In functions, global variables are variables at the outer level of some module (not in a function). It's generally accepted that global variables aren't a good way to pass data in or get results back (this is a complex issue we won't debate here). Changing mutable arguments can be just as bad: in both cases, the function produces side effects the caller may not expect.

Because of the danger of using globals, Python makes it harder to use global variables in a function than locals: in order to change a global variable, we need to declare it with a *global* statement first:

```
def sideEffects(x):
    global moduleVar
    moduleVar = x           # change a variable outside the function
```

As a rule, references can access local or global variables, but assignments always assume the variable is local (and create it locally if it doesn't exist yet), unless we declare it as global. This is really part of a larger issue, Python's name-scoping rules. For instance, functions can be nested (since *def* is just a statement):

```
def outer(x):
    def inner(y):
        return y+1
    return inner(x)          # same as: return x + 1
```

but this only creates a new, local function object and doesn't imply nested namescopes (as in Pascal); we'll defer more details on this topic until later in the book. In Python, functions never exist all by themselves: let's move on to modules.

# *Using Modules*

Although you could write entire programs at the command-line prompt, it's not really practical. Not only does the code you type go away when you quit the command-line interpreter, but there's also no way for you to edit and change the code you've already entered (you have to reenter it from scratch!). The command line is really intended for interactive testing of simple commands and code you've loaded from modules.

Modules address code reuse. Python modules are just text files containing Python statements, which may be loaded into other modules; they're normally written externally to Python using your favorite text editor. Since the interactive prompt is really the module `__main__`, you can load modules and test the objects they define interactively. Let's look at a simple example; the following code:

```
def printer(x):
    print x
```

is typed into a file called *hello.py* using a text editor.

*NOTE* One note on this process: most modern text editors can automatically indent lines according to the line before it. Since Python uses indentation to delimit blocks, it's worthwhile to find out how to do this in your editor. Spaces sometimes work better than tabs for indenting: some window systems change tabs on cut-and-paste operations.

This code can then be loaded and run as follows:

```
>>> import hello
>>> hello.printer('Hello world!')
Hello world!
```

Python source files have a *.py* suffix. Here, the *import* statement directs Python to:

1. Find the file *hello.py*.
2. Execute code in the file.
3. Load all the objects it defines into a new module namespace (*hello*).
4. Load module object *hello* into the current namespace (`__main__`).

We're then able to call the function from the importing module by qualifying it with the containing module's name (*hello.printer*); this dot notation is called an attribute reference. Alternatively, we can load objects in a module into the importer's namespace directly:

```
from hello import printer
```

which adds the name *printer* to the importing module. *from* follows steps 1 though 3 too, but replaces 4 with a copy of variables in the module. If we just want to grab all the objects in a module we use "*":

```
from hello import *
```

In both cases, the function becomes part of the importing module, as though it were typed in its file. We can then call the function directly without qualifying it by the name of the module it came from:

```
>>> from hello import printer
>>> printer('Hello world!')
Hello World!
```

Python looks for imported module files according to its search-path rules: we can define an environment variable, *PYTHONPATH* to include all the directories that we want Python to search for imported modules. The exact way to do this is covered in Chapter 3; most installations initialize the path to include the standard library directory, minimally. Normally, Python searches the current directory (the one where you started Python), so for now you can just start Python from the directory where your module files reside.

A word on code in modules: Python modules can include any sort of statement - *def* statements to create functions, *class* statements to define classes (we'll get to these in a minute), and other executable statements. When a module is imported the first time (by an import statement anywhere in the program), Python loads the module and executes its statements one after another. Some of these statements create new variables, functions, and classes in the imported module's namespace as a side effect. Others perform tasks needed to initialize the module. When the module is reimported later, its code is not reexecuted: instead, its existing objects are just made available to the importer's namespace.

An example will make this clearer: consider a simple implementation of a shared *stack* data structure (a common last-in-first-out list). The following code is typed into file *stack.py*:

*Example E-1: File: stack.py*

```
stack = []

def push(data):
    global stack                        # changes a global
    stack = [data] + stack              # add node to front

def pop():
    global stack
    top, stack = stack[0], stack[1:]    # delete front node
    return top

def empty(): return not stack
```

This module can be imported and used by any number of other modules; all modules will share the same stack:

*Example E-2: File: client1.py*

```
from stack import *
push(123)                    # 'stack' prefix not needed
```

*Example E-3: File: client2.py*

```
import stack
if not stack.empty():
    x = stack.pop()          # qualify by module name
stack.push(1.23)
```

The code that initializes *stack* to an empty list in *stack.py* is only executed once, by either the import in *client1.py* or *client2.py*, whichever is executed first. Executable code in modules is also useful for initializing module constants and to arrange for executing its contents automatically when it's imported or run on a Python command line:

*Example E-4: File: module.py*

```
def doStuff():
    print 'Bring out your dead...'

doStuff()
```

The function *doStuff* will be called automatically when *module* is first imported. Or, similarly:

*Example E-5: File: script.py*

```
def doStuff():
    print 'The owls are not what they seem.'

if __name__ == '__main__': doStuff()
```

Here, the function *doStuff* will be run automatically only when this module file is run as an immediate argument on a Python command line:

```
% python script.py
```

because each module gets a variable named `__name__` automatically, which is set to `__main__` when the module is loaded from a system Python command line like this (`__main__` refers to whatever is the top-level program). On UNIX systems, it's also possible to make a module directly executable by naming the path to the Python interpreter on the first line; these are usually called shell scripts (we'll see some later):

```
#!/usr/local/bin/python
<a python module>
```

To importers, modules are namespaces. They're perhaps best understood by realizing that they're just Python dictionaries internally. In fact, a module's dictionary can be accessed explicitly if desired. When a module is imported, Python creates a new dictionary and executes the code in the module. Any named objects created by the code (functions, classes, variables, even imported modules) are inserted into the module's dictionary as *'name':object* pairs, ready for access by importers.

The importers of a module either have the module itself inserted into their own module dictionary (*import module*) or have a set of dictionary entries copied over to their own dictionary (*from module import x*). And the module's namespace is itself the implicit global scope for name references in its own code. For instance:

*Example E-6: File: mod1.py*

```
x = 1
```

*Example E-7: File: mod2.py*

```
import mod1
```

*Example E-8: File: mod3.py*

```
import mod2
mod2.mod1.x = 2     # mod3 sets mod1's x
```

Here, the three modules have three namespaces, which are just three dictionaries. Qualification really just indexes the dictionaries associated with the module objects imported. Each module has a built-in attribute called `__dict__` which returns its dictionary, so the equivalence is as follows:

```
module.attribute        ⇔        module.__dict__['attribute']
```

and in the example above:

```
mod2.mod1.x             ⇔        mod2.__dict__['mod1'].__dict__['x']
```

Class attributes (to be discussed next) behave in roughly the same way.

Some more random points: when you start Python, there's a set of built-in modules ready to be imported. We'll look at all of these later, but one that's pervasive is *sys*: by importing the *sys* module, you can access information about the Python system. Some of what's available in the *sys* module:

*sys.path*
: Python's module search path, initialized to *PYTHONPATH*

*sys.argv*
: command-line arguments passed to a Python program

*sys.ps1, ps2*
: The interactive prompt strings (so you can change them)

*sys.stdin/out/err*
: Standard input, output, and error stream files (from C's standard streams)

*sys.modules*
: A dictionary giving all the modules already loaded

The *modules* attribute can be used to access any module, regardless of how or where it was imported:

```
module.attribute   ⇔   sys.modules['module'].__dict__['attribute']
```

To support incremental development, Python also includes a built-in function, *reload(<module>)*, which reloads a module already imported. Dynamic reloading leads to this sort of development cycle:

```
edit module file M.py
import M
repeat:
    test objects in M
    edit module file M.py
    reload(M)
until M works
```

*reload* has some limitations, but it's another useful tool to have: there's no need to stop Python each time you change a module file. There's also no need to stop a running program to reload one of its modules.

Wrapping up: modules are the largest program organization unit in Python programs. They're a level of grouping above functions and partition a program's set of functions into larger sets. Modules do the work of C's include files and also provide for dynamic linking in Python.

Modules can be implemented in Python or C (or any C-compatible language); when a module is imported, its objects are transparently linked into the Python image, whether it's written in Python or C. We discuss C modules in Chapter 14, *Extending Python*. Modules can also contain class definitions, and we turn to this topic next.

# Using Classes

In simple terms, Python classes are namespaces too, but support inheritance of attributes, and multiple instantiations (copies): each instance uses the class's data and has some of its own to record its state. Classes also don't correspond to an entire external source file; instead, classes (like functions) are defined inside a module. As in C++, classes are Python's basic object-oriented programming (OOP) construct. Let's start with a simple example:

```
class FirstClass:                   # class
    def printer(self, text):        # method
        print text

>>> x = FirstClass()
>>> x.printer('Hello world!')
```

We first define a class called *FirstClass*, using the compound *class* statement. We next create an instance of the class (*x*), by calling the class like a function. Finally, we call the *printer* method of the instance, by using the same "." qualifier syntax used for objects in a module, and our message is printed.

In this example, the *class* statement defines the class itself, *FirstClass*, with one method called *printer*. The class name becomes a constructor of instances of the class. It can be used to create any number of instances; each instance shares the class's symbols, and can get some of its own:

```
x = FirstClass()
y = FirstClass()
x.name = 'x'
y.name = 'Hello world!'
x.printer(y.name)              # prints 'Hello world!' again
```

Here, the instances *x* and *y* get a new attribute; each of them has its own local copy of *name*, which is not part of the class itself. In Python, attributes can be added and deleted dynamically. But normally instance members are created by being assigned in the class itself, instead of outside the class as in this example, to maintain consistency. We need a slightly bigger example to see how:

```
class SecondClass:
    def printer(self, text):
        print text
    def print_name(self):
        self.printer(self.name)      # get this instance's name
    def set_name(self, value):
        self.name = value            # set this instance's name

x = SecondClass()
y = SecondClass()

x.set_name('Hello world!')
y.set_name('Goodbye world!')

x.print_name()                       # prints 'Hello world!'
y.print_name()                       # prints 'Goodbye world!'
```

Here, we set per instance data in the class (*set_name*), not outside it. Since instance variable values can vary per instance like this, classes must qualify instance variable references by the instance itself. To support this, when an instance's method is called, the instance itself is automatically passed in as the implied first argument to the class method (and usually called *self*, by convention).

The reference to *self.name* in *print_name* fetches the instance's attribute, and the reference to *self.printer* gets the class's function (which is inherited by the instance). The value of *self.name* is different in *x* and *y*, the two instances of the class; by qualifying with *self*, we're sure to get the data in the instance that's the implied subject of a method call.

If *printer*, *print_name*, and *set_name* in *SecondClass* look familiar, they should: methods are just nested functions, with an instance argument added at the call. In fact, class statements simply introduce a new named namespace, just like modules: statements indented under the *class* statement header are executed when the class statement is, one after another. Some of them (*def*, variable assignments) create named objects in the class's namespace as a side effect, which become its methods and data members:

*Example E-9: File: feet.py*

```
class ShoeSketch:                      # make a new class object
    print 'making a class...'          # printed when the class is defined
    shoeSize = 7.5                     # class data shared by all instances
    def feet(self, value = None):      # make a method function
        if not value:
            return self.numFeet        # get my feet:  x.feet()
        else:
            self.numFeet = value       # set my feet:  x.feet(N)
    def worth(self):
        return self.numFeet * self.shoeSize
```

```
>>> import feet
making a class...
>>> x = feet.ShoeSketch()
>>> x.feet(3)
>>> x.feet(), x.worth()
(3, 22.5)
```

This is identical in spirit to modules, except that modules are a file of commands, and classes are not: more than one class can appear in a file. Functions (and hence methods) work differently: the statements indented under them aren't executed until the function is called; statements in classes and modules execute immediately.

In this example, *shoeSize* is a class member: it's shared by all instances made from the class. Classes don't normally include assignments outside methods for members that vary from instance to instance. But assignments inside class statements like this can be used to initialize constants, global counters, etc.

Python's distinction between classes and instances is important. When we create an instance, we're really making a new namespace that inherits the names in the class's namespace. A given class processes any number of instances: when a method is called, Python adds the instance to the front of the argument list automatically. The mapping from instance attributes to class members looks like this:

```
Instance.Method(args,...)    ⇔    Class.Method(Instance, args,...)
```

where Python determines the class implementing the method, according to the instance's inheritance paths. Unlike the implicit *this* argument in C++ methods, the instance in Python is always implicit at the call, but explicit in the method function: it's included in the class method arguments, and all instance data and class data must be accessed by qualifying it in method functions.

Python classes are designed to inherit members from other classes. This allows us to customize, override, and extend an existing class to do what we need. For example, we could have used inheritance in the example above to avoid a new *printer* method in *SecondClass*:

```
class FirstClass:
    def printer(self, text):
        print text

class SecondClass(FirstClass):            # SecondClass is a FirstClass
    def print_name(self):
        self.printer(self.name)
    def set_name(self, value):
        self.name = value

x = SecondClass()
x.set_name('Hello world!')
x.print_name()                            # both calls print our motto
x.printer('Hello world')
```

Here, we've made *SecondClass* a subclass of *FirstClass* (the superclass) by listing it in parentheses after the class name. Because of this, *SecondClass* inherits all the functions and variables in *FirstClass* unless it redefines them. The instance we create similarly inherits the union of the two classes' names and can change them locally as well. Like C++, Python also supports multiple inheritance (a class with more than one superclass listed in its header) and resolves conflicts by a depth-first search of the class hierarchy: the first occurrence of the attribute wins. We'll postpone discussion of this topic until later.

When we qualify a class instance's attribute, the type (class) of an object (instance) determines what that object's methods do. In Python, all methods and data members are virtual in the C++ sense, simply because all attribute references are looked up at run-time in the qualified object: *object.attribute* always depends on what *object* is bound to. Polymorphism really comes for free in dynamic languages like Python. Here's part of the classic (though artificial) *zooanimal* example in Python to illustrate:

```
class Animal:
    def reply(self):   self.speak()
    def speak(self):   print 'spam'

class Mammal(Animal):
    def speak(self):   print 'huh?'
```

```
class Cat(Mammal):
    def speak(self):    print 'meow'

class Dog(Mammal):
    def speak(self):    print 'bark'

class Primate(Mammal):
    def speak(self):    print 'Hello world!'

class Hacker(Primate):
    pass

>>> spot = Cat()
>>> spot.reply()
meow
>>> data = Hacker()
>>> data.reply()
Hello world!
```

Here, the call to *self.speak()* in the *Animal* superclass performs the *speak* method associated with the *lowest* class of the instance: *Animal* doesn't need to know what kind of animal the instance is. This set of classes defines a hierarchy (sometimes called a framework) that looks something like Figure E-2.

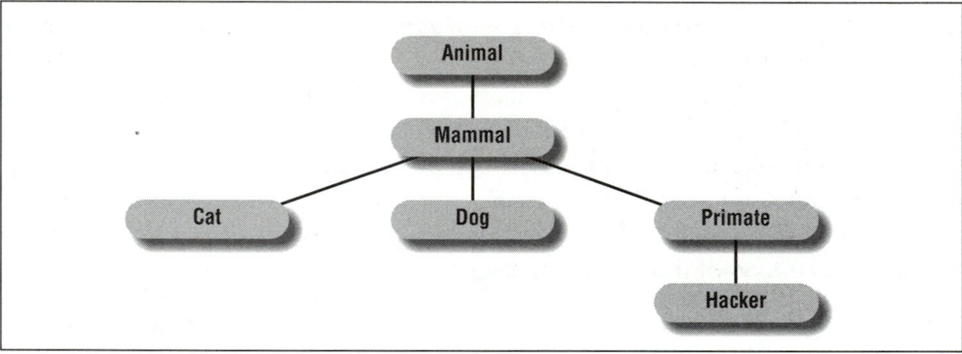


*Figure E-2: Zoo animal class hierarchy*

*Hacker* has no methods of its own, but inherits from *Primate*, which inherits from *Mammal*, which inherits from *Animal*. When we call the *reply* method of the *Hacker* instance, it runs *Animal*'s *reply*, which in turn calls the *Primate*'s *speak* method (*self.speak* finds the first *speak* by looking at *Hacker* and above). Finally, our message gets printed.

Of course, this is a contrived example, but the concepts apply to many programming scenarios. Graphical user interface (GUI) programming is a classic example: instead of animals, the hierarchy may contain *window* classes that inherit basic functionality and add some of their own (borders, containers, etc.).

Python classes also support most common OOP features. For instance, constructors and destructors are coded by defining the special method names `__init__` and `__del__`, respectively:

```
class Incarnation:
    def __init__(self):
        print 'Hello world!'
    def __del__(self):
        print 'Goodbye world!'

>>> x = Incarnation()
Hello world!
>>> x = 0
Goodbye world!
```

A class constructor is called when a new instance is created; this is a handy place to perform initialization tasks. The destructor, if present, is called when the instance is about to be reclaimed (which in Python, is usually when the last reference to the instance is removed). Apart from this automatic invocation, constructors and destructors are normal methods: they're inherited by subclasses, and constructors can take extra arguments for setting initial values. One implication of this is that (unlike C++) Python runs only one constructor or destructor automatically; sometimes, the invocation has to be passed along manually, by calling superclass methods:

```
class Mammal:
    def __init__(self, legs):
        self.legs = legs

class Primate(Mammal):
    def __init__(self, stance, legs):
        self.stance = stance
        Mammal.__init__(self, legs)     # call superclass init manually

class Hacker(Primate):
    def __init__(self, name):
        self.name = name
        Primate.__init__(self, 'upright', 2)

>>> x = Hacker('Data')            x has members 'name', 'stance', 'legs'
>>> print x.stance, x.name, x.legs
('upright', 'Data', 2)
```

In this example we called superclass methods directly from subclasses. Destructor calls can be passed to superclasses in this way too (destructors aren't as important in Python as in languages like C++ because we don't need to delete instance data manually: it's reclaimed by Python's garbage collection).

This example also illustrates the OOP paradigm of specializing superclass methods. Calling superclass `__init__` methods directly is just one way to extend a superclass. In general, superclasses define default behaviors, which can be replaced, enhanced, or customized in subclasses, by redefining methods that call superclass methods as part of their own action. Subclasses can also introduce completely new behavior, as new methods and variables. Here's a more comprehensive example.

```
class Mammal:
    def traits(self):
        return ['live-births', 'warm-blooded']

class Cat(Mammal):
    def lifespan(self):                  # inherit below
        return (10, 30)                  # add extra behavior

class Primate(Mammal):
    def traits(self):
        return ['large-brain'] + Mammal.traits(self)     # extend below

class Hacker(Primate):
    def traits(self):
        return ['enjoys-spam']                           # over-ride below

>>> data, cheetah, spot = Hacker(), Primate(), Cat()
>>> spot.traits()
['live-births', 'warm-blooded']
>>> cheetah.traits()
['large-brain', 'live-births', 'warm-blooded']
>>> data.traits()
['enjoys-spam']
```

Again, this is an artificial example, but the paradigm applies to real programming problems. For instance, a GUI program's window subclass might redefine a *draw* method which calls a superclass *draw* and writes some components of its own on top of those written by the superclass.

In OOP, there's an important distinction between inheritance and composition: inheritance deals with specializations and composition with compound objects. Composition is represented by embedding class instances in other class instances: one instance is made to contain another, by assigning an instance to another instance's attribute name:

*Example E-10: File: parrot.py*

```
class Actor:
    def line(self): print self.name + ':', `self.says()`

class Customer(Actor):
    name = 'customer'
    def says(self): return "that's one ex-bird!"
```

*Example E-10: File: parrot.py (continued)*

```
class Clerk(Actor):
    name = 'clerk'
    def says(self): return "no it isn't..."

class Parrot(Actor):
    name = 'parrot'
    def says(self): return None

class Scene:
    def __init__(self):
        self.clerk    = Clerk()                 # embed some instances
        self.customer = Customer()              # Scene is a composite
        self.subject  = Parrot()

    def action(self):
        self.customer.line()                    # delegate to embedded
        self.clerk.line()
        self.subject.line()
```

```
>>> import parrot
>>> parrot.Scene().action()
customer: "that's one ex-bird!"
clerk: "no it isn't..."
parrot: None
>>>
```

Here, a *Scene* contains three *Actors*: a Customer, Clerk, and Parrot. All three are independent classes (not subclasses of a Scene). When we ask a *Scene* to run its *action* method, it delegates the request to the embedded objects, which know what to say. Of course, this example is artificial too, but representative. In a GUI program, a window class may contain buttons, scrollbars, etc.; drawing requests are delegated to its components. In our example, Figure E-3 shows how the method call is passed off to contained class instances:

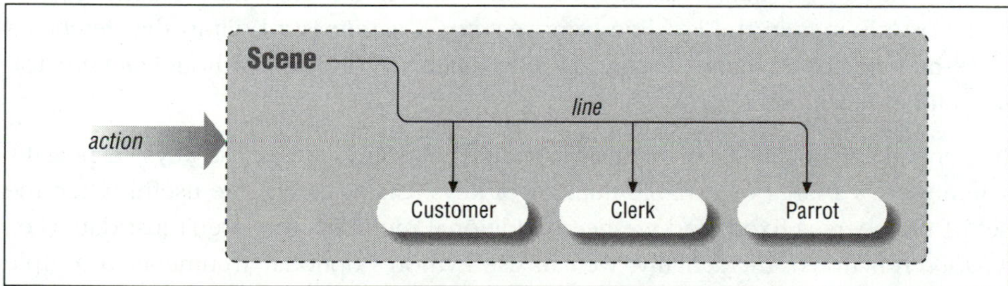


*Figure E-3: Composition—embedded class objects*

Earlier in this appendix, I promised to show how classes could be used to implement data records. Here's one way this can be done:

```
class Language:
    def __init__(self, name=(), disk=0, role=[]):
        self.author = name
        self.disk   = disk
        self.role   = role

table = { 'Perl':   Language(('Wall', 'L.'),       2, 'stuff'),
          'Tcl':    Language(('Ousterhout', 'J.'), 3, 'other-stuff'),
          'Python': Language(('van Rossum', 'G.'), 1, 'more-stuff')
        }
```

Fields can be fetched by qualification:

```
table['Python'].author              # ('van Rossum', 'G.')
table['Perl'].author[0]             # 'Wall'
table['Python'].role                # 'more-stuff'
getattr(table['Python'], 'role')    # 'more-stuff'
```

Fields are assigned in the same way:

```
table['Python'].role = ['system', 'extension', 'gui', 'rad']
```

---

*NOTE* In fact, the *Language* class can be used to create a table of persistent Python objects, which are retained between program executions. (See the discussion of *pickle* and *shelve* in Chapter 12, *Persistent Information.*)

---

Here, language details are stored as an instance of the *Language* class. If you compare this example to the earlier version, the similarity of classes and dictionaries stands out. In fact, the only major difference is that dictionary items are indexed, and class items are qualified: class attributes really are a dictionary internally. This is almost obvious in the last line using *getattr()*: *getattr* is a built-in that fetches a class member by its name *string*, just like dictionary indexing (though *getattr* follows inheritance paths too).

In general, dictionaries are better for simple mapping of data to keys, especially when there's a large or variable number of keys. Classes are more useful when the set of members is fixed, and we need additional members that aren't just data (i.e., *method* functions). Incidentally, we can use Python's optional arguments and tuple unpacking to make the __init__ method shorter here, if we don't need the defaults:

```
class Language:
    def __init__(self, *info): self.author, self.disk, self.role = info
```

Since Python allows class members to be added at run-time, we can also use empty classes to represent records, though we may run into fairly perplexing bugs if we're not consistent:

```
class Record: pass

x = Record()                          # like x = {}
x.author = ('van Rossum', 'G.')       # like x['author'] = ...
x.role   = ['sys', 'glue', 'rad']     # like x['role'] = ...
```

Unless the empty *Record* class inherits other functionality from another class, you might as well just use dictionaries for the records here; it's mostly a question of syntax: qualifying versus indexing (class representation may take up slightly more space). Let's move on to one last topic: exceptions.

# *Exception Handling*

Python has a simple facility for catching errors in an orderly fashion; this feature also turns out to be handy for implementing long jumps and alternative control flows in general. In Python, this all comes under the heading of exceptions, and is supported by two new statements: *try* and *raise*. To illustrate this topic, here's our running example again:

```
>>> printer = 'printer'
>>> try:
...     raise printer
...     print 'never reached'
... except printer:
...     print 'Hello world!'
...
Hello world!
```

The *try* statement defines a block of code that's to be executed as usual and a set of exceptions that are to be caught if they occur while the code block is running. The *raise* statement triggers an exception. In this example, the *raise* statement makes Python jump to the *except* clause immediately and print our message. After the *except* block executes, control then continues past the entire *try* statement. User-defined exceptions are any object; we define a string object (*printer*) to identify our exception.

Genuine program errors such as out-of-bounds indexes, division by zero, etc., cause Python to raise exceptions, and we can catch these with *try* too. The exception need not occur in the code of the *try* block itself to be caught: it can occur arbitrarily deep in a function-call chain started in the block:

```
def kaboom(list, n):
    print list[n]              # trigger IndexError
```

```
x = [0, 1, 2]
try:
    kaboom(x, 3)
except IndexError:
    print 'Hello world!'         # print 'Hello world!' the hard way...
```

The *try* statement is actually a lot more general than these examples suggest. For example, there may be more than one *except* clause, a selection list for an *except*, a default empty *except*, an *else* clause for exit if no exception occurred, and an argument on exceptions for additional information:

```
try:
    just_do_it()
except IndexError:                              # exception name
    print 'Out of bounds'
except SymbolNotFound, name:                    # name, info ('raise x, y')
    print "Name '%s' not found" % name
except (e1, e2, e3):                            # if e1 or e2 or e3 raised
    pass
except:                                         # default (for all other names)
    print 'Other error'; raise FatalError
else:                                           # if no exceptions occur
    print 'No errors.'
```

*try* statements can also be written with a *finally* clause:

```
file = open('data', 'r')  # open a file (discussed later)
try:
    stuff(file)           # the file has been opened here
finally:
    file.close()          # close the file no matter what happens in stuff
```

The *finally* part is executed on exit from the *try* block, regardless of whether an exception was raised or not. This is useful for clean-up tasks. *finally* can't appear in the same *try* statement as *except* and *else*; moreover, it doesn't clear the exception (it propagates higher, after the *finally* block exits).

Exceptions can *nest*: when one is raised, Python locates the closest (most recent) *try* statement that catches it. If it must be propagated, the *try* statement can *raise* it again:

```
speak = 'speak'

def hacker():
    try:
        raise speak               # go to hacker's except
        print 'not reached'
    except speak:
        print 'Hello world!'
        raise speak               # go to primate's except
```

```
def primate():
    try:
        hacker()
        print 'not reached'
    except speak:
        print 'Huh?'
        raise speak                    # go to mammal's except

def mammal():
    try:
        primate()
        print 'not reached'
    except speak:
        print 'Spam!'

>>> mammal()
Hello world!
Huh?
Spam!
```

There's more to say about exceptions than this; for example, they can be used to implement exotic control structures like backtracking (with a little more work to back out assignments).

One last note: like all dynamic languages, Python can't catch some common coding errors until run-time (misspelled variable names, type mismatches, etc.); if it did, it would sacrifice most of its flexibility. Luckily, Python also provides a powerful exception handling system that makes error handling simple.

# Conclusion

And that's a wrap for this brief tutorial. There's much we haven't covered yet; at this point you should probably proceed to read Part 2, (if you haven't already) for more information. The topics we touched on here are revisited and expanded on there. But the concepts and terminology we introduced here should make Part 2, and the bigger examples of Part 3, *Tools and Applications*, easier to grasp.

# F

# *Python Classes for C++ Programmers*

This appendix briefly summarizes some of the differences between Python and C++ classes. Python's *class* system can be thought of as a subset of C++'s. Though the comparison to Modula 3 is probably closer, C++ is the dominant OOP language today. But in Python things are intentionally simpler:

*Attributes*
: Although we've used both terms, there's no real distinction between data members and methods. In Python, both simply designate named attributes of instances or classes, bound to functions or other kinds of objects.

*"this" pointer*
: Python's equivalent of the C++ *this* instance pointer is the first argument added to method function calls (and usually called *self* by convention). It's usually implicit in a call but is used explicitly in methods: there's no hidden instance scope for unqualified names. Python methods are just functions nested in a *class* statement which receive the implied instance object in their leftmost parameter.

*Virtual methods*
: All methods and data members are virtual in the C++ sense: there's no notion of a compile-time resolution of attributes based on an object's type. Every attribute qualification (*object.name*) is resolved at run-time, based on the object's type.

*Pure virtuals*

Methods called by a superclass but not defined by it correspond to C++'s concept of "pure virtual" methods: methods that must be redefined in a subclass. Since Python is not statically compiled, there's no need for C++'s special syntax to declare this case. Calls to undefined methods raise a name error exception at run-time.

*Static members*

We don't need to declare *static* class data: assignments nested in a class statement make members associated with the class and shared by all its instances.

*Private members*

There's no notion of access restrictions for attributes: every member and method is public in the C++ sense. Attribute hiding is a matter of convention rather than syntax: C++'s public, private, and protected constraints don't apply.

*Const interfaces*

There's no equivalent of C++'s *const* modifier: nothing prevents an object from being changed in a method. Although methods can change mutable arguments (the *self* object, for example), Python again relies on convention instead of extra syntax.

*Reference parameters*

There's no direct analogue for C++'s *reference* parameters. Python methods may return multiple values in a tuple, and can change passed-in objects if they're mutable (for instance, by assigning to an object's attributes or changing lists and dictionaries in place). But there's no aliasing between names at the call and names in a function header: arguments are passed by assignment, which creates shared object references.

*Function overloads*

Python polymorphism is based on virtual method calls: the type of a qualified object determines what its methods do. Since Python arguments are typeless, there's nothing like C++'s function overloading for dispatching to different versions of a function based on the datatypes of its arguments. If needed, we can test types in methods, instead of writing separate functions for each type combination. Since dictionary keys may be type objects it's also possible to branch on types by indexing. (See Chapter 9, *Moving Menus to Classes*.)

*Multiple inheritance*

Python resolves multiple inheritance conflicts instead of treating them as errors. When multiple inheritance is used, Python takes the first appearance of an attribute during a depth-first/left-to-right search through the superclass tree.

*Virtual inheritance*

C++'s notion of virtual base classes isn't needed in Python. A Python class instance is a single namespace dictionary (with a class pointer for access to inherited attributes). Classes add attributes to the class-instance dictionary by assignment. Because of this structure, each attribute exists in just one place—the instance dictionary. For inherited class attributes, the search of the superclass tree resolves references unambiguously.

*Constructors*

Python only runs the one `__init__` method found by inheritance; it doesn't run all accessible classes' constructors automatically. We have to call other class constructors manually, if needed. But this is no harder than specifying superclass constructor arguments in C++. Python destructors (`__del__`) run when an instance is garbage collected (i.e., deallocated), not in response to *delete* calls.

*Scope operators*

In C++, a scope operator of the form *Superclass::Method()* is used to extend inherited methods and disambiguate inheritance conflicts. Python's equivalent is *Superclass.Method()*, a class object qualification. It isn't required for inheritance conflict resolution but can be used to override the default search rule.

*Other concepts*

We've seen that `__getattr__` works much like C++ -> overloading. Python class instances are generated by calling a class like a function and reclaimed automatically: there's no *new*, and Python's *del* just removes a reference, unlike C++'s *delete*. Finally, special method names are used to overload operators (`__add__`): there's no "operator+"-like syntax but the effects are similar.

Because C++ is a superset of C, all the comments in the text comparing Python to C apply to C++ too. For example, we can't overload = in Python as we can in C++ because assignment isn't an operator in Python. And pointers, central to much C and C++ programming, are completely absent in Python (though object references can have some of the same effects). Instead, Python programs use first-class objects, which are automatically allocated and reclaimed.

Naturally, Python has additional class features not found in C++, including:

- Metaobject protocols: `__setattr__`, etc.
- Bound and unbound method reference objects
- First-class class objects

- Dynamic method construction
- Dynamically typed method arguments and members
- Run-time access to implementation components: `__dict__`, `__class__`, *type()*, and so on.

See discussions in the main text for more details.

## *In Python, less is more*

And that's probably as many comparisons as we should try to draw with C++. Python is a very different kind of language: it's intended to be a simple tool which lends itself to writing programs *fast*—much faster than a static language like C++. Because of that characteristic, many of the ideas in C++ just wouldn't make sense in Python.

For example, the lack of private and protected access mechanisms may seem odd to C++ programmers. But in Python, they'd mostly just be extra noise: Python is not really meant for writing huge, multiprogrammer, ultra-efficient systems. Many of C++'s rules would probably get in the way in Python programming.

In fact, most of the differences noted above deal with C++ features that are the source of much of the confusion in C++ programming. In Python, most of these concepts are implemented in simpler form or are missing altogether.

C++ is a large, complex language, useful for writing efficient systems, using traditional development modes. While such a complex tool might make sense in C++'s intended domains, in a rapid development tool like Python the fewer language rules we have to deal with, the better.

# Bibliography

## Python Topics

Bauer, Jeff. *Introduction to Python.*

An overview article in the January 1996 issue of the *Linux Journal*

Conway, Matt. *A Tkinter Life Preserver.*

The essential reference manual for the Python/*Tk* GUI interface. Available on the CD-ROM and by anonymous FTP from *ftp.python.org* (currently in directory *pub/python/doc*).

Dubois, Paul, Konrad Hinsen, and James Hugunin. *Numerical Python.*

An article in the May/June 1996 issue of *Computers in Physics.*

Janssen, Bill. *Using ILU with Python: A Tutorial.*

Documents the ILU distributed object system interface. Currently at *ftp://ftp.parc.xerox.com/pub/ilu/ilu.html*, but see Python's FAQ for up-to-date sources. General ILU manuals are available from the same source.

Manheimer (original), Ken, Chris Hoffmann, and Anthony Baxter. *Quick Reference Documents.*

The Postscript *QuickRef* and ASCII *cheatsheet* versions are in the Python *Misc* directory. The HTML version of *QuickRef* currently appears at *ftp.python.org*, in the *pub/python/doc* directory.

van Rossum, Guido. *An Introduction to Python for UNIX/C Programmers.*

In the proceedings of the NLUUG (the Dutch UNIX users' group) najaarsconferentie 1993 meeting, November 1993. The PostScript files for this paper and also for the slides used for the accompanying presentation are currently available via anonymous FTP *ftp://ftp.python.org/pub/python/doc*, as files *nluug-paper.ps* and *nluug-slides.ps.*

———. *Slides for a Talk on Python.*

Presented at Usenix Symposium on Very High Level Languages in Santa Fe, NM, October 1994. Available as *ftp://ftp.python.org/pub/python/doc/vhll-slides.ps.*

———. *Python Reference Manuals.*

A Tutorial, Language Reference, Library Reference, and Extending Reference are available with the Python package, or individually by FTP from *ftp://ftp.python.org*. They're also available in hypertext form for browsing over the WWW, at *http://www.python.org*. The library manual is available in Emacs INFO form at: *ftp://ftp.python.org/pub/python/doc/lib-info.tar.gz.*

———, and Jelke de Boer. *Interactively Testing Remote Servers Using the Python Programming Language.* CWI Quarterly, Volume 4, Issue 4 , December 1991, pp. 283–303.

Watters, Aaron. *The What, Why, Who, and Where of Python.* UnixWorld Online, Tutorial Article No. 005 located at http://www.wcmh.com/uworld/archives/95/tutorial/005.html , 1995.

———, Guido van Rossum, and James C. Ahlstrom. *Internet Programming with Python.* M&T Books (MIS Press/Henry Holt and Co.) , Fall, 1996.

## *Tk Documentation*

The first source of *Tkinter* information is usually Matt Conway's *A Tkinter Life Preserver,* the manual referenced earlier. Beyond this, there are a number of *Tcl/Tk* books available, and *Tk* man pages. Since there's a fairly direct mapping from *Tk* to Python's *Tkinter,* the reader can extrapolate from *Tk* documentation to *Tkinter* use.

Ousterhout, John. *Tcl and the Tk Toolkit.* Reading, MA: Addison-Wesley.

This is the book by the inventor of both the *Tcl* language, and the *Tk* GUI extension.

———. *Tk* manpages.

Shipped with the *Tk* system. *Tcl* and *Tk* can be found at many FTP sites. One prominent current carrier: *ftp://ftp.sunlabs.com/pub/tcl.* See Chapter 3, *Getting Started,* for more details.

Welch, Brent. *Practical Programming in Tcl and Tk.* Englewood Cliffs, NJ: Prentice-Hall.

## Other Topics

*Compilers, Principles, Techniques, and Tools.* Reading, MA: Addison-Wesley.

Booch, Grady. *Object Oriented Analysis and Design with Applications.* Menlo Park, CA: Benjamin/Cummings.

Date, C. J.. *An Introduction to Database Systems.* Reading, MA: Addison-Wesley.

Kernighan, Brian and Rob Pike. *The UNIX Programming Environment.* Englewood Cliffs, NJ: Prentice-Hall.

Page-Jones, Meilir. *The Practical Guide to Structured Systems Design.* Englewood Cliffs, NJ: Prentice-Hall.

Rochkind, Marc J.. *Advanced UNIX Programming.* Englewood Cliffs, NJ: Prentice-Hall.

Sethi, Ravi. *Programming Languages, Concepts and Constructs.* Reading, MA: Addison-Wesley.

Tanimoto, Steven. *The Elements of Artificial Intelligence.* Computer Science Press.

## Other Languages

Budd, Timothy. *A Little Smalltalk.* Reading, MA: Addison-Wesley.

Cargill, Tom. *C++ Programming Style.* Reading, MA: Addison-Wesley.

Griswold, Griswold and. *The Icon Programming Language.* Englewood Cliffs, NJ: Prentice-Hall.

Kernighan, Brian and Dennis Ritchie. *The C Programming Language.* Englewood Cliffs, NJ: Prentice-Hall.

Lippman, Stanley B. *C++ Primer.* Reading, MA: Addison-Wesley.

Oualline, Steve. *Practical C Programming.* Sebastopol, CA: O'Reilly & Associates.

Sterling, Leon and Ehud Shapiro. *The Art of Prolog.* Cambridge, MA: The MIT Press.

Wall, Larry, Tom Christiansen, and Randal L. Schwartz. *Programming Perl, Second Edition.* Sebastopol, CA: O'Reilly & Associates.

*Lisp.* Reading, MA: Addison-Wesley.

# Glossary

**:-)**
A "smiley" symbol; it means something's supposed to be funny (See also YMMV)

**AI**
Artificial intelligence; also: a sound developers make after a disk crash

**API**
Application programming interface: the interface to a library or system

**assignment**
Binding values (object references) to variable names or data structure components

**attribute**
A named object, in an object that supports attributes: "b" in "a.b"

**Bob, Emily, Buddy**
Many of the names in the examples come from classic American television shows

**byte code**
A portable intermediate representation for programs in Python

**callback**
An event routed to a registered handler function

**class**
A template for creating instances and subclass trees; an object with attributes

**cohesion**
How components relate to the purpose of a program unit

**command line**
Words on the line of text used to invoke a program in a shell (*sys.argv*)

**compiler**
A program that translates another program to a more primitive representation

**composition**
Embedding objects in other objects.

**CORBA**
Common Object Request Broker Architecture: a distributed-object protocol

**coupling**
How program units are linked into bigger systems (obvious joke omitted)

**CPU**
Central processing unit; the busiest monkey in the machine

**dictionary**
A collection providing access by key (hashing)

**DLL**
Dynamically loaded library (object code file) on Microsoft Windows platforms

**DOS**
The basic disk operating system on most PCs

**dynamic typing**
In Python: objects without predefined type or size constraints

**emacs**
A text editor, and a whole lot more

**embedding**
Running Python code from within another system or language

**encapsulation**
Hiding object implementations behind well-defined interfaces; abstraction

**EOF**
End of File; a special case communicated by file processing interfaces

**exception**
Python's mechanism for communicating unusual events to programs

**executable**
A program that can be run by itself, from an operating-system shell

**extending**
Adding new functionality by coding Python programs, C modules, or C types

**FAQ**
Frequently Asked Questions file; a common public domain documentation tool

**FFI**
Foreign Function Interface; in Python, the C extensions API

**first-class objects**
In Python every object falls into the same generic category

**FOOD**
Just checking if you're awake

**framework**
A system of interrelated classes, allowing for extension and inheritance

**FTP**
File Transfer Protocol: a utility for copying files across the Internet

**function pointer**
A reference to (address of) a function in C

**garbage collection**
Strategies for reclaiming memory when it's no longer needed (but no sooner)

**globbing**
Filename expansion: collecting filenames in a directory that match a pattern

**grail**
A WWW browser, which may be extended in Python and/or C

**grammar**
A formal description of the legal sentences in a language (for parsing)

**GUI**
Graphical user interface: windows, buttons, etc.

**GUIDO**
A GUI for distributed objects (his idea, not mine :-)

**hierarchy**
See framework

**HTML**
Hypertext markup language; a standard language for designing WWW pages

**ILU**
CORBA-based distributed object system, with an interface for Python (See also CORBA)

**index**
To fetch a component in a collection, by offset (sequences) or key (mappings)

**inheritance**
Taking on the attributes defined in classes higher in a hierarchy

**instance**
A realization of a class (or built-in type) with a new attribute namespace

**integration tests**
Testing a system as a whole; the sum of its components

**Internet**
A network of linked computers, supporting FTP, mail, News, WWW, etc.

**interpreter**
A program that executes another program

**IPC**
Interprocess communication: pipes, sockets, signals, etc.

**list**
A variable-length, nestable, heterogeneous, array of object references (in Python)

**Makefile**
A build procedure, usually for creating compiled C programs or libraries

**mapping**
An unordered collection, supporting access by key, methods, etc.

**MDI**
A multiple document interface, usually under Microsoft Windows

**member**
A attribute of an instance that can be referenced

**method**
A callable attribute of an instance; a function with an implied first argument

**MFC**
The Microsoft Foundation Classes framework; a development API

**module**
A code packaging unit: a Python file or C extension; an object with attributes

**multiple inheritance**
When a class inherits from more than one superclass

**mutable**
An object that may be changed in place (without making a new copy)

**namespace**
A dictionary (usually) holding assigned variable names

**Ni**
From the Monty Python movie, *The Holy Grail*; sometimes spelled "Nee"

**number**
In Python: an integer, long integer, floating-point, or user-defined object

**Object**
A logic + data package; probably the most abused word in computer science

**OLE**
Object Linking and Embedding, a component integration system usually on Microsoft Windows platforms

**OOD**
Object-oriented design

**OODB**
Object-oriented database

**OODL**
Object-oriented dynamic language

**OOP**
Object-oriented programming

**OOPS**
Object-oriented mistakes

**OS**
Operating system

**parrot**
A reference to a Monty Python television sketch—and a very dead bird

**parsing**
Analyzing syntactic structure of a language sentence

**PDB**
The standard Python debugger

**Perl**
Larry Wall's system administration language

**persistence**
In Python: saving Python objects between program executions

**pickle**
Python's extension for serializing (nearly) arbitrary objects

**polymorphism**
Type-generic behavior; in Python: attribute access, and everything else

**protocol**
An interface, or set of conventions defined by a class or type

**prototyping**
Developing a system's functionality fast, with or without delivery constraints in mind

**PSA**
The Python Software Activity, currently sponsored by CNRI

**Python**
The most versatile language in the universe

**Python, the real definition**
Here's a much more precise definition of Python recently posted by Nick Seidenman on *comp.lang.python* . . .

*python*, (Gr. Myth. An enormous serpent that lurked in the cave of Mount Parnassus and was slain by Apollo) 1. any of a genus of large, non-poisonous snakes of Asia, Africa and Australia that crush their prey to death. 2. popularly, any large snake that crushes its prey. 3. Totally awesome, bitchin' language invented by that rad computer geek Guido van Rossum that will someday crush the $'s out of certain *other* so-called VHLL's ;-)

Well, I thought it was funny :-)

**qualification**
Accessing an attribute in an object's namespace: *object.attribute*

**RAD**
Rapid Application Development; note: backward compatible with "groovy"

**recursion**
When a function (or method) is called again before an earlier call exits

**reference counts**
Python's garbage collection strategy: objects carry reference counts

**regression test**
Running a program, capturing its results, and comparing them to the prior run's results

**regular expression**
A notation for specifying match patterns

**RPC**
Remote procedure call: a cross-network communication protocol

**scope**
A place where unqualified variable names exist: local, global, or built-in

**script**
An executable text file, written in an interpreted language

**self**
The conventional name given to the first argument in class methods (the instance)

**sequence**
An ordered collection, supporting slicing, concatenation, etc.

**shelve**
A dictionary-like table of pickled objects; a persistent object store

**shrubbery**
See Ni

**SIG**
Special interest group

**slice**
To extract a contiguous section of a sequence object

**smiley :-)**
A "smiley" symbol; it means something's supposed to be funny (See also YMMV)

**spam**
A delicious pork-based food; also: Python's *foo*; also: abusing the Internet

**SQL**
Structured query language: a standard way to access data in relational databases

**stdin, stdout, stderr**
Standard program data streams: input, output, error messages (module *sys*)

**stdio**
C's basic file system (and Python's file objects, made by the *open* function)

**string**
A collection (sequence) of characters

**subclass**
A class that inherits attributes from one or more superclasses ("derived class")

**superclass**
A class that provides attributes inherited by one or more subclass ("base class")

**Tcl**
John Ousterhout's string-based scripting language (pronounced: "tickle")

**The Meaning of Life**
A movie created by members of the Monty Python comedy troupe

**Tk**
A higher-level abstraction of the Xlib GUI API, integrated in Python as *Tkinter*

**Tkinter**
Python's class-based interface to the *Tk* GUI API

**tuple**
A collection that cannot be changed in place

**type descriptor**
A C *struct* used to hold function pointers for C extension type operations

**unit tests**
Testing a system in bits and pieces by running components in isolation

**UNIX**
A multitasking OS; various interpretations

**URL**
Universal resource locator: a standard address scheme on the Internet

**VHLL**
Very-high-level language; it takes less to do more

**WPY**
A portable GUI interface for Python based on the MFC framework

**WWW**
The World Wide Web; an information system based on the Internet

**YMMV**
Your mileage may vary; as in "That's what I think about C++, but YMMV"

# Index


& operator (shell), 117
* (asterisk)
    with from statement, 126, 149
    prefixing argument name, 162, 202
    repetition operator, 125
@ (at sign), 790
‵ (backquote), 160
\ (backslash), 100
! statement (pdb), 370
!= (inequality) operator, 91
{} (braces), 28, 100, 183
[] (brackets), 100, 124
    for slices (see slices)
: (colon), 817
, (comma), 161
$ (dollar sign), 790
" (double quotes), 103
= (assignment) operator, 88
= = (equality) operator, 92
# (hash mark), 84, 98, 816
< (redirect) shell operator, 113
< (less than) operator, 92
< > (inequality) operator, 92
> (redirect) shell operator, 113
> (greater than) operator, 92
() (parentheses), 100, 142, 161, 258
% for string formatting, 160, 775
| (piping) operator, 113
+ (concatenation) operator, 108, 265-271, 275, 827
? (question mark), 790
' (single quotes), 104
; (semicolon), 100-101
_ (underscore), variables starting with, 126
\0 for null character, 119

abstract object access API, 635, 752
abstraction, 347
access class attributes, 243
active code, reloading, 177
__add__ method, 265-267
administration, 81
    scripts for (see shell tools)
.after, .after_idle tools, 383
AI (artificial intelligence), 732
ampersand (&) shell operator, 117
anchors, 356
and keyword, 135
anonymous function objects, 214, 835
API, Python
    abstract object access, 635, 752
    embedded-call, 572-577
    errors, detecting, 577
    OLE, 723
    run-time, 515
    WPY and wxPython, 738-742
APP tags, 719
append(), 109, 267, 824
applets, 718-721
applications for Python, 7
apply(), 163, 205, 744, 753
arguments, 142-144, 154
    default, 143, 163
    lists of, 521

arguments (cont'd)
matching modes, 204
order of, 203
passing by assignment, 142
variable-length lists of, 162-164
arrays (see sequence objects)
associative (see dictionaries)
assignment, 88, 145-146, 760, 772, 816
instance attributes, 233-234
nested shelves, 401
passing arguments by, 142
tuples, 191-192
associative arrays (see dictionaries)
asterisk (*), prefixing argument name with, 162, 202
at sign (@), 790
attributes, 783, 854
object, 90, 199
special, 783
automatic
GUI construction, 330-347
language integration, 64, 630-636

background activities, 383
backquote (`), 160
backslash (\), 100
BASIC language, 701
batch mode, 165-167
bgen system, 634, 757
bidirectional IPC, 729-730
binaries (see source code)
binary
search trees, 480-484
operators, 458
bind(), 355
bison system, 656
blank lines, 101
block delimiters, 726
blocks, code (see code)
boolean operators, 190
bound methods, 257-258
braces {}, 28, 100, 183
brackets [], 100, 124
for slices (see slices)
branching, multiway, 159, 184
break statement, 129, 193-194
breakpoints, 366
browser(), 332
browser, Python-based, 718-721
browser, table, 393-424
bsddb module, 749
building Python from source code, 68
__builtin__ module, 776
__builtins__ module, 583
Button object, 26
buttons, 312, 355, 394, 679
byte-by-byte reading (see reading from files, read())

C language, 54-62, 474, 505
C extension modules, 170, 508-515
C extension types, 508, 532-568, 635
data conversion codes, 523-524
data types, 171
debugging, 364, 371
embedding Python in, 571-639
exceptions, 525
keyword argument values, 561
searching files for constants, 644
translating to Python, 757
(see also extensions)
–c option, python, 74
C++ language, 35, 624, 757, 854-857
calculator GUI, 675-684
__call__ attribute, 747
call routing, 516, 543-544
call statement, 121
callable object types, 258
callback handlers, 313, 319, 364-371, 377-380
scheduled callbacks, 383
capitalization (see case sensitivity)
cascades, 325
case sensitivity, 90
case statement (see elif clause)
catching exceptions (see exceptions)
CD-ROM with book, xx
CGI script, 735-737
character-by-character reading (see reading from files, read())
characters (see string objects)
circular module dependency, 171-173
__class__ attribute, 333
class methods, 227, 319
class statement, 227-230, 240, 244, 762
classes, 15, 220, 226-232, 250-253, 284, 383, 842-851
accessing attributes from methods, 243

classes (cont'd)
- buttons as, 679
- class instances (see instances)
- constructors, 235-238
- debugging with, 372-375
- globals for, 243
- graphs to, 487-489
- inheriting from multiple, 259-261
- menus as, 221-226
- mixin, 330-334
- namespaces, 238-248
- persistent instances, 426-436
- running in module files, 596
- set, 465-468
- sharing between languages, 624-630
- stack, 441-462
- subclasses, 27, 223, 287, 315-319, 338, 449, 683
- widget, 381
- wrapper, 421-424, 563-566, 625-630

clone(), 332
close(), 122
closures, 746-748
__cmp__ method, 443
code, xx, 133-135, 704
- #! line, 113
- active, reloading while, 177
- compounding lines of, 99
- GUI (see GUI)
- incremental development, 173-179
- indentation of, 98
- interactive coding, 114-117
- optimizing, 676-679
- reusing, 138, 684, 709
- trusted execution, 752

__coerce__ method, 458
coherence, 5
cohesion, 173
colon (:), 817
columns
- summing, 641
- text in, 49

combinations of sequences, 494-496
combo(), 494
comma (,), 161
command option, 312, 355
command-line arguments, 95
command-line interpreter, 72-74, 113
- –c option, 74

commands
- menu lists for, 186-195
- pdb debugging, 366
- shell, running in Python, 115

comments, 84, 98, 101, 726
communication, interprocess, 116
compacting code, 133-135
comparing, 91
- functions for, 498
- stacks, 550

compiled code, 294
completion (see globbing, filename)
complex numbers, 755
composition, 289, 848
compounding code lines, 99
concatenating, 108-110, 265-271, 827
- menus, 271, 274
- string objects, 47-50, 108

const modifier (C++), 855
constants, 644, 762
- mathematical, 790

constructors, 235-238, 413, 542, 847, 856
continuation lines, 100
continue statement, 193-195
converting
- between languages (see translating)
- data types, 576
- lists and tuples, 824
- sequence objects, 500-504
- to/from strings, 160
- wrapped objects, 627-630

copying
- copy module, 751
- lists and dictionaries, 267
- variables from modules (see from statement; import statement)

counter loops (see loops)
coupling modules (see dependency, module)
CPU time, 555
.createfilehandler tool, 384
csh (C shell), 23
customization, 30, 448-450

%d format code, 161
data conversion codes, 523-524
data entry dialogs, 353
data members (see members)
data sources, external, 16-18

data structures, 28-39
data types, 102-111, 196-198, 480-504, 763-769, 820-832
  in C modules, 171
  converting, 576
  declaring, 39
  dictionaries, 183-184
  integers, 559
  kjbuckets extension, 750
  sets, 462-479
  special attribute names, 783
  special class methods, 455-458
  stacks (see stacks)
  switching, 218-219
  testing for, 212
  tuples, 161-164
database systems, 388
dbm extension module, 69-70
dbm files, 39-41, 390, 410-417
dbx debugger, 364
dealloc operation handler, 546
debugging, 595
  Python debugger, 363-375, 750
declaring
  data types, 39
  variables, 85
DECREF (see Py_DECREF())
def statement, 141, 146, 214, 762
default
  argument values, 143, 163
  lambdas, 319
  menu values, 271
  shared mutable objects, 276-279
deferred calls, 319
__del__ method, 400, 458, 847
del statement, 399
__delattr__ method, 400
__delitem__ method, 400
__delslice__ method, 400
dependency, module, 168, 171-173
destructors (see constructors; __del__ method)
development
  cycle, Python, 697-713
  incremental, 173-179
dialogs, 320-321, 353
__dict__ attribute, 198, 246-248, 841
dictionaries, 25, 181-186, 197-198, 557, 766, 768, 822
  binary search trees versus, 483
  copying, 267
  instances as, 238
  keyword arguments, 202-207
  namespace, 246-248
  objects as keys, 312
  sets, 34-35, 469-472
  shelves, 390
  Tkinter and, 311
  (see also namespaces)
dir(), 199, 292
dmb module, 749
__doc__ attribute, 752
documentation, 71-72
  comments (see comments)
  strings, 752
  (see also help)
dollar sign ($), 790
double quotes ("), 103
downloading Python, 68
dumbdmb module, 7549
dummy modules, 591
dynamic
  binding, 518, 545
  interfaces (see GUI)
  menus, 264-279
  namespaces, 244
  typing, 39, 47

elif clause, 94, 159
  (see also if statement)
else clause, 190-192
  (see also if statement; try statement)
emacs text editor, 789
embedding Python, 62, 571-639, 676
  in C, 61-64
encapsulation, 15, 35, 282
ending statements, 100-101
environment variables, 66
EOFError exception, 132, 158
equality and equality operators, 91-92, 827
errors, 132, 151
  ErrorObject object, 525
  programming, 361-375
  stderr stream, 96, 117
  (see also exceptions)
escape codes, 119, 774

eval function, 49, 496-498, 674
eval statement, 200
event-driven programming, 314
events, window manager, 399
except clause, 131, 262, 852
exceptions, 22, 361, 489, 525, 530-532, 552, 574, 776, 851-853
  else clause, 190-192
  EOFError, 132, 158
  exception lists, 262
  handling with try statement, 131-132, 148
  parser, 673
  raise statement, 132, 151-152
  (see also errors)
exec function, 496-498, 674
exec statement, 200
execv(), 334
exiting
  code, 139
  exit statement, 139
  loops, 129
expand option, 339
expanding menus, 264-279
expect tool, 749
expressions, 760
extensions, 9, 54-64, 505-570, 749-750
  extension languages, 6
  filename (see suffixes, filename)
  granularity, 216-219
  installing, 69-71
  Python, future, 754-758
external
  data sources, 16-18
  files, 121-122, 125-126
  overriding modules, 208

%f format code, 161
FAQ, Python, 71
fastset (see sets)
file descriptors, 388
file methods, 118-121
file objects, 121, 125, 506, 765-767
  closing, 122
  dbm, 39-41
  filesystem structure, 97
  flat files, 387
  grep utility, 652-654
  opening for read/write (see open())
  processing differences, 656
  reading from (see reading from files)
  redirection (see redirection)
  scanning for, 16-18
File Transfer Protocol (FTP), 68, 72, 712
filenames
  globbing, 113, 115
  .py extension, 114
  suffixes, 520
files (see file objects)
fill option (windows), 339
filter(), 744
filters (see regular expressions)
finally clause, 132, 852
flat files, 387
floating-point numbers (see number objects)
flush(), 388
for loop, 93, 123, 128, 761, 819
fork(), 334
format
  formatting codes, string, 775
  string, 160
  text in columns, 49
FormGui class, 394-401
formtbl extensions, 417-420
forward references, 141
Frame class, 26
frame widgets, 314
frames, inheritance and, 317-319
freeware, 4
freeze tool, 294, 725
from statement, 24, 119-121, 126, 149, 169, 177, 179, 761
FTP (File Transfer Protocol), 68, 72, 712
functions, 91, 139, 141-144, 152-155, 776-778, 784, 832-837
  anonymous, 214, 835
  apply(), 163
  C, routing calls to, 516, 543-544
  comparison, 498
  in dictionaries, 185
  generating, 496-498
  generic, 248
  import statements in, 148
  keyword arguments, 202-207
  linking to callback handlers, 313
  mathematical, 790
  menu, 211-215

functions (cont'd)
- namespaces, 199
- None return value, 195
- overloading, 855
- POSIX, 787-789
- running in module files, 596
- scripts versus, 159-164
- set, 462-465
- variables in, 144-147

%g format code, 161
garbage collection, 122, 546, 766
- reference count management, 400, 526, 544, 585-586

gdb debugger, 364
gdbm (see dbm files)
generating
- exceptions (see raise statement)
- programs, 496-498

generic functions, 248
getargs( ), 522
getattr( ), 200, 543
__getattr__ method, 264, 417
getenv function (in C), 54
Get_Global( ), 593
__getitem__ method, 268, 411, 452, 458
getting binaries from Web, 71
getting source code, xx
global
- instance inaccess to, 243
- namespace, 144, 154, 241
- variables, 155, 837

global statement, 154
globbing, filename, 113, 115
Grail browser, 703, 718-721, 734
grammar, Python, 768-772
granularity, 216-219
graph searching, 484-491
graphical user interface (see GUI)
graphs of objects, 35
greater than (>) operator, 92
grep utility, 652-654
gridded mode, 351
grouping (see tuples)
GUI (graphical user interface), 24-28, 307-385, 507, 757
- automating, 330-347
- calculator, 675-684
- frame widgets, 314
- inheritance, 315-319
- menus and toolbars, 323-329
- PythonWin, 724
- table browser, 393-424
- updating windows, 379
- window layout, 339, 351, 380, 681-683
- window manager events, 399
- WPY and wxPython systems, 738-742

Guido van Rossum, 3, 72
GuiMaker class, 334-339, 343-347
GuiMixin class, 330-334

handling exceptions (see exceptions)
hash mark (#), 816
- for comments, 84, 98

__hash__ methods, 312
hash tables (see dictionaries)
has_key method, 184
header file, Python, 514
headers, searching for patterns in, 650-652
help, 71-72
hexadecimal constants, 103
history of Python, 3-4
holmes system, 643, 732
home page, Python, 72
HTML, Grail for, 718-722, 735

Icon language, 701
if statement, 94, 129, 159, 762, 816
ILU package, 634, 727, 730-732
image processing, 755
immutability, string, 106
implied-delimiter syntax, 101
import statement, 84, 93, 120, 126, 148, 168, 176, 520, 761
- circular module dependency, 171-173
- transitive, 177, 179-180
- (see also reload( ))

importing modules, 752
in operator, 111, 820
incremental development, 173-179
indentation of code, 98, 726, 817
index method, 190
IndexError exception, 151
indexes, sequence (see sequence objects)
indexing, 184, 267, 820, 830
- lists, 189

inequality (!=) operator, 91

inequality (<>) operator, 92
inheritance, 16, 26, 207, 229-232, 237, 280, 337, 845, 855
  frames and, 317-319
  from multiple classes, 259-261
  precedence, 232, 260
  widgets and, 315
__init__ method, 235-237, 443, 847
initialization function, 515
input/output, 127, 132
  raw_input(), 130-133
  redirection, 21-23, 113, 165-167
  stdin/stdout stream, 95-96
  (see also reading from files)
installing
  extensions, 69-71
  Python, 67-71
instances, 16, 230, 266, 410-417, 541, 543-544, 624-627, 844
  assigning attributes, 233-234
  configuring with constructors, 235-238
  as dictionaries, 238
  global inaccess, 243
  namespaces, 238-248
  persistent, changing classes of, 426-436
  self, 228-229, 270
integers, 559, 815
integration, 5, 53-64, 392, 505-639, 700
  automatic, 64, 630-636
  OLE, 723
interactive coding, 114-117, 833
interclass method calls, 253
interface, 152, 156-159
  API (see API)
  batch mode, 165-167
  calculator GUI, 679
  as class system, 250-253
  dictionary menus, 181-186
  GUI, 307-385
  keyed-access database, 749
  menu lists, 186-195
  OLE, 723
  shell tools, 356
  WWW/Internet, 732-737
Internet, Python tools for, 732-737
interpreter (see command-line interpreter)
interprocess communication, 116
intersection() (see sets)
intersections, set, 31
IPC tools, 729-730
is operator, 92, 550
item(), 503
items(), 824

Java, 703
join(), 167
joining strings, 47-50

key-value pairs, 183, 204
keyed-access database interface, 749
keys method, 184, 199
keyword arguments, 25, 202-207, 561
kjbuckets extension, 750
kwParsing system, 656

lambda statement, 134, 214, 319, 498, 744
languages (see programming languages)
layout, window, 339, 351, 380, 681-683
LEFT constant, 315
len(), 123, 831
__len__ method, 458
less than (<) operator, 92
LIFO lists (see stacks)
line-by-line input (see reading from files, readline())
linking namespaces, 245
Linux operating system, xix
list constants, 105
listboxes, 351
listdir(), 116
lists, 162, 820
  argument, variable-length, 162-164
  stacks as, 438
  tuples (see tuples)
load, system (see performance)
Load_Attribute(), 590
loading modules (see from statement; import statement)
Load_Module(), 590
local
  data in C extensions, 515, 540
  methods, 256-258
  namespaces, 144, 199, 241
  variables, 834
logging, 216, 285-290

logical operators, 190
long integers, 103
loops, 85, 93, 110, 123-125, 192, 818
  breaking, 129
  for, 93, 123, 128, 761
  while, 127-128, 761

Macintosh systems, 742
__main__ module, 73, 170, 366
mainloop(), 309, 359
makefile, embedding Python, 578, 604
manual searching of lists, 189
map function, 17
map(), 134-135, 502, 744
mapping, 106, 557-561, 786
  method calls to classes, 227
  mutable (see dictionaries)
  Tk/Tkinter, 382
matching patterns (see regular expressions)
math module, 790
matrix object, 755
members, 229, 234
__members__ method, 544, 549
membership (see in operator)
memory (see garbage collection)
menugui2 module, 352
menus, 181-209, 323-329
  cascading, 325
  as classes, 221-226
  concatenating, 274
  configuring data for, 233-238
  dynamic, 264-279
  functions for, 211-215
  GuiMaker class, 334-339, 343-347
  indexing, 267
  pull-down, 324
  tear-off, 325
  type-switching, 218-219
messages (see interclass method calls)
messages, error, 151
metaclass protocol system, 59, 271
metaprogramming, 200-201
METH_KEYWORDS (value), 561
method functions, 515
methods, 16, 91, 196, 227, 766
  accessing class attributes from, 243
  interclass calls, 253
  local, 256-258
  mapped to type descriptors, 566-568
  metaclass, 59, 271
  registering, 256-258, 620-622
  self instance and, 228
  special class methods, 455-458
  virtual, 854
__methods__ attribute, 200, 549
mixin classes, 330-334
modal windows, 355
modulator tool, 64, 630-633
modules, 13, 84, 168-180, 196, 207-209, 284, 778-782, 837-842
  C extension, 54-60, 508-515
  circular dependency, 171-173
  classes and, 225
  externally overriding, 208
  importing, 751
  loading (see import statement)
  overwriting names of, 119
  packaging with freeze, 725
  reloading, 173-180, 374-375, 591, 605, 842
  for reusing information, 138
  search path order, 519
  stacks as, 439-441
  statement order, 140
  using in C, 590-593
  wrapper, 57-60
  WWW/Internet, 718-721, 732-737
modules dictionary, 198
more than (see greater than)
mSQL system, 388
multiple inheritance, 232, 259-261, 337
multiple-line statements, 100
multiway branching, 159, 184
mutability, 106, 109, 154, 542, 831
  mappings (see dictionaries)
  objects, 276-279
  sequences, 787

n command (pdb), 368
\n for newlines, 119
__name__ module, 140-141, 840
named references (see variables)
names
  from statements and, 119
  Python library symbols, 527
  Python, source of, 65
  qualified, 90

names (cont'd)
  variables, starting with _, 126
namespaces, 90, 144-147, 179, 198-201, 238-245, 358, 772, 844
  dummy modules, 591
  dynamic, 244
  lambda statement and, 214
  linking, 245
  module, changing externally, 208
  nested, 244
  pdb and, 374
  scope versus, 240
  searching, 241
ndbm (see dbm files)
nested
  break statements, 193-194
  class statements, 244
  code blocks, 99
  continue statements, 194
  data structures, 188
  def statements, 146
  deleting nested items, 399
  exceptions, 852
  frame widgets, 315
  import statements, 148
  method calls, 253
  namespaces, 145-147, 244
  shelves, 401
  try statements, 132
Netscape plug-in, Python as, 743
newlines, 119
newsgroup, Python, 72
None (value), 121, 195, 824
notdone method, 326
null characters, 119
number objects, 103, 197, 557-561, 764, 786, 815
  complex, 755
  converting to strings, 161

object trees, 188-191
object-oriented programming, 5, 53, 207-209, 219-221, 253, 290, 705
  object-oriented databases (OODBs), 758
  wrapper classes, 563
objects, 13, 209, 220
  abstract object access API, 752
  anonymous, 214, 835
  attributes of, 90, 199
  in C, 515
  callable object types, 258
  classes (see classes)
  deep copies of, 751
  default shared mutable, 276-279
  as dictionary keys, 312
  file (see file objects)
  graphs of, 35
  indexing, 124
  list (see lists)
  numeric (see number objects)
  packaging, 279
  passing, 142
  persistent, 41-47
  stacks, 438-462
  string (see string objects)
  tuples of, 161-164
  wrapped, looking like Python, 627-630
octal constants, 103
OLE integration, 723
OLE scripting, Python for, 755
OOP (see object-oriented programming)
open( ), 85, 96, 133, 387
open architecture, 9
operations, 762
operators, 196, 785-787, 832
  binary, 458
  logical (boolean), 190
  overloading, 264-279
  precedence, 773
  regular expression, 648
  stack versus module, 443
optimization, 450-455, 753-755
code, 676-679
  sets, 34-35, 469-474
  (see also performance)
or keyword, 135
order (see precedence)
os module, 116-117, 388
output (see input/output)
overloading
  functions, 855
  indexing, 267
  operators, 264-279, 459
overriding modules externally, 208
overwriting module namespace, 119, 176

p statement (pdb), 370

packaging, 279, 294, 725, 751
pack(), 310
parentheses (), 100, 142, 161, 258
parsing (see processing)
pass statement, 158
passing objects, 142
PATH environment variable, 66
pattern-matching, 50
patterns (see regular expressions)
PC port for Python, 722-725
pdb debugger, 363-375, 595
percent sign (%) for string formatting, 160, 775
performance, 9, 622
  C extensions, 552-557
  compacting code, 133-135
  indexing, 191
  reading from files, 17
  scripts versus functions, 159
  sets, 466, 470-472
  stacks, 448-450, 454-455
  text filtering, 655
Perl language, 700
permutations of sequences, 494-496
permute(), 494
persistent-object stores (see shelves)
persistence, 41-47, 387-436, 507, 757
pickle module, 41-47, 392
pindent utility, 101, 726
pipe(), 729
piping input/output, 113
platforms, xix, 75, 519
  Macintosh, 742
  Windows, 722-725
polymorphism, 281
popen(), 116
pop() (see stacks)
pop-up dialogs, 320, 353
portability, 586, 722, 729
porting Python, 75
POSIX
  posix module, 388, 787-789
  regular expressions, 750
PostGres95 extension, 749
power, semantic, 5
precedence
  inheritance, 232, 260
  operator, 774
precompiled source code, 294
pregrex extension, 750
print statement, 85, 95, 130, 362, 445
printing, 762
private members, 855
procedures (see functions)
processing
  file objects, 656
  hand-coded parsers, 657-674
  languages, 52
  parser generators, 656
  rule strings, 642-644
  text, 47-53, 640-675
profile module, 467
programming, 697-700, 744-748
  errors, 361-375
  event-driven, 314
  generic functions, 248
  GUI (see GUI)
  incremental development, 173-179
  interactive, 834
  metaprogramming, 200-201
  object-oriented, 5, 53, 207-209, 219-221, 253, 290, 563
  simplicity, 195, 207
  structure, 13
programming languages, 6, 700
  C++, 35
  debugging and, 371
  integrating, 53-64
  processing, 52
  RAD, 375-380
  sharing classes, 624-630
programs (see scripts)
Prolog language, 192
protocol, 16
PSA (Python Software Activity), 4
pull-down menus, 324
  (see also menus)
pure virtual methods, 253, 856
push() (see stacks)
putenv function (in C), 54
.py filename extension, 114
PyArg_Parse(), 522, 576, 616
PyArg_ParseTuple(), 521, 576
PyArgs_VaParse(), 576
Py_BuildValue(), 522, 576
.pyc files, 294
Py_CompileString(), 576
Py_DECREF(), 527, 574, 585

PyDict_GetItemString(), 575
PyDict_New(), 575, 583
PyDict_SetItemString(), 527, 575
PyErr_Fetch(), 574
PyErr_IndexError(), 574
PyErr_Occurred(), 526, 574
PyErr_Print(), 574
PyErr_SetString(), 525, 530, 574
PyEval_CallObject(), 575, 581, 620
PyEval_EvalCode(), 576
PyEval_InteractiveLoop(), 576
PyEval_SimpleFile(), 575
PyEval_SimpleString(), 576
PyEval_String(), 576
Py_FatalError(), 527
Py_FindMethod(), 544
PyGres extension, 750
PyImport_AddModule(), 575, 581
PyImport_GetModuleDict(), 575
PyImport_ImportModule(), 575, 580-581
PyImport_ReloadModule(), 575
Py_INCREF(), 526, 574
PyInt_FromLong(), 576
PyMem_DEL(), 544
PyMethodDef(), 527, 576
PyModule_Check(), 574
PyModule_GetDict(), 527, 575, 580
PyObject object, 574
PyObject_DEL(), 577
PyObject_GetAttrString(), 574
PyObject_HEAD(), 577
PyObject_NEW(), 543, 577
PyObject_Print(), 574
PyObject_SetAttrString(), 574, 581
PyRun_File(), 573
PyRun_SimpleFile(), 573
PyRun_SimpleString(), 577
PyRun_String(), 573, 579
PySequenceMethods, 576
PyString_AsString(), 576
PyString_Check(), 574
PyString_FromString(), 576
Python
  abstract object access API, 635, 752
  debugger, 363-375, 595
  development cycle, 697-713
  embedded-call API, 572-577
  extensions (see extensions)
  FAQ on, 71
  functional structure, 290-294
  future of, 754-758
  history of, 3-4
  installing, 67-71
  interpreter (see command-line interpreter)
  as OLE scripting tool, 755
  profiler, 467
  release 1.2, 385
  release 1.4, 756
  run-time API, 515
  translating to/from, 757
  tutorial, 813-853
  where name came from, 65
Python Software Activity (PSA), 4
Python.h header file, 514
PYTHONPATH environment variable, 67, 520, 838
PYTHONSTARTUP environment variable, 67, 201
PythonWin, 722-725
_PyTuple_Resize(), 575
PyTuple_SetItem(), 575
PyTuple_Size(), 575
PyTypeObject, 577
Py_VaBuildValue(), 576
Py_XDECREF(), 527, 575
Py_XINCREF(), 527, 574

qualification, 85, 773, 841, 845
qualified names, 90
question mark (?), 790

r command (pdb), 370
RAD (Rapid Application Development), 375-380
__radd__ attribute, 275
raise statement, 22, 132, 151-152, 753, 762, 851-853
range(), 123-124, 493, 821
Rapid Application Development (RAD), 375-380
raw_input(), 130-133
reading from files
  readlines(), 17, 86
  readline(), 127-130
  read(), 85, 97, 130

recursive
  function calls, 836
  mainloop calls, 359
  sequence object reversal, 491
redirection, 21-23, 113, 165-167
reduce( ), 744
redundancy, 216, 219
ref parameters (C++), 855
reference count management, 400, 526, 544, 585-586
reference manuals (see documentation)
references, 88, 144, 774, 826
  arrays of (see lists)
  to instance attributes, 233
  named (see variables)
  simplified management of, 755
regex module, 50, 646
registering methods, 256-258, 515, 561, 620-622
registration table, 56
regression test script, 19
regsub module, 647
regular expressions, 50, 645-656, 750
relational algebra and sets, 474-479
reload( ), 173-180, 374-375, 842
reloading modules, 591, 605, 842
Remote Procedure Calls (RPC), 424
rename header file, 527
repetition, 125, 828
__repr__ methods, 443, 458, 565
reserved words, 89, 773
resizing windows, 339, 351
return statement, 142, 153, 762
  (see also functions)
reusing code, 138, 684, 709
reversing sequences, 491-494
RIGHT constant, 315
right-side variants, 458
Rivet library, 750
routing calls to C functions, 516, 543-544
RPC (Remote Procedure Calls), 424
rule strings, 642-644
Run_Function( ), 596, 616

%s format code, 160
scanning for files, 16-18
scheduled callbacks, 383
Scheme language, 700
scope (see namespaces)
scope operator, 856
scripting languages, 6
scripts, 159-164
ScrolledText class, 333
searching
  binary search trees, 480-484
  C files for constants, 644
  C header files, 650-652
  graphs, 484-491
  grep utility, 652-654
  inheritance, 232
  instance attributes, 233
  lists (see indexing)
  namespaces (scopes), 241
  search path, 66, 519
  strings, 646
self instance, 228-229, 270, 843
semantic power, 5
semicolon (;), 100-101
sequence objects, 106-110, 123-125, 541, 767, 787, 820
  converting, 500-504
  copying, 267
  dictionaries (see dictionaries)
  exception lists, 262
  indexing, 124, 189, 267
  lists, 104, 186-195, 197, 765
  map( ) with, 135
  permutations of, 494-496
  repetition, 125
  reversing, 491-494
  sorting, 498-500
  stacks and, 446
  tuples, 161-164
setattr( ), 415-417
__setattr__ method, 415-417, 458
Set_Global( ), 593
__getitem__ method, 268, 411
sets, 31-35, 462-479
  moving to dictionaries, 469-472
shared mutable objects, 276-279
shell tools, 12-23, 81-117, 159-164, 356, 507
ShellGui module, 349-351
shells
  command-line interpreter as, 74
  commands, running in Python, 115
  globbing and redirection, 113
shelve module, 41-47
shelves, 390

shortening code, 133-135
signals, 727
silent mode, 165
simplicity of programming, 195, 207
single quotes ('), 104
size, data types, 831
slices, 22, 86, 106-109, 128, 829
  slice assignment, 108
SmallTalk language, 701
sockets, 727-729
sort( ), 398, 500
sorting sequences, 498-500
source code
  #! line, 113
  building Python from, 68
  compiled/precompiled, 294
  getting from Web, xx, 71
  (see also code)
spawn( ), 332, 334
special
  attribute names, 784
  characters, 119, 774
speed (see performance)
split( ), 641
splitfields( ), 641
splitting strings, 47-50
stack_as_sequence struct, 542
stacks, 28-31, 438-462
  comparing, 550
  stack dump, 361
Stacktype struct, 542
statements, 13, 92-95, 759-761, 816-819
  implicitly ending, 100-101
  loops (see loops)
  multiple-line, 100
static
  binding, 517, 545
  language build cycle, 699
  members, 234, 855
  stacks class data, 450
stderr stream, 96, 117
stdin stream, 95, 132
stdio filesystem, 97
stdout stream, 95
stopping (see exiting)
__str__ method, 458
streams, redirecting, 21-23
string module, 641-645, 784
string objects, 47-50, 103, 197, 764, 825
  C extension modules, 509
  code (see embedding Python; extensions)
  comparing, 91
  concatenating, 108
  documentation, 752
  escape codes, 119, 774
  formatting codes for, 775
  formatting with %, 160
  immutability of, 106, 109
  regular expressions, 645-656
  repetition, 125
  rule, 642-644
structure, programming, 13
stub wrapper classes, 563-566, 625-630
subclasses (see classes)
subset( ), 494
substitution, string, 647, 656
substrings (see strings)
suffixes, filename, 520
summing columns, 641
SWIG system, 635
switch statement (see elif clause)
symbols, 744, 769
syntax, Python, 98
SyntaxError exception, 770
sys module, 84, 117, 841
system administration, 81
  scripts for (see shell tools)
system( ), 117
system load (see performance)

\t for tabs, 119
table browser GUI, 393-424
Tcl language, 69, 382, 700
tear-off menus, 325
testing
  data types, 212
  extensions, 529-532, 547-552
  FormGui interface, 402-410
  formtbl extensions, 417-420
  GuiMaker class, 337
  menu functions, 213
  mixin methods, 333
  sequence permutations, 495
  set classes, 465
  set functions, 463-464

testing (cont'd)
  unit testing, 173
  validation, 613, 618
text
  processing, 47-53, 640-675
  ScrolledText class, 333
this instance pointer (C++), 854
timer module, S, 454-455, 552
Tix library, 750
Tk language, 69, 382, 750
Tkinter module, 70, 307, 380-384
  GUI system, 742, 754
  Python debugger, 750
  Tix library, 750
  tkinter extension module, 69
tokens, 769
toolbars, 323-329
  GuiMaker class, 334-339
TOP constant, 311
traceback object, 753
transitive imports, 177, 179-180
translating
  conversion codes, 523-524
  Python to/from C, 520-524, 576, 757
  Tcl/Tk to Python/Tkinter, 382
trees, class, 27
troubleshooting, 71-72
  circular imports, 173
  reloading modules, 178
trusted code execution, 753
try statement, 22, 128, 361, 761, 851-853
  exception handling, 131-132, 148, 191
tuples, 161-164, 191-192, 197, 766, 823
  stacks and, 450-455
  tuple packing, 22
  (see also lists)
type(), 212
type descriptors, 541-542, 566-568
type methods, 258
types (see data types)
types module, 212

unbound methods, 257
underline option, 327
union() (see sets)
unions, set, 31
unit testing, 173
unparsing (see processing)
unqualified names, 199, 241-244
updating windows, 379
user interface (see GUI; interface)

validation, 216, 285-290, 609-620
van Rossum, Guido, 3, 72
variable-length argument lists, 162-164
variables, 88, 155, 198, 815
  declaring, 85
  environment, 66
  in functions, 144-147
  inheritance and, 229
  linking to entry fields, 355
  loading (see from statement; import statement; reload())
  Python module, in C, 593
  starting with _ (underscore), 126
vectors, 37-39
virtual inheritance, 856
virtual methods, 854
visual Python, 757

Watters, Aaron, 708
Web (see World Wide Web)
while loop, 127-128, 761, 818
whitespace, 50, 101, 654-656
  character escapes for, 119, 774
widgets, 26
windows, 25
  (see also GUI)
Windows port for Python, 722-725
World Wide Web
  getting binaries from, 71
  Python home page, 72
  Python tools for, 718-722, 732-737, 743
WPY system, 738-742
wrapper classes, 421-424, 563-566, 625-630
wrapper modules, 57-60
write(), 118
WWW (see World Wide Web)
wxPython system, 738-742

yacc system, 656

## *About the Author*

Mark Lutz is a practicing Software Engineer. He holds BS and MS degrees in Computer Science, from the University of Wisconsin. His experience includes working on FORTRAN compilers, C debuggers, scripting languages, C++ frameworks, and GUI programming environments. In graduate school, he dabbled with Prolog implementations. Most of his background involves UNIX development tools, though he's been known to admit to having programmed in COBOL on IBM mainframes, in a prior life.

## *Colophon*

Our look is the result of reader comments, our own experimentation, and distribution channels. Distinctive covers complement our distinctive approach to technical topics, breathing personality and life into potentially dry subjects. UNIX and its attendant programs can be unruly beasts. Nutshell Handbooks help you tame them.

The animal featured on the cover of *Programming Python* is a South American rock python, one of approximately 18 species of python. Pythons are nonvenomous constrictor snakes that live in tropical regions of Africa, Asia, Australia and some Pacific Islands. Pythons live mainly on the ground, but they are also excellent swimmers and climbers. Both male and female pythons retain vestiges of their ancestral hind legs. The male python uses these vestiges, or spurs, when courting a female. The pythons kills its prey by suffocation. While the snake's sharp teeth grip and hold the prey in place, the python's long body coils around its victim's chest, constricting tighter each time it breathes out. They feed primarily on mammals and birds. Python attacks on humans are extremely rare.

Edie Freedman designed this cover and the entire UNIX bestiary that appears on Nutshell Handbooks, using a 19th-century engraving from the Dover Pictorial Archive. The cover layout was produced with Quark XPress 3.3 using the ITC Garamond font. The CD design was created by Hanna Dyer. The inside layout was designed by Edie Freedman, Jennifer Niederst, and Nancy Priest. Text was prepared by Erik Ray in SGML DocBook 2.4 DTD. The print version of this book was created by translating the SGML source into a set of gtroff macros using a filter developed at ORA by Norman Walsh. Steve Talbott designed and wrote the underlying macro set on the basis of the GNU troff -gs macros; Lenny Muellner adapted them to SGML and implemented the book design. The GNU groff text formatter version 1.09 was used to generate PostScript output. The text and heading fonts are ITC Garamond Light and Garamond Book. The illustrations that appear in the book were created in Macromedia Freehand 5.0 by Chris Reilley. Whenever possible, our books use RepKover™, a durable and flexible lay-flat binding. If the page count exceeds RepKover's limit, perfect binding is used.

# More Titles from O'Reilly

## UNIX Programming

### POSIX Programmer's Guide

*By Donald Lewine*
*1st Edition April 1991*
*640 pages, ISBN 0-937175-73-0*

Most UNIX systems today are POSIX compliant because the federal government requires it for its purchases. Given the manufacturer's documentation, however, it can be difficult to distinguish system-specific features from those features defined by POSIX. The *POSIX Programmer's Guide*, intended as an explanation of the POSIX standard and as a reference for the POSIX.1 programming library, helps you write more portable programs.

### Programming with curses

*By John Strang*
*1st Edition 1986*
*78 pages, ISBN 0-937175-02-1*

*curses* is a UNIX library of functions for controlling a terminal'sdisplay screen from a C program. This handbook helps you make use of the *curses* library. Describes the original Berkeley version of *curses*.

### UML in a Nutshell

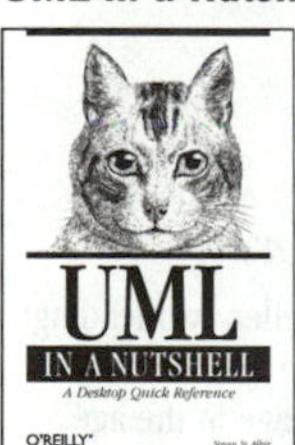

*By Sinan Si Alhir*
*1st Edition September 1998*
*290 pages, ISBN 1-56592-448-7*

The Unified Modeling Language (UML), for the first time in the history of systems engineering, gives practitioners a common language. This concise quick reference explains how to use each component of the language, including its extension mechanisms and the Object Constraint Language (OCL). A tutorial with realistic examples brings those new to the UML quickly up to speed.

### Power Programming with RPC

*By John Bloomer*
*1st Edition February 1992*
*522 pages, ISBN 0-937175-77-3*

RPC (Remote Procedure Calling) is the ability to distribute the execution of functions on remote computers. Written from a programmer's perspective, this book shows what you can do with RPCs, like Sun RPC, the de facto standard on UNIX systems. It covers related programming topics for Sun and other UNIX systems and teaches through examples.

### POSIX.4

*By Bill O. Gallmeister*
*1st Edition January 1995*
*568 pages, ISBN 1-56592-074-0*

A general introduction to real-time programming and real-time issues, this book covers the POSIX.4 standard and how to use it to solve "real-world" problems. If you're at all interested in real-time applications—which include just about everything from telemetry to transaction processing—this book is for you. An essential reference.

### UNIX Systems Programming for SVR4

*By David A. Curry*
*1st Edition July 1996*
*620 pages, ISBN 1-56592-163-1*

Presents a comprehensive look at the nitty gritty details on how UNIX interacts with applications. If you're writing an application from scratch, or if you're porting an application to any System V.4 platform, you need this book. It thoroughly explains all UNIX system calls and library routines related to systems programming, working with I/O, files and directories, processing multiple input streams, file and record locking, and memory-mapped files.

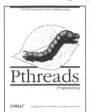

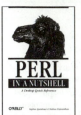

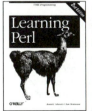

# Perl

## *Perl Resource Kit—UNIX Edition*

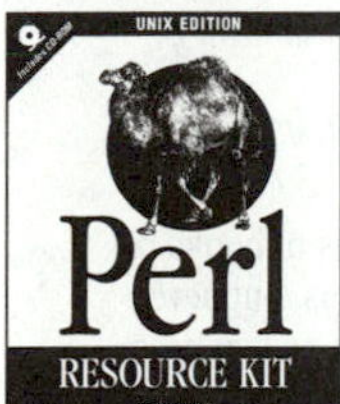


*By Larry Wall, Nate Patwardhan, Ellen Siever, David Futato & Brian Jepson*
*1st Edition November 1997*
*1812 pages, ISBN 1-56592-370-7*

The *Perl Resource Kit—UNIX Edition* gives you the most comprehensive collection of Perl documentation and commercially enhanced software tools available today. Developed in association with Larry Wall, the creator of Perl, it's the definitive Perl distribution for webmasters, programmers, and system administrators.

The *Perl Resource Kit* provides:

- Over 1800 pages of tutorial and in-depth reference documentation for Perl utilities and extensions, in 4 volumes.
- A CD-ROM containing the complete Perl distribution, plus hundreds of freeware Perl extensions and utilities— a complete snapshot of the Comprehensive Perl Archive Network (CPAN)—as well as new software written by Larry Wall just for the Kit.

**Perl Software Tools All on One Convenient CD-ROM**
Experienced Perl hackers know when to create their own, and when they can find what they need on CPAN. Now all the power of CPAN—and more—is at your fingertips. The *Perl Resource Kit* includes:

- A complete snapshot of CPAN, with an install program for Solaris and Linux that ensures that all necessary modules are installed together. Also includes an easy-to-use search tool and a web-aware interface that allows you to get the latest version of each module.
- A new Java/Perl interface that allows programmers to write Java classes with Perl implementations. This new tool was written specially for the Kit by Larry Wall.

Experience the power of Perl modules in areas such as CGI, web spidering, database interfaces, managing mail and USENET news, user interfaces, security, graphics, math and statistics, and much more.

## *Learning Perl on Win32 Systems*

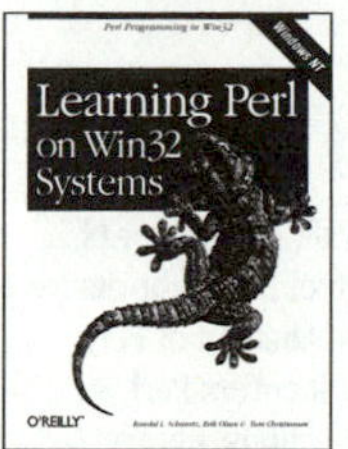


*By Randal L. Schwartz, Erik Olson & Tom Christiansen*
*1st Edition August 1997*
*306 pages, ISBN 1-56592-324-3*

In this carefully paced course, leading Perl trainers and a Windows NT practitioner teach you to program in the language that promises to emerge as the scripting language of choice on NT. Based on the "llama" book, this book features tips for PC users and new, NT-specific examples, along with a foreword by Larry Wall, the creator of Perl, and Dick Hardt, the creator of Perl for Win32.

## *Mastering Regular Expressions*

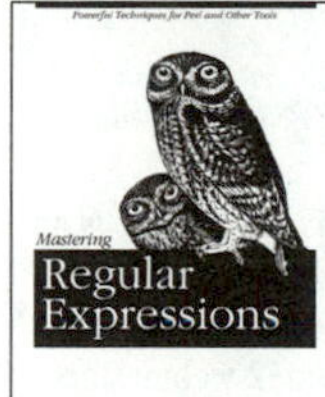


*By Jeffrey E. F. Friedl*
*1st Edition January 1997*
*368 pages, ISBN 1-56592-257-3*

Regular expressions, a powerful tool for manipulating text and data, are found in scripting languages, editors, programming environments, and specialized tools. In this book, author Jeffrey Friedl leads you through the steps of crafting a regular expression that gets the job done. He examines a variety of tools and uses them in an extensive array of examples, with a major focus on Perl.

## *Learning Perl/Tk*

*By Nancy Walsh*
*1st Edition January 1999*
*376 pages, ISBN 1-56592-314-6*

This tutorial for Perl/Tk, the extension to Perl for creating graphical user interfaces, shows how to use Perl/Tk to build graphical, event-driven applications for both Windows and UNIX. Rife with illustrations, it teaches how to implement and configure each Perl/Tk graphical element.

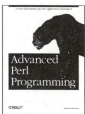

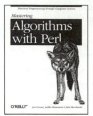

## Web Programming

### *JavaScript: The Definitive Guide, 3rd Edition*

*By David Flanagan & Dan Shafer*
*3rd Edition June 1998*
*800 pages, ISBN 1-56592-392-8*

This third edition of the definitive reference to JavaScript covers the latest version of the language, JavaScript 1.2, as supported by Netscape Navigator 4.0. JavaScript, which is being standardized under the name ECMAScript, is a scripting language that can be embedded directly in HTML to give web pages programming-language capabilities.

### *Learning VBScript*

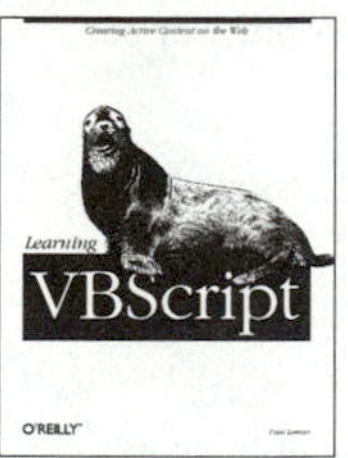


*By Paul Lomax*
*1st Edition July 1997*
*616 pages, includes CD-ROM*
*ISBN 1-56592-247-6*

This definitive guide shows web developers how to take full advantage of client-side scripting with the VBScript language. In addition to basic language features, it covers the Internet Explorer object model and discusses techniques for client-side scripting, like adding ActiveX controls to a web page or validating data before sending to the server. Includes CD-ROM with over 170 code samples.

### *Frontier: The Definitive Guide*

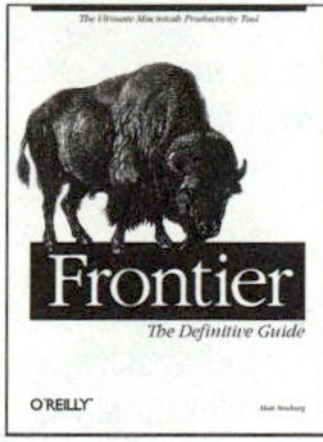


*By Matt Neuburg*
*1st Edition February 1998*
*618 pages, 1-56592-383-9*

This definitive guide is the first book devoted exclusively to teaching and documenting Userland Frontier, a powerful scripting environment for web site management and system level scripting. Packed with examples, advice, tricks, and tips, *Frontier: The Definitive Guide* teaches you Frontier from the ground up. Learn how to automate repetitive processes, control remote computers across a network, beef up your web site by generating hundreds of related web pages automatically, and more. Covers Frontier 4.2.3 for the Macintosh.

### *Web Client Programming with Perl*

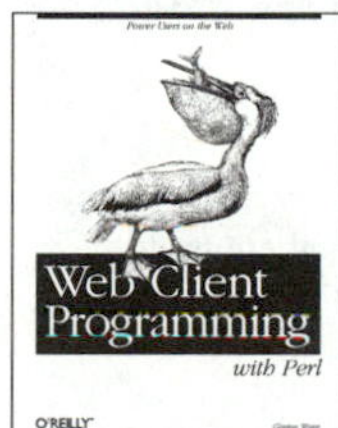


*By Clinton Wong*
*1st Edition March 1997*
*228 pages, ISBN 1-56592-214-X*

*Web Client Programming with Perl* shows you how to extend scripting skills to the Web. This book teaches you the basics of how browsers communicate with servers and how to write your own customized web clients to automate common tasks. It is intended for those who are motivated to develop software that offers a more flexible and dynamic response than a standard web browser.

# How to stay in touch with O'Reilly

## 1. Visit Our Award-Winning Web Site

**http://www.oreilly.com/**

★"Top 100 Sites on the Web" —*PC Magazine*
★"Top 5% Web sites" —*Point Communications*
★"3-Star site" —*The McKinley Group*

Our web site contains a library of comprehensive product information (including book excerpts and tables of contents), downloadable software, background articles, interviews with technology leaders, links to relevant sites, book cover art, and more. File us in your Bookmarks or Hotlist!

## 2. Join Our Email Mailing Lists

### New Product Releases

To receive automatic email with brief descriptions of all new O'Reilly products as they are released, send email to:
**listproc@online.oreilly.com**
Put the following information in the first line of your message (*not* in the Subject field):
**subscribe oreilly-news**

### O'Reilly Events

If you'd also like us to send information about trade show events, special promotions, and other O'Reilly events, send email to:
**listproc@online.oreilly.com**
Put the following information in the first line of your message (*not* in the Subject field):
**subscribe oreilly-events**

## 3. Get Examples from Our Books via FTP

There are two ways to access an archive of example files from our books:

### Regular FTP

- ftp to:
  **ftp.oreilly.com**
  (login: anonymous
  password: your email address)
- Point your web browser to:
  **ftp://ftp.oreilly.com/**

### FTPMAIL

- Send an email message to:
  **ftpmail@online.oreilly.com**
  (Write "help" in the message body)

## 4. Contact Us via Email

**order@oreilly.com**
To place a book or software order online. Good for North American and international customers.

**subscriptions@oreilly.com**
To place an order for any of our newsletters or periodicals.

**books@oreilly.com**
General questions about any of our books.

**software@oreilly.com**
For general questions and product information about our software. Check out O'Reilly Software Online at **http://software.oreilly.com/** for software and technical support information. Registered O'Reilly software users send your questions to: **website-support@oreilly.com**

**cs@oreilly.com**
For answers to problems regarding your order or our products.

**booktech@oreilly.com**
For book content technical questions or corrections.

**proposals@oreilly.com**
To submit new book or software proposals to our editors and product managers.

**international@oreilly.com**
For information about our international distributors or translation queries. For a list of our distributors outside of North America check out:
**http://www.oreilly.com/www/order/country.html**

O'Reilly & Associates, Inc.
101 Morris Street, Sebastopol, CA 95472 USA
TEL 707-829-0515 or 800-998-9938
(6am to 5pm PST)
FAX 707-829-0104